ISBN: 9781407770901

Published by:
HardPress Publishing
8345 NW 66TH ST #2561
MIAMI FL 33166-2626

Email: info@hardpress.net
Web: http://www.hardpress.net

Vassar Semi-Centennial Series

ELIZABETHAN TRANSLATIONS FROM THE ITALIAN. By MARY AUGUSTA SCOTT, Ph.D. (A.B. Vassar, 1876), Professor of English Literature in Smith College.

SOCIAL STUDIES IN ENGLISH LITERATURE. By LAURA J. WYLIE, Ph.D. (A.B. Vassar, 1877), Professor of English in Vassar College.

THE LEARNED LADY IN THE EIGHTEENTH CENTURY. By MYRA REYNOLDS, Ph.D. (A.B. Vassar, 1880), Professor of English Literature in Chicago University. [*In preparation.*]

THE CUSTOM OF DRAMATIC ENTERTAINMENT IN SHAKESPEARE'S PLAYS. By ORIE J. HATCHER, Ph.D. (A.B. Vassar, 1888), Formerly Associate Professor of Comparative Literature in Bryn Mawr College. [*In preparation.*]

INTRODUCTION TO THE STUDY OF VARIABLE STARS. By CAROLINE E. FURNESS, Ph.D. (A.B. Vassar, 1891). Professor of Astronomy in Vassar College.

MOVEMENT AND MENTAL IMAGERY. By MARGARET FLOY WASHBURN, Ph.D. (A.B. Vassar, 1891), Professor of Psychology in Vassar College. [*In preparation.*]

BRISSOT DE WARVILLE : A STUDY IN THE HISTORY OF THE FRENCH REVOLUTION. By ELOISE ELLERY, Ph.D. (A.B. Vassar, 1897), Associate Professor of History in Vassar College.

HOUGHTON MIFFLIN COMPANY

BOSTON AND NEW YORK

BRISSOT DE WARVILLE

Vassar Semi-Centennial Series

BRISSOT DE WARVILLE

A STUDY IN THE HISTORY OF THE FRENCH REVOLUTION

BY

ELOISE ELLERY, Ph.D.

Associate Professor of History in Vassar College

BOSTON AND NEW YORK

HOUGHTON MIFFLIN COMPANY

The Riverside Press Cambridge

1915

Published October 1915

PUBLISHED IN HONOR OF THE
FIFTIETH ANNIVERSARY
OF THE
FOUNDING OF VASSAR COLLEGE
1865–1915

TO

F. M. E. AND M. A. A. E.

PREFACE

THE main sources for the study of Brissot's life are his own works, including his early writings, his political pamphlets, his memoirs in the new and critical edition of M. Claude Perroud, his correspondence, also edited by M. Perroud, and especially the newspaper of which he was the editor, the *Patriote Fran-çais*. Other material of value is contained in the publications of the *Société des Amis des Noirs*, in the pamphlets and news-papers of Brissot's opponents, in letters and reports found among the correspondence between the French and English Foreign Offices, preserved at the *Ministère des Affaires Étran-gères* at Paris, in judicial and police reports at the *Archives Na-tionales;* and finally in the Craigie Papers among the Antiqua-rian Society collections at Worcester, Massachusetts, and the Scioto Papers in the collections of the New York Historical Society.

The writer desires to make grateful acknowledgment to the librarians and archivists of the various libraries where her investigation has been carried on, both in this country and abroad, for their help and unfailing courtesy. She is, moreover, especially indebted to Professor H. Morse Stephens, of the University of California, for assistance in the initial stages of her work; to the late Professor Ralph C. H. Catterall, of Cornell University, for untiring criticism and counsel; to her friend and colleague, Assistant Professor C. Mildred Thompson, for generous help in proof-reading, and above all to the inspiration and encouragement of Professor Lucy M. Salmon of Vassar College.

E. E.

VASSAR COLLEGE,
September, 1915.

CONTENTS

CHAPTER I

INTRODUCTION 1

The importance of Brissot.
Reasons why his life has never been written.
The diversity of his activities.
His connection with a defeated party.
Reasons why his life should be written.
New conception concerning the Girondins.
Brissot — a typical Girondin.

CHAPTER II

BRISSOT'S EARLY LIFE 4

Brissot's birth and family.
Limitations of his early environment.
Wide interests, large ambitions, and spiritual revolt.
Entrance on a legal career and removal to Paris.
Abandonment of a legal for a literary career.
Difficulties of the beginner.
First opening for journalistic work with Swinton at Boulogne.
Failure, return to Paris, entrance to literary and scientific circles.
Writings in the interest of reform.
Engagement to Félicité Dupont.
Journey to Switzerland and first contact with active revolutionists.
Establishment of the *Lycée* at London.
English friends and unfortunate acquaintances.
Failure of the *Lycée*, return to Paris and imprisonment in the Bastille for alleged libel.
Collaboration with Clavière and Mirabeau.
Schemes for reform work for the Duke of Chartres.
Establishment of the *Amis des Noirs*.
Journey to America.
Return to France at the beginning of the Revolution.

CHAPTER III

BRISSOT AS AUTHOR AND JOURNALIST BEFORE THE REVOLUTION 41

    Influence of Voltaire on Brissot.
    Influence of Rousseau.
    Influence of the humanitarian spirit of the age.
    Influence of the physiocrats.
    Influence of the institutions of the United States.
    His criticism of proposed reforms.
    His efforts to extend information and to educate public opinion.
    His difficulties with the censorship of the press.
    The reception accorded to his works.
    His faults as a critic.
    The permanent value of his works — their revelation of his character.
    Qualities seen in his works: earnestness, enthusiasm, ambition, and optimism.

CHAPTER IV

BRISSOT'S TRAVELS IN THE UNITED STATES 59

    Brissot's early interest in the United States.
    His defense of Chastellux's book.
    The Gallo-American Society.
    His book, *De la France et des États-Unis.*
    His plans for the journey to America.
    Their final success.
    His motives.
    His qualifications as an observer.
    The voyage across the ocean.
    Boston and its vicinity.
    His connection with the speculation in the American debt.
    His account of the simplicity and democracy of life.
    His account of Franklin.
    His account of Washington.
    His account of the Quakers.
    His account of the work for the negroes.
    His interest in the public debt.
    His interest in western settlement.
    Return to France.
    Connection with the land companies.
    Subsequent influence of his journey to America.

CHAPTER V

Brissot's Career as a Municipal Politician during the Constituent Assembly 91

Brissot's ideas concerning the organization and functions of the States-General.

His part in the electoral campaign; failure to secure election throws him into municipal assembly.

Questions at issue:

Internal organization of the city government.

Relation to the authority of the national government.

Size of the municipality.

Relation of the municipality to the policy of the National Assembly.

Rights of the people.

His interest in the development of provincial government.

His part in the *Comité des Recherches*.

CHAPTER VI

Brissot's Career during the Constituent Assembly. As a Journalist — "Le Patriote Français" 113

Part I. His Struggles to establish a Newspaper and his Attitude on Legislation.

Brissot's early journalistic experience.

Difficulties in establishing the *Patriote Français*, his struggles with the censorship.

The policy of the *Patriote Français*.

Its form and contents.

Its style.

Brissot's collaboration in the *Chronique de Mois*.

His collaborators in the *Patriote Français*.

His partner, the question of responsibility.

Desmoulins's attack.

Brissot's attitude toward the constitution; questions at issue.

One chamber or two.

The degree of independence of the legislative body.

The veto.

The right of declaring peace and war.

The relation of the ministry to the Legislative Assembly.

The democratic character of the constitution.

His attitude toward the judicial system.

His attitude toward freedom of the press.

Attacks made upon him.

His attitude toward the administrative work of the Assembly

Foreign affairs.

The Church.

Sale of church lands.

Financial affairs.

His interest in economic matters.

His use of the *Patriote Français* as an organ of the *Amis des Noirs*.

CHAPTER VII

BRISSOT'S CAREER DURING THE CONSTITUENT ASSEMBLY. AS A JOURNALIST — "LE PATRIOTE FRANÇAIS" 156

PART II. HIS ATTITUDE TOWARD POPULAR MOVEMENTS AND PUBLIC OPINION.

Popular movements.

The 4th of August.

The 5th and 6th of October.

The affair of Nancy.

Popular societies as a means of instruction.

Brissot's own connection with popular societies.

His democracy in relation to women.

His democracy in relation to socialistic tendencies and social customs.

His republicanism.

Pre-revolutionary utterances.

Continued support of monarchy in theory, but hesitancy as to actual change.

Attitude after June 21; connection with Republicanism.

Return to a more moderate position.

His part in the events leading to July 17.

CHAPTER VIII

BRISSOT AS A HUMANITARIAN — LA SOCIÉTÉ DES AMIS DES NOIRS 182

Brissot's incentive — an English organization against the slave trade.

Mirabeau's coöperation.

The organization of the society.

Its constitution.

Its decline during Brissot's absence in America.

Revival of interest on his return.

Efforts to interest the government in the work of the society.

Assistance of Clarkson.

Attacks on the society.

The question of the admission of deputies from the colonies to the States-General.

The question of the status of the mulattoes in the colonies.

The decree of March 8, 1790, against the mulattoes, and its results.

The decree of October 12, 1790, against the mulattoes, and its results.

The decree of May 15, 1791, in favor of the mulattoes, and its results.

The decree of September 24, 1791, against the mulattoes, and its results.

The question reopened in the Legislative Assembly.

The final struggle.

Results of the colonial policy of the *Amis des Noirs*.

Charges brought against the society and against Brissot.

CHAPTER IX

BRISSOT AS A MEMBER OF THE LEGISLATIVE ASSEMBLY . . 216

PART I. HIS ELECTION AND HIS RELATION TO THE WAR QUESTION.

Brissot's struggle for election; persistent attacks upon him, the accusations of Théveneau de Morande.

His election; how received.

His general position.

His views on the organization of the Assembly.

His election to the diplomatic committee.

His attitude toward diplomacy.

His attitude toward special questions:

The *émigrés*.

The princes who had protected the *émigrés*.

Cardinal de Rohan.

His position at the Jacobin Club.

His attitude toward the war question.

His relation to Narbonne.

His contest with Robespierre.

Desmoulins's attack on Brissot.
Division in the diplomatic committee.
Brissot's attack on Delessart.
Appointment of the Girondin ministry.
Attempt to secure an alliance with England and Prussia.
The declaration of war.
Support given by the other Girondins to Brissot's war policy.
Their motives in adopting this policy.

CHAPTER X

BRISSOT AS A MEMBER OF THE LEGISLATIVE ASSEMBLY . . 258
PART II. HIS INTERESTS AND INFLUENCE.
Brissot's policy toward financial problems.
His policy toward non-juring priests.
The Girondin ministry, Brissot's influence on its composition.
His influence over the policy of this ministry.
Change in his attitude; inconsistencies.
Attacks made upon him.
His attack on the "Austrian committee."
His defense of his alleged republicanism.
His attitude toward the King's vetoes and the dismissal of the
    Girondin ministry.
His attitude toward the events of the 20th of June.
His vacillating attitude from June 20 to August 10.
His position after August 10, and as a member of the Commit-
    tee of Twenty-one.
    Action toward Lafayette.
    Address to foreign powers.
    Radical legislation.
    Struggles with the Commune.
    Accusations against him.
His relation to the massacres of September.
Summary of his policy during the Legislative Assembly.

CHAPTER XI

BRISSOT AND THE CONVENTION 303
Brissot's election.
The abolition of royalty.

Quarrel with the Mountain.
   Question of the ministry.
   Question of the departmental guard.
Brissot's expulsion from the Jacobin Club.
His attitude toward the revolutionary propaganda.
His attitude toward the relations of France to Geneva and to the
   Swiss cantons.
His attitude toward Genet's expedition to Spanish America.
Question as to his attitude toward foreign war.
   His own contention that he was opposed to it.
   His attempt at alliance with England.
   His alleged motive for appeal to the people at the king's trial.
   His speech of January 14 in favor of war.
   His speech against the execution of the king on the ground that
     it would cause war.
   His attitude in the king's trial.
Brissot's interest in social equality.
Revival of the quarrel between the Girondins and the Mountain.
Attacks on Brissot.
His withdrawal from active control of the *Patriote Français*.
The popular movement of March 9.
Danton's efforts at reconciliation.
The desertion of Dumouriez and the final struggle.
Desmoulins's attack — *Histoire des Brissotins*.
Brissot's address to his *Commettans*.
The expulsion of the Girondins from the Convention.

BRISSOT AND FEDERALISM.
   Meaning of the word.
   Accusations of federalism and alleged proof.
   Accusations against Brissot.
   His defense.
   The defense of the Girondins as a whole.
   Origin of the change.
   Estimate of the value of the defense.

CHAPTER XII

ARREST, TRIAL, AND DEATH 351
   The situation of the Girondins in the crisis of May 31 to June 2,
     1793.
   Brissot's flight to Versailles.
   His efforts in company with Souque to seek refuge at Chartres.

His wanderings to Moulins.
His arrest at Moulins.
The perplexities of the authorities of Moulins.
His confession of his identity.
The decision to send him to Paris.
Accusations as to his conduct while at Moulins.
His arrival at Paris.
Report of Saint-Just.
Brissot's answer.
The writing of his memoirs.
Appeals to the Convention.
Amar's indictment.
The answer prepared by Brissot.
The preliminary examination.
The trial.
The verdict.
The execution.

CHAPTER XIII

BRISSOT'S FAMILY LIFE 387
Brissot's first acquaintance with Félicité Dupont.
Their engagement, a period of happy comradeship.
Their marriage.
Their life in London.
Financial troubles.
The birth of their first child.
Madame Brissot's literary productions.
Birth of two other children.
Difficulties of the wife of a revolutionist — poverty and loneliness.
Her character.
Members of the Dupont family and Brissot's connection with
    them.
    François Dupont.
    Madame Brissot's sisters.
    Madame Dupont.
Brissot's tardy recognition of his debt to his family.
Madame Brissot's arrest and imprisonment.
Her petitions for indemnification.
Her subsequent life and struggles.
The career of her children.
Her death.

CHAPTER XIV

Brissot's General Policy and Character 412

His policy in regard to democracy, liberty and sovereignty of the
people.
His patriotism, cosmopolitan character.
How far was he a typical Girondin?
How far was he a leader of the Girondins?
What was his character? Diverse opinions.
How far did he possess fitness for leadership?
Why, in spite of conspicuous faults, did he succeed so well?

Appendix 429

A. Letters by and to Brissot.
B. List of members of the *Société des Amis des Noirs.*
C. Accusation against Brissot in connection with the colonies.
D. Brissot's election to the Legislative Assembly.
E. Letter relating to connection of Brissot with war with England.

Bibliography 453

Index 509

BRISSOT DE WARVILLE

CHAPTER I

INTRODUCTION

THE life of Brissot has never been written. Considering the importance of the rôle which he played in the drama of the Revolution, this absence of a biography seems strange. At the beginning of the Revolution he already had considerable reputation as a writer, philanthropist, and traveler; he took a prominent part in reorganizing the city government of Paris; as founder of the *Amis des Noirs* he had a large share in shaping the colonial policy of the successive assemblies; he established one of the most influential newspapers of the period, and used it constantly to hold up American example to France; he, probably more than any one individual, was responsible for bringing on that foreign war which ended only with the fall of Napoleon; he was known as the leader of the Girondins, and indeed gave his name to a whole section of the party; and, when that party fell, he was brought to a trial known as that of "Brissot and his accomplices." A man of such prominence it might be supposed would be one of the first subjects of biographical study. That such has not been the case is accounted for by two reasons, which, while explaining why his life has not been written, at the same time suggest why it should be.

In the first place, the very diversity of his activities has made his career appear to lack unity and therefore interest. But though his activities were diverse, they all centered, to a degree unusual even among his contemporaries, upon a firm belief in the principles of liberty, equality, and the sovereignty of the people. Of these principles Brissot was one of the earliest and most ardent advocates, and in the external events which

turned those principles from theory into practice and transformed the bourgeois and limited monarchy into the democratic republic, he was one of the most active participants. His
early life was a struggle against despotism; his early writings
are permeated with revolutionary doctrines; his travels in the
United States were dictated by a desire to see such doctrines
in active operation; his part in building up a new city government for Paris was an effort to apply these doctrines to local
government; his founding of the *Amis des Noirs* witnessed his
zeal for liberty and equality for one particular class of the un-
free and the inferior; finally, through his paper, the *Patriote
Français*, he constantly protested against the inequality recognized by the limited suffrage, and, while grudgingly accepting
the constitutional monarchy, preached republicanism as a
theory and later upheld it in practice. In the legislature under
the monarchy, to which in spite of his republicanism he sought
election, he used all his influence to bring on foreign war, on
the ground that only by war could the counter-revolutionists
at home and abroad be defeated and liberty be preserved. Although not a leader in the final establishment of the republic
he joyfully accepted the result, claimed a share in the credit,
and was elected to the Convention, where, by preaching the
extension of the principles of the Revolution beyond the borders of France, he had a considerable share in involving
France in a general European war.

The failure of the armies of France in that war soon led to
the overthrow of the Girondins, and he fell with them in their
defeat in the Convention. That he belonged to the defeated
party is a second reason for the absence of a study of his life.
As the Girondins passed from the scene at the beginning of the
most dramatic phase of the Revolution, — among the first victims of the Terror, — they have been objects of pity, but have
aroused much less interest than their victorious opponents, the
leaders of the party of the Mountain, Danton, Robespierre,
and Marat.

But this conception of the Girondins, as the last representatives of a disinterested love of country and of opposition to bloodshed, has been given up. It has been shown that among the Girondins, as well as among the members of the Mountain, there were both idealism and selfish ambition; that the Girondins, after the overthrow of the king, sought to seize for themselves the power that had been wrested from the king by others; that they appealed to the provinces not against the principles, but against the power of the Mountain — an appeal which brought against them the accusation of federalism; that they, as well as the Mountain, forged the instruments of the Terror, but that they lacked practical ability to suppress internal dissension within their group and to control the situation which they themselves, by their instigation of foreign war, had had a large share in bringing about. Of this group Brissot is one of the most important because he is one of the most typical. He showed both the lofty idealism and the ambition and weakness of the Girondins. He was tremendously earnest in working for the principles of the Revolution, and he was also extremely anxious to be one of the agents through which they were to be put into operation; at one and the same time he upheld monarchy and made monarchy impossible. But when the democratic republic, which had long been his ideal, was finally established, he did not see that the war which he had furthered in order to maintain democracy and republicanism, and to extend them to other lands, demanded strong, vigorous measures. And thus he ultimately encountered defeat because of that inability to meet changing conditions — that lack of practical sense which was characteristic of the Girondins in general.

A study of his varied career as humanitarian, journalist, and political leader ought, therefore, to contribute to a better understanding both of the policy of the Girondins in the Revolution and also of the Revolution as a whole.

CHAPTER II

BRISSOT'S EARLY LIFE

LIKE many of his fellow revolutionists, Brissot was of humble origin, being the son of a restaurant keeper. He was born at Chartres, in the parish of Saint-Saturnin, in a house on what was then the *rue de la Boucherie*, number 16,[1] January 15,[2] 1754, and the same day was baptized Jacques Pierre.[3] The story of his childhood and youth is of significance in that it throws light on his later career, while the personal characteristics and external experiences and limitations of his early life explain Brissot the revolutionist.[4]

The most striking facts about his childhood, as he himself tells of it, were his mother's efforts to secure for him a good education and his almost abnormal love of study. In this effort to obtain for her sons opportunities for study, Madame Brissot found herself opposed by her husband, who did not favor anything like a liberal education for his children. His attitude was not to be wondered at, perhaps, in view of the fact that there were seven of them to be provided for,[5] but according to Brissot

[1] An article in the *Intermédiaire des chercheurs* of July 30, 1898, vol. II, in which it was asserted that Brissot was born at number 7 *rue des Vieux-Capuchins*, led to an investigation of the subject by the *Société archéologique d'Eure-et-Loir*. It was shown that this statement was a mistake, but that the real place of his birth was that given above, number 16 *rue de la Boucherie*, now *rue du Cygne*, number 6.

[2] See the record of Brissot's baptism given in Vatel, *Charlotte Corday et les Girondins*, II, 242.

[3] Not *Jean* Pierre, as given in the act of accusation before the revolutionary tribunal. The mistake must have been of earlier date, however, as Camille Desmoulins' pamphlet published in February, 1792, is entitled "*Jean Pierre Brissot démasqué.*"

[4] Practically the only source of information on Brissot's early life is his own memoirs. As far as possible his statements have been verified by other authority, but much still remains uncorroborated.

[5] Brissot (*Mémoires*, ed. par Perroud, I, 25) says that he was the third child

it was due to a narrow-minded fear that they might look down upon him with scorn if they were too well educated. Brissot's mother, however, was more ambitious. Not satisfied with the meager opportunities which Brissot had had in the little dame school to which he had been sent, she besought his father early and late till she finally obtained a reluctant consent to further schooling for her sons.[1]

Brissot was accordingly taken from this dame school and, in company with an elder brother, entrusted to an uncle, a priest in a neighboring town, to be prepared for a higher school. On the death of his uncle, three months later, he went back to Chartres to finish his preparation. He now began the study of Latin with the master of a boarding-school, and the following year, at the age of eight, he entered the college at Chartres, where he spent the next seven years of his life.[2] Here he received the usual classical training of the time, consisting of rhetoric, logic, Latin, and Greek.

As a consequence of the personal interest of one of his teachers, he devoted especial attention to Latin.[3] So eager was he to excel that he used to beg a candle from his sister when she went to mass at four in the morning, and with the aid of a dark lantern to conceal the light, that his father should not know what he was up to, he would pore over his Latin, quite as much a devotee to his books as his sister to her religion. In after life, when he became imbued with Rousseauism, he was wont to criticize the rigidity of the system by which he was taught. Although it did much to train the memory, it was not calcu-

and that there were four younger than he. Perroud (Brissot, *Correspondance et Papiers, Notice*, viii–x) says there were sixteen. In any case only seven lived beyond infancy. For details as to the career of those seven see, in addition to Perroud, an article by A. H. Gibon in the *Journal des Chartres*, September 30, 1899, quoted entire in the *Procès-verbaux de la Société archéologique d'Eure-et-Loir*, x, 121–23.

[1] *Mémoires*, i, 28–29.
[2] *Ibid.*, i, 32–34. Brissot speaks of this school as a college. But the so-called colleges of that time do not correspond at all to our colleges. They were scarcely of as high a grade as the preparatory schools of to-day.
[3] *Ibid.*, i, 33.

lated to inspire originality nor to develop the individuality of the student. Such evidences of spontaneity as he did show, far from being encouraged, were, he asserted, actually repressed. He declares that even as a child he had an uncomfortable sense of being cramped by a system which did not fit him, and a vague longing for better opportunities of self-expression.[1]

But the prevailing system of education at least gave him the habit of work and a well-trained memory. He showed an unusual fondness for study and seems to have been successful in all his classes.[2] His imagination, moreover, found satisfaction and stimulus in the contents of the library which one of his teachers kindly placed at his disposal. Here was a perfect mine of delight, and he fell upon it with avidity. "While reading the history of China," he wrote in his memoirs, "I was a conquering Tartar; when reading Plutarch, I was eager to be like Phocion. The hut of Philocles, pictured with all the charm of Fénelon, appeared to me more desirable than all the thrones of the world. . . . The reading of travels changed the course of my ideas; I became a traveler. I literally devoured the voyages of Magellan, of Anson, of Drake, and of Kempfer."[3] All in all, his school days were happy. When he returned home, exulting in his little triumphs, he was hurt by his father's coldness and lack of sympathy; but he found compensation for this disappointment in his mother's unfailing pride in his achievements and in her keen appreciation and constant encouragement.

At the age of fifteen he left the college and had to choose a vocation. After some hesitation he decided on the legal profession, partly because he had some inclination for the law, but chiefly, it must be confessed, because that career seemed to be the only one open to him. Having once made up his mind, he sought the best lawyer of Chartres, M. Horeau, began his studies under his direction, and threw himself, heart and soul,

---

[1] *Mémoires*, I, 35.

[2] Pétion, *Notice sur Brissot*, in Vatel, *Charlotte Corday et les Girondins*, II, 220. These notes by Pétion are evidently based on information derived from Brissot personally and therefore have not the value of an independent source.

[3] *Mémoires*, I, 42–43.

into the work. He was an indefatigable student in all branches
of the subject, — of canon, as well as of criminal and civil law.
He soon felt sufficiently sure of his knowledge to venture to
write a short treatise on canon law under the title of *Rome
démasqué, ou Observations sur le droit canonique*.[1] This he followed by an essay on theft and property, in which he argued
that in a state of nature there was no such thing as theft, —
a work which subsequently brought upon him much criticism.[2]

Nor were his interests confined to legal matters. After the
fashion of the time, he took all knowledge for his province.
M. Horeau's son possessed a library containing some works on
physics; Brissot immediately began to read on that subject.
Two Englishmen happened to be stopping at Chartres; he
seized the opportunity to take lessons in English.[3] A friend advised him to study Italian; he not only followed the advice,
but went on to the study of Spanish and Portuguese. And
finally, what was very unusual for a Frenchman of the eighteenth century, he even aspired to learn German.[4] According to
Pétion he was a veritable prodigy in learning foreign languages.[5]
At all events, he had unusual aptitude for such studies and made
considerable progress in a short time. He even planned a treatise on the *Théorie des langues de l'Europe et surtout de la langue
française*, but the appearance of Gébelin's learned work on this
subject prevented, perhaps fortunately, its publication.[6]

Still he was not a recluse. He enjoyed an occasional game of
billiards, took some part in social life, and made various friends;
among them, Blot,[7] to whom he remained deeply attached to
the day of his death. About this time the idea of marriage began to present itself to him in a form quite in accordance with

---

[1] *Mémoires*, I, 46–48.   [2] See p. 266.
[3] *Mémoires*, I, 48. Pétion, in his *Notice sur Brissot*, implies that Brissot carried on his studies without assistance. Vatel, II, 221.
[4] *Mémoires*, I, 53–54.   [5] *Notice* in Vatel, II, 221.   [6] *Mémoires*, I, 55–57.
[7] Blot, Pierre Charles, began his career as an ecclesiastic, gave up the Church,
married, entered the financial administration of the state at Lyons, and
became one of the leading revolutionists of that city. He came to be closely
associated with the Rolands and with Brissot. See p. 121.

his intellectual tastes. "I wanted a wife," he writes, "who, with external attractions, would combine good judgment and a philosophical spirit; who would prefer not the vain pleasures of the world, but those of solitude; who would be a good mother and a good wife; but who, at the same time, would be sufficiently well educated to be my friend, my second self, the companion of my studies." For so rare a partner he searched in vain, till his friend Blot, who shared his views, came to the rescue and told him of some one who, he assured Brissot, had all these qualifications which he had enumerated, and, moreover, a very strong character besides. But apparently before Brissot could even make her acquaintance she gave a peculiar evidence of her strength of character by killing herself.[1] Much disheartened, and perhaps alarmed by such possibilities, Brissot seems to have abandoned the search for a wife and flung himself back into his studies.

If his intellectual achievements and interests were abnormal, his religious experience was a more common one. Like many of his contemporaries, he began with extreme devotion to the Roman Catholic Church, passed through a severe struggle, and ended in deism. His early training was under the direction of priests and in an atmosphere of intense religiousness. He attended mass every day, piously confessed his faults, and displayed all the ardor of a zealous neophyte. In the simplicity of his faith he attributed all his success to his devotion to the Virgin, and on the eve of the distribution of prizes, his *Ave Marias* were very numerous.[2]

Out of this comfortable belief he was shaken by the sneers and ridicule of one of his schoolmates, Guillard,[3] who, as it happened, was not only exceptionally clever, but had enjoyed unusual advantages at home. He was accordingly much looked up to and his opinion had great weight with Brissot. The latter now began to read for himself Guillard's favorite authors, such as Rousseau, Voltaire, and Diderot. *La profession de foi du*

---

[1] *Mémoires*, i, 43–44, 62–63.   [2] *Ibid.*, i, 37.

[3] Afterward a poet of some note. See p. 11.

vicaire savoyard, to quote his own words, first caused the scales to fall from his eyes; but it was only after careful study of all the books within his reach that he definitely abandoned Christianity, and it was many years before he could entirely get rid of "the prejudices which had driven long, deep roots into his soul." [1]

Once during this struggle he was tempted to become a monk, not at all on account of any spiritual longing for peace, but because he craved the opportunity which the cloister afforded for a life of study. A mere subsistence and books were all he needed to be happy. From any such intention he was dissuaded by a certain Benedictine monk, who with much frankness pictured to him the restrictions of the monastic life in anything but glowing colors. This episode confirmed him in his opposition to Christianity. He even wrote a savage attack on the Christian religion, entitled *Lettres philosophiques sur la vie et les écrits de Saint Paul.* [2] The result of this experience was that he became a believer in deism and continued in that faith to the end of his days.

His struggle was all the harder because he had to fortify himself against the inevitable opposition of his family. He could not bear the thought of the strife that was sure to come, and for a long time concealed his changed views. For the sake of his sister he even continued to partake of the eucharist after he had lost all faith in its efficacy. It was the spiritual separation from his mother, however, which was hardest to endure. She had made possible his education, sympathized with him in his struggles, and stood between him and his unsympathetic father. But the break could not be avoided and was a tragedy for both sides — for Brissot because he was torn between sorrow for having wounded his family and irritation at what seemed to him the most narrow-minded dogmatism; and for his family because

---

[1] *Mémoires*, I, 38.

[2] Of the trenchant and dogmatic tone of this work he was afterward much ashamed. At the time it seems to have given him a reputation for cutting sarcasm which, to his regret, made the young women of his acquaintance rather afraid of him. (*Mémoires*, I, 61–62.)

they believed him lost to all eternity. As he himself well expressed it, he and his family had ceased to speak a common language.[1]

This religious difficulty made his home life unhappy and in consequence hastened his departure from Chartres. He suffered, too, from want of intellectual companionship. In the words of a modern writer, he felt himself cut off equally from the blessings of society and of solitude, and longed for life either in the country or in a large city. The chief reason, however, for his leaving Chartres was the consuming ambition which was one of his most marked characteristics. While still in school his plans for himself had gone beyond anything his native town had to offer; and when a kindly neighbor, thinking to flatter the boy, suggested that some day he would be like M. Janvier, one of the best lawyers of the place, he was actually displeased at the comparison,[2] and the more he studied the more Chartres seemed to him insupportable. His aspiration was all for a career in Paris, but it was only after four years of the study of law in Chartres that an opening presented itself. The opportunity came through a Paris lawyer, a M. Nolleau, who happened to be stopping at Chartres. On hearing of his arrival, Brissot seized the chance, wrote to him at once asking for a position, and accompanied the application with a copy of one of his legal essays. This production, according to Brissot's own account, happened to strike the fancy of M. Nolleau, who offered him the place of first clerk.[3]

While still living at Chartres he had added to his name " de Warville," the anglicized form of Ouarville, a little village where his father owned some property.[4] For this addition to his name he was afterwards much criticized, on the ground that it

---

[1] *Mémoires*, i, 28–39.   [2] *Ibid.*, i, 42.   [3] *Ibid.*, i, 63, 65.

[4] Brissot, *Réponse à tous les libellistes*, 5. The account which he there gives is incorporated by Montrol in his edition of Brissot's memoirs, a fact to which M. Perroud, in his edition, calls attention. (i, 53.) A writer in the *Intermédiaire des chercheurs et curieux* for January 25, 1876, says: *Warville n'est en effet que la corruption euphonique du mot Warvick [sic] laissé en France par Richard Nevil, comte de Warvick.*

betokened an unseemly hankering after aristocratic distinctions. Whether this criticism was justified or not, he continued to sign himself "Brissot de Warville," and by that name has long been known.[1]

It was in 1774 that he left Chartres.[2] The rest of his life, with brief intermissions, was to be spent in Paris. The occupations in which he engaged, and the connections which he made, both worked toward the development of the future revolutionist. He was now twenty years of age, abounding in hope and enthusiasm, and any regret which he might have felt at leaving Chartres was quite overbalanced by his delight at the prospect of life in the city which, with a not too modest opinion of his own ability, he regarded "as the center of science and a stage worthy of his efforts."[3]

Full of confidence in himself, he ventured, on the basis of a short acquaintance with the theater, to prepare a plan for a theater which should make a special business of presenting plays in English, Italian, Spanish, and German; and what was more, he had the temerity to seek out Linguet, the distinguished publicist, and present to him his plan.[4] Although warned by Linguet against a literary career, Brissot refused to be dissuaded, and influenced by the glowing pictures painted by his young friend, the poet Guillard,[5] of the delights of the life of a man of letters, he soon threw in his fortunes with the latter, and with a light heart started in pursuit of fame and fortune as a writer.[6] In order to prepare himself for his profession he devoted his entire time to study. Even on Sundays and holidays he would not leave his Locke, his Montesquieu, and his Montaigne,[7] and when Guillard would come in from his mid-

---

[1] See pp. 220–21.

[2] Brissot does not give the date of his arrival, but says he found the city in mourning for Louis XV. (*Mémoires*, I, 67.) As Louis died on the 10th of May, 1774, and the period of mourning for the king was three months, this would fix the date of Brissot's arrival some time between May 10 and August 10, 1774. (Franklin, *La Vie privée d'autrefois, les magasins des nouveautés*, III, 131–32.)

[3] *Mémoires*, I, 66.   [4] *Ibid.*, I, 82.   [5] See p. 8.

[6] *Mémoires*, I, 102–03.   [7] Pétion, *Notice sur Brissot*, in Vatel, II, 222.

night suppers he would find Brissot still poring over his Greek dictionary. Meanwhile he had to live, and he was not long in discovering that the path of a young man dependent on his pen for support was no easy one. He was obliged to ask his mother for money, but the amount which she could send him was not sufficient for his needs; the little pamphlets on matters of the day, from which he expected to make some money, were indeed accepted by a publisher, but the publisher failed to pay him anything for them; a spiteful satire, *Le Pot pourri*, which, in his disgust with the chicanery of the law, he wrote in collaboration with Guillard, brought on him the threat of a *lettre de cachet*; on account of some aspersions which it contained on the wife of a certain lawyer.[1] And to crown his misfortunes, just as he was threatened with the *lettre de cachet*, he was taken ill with fever, aggravated, if not brought on, by a combination of overwork, the excessive use of punch, and insufficient nourishment. Ill as he was, he was obliged to flee at once; and it was only after an illness of several months that he was sufficiently restored in health to return to Paris, weak in body and chastened in spirit.

As nothing better offered, he went back to Guillard. It was the same struggle to make both ends meet, and they were often in distress. But it was harder for Brissot than for Guillard, for the latter was a favorite in literary circles and was frequently relieved of the necessity of paying for his meals by an invitation to dinner, while Brissot, neither so popular nor so well known, had to provide his own dinner and find consolation by flattering himself, as he ate his bread and cheese alone, that he was above being a parasite.[2]

Meanwhile he was becoming more and more absorbed in plans for the reform of existing institutions. In the enormous scale of the works he undertook to write and in the audacious enterprise with which he brought them to the attention of distinguished men, he showed the same undaunted courage and large ambition which he had already displayed in his work on canon law [3] and in his plans for a theater,[4] and which he after-

---

[1] *Mémoires*, I, 104.   [2] *Ibid.*, I, 120.   [3] See p. 7.   [4] See p. 11.

ward showed throughout the Revolution. In addition to a satirical attack on the English cabinet, entitled *Testament politique de l'Angleterre*, he planned a *Théorie des lois criminelles*,[1] and sketched the outline of a work to be called *Pyrrhonisme universelle*. The last he ventured to send to D'Alembert and was much hurt that D'Alembert gave him only compliments when he wanted advice and encouragement. Wishing to print the letter which D'Alembert had written him, and having lost the original, he had the audacity to submit a copy to him and to ask for corrections.[2]

Voltaire seemed to be the one man who inspired him with awe. He yearned to present the introduction to his work on the *Théorie des lois criminelles* to Voltaire, but after having been actually admitted to the house where Voltaire was a guest, his courage suddenly failed him and he quietly stole out. Ashamed of this performance, he tried again, this time armed with a letter to present, but again he turned and rushed down the steps. But as it happened, he ran against Madame Du Barry, who was just coming away from her one famous interview with Voltaire, and Brissot summoned up courage to address himself to her. She good-naturedly took pity on his timidity, and called the master of the house. Thus Brissot was able to give his letter directly into the hands of Voltaire's host. He was still more delighted to receive from Voltaire a flattering reply, a part of which he inserted in the preface of his work.[3]

The plan for the *Testament politique de l'Angleterre* did not promise so well at first, though in the end it brought him good fortune. Vergennes, to whom he sent the manuscript, was so afraid of irritating the English that he forbade its publication, but Brissot managed to get it printed surreptitiously, outside of France. A copy happened to fall into the hands of Swinton, the publisher, who, in his *Courrier de l'Europe*, was making a specialty of English affairs. Being struck with Brissot's knowl-

---

[1] See p. 45. [2] *Mémoires*, I, 121–23.
[3] *Ibid.*, I, 145–47; also *Correspondance*, 3.

edge of the subject, he offered him a place on the French edition of the paper, published at Boulogne.[1] This was a godsend
to Brissot personally. Moreover, he looked upon it as an opportunity to better the character of the paper, — which, according
to his own account, was sadly in need of improvement, — and
thus to render a service to men of letters and to the cause of
political liberty.[2] Incidentally it would enable him to continue
his scientific and political studies. But most of all it was his
chance to break away from a kind of life for which his conscience had begun to trouble him. Having paid his debts with
money which Swinton advanced, he settled up his affairs and
set out in a state of blissful content for the scene of his new
labors, as delighted to leave Paris as he had been four years
before to arrive there.[3]

Brissot was forever an optimist. Each new enterprise, each
fresh start, was sure to be a success. The life at Boulogne, he
was confident, was to give him the opportunities he had hitherto
sought in vain. At first everything answered to his expectations. He was pleased with the English household of Swinton, in
which he was received on familiar terms, enjoyed the society of
various families to whom he was introduced, and was charmed
with the country walks in the beautiful surroundings of Boulogne and along the seashore. Besides all this, he was able to
complete his work on the *Théorie des lois criminelles*, a part of
which he presented in competition for a prize offered by the
Economic Society of Berne.[4] His main attention, of course,
was given to the *Courrier*, and into his new work he threw himself with enthusiasm, delighted to have a vehicle for the expression of his ideas. But his good fortune suddenly changed. According to his own account he expressed his ideas with too
much freedom, and in consequence brought down upon the
Courrier an order from the censor to confine itself to English

[1] *Mémoires*, i, 137–40.   [2] *Réponse à tous les libellistes*, 7.
[3] *Mémoires*, i, 139–40. See also Pétion, *Notice sur Brissot*, in Vatel, ii, 226.
Pétion evidently confuses Brissot's subsequent connection with the *Courrier*
at London with his work at Boulogne.
[4] *Mémoires*, i, 154–64.

news and to let French politics alone. His work being thus reduced to mere mechanical tasks, he began to lose interest in it.
At the same time Swinton, Brissot asserts, had become absorbed in some new scheme for the development of which he
needed to exercise greater economy. He accordingly sent word
to Brissot from London, where he was staying for the moment,
that he no longer needed his services, but he concealed the real
motive and tried to soften the abrupt dismissal by inviting
Brissot to visit him in his London home. In spite of his discharge, Brissot still had confidence in Swinton and accepted
the invitation, thus closing this chapter of his career with a
visit to England, — his first journey out of France.[1] This confidence, however, seems to have been misplaced, for, with
unpardonable simplicity, having left the settlement of their
financial arrangements to Swinton, he found that Swinton had
made the settlement very much to his own advantage.[2] This
account, of course, rests on Brissot's own statement. It is
quite possible there may have been another side to the story.
However that may be, from a business and professional point
of view his Boulogne experience had not been the success he had
anticipated.[3] It had, however, a lasting importance for him,
aside from the experience with newspaper work, as it was at
Boulogne that he made the acquaintance of the young woman
who was afterwards to become his wife — Félicité Dupont.

After a brief sojourn in London Brissot returned to Paris.
"Thrown back into the whirlpool," to quote his own language,
from which he had been so glad to escape, he had to find a way
to make his living.[4] While still at Boulogne he had appealed to

[1] *Mémoires*, i, 169–73.   [2] *Ibid.*, i, 173.
[3] How long he stayed at Boulogne, Brissot does not say. He apparently went
there in the spring of 1778 (see letter addressed to him at the time he left Paris,
by Voltaire, *Mémoires*, i, 147, and *Correspondance*, 3). According to Perroud
(*La Révolution Française*, xlvii, 127), he returned to Paris in the autumn of
1780, but as he seems to have been in Paris when he was summoned by his
father's last illness (*Mémoires*, i, 180), and his father died December 24, 1779
(*Notice* by Perroud in his *Correspondance*), his stay at Boulogne could have
lasted not more than a year and a half.
[4] *Mémoires*, i, 166–73.

his father, but received only a chilling response, written, Brissot was confident, under priestly influence, in which he spoke with pride of the first mass of another son, and made it uncomfortably plain to Brissot that he would give him help only on condition of his returning to the true fold.[1] Brissot evidently had nothing to hope from that source. He then applied to Linguet. But Linguet had been obliged to leave France on account of his quarrels with the encyclopedists, and was not in prosperous circumstances. The only work which Linguet would give him was the making of an index for three or four volumes of his *Annales*.[2] He also secured some hack work on a *Dictionnaire ecclésiastique de toute la France*, but he seems never to have received a *sou* for it.

In his discouragement and loneliness he began to think that it would be a comfortable consolation to have a wife to share his troubles. He had been greatly taken with Mademoiselle Dupont, whose family he had come to know at Boulogne, but the knowledge that she was already engaged had been an effectual check to his ardor. His thoughts now turned to a daughter of Swinton, but Swinton, who had higher ambitions for his children, would have none of Brissot.[3]

The one offset to these failures and disappointments was the kindness of Mentelle, the geographer. This Brissot owed directly to Madame Dupont, the mother of Félicité. She had spoken to Brissot of Mentelle as an old friend of the family, and when Brissot returned to Paris she recommended him to Mentelle. The latter responded most cordially, invited Brissot to his house, and introduced him to his friends.[4]

Just at this juncture he was called home by the last illness of

[1] *Mémoires*, I, 173–74.

[2] *Ibid.*, I, 93. Brissot eventually lost faith in Linguet, partly because he mistrusted that Linguet's kindness was not altogether disinterested and partly because of Linguet's quarrels with the encyclopedists. (*Ibid.*, I, 96–98.)

[3] *Ibid.*, I, 177–78.

[4] *Ibid.*, I, 178. See also p. 388. The one thing which Brissot did not enjoy at Mentelle's house was the concerts which Mentelle occasionally provided for his guests. Brissot admits that he not only had no taste for music, but that it was actually disagreeable to him.

his father. He was much touched, after their long estrangement, to receive his father's benediction,[1] but the softening influence of the occasion was marred for Brissot by the presence
at the deathbed of the priests to whom Brissot felt that the
estrangement was due. He felt, too, that he had further cause
for indignation. His mother had become subject to violent
attacks of insanity during which she imagined herself surrounded by horrible demons. This condition Brissot attributed,
in part, to the influence of the priests, who had wrought upon
her imagination with their pictures of the terrors of the next
world, and this conviction only increased his cordial hatred of
the Church.[2]

He now returned to Paris. Though he occasionally got into
difficulties due, if his own account is to be believed, to a too
great confidence in his fellow men, he was able to continue
extensive studies and to work out schemes for reform, this time
under pleasanter conditions and with happier results. The
legacy of four thousand francs which he received from his
father, small though it was, was of great help. The study of
chemistry, anatomy, and physics, which he now took up for
the first time, afforded him a fascinating field of investigation.[3]
Through Mentelle he secured the *entrée* to the best literary and
scientific circles; and his own scientific studies brought him
into connection with men of note, among them Chambon[4] and
Marat. The investigations of the latter in physics had attracted
his attention; and when Marat announced himself an apostle of
liberty, Brissot was ready to become his friend. With the im-
petuous zeal with which he always flung himself into any plan
for the extension of knowledge, Brissot set to work to extend
the reputation of Marat, both as a physicist and a physician,
only to be met, according to Brissot's account, by ingratitude

---

[1] His father died December 24, 1779. See article by M. A. H. Gibon, *ancien
greffier de Chartres*, in the *Journal de Chartres*, September 30, 1799, quoted entire in *Procès verbaux de la Société archéologique d'Eure-et-Loir*, x, 121–23.
1901.

[2] *Mémoires*, I, 181–82. [3] *Ibid.*, I, 181–88.

[4] Chambon, afterward Mayor of Paris.

and by demands for introductions which he felt he could not give.[1]

Brissot's interests were not confined, however, to matters scientific. Through Mentelle he was able to renew his acquaintance with Félicité Dupont. As her engagement was broken and there was now no obstacle to his suit, he lost no time in profiting by the circumstance, and they soon became engaged. Félicité was also interested in science, and they enjoyed a charming courtship while carrying on their studies together.[2]

He was most anxious to hasten his marriage, and as the small inheritance which he had received from his father would hardly enable him to support a family, he determined as a means of increasing his income to seek admission to the bar. He accordingly took up the study of law again. It was necessary to get certain degrees in the law school, but as that was a mere formality, he took the usual and shorter method of buying them, but he soon found insupportable the long novitiate through which he must pass before being admitted to full standing. Another cause was his lack of harmony with the lawyers of the Parlement of Paris, due, according to his own account, to the radical opinions he had expressed in his recent writings. He was disgusted, too, he declared, with the pedantry and formalism of the system. It is not unlikely, however, that indifferent success may have had something to do with his disgust. At all events, he threw up the whole business and went back to his scientific and philosophical studies. His practical experience only accentuated his interest in the theoretical side of the law and strengthened his conviction of the need of reform. During the three years of his second residence in Paris, he wrote much on this subject. He had already published, at the time of his admission to the bar, his *Théorie des lois criminelles*, and it was in part because of the ideas advanced therein that he did not receive a cordial welcome.[3] The work, however, was warmly

[1] *Mémoires*, i, 196–213; also *Correspondance*, 35–38.

[2] *Mémoires*, i, 185. For the details of this charming companionship, see chap. xiii.   [3] *Ibid.*, i, 194–95.

praised by various writers and brought him into pleasant, friendly relations with several prominent men. He also wrote two essays on the same general theme in competition for prizes offered by the Academy of Chalons-sur-Marne on the specific questions: *S'il était dû des indemnités par la société à un accusé dont l'innocence avait été reconnue;* and *Quelles pourraient être en France les lois pénales les moins sévères et cependant les plus efficaces pour contenir et réprimer le crime par des châtiments prompts et exemplaires en ménageant l'honneur et la liberté des citoyens.*[1]

His arguments against capital punishment and in favor of a more humane penal code, which were successful in winning the prizes, occasioned a furious assault from the *Mercure.* Brissot thought that he perceived in the assault the hand of Lacretelle,[2] but the satire proved to be the work of Garat.[3] Although he was much hurt at the time, the affair resulted in a pleasant personal acquaintance with both these writers. Another prize offered by the same academy for an essay on better education, for which Brissot likewise competed, led to his election to membership in the academy.[4] During this time he also wrote *Un Indépendant à l'ordre des avocats, sur la décadence du barreau en France,*[5] a direct attack on the French bar, and the outgrowth of his own experience. And influenced by his disgust at the quarrels and jealousy among men of letters, of which he had been a witness, he composed a treatise called *De la Vérité,*

[1] *Mémoires,* I, 228. He had already submitted an essay to the Academy of Besançon on *Des funestes effets de l'égoïsme,* but received only honorable mention. His indignant protests suggest that he himself was not altogether free from the malady of which he wrote. See his correspondence on the subject. *Correspondance,* 7–8.

[2] Brissot does not say which Lacretelle, probably Pierre Louis, who was born in 1751 and died in 1824, a prominent lawyer, writer, and politician, and friend of Garat, D'Alembert, and Condorcet. He was especially known for his *Discours sur le préjugé des peines infamantes.*

[3] Garat, Dominique Joseph, born 1749, died 1833. A writer and politician, was connected with the *Mercure,* and became a member of the Constituent Assembly. He was made Minister of Justice after the 10th of August, 1792, but his moderation in regard to the massacres of September led to a break with his old friends, the Girondins.

[4] *Mémoires,* I, 230–34.   [5] Brissot, *Bibliothèque philosophique,* VI, 344.

ou méditation sur les moyens de parvenir à la vérité dans toutes les connoissances humaines.[1] These essays he meant to serve, however, merely as prefaces to larger works; the treatise on criminal law was to be followed by a *Histoire universelle de la législation criminelle,* and the essay on *La Vérité* by a search for what was certain in all human knowledge. In the mean time, while waiting for an opportunity to carry out these ambitious plans, he began a compilation of material on criminal legislation, which ultimately reached ten volumes, and which he called a *Bibliothèque philosophique des lois criminelles.*[2] Not content with merely writing against abuses, he began to cogitate on methods of furthering the attack by organized effort. His idea, which he seems to have borrowed directly from La Blancherie,[3] was to assail despotism and to spread abroad ideas of political, as well as of legal reform, by means of an organization of the savants and reformers of all Europe.[4] This organization was to be called a *Lycée,* and was to consist of three parts, a correspondence between members, a special publication on the arts and sciences in England, and meetings which were to be held at the local office in London. From that center of freedom the members of the society were to "inundate Europe" with their writings against despotism.

But in order to "inundate Europe" Brissot needed coöperation and financial support. After some more or less cautious sounding of various persons on the subject, he found in a certain Villar [5] apparently just the man he wanted. Villar, although

[1] *Mémoires,* I, 189.

[2] *Ibid.,* I, 220, 226. See his correspondence with Droz, the secretary of the Academy of Besançon, on the subject. *Correspondance,* 11–19.

[3] La Blancherie was born in 1752 and died in 1811. He was known especially as the founder of the *Nouvelles de la république des lettres et des arts.* "*C'était l'organe d'une sorte de cercle artistique et scientifique destiné à fournir aux savants et aux artistes un centre de ralliement.*"

[4] *Mémoires,* I, 191.

[5] *Ibid.,* I, 239–42. Villar, Noel Gabriel Luce de, was born in Toulouse in 1748 and died in Paris in 1826. In 1791 he was made constitutional bishop of Mayenne and later was a deputy from that department to the Convention. His chief work during the Convention was as a member of the Committee of Public Instruction.

not a writer himself, had a wide acquaintance with men of letters and professed himself eager to use all his interest in Brissot's behalf. He had relations with all kinds of people and in
many countries. He was most optimistic. Russian counts,
Polish princesses, academicians and ambassadors alike, he was
sure, would hasten to support the project. D'Alembert had
written to Berlin, D'Argental to Tuscany; [1] some one else had
written to La Harpe,[2] and had recommended him to Russian
friends; Madame de Genlis [3] had spoken in his behalf to the
Duke of Chartres, who was just about to start for Italy and who
would further his plans there. Villar had audiences every day
with the ministers, and if need be he would speak directly to the
king. Finally, he introduced Brissot to Élie de Beaumont,[4] who
declared that he was enchanted with Brissot's plan, and that he
too was only waiting for the right opportunity to use his pen
and his fortune to overthrow despotism. They would found a
society, they would restore liberty to France, they would bind
each other by the strongest oaths, they would seal the project
with their blood.

Full of confidence in these promises Brissot immediately began to put his plans into operation. The first step was to provide for coöperation in Switzerland, and he accordingly set out

[1] D'Argental, Charles Augustus de Ferrol, comte, was born in 1700 and died
in 1788. He was a diplomat and man of letters and was chiefly known as a lifelong friend of Voltaire.

[2] La Harpe, Jean François de, was born in 1739 and died in 1803. He was
celebrated for his dramatic and literary criticism in the *Mercure* and for his lectures on literature.

[3] Genlis, Stéphanie Félicité du Crest de Saint-Aubin, comtesse de, born in
1746, died in 1830. At an extremely early age she showed great versatility. At
the age of sixteen she married De Genlis, who afterward became the Marquis
de Sillery, and, through her husband's connection with the house of Orléans,
she came to be charged with the education of the children of the Duke of
Chartres. With all her other natural endowments Madame de Genlis had the
gift of being a successful teacher, and carried on her work with originality
and great success. Having accompanied Madame Adelaide to England, she
was proscribed as an *émigrée*, but subsequently was allowed to return to
France.

[4] *Mémoires*, I, 240–41. Élie de Beaumont was a lawyer of some reputation,
chiefly known for his memoir on the Calas case.

for Neuchâtel.[1] But while on the way he received news from Geneva which changed his plans. A civil war had broken out in that city between the aristocratic and democratic factions, — a war complicated by the interference of the French on the side of the aristocratic party. It was now reported that the combined enemies of France — Berne and Savoy — were about to besiege the city, whereupon Brissot, getting excited by the chance of actually seeing a people in active revolt, set off posthaste for Geneva, only fearing that he might not get there before the siege should begin. He had been urged to come by D'Ivernais, the Swiss politician and economist,[2] who gave him a warm welcome and introduced him to the leaders of the popular party, among whom were Duroveray[3] and Clavière.[4] He was deeply impressed by the bravery of the people, and their efforts to gain their political sovereignty, and before he had been in the city forty-eight hours he had prepared an address to "its intrepid inhabitants to encourage them to a vigorous defense."[5] The lasting results of this experience upon Brissot were an account which he wrote shortly afterward, under the title of *Le Philadelphien à Genève,*[6] a lifelong enmity with Mallet du Pan,[7] and a lifelong friendship with Clavière.[8]

On his return to Paris he was quietly married, on the 17th of

---

[1] *Mémoires*, i, 244.

[2] *Ibid.*, i, 269. D'Ivernais, Sir Francis de, a Genevese politician and economist, born in 1757, died in 1842. He was exiled from Geneva in 1782 and went to England. At the time of the fall of Napoleon he returned and represented Geneva at the Congress of Vienna.

[3] Duroveray took a prominent part in the affairs of Geneva and drew up a code of laws for the city. He was afterward a friend and collaborator of Mirabeau.

[4] Clavière, Étienne, financier and politician, born in 1755, died in 1793. He wrote in collaboration with Mirabeau on financial subjects and became a lifelong friend of Brissot. He was made Minister of Finance under the first Girondin Ministry, and, after August 10, 1792, was one of the provisional executive council and from that time shared the fortunes of the Girondin party.

[5] *Mémoires*, i, 275.   [6] *Ibid.*, i, 271. Also see p. 25.

[7] See *Mallet du Pan and the French Revolution*, by Mallet, 50. Mallet du Pan, Jacques, born 1749, died 1800, was a Swiss publicist. He was connected with the *Mercure*, and in the Revolution espoused the royalist cause.

[8] *Mémoires*, i, 274.

September, 1782, to Félicité Dupont.[1] Félicité at this time was
employed under Madame de Genlis in the family of the Duke
of Orléans in the capacity of under-governess.[2] Until his establishment at London was well started, it did not seem best
for Félicité to accompany her husband, and partially with a
view to retaining her position in the mean time, the marriage
was kept a secret. Although Félicité had little influence on his
political life, in domestic life she never failed to be the good
comrade and helpful wife which her devotion in the days of her
engagement had promised. Moreover, in her family he found
the comradeship which he had missed in his own family circle,
and in her mother a real friend.[3]

The first proof of her friendship was to furnish him with
money for his new enterprise. For, although Villar and Beaumont were as voluble as ever in their promises of support, they
did not produce any ready money, and such funds as he had to
meet his immediate expenses were furnished by Madame Dupont.[4] The question of money aside, his undertaking was a decidedly presumptuous one for a young man, not yet thirty, who
was but little known in any part of the world, and particularly
in England. But with his usual sublime confidence in success
he set forth.

Aside from the outcome of the *Lycée*, his residence in England had two important results: it brought him into relations
with several discredited fellow countrymen which later turned
out to be most unfortunate, and, on the other hand, it gave
him the opportunity of meeting various Englishmen of note,
and of acquiring a knowledge of English political institutions.
Among these fellow countrymen of more or less unsavory reputation, Brissot made the acquaintance of an individual named
Pelleport, which was to cost him an accusation for writing a

[1] See record of the marriage in archives of the Department of the Seine.

[2] This connection was afterward made much of by Brissot's enemies, who
wanted to prove that he was devoted to the house of Orléans. See *Mémoires*,
II, 15.

[3] *Ibid.*, I, 300–01. For the character of Félicité and the details of their life,
see chap. XIII. [4] *Ibid.*, I, 300.

libel; of a certain Receveur, a spy in the employment of the French police, who, according to Brissot's account, was in part at least responsible for his imprisonment in the Bastille; and of the well-known libelist, Théveneau de Morande, to whom Brissot took a strong dislike and who afterwards became his bitter and persistent enemy.[1] His dislike for Morande was so intense that when the publicist, Swinton, his former employer,[2] offered him the position of manager of the *Courrier* on condition that Morande be his colleague, he refused the offer and broke with Swinton. According to the account which Brissot gives in his memoirs, his feeling was due to the extremely bad reputation of the latter as a libel writer,[3] but this explanation seems hardly adequate. A further and more satisfactory explanation is given by Pétion, who evidently obtained his information directly from Brissot, to the effect that certain articles had been inserted in the *Courrier* without his knowledge, articles which directly contradicted his principles, and for which he was made to appear responsible. The discovery that Morande was the author aroused his lasting hatred, and led to his refusal to have anything more to do with him. Whether or not this is the entire explanation, Morande in his wrath swore mortal hatred against Brissot, the result of which Brissot was later to know to his lasting sorrow.[4]

Meanwhile, through his journalistic work and his personal efforts he was making a number of more creditable acquaintances among people of note, among whom were Kirwan the chemist; Maty the scientist; Fanny Burney the novelist, whom he greatly admired; and Mrs. Macaulay the political pamphleteer and historian, with whose radical views he was already in sympathy.[5] He also met Priestly, Price, Mansfield, Gibbon,

---

[1] *Mémoires*, I, 318.   [2] See p. 14.   [3] *Mémoires*, I, 314, 317.

[4] Pétion, *Notice sur Brissot*, in Vatel, *Charlotte Corday et les Girondins*, II, 227.

[5] *Mémoires*, I, 349–59. Perroud suggests that these references to his acquaintances in London may have been drawn from the periodicals which Brissot published at this time, and that they did not form part of his actual memoirs. *Ibid.*, I, 354, note.

John Adams, David Williams, and Jeremy Bentham. The last
two he especially admired. "Williams," he declared, "of all
the Englishmen of letters seems to me the one who has the
most universal philosophy, who is the most free from all national prejudices." With Bentham he was on terms of some
intimacy, corresponded with him, and went frequently to see
him.[1] With such acquaintances he had unusual opportunities
for studying at first hand English political conditions.

In the midst of these manifold interests Brissot also found
time to publish a criticism of St. Paul, called *Lettres philosophiques sur Saint Paul*, and to complete *Le Philadelphien à
Genève*, the work inspired by his sojourn at Geneva during the
revolution.[2] Meantime he began to find the separation from
his wife insupportable, and in the summer of 1783 he sent for
her to join him in London.[3]

All this time he was struggling to put the *Lycée* on a firm
footing. The original promoters having left him in the lurch,[4]
money for the enterprise was finally furnished by a man named
Desforges, whom he had first met at Mentelle's.[5] According to
Brissot's own account, — with which, however, Desforges does
not agree, — it was Desforges who took the initiative and
eagerly pressed funds upon him, while Brissot himself, doubting
whether Desforges was capable of appreciating the noble motives which actuated him in the enterprise, hesitated. Brissot
further declares that from the first moment of his acquaintance with Desforges he was suspicious of him, though this may
be a case of being a "prophet after the fact." At all events,
they came to an understanding. It was agreed that Desforges
was to furnish fifteen thousand francs, of which, however, he
paid down only ten or twelve thousand, and a contract was

---

[1] *Mémoires*, i, 364–66. See also letters of Brissot to Bentham. *Correspondance*, 58, 59, 64. Later during the course of the Revolution Brissot was instrumental in getting the Legislative Assembly to declare both Williams and Bentham French citizens (*Moniteur*, August 28, 1792), and in having Williams
invited to come over to France to aid the committee of the Convention which
was engaged in drawing up a constitution. See also *Correspondance*, 305–06.

[2] See p. 22.   [3] See p. 390.   [4] See p. 391.   [5] *Mémoires*, i, 235–36.

drawn up, in which it was stipulated that the *Lycée* was to be continued for at least seven years, and was to consist of three branches, an assembly, a correspondence, and a journal of the arts and sciences in England.[1] But this "universal confederation" of the friends of liberty and of truth, as Brissot called it, was a complete failure. He had already printed a couple of volumes of the *Correspondance*, but the publisher absorbed all the profits of the edition printed in Germany, and not a single copy was allowed to enter France.[2]

He now announced the journal or magazine which was to be entitled *Tableau exact des sciences et des arts en Angleterre*, but unfortunately he scorned all the ordinary means of making a journal attractive, and too frankly announced that its one object was to be useful.[3] The newspapers did not mention the prospectus, and very few persons paid any attention to it. He was still hopeful, however, and in a vain attempt to attract subscribers he prepared a *Tableau des Indes*, which he distributed gratis to the few who did support the establishment. It remained to provide a place for the meetings of the society. The house where he was living contained no room sufficiently large for the purpose, but his friend David Williams offered to share with him the hall where he himself was then giving lectures. Unfortunately, however, Brissot had no money left with which to pay his share of the expense — nearly eight thousand livres. He accordingly applied to Desforges for the remainder of the fifteen thousand francs, which he had not yet paid, but to his consternation found him unwilling to pay.

Troubles now began to come thick and fast. He had no adequate means of providing for his family, recently increased by the birth of a son.[4] Desforges, who had arrived from France, proved at this juncture a most unwelcome guest. Moreover, Desforges was discontented with the lack of returns, and not only refused to furnish the remainder of the money promised, but requested a dissolution of the society, and loudly demanded the return of the money he had already invested; and to crown

[1] *Mémoires*, I, 339–42.   [2] *Ibid.*, I, 329.   [3] *Ibid.*, I, 339.   [4] *Ibid.*, I, 389–92.

Brissot's misfortunes, within a few days after the birth of his child, while his wife was still very ill, he was arrested at the instigation of his printer, and thrown into prison for debt. After a brief imprisonment, during which he suffered torturing anxiety lest his wife or child might die in his absence, he managed, through the help of friends and of Madame Dupont, to satisfy his creditors, and was released. But he was at the end of his resources in London, and, much as he hated to leave his wife, he had to set out for France at once, in order to try to raise funds.[1] As the climax to his misfortunes, shortly after his arrival in Paris, on July 12, 1784, he was arrested and thrown into the Bastille, charged with being implicated in the production of certain libels.[2] His first thought was for his wife, who, he feared, might not be able to survive the shock at hearing what had befallen him. In his distress he appealed to his mother-in-law. Madame Dupont was equal to the occasion. In order to forestall any possible reports which might reach her daughter, she refused to wait for the ordinary boat and risked crossing the Channel in a small launch. Though somewhat consoled by the presence of his mother-in-law with Félicité, he still feared the machinations of his enemies. His imprisonment he was sure was due to them — to the denunciations of Swinton, who had held Brissot's establishment responsible for loss of subscriptions to the *Courrier;* to Morande and Pelleport, who were in turn incited by Desforges, whose motive was to profit by Brissot's detention to settle to his own taste the affairs of the *Lycée.*[3]

Desforges had already accused Brissot of having swindled him, and had threatened, if he did not pay the sum demanded, to denounce him as a disseminator of libels. Meanwhile Brissot had accused Desforges of libel and of having insisted, in spite of strenuous objections, on taking up his abode in Brissot's house.[4] Desforges now carried out his threat and the result was two

---

[1] *Mémoires*, i, 391–95.
[2] *Ibid.*, ii, 5–7. See also Funck-Brentano, *Les Lettres de cachet à Paris*, 413.
[3] *Mémoires*, ii, 6–8.   [4] *Réplique de Théveneau de Morande*, 100–04.

suits; one in the civil, the other in the criminal courts. These suits were brought in 1784; and in 1791, when Brissot was a candidate for election to the Legislative Assembly, they were still pending.[1]

The whole affair was then raked up afresh by Théveneau de Morande.[2] He revived the charge made by Desforges and declared that it was true that Brissot had swindled Desforges out of fifteen thousand livres. Desforges was the dupe and the victim, he asserted. In the first place, Brissot had inveigled Desforges into investing his funds, and in order to do this he had deceived him as to the state of his own finances. In proof of this assertion Desforges adduced a letter of Brissot's, in which he declared that his father was worth two hundred thousand livres and that on his father's death he was sure to receive thirty thousand livres. Morande then put this letter in contrast with another letter of Brissot's, in which he admitted that he had nothing, and that he could count on nothing from his parents. Morande further declared that the *Lycée* never existed at all, that Brissot rented a house too small for the assembly which was to form so important a part of the *Lycée*,[3] and that he and his family lived at the expense of the society.[4] In substantiation of the last charge, Morande cited a statement from Brissot's accounts, in which the expenses of the society were set down in lump sums. As for the charge that Desforges had thrown himself upon Brissot's household, he had remained there only to prevent the sale of the furniture.[5]

In reply to these allegations Brissot declared that the anxiety to embark in the enterprise was all on the side of Desforges; that at first Desforges was ready to lend forty thousand livres, when he was asked for only ten thousand. The discrepancy in the two accounts of his prospects he explained by showing that one was written before, the other after, the death of his father.[6]

---

[1] Pétion, *Notice sur Brissot*, in Vatel, ii, 230–31, note.
[2] See p. 219.   [3] *Réplique de Théveneau de Morande.*
[4] *Ibid.*, 68; *Lettre aux électeurs*, 15.   [5] *Réplique*, 77, 94.
[6] Although in his memoirs the account of Brissot's connection with Des-

The charge that the *Lycée* never existed he met by declaring that it was agreed upon that the *Lycée* was to consist of three parts, and as two of the three — the *Correspondance*, and the *Journal* of arts and sciences — were established, the absence of the third —— the assembly — did not prove that the *Lycée* did not exist. As for his expenses, after having charged Desforges with juggling with the figures so as to convey a false impression, he produced an itemized account which very nearly covered the sum in question, and offered to show his receipts. That his family had lived at the expense of the society he absolutely denied.[1] He then accused Desforges of having libeled him, of having persisted in staying in his house during his imprisonment in the Bastille, and of having insulted his wife, mother-in-law, and sister-in-law.

The question is: In view of the evidence submitted on both sides, was or was not Brissot guilty of fraud? Of the charges there are two points on which he does not clear himself. The letter which he wrote to Desforges, setting forth his prospects, could hardly be justified, even on the plea of extreme optimism, since he was on bad terms with his father, and in any case was but one of a number of heirs. Again, his defense that the *Lycée* existed because the *Correspondance* and the *Journal* had been established, was in the nature of quibbling, since Morande had used the term *Lycée* to mean the assembly, which clearly did not exist. Moreover, there are two charges which he admits — that he did rent a house too small for the meetings of the assembly, though it served as an office; and that he furnished the house at the expense of the society.[2]

On the other hand, Brissot did succeed in showing that Desforges alone was to be responsible for the funds, and that, as he himself had contributed out of his own pocket, he was the creditor, not the debtor; that Desforges had refused arbitration and had approved his accounts.[3] It is also to be taken into

forges follows the account of the death of his father, there is nothing to show that he had not made his acquaintance before that time.

[1] *Réplique de Brissot.*   [2] *Ibid.*, 4–19.   [3] *Ibid.*, 4–8.

consideration that Desforges's side of the matter is presented by Théveneau de Morande, a professional libel writer.[1] Indeed, according to Vatel, Desforges tried to restrain Morande, and even disavowed some of his utterances.[2] And finally, if the arrangement was not a loan, but a partnership, as it had every appearance of being, and as it was evidently regarded, Desforges would have but doubtful claim to the money he had invested. That Brissot misused the money is probable, but that he deliberately planned to defraud Desforges is hardly credible.

That Desforges was directly responsible for Brissot's imprisonment in the Bastille is also a matter of doubt. The formal charge brought against him was that he had written libelous pamphlets against Marie Antoinette, and especially that he had had part in the production and circulation of a pamphlet entitled *Le Diable dans un bénitier*.[3] The latter did not concern

---

[1] In his early youth Morande was involved in various scandals and intrigues, which led to his imprisonment by *lettres de cachet*. On his release he fled to England; there he devoted himself to writing violent libels on various persons of prominence in France. His unexpected success suggested to him a new means of livelihood and he proceeded to engage in a system of blackmail. His most successful effort in this line was an infamous attack on Madame Du Barry, for the suppression of which he demanded a large sum from the French Court. He managed to foil the attempts of the police sent to arrest him, and as a last resource Louis XV entrusted the affair to Beaumarchais, who was obliged to pay Morande twenty thousand livres and a pension of four thousand livres for the suppression of the libel. Not long after this episode he was hired by Louis XVI as a police agent in England to suppress libels, evidently on the principle of "set a thief to catch a thief." During the Revolution he returned to France, where in 1791 he founded the *Argus patriote*, devoted to the interests of royalty, thus becoming the ally of the monarchy which, earlier in his career, he had insulted. See *Théveneau de Morande*, by Robiquet.

[2] Vatel, ii, 231, note.

[3] Brissot, *Réponse à tous les libellistes*, 40. See also *Mémoires*, i, 313–17; and Funck-Brentano, *Les Lettres de cachet à Paris*, 413. "Brissot de Warville (Jacques Pierre) avocat au Parlement. Entré le 12 juillet, 1784, sur ordre contresigné Breteuil. Pour libelles. Sorti le 10 septembre, 1784, sur ordre contresigné Breteuil." Also see Pétion, *Notice sur Brissot*, in Vatel, *Charlotte Corday et les Girondins*, ii, 228. "*Cette détention avait pour prétexte de prétendues liaisons avec un nommé belleport [sic], ce belleport avait publié à Londre un libelle infame contre la Reine de france et on voulut bien supposer que Brissot avait travaillé à ce libelle.*" Pétion evidently confuses here *Le Diable dans un bénitier* with the libels against the queen.

the queen, but was an arraignment of Receveur and Théveneau de Morande as spies of the French police and was afterward made much of by Morande in his attack on Brissot. The explanation given by Brissot was that Pelleport, in exasperation because Receveur had refused to pay the price demanded for a libel on Marie Antoinette which he (Pelleport) claimed to have in his possession, had published this satire, *Le Diable dans un bénitier*, against Receveur and Receveur's protégé Morande. But that he himself had any part, either in the libel on the queen or in the satire, Brissot indignantly denied. He asserted that, on the contrary, he had done his best to induce Pelleport to give up his traffic in libels and to suppress the satire.[1]

This explanation is in large part corroborated by certain reports at the *Ministère des affaires étrangères* at Paris. It seems that the affair of the libels against Marie Antoinette dated from the year before, and for some time Brissot's name figured in the reports of the police spies on the matter.[2] He was suspected of being the joint author,[3] and further was represented by Receveur in a report to Lenoir as the possible author also of some of the letters written by Pelleport in the course of his attempts to traffic with the Government.[4] Lenoir, however, was not inclined to put much faith in Receveur's suspicions.

[1] *Mémoires*, i, 321; also *Réplique*, 26. According to Robiquet (*Théveneau de Morande*, 64) the authorship of *Le Diable dans un bénitier* has never been definitely fixed and has even been attributed to Morande himself. At all events, the whole matter is of interest as throwing light on the police spy system of the Old Régime. Receveur and Morande, both men of more than doubtful reputation, and the latter himself a libelist, were hired by the French Government to find the sources of certain libels against the queen and to pay for their suppression. Brissot's statement that Receveur refused to pay Pelleport five hundred louis, seems probable in view of Robiquet's statement that Receveur had only two hundred guineas with which to make the purchase. See Receveur's own statement in his report to the French Ambassador, of May 22, 1783. (*Aff. étrangères, Angleterre*, 542, f. 278.) In the same report Receveur speaks of Pelleport having showed to Brissot this libel against the queen.

[2] See *Aff. étrangères, Angleterre*, 542, f. 278.

[3] See *Note faite à la hâte*, April 21, 1783. *Aff. étrangères, Angleterre*, 542, f. 79.

[4] *Lenoir au Comte de Vergennes*, May 4, 1783. *Aff. étrangères, Angleterre*, 542, f. 180. Also *Compte rendu par Receveur*, May 22, 1783, 542, f. 278.

Because Brissot was acquainted with various refugees, Lenoir declared, Receveur had jumped to the conclusion that Brissot was also a refugee. Receveur's suspicions, moreover, were perhaps quickened by the personal grudge which he bore against him. At all events, the affair blew over so far as Brissot was concerned till it was again brought up against him as a reason for his imprisonment in the Bastille.

As for *Le Diable dans un bénitier*, the whole evidence against Brissot consisted, first, in a certificate by a printer's assistant to the effect that Brissot had corrected the proofs of *Le Diable*, and second, in a letter written by a man named Vingtain, in which arrangements were referred to for the distribution of the pamphlet.[1] In answer, Brissot adduced a report of the matter made by the Minister Breteuil in which the certificate that Brissot had corrected the proofs was stated to be of doubtful value.[2] The other piece of evidence Brissot apparently did not try to disprove. Moreover, it is to be remembered that he cordially disliked both Morande and Receveur. It seems not improbable, therefore, that he was guilty of having assisted in the circulation of the pamphlet. Nor is it to be wondered at considering that they in turn cordially disliked him, that they may have had something to do with instigating his arrest.

But whether guilty or not, two months, which seemed to him two centuries, passed before he could obtain his release. All this time his family and friends — the number of whom was a tribute to the interest he had inspired — were exerting their utmost efforts in his behalf. Loyseau, the distinguished jurist, wrote to an influential woman of his acquaintance, asking her in turn to get the Prince de Conti [3] to write to the commandant, Delaunay; Mentelle urged Madame Genlis-Sillery to work through the Duke of Chartres, while various literary men, both in England and France, including Condorcet, Bernardin de

[1] *Réplique de Théveneau de Morande*, 58, 106.

[2] *Réponse de Brissot*, 19-20.

[3] Prince de Conti, Louis François Joseph, a member of the famous house of Conti, was born in 1734 and died in 1814, an ardent royalist and supporter of monarchy.

Saint-Pierre, Kirwan, Priestly, and Lord Mansfield, took up his cause and proclaimed their belief in his innocence.[1] Most of all his release was due, so he felt, to the efforts of his wife, who moved heaven and earth to secure it. The authorities, however, made what seemed to Brissot a hard condition, — he had to promise to give up his *Lycée*.[2] It is a significant fact that in enumerating those who aided him, Brissot omits altogether to mention the help received from the Duke of Chartres, afterward the Duke of Orléans,[3] and that he minimizes the help of Madame Genlis-Sillery,[4] and denies that he ever had any subsequent relations with her.[5] This is not to be wondered at, considering that one of the charges for which, at the time he wrote his memoirs, he was in prison and under sentence of death, was of adherence to the house of Orléans.

On his release from the Bastille, September 10, 1784,[6] Brissot found his finances in desperate condition, and was only saved from complete bankruptcy by the generosity of Clavière and of his mother-in-law.[7] For a time, at least, there were to be no more schemes for *Lycées* nor "universal confederations." He had all that he could do and more to provide for his family, soon to be increased by the birth of a second child.[8] He and

[1] *Mémoires*, ii, 10.

[2] *Ibid.*, ii, 24. See also *Biographical Dictionary*, ii, 9. Why this should be a hard condition, when the *Lycée* had already failed, is not clear. See further Brissot's account in his *Réponse à tous les libellistes*, 20.

[4] Charpentier, *La Bastille devoilée*, i, troisième livraison, 78 .

[3] See the account of the matter given by Madame Genlis-Sillery herself.

[5] According to her story she did help him subsequently to get employment in the household of the Duke of Orléans, but says that before his incarceration in the Bastille she had never even heard of him. In other particulars, too, her account contradicts Brissot's memoirs; for instance, she makes his imprisonment antedate his marriage. Her story is evidently not to be relied upon.

[6] Funck-Brentano, *Les Lettres de cachet*, 413.   [7] *Mémoires*, ii, 24.

[8] See *Archives nationales, F 1a 1570, 9 floréal, an IV*. Among the Roland papers at the *Bibliothèque Nationale* (n. ac. fr. mss. 9534, fol. 328) is a rough draft of a letter written three weeks after the birth of his child, asking for some sort of an appointment which would enable him to go to America. M. Perroud, in his *Notice sur la Vie de Brissot* (p. xl), in the *Correspondance* calls attention to the revelation contained in the letter of "*une vraie détresse morale et même matérielle, car, dans un coin du papier on trouve un compte de 'dépense pour la couche' s'élevant à la somme de six livres, six sols* [*sic*]."

Félicité lived with the greatest frugality, but in spite of rigid economy and unremitting industry, he had frequently to borrow from his friends.[1] His best friend seems to have been Clavière, who lent him money, took him into his house, and helped him out in difficulties.

While struggling with his own personal finances he began to write on financial subjects for Mirabeau. He had already had some correspondence with Mirabeau on behalf of the English Ambassador at Copenhagen,[2] and he was now brought into closer relations with him through Clavière. The latter was one of the men whose pen Mirabeau knew so well how to use for his own advantage, and Brissot was soon induced to lend his assistance. He and Clavière worked together on the *Caisse d'escompte*, which was published under Mirabeau's name.[3] They also wrote the *Banque de Saint Charles*, which they intended to publish themselves, and which was in fact out of the press when they were prevailed upon by Mirabeau to turn it over to him. Mirabeau had been asked to furnish such a work by Calonne, and promptly availed himself of this opportunity. According to Brissot,[4] Clavière paid the expenses and Mirabeau pocketed the profits. Brissot was probably mistaken in this, however.[5]

---

[1] "*Il étoit impossible d'être plus simple dans sa parure d'avoir des appartemens moins recherchés d'avoir une table plus frugal et de faire enfin moins de dépenses ; sa femme étoit également la simplicité même une excellente mère de famille uniquement occupée de ses enfans. Souvent brissot [sic] n'avoit pas six francs dans sa poche, il étoit obligé de faire à chaque instant de petits emprunts à ses amis et cet état de médiocrité a toujours existé pour lui cependant il ne dépensoit jamais un sou à ses plaisirs cependant personne ne travailloit plus que lui.*" Pétion, *Notice sur Brissot*, in Vatel, ii, 231–32.

[2] *Mémoires*, ii, 28–32.

[3] *Ibid.*, ii, 31. This statement throws light on Mirabeau's assertion that the work was written within four days after it was promised to Calonne, and published eight days after. Loménie, *Les Mirabeau*, iii, 630.

[4] *Mémoires*, ii, 31. Mirabeau, however, declared that he did not receive any money from Calonne. Loménie, iii, 633.

[5] The following letter tends to strengthen Mirabeau's assertion that Brissot was paid. The original is in the collection of the late M. Paul Arbaud, of Aix, in Provence, and for a copy of it the writer is indebted to Professor Fred Morrow Fling, of the University of Nebraska: "*Lettre de M. le Comte de Mirabeau à M.*

With the free-and-easy fashion with which Mirabeau took the credit of the work of other people, Brissot professed to be much shocked. Nevertheless, he himself did not seem to have very rigid ideas of the rights of authors, for, apparently without any thought of impropriety, he proceeded to have printed a manuscript bearing the name of Turgot, which had fallen into his hands, and which bore the title of *Plan des administrations provinciales*, whereupon Mirabeau, for some reason, which was not clear at the time, became very angry and threatened Brissot with a *lettre de cachet*. Later the reason became apparent. It seems that Mirabeau, who had previously had possession of the manuscript, had already sold it to Calonne as his own work.[1] Although Brissot had given the supposed author full credit and so had not been guilty of Mirabeau's sin of plagiarism, his action offered Mirabeau a point of attack. It was most unbecoming, he declared, for a man of his lofty principles not to recognize the sacred rights of property.[2] This accusation Brissot denied. He reminded Mirabeau that the author had been dead several years and that he himself had published the manuscript in the full persuasion that there was no one who had a right to claim it.[3]

le Cont*le* G*nl*. Paris, 30 Mai, 1785. Monsieur: J'attens vos ordres; la première ébauche de mon travail est faite et n'exige même plus que quelques notes, les dernières touches de l'écrivain et votre approbation. J'ai cru qu'il ne fallait pas un panflct qu'on ne lit point, mais un ouvrage (ex professo); et quoique fait trop vite, pour être bien rédigé, celui-ci contiendra au moins des principes sains et les faits principaux avec leurs conséquences naturelles. J'ai l'honneur de vous addresser la note des déboursés de l'édition que vous m'avez chargé de faire arrêter, tel que M. Brissot de Warville me la fait remettre et voila pourquoi le costume de cette note est si peu décent; c'est à lui ou à M. Clavière que vous voulez bien en faire remettre le montant, ce détail m'étant absolument étranger. Je crois l'ouvrage St. Charles très pressé; ainsi j'ose solliciter la faveur d'une prompte audience."

[1] The plan, although bearing the name of Turgot, was written, in part at least, by Dupont de Nemours-Loménie, *Les Mirabeau*, IV, 87. Brissot discovered the fact later. Calonne, it seems, showed the manuscript to Dupont, who "*lui apprit que ce manuscrit sur les Administrations provinciales n'appartenait même pas en entier à Turgot, et que c'etait lui qui en avait composé autrefois le plan pour le ministre.*" Brissot, *Mémoires*, II, 37.

[2] See the *Correspondance*, 94–95.

[3] As a governmental decree of August 30, 1778, gave the control of a man's manuscript after his death to his heirs, Brissot was legally in the wrong.

In spite of this quarrel, Brissot seems to have fallen again under the spell of Mirabeau's charms. At all events, he admired "his hatred of despotism and the courage with which he attacked it when he found it." At this time Mirabeau was planning to publish a paper with the innocuous title of *Analyse des papiers anglais*, in which he proposed to set before the French people certain truths which would not be welcome to the French Government, but unfortunately he was not any too familiar with the English language or with the state of England. Brissot could not resist this temptation and of his own accord offered his services to Mirabeau. But the views which Brissot expressed in his articles on the trial of Warren Hastings, and the situation of the English in the East Indies, led to disputes between Mirabeau and Mallet du Pan. In these disputes Brissot, who had already come into collision with Mallet on account of their opposing views on the Genevan revolution, took a not unwilling part — in some cases writing letters to Mallet which were published under Mirabeau's name.[1]

Meanwhile Brissot continued writing on his own account, and in the course of the four years from his release from the Bastille to his departure for America, published a considerable number of works. His three aims were to popularize knowledge, to attack abuses, and to further reform. To this end he continued the publication of the *Bibliothèque philosophique*,[2] and brought out his attack on canon law, *L'Autorité législative de Rome anéantie*, written some years before;[3] translated Mackintosh's *Travels in Europe, Asia and Africa;*[4] and published, besides, two letters to the Emperor Joseph II, on emigration and punishment for crime,[5] a criticism of the travels in America by the Marquis de Chastellux,[6] an attack on a new plan for an in-

[1] *Mémoires*, ii, 38.   [2] See p. 20.   [3] See p. 41.

[4] *Voyage en Europe, en Asie, et en Afrique.* 2 vols., London, 1786.

[5] *Un Défenseur du peuple à l'Empereur Joseph II, sur son réglement concernant l'émigration, ses diverses réformes*, etc. Dublin, 1785. And *Lettre à l'empereur sur l'atrocité des supplices qu'il a substitués comme adoucissement à la peine de mort. Bruxelles, aôut, 1787.*

[6] *Examen critique des voyages dans l'Amérique septentrionale de M. le Marquis de Chastellux.* London, 1786.

surance company,[1] and a denunciation of a threatened proposal of bankruptcy.[2] He also, with the assistance of his wife, translated a *History of England in a series of letters from a nobleman to his son;*[3] and in collaboration with Clavière, wrote what was up to this time his most important production, *De la France et des États Unis.*[4] The ostensible object of this work was solely to promote commercial and political relations between France and the United States; its real purpose was, further, to present so attractive a picture of the future prosperity of the Americans that his fellow countrymen would be tempted to imitate their conduct and to recover their own liberty.[5] But Brissot was never content with merely writing in the interests of reform; he must also be organizing. With the two objects in view just stated he now projected an organization to be called the *Société Gallo-Américaine*, but it seems never to have been carried out.[6]

In the midst of all this literary work Brissot somehow found time to take an interest in the discoveries which were being made in so-called animal magnetism. Learning that Bergasse was the chief exponent of these studies, he hastened to make his acquaintance and even wrote a pamphlet on the subject himself, *Un mot aux académiciens*, in which he told them in no flattering terms what he thought of them for their scorn of Bergasse's discoveries.[7]

[1] *Dénonciation au public d'un nouveau projet d'agiotage*, London, 1786, and *Seconde Lettre contre la compagnie d'assurance*, London, 1786.

[2] *Point de banqueroute ou Lettres à un créancier de l'état, sur l'impossibilité de la banqueroute nationale et sur les moyens de ramener la crédit et la paix*. Londres, 1787. See p. 39. The publication of this work brought upon Brissot a *lettre de cachet*, to escape the consequences of which he was obliged to flee to England. He soon returned to France. *Mémoires*, ii, 69.

[3] Published under the title of *Lettres philosophiques et politiques, sur l'histoire de l'Angleterre dépuis son origine jusqu'à nos jours. Traduis de l'anglais.* 2 vols. London, 1786.

[4] See p. 48.   [5] *Mémoires*, ii, 52.   [6] See p. 61.

[7] *Mémoires*, ii, 53. Bergasse, Nicholas, lawyer and politician, was born in 1750. He became known for his researches in animal magnetism, and later for his connection with the celebrated suit of Korman. In pleading the case of Korman against his wife, he attacked ministerial despotism and came into conflict with Beaumarchais who defended Korman's wife. Elected to the States-General he presented a draft of a constitution, but on its rejection retired in

He was delighted to find that Bergasse too was interested in political reform, and like himself was secretly working for it. "The time has arrived," Brissot quoted Bergasse as saying to him, "when France has need of a revolution. But to work openly for it is to fail; to succeed some mystery is necessary; men must be brought together under pretext of physical experiments, but in reality for the purpose of overthrowing despotism."[1] Brissot was also delighted to take part in these gatherings. They were held at the house of Korman,[2] which appears to have been a regular foyer of revolution.[3] According to Brissot's own account in his memoirs, he was the only one who preached there an out-and-out republicanism.[4] It is to be remembered, however, that at the time he wrote the memoirs it was to his advantage to appear to have been a republican at as early a date as possible.

Just at this juncture an unexpected chance was offered to Brissot to engage in practical work in philanthropy and reform. The Duke of Orléans, who had recently succeeded to the head of the house, determined for his own ends to encourage a spirit of political agitation and criticism. As a man known to represent this spirit Brissot was invited by the Marquis Du Crest, whom the Duke of Orléans had put in charge of the undertaking, to enter his service. That the opportunity came through his own reputation, and not as a result of Madame Brissot's early connection with the house of Orléans, Brissot was careful to emphasize.[5] He hesitated for a moment about accepting the offer, fearing that it might involve some loss of independence, but at the same time he felt that here under the guise of philanthropic effort was a glorious opportunity to make the palace of Orléans a center of revolutionary ideas, and to share in helping

disgust. His name was associated with Brissot's in the prospectus of the *Société Gallo-Américaine*. See p. 61.

[1] *Mémoires*, ii, 54.

[2] Korman, known for his suit against his wife, which became celebrated through the connection with it of Bergasse on one side and Beaumarchais on the other.

[3] *Mémoires*, ii, 56.   [4] *Ibid.*, ii, 54.

[5] *Ibid.*, ii, 14; also *Biographical anecdotes*, ii, 9.

to restore liberty to France. He accordingly accepted the offer, at a salary which was uncomfortably small, though he refused to add to it by any underhand means or even by ways usually considered legitimate.

To this enterprise Brissot not only devoted himself with ardor but enlisted the help of his friends. The Rolands assisted to found a *Maison philanthropique* at Villefranche.[1] Brissot's friend, Blot, became secretary of a similar institution at Lyons, and Pétion worked to found a third at Chartres. Meanwhile, he seems to have been laying plans for reform of a large and constructive order. Du Crest, it appears, was ready to denounce the existing ministry to the king, but Brissot assured him he must do more; that if he wanted both reform and glory, he must identify his cause and that of the house of Orléans with that of the people. He then proceeded to sketch a bold and comprehensive plan of procedure. They must form a party which should demand radical reform, and this party must find its support in the Parlement, which, in turn, must make every effort to gain popular support.[2]

These plans, however, were not carried out, and Brissot soon severed his connection with the house of Orléans. The immediate occasion of his withdrawal seems to have been a *lettre de cachet* with which he was threatened on account of his pamphlets on bankruptcy.[3] About this time, and perhaps because of the desirability of absence from France, he made a brief visit to England. Before leaving the service of the Duke of Orléans he had visited Holland also, just at the height of the republican rising against the stadtholder. Thus for a second time Brissot had the opportunity of seeing a people actually in revolt.[4]

[1] *Lettres de Madame Roland*, ed. by Perroud, ii, 730–31.

[2] *Correspondance*, 139, 160.

[3] The *lettre de cachet* was doubtless occasioned in part by the suspicion with which he was regarded as being connected with the schemes of the house of Orléans. See *Notice sur la vie de Brissot* by Perroud in the *Correspondance*, p. xlv. Pétion does not connect the severing of his connection with the house of Orléans with this *lettre de cachet*, but says it was due to his independence of spirit. *Notice* in Vatel, ii, 232.

[4] See Perroud, *Notice* in the *Correspondance*, p. xliv; also Brissot, *Mémoires*,

He now threw himself into another kind of reform. He had become deeply interested in the agitation, especially in England, against the slave trade, and, unmindful of his former failures in philanthropic schemes, proceeded to establish a society called the *Amis des Noirs*, whose object, as the name implies, was to work in behalf of the negro. The importance of this society, and of Brissot's influence in connection with it, demands treatment at some length, but the story can best be told in connection with Brissot's career during the Revolution, when the society was most prominently before the public.[1]

Meanwhile he had become so discouraged by the slowness of reform in France, that he began to think of the possibility of emigrating to America. The desire to obtain information on the state of the negro in America, and also to investigate that country as a possible place of residence for himself and his family, made him eager to undertake a journey to the new world. An opportunity soon presented itself. Some one was needed to carry on certain financial negotiations with the United States. Brissot was chosen, and in the spring of 1788 he set out.[2] He was still in the United States, at the close of 1788, when the news from France suddenly brought him to the realization that a revolution might be really at hand. A man who all his life had been working to bring about a revolution, was not going to miss the chance of being an active participant in it, and with all possible haste he hurried back to France.

II, 67. In his *Réponse* Brissot says that he fled to Holland on account of the threatened *lettre de cachet* and thence to England, but from his *Mémoires* it would appear that his trip to England antedated the *lettre de cachet*.

[1] See chap. VIII.

[2] For the story of these travels and of their subsequent influence on Brissot's career, see chap. IV.

CHAPTER III

THE external facts of Brissot's early life have been presented.
They show in some measure his ideals and aims and interests,
but the picture needs to be completed by a portrait of the man
as seen in his writings. During the fifteen years from 1774 to
1789, which were devoted in large part to literary work, he produced an enormous amount and on a great variety of subjects
from the customs of ancient India to the "search for truth."
All this work in its anti-Christian tendency, its emphasis on
natural rights, its gospel of humanitarianism and political reform, was typical of eighteenth-century thought. Moreover,
it throws light on Brissot's personal characteristics, plainly
revealing in the youth the father of the maturer man, and
forecasts the part which he was to play in the Revolution.

Brissot was at the same time the disciple of Voltaire, of
Rousseau, and of Montesquieu. The influence of Voltaire was
perhaps the least, but it is unmistakable in the general attitude and trenchant tone of his earlier works *L'Autorité législative de Rome anéantie* [1] and *Lettres philosophiques sur Saint
Paul*. The former was an attack on canon law. The whole system, Brissot declared, rested on an extremely shaky foundation.
The Holy Scriptures contained but little material on dogma or
discipline, the decisions of the councils were not infallible, the
decrees of the Popes had, in many cases, proved to be only a
tissue of falsehood, and the authority of the writings of the
church fathers was more than doubtful. And then, coming
nearer home, French canon law was drawn from sources which
were either uncertain or corrupt. In his *Lettres philosophiques
sur Saint Paul* he attacked the teachings even of Scripture.

[1] See p. 36.

The authority of his epistles was doubtful in the first place, and St. Paul himself was a dangerous fanatic, who deliberately invented stories of visions and miracles in order to gain power. His preaching, moreover, consisted of intolerant and harmful doctrines injurious both to the individual and to society. The doctrine of predestination Brissot held in special abhorrence. "The system of predestination," he declared, "destroys all noble ideas of courage and of patriotism; the soul plunged into a state of flabby inertia, expects everything from the hand of its God, favors on earth and salvation in heaven. This doctrine is therefore pernicious and enervating to society, in that it destroys all its energy; cruel to man, in that it makes him a mere slave; outrageous to the Supreme Being in that it makes him a capricious tyrant. St. Paul is, then, a dangerous dreamer, whose opinions ought to be proscribed." [1] Not only was St. Paul entirely wrong, but Christianity itself had done much harm. It was inevitable that it should work mischief, he asserted, because it was "contrary to the passions which nature has graven on the soul of man." Nature speaks with imperative command and legislators should take warning and deal much more leniently with those alleged crimes or vices, such as prostitution, adultery, and bigamy, which have their root in natural instincts.

Here Brissot was moved not so much by the rationalism of Voltaire as by the sentimentalism of Rousseau. He further held Rousseau's belief in man's natural goodness, or at least in his capacity for goodness, and in this belief he saw a further objection to predestination with its assumption of man's natural depravity. In language which was the very echo of Rousseau, he declared: "Man is naturally good, or at least he is born indifferent alike to vice and to virtue. Guide his steps in childhood by good example, by habits of justice, of social responsibility, of equality, and he will become just and upright." [2]

---

[1] *Lettres philosophiques sur Saint Paul*, 105–06. Had Brissot forgotten the Puritans?

[2] *Lettre à Barnave*, 61.

In his love of physical, as well as of human nature Brissot was also influenced by Rousseau. He was an indefatigable reader of Rousseau, especially of his *Confessions*, which he had read at least six times, and he was always quoting from his writings. Like Rousseau, he discoursed at length on the joys of solitude, and like him too, he was moved almost to tears by the beauty of a rustic life. But Brissot's assertion that they were much alike, not only in tastes but also in character, is amusing, considering that they represented the most divergent possible types, and proves either that Brissot did not understand Rousseau or that he did not understand himself.[1] But influenced he certainly was by Rousseau, and that influence is perhaps chiefly seen in his constant reference to a state of nature. In his work *Recherches philosophiques sur la propriété et le vol*, he undertook to show that in a state of nature there was no such thing as theft.[2] His argument was as follows: Everything is in movement; there can be no improvement without action; all action presupposes the application of one body upon another, and all such application means friction and hence destruction. Destruction, then, is the necessary consequence of movement; all things, therefore, are bound to destroy each other; and property is the right which one body has of destroying another body in order to preserve itself. But to preserve itself the body must satisfy its needs. The satisfaction of needs, then, is the end and cause of property. The right of property may be exercised upon animals as well as upon vegetables, and even upon man. There are no classes in nature. Each may live on his own species, if necessary. But as the cause of property is need, so the limit of property is the extinction of need. Hence there can be no exclusive property in a state of nature, neither can there be theft. The word "property" is erased from her code. She no more authorizes man to the exclusive enjoyment of the land than of air, or fire, or water.[3]

---

[1] *Mémoires*, I, 18–24, 249.
[2] See Goupil, *La Propriété selon Brissot de Warville*.
[3] *Recherches philosophiques*, in *Bib. phil.*, VI, 323.

After having stated these somewhat radical views, Brissot goes on to consider property in society. This kind of property, he declares, "has borrowed the features of property in a state of nature, and under this imposing mask has known how to secure for itself a veneration which it does not deserve, and defenders blinded by the desire for exclusive possession. It is this alleged property which is claimed by the rich financier who has constructed superb palaces at the expense of the public funds; by the greedy prelate who swims in opulence; by the lazy man of the middle class, who takes his ease while the day laborer is suffering. It is this alleged property which is claimed by that *seigneur* who, jealous of his rights, shuts his gates and closes his park and his gardens. . . . It is this property which has created locks and bolts and a thousand other inventions which separate man from his fellows and isolate him, and which protect the alleged right of exclusive possession, the curse of natural rights. The characteristic of property in a state of nature is that it is universal, while property in society is individual, special. People ascribe to these two things — property in nature and property in society — the same origin and the same attributes, but they are absolutely different." [1]

The doctrines and the conclusions to which these views inevitably pointed were sufficiently startling to evoke bitter criticism, of which Brissot apparently never heard the end. It certainly was not difficult to find in them a defense of cannibalism and a direct attack on property. When, therefore, early in 1792, the question of property rights was under discussion,[2] his enemies made haste to confront him with these early utterances. In defense he declared that he had not meant his statements to apply to organized society, and cited various passages from this and other early works in substantiation of this contention. It was indeed true that Brissot, like Rousseau, was frequently inconsistent; and like Rousseau too, frankly admitted the impossibility of the logical carrying out of his ideas.

[1] *Recherches philosophiques*, in *Bib. phil.*, vi, 323–24.
[2] The question of rights of property in negroes was involved. See p. 266.

For instance, in this very essay on property and theft in which he had savagely attacked property, Brissot says almost in the same breath that property must be protected; in the essay on the *Moyens d'adoucir en France la rigueur des lois pénales* he speaks with a sigh of regret of a proposition to distribute riches in a just proportion among all the citizens as a dream of the golden age, and in *Le Sang innocent vengé* he declares that the triple basis of the social contract is formed by liberty, security, and property.

But it was rather with the practical betterment of existing society than with theories concerning the state of nature that Brissot was chiefly concerned. He was imbued, not merely with the sentimentalism but with the humanitarian spirit of the age. Voltaire and Beccaria, Montesquieu and Filangieri, were pleading for a wider toleration, a milder penal system, and a more reasonable legal code. To this company Brissot joined his voice: "To better the penal legislation of all the peoples of Europe" was his somewhat comprehensive aim,[1] and it was to this end that he wrote treatises, compiled dictionaries, and founded societies. His fundamental premise, which, however, far from being original with him, was common to most of the humanitarians of the time, was that crime was in large measure a disease, the result of ignorance, oppression, and poverty. To imagine, therefore, that it could be lessened by severe and cruel punishments was sheer folly.[2]

The only effective way was to get at the root of the difficulty and to remove the causes of crime — in other words, make people happy and crime would almost disappear of itself. The particular means by which people were to be made happy, Brissot continued, — and here he showed the evident influence of Montesquieu, — depended in some measure on climate,[3] but in general he advocated lowering the taxes, raising the moral standard, which in turn would be furthered by a

[1] *Bib. phil.*, Preface, i, iv.
[2] *Moyens de prévenir des crimes en France*, in *Bib. phil.*, vi, 3.
[3] *Théorie des lois criminelles*, i, 113.

reform of national education, the encouragement of arts and letters, the extirpation of begging, and the establishment of better police protection, — in short, more liberty and equality.[1]

But the process of education was slow and existing crime must be dealt with. Here Brissot pleaded for greater moderation. The motives of the criminal should be taken into account, and a crime committed through fear of death or because of hunger or distress should be treated with more leniency than crimes committed through other motives. Theft, for example, so often occasioned by want and even by actual starvation, was punished far too severely. "It is not the poor starving wretch," he declared, "who deserves to be punished; it is the rich man who is so barbarous as to refuse to help his fellow man in distress who is worthy of condemnation."[2] Moreover, the end of punishment must be borne in mind, to make reparation to society or to the individual wronged, to warn by example and to prevent the guilty from doing further injury.[3] Any punishment which fails to fulfill these ends was unjustifiable. This was true, he declared, of the punishment of death, which not only did not prevent crime, but instead, by familiarizing people with the shedding of blood, offered an example of cruelty, and, moreover, involved the possibility of a fearful mistake.[4] Forced labor would act as a better deterrent and at the same time be more useful to society. Torture and mutilation were almost as objectionable as the death penalty, and for much the same reasons.[5] In fact, the severity of punishment should be moderated and in all cases the punishment should fit the crime, both in proportion and in kind. Crimes against the state should be punished more severely than crimes against morality, because they injure the public welfare,[6] and in this connection crimes against the dominant religion should be pun-

---

[1] *Moyens d'adoucir la rigueur des lois pénales.*
[2] *Recherches philosophiques,* in *Bib. phil.,* VI, 334.
[3] *Moyens d'adoucir la rigueur des lois pénales,* 83.
[4] *Ibid.,* 75–83; and *Le Sang innocent vengé.*
[5] *Bib. phil.,* IV, 179–80.
[6] *Théorie des lois criminelles.*

ished as anti-patriotic.[1] The state, moreover, should exercise control over punishment meted out by the ecclesiastical authorities, such as excommunications and exemptions, in so far as they applied to the individual citizen.[2] Imprisonment for debt should be abolished, and many offenses against morality might well be left to the scourge of an enlightened public opinion.

There was crying need, Brissot argued further, of a radical change in the procedure of the criminal courts. Forced confession should be abolished, proof by direct witnesses and by experts should be better regulated, circumstantial evidence should be surrounded by greater safeguards, more publicity should somehow be secured, a fuller communication of the charges should be made to the accused at an earlier stage in the trial, and he should always be given a lawyer for his defense.[3] All this would tend to prevent the conviction of the innocent, but, if in spite of all reasonable precautions, an innocent person should be convicted, provision should be made for reparation.[4] Above all, the accused must be separated from the convicted, and even among the latter there must be some division, according to the nature of the crime.[5] Furthermore, the bar itself was in a state of decadence. This was due to the poor education of the would-be lawyer, the obscurity of the laws, the insufficient pecuniary rewards of the profession,[6] and the narrow-minded spirit which pervaded the entire body of advocates. In short, in order to reform penal legislation the legal profession must be reformed.[7]

If Brissot's ideas on penal legislation show the influence of the humanitarians, his ideas on economic principles show the

[1] *Moyens d'adoucir la rigueur des lois pénales*, 72–74.
[2] *Théorie des lois criminelles.*
[3] *Moyens d'adoucir la rigueur des lois pénales*, 94–112.
[4] *Le Sang innocent vengé.* This work was severely criticized in the *Mercure* of August 3, 1782.
[5] *Théorie des lois criminelles*, i, 180–86.
[6] *Un Indépendant à l'ordre des avocats sur la décadence du barreau en France.*
[7] *Point de banqueroute.*

influence of the physiocrats. Like them he declared that the sole source of riches was in the soil, and not in money brought into the country in payment of exports; and that to try to enrich the country by so restricting foreign trade that the exports might always be greater than the imports and the balance of commerce be in favor of the home country, was sheer futility. These ideas he developed at length in the work which he produced in collaboration with Clavière, *De la France et des États Unis.*

France and the United States have need of each other's products, he argued. The latter being a new country must first develop her agriculture, and meanwhile she must depend for her manufactured articles on Europe. England is quite alive to this situation, and is bestirring herself to develop commercial relations with the United States. France will lose her opportunity. She ought to act quickly, for she needs commerce with the United States in order to develop her marine, and at the same time she stands in need of those very raw materials of which the United States has an abundance. To this end, protective duties should be removed, or at least lowered.[1] There must be liberty, and it must be as complete as possible. Freedom of trade also meant to Brissot freedom of internal trade, and, above all, abolition of monopolies. He was especially anxious to have the government monopoly removed on tobacco and salt.[2] Monopoly, he declared, might enrich some few individuals, but it was destructive of national commerce.

Many other evils, too, from which France was suffering were due, he maintained, to inherent injustice in the government itself. Rather than provide charitable institutions for the poor, he cried, do away with privilege, and you will find that there is little need of such institutions. Equality is the imperative need. In this connection, France might well learn from England where there exist much better resources against injustice

---

[1] *De la France,* 293. See also *Journal du Lycée,* 13. For a fuller statement, see p. 64.

[2] *De la France,* 86.

and oppression than in France.[1] At the same time, Brissot was no blind admirer of England, and while he was continually trying to extend in France information about English institutions, he by no means refrained from criticizing their defects. He recognized, of course, the superiority of England over France in that the English people through their representative institutions had a part in the government; but he agreed with David Williams in declaring that England had lost much of her vaunted political liberty because, as a matter of actual fact, the people had no adequate method of controlling either the legislative or the executive branch of the government.[2]

But if Brissot was lukewarm in his approval of England, he was most enthusiastic in his admiration for the United States. In fact, there was hardly a chapter in any of his works in which he did not allude to the importance of following American example. It was not in the formless and obsolete institutions of England, he asserted again and again, but in the free institutions of the new republic across the water that a people seeking to recover its liberty might find the true model.[3] There was to be found liberty, equality, and the sovereignty of the people. The Americans had done well, he declared, to avoid following too closely the example of England in their constitutions; and to illustrate his meaning he compared, point by point, the new constitution of Pennsylvania with the corresponding English constitutional provisions, much to the advantage of the former. If the people of Pennsylvania only showed the same wisdom, he added, in working out their system of legislation, they would be doubly happy.[4] In his theories regarding government Brissot was greatly influenced by Montesquieu, and a further cause of his admiration for the United States was that he saw there

[1] *Moyens d'adoucir la rigueur des lois pénales*, 36, and *Dénonciation d'un nouveau projet d'agiotage*, 47.

[2] *Lettres sur la liberté politique.*

[3] "*Je vis qu'on devait prêcher, aux sociétés, non d'adopter la charte informe et presqu'effacée des Bretons, mais le modèle simple, puisé dans la nature par les Américains.*" *Réponse à tous les libellistes*, 22.

[4] *Bib. phil.*, III, 254–58.

that system of checks and balances so warmly advocated in Montesquieu's *L'Esprit des lois ;* [1] but above all, he admired the United States because it was democratic in spirit and republican in government. He was a thorough-going democrat, and was constantly preaching equality. "There can be a real sentiment of patriotism," he declared, "there can be real public welfare only when the individual of the lowest class is happy and free." [2] "Political nomenclature itself must be changed and the word *people* substituted for the Gothic and disgraceful term *third estate.*" [3] If complete equality were impractical under a monarchical form of government, he would have at least civil equality, that is to say, equality before the law.

But however fully Brissot might adjust himself to existing conditions, at heart he was a republican. If he had carried out his theories, he would not have had monarchy at all. "Nothing that was unjust could be good politically," he maintained, and the inevitable limitations of equality under a monarchy were not consistent with the fullest justice. It did not always seem to him wise to proclaim his conviction, but he was certainly bold enough in the defense of the alliance of France with the republican party in Holland, in opposition to the stadtholder,[4] and in his criticism of the systems of provincial administration proposed by Necker and by Turgot, he came out with great frankness. The title itself of the latter work was courageous, *Observations of a Republican*, and the views which he expressed therein did not belie the title. "Authority is everything, the people is nothing," he declared; "this is true of all monarchical governments."[5] Again: "The methods of a republican government cannot be harmonized with the spirit and customs of a monarchy." And finally he declared it his opinion — an opinion of some importance, in view of his later attitude — that Turgot, in attempting to

---

[1] *Le Philadelphien à Genère,* 174.
[2] *Bib. phil. Discours préliminaire,* I, xxxiv.
[3] *Point de banqueroute,* 31.   [4] *Ibid.,* 80.   [5] See p. 253.

make a constitution without changing the form itself of the government, had undertaken an impossibility.

But putting aside the question of the theoretically best government and accepting the existing monarchy, he was convinced that the reforms advocated by Necker and Turgot were not thorough-going enough even for the actual situation. Both these reforms, though differing in detail, provided for provincial assemblies which should have power to discuss and to oppose the taxes. Brissot particularly objected to the limitations put upon these assemblies in Necker's plan; namely, that they were to meet but rarely, remain in session only for a limited time, and not to correspond with each other. In view of these restrictions he declared that Necker, instead of being a defender of the people, was really an advocate of absolute sovereignty. Turgot's plan, while it did oppose some check to the intendants, put the property qualification too high for electors of these local assemblies. Until a new system of taxation should be established, — that is, a tax laid on land only, — the consumer ultimately had a part in paying the tax and should be recognized. In short, every consumer of adult years should have a voice in choosing the men who were to control the apportionment of the taxes. Merely to apportion the taxes, however, was not sufficient, and both plans failed to go to the root of the evil in that they did not provide for any real *control* of taxation. To be of any practical use, the provincial assemblies must have the right to *refuse* to pay the taxes, and also the means of backing up their refusal. This criticism of the alleged conservatism of Necker and Turgot is interesting, in view of the fact that they both fell because they were thought to be too radical.

Meanwhile the existing taxes were proving more and more inadequate to meet the expenses of the government, the Parlement of Paris had resisted the imposition of new taxes, and the minister Brienne in despair had projected a declaration of bankruptcy. Apropos of this situation, Brissot wrote his essay *Point de banqueroute*, in which he upheld Parlement, vehemently opposed the declaration of bankruptcy, and declared that there must be no halfway measures, that thorough-going reform was needed. This included the determination of the deficit, the suppression of the particular taxes under discussion till the amount of the deficit should be ascertained and the said taxes consented to by the States-General, the establishment of a regular administration of the finances, a prompt calling of the States-General, and the abolition of *lettres de cachet*.

To bring about such reforms there were two methods: a slow process of education and actual revolt. Both of these methods Brissot advocated, though he laid more stress on the former. Indeed, a large part of his writing had for its direct and avowed purpose to extend information and to educate public opinion. Such was his purpose, it will be remembered, in the *Théorie des lois criminelles*,[1] *Un Indépendant à l'ordre des avocats*,[2] *De la Vérité*,[3] *Le Philadelphien à Genève*,[4] the *Correspondance universelle*,[5] *Lettres sur la liberté politique*, the *Journal du Lycée*,[6] the *Tableau de la situation actuelle des anglais dans les Indes orienteles*,[7] *Examen critique des voyages dans l'Amérique septentrionale de M. le Marquis de Chastellux*,[8] *De la France et des États Unis*,[9] and above all, in his *Bibliothèque philosophique*.[10] Like the encyclopedists, he would popularize knowledge. He would unite men of letters of all quarters of the globe in a single body, so that, to quote his own language, "a Laplander transplanted to Paris or Madrid would be as much at home as though he were a Frenchman or a Spaniard, since he would realize that as a man of letters he belongs to all countries." [11]

In this connection it is to be noted that Brissot went even further and advocated, not merely a universal brotherhood of savants, but of nations. In fact, he held ideas which to-day would place him among the leaders of the Peace Movement. In his arguments in *De la France et des États Unis*, against restrictive tariffs, he declared that nature evidently meant all

[1] See p. 13.   [2] See p. 19.   [3] See p. 20.   [4] See p. 22.
[5] See p. 26.   [6] See p. 29.   [7] See p. 26.   [8] See p. 36.
[9] See p. 48.   [10] See p. 20.   [11] *Journal du Lycée.*

men to be brothers,[1] and, apropos of the conclusion of peace between Great Britain and her former colonies, he wrote: "Let all men, English, French, Spaniards, Dutchmen, Catholics, Protestants, Jews, abjure the fatal prejudices which divide them. Let them hold out to each other the hand of friendship, let there be no more distinctions, no more of that national pride, no more of that antipathy which dishonors humanity and stains the earth with blood." [2]

This, however, was but a remote Utopia. Brissot's immediate aim was to bring about reform in existing governments. Education of both prince and people was necessary, but if it happened that the people were educated up to the necessity of reform while the prince was not, then revolt might be necessary. In fact, revolt occasioned by the vexatious acts of a magistrate who had abused his power in injuring the life or liberty of his people was not merely justifiable but a real duty. The revolutions in Holland,[3] in Geneva,[4] and in Hungary,[5] he held to be cases in point, and wrote at length in their justification.

In getting his works printed, Brissot had the usual struggle with the censorship of the press. This censorship was quite rigorous enough to justify Beaumarchais's famous satire. "They all tell me," Beaumarchais makes Figaro say, "that if in my writings I mention neither the government, nor public worship, nor politics, nor morals, nor people in office, nor influential corporations, nor the opera, nor the other theaters, nor any one who has aught to do with anything, I may print everything freely, subject to the approval of two or three censors." [6] The truth of this satire Brissot might well have realized when he secured permission to print his *Tableau des anglais dans les Indes* only on condition of submitting each number to the censorship of four ministers.[7] Considering the object of his work it is not to be wondered at that he was in

---

[1] See p. 49. [2] *Correspondance universelle*, i, 169.
[3] *Point de banqueroute.* [4] *Le Philadelphien à Genève.*
[5] *Un Défenseur du peuple à l'empereur* (Joseph II).
[6] See *Le Mariage de Figaro*, Act v, Scene iii.
[7] *Réponse à tous les libellistes*, 17–18.

continual difficulties with the censorship. These difficulties account, perhaps, for the anonymous publication of several of his works,[1] and explain why he took the usual expedient of having so many of his books printed outside of France. It by no means follows, however, because his books bore the imprint of a certain place, that they were actually printed there. All of his works, for example, which were marked Berlin came from the press of Neuchâtel.[2] But to get his works printed was but the beginning of his troubles; he then had the further difficulty of getting them introduced into France. When he did secure a permission, he could never be sure that it might not be withdrawn at any time.[3] The *Correspondance*, for instance, which he had tried to introduce clandestinely, was seized by the French government, so that he lost the whole edition and was forced to mourn at the same time the loss of ten thousand livres and the destruction of a work which he had hoped might hasten the reign of liberty in France. Taught by this lesson, he determined to be more cautious and to conceal the fact that his real object was reform; to quote his own expression, to substitute the mine for the open assault. The mine which he prepared was an account of the English constitution. "The French government, however, fearing to see much light thrown on the subject, was on its guard. Some deception was necessary. I therefore asked permission to print a journal which was to be called *Le Tableau exact des sciences et des arts en Angleterre*. There was nothing alarming about that title, and the support of certain influential persons secured me a permit, to which, however, was attached the condition that the journal must be written and printed in England, reprinted at Paris and submitted to a very rigorous censure."[4]

---

[1] At least three of his early works were published anonymously.

[2] "*Il y a des exemplaires de cette édition* [1781] *avec des titres ajoutés après coup, qui portent l'indication d'Utrecht. Tous des écrits de Brissot qui portent la rubrique de Berlin ont été imprimés à Neuchâtel d'ou ils étaient ensuite importés clandestinement en France.*" Edition of 1836 of the *Théorie. Avis de l'éditeur*, i, 1, note.

[3] *Mémoires*, i, 329.

[4] *Réponse à tous les libellistes*, 15.

The mine was, in fact, Brissot's favorite mode of attack and one which he employed in several other works. What would have been considered radical and dangerous doctrines if put into practice, he concealed, for example, in the case of the *Théorie des lois criminelles* in an apparently harmless treatise on the theoretical side of the subject; while the *Bibliothèque philosophique* was announced as a dictionary of information,[1] and the work, *De la France et des États Unis* as a treatment of commercial relations.[2] In short, the real object of all these works, as well as of most of his other writings, was to bring about radical reform — in the phraseology of the declaration of rights, liberty, equality, and sovereignty of the people — by peaceable means if possible, but if necessary by revolution.

The reception which these various works received differed. Some of them, such as the *Indépendant à l'ordre des avocats* and the *Examen critique des voyages dans l'Amérique septentrionale de M. le Marquis de Chastellux*, in part, perhaps, because of their polemic nature, attracted considerable attention and provoked the criticism of journalists and pamphleteers.[3] The work, *De la France et des États Unis*, though it was likewise criticized, seems to have had much success on its own merits.[4] Brissot, indeed, complains that the journals paid no attention to it, but at least it was translated into several languages.[5] Some of his other works apparently found but few readers besides the censors. According to Pétion, who, however, as Brissot's friend, was perhaps prejudiced, they deserved a better fate. *Le Sang innocent vengé*, he declared, was full of energy and eloquence, the letters to the Emperor Joseph were veritable masterpieces, and the *Bibliothèque philosophique*, if it

---

[1] *Mémoires*, I, 226.   [2] See p. 48.

[3] The *Indépendant à l'ordre des avocats* created a great furor among the members of the bar. A couple of pamphlets were written against it and steps taken to suppress it. *Bibliothèque philosophique*, VI, 344. On the *Examen critique*, see the *Journal de Paris* of November 16, 1786, for a defense of Chastellux's opinion of the Quakers.

[4] See the *Mercure politique* of June 30, 1787, for an attack on *De la France* and for the answers of Brissot and Clavière.

[5] See Bibliography.

had only been the work of a writer with an already established reputation, would have been celebrated far and wide.[1] As a matter of fact, Brissot's writings at best were comparatively little known, and were it not for their relation to his subsequent important political career, they might remain forgotten.

The reason for his failure as a writer is not far to seek. He was not original. What he said had, for the most part, been said before by such writers as Montesquieu and Rousseau, Diderot and Voltaire, Beccaria and Filangieri. Moreover, it had been said more effectively. The trouble with Brissot was that he was so absorbingly interested in knowledge for its own sake that he did not realize the necessity of clothing it in pleasing garb. He had a prodigious memory for all that he read [2] and so keen a relish for information as such that he sometimes forgot "that there is nothing so *bête* as a fact." His constant impulse to popularize knowledge, and to teach others what he had just learned himself, would, as M. Aulard remarks, have been pedantic if it had not been so generous and disinterested. But he was always in too much haste to popularize to pay sufficient attention to form. To quote M. Aulard again: "What Brissot lacks as a writer is style. . . . He is clear and fluent, but his pen runs along without any attention to form, his only care being to get down all he has to say." [3] At the same time his writing is simple and direct, but he was lacking in a light touch, the ability to make an abstruse subject attractive; and, moreover, he had absolutely no sense of humor. In one or two of his early works he made use of sarcasm, but he soon realized that sarcasm was not his forte, and abandoned it. His work, further, is unrelieved by imagery or imagination. Although he was sentimental to a degree, one can hardly conceive of him as a writer of real poetry. When roused by great emotion, his writing became forceful, but ordinarily it lacked force, for the same reason that it lacked finish.

But, although Brissot's writing is not of great importance

---

[1] Pétion, *Notice sur Brissot*, Vatel, II, 224–34.   [2] *Ibid.*, II, 222.
[3] Aulard, *Les Orateurs de la législative*, I, 223, 227–28.

as literature, in connection with his future career it is of the greatest importance. It shows, as has been seen, the interests of a reformer. It also shows a reformer who, on little provocation, would become a revolutionist. In the first place, he was tremendously in earnest. That he had a mission he did not doubt, nor did he lack a prophet's confidence in its righteousness. His *Bibliothèque philosophique*, to take but a single example, was to be useful to his own age and useful to posterity. In the variety of his interests and in his unceasing efforts for reform of all kinds, he suggests Benjamin Franklin, but unlike Franklin, he had not the vestige of a sense of humor, and took all the world, including himself, with profound seriousness. As a consequence, he was often unable to put himself in the place of others, and so did not come to an understanding of the men with whom he had to deal. But even men with whom he failed to make connections and who were inclined to mock at his seriousness could not help but admire his enthusiasm, even when it seemed to them misplaced to the point of absurdity.

This enthusiasm was not always disinterested. He was intensely ambitious for himself, as well as for his cause, and in whatever else he was lacking he did not lack belief in his own powers. From very early childhood he made large plans and was possessed of abundant confidence to carry them out. Nothing could daunt him. He was ready to write on the most abstruse subjects. While his companions were painfully struggling with the rudiments of a foreign language, or striving to master the elements of legal studies, or enjoying plays in their native tongue, Brissot was working out a theory of all the languages of Europe, writing treatises on canon law,[1] and laying plans for a theater for foreign plays.[2] Witness, too, his schemes for all-inclusive philosophical dictionaries, for international societies and universal brotherhoods, not to mention his temerity in bringing them to the attention of the most distinguished men of his time. With this ambition went an indefatigable perseverance. His faith in his ultimate success was such that

[1] See p. 7.   [2] See p. 11.

nothing could discourage him. If one distinguished critic disapproved of his work, he submitted it to another; if one edition of a book were suppressed, he prepared a second; if his cherished plans for a newspaper did not meet with a ready welcome, he sought new friends and began again.

His optimism equaled his ambition and his perseverance, with the result that he often undertook impossible schemes. He established newspapers for which there was no demand, he entered into unwise business arrangements for the publication of his works, and on the strength of the slightest encouragement he embarked with a light heart on undertakings from which more cautious people would have shrunk in dismay. With the same breath in which he expressed contempt for those vain persons who thought they could compile dictionaries and edit newspapers, he had the temerity to announce a dictionary and a newspaper of his own, in supreme confidence that he could succeed where others had failed.[1]

These qualities account both for Brissot's success and for his failure. It needs no prophet's vision to see in his earnestness, ambition, and optimism a leader in the approaching Revolution. But the defects of those very qualities — the over-seriousness, the stubbornness which would not abandon a hopeless scheme, and the optimism which would not see insurmountable obstacles — explain also why his career finally ended in failure.

[1] *De la Vérité*, 142–43.

CHAPTER IV

AMONG his many and varied interests no subject had for
Brissot a greater charm than the United States. It epito-
mized for him the liberty and democracy which he had longed
for in France, and furnished the ideal toward which he hoped
to see France progress. In pursuance of this ideal he was always referring in his writings to American example as a model,
not only for France, but for all Europe.

Works dealing with America had, therefore, a special fas-
cination for him. This was particularly true of Crèvecœur's
Letters of an American Farmer.[1] Crèvecœur, like Brissot, was
an admirer of America; and after reading his book Brissot felt
sure that he had found a congenial spirit and hastened to make
his acquaintance. It was Crèvecœur's criticism of slavery and
his appreciation of the Quakers which especially won Brissot's
heart; and when shortly afterward, the Marquis de Chastellux,
in his *Voyages dans l'Amérique septentrionale*, ventured to express opinions not altogether favorable to the negroes and the
Quakers, Brissot seized the cudgels in defense of Crèvecœur
and rushed into the arena with more zeal than discretion. His
weapon was a pamphlet which he called an *Examen critique*,[2]
in which he compared Chastellux most unfavorably with Crèvecœur, and boasted of his friendship with the latter.[3] Chastellux's book, Brissot declared, contained poison, for he had had

---

[1] Published in London early in 1782, and in France in 1784, under the title
of *Lettres d'un cultivateur américain. Saint-John de Crèvecœur*, by R. de
Crèvecœur, 295–96.

[2] *Examen critique des voyages dans l'Amérique septentrionale de M. le Marquis
de Chastellux, ou Lettre à M. le Marquis de Chastellux dans laquelle on réfute
principalement ses opinions sur les Quakers, sur les nègres, sur le peuple et sur
l'homme.*

[3] *Saint-John de Crèvecœur*, by R. de Crèvecœur.

the audacity to assert that the Quakers were guilty of Jesuit-
ism, were indifferent to the public good, and were averse to
shedding blood; though when it came to commercial profit they
were ready enough to sell provisions at a high price, to foe as
well as to friend. In answer Brissot maintained that Chastellux produced no evidence to substantiate his statements, and
that he did not know what he was talking about. The comparison with the Jesuits was most unfair, Brissot continued,
since the Quakers did not try to exert authority, had no ambition, and were decidedly tolerant. To furnish provisions to
both Americans and English was not a crime, neither was it a
crime to demand a good price for them. The Quakers had,
moreover, a high standard of morality, and their religion was
not, as Chastellux seemed to think, a subject for jest.[1] As for
their political ideas, Chastellux had asserted that they were
indifferent to the public good. If by that, Brissot retorted,
Chastellux meant that they were indifferent to the disputes of
sovereigns, it might be true, but indifferent to the interests of
humanity they certainly were not, as witness their work for
the negroes. On this latter subject, too, Brissot differed from
Chastellux, and took umbrage at his claim that the negroes had
not the sensitiveness of the whites; they *were* equally sensitive,
he maintained. Chastellux and he were once again in disagreement on the importance of the art of war. To pay it the attention which Chastellux did, Brissot declared, was to favor aristocracy. This, indeed, was the root of the whole difficulty.
Brissot and Crèvecœur in their attitude toward America were
in sympathy with democracy, and Chastellux was not. But
Crèvecœur was not willing to go as far as Brissot, and as Chastellux and Crèvecœur had common connections, Brissot's attack on Chastellux and defense of Crèvecœur put the latter
in a very embarrassing position, and involved him in a controversy much against his will.[2]

[1] Brissot admitted, however, it might be because Chastellux did not understand the English language that he found their service amusing.

[2] *Saint-John de Crèvecœur*, by R. de Crèvecœur, 130, 162. See p. 70. Also

Brissot's interest in the negroes and their protectors, the Quakers, as well as in the United States as a possible place for emigration, inspired him with an ardent desire to make a journey himself to the new world. One obstacle stood in the way, — he had no money. His first thought was to apply for a government position of some kind which would take him to America. He accordingly drafted a note to M. Colonne, setting forth the desirability of collecting information about the new world which might be useful to France, and stating as his special qualifications for such a mission his researches on the relation of England to India, his numerous works published with a utilitarian purpose, and his acquaintance with the English language and the English constitution.[1] It is doubtful whether this application was ever sent. At all events, it came to naught. The idea then occurred to him of getting some sort of a private endowment. He knew several persons, he wrote, who might be willing to join together for this object, and in general for "all projects tending to favor liberty and the progress of the light." To extend the connections of France in America would be the apparent object.[2] This frank avowal of his purpose made the scheme look very like an underhand attempt to further his own personal ends under the cloak of a public enterprise for the general good. And this would have been the case had he been working solely for his own interest, but though he may have had visions of wealth to be gained for himself through land speculation, the situation was saved by his firm conviction that in trying to bring about closer relations between France and the United States, he *was* working for the public good, and especially for the advancement of France.

To this end he called in his friends, Clavière, Crèvecœur, and Bergasse, and in company with them organized a *Gallo-Américaine* society. As the society was to be universal in its

Journal de Paris, November 16, 1786, where Philippe Mazzei, under the name of Ferri, defends Chastellux against the attacks of Brissot; and *Nouveau Voyage de Brissot,* II, 190.

[1] Draft of a letter to Colonne, April 4, 1786. *Correspondance,* 90–92.

[2] Rough draft of a plan for a voyage to America, *Correspondance,* 92–93.

scope, it was only fitting that there be no religious qualification required for membership in it, but that it be open to men of all faiths and creeds.[1] "To be useful to both the old world and the new," Brissot wrote, in speaking of their aims, such "is the purpose of this society. Everything which is connected with this end is to be the object of its attention. It is to be composed of men of every country, of every profession, of every religion, provided they are capable of devoting themselves constantly and seriously to the good of humanity."[2]

Their plans for universal good, irrespective of national differences, received a slight check from Philips,[3] Brissot's English friend, to whom he had written asking for information on the state of English commerce. In reply Philips wrote that while he could answer most of Brissot's questions, he gave him fair warning that he himself was too good an Englishman to sacrifice the interests of his country to friendship, and that, in consequence, he would undertake nothing which might tend to diminish English commerce.[4] Not at all daunted by this rebuff, they continued their plans. Persons possessed of ideas or information useful to them were to be sought out; English and American newspapers were to be secured, and the society in seeking the good of France was to devote itself not only to furthering the external relations of France, but also to improving its moral and economic condition within. It would be ill-advised, however, they decided, to speak too freely of their larger purpose. In their prospectus, therefore, they announced the society as an organization for the dissemination of information concerning France and the United States, with a view to promoting closer commercial relations between them. The membership was to be limited, consisting of twelve persons in Paris, twenty-four in the provinces, the same number in the United States, and of an indefinite number in other foreign

[1] *Procès-verbaux de la Société Gallo-Américaine. Correspondance*, 111.

[2] *De la France* (edition of 1791), 409, note.

[3] James Philips, an English Quaker and bookseller with whom Brissot was on terms of friendship.

[4] *Correspondance*, 107.

countries. For admission to resident membership a unanimous vote was necessary. Quality, rather than quantity, was thus emphasized, perhaps with a further idea of making the society attractive by reason of its exclusiveness. Although the members among themselves may have cherished large schemes for the universal good, their discussions were of a decidedly practical character. Brissot, for instance, presented a memoir drawn up by a member of the Royal Agricultural Society, giving a list of trees indigenous to America, which might, with profit, be naturalized in France. In turn he proposed to benefit America by introducing a new French process for the cheaper manufacture of paper.[1] The work of the society at home was soon somewhat interrupted by the departure of Crèvecœur for New York, where he went to take up his work as Consul of France. It was an opportunity, however, for the extension of the influence of the society in America, and Crèvecœur set out charged with the mission of spreading abroad news of its principles and purpose.[2]

As one contribution to this immediate end, that of establishing better commercial relations between France and the United States, Brissot had undertaken to write a book dealing with economic conditions in the two countries. That there was great need of such a book he was convinced.[3] He was equally convinced, at least at first, of his own ability to meet that need; but soon finding the task rather too much for him, he sought and secured the coöperation of Clavière. This work, *De la France et des États Unis*, was therefore published under their joint names.[4]

[1] *Procès-verbaux de la Société Gallo-Américaine. Correspondance,* 103–36.
[2] *Ibid.,* 134–36.
[3] As one excuse for his work, Brissot quoted a remark of Thomas Paine: "*Je remarquerai que je n'ai pas encore vu une déscription de l'Amérique faite en Europe sur le fidélité de laquelle on puisse compter.*" *De la France,* 7.
[4] *De la France et des États Unis, ou de l'importance de la révolution de l'Amérique pour le bonheur de la France ; des rapports de ce royaume et des États Unis, des avantages réciproques qu'ils peuvent retirer de leurs liaisons de commerce, et enfin de la situation actuelle des États-Unis.* See p. 90.
The title-page contains the following passage from a speech of Lafayette to

The argument — already referred to in connection with Brissot's writings — was developed with care, and was supported by much material drawn from documentary sources. It was as follows: France can derive much profit from the American Revolution, in the first place because that revolution has increased human knowledge and furthered the reform of social prejudices; and in the second place, because it has made people see the value of commerce. England is most alive to the latter point and is now bestirring herself to develop commercial relations with the United States. England is better informed on the subject than France, owing to the better understanding there of the theoretical science of commerce, and to the freedom of the press.[1] France also ought to bestir herself, but in the first place her ignorance must be dissipated.

Having thus sketched the end to be attained, Brissot and Clavière then proceeded to lay down general principles of commercial relations. Direct commerce, they argued, is better than indirect, and cheaper; mutual interest is the surest means of sustaining commerce between two nations; the prosperity of a nation does not consist in a cash balance in its favor; metals are not real riches; the only way of estimating correctly the increase of commerce is by the increase of the population.

Mutual interest, they continued, that most important factor in developing commerce, exists between France and the United States. France needs new markets in which to dispose of her superfluous productions, to encourage her manufactures, and to employ labor. Commerce with the United States would tend to better conditions in France, and moreover, all is ripe for it, for just as France needs a market for her manufactured

the American Congress: "*Le passé assure l'alliance de la France avec les États-Unis, l'avenir ne fait qu'agrandir la perspective, et l'on verra se multiplier ces rapports qu'un commerce indépendant et avantageux doit produire, en raison de ce qu'il est mieux connu.*"

The work is dedicated to the American Congress and the friends of the United States in both hemispheres.

[1] In this work Brissot made frequent comparisons between England and France, to the disadvantage of the latter.

articles, the United States needs those articles. As a new country, the latter must first develop her agriculture and depend on Europe for manufactured goods. At the same time, she can furnish in exchange her own raw products.

Among the things which she can obtain from France are wine, brandy, oil, olives, dried fruits, cloth, linens, silks, ribbons, and hats. France, on the other hand, needs the raw products of America, such as tobacco,[1] fish, whale oil, candles, grain, and materials for shipbuilding. All this commerce, Brissot and Clavière held, should be encouraged to the greatest possible extent; the old idea of maintaining a balance of trade was absurd and erroneous. Moreover, — and this was a pivotal point of their thesis, — there should be the least possible interference with trade on the part of the government. Freedom, not protection, was the law of nature. "It is a misfortune," they wrote, "that the United States was not able from the start to adopt so noble a system; that in order to pay the public debt, they were forced to have recourse to this miserable system of ancient governments — to tax foreign merchandise. Every other tax except that upon the soil is a source of error. It is in consequence of such errors that there has arisen in Europe that system of protective duties for national industry, whose effect is to mislead governments till they are persuaded that they have in their hands a creative force equal to that of the Almighty."[2]

Finally, they declared, there is no reason to hesitate to embark on this commerce on account of the condition of the United States. Despite reports to the contrary, it is by no means in a desperate condition. There is no anarchy; the war with the Indians will not last; the troubles over paper money are but local. There is, therefore, every reason why France

[1] Brissot here deals with the government monopoly of tobacco. He would have this removed, and would favor a plan proposed by Lafayette, by which leaf tobacco, coming into the country, would be subject only to a very moderate duty. Then if it were desirable, a further sum might be paid for permission to manufacture and sell.

[2] *De la France*, 293.

should profit by her opportunity, and, to the utmost extent of her ability, develop commercial relations with the United States.[1]

The investigations in which Brissot had engaged in order to write this work only increased his longing to make a journey to the new world, in order to see for himself the conditions which he had been describing. About a year after its publication the longed-for opportunity came, not through the government, as he had at first hoped, but through his friend Clavière, who, with two other gentlemen, had entered into an agreement to speculate in the American debt.[2] Some one was needed to go to America to investigate the matter, and Brissot was precisely the man they wanted. He was already in correspondence with the chief authors of the American Revolution; he was well informed on conditions in America, and he was deeply interested in the financial situation.[3] He was accordingly offered the chance, and he eagerly seized it.[4] Mr. Daniel Parker, who was connected with the operations of the American speculators, William Duer and Andrew Craigie, and who seems to have been back of the whole proceeding, wrote to the latter, in Brissot's behalf, and pointed out that in addition to Brissot's other qualifications, the fact of his having been known as a literary man would make him a safe agent as he would not be suspected of any financial schemes.[5]

[1] A contemporary criticism from an English point of view is of interest. It is from the *Monthly Review*, LXXVI, 593. "Messrs. Clavière and De Warville are spirited writers, but sometimes they are too violent. The ardor of liberty is liable to break out into the flame of licentiousness, unless restrained by the superior judgment of calm and unbiased reasoners. The authors are justly entitled to the united thanks of the French and the Americans; for they have plainly shown the mutual advantages that may accrue from a commercial intercourse between the two nations; and they have, at the same time, given a just view of a foreign trade and the benefits thence arising."

[2] The names of the two gentlemen were Stadinski and Cazenove, — the latter an Amsterdam banker. *Correspondance*, 179.

[3] For a letter to Jefferson making inquiries as ,to the public debt, see Appendix A.

[4] Pétion, *Notice*, in Vatel, *Charlotte Corday et les Girondins*, II, 236.

[5] Parker to Andrew Craigie, June 2, 1788, Craigie Papers, American Antiquarian Society. See Appendix A.

His contract provided that he was to start at the earliest possible moment, and on his arrival at New York he was to seek information on the following points: first, the present total of the domestic debt of Congress; second, the price at which contracts for that debt are sold; third, what are the best contracts; fourth, the way in which the interest is paid; fifth, the probable date of reimbursement; sixth, events in the United States — such, for example, as the ratification by the states of the new plan for a federal system — which might affect the stability of the debt; seventh, the debts of each of the states. As soon as he secured any useful information, he was to inform each of the three men respectively, and he was, moreover, not to give to any one else such information as might lead to rival speculation.   On the other hand, Clavière, Cazenove, and Stadinski agreed to pay Brissot ten thousand livres for the expenses of his journey and investigations, and to give him besides a commission on their purchase in American funds.[1]

This was to Brissot a heaven-sent opportunity. Though commissioned to study financial conditions, he now had the chance which he had long sought, to investigate the state of the negroes and to make connections between their benefactors, the Quakers, and the society of the *Amis des Noirs*, which he had just established in Paris;[2] and incidentally, perhaps, to substantiate his arguments against Chastellux.

In the second place, he wished to investigate the country as a possible place of settlement. He was thoroughly weary of the

---

[1] *Contrat de Brissot avec Clavière, Cazenove, et Stadinski, pour sa mission aux États Unis. Correspondance*, 179–81.

According to Pétion, he asked only that his expenses be paid. *Notice sur Brissot*, Vatel, ii, 236.

Brissot evidently took every means to inform himself on financial questions, as is evident by a rough draft of a *questionnaire* on matters pertaining to the debt of the United States. It consists chiefly of answers to questions previously propounded. *Correspondance*, 181–84. Similar notes, questions, and answers, including a list of questions *proposées par M. Stadinski*, are found in an interesting collection of Brissot's papers loaned to the writer by M. Charles Vellay, of Paris.

[2] See p. 184; *Mémoires*, ii, 74.

limitations imposed by despotism, and had formed a tentative plan with some of his friends, to emigrate to America. Brissot had a good deal of the frontiersman in his make-up, and the prospect of establishing a permanent home for himself on the borders of civilization appealed to his adventurous disposition. Before embarking on such an enterprise, however, some preliminary investigation was desirable. This Brissot now proposed to make.[1] He not only had a general plan, but was incidentally considering certain definite places as feasible for settlement, as is evident from the character of the information he was seeking. These, for instance, are some of the questions which he noted: "What kind of goods would one need to bring from France for family use?" "What part of the territory of the Mohawks is the best?" "Would it not be better to be somewhere along the Hudson?" "Would there be any hope" — and here crops up Brissot's never-ceasing desire to take part in public affairs — "for a Frenchman who settled there, of being elected to the county assemblies?" "What is the cost of the passage from France to New York for each person, — for a child?"[2] A third motive — one which at the time he naturally said less about — was to learn in America the means of bringing about a like revolution in France.[3]

For this task of investigating American conditions Brissot was well fitted. He had a fair knowledge of the language of the country; he was already in correspondence with some of its most famous men;[4] he had valuable letters of introduction;[5] and, moreover, he was possessed of considerable reputation as a writer on America — all of which gave him an unusual chance

---

[1] *Réponse à tous les libellistes,* 25. See also *Réplique de J. P. Brissot à Stanislas Clermont,* 9.

[2] This is a part of the same *questionnaire* in which financial matters are discussed. *Correspondance,* 184–86. Similar lists of questions on agricultural life in the United States are found in M. Vellay's collection, referred to above. ·

[3] *Projet de défense, Mémoires,* ii, 275.

[4] For instance, announcement is made in the *Charavay Catalogue* of 1858, of sixty-five letters addressed to Brissot by Americans. *Correspondance, avertissement,* 11. See Bibliography.

[5] Lafayette gave him a letter to Washington. *Correspondance,* 192.

to increase his acquaintance and to acquire further knowledge. He was, therefore, no casual traveler, jotting down whatever happened to strike his passing fancy. In his own opinion there were three requisites for the traveler whose journeyings were to be useful to others: he must be well informed regarding the country he is to visit; secondly, — to quote Brissot's own words, — he must have a "plan of observation"; and, thirdly, he must not be content with a superficial view, but must make a thorough investigation for himself.[1] All three of these requirements Brissot met fairly well. In preparation for his work, *De la France,* he had used all the books on the subject on which he could lay his hands; as for a "plan of observation," he was ready with a definite outline of points to be observed; and finally, his stay in America, although cut short by the beginning of the Revolution in France, was of sufficient length for him to make observations of thoroughness. Between his arrival in Boston in July, 1788, and his departure from America, at the end of the same year,[2] he traveled from Boston to Virginia,[3] visited numerous educational and philanthropic institutions, saw something of the workings of the government, and made the acquaintance of many men of note. Among these were John Adams; General Heath; General Hancock, Governor of Massachusetts; James Madison; Hamilton; Warren Mifflin; Colonel Duer; Griffin, the President of Congress; Franklin; Temple Franklin, his grandson; Miers Fisher; Crèvecœur; De Moustier, the French ambassador; and General Washington.[4]

---

[1] *Nouveau Voyage,* preface, xxxvi.   [2] See p. 85 and note.

[3] From the dates of his letters and other evidence, the following itinerary may be given: July 24 at Boston; from thence by way of Cambridge, Spencer, Brookfield, Springfield, Hartford, Wethersfield, Middletown, New Haven, Fairfield, Rye, New Rochelle, to New York, August 9. From New York, August 25, by way of Newark, Trenton, Bristol, to Philadelphia. By October 2 he was back in Boston. From there he visited Salem, Beverly, Newburyport, Portsmouth, and Andover. October 12, he left Boston for Providence, whence he went by boat to New York, and thence to Philadelphia, Chester, Wilmington, and Mount Vernon.

[4] *Nouveau Voyage,* i, 147–52, 242–48, 268, 281, 312; ii, 250.

Despite his advantages of language, information, wide interest, an extended acquaintance,[1] and the means of increasing it, Brissot nevertheless lacked one essential requisite for reaching sound conclusions concerning what he heard and saw. He was already prejudiced in favor of American institutions. To him America was the seat of liberty and the home of freedom, and it was extremely difficult for him to see anything but good in her customs and institutions. Moreover, having set forth in print views favorable to America, he was naturally anxious to substantiate his preconceived idea. To such an extent was this the case that, when certain foreign consuls who had lived in America for some time attempted to point out to him weaknesses and dangers in American life, he refused to credit their statements or to listen to their opinions.[2] It is to be remembered, too, that interest in furthering emigration to America led him to look on the situation with a favorable eye.[3]

But although Brissot observed to prove a thesis and wrote to set an example, he was never insincere, and always endeavored to set down conditions as he saw them. He usually saw them, however, in a rosy light. From the American point of view, this bias of Brissot's is not without compensation. The time of his journey was just at the end of the government under the Articles of Confederation; the new constitution had been drawn up and its fate was now hanging in the balance. The period was, in truth, a critical one in the history of the

[1] With but two exceptions Brissot seems to have been received everywhere with the utmost cordiality. These two exceptions were the French ambassador, M. De Moustier, and, strange as it may seem, Crèvecœur. See *Saint-John de Crèvecœur*, by R. de Crèvecœur, 162, note. As to the latter, we have only the details given by Brissot himself. Brissot says in his *Mémoires* (ii, 50) that Crèvecœur barely received him, kept him only one night, and gave him no introductions. This seems strange in view of their recent friendly relations in the *Société Gallo-Américaine*. Brissot says it was because Crèvecœur was dependent on the ambassador De Moustier. But the *Voyage* contains at least twenty times the praise of Crèvecœur, who must have aided him. Perhaps the account in the memoirs is colored by later events.

[2] *Nouveau Voyage*, preface, xxxix.

[3] See p. 88, note, for a criticism of his account of the Scioto Company as being too favorable for one interested in it.

United States, but the judgment of a man who saw in these conditions, not a comparison with earlier prosperity and later stable government, but a contrast with far worse conditions in France, served to show wherein those years, even at the worst, held hope for the future.

In the spring of 1788 Brissot set out for this new country, sailing from Havre on the *Cato*.[1] It was characteristic of his insatiable thirst for information, and of his desire to spread it abroad, that just before starting he should write an account of the country through which he had passed on his way, and of the city of Havre. Finally, on June 3, he sailed away on his voyage of discovery, pessimistic for the land which he was leaving, but full of enthusiasm for the future of America, and for his possible part in it. His experience on the sea was the common one of having moments of regret that he had ever left dry land, but he soon recovered his usual health and spirits, and also his characteristic interest in every new detail of his surroundings: the kind of food served, where it was obtained, the life of the sailors, and the fishing vessels they met. Much of his time was naturally devoted to reading and studying English. One outcome was a theory — a not unusual result with Brissot — that in order to bring different peoples nearer together, an effort ought to be made to produce a greater similarity in their languages, by incorporating the terms and phraseology of one in the other.[2]

Finally, after a voyage of fifty-one days, Brissot arrived at Boston, the 24th of July. It was to him a moment of supreme happiness. He was fleeing from despotism, and was about to enjoy the life of a people who were in the actual possession of that liberty and equality which everywhere else was regarded as a chimera. He was especially delighted to find himself in Boston, the first city to throw off the yoke of the English. He was charmed, he declared, to see how different it was from the

[1] Craigie to D. Parker, July 27, 1788. Craigie Papers, American Antiquarian Society.
[2] *Nouveau Voyage*, I, 91–108.

disagreeable, noisy whirlpool of Paris. He was especially impressed with the absence of that restless, busy seeking for pleasure which characterized his fellow countrymen; and "of that proud and haughty air of the Englishman." "Here was simplicity, goodness, and that dignity of man which is the possession of those who realize their liberty and who see in their fellow men only brothers and equals." [1]

He did not, however, allow the delightful novelty of his new surroundings to distract him from the business of the important commissions with which he was entrusted, and without delay he made connections with Andrew Craigie and other speculators to whom he had been especially commended.[2] They were only too ready to follow Parker's suggestion in his note of introduction,[3] and pay Brissot every attention, as it was with his assistance that they hoped to carry through a scheme of "great magnitude."[4] This scheme, the two parts of which were closely connected, consisted in a speculation in the American debt and in western lands, and the assistance of European agents was indispensable. They accordingly made much of Brissot. Indeed, their fear that he might be made use of by some one else, hastened the development of their plans,[5] while Brissot on his side was anxious to further profitable investments for his friends at home. The result of their common interests and ambitious undertakings was a contract, dated October, 1788, which reads in part as follows : —

Articles of Agreement entered into and fully agreed upon betwixt J. Peter Brissot de Warville for himself and Stephen Clavière of the Kingdom of France, and William Duer,[6] and Andrew Craigie of the State of New York, viz.:

The parties mutually agree and covenant with each other to use

[1] *Nouveau Voyage*, I, 110–11.
[2] Craigie to D. Parker, July 27, 1788. Craigie Papers, American Antiquarian Society.
[3] See above, p. 66.   [4] Duer to D. Parker, November 5, 1788. *Ibid.*
[5] Craigie to D. Parker, December 3, 1788. *Ibid.* See Appendix A.
[6] William Duer was born in England, in 1747. After serving with Clive in India, he gave up army life. Coming to New York on business, he settled there, and took the part of the colonists in the Revolutionary War. He was known as

their best exertions to form an association whose object of negotiation [*sic*] shall be as follows:

To obtain from the Court of France a transfer of the debt due to that crown from the United States;

To get such transfer ratified by the United States; and to obtain such a convention for the payment of the principal and interest due thereon, as shall be judged most advisable by the parties interested in the transfer;

To purchase from time to time as large a proportion of the domestic debt of the United States as they shall be able to procure, and on such terms as shall be agreed upon by the Company, or the parties interested in their behalf, to manage such speculation;

To obtain such loans of money as may hereafter be judged necessary by Congress, to enable them to pay the interest of their debt, foreign and domestic, and to discharge the other exigencies of the Union.[1]

It was further agreed that Mr. Daniel Parker should be authorized to accede to the agreement on the same terms as the subscribing parties. With the other plans of Craigie and Duer — the Scioto land speculation [2] — Brissot was not so immediately connected, and the carrying out of his part of the speculation in the debt he had to defer till his return to France.

Meantime, his personal interest in the development of the United States could not but be increased. One of the first things that struck him was the spirit of tolerance which prevailed. Judging from the *Lettres d'un cultivateur américain*, he had expected a "ferocious Presbyterianism," and was surprised to find, instead, a wide tolerance in practice, and little reference to dogma in the pulpit.

In their manner of life, especially in their picnics and their tea-drinkings, the Americans seemed to him to resemble the English.[3] Another thing which struck him was a growing spirit of commercial rivalry with England. It was this spirit which

a bold speculator and successful financier. After the resignation of Robert Morris as superintendent of finance, he became secretary of the treasury board. (See Belote, *The Scioto Speculation*, 14, note.)

[1] *Correspondance*, 208, 212. See also the Craigie Papers, American Antiquarian Society.

[2] See p. 85. [3] *Nouveau Voyage*, i, 112–16; 123–29.

was leading to so rapid a development of manufactures of all kinds. But he also remarked, as a natural corollary, in a country devoted chiefly to commerce, that the sciences had not reached a very high degree of development. Exception to the absence of intellectual life he found, however, at Cambridge, and with all that he saw there he was delighted — the quiet peace of the place, its proximity to Boston, the type of president and professors of Harvard, its library and equipment.[1]

With the men whom he met he was also much pleased, and especially with the simplicity in which they lived. To see men who had played a distinguished part in the American Revolution pursuing the occupation of farmers, seems to have caused him a momentary surprise, but he was none the less delighted that so simple a life was adopted by the nation's leaders. He was especially impressed with John Adams, as an example of a statesman who had returned to his plow from the court of kings. "I have seen Adams," he wrote, "occupied in the cultivation of his farm, forgetting the rôle which he played when he trampled under foot the pride of his king, that king who had set a price upon his head, and who was forced to receive him as ambassador from a free country. Such, surely," he added, rising to a comparison with classic times, "were the generals and ambassadors of the glorious epochs of Rome and Greece; such were Epaminondas, Fabius and Cincinnatus." Holding such an exalted opinion of Adams, he was distressed to find that he did not have great faith in the possibility of much liberty in France. "He does not even believe," Brissot adds sorrowfully, "that we have the right, according to our old States-General, of asking that no tax be laid without the consent of the people."[2]

But whatever view Adams might hold of the possibilities of a republican form of government for other nations, Brissot was ready to admit that Adams himself was a fine example of republican virtues. Nor was he the only notable example of such virtues. Brissot was also much impressed by General

[1] *Nouveau Voyage*, I, 130–36.   [2] *Ibid.*, I, 146–47.

Heath, Samuel Adams, and Hancock, the Governor of Massachusetts. "General Heath was one of those worthy imitators of the Roman Cincinnatus; for he does not like the American Cincinnati; their eagle seemed to him a gew-gaw, suitable only for children. . . . With what joy did this respected man show me all parts of his farm! What happiness he enjoyed there! He was a true farmer. . . . A glass of cider, which he presented to me in the spirit of good comradeship, seemed to me superior to the most exquisite wines." [1] Of Samuel Adams he said: "He has the republican virtues to an unusual degree, impeccable uprightness, simplicity, modesty, and above all, severity; he is unwilling to have any capitulation with abuses. He fears the despotism of virtue and ability as much as the despotism of vice. In spite of his love and respect for Washington, he voted to deprive him of his command at the end of a certain time." [2] In General Hancock, Brissot found another example of courage, patriotism, and democracy. This simplicity Brissot perceived was common to the people at large. It seemed to him the very basis of their high standard of morality, and he was never weary of calling attention to its various manifestations. The secret of this general high standard of morality, he, in common with Rousseau, attributed to a rural life,[3] and as substantiating his belief, he adduced the fact that nine tenths of the Americans lived in the country.[4]

After a stay of some two weeks in Boston and vicinity, Brissot set out for New York and Philadelphia. The journey from Boston to New York was accomplished in four days, but at the expense of a four o'clock start each morning.[5] The inconveniences of travel appeared to Brissot slight, however, in comparison with those of France. If the roads left much to be desired, the stage coaches seemed to him infinitely superior to

---

[1] *Nouveau Voyage*, i, 150.   [2] *Ibid.*, i, 152.

[3] *Ibid.*, Preface, xii. But see p. 83, where he attributes this high standard of morality to liberty.

[4] He excepted, however, the plantation life of the South, on account of the inequalities inseparably connected with slavery.

[5] *Ibid.*, i, 157.

the lumbering diligences of his own country. Moreover, the absence of any class distinctions between travelers delighted him beyond measure. "These carriages," he explains, "keep up the idea of equality. The member of Congress is placed by the side of the shoemaker who elected him; they fraternize and chat together. You see no person here taking upon himself those important airs which you too often meet with in France. In that country, for instance, a gentleman would blush to travel in a diligence; it is a common carriage; you never know with whom you may be thrown. . . . The artisan or the laborer who finds himself in any one of these stages with a gentleman, keeps still and attends to his own business, or, if he does take part in the conversation, he does his best to rise to the level of others." [1] At the inns, too, Brissot was pleased with the spirit of good-comradeship which existed between the tavern keepers and their guests, and by the absence of the spirit of servility, evidenced by the fact that the servants did not expect fees.

The contrast between American women and French women also greatly impressed him. On this subject Brissot, like every Frenchman, before or after him, who has come to America, had much to say. Like every Frenchman, too, he was struck with the freedom with which American women went about unattended. He often met them driving or riding alone on the country roads, and was constantly surprised that their doing so was taken as a matter of course, and provoked no comment or criticism. It argued well, he thought, both for the safety of the roads and the morals of the community. Wherever he went he was impressed with their freedom and lack of affectation — a forcible contrast to the manners of women in France. [2]

He noted with pain, however, beginnings of what he considered old-world luxury and formality. This was particularly true of New York, where the dress of the women, the elegant equipages and the luxurious tables betokened a growing taste for display. [3] The introduction of carpets, which, he com-

---

[1] *Nouveau Voyage,* I, 234–56.   [2] *Ibid.,* I, 183; see also 113, 255.   [3] *Ibid.,* I, 231.

plained, was due to English influence,[1] was one of the luxuries which he deplored. The increasing study of music also gave him concern, and he uttered a pious wish that the women of Boston might never be taken with the malady of desiring perfection in the musical art.[2] The prevalent use of the cigar disgusted him, though he thought that it had the advantage of assisting reflection by interfering with the smoker's immediate response to queries or arguments.

After the luxury of New York, it was a great relief to Brissot to visit the Quakers in Pennsylvania, among whom simplicity still reigned. He had solemnly espoused their cause, against the aspersions of Chastellux, and through their common interest in the slave trade, had made connections with some of their members. He naturally met a very cordial reception, and had the opportunity of seeing, at first hand, their mode of life, and of visiting various charitable institutions under their control. All that he saw only served to corroborate his former opinions, and in describing their virtues, he never missed the chance to give a fling at Chastellux, and to hold up his attitude to ridicule. Discussing two of their chief peculiarities, their refusal to take an oath and to bear arms, he declared that their objection to an oath was no indication of a wish to escape responsibility for their actions. He could wish, however, that since the war of the colonies against Great Britain was justified by that divine principle which authorizes resistance to oppression, they had seen fit to take part in it. But as they were consistent in their action, and as their neutrality did not mean a secret attachment to the British, he held that it was unjust to persecute them. It was their simplicity which most attracted him. He took pleasure in contrasting their worship with that to which he was accustomed; their life with that of the French. "What a difference," he writes, "between the simplicity of this and the pomp of the Catholic worship.

[1] For his aspersions on the English Brissot was sharply criticized in a review of the travels, in the *Monthly Review* for 1791, p. 531.

[2] *Nouveau Voyage*, i, 112; ii, 80.

Reformation in all its stages has diminished its formalities. It is thus that human reason progresses towards perfection." [1] And again: "Simplicity, candour and good faith characterize the actions, as well as the discourses of the Quakers. They are not affected, but they are sincere; they are not polished but they are humane; they have not that wit — that sparkling wit — without which a man is nothing in France, and with which he is everything; but they have good sense, sound judgment, upright hearts and honest souls." [2]

While at Philadelphia he also had the opportunity of visiting Franklin, for whom he had long cherished a profound admiration, and who seemed to him the very embodiment of all the virtues. "I have found in America," he wrote, "many enlightened politicians, many virtuous men; but I have seen no one who appeared to me to possess in so high a degree as Franklin the characteristics of a true philosopher." [3]

One reason for Brissot's keen interest in the Quakers was, as has been pointed out, their common enthusiasm in work for the abolition of the slave trade and of slavery. The societies formed by them seemed to him the most adequate agencies possible. Through his connection with the *Amis des Noirs*, in Paris, he was brought into relation with like societies in America, was everywhere received by them with cordiality, was shown every courtesy, and was elected an honorary member of several branches. The work which he saw accomplished in the growing sentiment against the slave trade, and in the North against slavery itself, encouraged him to hope for a like success on the part of his own society. In his enthusiasm he seems to have gone too far and to have displeased even the Quakers themselves by the extravagance of his praise, while the Pennsylvania Dutch, the Methodists, and others complained that

---

[1] *Nouveau Voyage*, i, 290.

[2] *Ibid.*, ii, 169. He followed the Quaker example of simplicity by leaving his hair unpowdered at a time when powder was the almost universal fashion. Quoted from *Beaulieu*, by Aulard, *Orateurs de la législative*, i, 219.

[3] *Nouveau Voyage*, ii, 312.

they too had worked against slavery, and that to ascribe all efforts in behalf of the negro to the Quakers alone was most unjust.[1]

In addition to organized societies, Brissot had two other means to suggest which would tend towards the abolition of slavery: the substitution of maple sugar for the sugar cane, and the emigration of negroes to Africa. The first, he claimed, would do away with the necessity of slave labor, and would, in itself, be a profitable enterprise; the second would add greatly to the happiness of the negro. It would, in turn, be directly advantageous to commerce, for the African negroes would be civilized by contact with the colonists from America, and the civilization thus established would create new markets for Europe.

He was most optimistic in regard to the capacity of the negro for civilization. The statement of Chastellux that "it is not only the slave who is beneath the master; it is the negro who is beneath the white man," he denied *in toto*, and asserted on the contrary that the reason why the negro had not risen was not because he lacked ability, but because the white man kept him down. In order to substantiate this opinion, Brissot made throughout his trip a special study of the condition of the negro. He visited numerous schools for colored children, and was always delighted whenever he was able to cite marked instances of ability. As a further confirmation of his belief that the difficulty with the negro was not heredity, but environment, he noted the contrast between the free negroes of the North and the slaves of the South.[2] His feeling on this subject was so strong that it prevented a full enjoyment of that part of his journey which lay south of Mason and Dixon's line. Even his admiration for Washington was clouded by the realization that he was a slave-owner. Brissot, indeed, in the course of a visit to Mount Vernon, tried to convert

[1] See letter of November 28, 1791, to Brissot, apparently from Francis Dupont. Scioto Papers, New York Historical Society.
[2] *Nouveau Voyage*, ii, 34.

Washington to his own views.[1] Washington, however, while protesting his sympathy for the movement as a whole, maintained that the time was not yet ripe in Virginia for radical action against slavery, to which Brissot retorted that he was mistaken, and that it would be a task worthy of Washington to begin the revolution and to prepare the way for emancipation. He failed, however, to convince him that the moment was favorable for the formation of an anti-slavery society.[2]

In all other respects Brissot greatly admired Washington. His was another example of the ideal private life of a great man. "You have heard him compared to Cincinnatus," Brissot wrote, "the comparison is well made. This celebrated general is nothing more at present than a good farmer, constantly occupied in the care of his farm, as he calls it, in improving the methods of farming, in building barns. . . . Everything has an air of simplicity in his home; his table is good, but there is no display, and everything in the domestic arrangements is well regulated. Mrs. Washington superintends the whole, and combines the qualities of an excellent farmer's wife with that simple dignity which ought to characterize a woman whose husband has acted the greatest part in the theater of human affairs." [3]

In the general economic problems of the United States, as well as in the special problem of the negro, Brissot was deeply interested. The treatment of the Indian involved certain difficulties, he admitted, but some of the trouble had been brought on, it seemed to him, by the whites, by their own conduct, and might have been avoided if all the whites in their dealings with the Indians had followed the example of the Quakers. The Indians might be led to accept European civilization, though it was, perhaps, not altogether desirable that they should; but at least with skill and forbearance on the part of the whites, more peaceable relations might be established.[4]

Not only a general state of peace was to be looked for, but

---

[1] Brissot was indebted to Lafayette for a letter of introduction. See p. 68.
[2] *Nouveau Voyage*, II, 44.   [3] *Ibid.*, II, 265-67.   [4] *Ibid.*, II, 427-31.

commercial prosperity. Commerce with the East Indies was being developed and both imports and exports were increasing.[1] This seemed to Brissot a hopeful sign, particularly in its bearing on the ability of the Americans to pay their debts. He was in fact much more ready to listen to the optimistic opinions of Adams as to the future of America than to the doubts of the French ambassador. It was, moreover, a favorable time for making a study of economic conditions. Western expansion was just beginning, and manufactures were springing up. Something of the future development of the frontier, as well as of the geographical lines along which it was to advance, Brissot seems to have perceived. He speaks, for example, of the commercial advantages which New York State would acquire through the connection of the Hudson and Mohawk Rivers with the Great Lakes by a series of canals;[2] and of the possibilities of expansion beyond the Mississippi. Unlike many Americans of the time, he saw no reason to fear that the Western states would separate from the Union. He predicted, on the contrary, that in case Spain were so foolish as to insist on closing the Mississippi, these states, instead of transferring their allegiance to Spain, would rise in their might and drive her out of her western possessions.[3]

This question of western expansion was not merely a matter of public interest to Brissot, it was also of vital personal concern, because of its bearing on a possible place of settlement for himself, his family, and his friends. The future of America was, after all, less important to him than the present and practical problems of a prospective settler. "What was the price of land?" "What were the wages of a farm laborer?" "Was it easy to get labor?" "How much land would it take to support a man, his wife, and two or three children?" These were some of the points on which Brissot was seeking information.[4]

Brissot's wife, meanwhile, was likewise preparing for life in America. He must not forget, she wrote to him, to let her know

---

[1] *Nouveau Voyage*, II, 364, 383, 397. [2] *Ibid.*, I, 224. [3] *Ibid.*, II, 432–35.
[4] See M. Vellay's collection of notes referred to above, p. 67 and note.

what they would need for the journey, particularly for the ocean voyage. What would life be like; how much comfort would they be likely to have; what must they bring with them?[1]

Although as a place for his own settlement the Mohawk Valley and Pennsylvania seem to have been the regions he most seriously considered, lands further west also claimed his attention. He was keenly alive to the difficulties of individual settlement, and welcomed, as a means of overcoming them, the formation of land companies.[2]

He foresaw with clearness something of the future of western expansion, but it would have taken a wiser man than he to foresee the material inventions which were to develop that western territory, by making its water-ways so tremendously important. The primitive steamboat which he saw being experimented with on the Delaware, seemed to him merely an interesting novelty; it was too expensive, too cumbersome, and required too many men to operate it, to be very useful.[3]

But if Brissot failed to perceive the means by which the country was to be developed, of its capacity for development he had not the slightest doubt. The taxes appeared to him to be low, at least in comparison with those of France. Large families were common; prices, if judged by the ordinary cost of living, and not by the tavern charges, were moderate; and, what seemed most remarkable of all, there were few signs of extreme poverty, except in the large cities. The striking exceptions to this prosperity were in Rhode Island and New Jersey, where, as a result of a craze for paper money, economic distress prevailed.

The existence of paper money was one of the few things which Brissot criticized in the United States. He was thor-

---

[1] *Correspondance*, 205.

[2] See the questions which he asked as to the relative merits of those two localities. *Correspondance*, 185–86. See also his notes in the collection of M. Vellay on the Illinois Company and the settlements made under its auspices.

[3] *Nouveau Voyage*, i, 340.

oughly convinced of the evils of this irredeemable paper currency, and considered it a signal merit of the new constitution
that, by taking away from the states the power of issuing paper
money, it relieved existing evils and gave promise of safety for
the future. Conditions in Rhode Island, on account of the paper
money, appeared to him especially bad. He also criticized the
constitution of that state, because it permitted too frequent
elections of the legislative body, and made the judicial body
too much subject to the control of the people.[1]

But with these few exceptions Brissot had nothing but warm-
est praise for America. And that American life was so simple
and wholesome, and the standard of morality so high, was due,
he declared again and again, to the liberty which formed the
basis of the government.[2] In his enthusiasm he was guilty of a
good deal of triviality. Liberty, in his opinion, accounted for
everything, from the good temper of the stage-driver to the
large size of the windows in the hospitals, — both of which,
he declared, would be exceptional in a land of despotism. To
liberty and equality was due the longevity of the people. To
the absence of entire liberty and equality in the case of women,
was due the greater prevalence of consumption among their
sex. "They are more susceptible to consumption," he explained, "on account of the absence of a civil existence. The
submission to which women are habituated, to which they are
condemned, has the effect of chains, which compress and gnaw
the flesh, cause obstructions, deaden the vital principle, and
impede the circulation." [3]

The constitution, which was to Brissot the tangible embodiment of liberty and equality, was the all-absorbing topic of
discussion at the time of his visit. At the date of his departure
from Havre, June 3, 1788, its fate hung in the balance. When

[1] *Nouveau Voyage*, i, 200–12.
[2] He had previously attributed all that was good in American institutions to
life in the country. See p. 75. The *Monthly Review*, for 1791 (p. 531), in
speaking of the *Voyage*, reminded Brissot that the excellent conditions which
he ascribed to liberty, were in existence under the British government.
[3] *Nouveau Voyage*, ii, 133.

he wrote his first letter from America, July 30, the acceptance of the constitution by New Hampshire, Virginia, and New York, had made the new government a certainty. In this political agitation Brissot took an absorbing interest, and through his letters of introduction he had the opportunity of meeting some of the men who had most to do with the formation and adoption of the new constitution. He visited Franklin, whom he had long admired for his part in the American Revolution; dined with Madison and Schuyler; and made the acquaintance of Hamilton, King, and Jay. In Hamilton he saw the "determined air of a republican "; in Madison, the " meditative air of a profound politician." He agreed with Madison that the refusal of North Carolina to accept the constitution would have little influence on the minds of the Americans, but he was inclined to lay more weight than Madison on the criticism with which that refusal would be received abroad. "People over there," he declared, "will not take the trouble to inquire into the motives which dictated the refusal, nor will they consider the small consequence of this state in the confederation. On the contrary, they will look upon it as a germ of perhaps lasting division." [1] The one blot upon the constitution was, in Brissot's mind, the recognition which it gave to slavery. He was hopeful, however, that the slave trade would soon be abolished, and that a growing sentiment against slavery would lead to the extinction of that evil.

Influenced by his belief in the future prosperity of America, he now came to a decision on the question he had been considering, and definitely made up his mind to settle in America, chose Pennsylvania as the place of his abode, and sent for his brother-in-law, who was then living in Russia, to come to join him.[2] In the midst of these plans his eye fell upon a notice

[1] *Nouveau Voyage*, i, 242, and *Correspondance*, 202.

[2] Pétion, *Notice sur Brissot*, in Vatel, ii, 237–38. See also *Réplique à Stanislas Clermont*, 9: "*Celle qui par sa grandeur et sa simplicité méritoit plus mon estime et mon attachment, la Pennsylvanie [sic] m'avoit adopté pour un de ses enfants.*" He seems to be speaking here only in a figurative sense. There is no record that the State of Pennsylvania bestowed citizenship upon him.

in the American papers, to the effect that the date of the meeting of the States General had been put forward from May to January. It seemed that revolution was to begin, and without even waiting the arrival of his brother-in-law, Brissot hastened back to France,[1] in the hope, as he says, of being useful to the cause of liberty.[2]

But though he unexpectedly ended his American travels and thus changed the whole course of his life, his experience in America continued to be an important factor in its influence both upon his private life and upon his public career. Immediately on landing he made connections with Parker, the agent of Duer and Craigie, with the purpose of furthering speculation in the American debt,[3] but he soon lost confidence in him. The operations in which they were engaged were not successful, and instead of immense gains the association appears to have come out of the transaction minus both glory and profit.[4]

Besides the speculation in the American debt, Brissot was also interested in the speculation in western land, particularly in the operations of Duer and Craigie in connection with the so-called Scioto Company. The situation was this: an association had been formed in America, known as the Ohio Company, which had obtained a grant of land from Congress. Taking advantage of this situation, Duer and his friends organized a private association — the Scioto Company — to buy land from Congress under the shadow of the Ohio Company's bargain.[5] The Scioto Company then intended to sell in Holland

[1] He sailed December 3, 1788, and "after a long, tedious and stormy passage of 41 days," disembarked at Falmouth, England. (Letter of Craigie to Dupont, February 2, 1789, Craigie Papers, American Antiquarian Society; and letter of Brissot to Duer, dated Falmouth, January 15, 1789, Scioto Papers, New York Historical Society.)

[2] *Réponse à tous les libellistes*, 25.   [3] See pp. 66–67.

[4] See the Craigie Papers, American Antiquarian Society; also Scioto Papers, New York Historical Society, especially letters of Craigie to Brissot, of June 13, July 28, 1789, and October 6, 1790; and letters of Brissot to Duer, of January 31, and April 28, 1789.

[5] "It was intended by the Scioto Company to make an immediate sale of its rights of preëmption in Holland and France. In both these countries large amounts of United States securities were held. These securities were then

and France its right of preëmption, and to this end they sent Joel Barlow to France to act as their agent. He arrived in June, 1788, just after Brissot had sailed for America, and promptly set to work to accomplish his task. He soon found, however, that it was very difficult to sell a mere preëmption in small lots to individual purchasers. To create public confidence a company was accordingly formed at Barlow's instigation, which took over the sale of the land, and which for the time being was successful; but the public soon lost confidence and it was thought necessary to organize a new company, the formation of which was made public in July, 1790. The operations of these several companies in many instances were not such as to bear the light, and the whole thing ended in failure.[1]

Just what was Brissot's relation to this affair is not clear. According to Todd, in his life of Joel Barlow, Brissot, before his journey to America, made some effort to sell the company's lands, but without success. There is no reliable evidence, however, to indicate any such attempt, and from the correspondence between Brissot and the American speculators at the time of his journey to the United States, it would not appear that they had had previous intercourse. Because of their association in connection with the American debt, he would naturally be connected too with their land schemes. He certainly advocated the formation of a European firm for the sale of American land. The land companies, he was persuaded, would make profit only if they developed a European market. It was necessary further, he argued, to open the lands for sale through a European house. People would lack confidence in any American house.[2] What was needed was a European con-

almost worthless. It was natural to suppose that their holders would gladly part with them in exchange for fertile lands in the west of the United States. The securities thus acquired could be used by the Scioto Associates to pay Congress for their lands. Since Congress would accept the securities at par while the Scioto Associates had received them at a greatly depreciated value, the latter would soon be able to pay for their lands and the sums derived thereafter would be clear profit." Belote, *The Scioto Speculation*, I, 20.

[1] *Ibid.*

[2] Observations on the scheme of lottery, respecting the contract of lands on

nection. How this should be worked out he set forth in what he called a "Plan of a society for promoting the emigration from Europe in the [*sic*] United States." There were many sober, industrious people in the various countries of Europe who, he was convinced, would be only too glad to emigrate to the new world if they could do so with safety and profit. But they were ignorant of the good opportunities which awaited them in the western lands; they lacked money and they did not know how to get there. This was a rare chance for an enterprising company. Such a company should buy lands, establish a house, or else enter into a partnership with a house already established in a "part of Europe: 1, not very far from home; 2d, in the center of Europe; 3d, in a free government where its operations should not be liable to be enquired into." [1] Such a society, he continued, ought further to distribute throughout Europe pamphlets in various languages, setting forth the physical, political, and commercial advantages to be enjoyed in the United States. It ought, moreover, to assist worthy emigrants with money, grants of land, and agricultural implements.

Whether these attempts of Brissot's to promote a European company were in the interest of the French Scioto Company or in opposition to it in order to further his own private interests, is not clear. But whatever may have been his relations to Barlow and the French Company up to the spring of 1789, it is clear that from that date he attacked the French Scioto Company most bitterly, and tried to divert interest from it to schemes of his own for American settlements. Witness the announcement in the *Patriote Français* of April 23, 1790, of a proposed French settlement in America, not connected — it is significantly added — with the Scioto Company.

the Mississippi (undated). Notes by Brissot in the collection of Brissot's papers belonging to M. Charles Vellay, referred to above.

[1] The plan is undated, but according to M. Perroud, it was probably drawn up about 1786 or 1787. It would fit in, however, he adds, with the announcement in the *Patriote Français* of April 23, 1790. *Correspondance*, 458–60. It is in Brissot's handwriting and in English, and incidentally shows how much grasp he had of the language.

The advantages of such a settlement, at this juncture, are portrayed in glowing terms, but at the same time persons intending to emigrate are warned that unless they are lovers of democratic simplicity and of liberty and equality, they will not be suited to the life of the settler. It is added that the possession of some means is also necessary. "From what has just been said," the writer continues, "it is evident that this establishment does not resemble at all that proposed by the Scioto Company. That company demands a considerable fortune, this one does not; that one carries on its operations in a country not yet inhabited, this one in a country already settled." Persons wishing further information are directed to write, care of the *Patriote Français*. A few months later the *Patriote Français* made a more direct attack on what it designated as the "so-called Scioto Company." This company, it was alleged, was victimizing French citizens.[1]

It was only the French Company, however, which Brissot had attacked; the original company he continued to defend, and with good reason, for he had been given power of attorney by Craigie for the sale of a tract of land on the Susquehanna,[2] and if suspicion were thrown upon the company, his own interests would suffer. In the published account of his travels, the *Nouveau Voyage*, which appeared in April, 1791, he accordingly spoke in the highest terms of the Scioto Company, and expatiated on the advantages of the western lands.[3] Indeed, his wish to portray the United States as a desirable place for emigration may have been quite as potent a factor in hastening the publication of the work as his endeavor to further liberty in France. Furthermore, just at this time he was brought into connection by an American friend, Miers Fisher, with American agents interested in the lands near the Ohio,

[1] *Patriote Français*, August 4, 1790.
[2] Craigie to Brissot, January 24, 1789. Scioto Papers, New York Historical Society.
[3] In a letter, apparently from Dupont, of November 28, 1791, Brissot is informed that he is criticized for speaking so highly of a company in which he is himself interested. Scioto Papers, American Antiquarian Society.

and asked to assist in the sales in company with Clavière at a commission of two and one half per cent.[1] He was also interested in the Illinois Company, and eagerly searched for information concerning its lands and settlements.[2] In all these various ways he tried to further emigration, sometimes, it would appear, with more zeal than discretion. That a man wanted to settle in America was sufficient for Brissot; whether he had the proper qualifications for a settler on the frontier mattered little. The letters of Madame Brissot at this epoch throw a side light on the matter. From them it is evident that Brissot's home was a rendezvous for would-be emigrants, not always of the most desirable character.[3]

He even thought of emigrating himself. Indeed, when he left America it was with the evident intention of returning,[4] but as political affairs more and more absorbed his attention, he gave it up. However, the charm of country life as he had seen it there still fascinated him and was probably one of the influences which led to his plans for the *Société agricole ou d'amis.* This was an association, which he tried to form in connection with the Rolands and other friends, for buying lands from the government and establishing a common life in the country.[5] The project, however, did not materialize.

But although Brissot never returned to America, he maintained an active correspondence with numerous friends there, both personal and professional. The settlement of his brother-in-law in Pennsylvania kept him in close touch with American affairs, while his connection with the land speculations influenced his ideas and activities.

[1] Letter of Miers Fisher to Brissot, February 2, 1791. *Correspondance*, 261, and another letter of November 3, 1790, in Scioto Papers, American Antiquarian Society.

[2] Notes in Brissot's writing communicated to the writer by M. Charles Vellay of Paris.

[3] *Correspondance*, 242–45.

[4] Letter of François Dupont. Craigie Papers, American Antiquarian Society.

[5] See p. 150. See also for the constitution of the society, *Correspondance*, 461.

The political influence of Brissot's travels was also of much importance and is seen throughout his career in the Revolution. Indeed, it was largely with the purpose of bringing American example before France that he decided in the midst of the turmoil of the Revolution to publish an account of his journey. Such an undertaking might seem out of place, he wrote in his preface, since "we also have acquired our liberty, but to acquire liberty is only the first step; we must learn from the Americans the secret of preserving it." That secret, Brissot continued, consisted chiefly in a high standard of morality. "I see with pain," he went on, "not only that we do not yet possess it, but that we are not yet persuaded of the absolute necessity of it for the maintenance of liberty. . . . Without private morality, no pure public morality, no public spirit, no liberty !" [1] To make the work more complete, he added the volume already published in collaboration with Clavière, — *De la France et des États Unis.* To round out the whole, a fourth volume was needed, dealing with political connections, but the time failed him for that.[2] Indeed, in order to publish the work at all, he was obliged to sacrifice polish; but the time was ripe, he was convinced, for just such information, and if he were to help France in her revolution he must publish the work as it was.[3]

Throughout the Revolution America continued to be his model. His constant appeals to American precedent in foreign affairs, his attempt to mould a constitution for France on the lines of the Constitution of the United States, his furtherance of Genet's appointment and of his mission to Spanish America, and, finally, his alleged adherence to federalism based on the ground of his admiration for the Republic across the water,[4] — all this is evidence both of the lasting results of his travels upon himself and also of the influence which, through him, was exerted upon the French Revolution by American institutions.

[1] *Nouveau Voyage,* preface, I, xii.   [2] *Ibid.,* preface, I, xxi, xxx.
[3] The work was published in April, 1791.
[4] See chapters VI, VIII, and X.

CHAPTER V

THE news of the rapidly rising tide of excitement at the approaching meeting of the States-General had cut short Brissot's travels in the United States and brought him back post-haste to France. He found that the country was indeed in a ferment of excitement, people everywhere were discussing the organization and functions of the States-General, and the press was pouring forth a flood of pamphlets on the subject. Here was his opportunity of applying his ideas of reform, and into this ferment he threw himself with characteristic ardor. He wrote pamphlets, organized committees, and made political addresses. In his friend Clavière he found active sympathy, and his house and Clavière's soon became centers for political discussion. According to Dumont who sometimes attended these meetings it was all useless chatter.[1] The active participants, however, were tremendously in earnest and felt that they were performing a most useful and indispensable work in drawing up declarations of rights and laying down principles for conducting the proceedings of the States-General. His own ideas on these subjects Brissot hastened to set forth in a pamphlet called *Plan de conduite pour les députés du peuple aux États-Généraux de 1789*, a production of considerable importance for the light it throws upon Brissot's attitude at this important epoch. Like most of the pamphleteers of the time, he began with a discussion of the system of voting. After considering various methods of voting, *par ordre, par tête*, by a number of bureaus, by two chambers, one of which should be composed of clergy and nobility, the other of members of the third estate,

---

[1] Dumont, *Souvenirs de Mirabeau*, 33; see also *Lettres de Mme. Roland*, ed. by Perroud, II, 737, Appendix Q.

he declared himself opposed to all these methods, and proposed instead voting by two chambers, each of which should be constituted as follows: clergy, 125; nobility, 125; third estate, 250. In case of failure to agree, the two chambers were to meet together as one body, and decide the matter by a majority vote. As for the powers and duties of the States-General, it should in the first place take steps to secure the inviolability of letters committed to the post, and also the liberty of its members; and in order to do its work uninfluenced by the court, it should remove to Paris. Further, in order that no able men should be shut out of the States-General, no matter what their financial condition, the members should be paid. "Not to pay a salary," he maintained, "would lead in France, as it has in England, to corruption." It would shut out from the assemblies men of talent who are not always in easy circumstances. They have had experience in this matter in America, and that is why the members of Congress are paid. The salary ought to be sufficiently large to provide for the daily expenses of the members, but not so large as to make the position of deputy sought for as a profession or profitable employment. The business of this body, he declared, was purely legislative. To make a constitution was outside of its province; it could only decree that the nation call a special body for that purpose. It would not be sufficient, however, to give to the States-General control of the taxes and of the army, as in England; there must be permanent, annual, and independent meetings of this body. Such meetings will serve to counterbalance the bad influence of the ministers, but they will not destroy monarchy. "On the contrary," he declared, "the true support of the French monarchy will be in annual meetings of the States-General. The present reigning family cannot have a surer and more invariable support." This statement was somewhat startling from a man who less than three years before had declared that no radical reform was possible under a monarchy. It shows that Brissot had either modified his ideas or else, in view of the possibility of election to the States-General, had modified their expression.

Meanwhile he actively engaged in the actual preliminaries of the elections. For electoral purposes, Paris had been divided into sixty districts. Each district was to choose delegates to the general electoral assembly of the third estate, and the general electoral assembly, in turn, was to choose twenty representatives to the States-General. In his own district, that of the Filles-Saint-Thomas, Brissot hardly arrived on the scene before he stepped into a place of prominence and was soon elected as its president. Even before the district had finished its legitimate business of choosing electors, he came forward with a plan, the object of which was to enable the districts to exercise some surveillance over the States-General, — in other words to enable the people to maintain their sovereignty. This was to be accomplished by means of committees of correspondence between the districts, the electors, and the deputies of Paris. If the two orders should fight for their pretensions, he argued, the third estate would fight for its "inalienable rights." In case a schism should result, the deputies would return to their constituents, the inhabitants of the districts. The districts, therefore, should remain in readiness to assemble, and the only means of assembling the people was by a committee of correspondence always in activity. As a result of his argument, his district appointed such a committee, with Brissot himself at its head, and invited the other districts to take like action.[1] The invitation met with a speedy response, and there was thus created, largely through Brissot's instrumentality, permanent organizations, which were to have an important part in the development of the future government of Paris.[2]

He next proceeded to draft a statement of grievances for the use of the electoral assembly in drawing up its *cahier* of complaints. Although not a member of this assembly he did not hesitate to offer his advice. They would do well, he wrote, to

---

[1] *Observations sur la nécessité d'établir, dans les différents districts et dans l'Assemblée générale des électeurs de Paris, des comités de correspondance avec les députés de Paris aux États-Généraux, 2 avril, 1789.*

[2] Chassin, *Les Élections*, ii, 403.

limit their instructions to their deputies to four subjects — the organization of the States-General, and the manner of its deliberation, a declaration of rights, the consolidation of the debt and temporary means of payment. Then after summing up what he had already said on these subjects in his *Plan de conduite*, he reiterated with especial emphasis his previous statement that until fundamental rights were established, Paris had better be silent as to her own special grievances.[1]

While dealing with the principles to be upheld by the electoral assemblies and by the States-General he was quite as vitally interested in the persons to be elected. One may be sure that the frequent excited gatherings at his house and the hurried notes which he and his friends were constantly sending to each other were not concerned with principles alone, but also with the interests of individuals. One may be sure, too, that all this activity of Brissot's was not entirely disinterested. He looked forward to the States-General as a means of overthrowing various forms of despotism which he had long and vigorously attacked, and he was desperately anxious to have a part himself in the final assault. The 25th of April he wrote in English to a friend: "We are in the electioneering fire. There is some chances [*sic*] for me. I have preached very successfully [*sic*] the people. However, there are so many intrigues that I am quite desponding." [2] His friends at Chartres, among whom were Pétion and the Countess de Seinie, were specially active in his behalf and put him forward as a candidate for deputy from his native place.[3] But their efforts were unsuccessful, and at Paris, notwithstanding his prominence in his district, for some reason he was not chosen even to the electoral assembly.[4] Although discouraged, he still hoped that he

[1] *Précis adressé à l'Assemblée générale des électeurs de Paris pour servir à la rédaction du cahier des doléances de cette ville*, May, 1789. See Chassin, III, 211.

[2] *Correspondance*, 230. This note shows the extent of his knowledge of English.

[3] *Ibid.*, 225-28.

[4] In his *Précis adressé à l'Assemblée* he alluded to the singular circumstances which prevented his election. See also his *Discours prononcé à l'élection du district des Filles-Saint-Thomas, le 21 avril, 1789*. Note also that some light is

might be chosen to the States-General, and it was, undoubtedly, as much to further his own cause, as to set forth his principles, that he drew up the advice as to the *cahier*. Indeed, this draft of a statement of grievances was in part at least the expression of his own grievance in not being elected, and an excuse for calling the attention of the electors to the fact that in choosing the deputies they were not limited to their own number.[1]

His reputation as a pamphleteer and a humanitarian helped his cause, and his name was inserted fourth in a list of "twenty-one friends of the people who deserve to be the choice of the electors of Paris." The document in which this assertion was made further declared that "there had been distributed in Paris lists in which celebrated names were mixed with the names of obscure and dangerous men." But in *this* list, the public was assured, were inscribed "only those persons who had made open profession of defending the cause of the people." [2] But in spite of all these efforts, he was not elected, a result which he afterward declared was due in part to the influence of the Duke of Orléans against him, though his reason for the supposition is not clear.[3] He was naturally bitterly disappointed, but a man

thrown on the matter by Étienne Dumont. He says: "*J'étais à la section des Filles-Saint-Thomas ; c'était un quartier central, occupé par la classe la plus opulente : pendant long-temps il n'y avait pas deux cent individus. L'embarras de se mettre en action était extrême ; le bruit était affreux. Tout le monde était debout, tous parlaient à la-fois ; les plus grandes efforts du président n'obtenaient pas deux minutes de silence. Il y eut bien d'autres difficultés sur la manière de prendre les suffrages, et de les compter. J'avais recueilli plusieurs traits curieux de cette enfance de la démocratie, mais ils sont a-peu-près effacés de ma mémoire, ils revenaient tous à l'empressement des hommes à prétention, qui voulaient parler pour se faire connâitre, et se faire connâitre pour être élus.*

"*On voyait les premiers essais de l'art des intrigues et des cabales pour faire tomber les nominations sur ceux de son partie. On ne voulait point de listes de candidats ; tous étaient appelés à choisir sur tous. Les voix se dispersèrent tellement dans les premières operations, qu'on ne pouvait obtenir la majorité absolue pour aucun des designés. Il fallut réitérer l'élection jusqu'à ce qu'enfin on obtint le résultat nécessaire.*" Dumont, *Souvenirs*, 39–40.

[1] *Précis adressé à l'Assemblée générale des électeurs de Paris.*

[2] Chassin, ii, 312.

[3] *Mémoires*, i, 119. It must be remembered that at the time Brissot wrote

of his interests and ideas was not going to sit quietly by and let
reform go on under his eyes without taking some part in it.
Though cut off from participation in legislation, he was by no
means cut off from exercising influence upon it. There were
other opportunities, and he seized upon them, threw himself
heart and soul into the work of the *Amis des Noirs*, and
made it a factor with which the States-General had to deal.
He established a newspaper — the *Patriote Français* — which
helped to create public opinion, and so, in turn, influenced
legislation, and if he could not be a leader in the reorganization
of France, he played a very important part in the reorganization of Paris, in establishing its liberty, and in transferring
authority from the central government to the people.

"The Revolution made Paris a commune before it made
France a nation," says M. Monin.[1] The old government of
the city was divided between the *parlement*, the *Châtelet*, the
ministry of Paris, the lieutenant-general of the police, certain
guilds, the *hôtel de ville*, the church, and the university. "It
was a chaos of competing authorities, a tangle of obsolete privileges, and a nest of scandalous abuses. Anomalous courts
jostled and scrambled for jurisdiction, ancient guilds and corporations blocked every reform, atrocious injustice and in-
veterate corruption reigned high-handed in the name of king,
noble or church." By a single event, the storming of the Bastille, this ancient municipal régime was swept from power and
a clear field was left for the development of a modern city government in Paris. But to tear down was one thing; to build up
quite another. Immediately on the fall of the Bastille and the
flight of the constituted authorities, the instinct for law and
order asserted itself and led to the acclamation of Bailly as

his memoirs, it was to his interest to show that there was no connection
between him and the Duke.

[1] *L'État de Paris en 1789*, 27. A comparison of the present government of
London and of Paris makes clear the advantage which the latter gained in the
Revolution. Whereas London still suffers from the overlapping of authorities and from antiquated tradition, the government of Paris is clear cut and
thoroughly modern.

Mayor of Paris and of Lafayette as commander of the national guard, but it was not until October, 1790, after several unsuccessful experiments and organizations, that anything like a permanent and legal form of municipal government was established. In the actual attack on the Bastille, there is no record that Brissot took any part, but with the resulting events he was closely connected. As the president of the district of the Filles-Saint-Thomas he had the honor of receiving the keys of the fortress,[1] he is said to have been prominent in putting forward Lafayette [2] as commander of the national guard, and in the slow process of building up the new city government, he was one of the leaders.

The machinery for forming a new government was set in motion by the electoral assembly. This assembly had been chosen in the spring of 1789 and was charged solely with the duties of drawing up a general *cahier* and of electing the deputies of the third estate of Paris to the States-General. After performing these duties it had no further legal warrant for existence, but nevertheless it did not dissolve; and, when on July 13 and 14 the old city government fell to pieces, it slipped into the vacant place, and with the assistance of the electoral organizations of the districts, proceeded to take upon itself the government of the city. The district assemblies, like the general assemblies of the electors, were formed with the one

---

[1] This rests on Brissot's own statement given by Charpentier in *La Bastille dévoilée*, I, *troisième livraison*, 78. It is also mentioned in the introduction to the *Moniteur*. But the original *Moniteur* was not published till November, 1789, and the edition containing the introduction was not published till 1796. This reference is therefore not contemporaneous and is probably derived from Brissot's own statement. A key of the Bastille was sent to Washington by Lafayette (*Washington's Writings*, ed. by Ford, XI, 493). It is possible that Lafayette may have received the key from Brissot.

[2] "*On se rappelle que c'est lui* [Brissot] *qui appuya à la Maison Commune, la motion faite par le flagorneur Fauchet, de nommer le sieur Mottié, généralissime des guardes nationale.*" Note of Delacroix in *L'Intrigue dévoilée, ou Robespierre vengé des outrages et des calomnies des ambitieux*, quoted in *Annales révolutionnaires*, I, 338–39, April, 1908. This is very doubtful authority, however, as it was to the interest of Delacroix to make out Brissot as closely connected with Lafayette.

purpose of carrying on the election, and on the completion of that work should have dissolved. Instead, they proceeded to effect a more or less permanent organization and to take part in political discussion. This was due to Brissot, who with his plan of committees of correspondence, furnished the means for permanency. There was thus created a number of local organizations to which the electoral assembly could appeal. This assembly was perfectly aware of the irregularity, not to say the illegality of its position as a city government, and within a few days after the fall of the Bastille it suffered the districts to make formal choice of a regular central assembly. The municipal government thus created was called the assembly of the representatives of the Commune and met for the first time, July 25, 1789.[1]

As the president and most prominent representative of the district of the Filles-Saint-Thomas Brissot was elected to the new municipality, and thus he found his first real opportunity of applying his political theories to the solution of practical problems. These theories, as has been seen, tended toward democracy and popular sovereignty. The first problem which presented itself was that of providing a permanent municipal organization. Where, for instance, was the balance of power to be, — with the district, or with the central administrative body? — a question of sovereignty. In the formation of a municipal constitution how far was the city to act independently of the National Assembly? — a question of liberty or sovereignty under another aspect. Was Paris, like other cities, to be included in a department, or was it to form a government by itself? — a question of equality.

To each of these questions Brissot had a ready answer, but

[1] The successive stages of the development of this city government may be very briefly stated as follows: (1) the assembly of the electors of Paris from July 14 to July 25, 1789; (2) the temporary Commune which lasted from July 25 to September 18, 1789; (3) the second temporary Commune from September 25, 1789, to October 8, 1790; (4) the permanent Commune which was established October 8, 1790. See Lacroix, *Actes de la Commune de Paris, pendant la Révolution;* Introduction, I, II.

as he was not elected to the constitutional committee of the municipal assembly, it seemed at first that he was to have little chance to exert his influence. A general laxity in the management of committee business, however, had made it possible for persistent outsiders to take part in the discussions and influence the decisions. Taking advantage of this state of things, Brissot succeeded in attaching himself to the committee as a kind of unofficial member, and in exercising considerable influence upon its conclusions. For instance, the plan for a constitution as it had been originally presented to the committee had contained no declaration of rights. This seemed to Brissot so glaring an omission that he promptly drew up a municipal charter which did contain such a declaration and submitted it to the committee. The declaration asserted that cities had the right to form their own government, subject to the general supervision of the central government; that Paris, as a unique city, ought to have a special form of government and be considered both a city and a province; that all citizens ought to have part in the elections; and that the preponderance of power should lie with the central city administration and not with the districts.[1] Brissot unfortunately does not seem to have been consistent, for in his *Motifs des commissaires pour adopter le plan de municipalité* he makes the suffrage depend on the payment of a direct and personal tax.

The plan itself provided for the division of Paris into sixty districts; for a central legislative body of three hundred members, five from each district; for the renewal of one fifth of the legislative body each year; and for a *conseil de ville* of sixty members, the majority of whom were to be chosen by the legislative body of the municipality. Its fundamental principle, the concentration of power in the legislative body of three hundred, was certainly not in harmony with the declaration of rights nor with Brissot's ideas of democracy, and was a decided contrast to other plans which gave more power to the

---

[1] *Observations sur le plan de municipalité de Paris, suivies du plan original et d'une déclaration des droits des municipalités.*

mayor or to the districts. Two of its features suggest the arrangements frequently carried out in a modern city government: the close relation of the districts to the central government, secured by making the president of each district a member of the legislative body; and the system of partial renewal of that body. This concentration of power naturally met with much opposition on the part of the districts. It was asserted that places would be open only to the rich. In consequence the municipality would degenerate into an aristocracy, and finally, these class distinctions could be avoided only by such general periodic renewals in the assembly as would leave at each renewal only a minority of former members in office. The districts also claimed that the choice of the *conseil de ville* belonged of right to them, and not to the legislative body; and further, that one member should be chosen to this council from each district, — a claim which suggests the modern question of ward representation.[1] Brissot's plan was accordingly modified in this particular, the choice of the *conseil de ville* being transferred to the districts.[2] Nevertheless, the essential part of his plan was accepted and formed the basis of the successive provisional organizations under which Paris was governed from September, 1789, to October, 1790. Brissot was elected to the assembly of the representatives under this new government and endeavored to take an active part in municipal affairs.

The second important question in regard to the new city government, the proper relation of the national government to municipal government, Brissot answered quite in accord with his principles of democracy and with the most modern ideas of "home rule for cities."[3] Municipal and provincial assemblies, he declared, ought, as far as their objects and their power are concerned, to be entirely distinct and separate from the national legislative assembly. The function of the latter was merely to give its sanction to every municipal and provincial constitu-

---

[1] Robiquet, *Le personnel municipal*, 147–148, note; 162.   [2] *Ibid.*, 162.
[3] *Discours prononcé par Brissot de Warville au district des Filles-Saint-Thomas*, July 21, 1789. Lacroix, *Actes de la Commune*, I, 292.

tion. In short, cities ought to have the right to form their own municipal governments; to the central government belonged only the veto power over the clauses of the municipal constitutions. Indeed, Brissot was so jealous of the rights of the new government of Paris that when Mirabeau, in speaking of the rights of local civil authorities, criticized the municipalities as being aristocratic and despotic,[1] he saw in Mirabeau's remarks an attack on Paris and immediately proceeded to arraign Mirabeau in a letter published in the *Patriote Français* in which he reiterated his former arguments, declaring again that it was the province of the municipalities to draw up their own system of government, and that the legislative power had only the most limited control over their charters. He soon discovered on reading a fuller report of the speech in question that Mirabeau had really cast no aspersions on Paris. He was therefore obliged to retract his too hasty criticisms.[2]

The third important question was that of the advisability of including Paris in a department of the same size as other departments, or of forming it into a department by itself. Here Brissot took what has proved to be the modern view, advocating a special form of government for Paris and claiming that it was not a violation of equality since Paris was a unique city. In a speech before the city council he advanced the argument, since justified by experience, that the exceptional conditions of a large city require a particular kind of government, and that to make such a city dependent on a department in just the same manner as smaller cities were dependent, is to work against the interests of its inhabitants.[3] In this case, however, Brissot was not altogether successful, for although the Department of the Seine was so constituted as to include but little territory outside of Paris, yet the Commune of Paris did not secure an independent government but was made subordinate to this departmental government.[4]

---

[1] *Moniteur*, August 10–14, 1789.   [2] *Patriote Français*, August 17–18, 1789.
[3] *Opinion de J. P. Brissot de Warville sur la question de savoir si Paris sera le centre d'un département*, December 15, 1789.
[4] Lacroix, *Actes de la Commune*, iii, Introduction, and p. 197.

Meanwhile, in the administration, as well as in the organization of the city government, he was taking an active part. He served on committees, made speeches both in his district and section, and in the central assembly, drew up addresses, and at the same time, by means of his newspaper, the *Patriote Français*, kept the public informed of municipal affairs and of his own views upon them. Especially on occasions when the municipality had a communication to make to the National Assembly or undertook in other ways to make its influence felt in national affairs, Brissot was sure to appear at the front, if he did not himself take the initiative. For example, on the bringing of the king and queen and the National Assembly to Paris, he was appointed as one of the committee to draw up an address to be sent to all the municipalities of France,[1] and on another committee to draw up and present an address to the National Assembly on the same occasion. Both addresses appear to have been Brissot's own work and were skillfully expressed. They minimized the actual events of October 5 and 6, dwelt on the advantages of the removal to Paris in that the Assembly would be more under the influence of the people, and assured the Assembly that the municipality of Paris would take all measures in its power for its protection. Again when it was a question of stating the opinion of the municipal government on toleration for the Jews, Brissot was appointed to examine a work on the subject.[2] And once more when the very important matter of the ecclesiastical property was under discussion he was named on the committee to present an address to the National Assembly.[3] In this case it was strange that Brissot should have been put on the committee, for, in a recent address, he had expressed views with which the municipal assembly was not in sympathy. The National Assembly had offered to the municipalities of France the opportunity to purchase the lands of the Church, to re-sell them, and to keep a generous share of the proceeds. This opportu-

[1] Lacroix, *Actes de la Commune*, ii, 245–47.
[2] *Ibid.*, v, 498.   [3] *Ibid.*, vi, 130.

nity, Brissot declared, ought to be confined in the case of each municipality to ecclesiastical territory within its own limits, for, he argued, municipalities were local administrations; they could look after distant property only with great inconvenience and expense; and finally, the conflicting interests which would inevitably arise would put a severe strain upon the spirit of fraternity. Furthermore, if the municipalities were really disinterested, they would also give up the profits accorded to them by the re-sale. Paris, he added, had had a fine chance to offer to all the other municipalities of France an example of patriotism.[1] This opportunity Paris declined to avail herself of, on the ground that a large part of the ecclesiastical property in the city of Paris was unproductive, and that as it might be years before she could re-sell, her interests would be sadly injured if she were limited in her acquisitions to Paris itself.[2]

Meanwhile, the city had a more pressing difficulty to meet in the scarcity of currency, and on this question, too, Brissot had something to say. The trouble, he declared, was due to the suspension of payment of its notes by the *caisse d'escompte*. This institution was a bank of issue founded during the reign of Louis XV, and reëstablished under Turgot. It had not been sufficiently controlled by the government, had gotten into difficulty and suspended payment. The remedy, according to Brissot, was not to lessen the difficulty for Paris by circulating the bills of the *caisse* in the provinces, neither was it to issue small notes, but solely to limit its privileges by making the *caisse d'escompte* redeem all its bills in cash. Every bill, he declared in terms which were hardly consistent with his arguments in favor of assignats, which was not instantly convertible into specie, was a dangerous kind of paper. The municipality ought to appeal to the National Assembly to forbid a further suspension of payment of the *caisse d'escompte*, and to

---

[1] *Motion sur la nécessité de circonscrire la vente des biens ecclésiastiques aux municipalités, dans leur territoire. Présentée à l'Assemblée générale des représentants de la Commune de Paris,* May 22, 1790.

[2] Lacroix, v, 457, 500; vi, 51, 59, 130.

make all possible haste to discover and announce the real state of the finances.[1]

The finances were not the only branch of the administration which Brissot felt the people of Paris ought to censure, and in a speech before the general assembly of the section of the *Bibliothèque*, the 24th of October, 1790, he emphasized his ideas of popular sovereignty and made an appeal for the dismissal of the entire ministry, including the first clerks. The request for the dismissal of the ministry had already been made, but hitherto without result. "The National Assembly has succumbed," he cried; "it is now time for the people to triumph, it is time for them to make their voice heard. The ministers of the army and navy have protected aristocratic officers; the minister of foreign affairs has protected officers who have not taken the oath, the minister of finance has badly mismanaged the finances. They should all be dismissed." In this case Brissot was successful, at least to the extent that a resolution was passed urging their dismissal and sent to the National Assembly.[2] According to the *Journal général de la cour et de la ville*, he was not content with his success in the section of the *Bibliothèque*, but had thousands of copies of his address printed and distributed throughout Paris.[3] Meanwhile, he was standing for the right of the people to criticize, not only the ministry but their own city officers. He also boldly upheld Marat and Danton who represented the democratic party in their attacks on the moderates and aristocrats, as represented by the mayor, Bailly. Brissot thus allied himself, not only with freedom of speech, but with democracy.

But Brissot by no means confined his attention to Paris and the influence of Paris on the National Assembly; he was equally interested in the development of local government throughout

---

[1] *Discours sur la rareté du numéraire et sur les moyens d'y remédier, prononcé à l'Assemblée générale des représentants de la Commune de Paris, le 10 février, 1790. Le Patriote Français*, February 15, 1790.

[2] *Discours prononcé à la section de la Bibliothèque dans son Assemblée générale le 24 octobre, 1790, sur la question du renvoi des ministres.*

[3] *Journal général de la cour et de la ville*, November 9, 1790.

France. He was a member of the society of "patriotic electors" whose object was to further the election of good local officers and of the *Société des anciens représentants de la Commune* who through their *comité de surveillance* kept up a correspondence with the directories,[1] while in the columns of the *Patriote Français* he devoted much space to local municipal affairs and gave frequent advice as to the dangers to be avoided. For example, in the issue of the 8th of June, 1790, he warned the electors to be cautious in the choice of their officers and to avoid all frivolous and vain persons who were incapable of understanding the meaning of the word equality. On a previous occasion he had been more precise and inserted an article which advised the electors in organizing a new government not to choose the present officers, nor, in short, any person who belonged to the old order of things. Such advice naturally did not escape the attention of the proscribed classes and was the occasion of an acrimonious pamphlet directed against the *Patriote Français* by one of their number.[2]

Throughout his career as a municipal politician, Brissot showed himself thoroughly radical in his hostility to the old régime and in his approval of the new. He even tried to use his position of influence in municipal affairs to further a new colonial régime. He endeavored to interest his fellow politicians in the cause of the negro, and sent copies by the hundred to the central municipal assembly of addresses of the *Société des Amis des Noirs*. These addresses were apparently favorably received, but when he attempted to bring the cause before his district, his constituents told him plainly that his advocacy of the anti-slave trade propaganda was untimely, refused to support his

---

[1] *Réflexions sur l'état de la société des électeurs patriotes sur ses travaux, sur les formes propres à faire de bonnes élections, — lués à l'assemblée de cette société, dans la séance du 21 décembre, 1790, par J. P. Brissot, électeur, Paris, 25 décembre, 1790.*

[2] *Lettre à M. Brissot de Warville sur ses Réflexions importantes relatives aux électeurs futurs des municipalités contenus dans le supplément du No. CLXIV de son Journal intitulé Le Patriote Français, par Verney, avocat Lyon,* January 30, 1790.

measures in favor of the negro, and expressed their strongest disapproval of any steps which might interfere with colonial commerce.[1] Meanwhile, he was sharply criticized by the press for dragging such a topic into the discussion, while the real business of the municipality, the formation of a permanent government, was still unfinished.[2]

Brissot's main work, however, in the new city government, that in connection with which he was best known and most severely criticized, was as a member of the *Comité des Recherches*. This committee was organized October 22, 1789, and the same day Brissot was chosen a member. Its functions — " to receive denunciations and depositions of intrigues, plots, and conspiracies, in case of necessity to keep under surveillance the persons denounced, to examine them, to collect proof " [3] — were not unlike those of the governmental police under the old régime. The very nature of such functions, involving of necessity a certain amount of secrecy and arbitrary action, was sufficient to bring the committee into disfavor and to arouse bitter criticism.[4] They had to meet the impossible problem of reconciling the methods of a special tribunal with the new democratic ideas of liberty and equality. But to stand for law and order, and at the same time to show their abhorrence of the old régime and all its works, was a matter of some difficulty. For example, it was apparently their business to investigate the disorder of the 5th and 6th of October at Versailles and punish the authors of it; but they were obviously afraid to

---

[1] Lacroix, III, 366, 370, note 2; IV, 100; also *Extrait des registres des délibérations du district des Filles-Saint-Thomas. Supplément au procès-verbal de l'assemblée nationale, Colonies*, I; *Traité des Nègres*, II.

[2] *Les Révolutions de Paris*, February 13–20, 1790.

[3] Lacroix, II, 376–77.

[4] A report of the work of the committee, made November 30, 1789, only a little more than a month after its formation, will serve to indicate the kind of work in which it was engaged. "The committee," says the report, "finds three kinds of plots to deal with: (a) those attributed to the aristocratic party; (b) such abnormal excesses as those committed in the Château of Versailles; (c) schemes for frightening the people, — such as incendiary motions and seditious writings." Lacroix, III, 76–81.

do so lest they might be thought to be on the side of royalty against the people. They had no such scruples, however, about attacking representatives of the old régime, no matter what their rank or official position.

The prominence of the persons thus accused made the committee and its methods very conspicuous. It was a situation of which the royalist newspapers were not slow to take advantage. They defended the victims of the committee and assailed its principles. "You may pride yourselves," they said, "on your democratic principles; you may put these principles into practice by attacking representatives of royalty, but in spite of your pretensions, you yourselves are using power nothing short of despotic; and, while bringing accusations against the old régime, you are employing its very methods." On account of his reputation as an opponent of despotism, Brissot was the most conspicuously inconsistent member of the committee and was accordingly singled out for special attack. "We know very well," declared the *Actes des Apôtres*, "that no *Comité des Recherches* has the right to hold citizens accountable for their ideas or for their opinions; that *Comités des Recherches* and municipalities are not tribunals instructed to judge such matters; that there is no law in existence against the liberty of the press. We know all this, and if we did not know it M. Brissot de Warville, the president of the *Comité des Recherches*, would tell us." Nor was such criticism confined to the royalist journals. So advanced a paper as the *Révolutions de Paris* also called Brissot to account. "A longer exercise of power," it declared, "might become fatal to the virtues of that committee. The decemvirs oppressed no one at the beginning of their magistracy; it was only as they became familiar with the power with which they were clothed that they became tyrants. . . . It is time that they abdicated. The spirit of the inquisition seems to have already destroyed the good principles of that member of the committee who, a martyr of liberty under the ministerial régime, we thought, was going to be its defender under the coming new régime. 'Some authors of incendiary writings have been arrested,' says M. Brissot de Warville in his paper of November 8. . . . Before going further we ask M. Brissot de Warville, the journalist, by what rule M. Brissot de Warville, the member of the *Comité des Recherches*, decides whether a certain piece of writing is incendiary or whether it is not." [1]

These general charges received a special and damaging application in the affair of MM. Dhosier and Petit-Jean. The case itself was of little moment, but it was important in the accusations to which it gave rise, and because it provoked a defense of the committee of which Brissot was the author.[2] MM. Dhosier and Petit-Jean were two men who had appeared at the Château of Saint-Cloud, June 29, 1790, and aroused suspicion by their peculiar actions. On being questioned, they produced a paper purporting to contain directions from the Virgin Mary to the king, which they declared was given to them by Madame Thomassin, who, while in a state of somnambulism, had received it directly from the Holy Virgin. This paper, which at first sight appeared to be the production of some weak-minded individuals, seemed to the authorities to contain evidences of a conspiracy. Madame Thomassin and her friend Madame Jumilhac were accordingly arrested, and after examination the committee reported to the effect that although there were suspicious circumstances, the affair was not worth investigation.[3]

This report was taken up by Stanislas Clermont,[4] who made it the basis of an attack on the *Comité des Recherches*. He accused the committee of the following offenses: [5] they arrested Madame Jumilhac on insufficient evidence; they did not make any effort to obtain the *corpus delicti*; they used an unneces-

---

[1] *Les Révolutions de Paris*, November 8–14, 1789.

[2] Brissot, *Rapport dans l'affaire de MM. Dhosier et Petit-Jean . . . le 29 juillet, 1790.*

[3] *Brissot . . . à Stanislas Clermont*, 39.

[4] Stanislas Clermont was a leader of the liberal nobility.

[5] *Réflexions sur l'ouvrage intitulé : "Projet de contre-révolution par les somnambulists ou rapports dans l'affaire de MM. Dhosier et Petit-Jean," août, 1790.*

sary display of force in order to arrest her; they did not confront her with the accuser; they neither acquitted nor condemned her. The committee, in short, was a tribunal which considered itself above law, arresting, imprisoning, punishing, according to its will — a veritable inquisition. To these accusations Brissot made a formal reply [1] to this effect: that the paper in question *was* of a treasonable nature, and that there was, therefore, due reason for Madame Jumilhac's arrest; that the order for her arrest came from the *Comité des Recherches* of the National Assembly; that the high rank of Madame Jumilhac afforded no ground for treating her with more consideration than other people; that a large force was necessary in arresting her to prevent opposition by her friends and servants; that the verdict was necessary from the circumstances of the case. The general charge that the committee was an inquisitorial body, Brissot denied most emphatically. This tribunal was not an inquisition, he declared, for it was not secret; the same proofs were required as in ordinary tribunals; the prisoners were not refused permission to see their friends, and were not kept in solitary confinement. Surely such a committee was necessary in time of crisis. Very much the same accusations had been made by the Chevalier de Pange, in answer to whom Brissot had already made a formal defense of the committee, in which he declared that there was no such thing as *délation* under a free government. [2] To the accusation that the committee was simply the old police under a changed name, he answered that although it might have the same powers, it was like the old police neither in function nor in spirit. It did not work in secret nor pronounce sentence, but merely sent the accused to the proper tribunal; further, its object was not, as with the old police, "to support despotism, but to defend the temple of liberty." While Brissot was undoubtedly justified on account of the extraordinary circumstances of the time in

---

[1] *J. P. Brissot . . . à Stanislas Clermont,* and *Réplique à Stanislas Clermont.*

[2] *Lettre de Brissot à M. le Chevalier de Pange, 1790.*

making these distinctions, he showed a perverse tendency to exaggerate the importance of a change of motive, especially in his assertion that a committee of inquiry might justly use the machinery of despotism provided it were done in the interests of liberty.

The real justification for such a committee was in the necessities of the time. As early as October, 1790, when conditions seemed to have become more normal, the question of its dissolution was discussed and the motion for its continuance passed by a very small majority.[1] Brissot himself shortly afterward withdrew from the committee.[2] A year later, the committee as a whole resigned, on the ground that "the Revolution was ended and the reign of law established." [3]

Meanwhile Brissot had aroused opposition of another kind, on account of his principles regarding the distribution of authority in the city government. The form of government which went into effect in September, 1789, was, after all, only provisional, and the city council still had, as its chief work, the formation of a permanent organization. The main issue was, as before, the balance of power between the central council and the districts. Brissot continued to support the central council, and thereby came into renewed conflict with the districts. The 30th of November, 1789, he made a motion in the city council that they should ask the National Assembly to authorize its constitutional committee to consult with the committee chosen by the city council for the purpose of presenting a plan of organization for Paris. In this motion Brissot appeared to be desirous of confining all collaboration in the matter to a committee of the council to the exclusion of the council itself, not to mention the districts.[4] Such a proposition was naturally opposed by large numbers of the council, while numerous representatives of the districts appeared to express their vehement disapproval, and after much discussion it was voted

---

[1] Lacroix, *Actes de la Commune*, 2d series, i, 125.
[2] Robiquet, *Le personnel municipal de Paris*, 441.   [3] *Ibid.*, 465.
[4] Lacroix, *Actes de la Commune*, iii, 82, 89–90.

down. The affair seems to have provoked great excitement. Brissot was called to account for not having given a correct report of it in the *Patriote Français*, whereupon he promised to set the matter right and at the same time protested that he had not intended to deprive the districts of all voice in the matter.[1] But the districts were not to be convinced. He soon stirred up the enmity of his own district by an unwise advocacy of his propaganda against the slave trade.[2] Furthermore, in the matter of the administration of the sale of ecclesiastical lands, he aroused not only his own, but all the districts. The management of these sales was claimed by the districts, — a demand which Brissot opposed on the ground that the districts were not administrative bodies. The management belonged therefore not to them but to the *bureau de ville*, the administrative branch of the general city government.[3] The districts had their revenge when, in the establishment of the permanent municipal government, in October, 1790, they refused to elect Brissot to the municipal council or to any other office. His active part in the municipal politics of Paris thus came to an end.

In view of his later mortal combat with the municipal government of Paris, his early connection with it is of special interest. In view, also, of the ground of that combat, — the strife between the provinces and Paris, — his early insistence on the importance of Paris is noteworthy. Because it was so important he argued it must have a special form of government. But also because of its importance it must recognize its duties. For this reason — because it was the foremost city — he had insisted that it ought not to state its own grievances till the general grievances were adjusted, that it ought not to lessen its own burdens by floating the notes of the *caisse d'escompte* on the country at large; and on the other hand that it should

[1] Lacroix, *Actes de la Commune*, III, 124; and *Les Révolutions de Paris*, November 28 to December 5, 1789.

[2] See p. 197.

[3] *Motion sur la nécessité de circonscrire la vente des biens ecclésiastiques aux municipalités*, May, 1790.

set a good example to France by a disinterested policy in the matter of church lands. In short, Paris must take her place as the first city of France.

While remaining true to his ideals of equality and government by the people, he found it necessary to modify them somewhat in practical politics; for example, in limiting the power of the districts and in the case of the *Comité des Recherches*, while continuing to preach liberty he had not hesitated to use despotic power to preserve it. If his interests subsequently changed, and if from being an enthusiastic representative of the municipality of Paris he became one of its most bitter foes, his fundamental policy did not change, and in his future work as a legislator in helping to transform France the limited monarchy into France the republic, he showed the same ideals and the same policy that he had shown in his work as a municipal politician in changing Paris of the old régime into Paris the modern city.

CHAPTER VI

PART I

His Struggles to Establish a Newspaper and his Attitude on Legislation

BRISSOT had failed to be elected to the Constituent Assembly,[1] but he was none the less to exert an important influence during its session, not only as a municipal politician, but to a greater degree as the editor of one of the chief newspapers of the period, — the *Patriote Français*. In starting this journal Brissot was a pioneer in two respects. In the first place he established one of the first real newspapers in anything like the modern sense of the term. Up to the time of the French Revolution such periodic publications as existed were more like series of essays or pamphlets, "periodic books" — to use Brissot's own phrase. In the production of this kind of literature Brissot himself had had some experience in his work on the *Annales* of Linguet and the *Courrier* of Swinton and in his own *Correspondance Universelle*. The French Revolution now brought about a great and sudden change. It converted the pamphlet into the regular newspaper, and led to the founding of a large number of daily journals of every shade of opinion and of every degree of excellence. Of these new journals Brissot's *Patriote Français* was practically the first. In the second place he took the lead in a valiant struggle against the censorship of the press,[2] — a struggle which brings into high relief a picture of the gradual crumbling of the old régime and the slow and painful building up of the new.

---

[1] The name afterwards given to the body summoned as the States-General.

[2] Note also the part taken by Mirabeau in this struggle in his attempt to establish his newspaper, the *États-Généraux*.

It was a courageous attempt that he made, in view both of his own unfortunate encounters with government repression and of the existing restrictions on the press. On March 16, 1789, he issued his first prospectus, in which, after portraying the advantages of the newspaper over the pamphlet, he stated his intention of founding a newspaper which should further revolution in France, just as the newspaper had furthered revolution in America. He declared, moreover, in unmistakable terms that he proposed to make that newspaper not only truly national and free, but also independent of the censorship and of every kind of influence. As to the details of the publication, he stated that the paper would appear about the first of April and that the price of subscription would be 24 livres a year.[1] A few days later he published a second prospectus, in which he announced that the paper would be published four times a week instead of twice, as at first stated; that subscriptions might be left with the bookseller, Buisson, and that the first number would appear about April 20.

This seemed to the authorities "the last degree of audacity," and they immediately took steps to show Brissot that he had made a serious mistake in assuming that any such ideas could be carried out. The lieutenant of the police and the director-general of the book trade first warned the authorized journals to make no announcement of the prospectus in question. They then dispatched a circular letter to the inspectors of the book trade, urging them to take all measures within their power to stop the circulation of the prospectus and the printing and distribution of the journal.[2] These measures were effective at least in frightening Buisson who, it had been announced, was to receive the subscriptions, for he promptly disavowed his connection with Brissot's newspaper and declared that his name had been used without his consent.[3] He seems subse-

---

[1] See the prospectus as quoted in Tourneux, *Bibliographie de l'histoire de Paris pendant la Révolution française*, II, 500.

[2] *Lettre de Maissemy, Archives nationales*, v[1], 551.

[3] This claim appears to be true, for, in his protest to Maissemy, of April 13 (*Archives nationales*, v[1], 551), he, Buisson, incloses a copy of a letter which reads

quently to have recovered from his fright, for when the paper began to appear regularly, it was at his shop that subscriptions were received.[1]

Brissot himself was not at all daunted, and on the 6th of May he boldly published the first number of the *Patriote Fran-çais*. It appeared as a tiny sheet of eight duodecimo pages and consisted of two parts: an account of the opening of the States-General at Versailles, and a discussion of the *cahier* of the third estate of Paris, in which the public was urged not to be discouraged in spite of the attitude of the king and Necker toward the third estate. Meanwhile Brissot's cause was becoming a general one. Other newspapers were being established and the authorities thus had to contend with a rapidly rising tide of opposition to their power. To meet it, they re-inforced the circular to the inspectors of the book trade, which was directed especially against Brissot, by a general decree of the royal council which forbade the unauthorized announcement for distribution of any new newspaper whatever.[2]

This decree Brissot could not ignore, as he had the previous orders. To continue the publication of his paper was for the moment clearly impossible, and he reluctantly addressed a letter to his subscribers, informing them that the publication of the *Patriote Français* was stopped. But, he assured them, the suspension would be but temporary; he was preparing a memoir to the States-General on the subject, and the first thing the States-General would do, as soon as it was organized, would doubtless be to establish freedom of the press. In this memoir he made

in part: "*Ci-joint M[onsieur] le prospectus d'un J[ourn]al sur lequel j'ai cru devoir imprimer votre nom pour recevoir les subscriptions et que je vais faire distribuer. Je ne pense pas qu'il puisse éprouver aucune difficulté puisque'en y destinant moi même mon nom, je me rends responsable de tout ce qui sera imprimé dans ce journal.*"

[1] They soon came to a break, however. For the dissolution of their connection, see *Archives nationales*, v[1], 553; also the *Patriote Français*, September 14, 1789. *Avis important de M. Brissot de Warville aux souscripteurs de ce journal.*

[2] Quoted in Tourneux, *Bibliographie*, ii, 502. See also *Lettre aux souscripteurs*, May 12, 1789.

an ardent plea for such freedom. There could be no free constitution without it, he declared. Moreover, it was a natural right necessary for the States-General and necessary for the government. To be effective it must be given freely and fully, and all newspapers ought to be allowed to be sent by post without any previous permission. In giving such freedom there was no occasion to fear its abuse, for too great license could be prevented by special laws. Their execution, moreover, should be intrusted to independent tribunals and not left to arbitrary rules of the ministers. Finally, in view of these principles, he demanded freedom to publish the *Patriote Français*.[1] Although he did not receive a formal decision from the States-General in his favor,[2] the events of July established freedom of the press *de facto*, and without waiting for its establishment *de jure*, on July 28 he again started his newspaper, and issued the second number, the first of the uninterrupted series.[3] Thus was established the *Patriote Français*, one of the most important newspapers of the period of the French Revolution. It was true to the motto printed at the head of each number: "A free newspaper is a sentinel who always stands on guard for the people." Indeed, to quote the ardent republican, Manuel, it "was the *first* sentinel who cried Constitution, Truth, Liberty."[4]

Of liberty in all its forms the *Patriote Français* was consistently the champion. Throughout the session of the Constituent Assembly it opposed those who would emphasize the constitution at the expense of the declaration of rights, and maintained that the declaration of rights was, on the contrary, the ideal to which the constitution ought to conform. Under

[1] *Mémoire aux États-Généraux*, June, 1789.

[2] On May 19, Maissemy, the director-general of the book trade, made what was virtually a confession of complete defeat on the part of the authorities, by issuing an order which permitted newspapers to publish the proceedings of the Assembly but forbade them to make any commentary or reflections. Avenel, *Histoire de la presse française*, 48.

[3] The delay was probably due in part to the active rôle which he had played in the election of representatives of the third estate in Paris. Tourneux, II, 503. See also p. 94.

[4] Quoted in Hatin, *Bibliographie de la presse périodique*, 142.

the Legislative Assembly and the Convention it became the leading organ of the Girondins in opposition to the Mountain, and finally came to an end with the fall of the Girondins. It was at the same time "the scourge of the court and the terror of the terrorists." [1]

In its form and content the *Patriote Français* compared favorably with the best newspapers of the time. Despite the legal difficulties encountered and despite numerous other hindrances then incident to the publishing of a first-class journal, Brissot not only managed to continue his newspaper without interruption but to make some improvements in his original plan. Instead of appearing only four times a week as was announced in the original prospectus, it was published every day but Sunday, and from November 1, 1789, on Sundays also; and instead of a duodecimo sheet, it came out as a large quarto of four pages to which supplements were frequently added. [2] From the first it paid particular attention to the National Assembly, and while not attempting to give verbatim reports, devoted much space to comments and observations upon its proceedings. Even this did not satisfy some of Brissot's readers and he was reproached for not giving more details. In reply he urged the wide scope of his journal as an excuse and complained that it was unfair to compare his newspaper, "which embraced all that patriotism embraced," with the *Moniteur* which made the reports of the debates its almost exclusive business. His aim certainly was extensive. He proposed, according to both his announcements, to do five things: (1) to set forth facts faithfully; (2) to reproduce all the publications of the government and to outline the debates of the States-General; (3) to register the transactions of the provincial assemblies; (4) to discuss current questions, and (5) to review political pamphlets. In his second prospectus he announced further that he would include in his newspaper the results of his researches on the constitutions of England and of the United States. After the first

---

[1] Hatin, *Bibliographie de la presse périodique*, 143.
[2] January 1, 1791, the size was enlarged.

few months he was able to carry out fairly well this extensive plan, and about the first of February, 1791, he made still further improvements, and included regularly a column on the money market and a list of the current plays. Besides its extensive reports of the proceedings of the National Assembly, the *Patriote Français* paid much attention to the municipal affairs of Paris. This was particularly true during the period of Brissot's career as a municipal politician, when the concerns of the city government naturally occupied a large share of his interest. A special column was devoted to Paris; the proceedings of the municipal assemblies were reported and the policy of the city government defended, especially in the case of the *Comité des Recherches*. But the *Patriote Français* by no means confined its attention to Paris. It also took a keen interest in the course of the Revolution in the provinces and followed the development of local government throughout France. In these particulars it was not so different from some of the other journals, but in the amount of attention it paid to the cause of the negro and to American affairs it stands alone. It was in fact the organ of the *Société des Amis des Noirs*, publishing its addresses, defending its policy, and attacking its opponents. As for his interest in the new world Brissot had already pointed out in his prospectus that the *Patriote Français* was to be the means for spreading abroad information about America and for impressing upon the public the ideas that he had gained from his own experience. Hardly a number appeared in which he did not make some reference to the United States. He covered the whole range of the subject, from an advertisement by a man who was looking for a partner in his Kentucky lands to a discussion of the fundamental principles of the American constitution. In everything connected with the establishment of the new government of the United States he was especially interested. He approved of Washington's cabinet appointments,[1] printed a copy of his first Thanksgiving proclamation,[2] and reviewed the proceedings of Congress at Philadelphia. Yet

---

[1] *Patriote Français*, November 26, 1789.   [2] *Ibid.*, January 18, 1790.

it was not as a matter of merely abstract interest that Brissot referred so frequently to America; it was rather that its recent history might serve as a precedent to France. He praised the democratic spirit of the United States in proscribing all titles of nobility; he commended their tolerance for establishing freedom of religion;[1] when plans for the municipal government of Paris were under discussion, he argued, from the separation of national, state, and city affairs in the United States, that the drawing up of the plan belonged not to the National Assembly, but to the city itself; and when, at the opening of the Legislative Assembly, the question was raised whether they should have few or many committees, he made use of the example of the American Congress as a weighty argument in favor of having as few as possible.[2]

This wide range of contents appealed to a variety of readers, and the *Patriote Français* became very popular. Its style was perhaps not equal in merit to its contents. Like his other works it showed a lack of a sense of humor and of a light touch; but if wanting in the wit and brilliancy of Desmoulins's *Révolutions de France et de Brabant* or the virility of Prudhomme's *Révolutions de Paris* it was a decided improvement on Brissot's earlier writings, both in force and vigor. He was obliged, however, to defend himself against the charge of too great seriousness. "People have said to me," he wrote, "that I was too serious; they want me to make fun, to chaff and to draw caricatures. That rôle does not suit me; one must be himself, and if the French people fall again into the taste for political and literary buffooneries, a writer whose only desire is to be useful, ought never to lend himself to such things."[3] Brissot might indeed be charged with a lack of humor, but he certainly could not be accused of the scurrility and personal invective which marked the *Père Duchesne* and the *Ami du Peuple*. Whatever the *Patriote Français* was or was not, it never, at least, lacked

---

[1] *Patriote Français*, May 7, 1790.
[2] *Discours sur l'organisation des comités*, October, 1791. See p. 226.
[3] *Patriote Français*, April 9, 1790.

in dignity. Its radical stand naturally brought it into conflict with the conservative press, but although it had numerous sharp controversies with royalist and moderate journals, when it concerned personalities, it was generally inclined to limit itself to the defensive. In matters of general policy it could count on the invariable support of the *Courrier des Départements* and the *Chronique de Paris* and the invariable hostility of the *Actes des Apôtres*, the *Journal de Paris*, the *Journal général de la cour et de la ville*, and later of the *Ami du Peuple;* while the *Révolutions de France et de Brabant* and the *Révolutions de Paris* approved and criticized in turn. His most serious conflicts arose from his zealous attacks on despotism and more than once led to accusations for libel.

Besides carrying on the *Patriote Français*, Brissot was one of the collaborators of the *Chronique du Mois*. This publication which appeared monthly from November, 1791, to July, 1793, was not, properly speaking, a newspaper at all, but merely a series of essays.[1] It was founded, so the prospectus set forth, to further the public good. It might more truly have been said, to further the interests of the Girondin party. To this periodical Brissot made a number of contributions, but they consisted chiefly of reproductions of articles which had already appeared elsewhere, and hence do not add materially to the knowledge of Brissot as journalist or politician.[2]

---

[1] *La Chronique du Mois ou Les Cahiers patriotiques de E. Clavière, C. Condorcet, L. Mercier, A. Auger, J. Oswald, N. Bonneville, J. Bidermann, A. Broussonct, A. Guy-Kersaint, J. P. Brissot, J. Ph. Garran de Coulon, J. Dussaulx, F. Lanthenas, et Collot d'Herbois*, November, 1791, to July, 1793.

[2] Each number was headed by a full-page portrait of one of the collaborators of the paper or of some man prominent in public affairs. Brissot's portrait appears in the number for July, 1792. His part, advertised to consist of "some of his eloquent speeches upon our rights which he knows so well how to defend," was made up of nine contributions as follows: —

(a) *Sur les reproches qu'on fait à l'Assemblée nationale*, March, 1792.

(b) *Sur la justice de la guerre contre l'Autriche*, May, 1792.

(c) *Observations sur Helvetius*, July, 1792. A criticism of Helvetius' theory — that all passions have their origin in the physical senses, in love of pleasure, or in aversion to pain — as being on too low a plane.

(d) *Politics de Paul*, August, 1792. An extract from his work: *Lettres sur Saint Paul.*

In carrying on his own paper Brissot was in turn assisted by numerous collaborators: by Clavière, with whom he had long been on terms of intimacy; by Grégoire, his fellow worker in the *Société des Amis des Noirs;* by Pétion, the Mayor of Paris; [1] Thomas Paine, the Anglo-American; and, above all, by the Rolands and a little group of friends who centered around them and which included Blot, the friend of Brissot's childhood,[2] Lanthenas,[3] Bosc,[4] and Bançal des Issarts.[5] According to M. Perroud something over one hundred contributions to the *Patriote Français* may be attributed to members of this group. Brissot's acquaintance with the Rolands dated from the publication of his book *De la France et des États Unis.* In this work Brissot frequently quoted from Roland, praised his learning and courage, and when the book was published sent him a copy. There resulted a lively correspondence between Brissot and the Rolands. Through Bosc and Lanthenas, whom

(e) *Sur les motifs de ceux qui défendant la monarchie et qui calomnaient le républicanisme. J. P. Brissot à N. Bonneville,* October, 1792.

(f) *À tous les républicains de France : sur le Société des Jacobins de Paris, 1792,* already published in pamphlet form.

(g) *De la marche des agitateurs,* January, 1793.

(h) *Sur le tems* [sic]. March, 1793.

(i) *De quelques erreurs dans les idées et dans les mots relatifs à la révolution française,* March, 1793.

[1] *Pétion y faisait paraître les lettres, avis, observations qu'il avait à publier comme maire de Paris.* Vatel, *Charlotte Corday et les Girondins,* I, 240, note.

[2] See p. 7.

[3] *François Lanthenas,* a physician and author of numerous political pamphlets, was born in 1754 and died in 1799. He was a friend of the Rolands, and under the first Roland ministry was given the first place in the department of public instruction. Although arrested with the Girondins he escaped proscription and was elected to the Council of 500.

[4] *Louis Augustin Guillaume Bosc* was a French naturalist, born in 1759 and died in 1828. He was a friend of Madame Roland and one of her correspondents, and under the Roland ministry became director of the post-office. He remained attached to Madame Roland, risked his life by visiting her in prison, and preserved the manuscript of her memoirs. He escaped the guillotine and under the Directory was sent on a diplomatic mission to the United States.

[5] *Jean Henri Bançal des Issarts* was born in 1750 and died in 1826. He represented Auvergne in the National Assembly and founded a society of the Jacobins at Clermont. Later, he became a friend of Madame Roland and an avowed republican and an ally of the Girondins.

Brissot came to know at Paris, he was brought into still more friendly relations with them though without ever having seen them; and when he projected his newspaper, he found his new friends ready to sympathize with his plans and to help him by their correspondence. They lent copies of the *Patriote Fran-çais* to their friends, tried to increase its circulation, and sent him articles for publication on the course of the Revolution at Lyons. He seems to have been especially delighted with the contributions of Madame Roland, who was, he declared, "both well informed and of a truly strong character." He even ventured to insert in his newspaper passages from her letters to Bosc and Lanthenas which had been passed on to him; [1] and when at a later period she criticized him for not being sufficiently radical, he took the criticism with good grace and attacked the royalist party in Lyons with more vehemence. [2] While the Rolands were writing for the *Patriote Français* of the struggle in Lyons against despotism, Lanthenas was writing against despotism in general, his chief articles being on the freedom of the press and on the organization of popular societies. [3] Bançal meanwhile kept the *Patriote Français* informed of events in Clermont. In turn, Brissot supported the interests of his friends in local and national elections. [4]

The Rolands were his chief correspondents, but the financial support for his journal came from a man named LePage, to whom, apparently, he left much of the business management. LePage is said to have made money out of it for himself, but Brissot, according to Madame Roland, instead of likewise profiting, was content with the small salary allowed him by his partner and came out of the enterprise as poor as when he

[1] For the details of their early correspondence, see Perroud, *Lettres de Madame Roland*, II, 55 and note, 61, 64 and note, 77, 78, 95, 114; *Mémoires de Madame Roland*, I, 61, 191, 192, and *Brissot et les Roland, Collaboration des Roland au Patriote Français*, in *La Révolution française*, XXXIV, 403, May, 1898.

[2] *Lettres de Madame Roland*, II, 174, 175, note.

[3] See, for example, the *Patriote Français* of February 5, 14, 28, 1791.

[4] See article by Perroud in *La Révolution française*, XXXIV, 403–22, May, 1898.

went into it.[1] In true French fashion the members of his family assisted in the business, his mother-in-law and one of his sisters-in-law helping in the office.[2] His main collaborator, and most of the time his partner, was Girey-Dupré,[3] a young journalist of Girondin sympathies. On several occasions Brissot turned over to Girey-Dupré a considerable share in the responsibility for the newspaper. The first time was at the opening of the Legislative Assembly, when, quite overcome by the responsibilities of his new position as legislator, he announced that "in order to devote himself entirely to the important functions to which the choice of his fellow citizens called him," he would abandon the chief editorship to his colleague.[4] But it was not long before he realized the importance of the post he had surrendered, and re-assumed control of that part of his paper dealing with the reports of the National Assembly.[5] Again, during the trial of the king it was Girey-Dupré who was entrusted with the reports on the ground that Brissot while acting as judge had no right to express his opinions editorially.[6] Finally, when the decree of the Assembly on March 9, 1793, forbade the members of the Convention to conduct newspapers,[7] Brissot definitely turned over the management of the paper to his partner. Three months later, with the fall of the Girondins and the flight of both Brissot and Girey-Dupré, the *Patriote Français* came to an end. The partnership in the conduct of the journal naturally raised the question of respon-

[1] *Mémoires de Madame Roland*, i, 197–98. Brissot felt that LePage did not always treat him fairly. See, for instance, a letter of Madame Brissot, of October 22, 1791 (*Correspondance*, 276). Again, in writing to her brother, January 15, 1792, she says, "*Le Journal ne rapport que 4,000 livres et mon mari a dépensé en impressions 100 louis.*" *Correspondance*, 279.

[2] Article by M. Perroud, *La Famille de Madame Brissot* in *La Révolution Française*, LIX, 270–74, September, 1910.

[3] Joseph Marie Girey-Dupré was born in 1769. He cast in his fortunes with Brissot and the Girondin party and, after May 31, 1793, was proscribed, and was executed November 21, 1793, for his connection with the *Patriote Français*. See pp. 233 n., 329.

[4] *Patriote Français*, September 23, 1791.

[5] *Ibid.*, January 1, 1792.

[6] *Ibid.*, December 12, 1792.

[7] *Moniteur*, March 11, 1793.

sibility. It came up apropos of an article which had appeared in the *Patriote Français* reflecting on Camille Desmoulins, who proceeded to call Brissot to account. His defense was that the article under discussion was Girey-Dupré's. To this Desmoulins replied, with his *Jean Pierre Brissot démasqué*: "It is of no use to say that the diatribe is not yours, that it is acknowledged and signed by Girey-Dupré. The master is responsible for the misdemeanor of the servant. It is convenient for a journalist to take M. Girey thus on the croup to cover his back, but I jump to seize the bridle because it is really you who hold it and it is you who gave me that dressing."

Desmoulins was right. Whoever may have been technically and legally responsible for certain numbers, the fact remains that from first to last the *Patriote Français* represents Brissot's own ideas as a politician and his influence as a journalist. The period of its greatest influence was perhaps that of the Legislative Assembly, but during the session of the Constituent it was the center of Brissot's interest and his chief means of expression. In the *Patriote Français*, therefore, can be traced Brissot's attitude toward the constitution in the making, his views on the destructive and constructive work of the National Assembly, his relation to the progress of the Revolution, his part in the republican crisis of 1791, and finally, his acceptance of the constitution and of constitutional monarchy.

In his *Plan de conduite* Brissot had declared that the making of a constitution was not within the province of the States-General, but the opposition of the court had changed the situation; and if Brissot had been a member of the States-General, — now become the National Assembly, — he would most certainly have joined in the oath taken by the members not to separate till they had made a constitution for France. The drawing-up of this constitution was now the chief work of the Assembly, and party divisions, already outlined, began to show themselves more distinctly. They turned on the fundamental question whether reform should be brought about by modifying the old system of government or by developing an entirely new system. In this tremendous task Brissot's sympathies were with that section of the left well toward the extreme which at first had supported the monarchy, on condition that the king's power be strictly limited, but which now began to incline toward a republic. He took an absorbing interest in the proceedings of the Assembly, reported the debates at length, especially those which represented his own views, and sought in every way to influence public opinion. He was especially active in urging American, rather than English example upon France. The Constitution of the United States seemed to him a well-nigh perfect model, and the necessity of drawing up a new form of government for France gave him the chance to plan for a French adaptation of that model. He was also interested in the state constitutions, and his admiration was shared, though perhaps in a less degree, by many of the leaders of the Assembly. Editions of these American constitutions, both state and national, had been published in France, and there had grown up a strong feeling among such men as Lafayette and De Saint-Étienne [1] that in the fundamental principles of her proposed constitution France could find no better model than America. While these men were supporting American ideas by their votes in the National Assembly, Brissot was guiding and directing public opinion toward the same end. The recent American experience in constitution-making was a subject in which every one was interested. As Brissot had enjoyed the advantage of travel in America, he was regarded as an authority, and his opinions were listened to with respect, even where they were not followed. As a recent writer has pointed out, the precise extent of American influence is not susceptible of measurement; [2] its working, however, may be observed with profit.

[1] Jean Paul Rabaut Saint-Étienne, born in 1743, was a Protestant pastor. He was a member of the States-General and of the Convention, and stood always for moderation and tolerance. As a member of the committee of twelve, which provoked the revolution of May 31, he was outlawed and fled. On his discovery he was executed.

[2] Aulard, *Histoire politique de la Révolution*, 19–28. See the article by

The first subject of discussion was a declaration of rights: what rights should be included and whether there should be a declaration at all. That any one should question for a moment such a necessity seemed to Brissot absurd. "A declaration of rights," he declared, "is a chapter as necessary for a constitution as a foundation for a house. The constitution may change; the declaration of rights ought never to change." [1] He also objected strenuously to Mirabeau's proposition that the consideration of the declaration of rights might well be put off till the constitution was finished. If the declaration were the foundation it must of necessity be laid first.[2] Mirabeau, if not convinced, yielded to the pressure of opinion and presented a draft of a declaration. This draft met Brissot's approval in that it was short and clear; he objected, however, to a statement that it was drawn up in the name of the representatives. It ought to be in the name of the French people. And the whole thing ought, he complained, to be drawn up more rapidly. Why could not the Assembly take example from the promptness with which the Americans produced their Declaration of Independence? [3]

The two most important problems in the formation of the constitution itself concerned the distribution of power between the king and the legislative body and the extent to which democracy was to prevail. The former involved the question of one chamber or two, the degree of independence of the legislative body, the veto, the right of declaring peace and war and the relation of the ministry to the legislature.

On the question of a bicameral versus a unicameral system, Brissot supported Buzot's plan for a single chamber divided into two sections. He was careful to explain, however, that in so doing he was not advocating anything which resembled the English parliament. The ignorant and the unreflecting, he de-

Henry E. Bourne, entitled "American Constitutional Precedents in the French National Assembly," in the *American Historical Review*, April, 1903, viii, 466–86.

[1] *Patriote Français*, August 1, 1789.
[2] *Ibid.*, August 20, 1789.   [3] *Ibid.*, August 24, 1789.

clared, had raised the cry that it would mean two chambers. Their assertion, he argued, was not true. Aside from the number two there was nothing in common between the two sections proposed and the two chambers of the English Parliament. In the first place the members of the House of Lords and of the House of Commons were not drawn from the same classes, and the division was permanent; whereas the members of the two sections in the proposed French legislature were drawn from the same body and the division into two sections would be but temporary, being made every two months and by lot. Hence there would be no reason to fear intrigue or any *esprit de corps*. In the second place the object of the two chambers was both to discuss and to vote; whereas the object of the two sections would be only to discuss, the voting being done in the united assembly. In the third place the House of Lords had a veto on the House of Commons; whereas in the plan of the sections neither would have a veto upon the other.[1] But whatever the number or the division of the chambers, Brissot stood firmly for the permanency of the legislative assembly, by which he meant annual meetings which should convene regularly without being called.[2]

Closely connected with the question whether there were to be two chambers — one to have a veto on the other — was a question of another kind of veto, that exercised by the king upon the legislative body. This brought up the whole subject of the relative proportion of power to be given to the king and to the Assembly. Opinion was sharply divided: one section demanded that the power of the king be reduced to the narrowest possible limits, while the other stood for a strong executive. Of the former section Brissot was one of the most ardent advocates, while the other was ably represented by Mirabeau, who declared that in order to make the constitution workable, the executive must be given considerable power. To this end Mirabeau proposed to give the king an absolute veto and some

---

[1] *Patriote Français*, May 24, 1791.
[2] *Observations sur la nécessité d'établir . . . des comités de correspondance*, 6.

real influence in making peace and declaring war as well, and also to have the ministry chosen from the legislative body. "The absolute veto," he maintained, "would not give too much power to the king, because any long-continued and persistent opposition to the wishes of the people would result in revolution, and therefore public opinion might safely be trusted as a sufficient check to the apparently arbitrary power involved in giving the king an absolute veto." This opinion Brissot vigorously combated in the *Patriote Français*. In the issue of September 15, 1789, he took up a speech by Mirabeau on the subject and assailed it point by point. His argument deserves quotation at length, not only on account of the importance of the subject, but also because of the frankness with which he expressed republican sentiments.

"Mirabeau," the *Patriote Français* declared, "begins by saying that the greater a nation is the more active ought the executive power to be: from which comes the necessity of a monarchical government in large states. . . .

"This is an error sanctioned by Montesquieu, of which one is disabused if one reflects on the history of America. It is not the number of individuals nor the extent of country which demands a monarchical government. The moral state of a nation is the only thing which ought to decide its government. If America had fifty million inhabitants of whom four fifths were laborers, as is the case to-day, the republican form of government would be the natural one for it. Moreover, a republic like that of the Americans has no need of this great activity in the government, because it is a government of peace in harmony with society, while in a monarchy, the government is constantly at war with society, and consequently needs great strength. I do not say on this account that France ought not to have a monarchical government, but I do say that it is not on account of its population but because of its moral maladies.

"*The prince is the protector of the people.*[1]

[1] In this and the following *italicized* statements Brissot is citing Mirabeau.

"He may and he may not be. The representatives may be and they may not: they are under the hand of the people.

"*If the king does not have the sanction he will be obliged to use armed force against the people.*

"Rarely, and if he does have it, he will turn it against them very often. Why? For the same reason that for six centuries has kept us in slavery. The man who does not take an unfair advantage when he can do it with impunity is an angel.

"*The representatives may be badly chosen.*

"But they are chosen everywhere at the same time. They are changed at the end of two years, and if they have made a bad law, their successors change it. The prince, on the contrary, is not chosen; he holds his office for life.

"*The grandeur of the prince depends on the prosperity of the people.*

"A political fable on which we have been brought up since the making of books began. These protectors of the people have even amused themselves (with the exception of a few) in heaping up debts, taxes, vexations . . . the true protection of the people is in its representatives and especially in the constituent power frequently exercised.

"*The prince is the perpetual representative of the people, as its deputies are its temporary representatives. Why not give them the same part in the law?*

"Because the one is a perpetual representative and not chosen, and the others are chosen and for short terms, and are consequently less dangerous; because the latter have only one kind of power, and the other, if he had a veto, would have a terrible power joined to the most terrible of all powers — the executive.

"*If the prince has not the veto, what will prevent the representatives from prolonging their authority and holding it indefinitely?*

"The constitution, which preserves in the hands of the people the right of reforming it and of choosing special assemblies at fixed terms and thus putting a stop to the usurpations of its representatives. . . .

"What is there to fear from the royal veto if the taxes and the existence of the army are provided for annually?

"Everything, for the people will never dare to stop the payment of the taxes, or to dismiss the army. The evil which will result from this state of things will fall more upon the people than upon the king.

"Finally, if the Prince does not have the veto, and if he is obliged to sanction a bad law, the only remedy is in insurrection.

"An error. The representatives who follow can change the law, according to the will of the people."

Brissot objected also to the alternative involved in a suspensive veto which would necessitate the reënactment of any vetoed measure by the next two legislatures. In opposition to both alternatives, he proposed a veto like that given to the President of the United States, which would check legislation, but only temporarily. If ever Brissot longed to have a voice in the Assembly it was that he might plead for this American veto. Lacking such opportunity, he tried through the columns of the *Patriote Français* to arouse public opinion on the matter. It was so reasonable, he urged; it prevented hasty and ill-considered legislation on the one hand, and on the other gave no dangerous power to the President. It only necessitated further discussion and could not prevent the passing of any law which was really good and widely demanded.[1]

On the question of the right of declaring war and making peace, Brissot and Mirabeau again came into clash. As in the matter of the veto, Mirabeau exerted all his energy to securing some effective authority for the king. Realizing that it was hopeless to propose that the king alone should have the right of declaring war, he contented himself with a compromise, and proposed instead that the right of making peace and declaring war belonged to the nation, but that in the case of threatened hostility the king should be allowed to make preparation for war and afterward to appeal to the legislative body for sanction of his course of action.[2] This proposal to leave a virtual

[1] *Patriote Français*, September 4, 1789.   [2] *Moniteur*, May 21, 1790.

initiative to the king, aroused great indignation, which Brissot was one of the first to voice. Mirabeau's plan, he declared, was not clear, since it did not make sufficiently plain the line of demarkation between the executive and the legislative, and it ignored the rights of the nation. The debates on this subject Brissot reported at length, but with perhaps more than usual partisanship. He spoke, for instance, of the miserable subtleties of a Malouet who pretended that "almost all wars were undertaken in the interests of the people rather than by the caprices of kings," and supported Pétion in his argument that under a king who exercised the right of making war, liberty could not long exist.[1] In spite of this opposition Mirabeau secured the adoption of the fundamental principle of his bill.

On the question of choosing the ministry from the legislative body Brissot was again opposed to Mirabeau. To establish such a connection would obviously bring about greater harmony between the executive and the legislative departments of the government, but Brissot strenuously opposed it, on the ground that it savored too much of the English constitution and that in any case it would give too much power to the executive. In answer to Mirabeau's argument that under existing conditions such separation would result in anarchy, he pointed to the example of the United States. "Admit the ministers to the Assembly," he declared, "and you will give them the means of executing the schemes which they have devised in their cabinets. . . . Such is the history of the parliament of England [ministerial corruption]. It is because the United States were familiar with that daily experience that they have forever excluded the secretaries of state from the meetings of Congress. If, then, in a country where there is little opportunity for corruption, and where there are no pensions or lucrative places, and where assemblies are frequently renewed . . . If, I say, in that country the influence of ministers is feared, how much more ought it to be feared in a country where corruption and the most frightful luxury reign?"[2]

[1] *Patriote Français*, May 18–21, 1790.   [2] *Ibid.*, November 8, 1789.

"Further," he argued, "ministers not only should be allowed no chance for control of the legislative body; but, on the contrary, the legislative body should have that control over the ministers which would come from some voice in choosing them. The choice and dismissal of the ministers and ambassadors ought not to be left to the king alone, the representatives of the people should have something to say in the matter. Leave to the king, for instance, the right of naming three or four persons for each vacancy, and then let the National Assembly choose one from this list. Under the new régime," he added, "it would not be difficult to find sufficiently able ministers." Now that many of their former functions had been taken over by the legislative body no extraordinary ability was needed to fill the office. Ordinary intelligence, some knowledge of affairs, dignity and diligence were quite sufficient.[1]

In the method of amending the constitution Brissot was not quite so anxious to follow American example. Indeed, this seems to be one of the few cases where he realized that a difference in conditions might require a modification in the model followed. France, not being a federation of states and having a legislative body of one chamber instead of two, lacked the machinery for amending the constitution which was employed in the United States. However well it might work there, Brissot feared giving an initiative in changing the constitution to the legislative body. As it was not practicable for the people themselves, gathered in primary assemblies, to change the constitution, conventions should be called. And, as it was not desirable to leave the calling of conventions to the very powers they were summoned to censure, they ought to be periodic. If it were objected that conventions might dare to change the fundamental principles of the constitution, this danger, Brissot replied, would be slight compared with the evils which would result from the absence of conventions altogether. One method of preventing it would be to take a hint from the method employed in the United States, and, while rejecting

[1] *Patriote Français*, September 26, 1790.

the initiative of the legislative body, allow that body to veto amendments by a two-thirds vote.[1] The arrangement for proposing amendments only on the demand of three successive legislatures would, on the contrary, he declared, be absolutely ineffective, since three successive legislatures would never want the same thing.[2] Brissot's ideas did not prevail on all these important questions — a unicameral system being adopted instead of the two-sectioned chamber, a really suspensive veto instead of the modified American system and a method of amendment which did not provide for elections at fixed periods. On the other hand, his ideas did prevail in the manner of choosing the ministers, and on those points where his views were not carried out he assisted in forcing a compromise, and in preventing the complete adoption of Mirabeau's plans. The constitution in its solution of the relation between the king and the legislature conformed far more closely to the ideas of Brissot than to those of Mirabeau. This was unfortunate, as the outcome proved.

With the solution of the other main question — how far the constitution should be democratic in character — Brissot was far from satisfied. As might have been expected from his attitude in his early writings, he not only demanded that the power of the king be weakened, but that democracy prevail to the greatest possible extent. To this end he supported with all his might that small section of the left of the Assembly which stood for a democratic as opposed to a bourgeois constitution. In his *Bibliothèque philosophique* he had said that under a monarchy he would be content with civil equality,[3] but he now demanded political equality. Indeed the division into active and passive citizens seemed to him not only unwise, but positively iniquitous, and through the columns of the *Patriote Français* he strenuously and repeatedly objected to all legislation based upon it. To withhold the right of suffrage from passive citizens was, he

[1] *Discours sur les conventions, 8 août, 1791.*
[2] *Patriote Français,* September 5, 1791.
[3] *Bibliothèque philosophique,* iii, 235.

declared, a violation of the principle laid down by the Assembly that a man can be subject only to those laws to which he or his representatives have given their consent. Can the Assembly thus violate that principle with regard to any one class of citizens without hopelessly contradicting itself? he asked. Why, to take a particular instance, should domestics be specifically excluded? Were they not men? They were in a state of dependence, it was asserted; but that was true of many professions.[1] Another vicious law, he declared, was that providing that the national guard should be composed only of active citizens, and to enforce his point he published, though with some omissions, a vehement letter of Madame Roland in protest.[2] He even went so far as to assert that some of those who had striven for this division into active and passive citizens, had done it with malice aforethought, with the secret purpose of creating in the passive citizens an agency which might be used in the interests of despotism.

A representation which rested on territory and taxes, as well as on population, he assailed as likewise undemocratic and quoted at length Pétion's arguments to prove that since men alone were represented, population should be the sole basis for national representation.[3] He objected also to the indirect method of election to the legislative body; it was better than destroying the influence of the people by two intermediary degrees in the elections, but it would have been better yet to follow the example of England and America, and have elections directly by the people.[4] While arguing for the rights of the people in the matter of elections, he took up the cause of the Protestants, Jews, and actors, and was one of the first to plead, both in his newspaper and before the city council, that they be given civil

---

[1] *Patriote Français*, October 24, 1789.

[2] Madame Roland wrote: "*J'ai vu aujourd'hui cette assemblée qu'on ne saurait appeler nationale (c'est l'enfer même avec toutes ses horreurs), la raison, la vérité, la justice y sont étouffées, honniés (conspuées).*" The words between the parentheses are omitted in the *Patriote Français*. See *Lettres de Madame Roland*, ii, 269–71 and note, 271; also *Patriote Français*, April 30, 1791.

[3] *Patriote Français*, November 10, 1789.   [4] *Ibid.*, November 18, 1789.

rights.[1] The power accorded to an hereditary, immovable, and non-elective regency he also objected to, as another thoroughly undemocratic feature of the constitution, criticized Barnave severely for supporting it, and praised Pétion warmly, as the one man who had opposed it.[2]

In spite of the efforts of the left in the Assembly, represented by such men as Pétion, and by such journalists as Brissot, a constitution was finally adopted which, if it greatly limited the power of the king, was far from being democratic, and it was further decreed that it should go into effect without being submitted to the people. To such a decision Brissot had been constantly opposed as another evidence of an undemocratic spirit. In his *Plan de conduite* he had spoken in favor of the submittal to the people,[3] and when the constitution was first discussed he published an excited letter of Madame Roland on the subject,[4] and wrote himself with much spirit that not to submit the constitution to the people seemed to him so dangerous, so destructive of a free constitution, that he could not conceive how such an idea could find partisans in the Assembly, and especially among the defenders of the people.[5] But in view of the crisis of the summer of 1791, he came to doubt the advisability of submitting this particular constitution to the people at a time of such general disturbance, and in his *Discours sur les conventions* of August 8, 1791, he wrote that "a ratification just now would be impossible, impolitic and dangerous. In fact, the people are just emerging from a long period of slavery; they are emerging from the tomb. Their eyes are barely open to the light. They

---

[1] *Patriote Français*, December 24, 26, 1789, and June 15 and 17, 1790.
[2] *Ibid.*, March 23–26, 1791. [3] See p. 92.
[4] Letter to Brissot of August 3, 1789, printed in the *Patriote Français* of August 12: "*Au nom de Dieu! gardez-vous bien de déclarer que l'Assemblée Nationale peut fixer irrévocablement la Constitution; il faut, si elle en trace le projet, qu'il soit ensuite envoyé dans toutes les provinces, pour être adopté, modifié, approuvé par les Constituants.*
"*L'Assemblée n'est formée que de constitués, qui n'ont pas droit de fixer notre sort, ce droit est au peuple, il ne peut ni le céder, ni le déléguer.*" *Lettres de Madame Roland*, ii, 55.
[5] *Patriote Français*, September 9, 1789.

need to learn how to use their organs before judging with them."

Closely connected with the constitution, though not an actual part of it, was the new judicial system. The reform of justice had been the subject perhaps dearest of all to Brissot's heart, and he now watched the development of the new judicial organization with the keenest interest, throwing his influence always in favor of such organization as would provide for the fullest equality and the greatest power in the hands of the people. Three general plans were proposed by Thouret, Duport, and Sieyès respectively: Thouret's plan was rather a modification of the system existing under the old régime than a new system and allowed the king considerable power in choosing the judges. It provided, however, for a jury only in criminal cases. Duport on the other hand suppressed all vestige of the past, and in building up a new system followed largely English example. He provided for juries in civil, as well as in criminal cases, and gave the nomination of the judges to the directories and their final choice to the people. Sieyès's plan also provided for a thoroughgoing change, its most distinctive feature being the organization of juries composed of members of the bar.[1] In criticizing these plans Brissot spoke with rather more caution than usual. He objected to Thouret's scheme as savoring too much of the old régime,[2] approved of Sieyès's plan in the abstract, but declared with an apt quotation from Montaigne, that everything that emanated from Sieyès would fit in a new world, but was less suited to a world where custom was already fixed.[3] Duport's scheme, therefore, as involving both thorough reform and practicability seemed to him the best. Brissot admitted that the English had had some difficulties with the jury system, but thought that they had been exaggerated, and declared himself in favor of the jury for civil as well as for criminal cases. The whole matter seems to have been decided with less acrimonious discussion and with more unanimity than usual and

---

[1] See Seligmann, *Le justice révolutionnaire.*
[2] *Patriote Français,* March 25, 1790.   [3] *Ibid.,* April 7 and 30, 1790.

on the whole to have met Brissot's approval. There were other features of the proposed judicial system, however, which gave rise to considerable debate, namely, the question of tenure of office and of circuit judges. To the proposition for life office, Brissot objected as a flagrant violation of equality, and rejoiced when it was rejected. At the same time he would give judges a longer term of office than ordinary administrators, and make them reëligible, requiring, however, an interval before they could be reëlected. This constant reëligibility he declared was the one fault in the American Congress and ought to be avoided in France.[1] He was consequently much disappointed to find that the reëligibility of the judges was voted with no provision for an interval. He also regretted the decision in favor of sedentary judges instead of judges on circuit, which, in spite of some English opinion against it, seemed to him decidedly preferable.[2] But in the main the new system meant equality and real justice, and Brissot was fairly content.

With the development of liberty in relation to the freedom of the press, he was less content. As a pamphleteer and journalist it had long been to him, and throughout his career in the Revolution it continued to be, not only a matter of principle but also of vital personal interest. He was no mere onlooker, but from the moment when he boldly announced his journal and, in the face of ministerial opposition, appealed to the States-General,[3] he was an active combatant in the forefront of the battle. The decree of May 19, by which Maissemy, the general director of the book trade, permitted newspapers to publish the proceedings of the Assembly, was a virtual recognition of freedom of the press, though he tried to save appearances by adding that no reflections or commentary on the debates would be allowed,[4] and the events of July 14 made its *de facto* establishment complete. It was some weeks, however, before the action of the Assembly provided for freedom of the press *de jure*.

[1] *Patriote Français*, May 4, 1790.
[2] *Ibid.*, March 31, May 2, 4 and 26, 1790.
[3] See p. 115. [4] See p. 116.

This delay Brissot found very trying and complained bitterly that the Assembly was altogether too slow in recognizing already existing facts. He was therefore delighted when, on August 24, the Assembly voted article eleven of the declaration of rights, "that the free communication of his thoughts and opinions was one of the most precious rights of man and that every citizen was at liberty to speak, write and print freely whatever he pleased, being answerable only for the abuse of that liberty in the cases determined by law." This was merely a declaration; there remained the difficult and delicate task of formulating the law which was to carry it out.[1] In January, 1790, Sieyès came forward with the proposition for a law to the effect that if a certain work should excite the people to use violent means in order to obtain their demands, the persons responsible could be declared guilty of sedition and punished; and further, if an article printed within eight days before a seditious outbreak should contain false allegations which had excited the sedition, the persons responsible should be pursued and punished as themselves guilty of sedition.[2] This law Brissot criticized severely, chiefly upon the ground that sedition itself had not yet been defined.[3] Moreover he did effective work in preventing its passage, by publishing frequent articles against it.[4] Just at this juncture the quarrel between the Châtelet on the one hand and Marat and Danton on the other came to a head and gave special point to the discussion of freedom of speech. On account of his violent attacks on the moderate party, particularly on Bailly, Mayor of Paris, the Châtelet had ordered the arrest of Marat. It now turned upon Danton for having resisted that court as illegal and more especially for having himself, in the local assembly, threatened resistance to the authorities of Paris. Desmoulins in his paper took up the cause of Danton and was ably seconded by Brissot. Freedom of thought

[1] For a discussion of this subject see Söderhjehm, *Le Régime de la presse.*
[2] *Moniteur*, January 23, 1790.   [3] *Patriote Français*, January 31, 1790.
[4] See, for example, the quotation from an article by Kerolio in the *Patriote Français* of February 3, the address of Robert Pigott in that of February 10, and the letter from Chaveau de la Garde, February 15, 1790.

would cease to exist, declared the latter, if speeches, whatever their character, which were made in the course of a discussion in a legislative body could be travestied into flagrant misdemeanors.[1] And when, a few days later, apropos of an article of Marat calling the people to arms, and an article of Desmoulins comparing the fête of the federation with a triumph of Paulus Emilius, the Assembly ordered an accusation of high treason against the journals which had incited insurrection, he cried out with horror that the Assembly should have dared to pass such a decree against alleged libelists before it had even decided in what a libel consisted. And even if they had laid down definite principles, they were taking action without first inquiring whether the persons accused were the authors of the articles in question, and if so, whether the principles applied to them. Though he was far, he added, from approving of the fury of Marat, he could not help feeling that his case had done good service in repressing the enemies of the Revolution, and in any event so long as there existed no definite law against libels, nor special tribunals to deal with them, any accusation of the kind in question was a violation of the rights of man, of the rules of common sense and of the constitution, and was liable to lead to the most monstrous iniquity.[2]

Meanwhile Brissot had gotten into trouble himself. He had published a letter in which a chapter of women at Remiremont was accused of aristocratic tendencies, of hindering the prosperity of the city, and of using its influence against the Revolution. These allegations produced a tempest of excitement at Remiremont and stirred up a veritable wasps' nest for Brissot. Three citizens of Remiremont declared that they were in danger of losing their lives under suspicion of having written the letter, and begged him to reveal the name of the real author; and a deputation of the municipality and of the national guard made formal complaint against him before the National Assembly.[3]

---

[1] *Patriote Français*, March 26, 1790.   [2] *Ibid.*, August 2, 1790.
[3] *Procès verbal de l'Assemblée nationale*, August 5, 1790. See also Lacroix, *Actes de la Commune*, VII, 268, note.

M. Bexon, a Paris lawyer, took up this cause, haled Brissot before the police, and had the number of the *Patriote Français* in question placarded as a libel. In reply, Brissot declared that the matter was outside of the jurisdiction of the police; that M. Bexon was not qualified to plead; that the placard against the letter was itself a libel but that the letter was not libelous. Libel, he declared, must involve a false accusation of an overt act of which the law could take cognizance; to accuse a person of pride, or lack of patriotism, or other fault of character not within the purview of the law, could not possibly be construed as libel.[1]

Meanwhile no definite law against libels was enacted by the Assembly, but with the growing disturbances of the summer of 1791, the matter again came to the front. Brissot was more and more inclined to believe in complete liberty. He published extracts from Lanthenas's work on the subject, quoted Pétion's speeches, and declared that much as he abhorred any incitation to murder or assassination, he did not believe it possible to frame a law which would effectively prosecute libels and at the same time not serve as a pretext for injustice. It was equally impossible, he added, to frame one which could not be easily evaded, and of which the benefit to the persons injured would not be overbalanced by injury to the public welfare. In any case, the law should take cognizance only of the calumnies directed against citizens as private individuals.[2] The law of August 22, as passed, therefore seemed to him dangerous, and he warmly commended Robespierre's objections to it. In providing for action against those who purposely provoked disobedience to the laws and the degradation of constituted authorities there was danger, he asserted, of checking free discussion of public affairs, and especially legitimate criticism directed against public men.[3] His attack was met by the supporters of the law with the assurance that by constituted authorities it was not intended to include the men who exer-

---

[1] *Précis pour M. Bexon.*   [2] *Patriote Français*, August 18, 1791.
[3] *Ibid.*, August 23, 1791.

cised the authority, and that freedom was further guaranteed
by the provision that accusation against the press must be
tried by a jury.[1] As the Revolution progressed, however, libel
came to be applied with great elasticity, both to opposition to
persons in power and to the policy they represented. As early
as January, 1792, Bertrand de Moleville, the minister of marine,
attempted to get a decree of the council against Brissot for
"atrocious and calumnious imputations" against Louis XVI,
but it was too late, the royalist and the moderate party had lost
their power and the attempt failed.[2] After the 10th of August
there was no longer freedom of speech for the royalist journals,
and when the Girondins in turn began to lose influence, their
journals were likewise denounced as libelous, and on March 10,
1793, on the pretext that a member of the Convention should
not at the same time conduct a journal, Brissot was obliged
to give up the editorship of the *Patriote Français*.[3]

The work of constitution-making and of passing fundamental
laws on the judicial organization and on freedom of speech was
not the only task of the National Assembly. Owing to its distrust of the king and his ministers, it gradually assumed a large
share of the administration of the government. With every
step in this direction Brissot was delighted. The sovereignty
of the people might not be complete in that they did not choose
the executive, but he would have it as complete as possible in
controlling the actions of the executive. Holding such views,
he naturally resented the assertion of the *Moniteur* that the
ministers had the right to order the coining of money without
consulting the Assembly; declared that the ministers must be
held accountable for their conduct;[4] that the Assembly was too
ready to leave in office men attached to the old régime;[5] and
that in the conduct of foreign affairs they must be particularly

[1] *Patriote Français*, August 24, 1791. For the danger of resisting freedom
of speech in making laws against the refractory priests, see p. 146.

[2] Bertrand de Moleville, *Histoire de la Révolution de France*, vii, 54.

[3] *Moniteur*, March 11, 1793. See also p. 329.

[4] *Patriote Français*, October 21, 22, 1790.

[5] *Ibid.*, November 4, 1790.

careful to choose men whom they could rely on as attached to the principles of the Revolution.

As regards foreign affairs the Assembly was only too ready to take the control into its own hands and to adopt most radical measures. Here again, as on the constitution, Brissot was diametrically opposed to Mirabeau, and again he used the influence of his paper to press what he considered the example of the United States and to uphold the power of the people as against that of the king. Mirabeau, as chairman of the diplomatic committee of the National Assembly, held a position of influence which gave him great authority in foreign affairs. With all the power of tongue and pen at his command he tried to prevent the headstrong policy of the Assembly from ending in war. In the case of Avignon there was special need of his restraining hand, for France regarded with covetous eyes this ancient possession of the Papacy. In Avignon itself a French party had been created which demanded annexation to France, and this policy was powerfully supported by a large number of deputies in the Assembly. Mirabeau had succeeded in deferring the decision for a time, but upon the outbreak of a revolution in Avignon the Assembly dispatched troops there, and the radical party made this circumstance an added argument for annexation. This policy Brissot ardently supported. When the request for annexation was referred to the king he was very anxious lest the king might refuse his consent, and found in the danger of this situation an argument against giving to the executive power the sole initiative in foreign affairs. That Avignon belonged to the Pope, and that its annexation would involve a flagrant breach of international law, counted for little in his estimation. To await the consent of the Pope he considered a recognition of diplomatic usage which the United States never would have sanctioned, and following what he supposed to be the example of the United States, he declared that diplomacy must be disregarded. Mirabeau's statement, that even if Avignon were free to give herself, France had no right to accept the offer, he denounced as involving both a violation of the natural rights of man and a recognition of the power of the old diplomacy.[1]

Another important international question was the affair of Nootka Sound — and here Mirabeau and Brissot upheld the same policy, though for different reasons. Spain had seized property claimed by England in Nootka Sound, off Vancouver Island, and, when England threatened war, Spain appealed to France for aid. She based her appeal on the *Pacte de Famille*, the offensive and defensive alliance concluded between France and Spain in 1761. In answer, the Assembly, led by Mirabeau, while not refusing Spain's appeal for assistance, practically nullified that assistance by taking steps to dissolve the *Pacte de Famille* on the ground that its further continuance would be inexpedient and dangerous for France. The Assembly proposed instead to substitute for it an ordinary treaty of alliance. With this action Brissot was fully in sympathy, not on the ground of expediency, but because the family compact was a reminiscence of the old régime and as such should be destroyed.[2] "The court of Spain does not know," he wrote, "that since the revolution a king *of the French* is not under obligation to execute the treaties of the king *of France;* that kings in a free government have no family; that France hereafter will have compacts only with the great family of the human race." [3]

In this case Brissot and Mirabeau agreed, but agreement between them was the exception. As in the formation of the constitution, Mirabeau's object was to produce a constitution which should be practicable, so in the management of foreign and financial affairs he was guided by expediency. Brissot, on the other hand, was predominantly influenced by theory and considerations of abstract right, and failed both to appreciate

---

[1] *Patriote Français*, November 18, 1790, where he supported Pétion in his contention that Avignon had the right to unite herself to France. See also *Patriote Français* of November 22, 1790.

[2] *Ibid.*, June 21, 1790. See also Manning, *The Nootka Sound Controversy*, in the *Annual Report* of the American Historical Association, 1904, pp. 424, 428.

[3] *Patriote Française*, May 12, 1790.

Mirabeau's regard for the practical necessities of the moment and to recognize the real greatness of the man. Mirabeau's death therefore did not seem to him an unmitigated calamity. Mirabeau, he wrote, hated despotism more than he loved liberty. He did not love the people, he never really knew the people, he only made use of the name of the people, in order to secure his own purpose, which was to oust the ministers and to slip into their place. His death was thus a good thing for liberty.[1]

Besides foreign affairs, the Assembly assumed control of the Church. On this subject Brissot was, in the main, in harmony with the majority and represented moreover the radical opinions which might be expected from a deist. The first step of the Assembly with regard to the Church was taken on the 4th of August, when in its orgy of decrees it declared the tithes paid to the Church abolished without compensation. This case was an exception to Brissot's general agreement with the policy of the Assembly on ecclesiastical matters, and when Sieyès, who was the only member who apparently realized that the Assembly was merely making a present to the landholders, raised his voice against the measure, Brissot was the sole journalist who ventured to support him.[2] With the pivotal policy of the Assembly toward the Church, the assumption of the church lands, Brissot was in full sympathy. The Assembly was in a difficult position. It was warned not to imitate the monarchy in perpetual appeals to credit, and, at the same time, was urged to diminish the public debt. It was not possible to borrow or to increase the taxes.[3] That the state needed the wealth of the

---

[1] This expression of opinion was most pleasing to Madame Roland. In a letter to Bançal she wrote: "*Tous les journalists se sont emparés de sa mort comme d'un morceau précieux, riche et pathétique dont chacun tire parti suivant ses talents. Je ne connais que Brissot qui ait eu la sagesse d'éviter l'idolâtrie, avec le prudence de ne pas offenser l'opinion.*" *Lettres de Madame Roland*, II, 257.

[2] "*Elles [les dîmes] sont supprimées sans indemnité chez l'ecclésiastique ; un seul membre s'est levé contre la rédaction de ce dernier article seutement, et il desoit en lui-même : Ils veulent être libres, ils ne savent pas être justes.*" *Patriote Français*, August 13, 1789.

[3] Gomel, *Histoire financière*, I, Introduction, xxiv.

Church was thus evident; that she had a right to take it was more doubtful. But to Brissot the right was as obvious as the need. The clergy, he declared, quoting the speech of M. Chassé, were not proprietors, only depositaries; they could with perfect propriety be paid in some other way than by giving them the use of the property.[1] Furthermore, the church property had been given to the clergy only on condition that they were useful to society; if they ceased to perform useful functions they could be despoiled of it.[2] These arguments, reinforced by the very practical one of financial necessity, prevailed, and the property was taken, — "assumed" said the majority of the Assembly, "confiscated" said the Church.

The Assembly had thus torn down. It had now to build up, and in this process it had to deal with questions of religion and religious tolerance, as well as with ecclesiastical organization. A question of this kind first came up in connection with the declaration of rights. Should the name of God be inserted and God be declared the first cause of all those rights? Contrary to what proved to be the opinion of the majority, Brissot argued against it. "God is indeed the first cause of these rights, as He is of everything," he wrote; "but the true first cause of the rights of man is man's existence. He ought to be free because he exists." [3]

A more serious matter from the practical point of view was that brought up by Dom Gerle's motion that the Catholic, Apostolic, and Roman religion should always be that of the nation. This was clearly a violation of tolerance and, after a stormy debate, was rejected as such. According to Brissot even to deliberate on such a proposition was a crime. "To say that one believes in the Catholic religion is to make a profession of faith; but to authorize only that religion, is to interfere with other religions, to persecute them; it is to force people to believe and to practice Catholicism alone; and such intolerance is a crime against Christ himself, who allowed himself to be

[1] *Patriote Français*, October 24, 1789.
[2] *Ibid.*, September 11, 1789.   [3] *Ibid.*, August 20, 1789.

crucified and who crucified no one." [1] And consistently with this spirit of tolerance he argued that civil rights be given to Protestants, Jews, and actors. But though strongly against the establishment of the Catholic religion to the exclusion of all others, he was heartily in favor of the Catholic Church as the State Church, and supported the radical policy involved in the election of the bishops and priests by the people, the regulation of the salaries of the clergy by the government, and the demand from every priest of an oath to support the civil constitution of the clergy.[2] The priest was a state functionary, he declared, and quoted Voltaire to the effect that priests in the state were very much like tutors in the home, agencies for teaching, preaching, and furnishing a good example.[3] He even went so far as to say that there was reason in the idea of the Quakers in abolishing the priesthood altogether. At the same time, he admitted that ideal as that might be, France was not yet ready for such a step. He added, however, that the example of the Quakers should be imitated to the extent of proscribing all useless priests, in which number he included all archbishops and bishops. He also advocated the radical policy of the marriage of the clergy, but acknowledged that this idea must be presented with caution, as the people were not yet educated up to it.[4] At all events he would do away with monastic vows, and was therefore greatly pleased at the decree suppressing religious orders.[5]

Above all, he preached tolerance, and like most of his contemporaries did not seem to realize that in upholding the oath of obedience to the new constitution which it was proposed to require of the clergy, he himself might be guilty of rank intolerance. To take this oath involving adhesion to the principle of election of priests without any confirmation by the Pope, was to many churchmen a violation of their conscientious scruples. The Pope certainly regarded it as such, for he threatened with

[1] *Patriote Français*, April 13, 1790.
[2] *Ibid.*, August 12, 13, 1789; June 1, 1790.   [3] *Ibid.*, May 30, 1790.
[4] *Ibid.*, June 1, 1790; July 27, September 4, 1792.   [5] *Ibid.*, April 7, 1792.

excommunication all ecclesiastics who took the oath. The authority of the Pope Brissot had already assailed in *L'Autorité législative de Rome anéantie*, published a few years before.[1] He now seized the occasion to bring out a new edition, entitled *Rome jugée et l'autorité législative du pape anéantie*, with a new preface in which he stated that he proposed "to prove that the popes are only usurpers, total strangers to French Christians, and that for free Frenchmen a pope who excommunicated them was only an enemy who ought to be punished if he had any power, but that as he was a mere phantom, he need only be scorned. The timid fear that interdict; rogues exaggerate the danger. The former must be enlightened, the latter unmasked." That this whole attitude on the part of the Pope and the clergy might be a matter of conscience Brissot refused to consider, and ridiculed as absurd the suggestion of Abbé Maury that the civil constitution of the clergy ought to have the sanction of a national council or of the Pope, and that the government "ought not to violate timorous consciences."[2] However much matters of religion seemed to the clergy to be involved, to the majority of the Assembly it was a matter of political import only. Their attitude toward the Church had been directed in the first place, not by any burning zeal for religion, but by the need of money, and the land of the Church had been taken not with the idea of making the Church less secular, but as a financial resource in dire distress. To oppose the new organization which had been devised in consequence seemed therefore to Brissot, as to many other revolutionists, merely perverse objection to the principles of the Revolution.

On the financial, as well as on the ecclesiastical policy of the Assembly, Brissot was on the radical side. In his early writings he had frequently discussed financial questions, and he now had a chance to make his influence felt directly through his journal. He accordingly devoted much space to the subject. He wished

[1] See p. 36.
[2] *Patriote Français*, November 29, 1790. See also issues of January 8, 19, 24, and February 18, 1791.

to get rid as fast and as far as possible of the influence of the old régime, prevent any introduction of its methods into the new régime, reduce the power of the king and ministers in financial matters to its lowest terms, substitute for it the authority of the Assembly, instead of temporary expedients for raising money, adopt the most thoroughgoing measures, and finally introduce a system of taxation which would be both just and democratic. One of the first abuses of the old régime to which the Assembly turned its attention was that of pensions. To Brissot they seemed an unmitigated evil, and when it was suggested that a pension was an acquired property, and that to abolish the pension without restriction might be a violation of the declaration of rights, he expressed great astonishment. There was practical agreement, however, that the pension list should be revised, but when it was proposed that the revision should be made by the executive power Brissot again uttered protest. "It would be to put in charge of curing the evil," he objected, "the very persons who were profiting by it." [2] This objection seems to have had some influence, for when the law against pensions was brought forward it provided that the revision should be made not by the king, but by a committee of the Assembly. With this decision Brissot was greatly pleased, as also with the further clause that no pension or salary should be paid to Frenchmen who had left the realm without the authorization of the government.[3]

Of the general financial policy of the ministry as represented by Necker, he was a constant and severe critic. In his *Observations d'un républicain* he had declared that Necker was not a defender of the people but an upholder of despotism, but in the *Plan de conduite* he had in a measure retracted his earlier statements and appealed to the public to rally to Necker's support. He now apparently went back to his former opinion, and till the retirement of Necker in September, 1790, there were few numbers of the *Patriote Français* in which he did not assail him

---

[1] *Patriote Français*, January 6, 1790.   [2] *Ibid.*
[3] Gomel, II, 16.

for some sin, either of omission or commission. He criticized him for his unwillingness to produce the *livre rouge*,[1] "that infernal cavern,"[2] to use Brissot's own term; maintained that in face of the decree of the Assembly, the expenses must be reduced sixty millions (Necker had declared it possible to reduce them only thirty millions); found fault with him for encouraging the lottery,[3] and objected strenuously to his plans for transforming the *caisse d'escompte* into a national bank.[4] To this institution Brissot was particularly opposed. The Assembly must exercise greater control over it, he argued both in his speech before the municipal council and in his journal; on the other hand it must not accord it greater privileges. Brissot was by no means alone in his hostility, and the general opposition resulted in the defeat of Necker's plan, and in demands on the *caisse d'escompte* on the part of the Assembly which weakened what credit it still had.[5] In taking this step the Assembly weakened a source of its own support, and as the patriotic contribution of one fourth of the revenue, from which much had been expected, had not been productive,[6] the government was under more urgent necessity than ever for providing financial resource. That resource, according to Brissot, and, as it proved, according to the majority of the Assembly, was to be found in assignats issued on the church lands. In the measures for the sale of these lands Brissot seems to have been more prudent than the majority of his fellow politicians and journalists, and even at the risk of offending his constituency urged that

[1] The book of secret expenses of the royal government under Louis XV and Louis XVI. *Patriote Français*, April 22, 23; May 2, 1790.

[2] *Ibid.*, April 8, 1790.

[3] "*Comment peut-il croire à l'existence des loteries sous le règne de l'ordre public? une loterie n'est-elle pas le jeu le plus immoral, le plus contradictoire avec l'esprit et les mœurs d'une constitution libre et d'un peuple qu'on veut régénérer? Le profit de l'état sur les loteries n'est-il pas un vol infame, fait à la partie la plus misérable du peuple qu'on abuse? La misère a dû faire la gabelle: la morale doit faire abolir la loterie.*" *Patriote Français*, June 5, 1790.

[4] See p. 103.

[5] *Patriote Français*, September 23, October 3, December 19, 1789; also Gomel, I, 516.

[6] *Ibid.*, March 14, 1790.

the municipalities renounce a share of the rather large part of the proceeds which had been offered them.[1]

He not only supported the assumption and sale of church lands by the state, as a financial measure, but was also enthusiastic over the opportunity it offered to him personally to further the interests of an association of which he was one of the promoters and probably the originator. The plans for this association were drawn up in Brissot's own hand and apparently just after the decree of November 18, 1789, which placed on sale the property of the Church.[2] The plan, which showed the influence both of Rousseau and of Brissot's American experience, provided for an association founded on ideas of democratic equality, something after the style of the Moravian Brethren.[3] It was to be called the *Société agricole ou d'amis* and was to have for its object the regeneration of society by means of rural education. It was to purchase, in the first place, property of sufficient size to provide for about twenty families, and in a locality where further purchases could be made as the society grew. In order to fulfill its educational purpose its members were to engage in teaching a system of the purest morality, the simplest religious opinions, and manual labor, and by a method entirely different from that which was usually followed. When the society was well established it was to undertake such manufactures as could be easily carried on in the country. It was also to have a printing establishment, in the first place for its own use and in the second place for extending its teachings throughout France. There was to be provided further a common library and a common meeting place, though each family was to have its own house, which must be simple and without unnecessary luxury or ornamentation. New members were to be admitted only after having passed through a novitiate and would be required to subscribe in advance to the form of government

[1] See p. 103.

[2] *Lettres de Madame Roland*, ii, 77. See also Perroud, *Un Projet de Brissot pour une Association agricole*, in *La Révolution française*, March, 1902; xlii, 260–65.

[3] See p. 89.

established. Active members would be expected to subscribe from twelve to fifteen thousand francs, though provision was made for loaning money to those who had little or nothing, and for receiving special gifts from those who were willing to give more than the required amount.

The ideas set forth in this scheme Brissot communicated to Lanthenas, who in turn explained them to the Rolands, and they in turn together with Champagneux,[1] Blot, and Bançal des Issarts,[2] joined in planning the association.[3] Brissot meanwhile approached his friend Robert Pigott, the English Quaker, from whom he hoped financial backing for the enterprise. Of all his friends Brissot found Lanthenas his most active supporter, and during the fall of 1790 they had much correspondence as to ways and means.[4] It was proposed at first to buy property in the vicinity of Lyons, but Brissot found the neighborhood was too aristocratic and recommended purchase elsewhere. But apparently before any purchase could be made the ardor of his friends began to cool. Pigott, on whom he had staked his hopes, withdrew; Bançal des Issarts departed for England, not improbably with the motive of disengaging himself from what he had evidently come to regard as an impracticable scheme; and even the enthusiastic Lanthenas ventured to express doubt whether Brissot had adequately gauged the difficulties of the enterprise.[5] Thus another of Brissot's schemes for brotherhood and social regeneration came to an end, this time before it was even inaugurated.

Meanwhile, Brissot continued to fill the columns of the *Patriote Français* with arguments in favor of the assignats. The assignats were very different, he declared, from the paper of the *caisse d'escompte*. There would be much more confidence in this kind of paper, bearing interest, based on the goods of the clergy and other property of the state, limited in purpose

[1] L. A. Champagneux, the friend of the Rolands and editor of Madame Roland's works.

[2] *Correspondance*, 252–53.

[3] *Lettres de Madame Roland*, ii, 743; Appendix O.

[4] *Correspondance*, 255.   [5] *Lettres de Madame Roland*, ii, 179.

and in quantity, and payable at a fixed time, than there
would be if it were connected with the operations of a discredited *caisse*, whose condition was unknown and whose decrees of suspension of payment proved its embarrassment.[1]
The proposed issue of four hundred millions he declared too
small, and urged that six hundred millions was not too much.
In spite of some protests, these demands prevailed and the
assignats were voted, though the amount was at first limited to
four hundred millions. But as it did not bring the money expected, another issue was soon called for. This issue also Brissot advocated as a necessary expedient and resented any suggestion of evil consequences. He reported with satisfaction
that the chambers of commerce of Nantes and of Bordeaux
had unanimously demanded it, and that similar bodies in other
parts of France were going to take like action; attacked collec-
tively and by name opponents of the measure, including Necker,
Talleyrand, and Bergasse;[2] retorted to the objection that the
assignats could not be used in foreign commerce, that no one
claimed they could, but that they would greatly facilitate it by
taking the place of coin which would be used for that purpose.
And when some one turning to Brissot's favorite example ventured to suggest the warning that might be drawn from the
experience with paper money in America, he declared that the
cases were not at all parallel. The American money had no
foundation; was issued in the midst of war, and was thirty or
forty times greater than the coin in circulation; as for the assertion that the effect of paper money in America had been
to raise the price of provisions, he replied that that rise was
not the effect of paper, but of doubled consumption and lessened production. "How can any one have the bad faith," he
asked, "to compare the certificates of America, founded upon
unsalable land lacking purchasers and cultivation, with assignats based on lands of great value for which there is a ready

---

[1] *Patriote Français*, December 18, 1789, and *Discours sur la rareté du numéraire.*
[2] *Patriote Français*, March 12, May 17, June 23, 1790.

sale?" [1] And, when coming nearer home, the example of Law's paper money was cited, he again replied that the cases were not parallel, and forgetting as he did on other occasions that a change in the form of government did not change the laws, either of political economy or human nature, added that the paper of Law was manufactured by despotism, and was therefore a very different thing from the assignats issued by a free nation.[2] In spite of the protests from Talleyrand and a few others who foresaw the destruction to which such opening of the dikes would lead, these and like arguments prevailed and a new issue of assignats was voted.

With the issue of the assignats the control of the finances passed more and more from the ministry to the Assembly. Of this new administration Brissot was as critical as he had been of the old. On January 21 he published an open letter to Camus,[3] in which he censured him for reporting in favor of the claim of the Duke of Orléans to a *dot* promised by Louis XV to the daughter of the regent, a part of which had not been paid. It would be like giving to a thief the little that remained in your purse after he had robbed you, and would hark back to the methods of the old régime. There was already too much, he added, of that spirit in the operation of the treasury.[4]

It was now proposed to put the administration of the treasury into the hands of a committee chosen from the Assembly. When a like proposition had been made by Necker a year before, Brissot had vigorously opposed it on the ground that it would mean the confounding of two distinct powers.[5] Now, conditions having changed, he was in favor of it, and in the face of his former argument declared that to give the choice of the

---

[1] *Patriote Français*, April 10, September 26, 1790.   [2] *Ibid.*, April 16, 1790.

[3] Armand Gaston Camus (born 1740, died 1804) was an enthusiastic supporter of the Revolution and a deputy of Paris to the States-General. He took a prominent part in the debates on financial questions and was one of the chief advocates of the civil constitution of the clergy. He was also a member of the Convention, and of the committee of public safety, and under the Directory was offered the place of minister of finance.

[4] *Lettre à M. Camus*, January 21, 1791.

[5] *Patriote Français*, March 17, 1790.

administrators to the legislative body instead of to the king would not make the legislative body in any sense an executive body.[1] It was decreed, however, that the choice should be made by the king. With the personnel of the committee, as well as with the manner of choice, Brissot was ill satisfied, because it included, he was convinced, either men who were opposed to the assignats or who knew little about finance. On the latter ground he ventured to criticize even Condorcet, whom in most respects he greatly admired, and published a letter to him in the *Patriote Français* in which he calmly told him of his shortcomings for the position.[2] Lavoisier, another member of the committee chosen by the king, he criticized because of his offer to serve without pay. The offer was actuated by the best motives, he admitted, but its effect would be to humiliate those who had to depend on their pay for their livelihood. Moreover it was not seemly under a free government.

In all economic matters Brissot was also greatly interested. If in things political, equality was his watchword, here it was liberty, and to questions where liberty was in any way involved he gave especial attention, such as the price of grain, its free circulation, the provisioning of Paris,[3] the free cultivation of tobacco, its free importation or at least low duties on it,[4] and the extension of foreign trade, especially with America.[5]

But the subject to which above all others he devoted the columns of the *Patriote Français* was the cause of the negro. He stood for his liberation from slavery, and for the extension of a greater measure of equality to the mulattoes. To this end he supported the *Amis des Noirs*. Indeed, as has been pointed out, he made his paper the organ of that society, upheld its policy, and as colonial problems occupied more and more attention in the Assembly, devoted an increasing amount of space to their discussion. In fact, most of the controversies in which

[1] *Patriote Français*, March 10, 1791.   [2] *Ibid.*, April 10, 1791.
[3] *Ibid.*, July 30, August 7, 10, 18, 27, September 12, 1789.
[4] *Ibid.*, November 17, 1790; January 30, 1791.
[5] *Ibid.*, February 14, 15, 1790.

the *Patriote Français* became involved either with individuals or with other journals grew out of his championship of the negro, and of the *Amis des Noirs*. A discussion of Brissot's attitude on this subject belongs, however, rather with the history of that society than with his influence as a journalist.

CHAPTER VII

PART II

His Attitude toward Popular Movements and Public Opinion

THE work of the Assembly, both in the formation of the constitution and in the administration of the government, was modified and profoundly influenced from time to time by popular movements. Of the importance of such movements and of their influence on the Assembly Brissot was keenly aware. What was being done and said outside of the Assembly was, he realized, of the greatest moment, and he gave much space in the *Patriote Français* to its discussion. At first the Assembly had paid little attention to external events and had gone calmly on debating a declaration of rights, syllable by syllable, till it was brought down from the clouds by Salomon's report. The result was the sudden and enthusiastic vote against feudal privilege of every description known as the "orgy" of the 4th of August. Although Brissot spoke with approval of the "generous enthusiasm" of the privileged classes,[1] he was not so enthusiastic over this particular onslaught on depotism as might have been expected; but his objection was not to the decrees themselves, but to the headlong haste with which they were passed, and may perhaps have been colored by his disappointment that the articles voted did not include liberty of the press.[2] In his opinion, there was crying need of another constructive measure which ought to be taken without waiting till the constitution was finished, — namely, the establishment of a provisional national tribunal. "It is not with promises," he warned the Assembly, "that the fury of the people can be

[1] *Patriote Français*, August 6, 1789.   [2] *Ibid.*, August 7, 1789.

stopped. They clamor for deeds, they want to be satisfied immediately. Perhaps if such a tribunal is not established more blood will be shed. One must be created which, in the midst of chaos and anarchy, will execute prompt justice upon a few agents of despotism, and thus force the others to abandon their posts." [1]

As Brissot predicted, disorder continued and culminated in Paris on the 5th and 6th of October, when a mob rushed out to Versailles, insulted the dignity of the Assembly, broke into the palace, murdered members of the king's guard, and forced the king and queen to remove their abode to Paris. Lafayette, who as the commander of the national guard was responsible for order, arrived late on the scene and eventually quelled the disturbance, but it was felt by many people that if he had acted with promptness and vigor the outbreak might have been prevented altogether. In judging of this unfortunate affair Brissot did not take a very decided or radical stand. While deploring the acts of violence and the shedding of blood, he was not one of those who held Lafayette responsible, but on the contrary commended his "prudence and courage." As a member of the *Comité des Recherches* of the Commune he had to take action against the alleged instigators of violence, but at the same time he joined his fellow members of the committee in a declaration that in taking such action they were only fulfilling their duty and that they had nothing to do with ulterior causes — which was equivalent to saying that they were in sympathy with the movement as a whole.[2] Moreover, this censure was rather offset by the fact that when Brissot wished to show that the people were really not "ferocious" he made the singular choice of the events of October 5 and 6 as an example with which to prove his point, and complacently remarked that the mob did not do all the harm it might have

---

[1] According to Jaurès (*Histoire socialiste*, i, 288) Brissot's criticism was from the point of view of a doctrinaire and a pedant who wanted long discussion of theories and not immediate action.

[2] Lacroix, *Les Actes de la Commune*, v, 134.

done. With the incidental result, the transfer to Paris of the National Assembly, he was greatly pleased. In his *Plan de conduite* he had pressed upon the States-General the advisability of such a step, and now that it was taken he was in the forefront in presenting congratulations and promises of support on the part of the municipality of Paris.[1]

In the affair of Nancy, when many of his fellow citizens hesitated, he was more decided and was one of those who expressed open sympathy with the mutinous soldiers. The revolt which culminated at Nancy grew out of the suspicion with which the army was regarded. A large part of the Assembly doubted its adherence to the Revolution and thought of it as a possible means by which the king might reëstablish his authority. Influenced by their fear of its power and by their own ideas of fraternity and equality, they had passed various decrees which were utterly destructive of discipline. The result was disorganization everywhere, culminating on August 31, 1790, in an open mutiny at Nancy which was suppressed by the Marquis de Bouillé. The Assembly was in an embarrassing position: it did not wish to uphold what might be considered a despotic exercise of power; at the same time it could not encourage mutiny, even though that mutiny were the result of its own action. The outcome was that the majority officially approved of Bouillé's action; but a considerable minority, joined by many outside of the Assembly, did not hesitate to declare that the mutinous soldiers had right on their side and that Bouillé had been guilty of an act of tyranny. Believing that soldiers were justified in protesting against orders of which they did not approve,[2] even this illustration of the result of such doctrine did not open Brissot's eyes nor prevent him from criticizing M. Bouillé severely. "The triumph of M. Bouillé," he wrote, "the death of four hundred citizens, has caused general indignation." The soldiers were rebels, he admitted, but those rebels were their brothers, and the blood of their brothers should be shed sparingly. Bouillé ought to have

---

[1] See p. 91.   [2] *Patriote Français*, April 26, 1791.

reasoned with them as a father, and, like those entrusted with putting down Shays' Rebellion in Massachusetts, have avoided the shedding of blood till the last extremity.[1] A little later he expressed himself even more emphatically, laying blame on the municipality of Nancy, the department, M. Bouillé, and the Swiss officers; in short, on every one but the soldiers. "Should the soldiers be blamed?" he demanded. "Doubtless they did make mistakes, but their excuse is in the revolution, their own patriotism, the aristocracy of their officers and the loyalty with which they are inspired."[2] For the time being Brissot was in advance of public opinion in his condemnation of Bouillé and represented only the minority, but that minority was strong enough to stop the persecution of Bouillé's French prisoners,[3] and eventually Brissot's point of view prevailed, and Bouillé, instead of being honored as a military hero, came to be popularly regarded as a cruel tyrant of the old régime.

Brissot's decidedly unmilitary idea of discipline was again evident in the matter of the disobedience of the soldiers to Lafayette when they prevented the king from going to Saint-Cloud, on April 18, 1791. Passive obedience, he admitted, might be necessary for discipline, but it was one thing to obey blindly orders concerning discipline and tactics, and quite another thing to obey commands which seemed to be unjust, contrary to law and liberty.[4]

Brissot was indeed a thorough democrat in his sympathy with the people. He naturally, therefore, upheld the right of petition and resented any limitations upon it. He went further, and upheld popular movements not only in the specific cases referred to, but in general. "The instinct of the people is worth more than all your dialectics," he cried; "it has saved you ten times over and it will continue to save you." Popular movements were to be expected and desired among a people

---

[1] *Patriote Français,* September 3, 4, 1790. [2] *Ibid.,* December 9, 1790.

[3] The Swiss soldiers, however, over whom the jurisdiction of the French law did not extend were tried by court-martial created by their own officers.

[4] *Patriote Français,* April 26, 1791.

whose constitution was not yet finished, as a means of frightening conspirators and false patriots, and especially among a
people, a large part of whom were excluded from a share in
making the laws. To require a people to submit without question to all the laws, it would be necessary that all people should
have a share through their representatives in making the laws.
But owing to the distinction between active and passive citizens
half of France was not represented, was in a state of subjection.
When that half once realized the uselessness of petitions as a
means of securing redress, insurrection would be its natural
weapon.[1]

But that the people might not become the prey of unscrupulous agitators they needed to be instructed. He therefore welcomed the growth of popular societies. Such societies, the
distinctive feature of which was that, unlike the Jacobin Club,
they were open to passive as well as to active citizens and to
women as well as to men, began to come into existence in the
autumn of 1790, and by the spring of 1791 they were numerous
and flourishing. With this movement Brissot was delighted
and did all in his power to encourage and foster it; he published
articles by Lanthenas on the subject, declared that such organizations were the secret of peace and social order, and urged
their establishment everywhere.[2]

Of one of the societies — that at Lons-le-Saunier — he became the special champion. Another society of aristocratic
character had been formed at the same place, and both claimed
affiliation with the Jacobins at Paris, which, under the leadership of Theodore Lameth, decided in favor of the latter.
Whereupon Brissot took up the cudgels in behalf of the democratic society, opened the columns of his newspaper to their
complaints, and attacked Lameth in unsparing terms. The
cause of the democratic society, he declared, was the cause of

[1] *Patriote Français*, May 12, 1791. See also Aulard, *La Formation du parti
républicain*, in *La Révolution française*, xxxv, 318–22.
[2] *Patriote Français*, February 14, 1791. Of the societies for women he
apparently did not approve unreservedly.

patriotism and of justice. Whoever was indifferent to the complaints of their brave brethren of Mont-Jura was unworthy of liberty; whoever would stifle these complaints was a traitor to patriotism.[1]

While defending popular societies in general, he became a member of one of the most prominent of such societies at Paris — the *Cercle social*. This society, a little group of municipal politicians gathered around Fauchet, was in part made up of the former representatives of the Commune. It was based on a kind of free-masonry, and was somewhat socialistic as well as democratic in character. With the idea of extending its activities it proceeded to develop an organization known as the *Confédération des amis de la vérité*, whose purpose was to preach the rights of man as an end, and as a means to this end to further universal brotherhood.[2] In spite of some practical work this confederation seems to have been too theoretical to have altogether satisfied Brissot with his never quenched desire for active propaganda; and with the aim, apparently, of educating public opinion more directly, he engaged in company with his friends, Lanthenas, Bançal, and the Rolands, in trying to form a federation of philosophers. Like his previous enterprises, this was not to be primarily a money-making scheme, and was therefore to be carried on by such persons as would be content to get only a bare living out of it, and would concentrate all their energies on making it useful to humanity.[3] As in the *Association agricole*, he hoped to get help from the English Quakers, and here again he found in Lanthenas his most active supporter.[4] Lanthenas, however, feared Brissot's over-zealous ardor, and apparently with good reason, for Brissot in his

[1] *Patriote Français*, February 25, March 13, 1791.
[2] Lacroix, *Les Actes de la Commune de Paris*, VII, 416, 452, 607.
[3] *Lettres de Madame Roland*, II, 253–59; April, 1791.
[4] At the time that this project was on foot, Madame Roland was corresponding with Bançal as to the possibility of his acting as agent for the *Confédération des amis de la vérité* at Paris, and forming a like society at London, but the plan seems to have fallen through. It is possible that Brissot's plan was connected with this. *Lettres*, II, 248, 262.

anxiety to get money kept running after Lafayette, and failed to see what to Lanthenas seemed self-evident, that Lafayette was playing with him, and that he was being blinded to Lafayette's real political sentiments.[1] This accusation is naturally not susceptible of proof, but at all events Lafayette apparently gave him no money, and as very few other people seem to have either, the enterprise fell through.

In connection with Brissot's democracy two interesting questions arise: did it extend to women, and was it socialistic in character?[2] As to the first question, he certainly approved of the admission of women to the popular societies, showed his sympathy with a society of women known as the *Amies de la vérité*, by sending them a letter of congratulation, and spoke with satisfaction of the women's clubs formed at Bordeaux, Allais, and Nantes.[3] But it cannot truthfully be said that he was very enthusiastic on the subject. The place of woman, he declared apropos of Talleyrand's outline of a plan for national education, was in the home. She should, therefore, be given an education which would suit her for private, not for public life. His inmost feelings on the subject are best seen in his memoirs, where he declared that a woman devoted to politics seemed to him a monster, or at least a "*précieuse ridicule*" of a new kind.[4]

As to the socialistic character of Brissot's democracy, the answer is not so easy. No scheme for the suppression of private property or for its wholesale redistribution apparently ever crossed his mind, yet some of his ideas might be characterized as socialistic in the broader sense of the term, his advocacy, for instance, of the abolition of primogeniture. To permit this inequality in bequests of property, he wrote, was to accumulate

---

[1] "*Lanthenas écrivait déjà à Bançal en avril, en lui exposant ses plans de propagande (Bib. nat. 9534, fol. 200–01): Brissot va ce matin, chez M. Lafayette pour éprouver ses intentions. Il a offert plusieurs fois l'argent pour quelque entreprise qui tendît à garantir la Constitution contre les dangers qui de tous côtés la menacent. Si nous pourrons le déterminer pour ce projet des Sociétés populaires.*" *Lettres de Madame Roland*, ii, 273, note.

[2] Lacroix, *Les Actes de la Commune de Paris*, vii, 622.

[3] *Ibid.*, and *Patriote Français*, April 1, 1791.   [4] *Mémoires*, i, 272–73.

property in the hands of a few privileged persons. The division of property, on the other hand, was the most fruitful source of public prosperity.[1] Further, he was a constant champion of the poor. For example, in connection with the subject of finance, he argued for the small assignat, on the ground that it was needed by the poor workmen;[2] and on the subject of taxation he argued against the octroi because it weighed with especial heaviness on the poor.[3] Nor did he hesitate to publish an article *Sur le peuple* in which the vices of the rich and the virtues of the poor were frankly contrasted,[4] and in the *Patriote Français* of July 18, 1791, he declared that the amount of money paid in taxes by the poor was not as small as it seemed; that, on the contrary, if the value of their work was considered, they really paid more than the rich.

Though he preached no immediate change in fundamental social relations, he would do away at once with undemocratic social forms. It was not only an undemocratic reminiscence of past distinctions, he maintained, but quite useless as well to address your letters to your neighbor "Monsieur" or "Madame" and to sign yourself "his most humble and obedient servant." It would even be better, provided one could change all his habits at once, to substitute for the formal second person of the plural the *tu* forms of the singular.[5] People should certainly drop the aristocratic *de* from their names, though in order to avoid confusion the patronymic would better be kept.[6] Not even the king should be excepted in this abandonment of aristocratic titles. The king was no longer the sovereign, he declared; he should therefore not be given the name,[7] while to call him "Louis by the grace of God" was positively obnoxious, as absolutely out of harmony with the acknowledged fact that

---

[1] *Patriote Français*, March 14, 1791; also August 14, and December 6, 1790.
[2] *Ibid.*, May 6, 1790.   [3] *Ibid.*, February 13, 1791.
[4] *Ibid.*, February 5, 1791.   [5] *Ibid.*, June 23, 1791; also July 4, 1790.
[6] *Ibid.*, July 1, 1790. Note the way in which he followed his own advice. In the *Patriote Français* of October 7, 1790, he gives a list of the works of "J. P. Brissot," then below in smaller type is printed "*ci-devant de Warville.*"
[7] *Ibid.*, September 24, 1790.

Louis was king solely by the will of the people.[1] Indeed, Brissot felt so strongly on the matter that when at the theater people shouted, "*Vive le roi*," he found his pleasure completely spoiled. One comparatively trivial evidence of aristocratic exclusiveness on the part of the king irritated him extremely, namely, that during the presence of the king at the Tuileries the garden was kept shut till one o'clock, and when it was open, workmen and people shabbily dressed, or carrying packages, were not allowed to enter. The garden, as well as the Champs Élysées, he maintained, should be freely open to the public irrespective of occupation or attire.[2]

Also in more serious matters Brissot wished to do away with the privileges accorded to the king and to reduce him to a plane of democratic equality with other citizens. He rejoiced, for example, when the right of pardon was taken from him,[3] objected to his control of so many domains [4] and so large a pension fund, his inviolability as a private citizen [5] and his private guard.[6] In fact, in every possible way and in the strongest terms Brissot showed his desire to lessen the power of the king.

But did he wish to do away with the king altogether? He was a thorough democrat, but was he also a republican? To compare his utterances on this subject at various times, as his opponents were not slow to do, would make him out to be both changeable and inconsistent, but a closer examination shows that while he was invariable in his adherence to republicanism as the best government in theory, he only varied in his opinion as to its immediate practicability. Hence he is found at one moment proclaiming the advantages of a republic — especially one like the United States — and the next supporting monarchy. For instance, his pamphlet on systems of provincial administration proposed by Necker and Turgot, he boldly entitled *Observations d'un républicain*, and in it did not hesitate to declare that thoroughgoing reform was impossible under a

---

[1] *Patriote Français*, October 10, 1789.
[2] *Ibid.*, August 29, 1790.
[3] *Ibid.*, June 5, 1791.
[4] *Ibid.*, August 20, 1790.
[5] *Ibid.*, December 23, 1790; March 30, 1791.
[6] *Ibid.*, November 12, 1790.

monarchy. But when once the monarch gave serious evidence of a willingness to further reform by calling the States-General, Brissot, with other theoretical republicans, seems to have realized that the "half might be better than the whole," and stopped talking about republicanism. If the king were really in earnest, he held that it might be well to give him a chance, and both in the prospectus to his journal and in his *Plan de conduite* he spoke of the king as the "friend of the people," and of the States-General as the "support of monarchy." It is to be borne in mind, however, that in writing these pamphlets he was anxious, on the one hand, not to offend the government, whose sanction he needed for his newspaper; nor, on the other hand, the people, whose votes he wanted for his election.

As the Revolution progressed he not only continued his criticism of the prerogatives of royalty but became more open in again stating his admiration for the republican form of government, as such. "I hate royalty," he wrote in the *Patriote Français* of September 24, 1790, "and I have hated it from the moment I began to reflect. Nothing seems to me more degrading to man. I adore the republican government, but," he added, "I do not believe the French are worthy yet of this holy régime." He would not for a moment admit, however, that they could not become ready for it, and when Clermont-Tonnère upheld monarchy as in itself the best form of government, Brissot attacked him almost with rage. Since France had now a representative legislative body and elective judges, it was republican, Brissot declared, in two thirds of its elements, and could not, therefore, any longer be considered a monarchy at all, in the sense meant by the monarchists. He then took up, one after the other, the statements of Clermont-Tonnère, and denied in the first place that a monarchy was necessary to the prosperity of France; in the second place, that the extent of its territory precluded the establishment of a republic; and in the third place, that the national character was unsuited to a republic. He maintained, on the contrary, that France was in slavery under the old régime; that she was now only half free, and that she would never be wholly free as long as she had a king; that this doctrine, far from being abominable, was the only one in conformity with reason, religion, and a sane policy; and that it was the doctrines of Clermont-Tonnère, on the contrary, which were cruel and degrading to the human race and which deserved to be called abominable. But even while upholding republicanism with almost unseemly ardor, Brissot did not advocate the immediate establishment of a republic. A little later, in defending Robert's [1] famous pamphlet *Le Républicanisme adopté à la France*, he expressed himself with more calmness. "That the republican government is preferable to monarchy," he wrote, "is a statement that is doubted only by people who have no initiative, by the weak, the unthinking and corrupt; but whether the republican government can be adapted alike to all countries, to all peoples, is a problem very difficult to solve. There is, in France, too much ignorance, too much corruption, too many cities and manufactures, too many men and too little land. . . . I scarcely believe that republicanism could maintain itself side by side with these causes of degradation." But, while admitting that personally he did not consider France ready for a republic, he declared that whenever the people themselves were convinced that it was time to abolish the monarchy and set up a republic they had a perfect right to do so, and that consequently Robert, or any one else, was free to preach republicanism. Moreover, to deny that right, he asserted, was to make the declaration of rights a dead letter.[2]

In spite of this explanation, Brissot was soon accused by Choderlos de Laclos in the *Amis de la constitution* of being guilty jointly with Robert of preaching republicanism. "Our constitution," declared Choderlos, "has two kinds of enemies

---

[1] Pierre François Joseph Robert (born in 1763, died in 1826) was an active member of the Club of the Cordeliers, secretary to Danton during his ministry, and afterward a member of the Convention. He was accused by the Girondins of buying up a quantity of rum contrary to the law, and eight casks found in his cellar were confiscated. In consequence of this affair he was dubbed with the name of "Robert Rhum."

[2] *Patriote Français*, December 19, 1790.

in France: the one wish a democracy and no king, the others a king and no democracy. Messrs. Robert, Brissot, etc., write for the first." [1] In answer, Brissot did not deny that he believed royalty was a curse, "but," he maintained, "to hold that opinion as a matter of political philosophy and in practice to reject the king adopted by the constitution were two entirely different things." [2]

Such an attitude might well give opportunity to those who were looking for ground for criticism. Brissot, they could declare with some point, was trying to be on both sides of the fence at once, only waiting the course of events to take his stand openly with the winning side. His attitude toward the whole affair of April 18 was a case in point. The king on that day had essayed to go out to mass at Saint-Cloud, but had been prevented by the national guards who had refused to obey Lafayette's command to allow the king to proceed. Lafayette had, thereupon, handed in his resignation, but on pressure had withdrawn it. In commenting on this event, Brissot asserted that the soldiers were right in disobeying Lafayette but that Lafayette was at fault in resigning. His resignation, he added, was a real calamity.[3] These opinions fell under the sharp eyes of Desmoulins, who criticized them severely, adding significantly that Brissot was not alone in asserting that the resignation of Lafayette was a calamity, as that was just what the aristocratic journals were saying.[4]

In reality, however, Brissot, in spite of his leaning toward Lafayette, was on the side of the people against the king, but during the next few weeks he seems to have made up his mind

[1] No. 19, given in *Buchez et Roux*, as quoted by Brissot, IX, 433–41.
[2] *Patriote Français*, April 9, 12, 1791. [3] *Ibid.*, April 22, 1791.
[4] *Révolutions de France et de Brabant*, no. 74. Desmoulins quotes Brissot as saying that the soldiers were right in disobeying, that a general who was disobeyed ought to resign, and that Lafayette was wrong in resigning. Such a statement, as Desmoulins pointed out, involved a flat contradiction. What Brissot actually said was: "*M. Lafayette a donné sa démission de commandant-général. Il a été désobéi par ses troupes, et un général désobéi doit quitter : voilà son motif ; nous croyons qu'on a eu raison de désobéir à M. Lafayette ; nous croyons qu'il a eu tort de donner sa démission.*" *Patriote Français*, April 22, 1791.

more firmly to support the monarchial constitution, and, on June 9, 1791, he expressed himself emphatically on the subject. After stating, as he had done before, his belief in a republic as the ideal form of government, he added: "As for the present state of things, I regard as criminal every man who does not submit to the constitution decreed and who thinks of changing any part of it whatever by other than constitutional means."

The flight to Varennes considerably modified these views. Suspicion, which had been grave since the 18th of April, was now transformed into certainty. There could no longer be any doubt that the king was opposed to the Revolution. Some decisive action must be taken at once in regard both to the king and to the constitution. As to what that action was to be there was wide difference of opinion. The Assembly was divided. Some wished to try the king; others proposed to follow the principle of the English law, which was embodied in the nearly finished constitution, that the king can do no wrong, and try only his subordinates. Some members of the Assembly felt that the king was in a measure justified in his refusal to submit to a constitution which had reduced his power to so extremely narrow limits, and that the real remedy was to be found in so altering the constitution that it would give him real power. To others this seemed virtual suicide to the Revolution. The king, they argued, had proved that he could not be trusted and he must be deposed, if only to prevent further mischief. And not only this, but the form of the government must be changed. There, for the first time, a republic was suggested as an immediate practical solution.

In this crisis, which promised the fulfillment of his long-cherished republican ideas, what was Brissot's attitude? On the news of the king's flight he hurried off to the home of his friend Pétion where he met Desmoulins, Robespierre, and Madame Roland, all gathered in great excitement. Robespierre, according to Madame Roland, was sure that the royal family had not fled without the help of a formidable party in Paris and that they, the patriots, might all expect to be murdered in a second

St. Bartholomew. Pétion and Brissot, on the other hand, were delighted; they were sure the king had effectually destroyed any remnant of authority he might still possess, and had made it evident beyond a doubt that he was opposed to the constitution. Here, therefore, was their opportunity to make a better one and to prepare people for a republic.[1] Some one apparently suggested that Lafayette might have to be reckoned with, but Brissot, still unheedful, in spite of Desmoulins's warnings, of the attitude of Lafayette toward the king on the 18th of April, declared that if Lafayette had favored the flight of the king, it was with the express purpose of giving France a republic.[2] Meanwhile, the capture of the king put another face on the situation. Robespierre was greatly relieved, but to the others it meant the return of the main source of trouble, with resulting complication and intrigue.

Brissot, who was regarded as one of the leaders of the republican party, was one of the first to be accused of republican conspiracy. In company with Clavière he was charged with having sent out messengers on the 25th of June to all the eighty-three departments bearing dispatches calculated to stir up the people in favor of republicanism. This accusation Madame Roland indignantly denied. At the same time she was not satisfied with Brissot's attitude in the *Patriote Français*, evidently because it was not republican enough.[3] To be sure, he had seized the occasion of the king's flight to attack the moderate party in the most severe terms. He did not use the word republican, but his implication was evident enough. "Will they still come to us," he asked in the *Patriote Français*, of June 22, "with their enthusiastic boasts of the good faith of kings?

---

[1] *Mémoires de Madame Roland*, i, 205, note.

[2] Desmoulins in no. 82 of *Les Révolutions de France et de Brabant* says, apropos of the arrival of the courier from Varennes: "*La scène change. Brissot, qui trois heures auparavant me disait chez Pétion, soyez sûr que si Lafayette a favorisé l'évasion du roi, c'est pour nous donner la république, Brissot ne peut plus nous endormir de ce conte bleu, puisque Bouillé son cher cousin, son complice ne conspiroit pas sans doute pour la démocratie.*"

[3] *Lettres*, ii, 311–12.

Will they vaunt the patriotism of our king, his attachment to the constitution? Citizens, you were all there, you heard the speeches made by the king to the National Assembly and the democratic Manifesto which he sent to all the courts of Europe. People put confidence in these fine protests; it was a crime even to doubt the word of a king. Ah, well! that patriotic king has fled! Louis XVI has himself broken his crown. . . . We must not merely half profit by the lesson." The next day Brissot wrote again: "A king after such perjury is not compatible with our constitution." Even in speaking of the flight he would have no terms used which might suggest a palliation of the offense, such as the proposed statement that the "king had been carried off." He approved, instead, the more equivocal phrase which was substituted, "that he had deserted the realm." [1] But Madame Roland wanted not merely comment on facts, but definite expression as to a constructive policy. This criticism evidently had weight with Brissot, for the next day he spoke with greater frankness and won the approving comment from Madame Roland that he was doing better.[2] "It is evident," he wrote, "that the king cannot possibly be the king of the new constitution. Even if he wanted to be now, even if he appeared to repent, to regret his perjury, to acknowledge his crime, would it do to allow him to keep the crown? [3] Would there not be danger still, that some day when he had sufficient force under his control, he might declare that his repentance was forced, and retract it?" Brissot regretted, he went on to say, that republicanism had not as many friends as might be expected. He wondered too, he added, why people were unwilling to give its real name to a condition which practically existed.

Besides preaching republicanism in his own journal, Brissot was actively interested in trying to establish a new journal which was to have the defense of republicanism as its sole

[1] *Patriote Français*, June 24, 1791.
[2] *Lettres de Madame Roland*, ii, 314; June 25, 1791.
[3] *Patriote Français*, June 25, 1791.

purpose. The project grew out of discussions among the little republican group which was accustomed to gather at the home of Pétion to talk over the situation. It included, besides Brissot and Pétion, Condorcet, Clavière, Buzot, Thomas Paine, and Du Chastellet.[1] Of this group Du Chastellet seems to have been the most enthusiastic and the most ready to take revolutionary action. As a result of his ardor the members of the National Assembly were surprised one morning to find posted up at the doors and in the corridors of their place of meeting the following prospectus drawn up by Thomas Paine, but signed by Du Chastellet:[2] —

"The perfect tranquillity, the mutual confidence which reigned among us during the flight of the former king, the profound indifference with which we have seen him brought back, are the unequivocal signs that the absence of a king is worth more than his presence, and that he is not only a superfluity but a very heavy burden which weighs upon the entire nation. . . .

"Animated by the ideas expressed above, a *Society of Republicans* has resolved to publish in detached sheets a work under the title of *Le Républicain*. Its object is to give people information upon this republicanism, which is calumniated because it is not understood; upon the uselessness, the vices and the abuses of royalty which prejudice is obstinate in defending, although they *are* understood."

According to Dumont, Du Chastellet in posting this notice was acting on his own responsibility and did not have the approval of the rest of the group; but as Dumont evidently wished to minimize his own part he is perhaps not to be credited.[3] At all events, the moderates in the Assembly regarded it as a most audacious proceeding and threatened to bring the authors before the courts.[4] In spite of this threat, several

---

[1] Achille Du Chastellet (born 1759, died 1794), a distinguished officer closely connected with Brissot and the Girondins.

[2] Dumont, *Souvenirs*, 321–26; also Madame Roland, *Mémoires*, I, 204–05, and notes.

[3] *Souvenirs*, chap. XVI.

[4] *Mémoires de Madame Roland*, I, 204–05, note.

numbers were published, but with the reëstablishment of the king the publication naturally came to an end.[1] As long as it lasted Brissot gave it his full support in the *Patriote Français*, quoted in full the prospectus, derided the demand of Malouet that its authors be haled before the courts, and printed the letter of Du Chastellet in reply to his critics.[2]

Meanwhile he was constantly publishing other material most suggestively republican, such, for example, as an address of Bançal at Clermont in which the latter declared that liberty was incompatible with an hereditary monarchy;[3] an article on the abolition of royalty at Athens, which pointed out that its partial failure was owing to the fact that the first archon was the eldest son of the king;[4] and the announcement of a prize of three hundred livres for the person who could prove that a republican and a free citizen were not two inseparable things.[5] He continued also himself to write in defense of republicanism, spoke in highest terms of Condorcet's speech on republicanism before the *Cercle social* on July 9,[6] and hotly resented the suggestion afterward the basis of most violent attacks on the Girondins — that to make France a republic was to make it a federation of eighty-three republics.[7]

However, he soon began to realize that public opinion was not ripe for so radical a change, and, while continuing to defend republicanism with vigor, he gradually moderated his demands as to the immediate action to be taken, and skillfully suggested that if it were thought that France were not ready for a republic in its complete form, the essentials of that kind of government might be gained in another form. "If you keep royalty," he wrote, "let the executive council be elective, chosen by the departments and removable. We shall gain all if this point is gained and liberty will no longer be in danger. . . . This is the

---

[1] *Souvenirs*, chap. XVI. According to Dumont the republicans went so far in their attack on monarchy that they changed an article he sent them from London, with the view of making it more radical.

[2] *Patriote Français*, July 2 and 4, 1791. [3] *Ibid.*, July 3, 1791.
[4] *Ibid.*, July 9, 1791. [5] *Ibid.*, July 4, 1791.
[6] *Ibid.*, July 17, 1791. [7] *Ibid.*, July 9, 1791.

idea which seemed to win the support of the majority of the Jacobins. It was proposed at first by M. Danton. The Jacobins are willing to have a king only on this condition. At the same time they are not willing to be thought republicans. Let us not dispute over terms. I ask for no better republic than such a monarchy. The Jacobins are republicans without knowing it. Like M. Jourdain they make prose without being aware of it. No matter! The prose is excellent." [1] A day or two later Brissot repeated this suggestion in modified form. Let the king be dethroned temporarily by the Assembly, which would then appeal to the primary assemblies on the question of his permanent dethronement. The crown would then pass to his son, a minor, who should be given an elective council chosen by the departments. [2]

Again, going back to the idea of retaining the king himself, he set forth his general idea in a series of articles entitled "*La profession de foi sur la monarchie et sur le républicanisme,*" which appeared first in the *Patriote Français* and was subsequently republished in pamphlet form. [3] It was an extremely skillful piece of work, well calculated to conciliate the opposition and to present republicanism in its best light. The importance of the profession as showing Brissot's views at this critical time justifies quotation at length. He began by declaring that the monarchists and the republicans were really in closer agreement than people thought. They wanted peace and good order, and it only needed a frank discussion to show how much they had in common. He then proceeded to define a republic as a government in which all the powers were representative, that is to say, delegated; all the authorities temporary or removable and elected by the people directly or indirectly. Taking this definition as a basis he declared that five sixths of the authorities provided by the constitution were already representative, elective, and removable, and that the last sixth (the king) was,

---

[1] *Patriote Français*, June 29, 1791. [2] *Ibid.*, July 1, 1791.
[3] It originally appeared in the *Patriote Français* of July 5 and 6, 1791, and was republished in pamphlet form under date of July 17.

by a fiction of the law, also representative and elective. The only question which divided the monarchists and the republicans was whether the last sixth should be made representative in reality. The republicans said yes; the monarchists, no.

"The republicans believe," he continued, "that royalty can be and ought to be abolished immediately. It can be abolished, they say, without violating the decree which preserves the monarchy, because a monarchy can exist without an hereditary king. Again, it can be done without violating that decree because he who held the position of royalty, having protested against the constitution, has by that very fact abdicated and left us where we were before we declared the monarchy hereditary. It ought to be done because to preserve royalty would only be to preserve a source of calamity and disorder. . . .

"The republicans maintain that royalty ought to be abolished," he went on to say, "because chance is as likely to call to the throne an idiot or a rogue as a capable and good man; because royalty involves a heavy weight of expense upon the nation, and because a good executive power and an energetic administration are possible without a king. But it may be objected that the office of king is necessary in the present crisis. In answer, let it be remembered that the office has practically been suspended for two years and legally for two weeks and society has not gone to pieces." Finally, he concluded, republicanism was much less likely than monarchy to bring about anarchy. For, if the people chose all their departments of government, they would have confidence in them. They would obey them with pleasure.

But, while maintaining the superiority of a republic over a monarchy in the abstract, Brissot admitted that these arguments might not be sufficient to lead to the establishment of a republic immediately. As a practical substitute, he proposed a king with an elective and removable council.[1] In the *Patriote Français* of July 1, he outlined a method for the formation of this council. The electoral assembly of each department should

[1] Again taken up in the speech of July 10.

choose one citizen and these eighty-three citizens should choose the council from their own number.[1] It was only as a substitute, Brissot was careful to add: the real and lasting remedy was to be a republic.[2] In short, to quote M. Aulard, he changed his tactics but not his principles.[3]

As to the concrete question involved: "Was the king to be held responsible for his recent action?" Brissot kept firmly to his former opinion. In numerous articles in the *Patriote Fran-çais*, he inveighed against that section of the Assembly led by Barnave which upheld the inviolability of the king.[4] And on July 10 he made a notable speech on the subject at the Jacobin Club.[5] He began by defending the Jacobins against the accusation of republicanism, and declared that, while they demanded that the king be tried, they were at the same time defenders of the constitution. Then, passing directly to the question of the inviolability of the monarch, he asserted that such a claim was entirely without foundation. The sovereignty of the nation, he argued, recognized no one above itself, hence if the people were

[1] This method of choice by the departments suggests the federalist idea. See chap. xi. It is interesting to note that in a letter to Bançal des Issarts, dated July 1, 1791, Madame Roland speaks of an elective council and urges Bançal to work for it. She says: "*Vous ferez une chose excellente si vous pouvez porter vos assemblées primaires à délibérer que, les circonstances requérant un novel examen de la chose publique, elles ont voulu connaître quels changements il convenait d'y apporter, et, d'après une sage discussion, ont arrêté sur telles considérations que l'Assemblée nationale serait priée de convoquer toutes celles du royaume pour avoir leur vœu sur la formation d'un conseil électif et temporaire, auquel serait confié le pouvoir exécutif.*" *Lettres de Madame Roland*, ii, 319.

[2] According to De Lacroix (*L'Intrigue dévoilée*), it was this production which finally gained Brissot his election to the *Législative*.

[3] *Histoire politique*, 134.

[4] The question was discussed either editorially or in the form of communicated articles in almost every issue, from the time of the king's flight to July 11.

[5] *Discours sur la question de savoir si le roi peut être jugé 10 juillet, 1791*. Brissot had become a member of the Club some time between December 21, 1790, and May 11, 1791, but the exact date of his admission does not appear. In the list of members drawn up December 21, 1790, his name is not included (Aulard, *Les Jacobins*, i, Int., xxxix) and the first mention of his participation in the meetings of the Club was May 11, 1791, when he made a speech. Aulard, *Les Jacobins*, ii, 412.

not inviolable, the king could not be inviolable; and, according to the declaration of rights, all men were equal before the law. Further, the inviolability of the king would only mean anarchy. Again, to take example from foreign experiences, the responsibility of the President of the United States worked no harm, but acted rather as a preventive; and in England, although the people admitted the inviolability of the king theoretically, they denied it practically whenever they wished to overturn the constitution. After having considered the question in the abstract, Brissot turned to the concrete objection that to hold the king accountable would bring down on France the vengeance of foreign powers, and tried to show, by taking up in detail the condition of each country, that there was no possibility of any of them making war upon France. But if they did make war, he continued, with his unfailing optimism, France, as a free country, would easily be victorious.

According to Madame Roland, Brissot fairly outdid himself in this speech. "He was no more a mere orator," she wrote in one of her letters; "he was a free man, defending the cause of the human race with the majesty, the nobility, and the superiority of the very genius of liberty. He convinced people's minds, he electrified their souls. . . . Three times the Assembly . . . rose in a body and threw their hats into the air in an irrepressible enthusiasm."[1] And Desmoulins, who was not overready to praise Brissot, declared that he had exhausted the subject. Others had made speeches, but he had left nothing more to be said. His speech ought to be given the widest publicity.[2] The Jacobins were evidently of the same opinion, for they decreed that the speech be printed and copies sent to the National Assembly and to all the departments.[3]

---

[1] *Lettres*, ii, 326.   [2] *Révolutions de France et de Brabant*, no. 85.

[3] Aulard, *Les Jacobins*, iii, 628. The following is an English appreciation of the speech (*Diary of the Second Viscount Palmerston in France*, July 6 to August 31, 1791; describes meeting of Jacobin Club; about one thousand present): —

"Brissot read a speech very violent and inflammatory, to prove that the king's person was inviolable only for those Acts of Government which are

A few days later the Club petitioned for dethronement, and, as an evident recognition of his influence, Brissot was appointed a member of the committee which was entrusted with the drawing up of the petition.[1] This petition closed with a request that the National Assembly receive in the name of the nation the abdication which Louis XVI had already made on June 21, and that it use all constitutional means to provide for filling the vacant places. This last clause was violently opposed by the avowed republicans on the ground that it both upheld the throne and implied a desire to put on it a member of the Orléanist family. After a heated debate, the Jacobins finally decided to retain the clause in question, and although such action did not necessarily imply that they were Orléanists, it did show that they were not willing to lead in the immediate establishment of a republic. This petition had already been presented for signatures on the Champ de Mars, when news came that the Assembly had decided that the decree suspending the king should remain in force till he should accept the constitution. The Jacobins, accordingly, withdrew their petition and appointed another committee, of which Brissot was a member, to draw up an address to the affiliated societies, explaining and defending their position.

According to Brissot's own account, his authorship of the petition had been made known by Laclos.[2] At all events, his membership in these two committees was a public acknowledg-

transacted through his Ministers; that there was a case in which he was personally answerable; that he ought to be tried for his conduct, and that there was no danger to be apprehended from foreign powers on that account. His speech was lively and full of declamation, well suited to the temper of his audience, who received it with such continued bursts of applause as almost deafened me for the rest of the evening. He was very deficient in point of argument and totally passed over what are considered as the most material grounds by those who hold the other opinion. . . . Monsr. Brissot's speech, however, was perfectly satisfactory to his audience, and the shouts of applause given by so many hundred people on such a subject, showed a kind of ferociousness of disposition which was infinitely disgusting to a moderate mind. It was ordered to be printed and distributed over the country, which I doubt not will be much inflamed by it." *July 10, Dispatches of Earl Gower*, 287–88.

[1] Aulard, *Les Jacobins*, III, 19.   [2] *Projet de défense, Mémoires*, II, 282.

ment that he had retreated from the advanced republican position which for the last four weeks he had openly held, though with some wavering. His enemies hastened to say that it was also an acknowledgment that he was an Orléanist, a charge which his friends, in turn, hastened to deny.[1] From his statement, later, that when urged by Laclos to present the petition he refused, on the ground of pressing business elsewhere, it looks as if he did not wish to make his part in the event too conspicuous.[2] At the time of his trial this charge of being a partisan of the house of Orléans was again brought up, and with more serious import. The debated clause, "*et a pouvoir à son* [the king's] *remplacement par tous les moyens constitutionnels*," was adduced as a strong link in the alleged chain of proof that he was a royalist and Orléanist, and that, while ostensibly supporting republicanism, he was and always had been, its enemy. In his *Projet de défense* he admitted having yielded to the persuasions of Laclos to draw up the petition, but declared most emphatically that the last clause was afterward added by Laclos and that he was himself in no way responsible for it.[3] According to Madame Roland, who apparently derived her information from Brissot, Laclos openly proposed to him the addition of the clause, and on his strenuous objection agreed to withdraw it, but covertly managed to slip it in afterward.[4] Despite Brissot's apparent failure to explain himself at the time, his later defense is borne out by the fact that Laclos was a known Orléanist and opposed to Brissot's republican ideas.[5]

---

[1] Bonneville, a friend of Brissot and an enemy of Laclos, came to the rescue of the former (Dard, *La Général Choderlos de Laclos*, 323), and in the *Bouche de Fer* of July 17, wrote: "*Sur le nom du rédacteur le patriote Brissot, nous différons de rendre compte des violens soupçons qui se sont élevés à la lecture (arrières-pensées Orléanistes) nous ne les partageons plus. Brissot est un patriote intègre.*" Quoted in *Bouchez et Roux*, x, 447.

[2] *Mémoires*, ii, 282.   [3] *Ibid.*, ii, 282–83.

[4] "*Ce même Laclos proposait d'insérer un article qu'il annonçait d'un air sans conséquence, mais qui eût été favorable à d'Orléans, que Brissot le rejeta avec indignation, en mettant à la place celui qui invitait à la République pour laquelle ce moment était le véritable et eût été bien précieux.*" *Mémoires de Madame Roland*, ii, 285.

[5] Dard, 158, 275.

It receives further substantiation from Dard's [1] assertion that the clause in question was in an unknown hand.[2]

The events which followed the withdrawal of the Jacobin petition are well known: the preparation by the dissatisfied radical societies of another petition, which said nothing about constitutional means of filling the throne; the proclamation of Bailly, the Mayor of Paris, and Lafayette, the commander of the national guard, both of whom were adherents of monarchy, forbidding any gathering in the Champ de Mars; the assembling of the crowds in spite of the proclamations and the firing on them by Lafayette's troops. In the conservative reaction which followed, an attempt was made to punish the instigators of the republican movement. Brissot, with other republicans, was accused of being in the pay of foreign powers, but for some reason, he himself was not arrested; a fact which was afterward alleged against him as another evidence that he was a royalist and had a secret understanding with the reactionaries. His escape seemed to be accounted for, in part, by the fact that the petition presented was not the one with the drawing up of which he was connected; and in part because, when it came to the actual presentation of the latter petition for signatures, he remained behind the scenes. At all events, he stood his ground fairly well, considering the dangerous position in which he was placed, and he did not suspend his journal nor flee from Paris. But while he admitted that he had held republican opinions and preached them in his journal, he denied that he had had any part in the active republican movement. Nor were the people to blame, he declared with his usual readiness to defend the democratic against the bourgeois element. They had merely been deceived by a few seditious leaders.[3] But even

---

[1] The biographer of Laclos.

[2] In the judicial investigation, which was held immediately after the affair of the 17th of July, Brissot testified that he had had nothing to do with the printing, distributing, or signature of the petition. M. Mathiez, in commenting on this testimony, calls attention to the fact that Brissot took good care not to say anything as to the *drawing up* of the petition. Mathiez, *Le Club des Cordeliers*, 262, and note.

[3] *Patriote Français*, July 20, 1791.

Brissot, wrote Madame Roland, in terms which showed her high opinion of his courage, did not dare to tell the entire truth about the events of the last few days. To do so would only be to bring down the knife which was suspended over the heads of the republicans.[1]

He was certainly bold enough in denouncing Lafayette. "The deed was done," he wrote, "by a man who has told me a hundred times that he was a republican; who called himself the friend of the republican Condorcet; who told me that he cordially detested the vile persons with whom he is to-day connected. . . . There is from now on nothing more in common between him and me." [2] Brissot also denounced the Assembly for its proposal to send his fellow republicans before a special court. Such a court, he declared, was nothing short of a star chamber, or the rule of the Thirty at Athens; the courageous friends of liberty might as well prepare to drink hemlock.[3] Meanwhile, as the conservative reaction had decided that the proposed constitutional monarchy was not to give place to a republic, the constitution was once more brought up for discussion. And once more Brissot opposed with all his might the tendency to strengthen the power of the executive, and urged provision for periodic conventions as a means of amendment, though he now opposed, in view of the disturbed conditions of the country, the submittal of the present constitution to the people.[4] Of one important change that was made, the lowering of the qualifications for the position of deputy, he thoroughly disapproved, supporting Robespierre, Pétion, and Buzot in their opposition, on the ground that it was only an ostensible concession to democracy, since at the same time the qualifications for electors were raised. As the electors would be apt to choose deputies from among their own number, democracy had lost rather than gained by the change.[5]

---

[1] "*Toutes les relations des faits de dimanche sont fausses, à commencer par le procès-rerbal de la municipalité; personne n'ose faire les véritables, même B'st* [Brissot], *car ce serait de plonger le couteau sous lequel on est tenu.*" *Lettres*, II, 341.

[2] *Patriote Français*, July 18, 1791.   [3] *Ibid.*, July 23, 1791.

[4] See p. 135.   [5] *Patriote Français*, August 12, 1791.

The constitution, as thus completed, satisfied neither the conservatives who wanted the power of the king strengthened, nor Brissot and his friends, who wanted it lessened; but both agreed for the time in supporting the constitutional monarchy as thus established. Brissot soon obtained a seat in the legislative body under this new government and a chance to take a more direct part in political life. His success was due largely to the reputation he had gained as editor of the *Patriote Français*. In this capacity his writings on the formation of the constitution and on the events of the day had made him widely known, and decidedly influential as a supporter of the extreme left and an opponent, not only of the royalists, but also of the moderates, the advocates of constitutional monarchy such as Barnave and Lameth. In short, though he had in the end accepted an undemocratic monarchy he had made a name for himself as an upholder of the practice, as well as the principles, of democracy and sovereignty of the people.

After his election to the Legislative Assembly he still kept the direction of his journal,[1] and thus commanded a double portion of influence. Through the *Patriote Français* he continued to stand for humanitarian principles, to uphold American precedents, and to preach democratic republicanism as a theory,[2] — even though he wavered in regard to republicanism in practice. At the same time that Brissot was coming to be recognized as a leader of the Girondins, he made his paper more and more the organ of that party in the Legislative Assembly and later in the Convention; and as such it vehemently advocated the war, attacked Robespierre, denounced the Commune for its opposition to the Girondins, and fell with the Girondins in their defeat. During this later period interest is focused on Brissot as a legislator, rather than as an editor. The later history of the *Patriote Français* may, therefore, best be studied in connection with the Legislative Assembly and the Convention.

[1] He did give it up for a brief time but soon resumed it. See p. 361.

[2] A dispatch of Earl Gower of September 16, 1791, speaks of the *Patriote Français* as the most republican journal published in Paris.

CHAPTER VIII

BRISSOT AS A HUMANITARIAN

La Société des Amis des Noirs

IF any Frenchman in public life had been asked, up to the close of the Constituent Assembly, for what Brissot was best known, he would undoubtedly have answered without hesitation, for his work as the leader of the *Amis des Noirs*. Indeed, to his connection with this society which had so large an influence on the colonial question and which was so intensely hated by the white planters, Brissot owed a large share of his reputation for good or for ill. He was one of the most zealous humanitarians of the eighteenth century. But of all his many and varied humanitarian interests the cause to which he was most devotedly attached was that of the negro. In his ardent desire to extend to this oppressed and inferior race some measure of the liberty and equality which Frenchmen were claiming for themselves, and particularly to abolish the slave trade, he established *La Société des Amis des Noirs*.

His immediate incentive to this undertaking was the energetic work of an English organization directed against the slave trade. As early as 1727 the English Quakers had expressed their disapproval of that trade; and in 1761 they agreed to exclude from their society all persons who should be found to be concerned in it. In 1772 their cause was furthered by the famous judicial decision of Lord Mansfield, that as soon as a slave set his foot on the shores of England he became free.[1] In 1783 they formed an association "for the relief and liberation of the negro slaves in the West Indies and for the discourage-

---

[1] "The air of England has long been too pure for a slave and every man is free who breathes it. Every man who comes into England is entitled to the protection of the English law." Somerset *v.* Stewart, *Lofft's Reports, State Trials*, I, 201.

ment of the slave trade on the coast of Africa." The interest
aroused by the Quakers led Dr. Pinkard, the Vice-Chancellor
of the University of Cambridge, to propose as the Latin prize
essay at Cambridge for the year 1785 the subject *An liceat
invitos in servitutem dare*. The prize was won by Thomas Clarkson, who published his work in English in 1786 in an extended
form, under the title of "Essay on the Slavery and Commerce
of the Human Species." The publication of this essay marked
an epoch in the struggle against slavery. Clarkson was joined
by Wilberforce and Granville Sharp, and under the presidency
of the latter a committee was formed in 1787 for the suppression of the slave trade.[1]

Just at this juncture Brissot arrived in England, whither
he fled to avoid the *lettre de cachet* threatened on account of
his pamphlet, *Point de banqueroute*, and through his previous
affiliations with the Quakers was brought into connection with
the work of the committee now just getting under way.[2] He
was already greatly interested in the negro and had rushed to
his defense against the strictures made on him by the Marquis
de Chastellux.[3] He now returned to France, thrilled with the
idea of participating in so noble a cause.[4] He stirred up his
friends to interest in the subject, after his usual fashion laid
plans for disseminating knowledge by providing for the translation of books and pamphlets, and appealed for help to Mirabeau. As it happened Mirabeau had just secured government
permission for the publication of his *Analyse des papiers anglais*. Moved doubtless, in part, by the probable advantage to
himself, he not only agreed to convince the government of the
utility of allowing him to include translations of works on the
slave question as a kind of supplement to his journal, but offered Brissot very advantageous business terms for the arrange-

---

[1] Clarkson, *History of the rise, progress and accomplishment of the abolition of the African slave trade*, I, 257.

[2] See p. 39.   [3] See p. 59.

[4] "*Ce qui est certain c'est que ce club était une importation anglaise, qui ne nous a pas été moins funeste que les autres marchandises arrivées de la Grande Bretagne*." Beaulieu, *Essais historiques sur la Révolution française*, II, 489, note.

ment.[1] This arrangement he seems to have faithfully carried out, for as long as the *Analyse* lasted, it continued to be the organ of the *Amis des Noirs*, fulfilling the function which was afterward taken up by Brissot's own newspaper.

Meantime Brissot had written a letter to the English society in which with a superb disregard of international barriers he offered to act as their agent in France and promote a subscription there. At this proposition the English society was somewhat alarmed, and while thanking him warmly and electing him and Clavière honorary members and correspondents, made haste to decline his offer of raising funds, and suggested that a better method would be to organize in France a separate society.[2]

Whereupon Brissot through *L'Analyse des papiers anglais* promptly announced the proposed formation of such a society and begged for the coöperation of all the friends of humanity. As a result of his efforts, on February 19, 1788, a handful of men gathered at No. 3 rue Française to effect an organization.[3] Brissot counted eleven besides himself among the founders, but according to the records of the society they numbered eight, including, besides Clavière and Mirabeau, Valady and Carra, afterward associated with Brissot and the Girondins. To this little company Brissot made a stirring appeal, setting forth in eloquent terms the work to be done in bringing about the abolition of the slave trade and of slavery, and the urgent need of organized effort. Although the task seemed beyond their powers, they might well be encouraged by what had already been accomplished in America and in England. In order to achieve

---

[1] In the number of *L'Analyse des papiers anglais* of February 29 to March 6, 1788, Mirabeau announced the publication of works on slavery — at a reduced price to those who subscribed for them in connection with his paper. See also Brissot, *Mémoires*, II, 79. See also the *Extrait du registre* referred to below.

[2] Proceedings of the committee for the abolition of the slave trade, 1781–1819, 3 vols., British Museum, Mms. 21254–21256.

[3] See *Extrait du registre de la société* at the Institute, Paris, papers of Condorcet; also article by Cahen: *La Société des Amis des Noirs et Condorcet* in *La Révolution française*, June, 1906.

like results he recommended that they translate and publish
English works on the subject, make appeals through the newspapers, correspond with the English society and carry on researches on the condition of slavery in the French colonies.[1]
The eight accordingly proceeded to action, drew up the outline
of a constitution, and unanimously chose Clavière president.
Thus was formed *La Société des Amis des Noirs.*[2]

A part, at least, of the plan was immediately carried out,
for there began to appear in *L'Analyse des papiers anglais* of
Mirabeau works on slavery. Their zeal seems to have startled
the English society, for, a few weeks later, the latter felt obliged
to issue a formal statement in reference to a wild rumor that
was abroad to the effect that it was trying to bring about the
immediate abolition of slavery in the English colonies. It had
no such intention, it declared, and in order to make perfectly
clear what its intentions actually were it wished to state pub-
licly its purpose of keeping strictly to its main aim — the abolition of the slave trade.[3] It is not improbable that this declaration was provoked by Brissot's speech at the founding of the
Amis des Noirs which was printed under the title *Discours sur
la nécessité d'établir à Paris une société pour concourir avec celle
du Londres, à l'abolition de la traite et de l'esclavage des nègres.*
At all events, the English society issued the above protest, and
whether or not the French society really felt itself to blame, it
decreed that the protest should be sent to all the journals of
France. If it issued a like declaration on its own behalf there
appears to be no record of it.

Meanwhile Brissot was zealously seeking to attach to the
society persons to whose humanitarian interests it would seem
to appeal, particularly those whose position and influence
might be of help to them. He tried to secure the adhesion of

---

[1] Although Brissot's name does not appear in connection with this speech, it
was undoubtedly his, as he says in his memoirs (ii, 78) that the speech which
he made at the opening meeting was printed by Mirabeau, and this is the only
speech made on that occasion printed by him.

[2] *Extrait du registre.* For a list of the members see Appendix B.

[3] *L'Analyse des papiers anglais,* i, April 4, 1788.

Bernardin de Saint-Pierre, and of Hérault de Séchelles, a celebrated lawyer in the service of the government,[1] and even
ventured to write to Thomas Jefferson. But in these cases he
was not successful. The first declined on the ground of ill
health; Hérault de Séchelles felt that on account of his official
position it would hardly be seemly for him to appear to be the
accomplice of a society preparing for revolution; and Jefferson
also, while professing the greatest interest in the work, explained that as the official representative of the United States
he too was precluded from active coöperation.[2] Others, Brissot
was more successful in persuading to join the society. Among
them were Lubersac,[3] Bishop of Chartres; Brach, royal censor
and director general of exports; the Marquis of Beaupoil de
Saint-Aulaire,[4] the Marquis of Pampeluna,[5] Lanthenas,[6]
Crèvecœur;[7] and the Englishman, Pigott.[8] Of the various people to whom he appealed, Lafayette seems to have been of the
greatest help. He had responded cordially to Brissot's invitation to become a member of the society, and though he was
not present at the first meeting he was considered one of the

[1] Marie Jean Hérault de Séchelles (born 1759, died 1794) was a writer and
lawyer of considerable reputation on account of his oratorical powers. He was
elected to the Legislative Assembly, where he took his place on the extreme
left, and afterward to the Convention, of which he was twice president. The
constitution drawn up under the leadership of the Mountain in the summer of
1793 was chiefly his work. He followed the policy of Danton and perished with
him.

[2] Brissot, *Correspondance*, 165–66.

[3] Jean Baptiste Joseph, Baron de Lubersac (born 1740, died 1822), became
Bishop of Chartres in 1780 and was elected as deputy of the clergy of Chartres
to the States-General. At first he showed liberal tendencies, but refused to
accept the civil constitution of the clergy, emigrated and returned to France
only after the Concordat.

[4] Martial Louis Beaupoil de Saint-Aulaire (born 1719), was a bishop of Poitiers and was elected by the clergy of Poitiers to the States-General, where he
sat among the royalists. He subsequently emigrated to England where he died.

[5] Probably Jacques Joseph de Guyon de Geis, Baron de (born 1748, died
1789), *député suppléant* to the States-General.

[6] See p. 121.   [7] See p. 59.

[8] Robert Pigott was one of the English Quakers who had so large an influence
on Brissot. Various articles by him were inserted by Brissot in the *Patriote
Français*.

founders, and took it upon himself to set forth the purpose of the society in as favorable a light as possible before the minister Brienne. If he could not convince him of its usefulness, he would at least try to persuade him that it was innocuous. Brienne did not seem to have been altogether persuaded, however, for he warned Lafayette that it was a delicate question which the *Amis des Noirs* were essaying to settle and that they needed to handle it with great care. But at any rate he let the society alone. This freedom from molestation under a despotic government meant much to them, and Brissot, even after he had come to regard Lafayette as a traitor to the Revolution, never forgot what the *Amis des Noirs* owed to his protection and assistance.[1] It was also indebted to him for introducing Condorcet, who was an especially valuable acquisition, as he joined with Lafayette in bringing in other persons of note and influence.[2]

Besides bringing in new members Condorcet did good service to the society by drawing up a constitution. This document was divided into eight chapters and sixty-four articles, of which the most important were as follows: Membership was unlimited as to numbers and was open alike to men and women, Frenchmen and foreigners; but as it was stated later that ladies would be welcome to the social semi-annual meetings when reports of the work of the society would be made, it was obvious that they were *not* welcome at the ordinary meetings, nor expected to take part in the public work of the society. No one would be admitted to membership, however, except on presentation of a member who would stand sponsor for him and who was supported by four other members. The annual dues were two louis, but the members *might* give more. Meetings were to be held regularly on Tuesday, and besides the regular meeting a special meeting was held at the end of each semester to hear reports of papers. Members were to be notified in advance of the meetings and of the subjects to be discussed. The officers were to be a president, a secretary, a treasurer, and a general

---

[1] *Mémoires*, II, 76-78.   [2] *Ibid.*, II, 86.

committee, for the election of each of whom a different method was provided. The president was to be elected from the general assembly by a majority vote from members of the committee present, to serve three months, and then be reëligible only after an interval of three months. For the election of the secretary, evidently the most important officer, the assembly in the session preceding the one in which the secretary was to be elected, was to add five members to the committee. The body thus constituted was to choose at least four names to present to the assembly, by whom the choice was to be made. The term of office was to be two years, but the secretary might remain in office another two years if he were supported by two thirds of the members, and still another two years if supported by three fourths. Even if he did not receive the requisite majority, he nevertheless continued to be reëligible, but in competition with others. His salary, which he might refuse, was to be eight hundred francs, besides expenses of the office. He was also to have a clerk with a salary of six hundred francs. The treasurer was to be elected by the assembly at large, the term to be two years, with continued reëligibility. The committee, consisting of twenty-one members, including the president, secretary, and treasurer, *ex-officio*, elected for three years, seven at a time, was to have charge of the business of the society and particularly of preparing translations. Numerous other rules providing for the procedure in the meetings suggest that the society looked forward to vigorous, not to say acrimonious, discussions.[1]

The most striking thing about the whole constitution is the faith which it indicates on the part of the founders in the growth of their organization and the seriousness of their undertaking. Brissot's apparent failure to have part in it is explained by the fact that it seems to have been drawn up during his absence in America.[2] The society was hardly organized when

---

[1] The manuscript of the *Réglements* is found at the library of the Arsenal. It is printed in a pamphlet at the *Bibliothèque nationale* and also by M. Cahen in the article referred to above in *La Révolution française*, June, 1906.

[2] Article by M. Cahen, referred to above.

he set out upon his travels. Indeed, one part of his purpose in making this journey was to study the problem of slavery in the new world. Before starting he wrote to the English society of his intention, — whereupon they commended him to like societies at Philadelphia and New York and asked them to aid him in collecting information.[1]

In spite of the formation of the constitution, the French society, if Brissot's own account is to be believed, languished and nearly perished during his absence.[2] There certainly seems to be no evidence of great activity on its part till the spring of 1789, when, after Brissot's return from America, it became extremely active. In the month of February a meeting was held to listen to his report of the slavery problem as he had seen it in America. This report included a statement of what had been done with regard to the importation of slaves, with regard to slavery, the steps taken for the education of the negroes and an explanation of the compromises in the constitution of the United States on the subject, and a firm expression of belief in the capacity of the negro.[3]

The opportunity now offered to all classes of the French people to draw up statements of their grievances was also the opportunity of the *Amis des Noirs*, and they lost no time in preparing an address to be sent to all the *bailliages* of the kingdom. In this address the *bailliages* were begged to instruct their deputies to try to induce the States-General to consider means of abolishing the slave trade and to prepare the way for the abolition of slavery itself.[4] At the opening of the States-General they appointed a committee, of which Condorcet and Brissot were members, to keep track of legislation and to

---

[1] British Museum, *Proceedings of the committee*, Mms. 21254-21256.
[2] *Mémoires*, ii, 74.
[3] *Mémoire sur les noirs de l'Amérique septentrionale, lue à l'assemblée de la Société des Amis des Noirs, le 9 janvier, 1789.*
[4] The minutes of the English committee for April 21, 1789, state that a translation of the address of the society in France to the *bailliages* of that kingdom had been sent to some of the public papers and that it was resolved that two thousand copies of the said address be printed.

defend the interests of the negro whenever they were in question. They further drew up a letter to M. Necker in criticism of certain statements which he had made in a speech to the States-General on the slave trade.[1]

A letter was also addressed "to the deputies of the three orders to urge them to follow the example of the English and choose a committee charged with examining the cause of the negro." It was signed simply "*Un ami des noirs*," but may possibly have been the work of Brissot. The slave trade, the writer argued, should be abolished at once, and for six reasons: (1) it was the only cause of most of the wars between negro princes, and its abolition would save the life of a considerable number of sailors and of infinite numbers of negroes; (2) the continuance of the slave trade was ruinous to the nation; (3) the colonies could get along without the slave trade, as experience had demonstrated; (4) it was necessary to abolish the slave trade if the colonies were to be preserved and numberless abuses remedied; (5) the negroes were sadly maltreated, and the abolition of the slave trade was the only means to ameliorate their condition; (6) it would be easy to manage the revolts which the planters predicted would be the result.

In attempting to carry on its work the society was now assisted by Clarkson, who was sent over to help them by the English society. The latter, evidently mindful of Brissot's quixotic schemes of coöperation at the time of the founding of the *Amis des Noirs*, feared that his enthusiasm might not be properly balanced with caution; and, when the proposition was made that the two societies combine their efforts to induce the governments of their respective countries to take concerted action against the slave trade, the English society perceived that any such proposition coming from the English side would be regarded by the French government with suspicion. Clarkson was accordingly warned to beware of involving the English society in political complications.[2] When he arrived at Paris

---

[1] *Lettre à M. Necker.*
[2] *Life of Wilberforce* (ed. by R. I. and S. Wilberforce), I, 231.

in July, 1789, he found that the enthusiasm of many of the members of the *Amis des Noirs* had somewhat died down.[1] It would, perhaps, be more correct to say that they were so actively engaged in actual revolution that they had no time left to think of a reform which was not a matter of immediate and pressing importance. Those members of the society who were also members of the National Assembly were almost constantly engaged at Versailles, those who were connected with the municipal government were absorbed in their work at the *hôtel de ville*, while others were occupied in learning the use of arms or in doing guard duty. Attendance at the meetings of the society naturally fell off, and although Clarkson had been introduced to the Duke of Rochefoucauld, Condorcet, Pétion, Clavière, Brissot, and Lafayette as active workers, when he came to attend a meeting of the committee, he was surprised to find that Brissot was the only one of those mentioned who was present.

The zeal of those who were there was unabated. They decided to seek an audience with M. Necker, through Clarkson who was to be accompanied by Condorcet, De Bourges, and Brissot; also to write to the president of the National Assembly, asking him to appoint a day to hear the cause of the negro. They further proposed to recommend to the committee in London to draw up a petition to be signed by as many as possible of the friends of the cause in England, and addressed to the National Assembly of France, praying for the abolition of the slave trade by the French government. As delicately as he could Clarkson insinuated the impropriety of the last motion, but the committee would not listen to him for a moment. "The National Assembly of France," they declared, "would glory in going contrary to the example of other nations in a case of generosity and justice." Finding his protests in vain, Clarkson could only reply that he would communicate the measure to the

---

[1] Clarkson, *History of the rise, progress and accomplishment of the abolition of the African slave trade*, II, chap. II. What follows concerning the work of the society and its friends till the end of 1789 is also from Clarkson.

committee in London, but that he could not answer for the part that they would take in it. He was soon proved to be right in his assumption as to the attitude of the English committee, for they refused unequivocally to have anything to do with such a petition. Neither did the other measures taken at this meeting come to anything, for, though Necker did grant the delegation a very brief interview, he had far too overwhelming responsibilities of his own in trying to manage the finances, to give any attention to the African slave trade; and if the president of the Assembly answered their letter, they never received it.

At the next meeting they decided to write again to the president of the Assembly. A new president had come into office and might be more friendly to their cause. Furthermore, it was necessary, they declared, to bestir themselves in order to meet the machinations of the merchants, planters, and others interested in the slave trade, who were holding daily meetings to watch and thwart the plans of the *Amis des Noirs*. As no answer was received to this letter either, they made up their minds that it had been intercepted. They seem to have had some reason for their suspicions, for, at the following meeting, Clavière produced anonymous letters which he had received and in which it was stated that if the society did not dissolve he and the rest of the members would be stabbed, and that three hundred persons had banded together prepared to carry out these threats. Clarkson had also received similar letters, which, on examination, proved to be written by the same hand as those received by Clavière. Not content with threats, the enemies of the *Amis des Noirs* attacked them through the press, charging them with the intention of sending twelve thousand muskets to Santo Domingo in order to promote an insurrection in that island.[1] These rumors were so industriously circulated

---

[1] It was also charged that the society was run by foreigners. See *Lettre aux bailliages de France*, December 1, 1789. "*Les sieurs Clavières* [sic] *et du Rovray sont les chefs de cette Secte infâme, ce sont deux Génevois qui ont été chassés de leur Patrie pour sédition. Le nommé Clarkson, Anglois, est aussi à Paris depuis quelques mois, s'il y répand l'argent de l'Angleterre, celle-ci n'y perd rien; c'est semer*

that soldiers were sent to search the committee rooms. When, however, they found only two or three books and some waste paper, they retired in much disgust. Meanwhile, Clarkson realized that his prominence in the movement put him in very real danger. He therefore moved from his first lodgings to a hotel near Lafayette, in order to be within reach of his protection, and it was agreed that if any unusual gathering about the hotel seemed to portend danger, Lafayette should be notified at once, when he would send a detachment of his troops to the rescue. The danger may have been exaggerated, but its evident existence is a proof of the influence which the *Amis des Noirs* were supposed to possess.

As to the extent of their possible influence upon legislation they themselves seem to have been somewhat doubtful; and, when at one of their meetings the question was raised whether a proposition for the abolition of the slave trade could be made in the existing Assembly with any hope of success, or whether it would be better to wait till the next one, there was much difference of opinion. Of those who were for its presentation in the present Assembly, Mirabeau was the most enthusiastic and prepared with ardor to be the spokesman of the cause.[1] He wrote a speech on the subject, begged Clarkson to furnish him with facts and details, went about sounding opinion on the matter, and assisted in the distribution of literature calculated to arouse sympathy for the negro. This was furnished largely

---

pour recueillir, à ces Étrangers s'est joint le sieur Brissot de Warville, fils d'un Pâtissier de Chartres, chassé de chez ses parens à cause de son esprit bouillon et séditieux. Il a ajouté le nom de Warville au sien, pour mieux fraterniser avec les Anglois nos ennemis. Le sieur Brissot de Warville reçoit chaque jour le salaire de son adoption. Lecteurs, observez que son rôle est absolument l'inverse de celui du sieur Clarkson, l'un donne de l'argent pour enricher sa Patrie, l'autre en recoit pour la ruiner."

[1] Clarkson quotes Lafayette as saying: "Mirabeau is a host in himself and I should not be surprised if by his own eloquence and popularity only he were to carry it; and yet I regret that he has taken the lead in it. The cause is so lovely that even ambition, abstractedly [sic] considered, is too impure to take it under its protection, and not to sully it. It should be placed in the hands of the most virtuous man in France. This man is the Duc de la Rochefoucauld." *History,* II, 146.

by Clarkson and included a thousand copies of a slave ship —
that horror so well described by Mirabeau as a long coffin —
and five hundred engravings which were distributed by the
members of the society. It did arouse sympathy, but it also
aroused the colonial planters and traders whose interests were
at stake.[1] The latter immediately began a counter agitation,
circulated literature in their own interest, offered money to
Mirabeau, and worked to so good an effect in stirring up public
opinion in their favor, that, when Mirabeau came to canvass
the Assembly with a view to discovering how much support he
could count on for a measure to abolish the slave trade, he
found that a like canvass had already been made by the representatives of the planters and that the cause was for the time
being hopeless. Perceiving that further immediate action, at
least on this particular phase of the negro question, was not
probable, Clarkson soon returned to England.

The planters had already increased their strength by organizing themselves into a club named the *Club des Colons Blancs*,
or as it soon came to be known from its place of meeting, the
Club de Massiac, formed for the express purpose of fighting the
Amis des Noirs. From the summer of 1789 there was constant
combat between the two organizations.[2] The ranks of the latter continued to be led by Brissot, who was untiring in his zeal
in behalf of the negro and mulatto. He wrote addresses in the
name of the society, presented the cause at the Jacobin Club,[3]
tried, though unsuccessfully, to work through municipal organizations,[4] denounced the leaders of the opposition, and above all
made the *Patriote Français* the champion of the negro. In fact,
his newspaper may be said to have been the official organ of the
Amis des Noirs. From almost the first issue he devoted a large
amount of space to the affairs of the society and to the objects
for which it was working. He dwelt on the horrors of the slave

---

[1] The king, it seems, had some time before been approached and asked to
dissolve the society, but had refused. See report of a speech of Wilberforce in
the House of Commons, May 21, 1789. *Courrier de l'Europe*, May 22, 1789.

[2] Challamel, *Les Clubs contre-révolutionnaires*, 67–69.

[3] Aulard, *Les Jacobins*, ii, 412.   [4] See p. 105.

trade, published a list of books advocating abolition, gave reports of meetings of the society, entered into sharp controversy with hostile newspapers, and at epochs at which colonial questions were under discussion filled his columns with reports on this subject to the exclusion of almost everything else.

The opening of the States-General had raised new problems regarding the situation in the French colonies. The *Amis des Noirs* thus had to deal not only with the slave trade but also with questions of more immediate policy. The situation was this: The population of Santo Domingo — the largest and most important of the French colonies — was divided into three distinctly marked classes: the whites, including the planters and the merchants of the cities, the mulattoes, and the slaves. The whites were aristocratic in spirit, if not by birth, and looked down with scorn both upon the negroes and upon the mulattoes. The latter were for the most part the free descendants of white settlers and their negro slaves, in many cases they were themselves slaveholders, but they were regarded as colored men. All three classes alike were eager to seize upon the liberty promised by the Revolution, but, as a recent writer has well said, each class wanted to put upon that magic word its own interpretation.[1] To the whites it meant local government with as little interference from France as possible; to the mulattoes it meant participation in that local government; to the negroes freedom. In order to secure their own ends, the whites decided to send to the States-General at Paris delegates who would represent them alone; and in spite of the prohibition of the governor of Santo Domingo, assemblies were formed to hold the elections. But to gain admission for these representatives they found a difficult matter. As the delegates from Santo Domingo represented only a small section of the population — a section which did not include even the mulattoes — the question was at once raised whether they could rightfully be considered as representatives at all. This, in turn, involved the fundamental question: were the principles of the declaration

[1] Mills, *Early Years of the French Revolution in San Domingo*, 24.

of rights — liberty, equality, and popular sovereignty — really applicable to the colonies? In other words, how far had the colonies a right to local government? should the slaves be ultimately freed? and in the mean time should the mulattoes be admitted to the rights of citizenship?

The immediate question was settled tentatively by the admission to the States-General of six of the deputies from Santo Domingo. Against this measure Brissot protested vigorously. The colonies were too far away, he declared, their interests too different from those of the mother country, to permit them to be governed by the same system. And, in this particular case, the election of the deputies was neither free nor valid; and even if it were, the number of deputies was too great; the same proportion should be followed as in France, which would give them only one. Furthermore, the admission of too large a number of such deputies from the colonies would prejudice the interests of the negro and mulatto.[1]

The other fundamental questions involved were the admission of the mulattoes to rights of citizenship and the measure of self-government to be allowed the colonies. These two questions were closely connected, for to give the colonies full legislative independence meant inevitably that they would act against and not for the mulattoes. The most active support for the latter came from the society of the *Amis des Noirs* and the most bitter opposition from the *Club des Colons Blancs*. In regard to the question of self-government there were many shades of opinion, both as to its extent and the way in which it should be exercised. The extreme royalists held that the colony should remain under the absolute and exclusive rule of the king; the *Club de Massiac* thought that the king and a colonial assembly composed exclusively of whites should govern; the *Amis des Noirs* demanded a local government in which the rights of the mulattoes should be guaranteed; the delegates themselves

---

[1] *Réflexions sur l'admission aux États-Généraux des députés de Saint-Domingue.* See also the *Moniteur* of July 4, 1789. Twenty was the number asked for, twelve had been admitted previously. *Moniteur*, session of June 27, 1789.

wanted to keep the power in their own hands as much as possible and to govern with the aid of a committee appointed by the National Assembly; while the greater part of the Assembly was suspicious of all these factions and desired to keep the colony under its own immediate control.[1]

Meanwhile the mulattoes were clamoring for equal rights with the whites. They had even sent deputies from their number to beg for admission to the National Assembly. One of them, M. Joly, presented himself to the Assembly of the representatives of the Commune, asking for their support. This demand was enthusiastically backed by Brissot, who thus brought upon himself a sharp reprimand from the *Révolutions de Paris* which inquired tartly why he was diverting the municipal assembly from its proper business of drawing up a city charter.[2]

At the same time that Brissot was defending the cause of the mulattoes before the municipal assembly, he did not for a moment relax his efforts against the slave trade,[3] urged the *Amis des Noirs* to renewed efforts,[4] and carried on his propaganda through the press. The 8th of January, for example, the *Patriote Français* wrote: "The Assembly, by its decree that we men are born and remain free and equal, has it not declared war on every kind of inequality, oppression and tyranny, has it not declared that no man can ever be bought or sold or kept in slavery? The hatred of the Assembly for all kinds of injustice, its zeal in destroying all sorts of abuses, even those which might be useful to it, the spirit of justice and humanity by which it is dominated, are not these guaranties for the proscription of the slave trade?"[5]

In defense, the planters and their friends declared that the

[1] Mills, *Early Years of the French Revolution in San Domingo.*
[2] *Révolutions de Paris,* February 13–20, 1790.
[3] *Patriote Français,* January 27, 1790.
[4] Address by Brissot to the *Société des Amis des Noirs.* The society passed a vote of thanks to Bernardin de Saint-Pierre, for his defense of the negro in his work *Vœux d'un Solitaire. Patriote Français,* January 19, 1790.
[5] *Patriote Français,* January 8, 1790.

Amis des Noirs were acting on entirely wrong premises. The so-called philanthropists talked about the horrors of the slave trade and of slavery; they would do well to consider how much better off the negroes were as slaves in the French colonies than at home in Africa, and indeed than many a French peasant.[1] Instead of bettering conditions, the schemes of the *Amis des Noirs* would only make them worse. Indeed, their talk of abolishing the slave trade and slavery had already occasioned an insurrection in Martinique which threatened to spread and do incalculable harm.[2] So persistent was this rumor that the *Amis des Noirs* were working for the immediate abolition of slavery as well as of the slave trade, that the society was moved to make formal and official denial of any such intention. This statement was drawn up by Brissot and presented to the National Assembly, January 21, 1790.[3] No such idea, he declared, had ever entered their minds. They were only too well aware that the immediate freeing of the negroes would not only be a fatal step for the colonies but also a fatal present for the negroes themselves.

In issuing this clear and emphatic statement as to their immediate purpose, the *Amis des Noirs* made it equally clear that the abolition of slavery was still their ultimate purpose, nor did they retreat a step from their position on the abolition of the slave trade. Indeed, the above protest was coupled with a plea for such abolition. It had been asserted again and again that to do away with the slave trade would be to ruin the French colonies and seriously injure the French marine and French manufacturers. This the *Amis des Noirs* strenuously denied. Even if such claims were true, what weight, they asked, are the mere gains of commerce, when compared with

---

[1] *Lettre de M——— à Brissot de Warville, président de la société des Amis des Noirs.*

[2] See *Journal de Paris*, December 28, 1789, *Lettre de M. Mosneron.*

[3] *Archives parlementaires*, XI, 271–77. This probably is the address of which Brissot presented two hundred copies to the municipal assembly January 5, and eight hundred more copies February 13. Lacroix, *Actes de la Commune*, III, 366, 370; IV, 100.

the blood of thousands of men shed every year? But they were not true. The small number of vessels engaged in the slave trade could be put to other uses, the lives of great numbers of sailors would be spared, the *bonus*, now a heavy drain, would be saved; and, as for the slaves, if their number could not be augmented, they would be treated with more humanity and so would increase faster, and the colonists would not have to contract heavy debts in order to buy slaves. Furthermore, French manufacturers would reap advantage, for some of the money hitherto spent for slaves would be spent in buying French products. What if a temporary disturbance did result? France had not hesitated for that reason to make sweeping reforms at home.

These arguments failed, however, to convince the Assembly, for within a couple of weeks when the question of the rights of the mulattoes and the powers of the local colonial assemblies again came up it passed decrees which, while they did not mention the slave trade by name, were distinctly contrary to the spirit of the above demands. The measure as finally passed March 8, 1790, was pushed through largely by the efforts of Barnave and represented a compromise between many conflicting claims and interests. By its terms each colony was allowed to make known to the National Assembly its wishes in regard to a constitution and form of administration, and colonial assemblies were given the right to offer suggestions on decrees passed by the National Assembly concerning municipalities and administrative assemblies. Finally, the colonies were assured that no radical changes in regard to commerce were contemplated and that they and their property were under the protection of the Assembly. These provisions, by which the colonies were given at least some show of power, were sufficiently ambiguous to satisfy both the *Club de Massiac* and the representatives from Santo Domingo, as well as the majority of the Assembly. But to the hopes of the mulattoes and to the *Amis des Noirs* this decree was a decisive blow. It virtually put colonial affairs under the control of the whites in the islands, and the mulattoes did not need an interpreter to tell them what that meant.

Brissot was almost broken-hearted. A few days before the decree was passed he had declared that on account of the hatred which the whites manifested for the mulattoes, it would be extremely dangerous to give over to the former the task of drawing up a colonial code. That code should be made in France by a disinterested Assembly.[1] He now bitterly upbraided Barnave and declared that he could not conceive how Barnave could have consented to further such a measure. This measure, Brissot maintained, was obviously unfair to the mulattoes; furthermore, by its provision for criminal proceedings against any one who should work to bring about risings against the planters, it opened the way for rank injustice to the *Amis des Noirs*.[2] He saw some hope, however, in the instructions drawn up for the formation of local colonial assemblies, which provided that all persons twenty-five years of age, who were proprietors, or who had lived two years in the parish and paid a tax, should form the parochial assembly. The mulattoes must be held to be included in this decree, he declared, though they ought to have been specifically named; and from the fact that they were not, he predicted trouble between the whites and the mulattoes.[3]

Trouble soon arrived for the *Amis des Noirs*. As Brissot had foreseen, the clause of the decree of March 8, which had declared criminal all attempts to excite risings against the planters, was invoked to stop the work of the society. The *Amis des Noirs* accordingly drew up another address to the Assembly, in which they protested against this interpretation and declared their confidence that such had not been the intention of the Assembly.[4] Meantime, they proceeded to show not only that

---

[1] *Patriote Français*, March 1, 1790.

[2] *Ibid.*, March 9, 1790. [3] *Ibid.*, March 29, 1790.

[4] *Seconde adresse à l'Assemblée nationale par la société des Amis des Noirs, 9 avril, 1790.* Presented to the National Assembly the 10th of April, according to the *Archives parlementaires*, XII, 627. The Assembly apparently took no action on this address.

"the decree of March 8 had not closed their mouths" but that they were going to make themselves heard even more plainly than before. To this end, they issued an outline of the work they proposed to do, addressed this time not to the Assembly, but to the "friends of humanity."[1] Considering the circumstances under which it was written, it was nothing short of a blast of defiance.

Despite the efforts of the *Amis des Noirs* they seemed to lose rather than to gain ground, for on October 12, on the proposition of Barnave, a decree was passed which interpreted the previous decree of the Assembly as a virtual promise to take no action on the status of any of the inhabitants of the colonies except on the request of the colonial assemblies. In other words, the status of the mulattoes was left to the whites in the colonies, which meant, of course, that they would certainly not be given the rights of citizens. If Brissot had spoken of Barnave's attitude toward the March decrees with grieved surprise, he now attacked him with venom and denounced his entire colonial policy as worthy of execration. The rights of man were involved, Brissot declared, and the Assembly had no power to pass any decree upon the rights of man, whether in France or in the colonies; it could never make them the subject of a constitutional article; they were fundamental and preceded all constitutions. Moreover, "nothing that was unjust could be good politically," as was proved by recent events in the colonies. All their evils were due to the decrees of March and October, and unless these decrees were changed the colonies would become independent. Furthermore, Barnave had not only furthered a bad policy but he had done it in bad faith.[2]

[1] *Journal de Paris*, June 15, July 27, 1790. *Patriote Français*, July 1, 1790.

[2] *Lettre à M. Barnave*. Brissot subsequently accused M. Trémondrie, the president of one of the colonial assemblies, of having misquoted instructions with regard to primary elections, so that they appeared to have discriminated unjustly against the mulattoes. That he had done so M. Trémondrie denied and declared that his assertion would be found to be true if his instructions, which Brissot had cited only in part, had been cited in full. *Journal de Paris*, December 1, 1790. *Lettre à Barnave*, 32, note 2. The *Patriote Français* ridiculed M. Trémondrie's explanations.

The assertion contained in the preamble, that the Assembly did not intend to take action on the status of the inhabitants of the colonies except at the instigation of the colonial assemblies, Brissot declared to be "at the same time a lie and a base abandonment of all principles of humanity, liberty, justice and prudence." Such an assertion not only was infamous, but the way in which the decree was passed was an outrage, for there was no discussion, and the Abbé Grégoire, Pétion, and Mirabeau, who wanted to speak, were prevented. "Enemies of liberty and humanity," he cried, addressing Barnave and the other partisans of the measure, "you shall not triumph forever. It is impossible that Heaven which has wished us to be free should not desire justice for all men. . . . Thus the names of those who have contributed to iniquity shall be branded forever in public opinion; such is the lot which awaits M. Barnave."

By passing this constitutional decree the Assembly evidently regarded the matter as settled. But Brissot did not propose to consider it settled. He wrote to his friend Lanthenas, begging him to return to Paris to help him defend the cause of the mulattoes,[1] assailed their enemies in the columns of the *Patriote Français*, and entered upon a vigorous campaign for the repeal of the decrees of March and October. He even upheld the mulatto insurrection which had broken out under the leadership of Ogé; and, in an article, which considering the circumstances was more eloquent than timely or politic, made a stirring appeal in their behalf. "I implore those planters resident in the islands," he wrote, "who have a real interest in their prosperity, to look upon the mulattoes as their best support, their friends, their brothers; I implore those French capitalists who have immense mortgages upon our islands to reflect that the payment of those debts depends on the general prosperity; that prosperity cannot exist under oppression because of the

---

[1] See letter of Lanthenas to Bançal, November 30, 1790. "*Brissot me presse de retourner à Paris cet hiver, pour défendre les noirs.*" *Lettres de Madame Roland*, ii, 204.

ever present danger of insurrection. . . . I implore the French merchants who supply the islands with provisions to reflect that it is to their interest to increase the number of well-to-do consumers, to multiply the population." The obvious means to this end, Brissot declared, was to render justice to the mulattoes.[1] As for Ogé's attempt to wrest justice from the planters by force, instead of condemning him for inciting an uprising, Brissot praised his moderation and pointed out that he had made no demands in regard to slavery. The deed for which Ogé was counted as a criminal, he declared, far from being a crime "was an act of virtue, a duty, a sacred duty." "The conquerors of the Bastille," he added, "are heroes, and for a like act of heroism M. Ogé is to be condemned."[2]

Such doctrines on Brissot's part, backed, as it was felt they were, by the *Amis des Noirs*, aroused the planters and their friends to angry opposition. Gouy D'Arsy, a colonist of title and importance, declared that the negro slaves were well off and would themselves resent the efforts in their behalf, and that in espousing the cause of the mulattoes Brissot was seeking merely his own glory, and that he and the other *Amis des Noirs* were actuated by motives of cupidity.[3] Further, Arthur Dillon, a deputy from Martinique, made a speech before the Assembly, in which he accused the *Amis des Noirs* of deliberately provoking the disasters in the colonies by their publications,[4] and insinuated that they were in the pay of foreign powers. A movement was set on foot at Bordeaux to petition the Assembly to change the preamble of the decree of October 12 into a constitutional article;[5] an address from Nantes demanded not only that the decree of October 12 be maintained, but that the most absolute silence be imposed on all those pretended reformers, whether or not members of the society of the *Amis des Noirs*, who were attempting to decide

---

[1] *Patriote Français*, January 5, 1791.   [2] *Ibid.*
[3] Gouy D'Arsy, *Première et dernière lettre.*
[4] *Patriote Français*, March 4, 15, 1791.
[5] *Extrait des lettres de Bordeaux*, February 22, 1791, in the *Patriote Français*, March 2, 1791.

matters in which they were in no degree experts;[1] while Moreau de Saint-Méry, one of the most important colonists, in a lengthy pamphlet, addressed to "the true friends of the peace and happiness of France on the occasion of the renewed agitation of the so-called *Amis des Noirs*," denounced the society as responsible for everything which had happened in the colonies, charged that they had desired, advised, and preached a revolt of the slaves, and that Brissot at best was a delirious creature who pretended to be a philosopher.[2]

Under these accusations and attacks, which certainly showed that the *Amis des Noirs* had made themselves a force to be reckoned with and had thoroughly frightened the planters, the former naturally did not remain silent, either as individuals or as a society. Brissot was cut to the quick by Gouy's insinuations of personal motive, as is evident from the vituperative terms of his answer. Gouy was a wretch, he declared, with his lies and impertinence, a dangerous wretch without credit or standing; while he (Brissot) was a Cato, or a Cicero denouncing Catiline.[3]

As for the accusation of Dillon, the society of the *Amis des Noirs* in its wrath laid formal complaint before the Assembly, in which they demanded that the Assembly either censure M. Dillon or that it allow the society to hale him before the courts for libel. As was promptly pointed out, this came dangerously near infringing the inviolability of members of the legislative body. The society maintained, however, that such inviolability concerned only matters of opinion and ought not to be used as an excuse for calumniating private citizens. From the necessity of deciding this delicate point the Assembly was rescued by an explanation made in behalf of M. Dillon by one of his friends, to the effect that he did not intend to inculpate the entire society — an explanation which the Assembly accepted

[1] *Perfidie du système des Amis des Noirs*, Nantes, February 23, 1791.

[2] *Considérations présentées aux vrais amis du repos et du bonheur de la France à l'occasion des nouveaux mouvements de quelques soi-disant Amis des Noirs.*

[3] *Réplique de J. P. Brissot.*

as sufficient, though it by no means satisfied the *Amis des Noirs*.[1]

The society next proceeded to issue a general statement of its principles — a kind of campaign platform — the immediate occasion for which was a renewed demand on the part of the planters that the decision of colonial affairs be left to the whites alone. It was drawn up by Clavière and addressed to the National Assembly, to all the commercial cities, to all manufacturers, colonies, and societies and friends of the constitution. It began by an attack on a lengthy pamphlet of Moreau de Saint-Méry's, which it characterized as a diatribe of the worst order, and its main allegation, that the *Amis des Noirs* were responsible for the evils in the colonies, as a glaring falsehood. This pamphlet, it declared further, had been announced as coming from the national printing shop, in order to make it appear to have the seal of the approval of the Assembly. The address then attacked the demand of the whites to be assured of the control of affairs. Such a demand should be refused, as it was not fair or just to leave the fortunes of the colony to one class, whose interests were opposed to the interests of all other classes. Injustice had already been done in not observing the terms of the decree of March 28, which based the suffrage on a general property qualification and did not expressly exclude the mulattoes, whereas in administering the decree they had been excluded. The address then went on to deny that the mulattoes were unfitted to rule, or that to give them the suffrage would result in a slave insurrection or in a falling off in commerce; and closed with a reiteration of the general principles of the *Amis des Noirs;* that though they were opposed to slavery, root and branch, as contrary to the natural rights of man, they did not advocate its immediate or sudden abolition; that they believed that the constitution ought to be applied in full to all the colonies as provinces of the realm; that the slave trade should be abolished; and that there should

[1] *Patriote Français*, March 4, 15, 1791. See also *Le Courrier de Provence*, March 6, 8, 1791, and the *Moniteur*, March 7, 1791.

be the greatest possible freedom of trade allowed to the colonies.[1]

Meanwhile, Brissot continued his campaign in the *Patriote Français*, printed an address of the Jacobin Society of Angers to all the patriotic societies of the realm, in favor of the mulattoes,[2] also a petition of the mulattoes themselves to the Assembly,[3] wrote at length on the fearful punishment of Ogé,[4] interested his friend, Madame Roland, in the cause,[5] and took steps to consult with the English society as to ways and means of providing funds for the campaign.

Notwithstanding the vigorous fight made by the representatives of the colonial interests, the *Amis des Noirs* finally succeeded in inducing the Assembly to modify the decree of October 12, and on May 14 and 15, 1791, the Assembly voted that it would never take action regarding the state of mulattoes who were born of free fathers and mothers, except on demand of the colonies themselves; that the existing colonial assemblies should be maintained; but that in the future, mulattoes who were born of free fathers and mothers should be admitted to the parochial and colonial assemblies if they had the other qualifications necessary.[6] Considering the large majority with which the decree of October 12 passed and the strength and influence of the opponents of the *Amis des Noirs*, this was a considerable victory, though it was not by any means what they hoped. They still feared, and with some reason, that it might not be executed.[7]

But this decree, which was so great a source of satisfaction to the *Amis des Noirs*, seemed to the planters, and indeed to

---

[1] A second edition of the address contains also a justification of Ogé, and letters of different *sociétés des amis de la constitution*, claiming rights for the mulattoes.

[2] *Patriote Français*, March 25, 1791. *Lettres des diverses sociétés des amis de la constitution qui réclament les droits de citoyen actif en faveur des hommes de couleur des colonies.* March 8, April 17, 1791.

[3] *Patriote Français*, March 25, 1791.   [4] *Ibid.*, May 1, 1791.

[5] *Lettres de Madame Roland*, ii, 276.

[6] *Moniteur*, May 16, 1791.

[7] *Patriote Français*, June 3, 1791.

almost every one who had a first-hand knowledge of the colonies, the height of folly, and they went to work most energetically to bring about its repeal. At the same time the friends of the mulatto took up its defense and protested against the possibility of evil consequences arising from it. In a speech at the Jacobins the 12th of September Brissot reiterated his former arguments in favor of the civil rights of the mulatto, and in the face of strong indications to the contrary, denied that the slaves had revolted, that all commercial cities were against the decree of May 15, and that civil war had broken out. Even if it had, he declared, it was due, not to the decree of May 15, but to the failure to execute it.[1] Rumors from the colonies, however, offset these protests, and on September 24, on the very eve of the dissolution of the Constituent Assembly, the measure of May 15 was virtually repealed by a law which gave to each colony the right to regulate its own internal affairs. Brissot and his friends were naturally greatly depressed, but they had no intention of considering this decree as final, and on the opening of the Legislative Assembly they took up the struggle with renewed vehemence.

Meanwhile, the election of Brissot — the heart and soul of the *Amis des Noirs* — to this Assembly gave him a new opportunity and shifted the center of the combat to that body. His influence on colonial questions during this period is so closely related to his previous work on the same subject that it may best be considered here instead of in connection with his other work as a legislator. As a deputy to the Assembly he now had the chance of exercising directly upon legislation that influence which, in the case of the former decrees, he had exercised only indirectly through the *Amis des Noirs* and through the columns of the *Patriote Français*. The part of the society in this new phase of the struggle is not clear, but in the absence of records to the contrary, it must be assumed that they left the struggle largely to Brissot. And into the combat he threw himself with

---

[1] *Discours sur la nécessité de maintenir le décret rendu le 15 mai, 1791, en faveur des hommes de couleur libres, prononcé le 12 septembre, 1791.*

all his accustomed ardor. According to Paganel [1] he sought influence in the Assembly, solely that he might be in a better position to defend the mulattoes, and for this reason allied himself with the party of Gensonné and Guadet.[2] Hardly had the new assembly assumed power before alarming reports began to come in of a slave insurrection in Santo Domingo. News was also brought that the mulattoes, when they had learned of the rights given them by the decree of May 15, had, on September 20, extorted from the whites a formal agreement by which the whites recognized and guaranteed these rights.[3] Whereupon, the colonial committee proposed, in case the reports of the insurrection should be confirmed, to send out an armed force. At this point Brissot expressed himself vigorously upon what he considered the cause of the trouble, though he protested that the extent of the insurrection had been much exaggerated. The cause was to be found, he asserted, in the law of September 24, which humiliated and debased the mulattoes. This, Tarbé of the colonial committee replied, could not be true, because the insurrection began before the September law was passed. The real cause, in his opinion, was the original decree of May 15, 1791. While accepting Tarbé's correction as to the date of the insurrection, Brissot denied absolutely that the decree of May 15 was responsible for it. He maintained, on the contrary, that the whole trouble was stirred up, not by the decree of May 15, but by its non-enforcement, and further he demanded a speedy consideration of the whole question. The colonial committee was instructed to report, but the tardiness with which news arrived delayed its action for some weeks. Delay was intolerable to a radical like Brissot, who undoubt-

---

[1] Pierre Paganel (born 1745, died 1826) was a French politician, a deputy from the department of the *Lot et Garonne* to the Legislative Assembly and to the Convention, a deputy on mission in 1793 and afterward general secretary of the ministry of foreign affairs.

[2] *Essai historique et critique sur la Révolution française*, ii, 228: *Il servait le parti des Gensonné, des Guadet, etc., dans l'espérance de fortifier de leur crédit et de leur influence la cause des noirs.*

[3] Garran de Coulon, *Troubles de Saint-Dominique*, ii, 284–85.

edly suspected the good faith of the committee and attributed delay rather to design than to the cause alleged. He finally lost all patience, and on November 20 declared to the Assembly that if the committee did not make a report on the colonies, he would.[1] Already fuller information had come in. It was now known that the situation was desperate. What the planters had predicted had come to pass. A slave insurrection of unspeakable horror was in progress, and the island was being devastated with fire and rapine.

Such was the condition of affairs in Santo Domingo when, on December 1, Brissot made his promised speech, one of his longest and most eloquent efforts. He argued that the real cause of the trouble was the machinations of the disloyal whites, who had refused to obey the decree of May 15, and had actually disarmed the mulattoes. The accusation that the *Amis des Noirs* had in any way been instrumental in causing the insurrection he hotly denied. "Produce a single scrap of evidence of correspondence between the society or its individual members and the colonies," was his challenge; "show me a single emissary to the colonies, and we will march to the scaffold." As for the remedy, he had no faith in the formal agreement of September 20. It was forced from the whites almost at the moment when the National Assembly was passing the law of September 24 which gave to the whites power to decide on the status of the mulattoes. If the whites had known this they would never have consented to the agreement, and now that they had despotic power legally in their hands, they would use it despotically and disavow the agreement. The one reasonable thing for the Assembly to do was to repeal the law of September 24 and by its own action assure to the mulattoes their rights. To this end he proposed a series of radical measures. The most important were the arrest and trial before the high national court of the members of the general assembly of Santo Domingo, and of the governor, M. Blanchelande; the calling of a new colonial assembly without distinction of color and the

[1] *Moniteur*, November 21, 1791.

sending to the islands of civil commissioners and troops.[1] The
Assembly evidently was not ready for such measures, but one
thing was clear even to Brissot's opponents: troops were imper-
atively needed in the island and at once. The task of Brissot
and his friends was now to win the passage of a decree which
would insure that the troops should not be used against the
mulattoes. To this the colonists vehemently objected and the
debates became tempestuous. In the struggle Brissot had
the support of his Girondin friends in his main purpose, though
they differed as to the means by which it was to be attained.
Guadet and Vergniaud each had a different wording for the
definitive clause of the decree; Vergniaud's, providing that the
troops could be used only on the requisition of the civil commissioners, was the more conciliatory; while Guadet's stated
that the king should use the troops for the provisional maintenance of the agreement made by the whites. This latter
proposition aroused fierce debate; since, by dictating the action
of the colonial assemblies it took away the freedom granted
by the September law. The fundamental question of the status
of the law was thus raised. It had been passed as an *acte constitutionnel sur les colonies* and the question was: Did it fall
under that provision of the constitution which declared that
the next two legislatures could not propose the change of any
constitutional article? As a constitutional article had unfortunately not been defined, there was room for endless argument.
The colonial committee declared that the law under discussion
was to all intents and purposes a part of the constitution and
so could not be changed, while Brissot stoutly maintained that
it was not a part of the constitution and therefore could be
changed.[2] In spite of intense opposition, Brissot won a victory
on the immediate question of the use of the troops which were
to be sent to Santo Domingo, it being provided that they could
be used only to put down the revolt of the negroes and not to
the prejudice of the rights of the mulattoes, as established by
the agreement entered into by the whites.

[1] *Moniteur*, December 2 and 4, 1791.   [2] *Ibid.*, December 8 and 9, 1791.

But the definite settlement of the fundamental question of the status of the mulattoes, and the relation of the colonial assembly to it, was put off for some time. Finally, on March 21, Brissot demanded that the discussion of the subject be begun at once and be continued without interruption until it should be settled. He then made a lengthy speech, in which he reiterated his former assertion that the difficulty was due not to the decree of May 15, but to its non-enforcement; pictured in glowing colors the moderation and the patriotism of the mulattoes in the face of wrong and oppression; accused the colonial assembly of plotting for the independence of the colonies; and declared that the only just and adequate solution of the problem was the revocation of the decree of September 24.[1] These arguments were answered by Tarbé, of the colonial committee, who declared that the evidence on which Brissot based his charges against the colonial committee was ill founded, drew a lurid picture of the cruelty of the mulattoes, — a ghastly contrast to Brissot's presentation, — and vehemently opposed the revocation of the September decree.

The question of the constitutional character of this decree was taken up by Gensonné and Guadet, both of whom argued against its constitutionality on the ground that by giving so much authority to the colonial assemblies it violated the indivisible sovereignty of the people.[2] The further argument was adduced by Gensonné that it could not be considered constitutional, because it was passed after the constitution had been declared finished. After a stormy debate Girondin influence finally prevailed, and on March 24 Brissot and his friends won a decisive victory in the passage of a law which practically re-enacted that of May 15, by giving civil rights to the mulattoes.

Brissot was fairly carried off his feet with delight at the success of this measure, and, in an editorial in the *Patriote Français*,

---

[1] *Moniteur*, March 22, 1792.

[2] *Ibid.*, March 23 and 24. The *Patriote Français* of March 23 said of Guadet's speech: "*Sensibilité, énergie, logique, et plaisanterie, il a su fondre toutes les couleurs avec l'art le plus délicat.*"

gave vent to a perfect pæan of joy — an editorial which showed his absolute inability to understand that there were two sides to the question or to credit his adversaries with honest conviction and sincerity of motive. There was nothing left for them, he declared, but opprobrium, ineffaceable opprobrium. Their souls were hardened, ossified; they were dead to liberty and humanity.

This decree which so moved Brissot was the last colonial legislation of importance during his career, but the spirit of his measures was followed out, two years later, by a decree abolishing slavery. The insurrection, meanwhile, was not permanently quelled, and under Toussaint l'Ouverture Santo Domingo practically secured her independence. That the *Amis des Noirs* had any part in this subsequent legislation is not proved by any records known to the writer. The résumé of the proceedings of the society, found at the Institute among the papers of Condorcet, stops with the meeting of June 8, 1790, but the existence of the society as late as July, 1792, is attested by the records of the English society. It is not unlikely that, after the victory of March, 1792, when other interests absorbed the time and attention of its leader, it abandoned further immediate efforts and became less and less active.

The responsibility for the initiative of this colonial policy was universally laid at the door of the *Amis des Noirs*, and from the time when they opposed the admission to the Assembly of the deputies from Santo Domingo to the passing of the decree of March 24, 1792, accusations were heaped up against them. These accusations came from at least three sources: the commercial class, both in the colonies and in France, who declared that they would be ruined if the slave trade were destroyed; the planters, who, in addition to commercial ruin, feared the horrors of a negro insurrection; and the more conservative element in the Assembly, who, while they were not personally involved, foresaw the dangers which might result from too radical action.[1]

[1] See, for example, a cut which appeared in the *Actes des Apôtres*, vol. XI, no.

The charges brought against the *Amis des Noirs* by these various enemies went all the way from a simple allegation that they had been guilty of bad judgment in trying to bring about the abolition of the slave trade and of slavery to the accusation that they had deliberately stirred up revolt for treasonable purposes. One of the most violent denounced the society as a sect which carried with it the destruction of all religions, of all forms of government. The majority of these attacks accused the society, at most, of bad judgment, and were based on the general argument that the colonies could not exist without the slave trade and that the result of its suppression would be weakness and poverty.[1] "Such is the natural result," wrote Saint-Cyran, "of the ideas with which a multitude of lazy people, who know very little about our colonies and our commerce, are trying to buy celebrity at any price. We ought, no doubt, to consider these humanitarians as fanatics who are acting in good faith, although appearances are to the contrary." [2]

As might be expected, many of the attacks were directed especially against Brissot. He had at least twice held the office of president of the society of the *Amis des Noirs*, — in February, 1789, and again in January, 1790; during a large part of 1790 and in 1791 he filled the more important post of secretary and was known as the founder and most active member.[3] He was accused of being from first to last the author of the trouble in the colonies and of having acted as the agent of the English government with the deliberate purpose of bringing about their ruin. Such charges, in various forms and in various degrees of

306, about January, 1792, representing in the background the city of Bordeaux and in the foreground Vulcan chained, a broken anchor, and a wrecked ship with this inscription: "*Actirité constitutionnelle du commerce de Bordeaux, cette estampe est dédiée à la Société des Amis des Noirs et recommandée particulièrement à Mm. [sic] Condorcet et Brissot.*"

[1] De Pons, writing to Barnave, *Observations sur la situation politique de Saint-Domingue*, November 27, 1790.

[2] *Réfutation du projet des Amis des Noirs sur la suppression de la traite des nègres et sur l'abolition de l'esclavage dans nos colonies*, par M. de Saint-Cyran, 1790.

[3] See the signatures of the officers attached to various addresses of the society.

intensity, were repeated again and again during the period when colonial affairs were under discussion and were brought up once more during the trial of the Girondins, both openly and anonymously.[1] One anonymous writer, for example, denounced Brissot to this effect: He fled from home some years before and came to Paris, where he was shut up in a house of correction on account of many scandalous libels, of which he was recognized as the author. Forced to leave the kingdom, he embarked for New England as a cabin boy. By means of a certain amount of talent, especially a talent for intrigue, and his pleasing appearance and manners, he succeeded in making the acquaintance of some Frenchmen in New York who provided for his support. They were all deceived. A blunderer by nature and vicious besides, he stirred up trouble, in which he compromised his friends. They made haste to get rid of him. No one would have anything to do with him, and he was forced to embark for England. In this wretched condition, to which he was reduced by his wickedness, without refuge, without support, he applied to the Revolutionary Club at London. They took him into their service in their plan of vengeance against France.[2]

These charges are manifestly so absurd as to need no refutation. As for the charges against the society, it is to be remembered that in many cases they were made by persons interested; at the same time it is to be observed that in several instances, at least, they were made by men who had been in the colonies and knew whereof they spoke — as the *Amis des Noirs* did not. The accusation that they stirred up rebellion for treasonable purposes is certainly without real foundation, although in one case circumstances seemed to connect them directly with disorder in the colonies. Ogé was affiliated with the society.

[1] See a paper found among the papers of the colonial committee [A. N. A. A. 54, 1509], unsigned and undated. It consists of a long list of accusations — thirty-two counts in all — supported in almost every case by a citation from the *Patriote Français*. See Appendix C.

[2] *Découverte d'une conspiration contre les intérêts de France*, without date or signature. Printed in *Supplément aux procès-verbal de l'Assemblée nationale, colonies*, I, *traite des nègres*, part II.

After his stay in Paris he went directly back to Santo Domingo and raised an insurrection. But even in this instance it can hardly be asserted that the society deliberately instigated rebellion, although they certainly sympathized with its ends. They also sympathized with all efforts for the ultimate abolition of slavery; but the charge that they were trying to bring it about immediately is without proof.

At all events, their efforts to extend the principles of liberty and equality to the colonies were attended with disastrous results. The *Amis des Noirs* may not have been responsible for the consequences, but their principles were embodied in the decrees which had these deplorable results. The members of the society, and Brissot in particular, thought that they understood the subject, but they had not lived in the colonies and were really meddling in a matter that they knew nothing about. Robert-Dubayet put the matter very well when he declared that "the experiences of all time teach us that there are moments when it is not desirable to publish, much less to put into practice, political maxims of eternal truth, especially when the premature application of a principle means the ruin of many thousands of individuals."[1] This is practically what the *Amis des Noirs* had done under the leadership of Brissot. As a French politician of the time declared: "Our colonies became the prey of their humanity."[2]

[1] *Moniteur*, March 24, 1792.

[2] Paganel, *Essai historique*, ii, 229. Paganel says: "*Brissot se proposait de venger la nature et de rétablir dans ses droits la moitié de l'espèce humaine. Que fit-il, en effet? Il assimila dans l'ordre politique et civil à tous les Français des hommes qui leur étoient absolument dissemblables par les habitudes, leurs mœurs, et la privation de toute lumière; il déversa tout-à-coup dans l'harmonie sociale l'indépendance sans régulateur et les passions sans frein. . . .*

"*La philosophie eut dans les premières législatures ses dévots, et la liberté ses fanatiques. Il n'est pas plus permis, disait Brissot, de composer avec les principes qu'avec les devoirs. Juges et parties, les blancs ne sauroient, sans crime et sans honte, proroger la servitude des noirs.*

"*Ainsi Brissot et son parti opposoient la nature à l'intérêt particulier, la raison à la violence, le droit au privilège, le perfectionnement de l'espèce humaine à l'orgueil de la couleur, enfin au système colonial, le système éternel d'ordre et de justice fondé par le père commun des hommes. . . .*"

CHAPTER IX

PART I

His Election and his Relation to the War Question [1]

A FEW days before it dissolved, the first National Assembly had declared that the one object of the Revolution was to give the French people a constitution, and that as the constitution was completed, the Revolution was ended. To those who believed this declaration, the period of the Legislative Assembly furnished a complete disillusion. At its beginning France was a bourgeois monarchy at peace with all its neighbors; before its close she had entered upon a war which was to end only with the fall of Napoleon; and she had become in all but name a democratic republic. In both these changes Brissot took an active part. He was influential in bringing about the overthrow of the monarchy, and for the war he, more than any other one man, was responsible. The period of the Legislative Assembly was indeed the most important epoch of his life and the time of his greatest influence.

In spite of his avowed republicanism, he had no hesitation about accepting the position of deputy under the constitutional monarchy. On the contrary, he was eager for the opportunity to sit in the Legislative Assembly, and it would have been a keen disappointment to him if he had failed of election, as he had two years before to the States-General. Quite aside from his own personal interest, the approaching elections were to him a matter of the deepest concern. It was of vital importance, he felt, that the right sort of men should be chosen, and in the *Patriote Français* of June 14 and 15 he gave his advice at length on the subject. Exclude former princes and members of the high nobility and the high clergy, he urged. Mistrust those men who have been connected with great houses, exclude not only those who have had pensions from the government, but also those who are holding public and lucrative places, of whatever nature, for it may be regarded as a sacred maxim that no one can fill two offices at a time. Mistrust bankers; men who have belonged to the old parliamentary magistracy; men of letters, who have been the champions of the ministry; almost all academicians, men who have passed their lives in the midst of the great; and finally, both the men who are always preaching moderation and those who defend the cause of the people with frenzy. Barring out such men, the safest classes from which to choose are first of all political writers, and then in order doctors, lawyers, and business men. In making these recommendations, Brissot, while obviously sincere, was perhaps not altogether disinterested.

His own chances were certainly better now than they had been at the opening of the States-General, partly because the self-denying ordinance, by making ineligible to the Legislative Assembly all members of the first Assembly, had removed from the field of competition many prominent men, who might otherwise have been his rivals; but chiefly because he had won for himself a considerable reputation as a municipal politician, leader of the *Amis des Noirs*, and most of all as editor of the *Patriote Français*. On the other hand, these very activities which had proclaimed him a partisan of an equality which extended even to the negro, and of a sovereignty of the people which would overthrow the king, had made him many enemies among the colonists, the aristocrats, and the royalists. It was not a question of "accepting" the position of deputy, but of fighting a long and arduous battle to gain it.

The attack against him was led by royalist journals, such as the *Actes des Apôtres*, the *Journal de la cour et de la ville*, the *Ami du Roi*, the *Argus Patriote*, the *Babillard*, and the *Chant du Coq*.[1] While these papers could not be compared to the revo-

---

[1] " *Le Chant du Coq semblait n'avoir été créé que pour mener une campagne acharnée contre Brissot.*" Charavay, *L'Assemblée électorale de Paris*, 1791–92,

lutionary journals for the weight and force of their arguments, in wit and ability to make their antagonist ridiculous they were disconcertingly successful. Brissot's candidacy was no sooner announced than they began their fusillades. Among these attacks the most noted and the most effective was that of the *Journal de la cour et de la ville*. In the midst of the election it came out with this epigram: —

> Mons Bris . . . ressemble au fripon
> Qui, dans la crainte de la gcôle,
> Va partout criant : Au larron !
> Et pendant ce temps-là vous vole.[1]

The accusation of theft hinted at in these lines is said to have first been made by Théveneau de Morande, the editor of the *Argus Patriote*, who is held responsible for coining the word *brissoter* as an equivalent for steal.[2] It was immediately seized upon by the royalist journals, who lost no time in putting it into circulation, as an equivalent for *escroquer*, to steal, nor did its use cease with Brissot's election. For example, the *Journal de la cour et de la ville* of September 25 made this edifying statement: "When Mr. Burke learned that it was sufficient to know how to *brissoter* neatly in order to be chosen as deputy to the new legislature, he said: 'I hope that Mr. Pitt will not continue to send the *brissoteurs* of London to Botany-Bay, since he can now settle them so well with our neighbors; those clever pickpockets will find themselves at home there.'" Again a few days later the same journal, apropos of a theft, alluded to a *brissotement* that had been perpetrated upon an Englishman in one of

Introduction, xxii. The editors of the *Babillard* were cited by Brissot before the courts. Their defense was that they had merely borrowed from Théveneau de Morande. At all events, the suit came to nothing. *Bouchez et Roux*, xii, 15–17.

[1] Charavay, *L'Assemblée électorale de Paris*, Introduction, xxii–xxv.

[2] No. 2, of September 17–18, p. 52. Claretie in his biography of Desmoulins (p. 180) credits him with coining the word in his *Jean Pierre Brissot démasqué*. But this pamphlet did not appear till February, 1792, and the word *brissoter* was used in the *Journal de la cour et de la ville* of September 10, 1791 (Charavay, *L'Assemblée électorale de Paris*, 1791–92, Introduction, xxvii, note). According to Beaulieu, *Essais historiques*, 47, it was Théveneau de Morande in the *Argus* who was responsible.

the chief gambling-halls of the Palais Royal.[1] According to Beaulieu, the use of the word became so common that even the children in the streets took it up. Instead of saying, "You have stolen my ball or my top," they would say, "You have *brissoté* my ball or my top."[2] The stigma involved clung to Brissot to the end of his days.

Théveneau de Morande, mentioned above as the originator of this libel, was Brissot's most bitter and persistent enemy. It will be remembered that they had come to serious disagreement during Brissot's residence in London in 1783, when they both worked on the *Courrier* for Swinton,[3] and that Morande had subsequently accused him of swindling Desforges, Brissot's partner, in the *Lycée*, in consequence of which Brissot had brought a suit against him which was still pending.[4] Morande had now renewed his attacks. According to Madame Roland, he was one of three or four scribblers paid by Montmorin to run down Brissot, and had been called from London expressly for this purpose. At all events, whether on his own account or in the pay of others, he denounced Brissot unsparingly. Not content with heaping up accusations in his journal, he now published them enlarged and embellished in pamphlet form, with the object of reaching a larger audience, and thus inflicting all possible damage. To these attacks Brissot replied by similar pamphlets and through the columns of the *Patriote Français*. Though waged for political reasons, the combat was not on questions of political policy but of personal conduct. Neither party scrupled to drag in the details of the private life of the other, and their mutual recriminations were far from edifying.[5]

---

[1] *Journal de la cour et de la ville*, October 12, 1791. The same paper made a wretched pun declaring that the name was really *Tressot*. It also declared that Brissot's schoolmates had sought the origin of his name in Greek roots and found it to be the future of the verb *britho*, that is to say, "*Je suis sur le voie d'être pendu.*" December 21, 1791.

[2] "*Cette méchanceté fit fortune. Les enfants, dans leurs jeux, ne disaient plus: 'Tu m'a pris ou volé ma boule ou ma toupie,' mais 'Tu m'a brissoté ma toupie, tu m'as brissoté ma boule.'*" Beaulieu, ii, 47.

[3] See p. 24. [4] See p. 28.

[5] (a) *Réplique de Charles Théveneau Morande à Jacques Pierre Brissot sur*

Morande's accusations were not so well founded as Brissot's, but he was extremely skillful in making the worse appear the better reason, and pertinacious in supporting his accusations by plausible arguments and by suppositions which seemed to the uninitiated additional proof. He raked up every unfortunate accident or unhappy circumstance of Brissot's past life and adroitly interpreted them to Brissot's disadvantage, presenting even the most innocent facts in such dark and damning colors that Brissot himself might well have doubted his own integrity.[1] He dwelt at length on the fact that Brissot was of insignificant birth, the son of an eating-house keeper, and when Brissot retorted that Demosthenes was the son of a blacksmith, Massillon of a shoemaker, and Diderot of a cutler,[2] Morande declared that he had almost died of laughter at the audacity or rather the simplicity of the comparison. The addition of *de Warville*, which Brissot had made to his name before leaving Chartres, Morande alleged as evidence of aristocratic tendencies,[3] and Brissot's efforts in behalf of the negro as evidence that he was in secret and treasonable collusion with England for the purpose of ruining French commerce and destroying the French colonies.[4] Morande declared further that Brissot had "forgotten" for six months to restore to the treasury of the

---

les erreurs, les oublis, les infidélités et les calomnies de sa réponse. August 26, 1791. The title evidently makes allusion to the earlier phase of the contest which had been carried on in the respective newspapers of Morande and Brissot.

    (b) *Lettre aux électeurs du départment de Paris sur Jacques Pierre Brissot*, par Charles Théveneau Morande. September 3, 1791.

    (c) *Supplément au No. 25 de l'Argus Patriote. Réponse au dernier mot de J. P. Brissot et à tous les petits mots de ses camarades.* September 6, 1791.

    [1] (a) *Réponse de Jacques Pierre Brissot à tous les libellistes, qui ont attaqué et attaquent sa vie passée.* August 10, 1791.

    (b) *Aux électeurs du département de Paris.* August 26, 1791.

    (c) *Réplique de J. P. Brissot à Charles Théveneau Morande.* August 30, 1791.

    [2] *Réponse de Jacques Pierre Brissot*, 3. A keener sense of humor would have prevented Brissot from making such a comparison. It was very characteristic that he did not realize how this would sound.

    [3] *Réplique de Charles Théveneau Morande*, 47–48.

    [4] *Lettre aux Électeurs*, 19–20.

district of the Filles-Saint-Thomas five hundred and eighty livres with which he had been entrusted as president of the district,[1] and finally, returning to his earlier charges, he dwelt at length on the accusation that Brissot had had part in the distribution of the *Diable dans un bénitier*,[2] and that he had swindled his partner Desforges out of fifteen thousand livres.[3]

These charges were supported by insufficient evidence. It is true that he habitually signed himself *Brissot de Warville*, and even became known as *Monsieur de Warville*,[4] but that this was an evidence of aristocratic tendencies Brissot emphatically denied. He added the *de Warville*, he declared, in early life, simply in order to distinguish himself from his brothers, and then having published works under that name, it seemed better to keep it. It is to be remembered, moreover, that Brissot was not the only revolutionist who bore a title without being of the nobility or having the least desire to be.[5] But although it showed a little human weakness, and certainly gave a handle to unfriendly criticism, it was really no proof of opposition to the democratic principles of the Revolution.[6] As for the charge that he was sold to England, an accusation of like venality was made, at one time or another, against almost every public man in France. The cry was raised that Mirabeau was sold to the court, Condorcet to the king, Danton to the foreigner, but, lacking unquestionable proof, such charges may be dismissed as unworthy of consideration. The accusation that Brissot kept back money belonging to his district falls to the ground, since he was able to produce a receipt for the money.[7] On the last two charges, that of complicity in the authorship of the *Diable dans un bénitier* and of having swindled Desforges, Brissot, as has already been seen, was not able to clear himself so

[1] See Brissot, *Réplique*, 26. [2] See p. 30. [3] See p. 28.
[4] He was known as *De Warville* in America. See letters addressed to him by Americans, in Craigie Papers, American Antiquarian Society, and Scioto Papers, in New York Historical Society.
[5] Brissot, *Réponse à tous les libellistes*, 5.
[6] *Notice sur Brissot*, in Vatel; *Charlotte Corday et les Girondins*, ii, 244.
[7] *Réplique de Brissot*, 26.

completely;[1] but at least if evidence of his perfect innocence is lacking, so is evidence of his guilt. It is a case of "not proved."

But if Morande's facts were doubtful, his skill in presenting them was great. With a deft touch and a clever turn he had brought out the weak points in Brissot's career. He showed that Brissot, if not himself a writer of libels, had been closely connected with people who did write them, pointed out Brissot's failures as a man of letters, and held up to ridicule his impracticable schemes.[2] The very bitterness of the attack was, on the other hand, a tribute to Brissot's position, for had he not been a man of prominence he would not have been so vigorously opposed.

Brissot's cause was meanwhile supported by his friends, his section, and his native city. In answer to the allegations of the *Babillard*, borrowed from Morande, that he had not accounted for money belonging to his district, certain important members of the section of the Bibliothèque posted two certificates which showed that the money had been duly paid,[3] and the citizens of Chartres, Brissot's native place, sent to the electors of Paris an address in which they asserted their belief in his innocence and denounced the accusations made against him as atrocious calumnies.[4] The district of Lyons also sent an ardent address in his behalf.[5] Brissot himself, in addition to his defense against specific charges, wrote an exhortation to the electors which, while general in its terms, was really an appeal for personal support. The fate of the constitution, he reminded them, depended in large part on the future legislature. Its members should, therefore, be chosen with the utmost care. Calumnies against the candidates instead of being lightly accepted should

---

[1] See pp. 28, 30.   [2] *Réplique de Brissot*, 39, 51.

[3] *Bouchez et Roux*, XII, 15–17. Whereupon the *Babillard*, in another issue, questioned the worth of these certificates and added that Brissot had taken the sum twice, but this seems hardly probable.

[4] Charavay, *L'Assemblée électorale de Paris*, 1791–92, pp. 202–03. The instigators of this letter were the members of the local Jacobin Club. Their support of Brissot may, therefore, have been due more to his popularity with the Jacobin Club at Paris than to the fact that he was a native of Chartres.

[5] *Archives Nationales*, B¹ 11.

be carefully sifted. Proved patriotism, courage, good judgment, and uprightness were the indispensable requisites.[1]

Despite all the efforts in his behalf, it looked for some time as though Brissot's opponents were going to be successful in keeping him out of the Legislative Assembly. Proposed again and again in the Electoral Assembly of Paris he was again and again defeated, and it was only after repeated attempts that on September 14 he was finally elected twelfth deputy from Paris out of twenty-four.[2] His election under such circumstances was a decided victory for the advanced party, and was hailed with great rejoicing by the citizens of Chartres, by the Jacobin Club of Paris, by various local Jacobin clubs,[3] by the radical press,[4] and by his personal friends. Madame Roland had been among those who had followed the course of the elections with the deepest interest. She was distressed at his defeats,[5] but greatly delighted at his ultimate success. Her hope for him was that he might be able to do the good that he longed to do.[6]

The Assembly was composed, for the most part, of young men, and, as a result of the self-denying ordinance passed by the Constituent Assembly, of inexperienced men. It thus offered an unusual opportunity to Brissot, one of the few members who had already made a name for himself. To a man whose most absorbing interest for years had been political reform, now to have a share in actual legislation was both a reward for past work and a stimulus to further effort. And he threw himself into his new task with all his heart and soul. He

[1] *Patriote Français*, August 23, 1791.

[2] Charavay, *L'Assemblée électorale de Paris*, 1791–92, pp. 133–227. See also Appendix D.

[3] *Lettres de félicitation des Sociétés des Amis de la Constitution de l'Yonne et de Saint-Denis, et de plusieurs électeurs du district de Lyon, pour le choix de Brissot, 19, 20, 28 septembre, 1791. Originaux signés A. N. B¹ 11.*

[4] Charavay, *ubi sup.*, Int., xxix.

[5] Madame Roland to Bançal, September 3: "*Brissot est terriblement balotté; s'il ne passe pas aujourd'hui; je tremble pour lui.*" *Lettres*, ii, 368.

[6] *Ibid.*, ii, 384. "*La nomination de Brissot fut célébrée par toute la presse patriote. C'était le premier candidat de la fraction la plus avancée de l'Assemblée qui réunit la majorité.*" Charavay, *ubi sup.*, Int., xxix.

gave up for the time active participation in the editing of his journal, "in order that he might devote himself more fully to the important functions to which the choice of his fellow citizens called him."

His candidacy had been well supported by the radical press. The only democratic journalist who expressed doubt as to his political policy was Marat, who was unable to forget or to forgive Brissot's support of Lafayette; and with his usual penetration, he pointed out the weakness in Brissot's position. Brissot, he declared, by trying to conciliate incompatible interests, had displeased both parties; clear-sighted patriots lacked confidence in him, while the enemies of the country distrusted him.[1] Brissot's opposition to the constitution and outspoken admiration for a republic, followed by his acceptance of the constitution, certainly did give ground for suspicion, on the part both of the conservatives and of the radicals. And when, on the opening of the Legislative Assembly, he took the oath to the constitution, the royalist journals indulged in sarcastic comment at his expense. *L'Ami du Roi*, for example, in referring to the oath taken by the deputies, declared that "among the orators of that pious opera the one who made the greatest sensation was M. Brissot, who was received with exaggerated and ironic applause. People supposed that it would cost that famous republican much effort to swear *fidélité* to the king; but it must be admitted that M. Brissot carried it off with a very good grace. The pleasure of seeing himself . . . seated upon one of the national thrones made him swallow the pill of the oath without a grimace." [2]

The possible effect of this inconsistency Brissot had not failed to appreciate, and in an address to the Electoral Assembly just after his election, he had attempted to set himself right. "I have been pictured to you as an enemy to the constitution," he declared. "Far from me that horrible character. To wish to improve it while it was still unfinished, was that to be an

---

[1] *L'Ami du peuple*, September 11, 1791.
[2] *L'Ami du Roi*, October 6, 1791. Quoted in *Bouchez et Roux*, XII, 51.

enemy of the constitution? Finished, entire, to-day it commands respect, and its worship is in my heart; it is in the heart
of all patriots." [1]

But, in this same address, in speaking of the difficulties with
which the legislature would have to contend, he declared that
the executive power was without energy and without confidence, — a statement, which, while it might be taken to refer
to the ministry, might at the same time be suspected of imply-
ing distrust of the king himself, and of containing the germ of
opposition to the whole executive department as provided for
in the constitution. The royalist journals were fundamentally
right. The above declaration as to his devotion to the constitution, while not untrue, was not the whole truth. Brissot's
ardor was for the new constitution only so far as it represented
a victory over the old régime; for it, as a finished and unchange-
able form of government, his ardor was much less; and in the
new legislature he took his seat, not with the right, which
wanted to maintain the constitution, the whole constitution,
and the constitution at any cost; but with the left, which,
while not openly opposing the constitution, by no means accepted it as the climax of the Revolution and which was not in
the least inclined to regard the Revolution as finished. It was
with the deputies from the Gironde, Vergniaud, Gensonné, and
Guadet, who formed the nucleus of that group afterward to be
known as the *Girondins*, with whom he especially allied himself.
According to Paganel, his motive in connecting himself with
them was that he might have their support in his contest in
behalf of the mulattoes.[2] At all events, his opinions soon acquired much weight with them, and he became so important
and influential a member of the Assembly that his political
adherents, both within the Assembly and without, were known
as *Brissotins*. As has been said, this was the period of his greatest influence. This influence was due in part to his numerous
speeches before the Assembly. He always spoke with clearness

[1] *Patriote Français*, September 17, 1791.
[2] Paganel, *Essai historique*, II, 228.

and some force, and occasionally with eloquence, but he was not a great orator. His real strength lay in the tremendous earnestness with which he worked, in his untiring perseverance, and in his zeal in organizing and directing affairs outside as well as in the Assembly itself.[1]

The first business of the Assembly was to provide the necessary machinery for work, and it had hardly begun the task when Brissot, with his usual readiness, came forward with a plan for the organization of committees; but, although he made every effort to be heard, he could not obtain the floor. Undaunted by this failure, he gave the speech at the Jacobin Club and had it printed. It was a clear and forcible argument in favor of having as few committees as possible. Committees were necessary, he admitted, but to create many committees was to increase ministerial influence, to hinder freedom of opinion, and to encourage the despotism of individuals. He would even dispense, in time of peace, with a separate diplomatic committee, but would unite it with the committees on military and marine affairs, under the general name of the committee of safety and defense.[2] A diplomatic committee was nevertheless formed on October 25, and Brissot's reputation for an extended knowledge of foreign affairs secured his election to it.[3]

As the body to which foreign affairs were referred, the diplomatic committee was one of the most important, if not *the* most important, of all the committees; and Brissot, by virtue of his position as its best known member, with the possible exception of Koch, the learned professor of international law at the

---

[1] See p. 420.

[2] *Discours sur l'organisation des comités destiné à être prononcé à l'Assemblée nationale le 12 octobre 1791, prononcé aus Jacobins le 14 octobre.* See his preliminary note. Many of his later speeches, both at the Club and at the Assembly, were printed for him by these respective bodies.

[3] *Procès-verbal de l'Assemblée nationale,* I, 232. See also *Ibid.,* October 18, 1791. He was elected secretary on that date. There were six secretaries, renewed by half every two weeks. The committee was in part renewed (by lot) March 2, but Brissot remained in the committee. He withdrew on June 6, and was reëlected July 17.

University of Strasbourg, was thus able to exercise a dominating influence upon foreign affairs.[1] In view of his previous
utterances the general policy which Brissot would follow was
not difficult to predict. In his opinion, diplomacy was an
adjunct of the old régime, and since the old régime was an evil,
diplomacy was an evil. He failed even to appreciate the possible
use of diplomacy as a means of avoiding war, and urged France
to follow the example of the United States with regard to the
diplomatic corps. He especially urged that the number of persons employed be diminished and that the salaries of those who
were retained be reduced. Such measures, Brissot protested,
would only tend toward peace.[2]

The immediate diplomatic problems which confronted the
Assembly in its opening days involved the relation of France
both to the *émigrés* and to the German princes along the Rhine,
to whom many of the *émigrés* had fled. The revolutionists were
incensed against these princes for the support they had given
to the anti-revolutionary party; and the German princes, many
of whom had property within French territory, were incensed
against the revolutionists on account of the recent abolition of
feudal rights. Alleging that they still held their feudal privileges from the emperor, they appealed to him to redress their
wrongs.[3] At the same time they continued to aid the *émigrés*,
who, in turn, were stirring them up against France. What was
to be the attitude of France toward these *émigrés* and toward
the princes who were supporting them? This, in turn, involved
the question of the attitude of France toward the *émigrés* in
general. To these questions Brissot had a ready answer, and
on October 20, in a speech before the Assembly, set forth his
views at length. Its most notable feature was its attempt to
carry out to the fullest extent the liberty guaranteed by the

[1] For an extended consideration of the subject of Brissot's influence on foreign affairs see H. A. Goetz-Bernstein, *La Diplomatie de la Gironde, Jacques
Pierre Brissot*, Paris, 1912.

[2] *Patriote Français*, November 16, 1789.

[3] The feudal relation of "the immediates" in Alsace was "ambiguous,
obscure, and litigious." Sorel, *L'Europe et la Révolution française*, II, 78.

declaration of rights and at the same time protect France from the dangers to which that liberty might give rise. The laws against the *émigrés*, he maintained, had been confused with the laws against revolt. The declaration of rights proclaimed freedom to every one to go wherever it seemed good unto him; from which it resulted that the citizens ought to be entirely free to emigrate. Then, coming down to more practical considerations, he drew example from the emigration of the Protestants under Louis XIV, and argued that if that powerful monarch, with his hordes of spies, priests, and soldiers, was not able to prevent emigration, it would be quite useless for France, under existing conditions, to attempt it. He therefore proposed that all *émigrés* should be exhorted to return to France, but that in meting out punishment, a clear-cut distinction should be made between princes and public functionaries on the one hand, and ordinary citizens on the other. As for the foreign princes who were encouraging the *émigrés*, here it was no longer a question of liberty, but one of self-defense; France must act with firmness and dispatch. Though these princes had universally opposed the Revolution, they were not to be feared, even though their intentions were hostile. But, he declared, they ought to be asked what their intentions really were, and if they refused to stop protecting the *émigrés* or if they insisted on armed mediation, France must not wait for them, but must be the first to make the attack.

This, Brissot's first speech of importance before the Legislative Assembly, was a great success. He was vigorously applauded and the applause continued as he made his way down from the tribune till he reached his seat.[1] Outside of the Assembly it was received in quite different ways by different factions of the press. According to the *Journal de la cour et de la ville*, it was "a ridiculous harangue and consequently obtained the honor of being printed." "We will not speak further of it," added the same journal, "except to say that the constitution had already deprived *le sieur Brissot* of his surname *de*

---

[1] *Moniteur*, October 22, 1791.

Varville [*sic*]. This speech ought surely to make him lose the first three letters of the name which are left."[1] *Les Révolutions de France et de Brabant*, on the other hand, spoke of it as a superb speech and his draft of a decree as cutting the evil at the root.[2]

After a discussion of several weeks, a decree was finally passed, November 9, which, while modifying somewhat his proposal, accepted the distinction between classes which he laid down, severe penalties for flight being imposed only upon princes and public functionaries, and upon those bearing arms against France.[3]

While the king still had this decree under advisement, Brissot, on November 15, informed the Assembly that the committee was ready to report upon the action to be taken with regard to the foreign powers who had aided fugitives, and asked that the matter be placed on the calendar for early discussion.[4] The subject did not, however, receive the prompt attention Brissot wished, and when the report was presented it was by Brissot's more conservative colleague, Koch.[5] Although admitting that the German princes of the empire were in the wrong in harboring and protecting the *émigrés*, Koch showed his moderation by suggesting that it was not improbable that firm and immediate action might be successful in averting war. There was no need to despair, he maintained, of making those German princes understand that it was neither to their interest nor to their glory to intrigue with a few fugitives. To bring these princes to a realization of their duty to a neighboring nation and to the empire was by no means impossible. Again, on November 29, he spoke in the same tone, and while accepting the substance of a motion of Daverhoult's to the effect that a committee of twenty-four be appointed to request the king to communicate with the German princes, asking them to state their intentions, he objected to that part of the motion which limited to two

---

[1] Number of October 22, 1791. [2] No. 98.
[3] *Moniteur*, November 10, 1791.
[4] *Ibid.*, November 16, 1791. [5] *Ibid.*, November 23, 1791.

weeks the time within which the princes should be required to dismiss the *émigrés*. Such a demand, he insisted, was unreasonable and it savored too much of an ultimatum. More time should be given the princes.[1]

The conciliatory tone of Koch's speech was very different from the warlike and immoderate tone of Isnard's reply. "Let us say to Europe," he cried, "that if the French people draw the sword they will cast the scabbard behind them, and that they will sheathe the sword again only when they return crowned with the laurels of victory; and that if, in spite of their might and courage, they should be vanquished in the defense of liberty, their enemies will reign only over corpses. Let us say to Europe if the cabinets of foreign courts excite a war of kings against peoples we will excite a war of peoples against kings."[2] This language was not exactly calculated to calm the feelings of the kings in question, and, as the *Patriote Français* remarked, was indeed "the sword suspended over the head of Damocles."[3] It is to be observed, however, that it is the language of which the *Patriote Français* approved, and of which it showed its approval by noticing at some length the speech of Isnard, while it had not a word to say of that of Koch. But in spite of the eloquence of Isnard, Koch's arguments prevailed and Daverhoult's motion was amended so as to omit the fixed limit within which the princes must reply. As passed, it simply provided that the king be requested to make evident by all proper means to the princes along the Rhine the absolute necessity of withdrawing all assistance from the French *émigrés*.[4]

Meanwhile, the king had vetoed the decree against the *émigrés*, a step which Brissot did not hesitate to denounce in severe terms. "The veto put by the king upon the decree against the *émigrés*," he declared, "is contrary to the spirit of the constitution, because, in the first place, it was demanded and sanctioned by public opinion and because the king hastened to give his veto without awaiting the expiration of the

---

[1] *Moniteur*, November 30, 1791.   [2] *Ibid.*, December 1, 1791.
[3] *Patriote Français*, November 30, 1791.   [4] *Moniteur*, December 1, 1791.

time allowed him by the constitution in which to consult public opinion." [1]

The general discussion of the subject of the *émigrés* now gave place for a moment to the discussion of a special case. It was a question of action against Cardinal de Rohan, who was charged with complicity in the plot to deliver Strasbourg to the *émigrés*. Again the *Patriote Français* supported the radical side, represented in this case by Ruhl, and declared that it was their right and their duty to present a decree against the cardinal as a French rebel. [2] Koch in reply reminded the Assembly that since Cardinal de Rohan, by abandoning his domicile in France, had lost his status as a French citizen, they could not indict him without exposing themselves uselessly to the danger of arousing the empire. Koch thus succeeded in checking the zeal of the Assembly.

With such an appeal to the fear of war Brissot was not in sympathy. For some time he had maintained that the possibility of war was no cause for alarm; if France were timorous the example of America might well give her courage. "What soldiers of despotism," he cried, "can for any length of time withstand the soldiers of liberty! The soldiers of tyrants are after pay, they have little fidelity, and desert on the first occasion. The soldier of liberty fears neither fatigue, danger, nor hunger — he runs, he flies at the cry of liberty, while despotism is scarcely taking a few tottering steps. . . . Oh, you who doubt the prodigious and supernatural effects which the love of liberty is able to inspire in men, think what the Americans did to gain their independence! Think, for example, how Dr. Warren, who had never handled a musket, defended Bunker Hill with a handful of Americans, badly armed and badly disciplined! . . . Follow General Washington making head with three or four thousand peasants against thirty thousand Englishmen!" [3]

---

[1] *Patriote Français*, December 12, 1791.

[2] *Ibid.*, December 17, 1791; and *Moniteur*, December 18, 1791.

[3] *Discours sur la question de savoir si le roi peut être jugé*, July 10, 1791. See Aulard, *Les Jacobins*, ii, 619–20.

But Brissot not only maintained that war was not to be feared, but that France should take the initiative.[1] There were many who argued with him that the equivocal attitude of the German princes in regard to the *émigrés* and their openly expressed sympathy with the anti-revolutionary party in France ought not to be tolerated. Yet a large section, both of the Assembly and of the Jacobin Club, held that the trouble could be settled by negotiation and diplomacy; that France was not ready for war, and that to drag her into a war for which she was not prepared was sheer folly. Between the war and the anti-war factions, led respectively by Brissot and Robespierre, a prolonged struggle now began.[2] It was an uneven contest. The traditional and long-continued enmity toward Austria, which in the minds of many Frenchmen the treaty of 1756 had formally but not really ended, gave to Brissot a decided advantage.[3]

The personal contest with Robespierre was carried on at the Jacobin Club, where Brissot was just at the height of his popularity.[4] The combat began on December 16, when Brissot in one of his longest and most eloquent speeches advocated immediate war. He began by declaring that, for a people who had

[1] *Moniteur*, October 22, 1791.

[2] Their previous relations had not been unfriendly. Brissot had been in sympathy with Robespierre's democracy and especially with his opposition to the repeal of the decree of May 15, but Robespierre had been much less inclined toward republicanism than Brissot.

[3] Glagau, *Die französische Legislative und der Ursprung der Revolutionskriege, 1791–92*, p. 87.

[4] His popularity seems to date from his speech on the dethronement of the king (see pp. 175–176). The Club watched with keen interest his struggle for election to the Assembly and received the news of his success with great delight. Aulard, *Les Jacobins*, iii, 128, 135. His first appearance at the Jacobin Club after his election was greeted with enthusiastic applause, and in response he made a brief but telling speech, in which he told the Jacobins that he knew what they wanted was deeds not words, and assured them that they would always find him at the tribune of the National Assembly under the flag of liberty. A few days later he was elected president of the Club. See Aulard, *Les Jacobins*, iii, 195. The exact date of his election is not given, nor is the date of his retirement. He is mentioned as president October 3, and his retirement could not have been later than October 19.

just acquired their liberty after a dozen centuries of slavery, war was necessary in order to establish that liberty on a firm basis, in order to test it, to discover whether people were worthy of it. It was necessary, moreover, in order to purge away the vices of despotism and to get rid of men who might still be a source of corruption. He then went on to argue that France had already had sufficient provocation; that if she did not make the attack, other nations would think her weak and would perpetrate further outrages; that the war would not injure commerce, and that it was the very best means of striking at a single blow the very center of the revolutionary movement, "the criminals at Coblenz." Finally, he declared that there was not the slightest danger that the king could make use of the army to recover his former crown. The day had gone by when the soldiers would lend themselves to any such dishonor. At every step in the argument Brissot cited American example which he seemed to think conclusive. America has passed safely through the crucible of war, he argued, why should not France? [1]

At the same time that Brissot was arguing at the Jacobin Club for war, the *Patriote Français* was also clamoring for it. "War! War! Such is the cry of all French patriots," it declared; "such is the desire of all the friends of liberty scattered all over Europe, who are only awaiting that happy diversion in order to attack and overthrow their tyrants. It is that expiatory war which is to renew the face of the world and plant the standard of liberty upon the palaces of kings, upon the seraglios of sultans, upon the châteaux of petty feudal tyrants and upon the temples of popes and muftis." [2]

Meanwhile, the war question entered a new phase. The king had called Narbonne to the ministry of war and the latter had instigated a vigorous war policy. This was like stealing their

[1] *Discours sur la nécessité de déclarer la guerre.*

[2] *Patriote Français*, December 17, 1791. The immediate direction of the *Patriote Français* at this period, it will be remembered, had been abandoned by Brissot in order that he might devote himself more entirely to the work of a legislator, but there is no doubt that it continued to represent his sentiments.

powder and was decidedly disconcerting to Brissot and his friends. Brissot had declared the center of the counter-revolution to be the camp of the *émigrés* at Coblenz, and, by his censure of the king for leniency toward the *émigrés*, had pretty plainly insinuated his connection with the counter-revolution and the anti-war faction. Now to find the king appearing as the champion of war decidedly weakened his arguments. This was a situation of which the opponents of war were not slow to take advantage. On December 18, Robespierre made a speech on the subject at the Jacobin Club, in which he pointed out that as the ministry desired war, to bring it about would only be playing into their hands. "War," he declared, "is always the first desire of a powerful government which desires to increase its power. I need not say that it is during war that the ministry succeeds in exhausting the people and wasting the revenues; that it covers its depredations and its sins with an impenetrable veil. I will not speak to you of what touches most directly the heart of our interests. It is during war that the executive power displays the most dangerous energy; that it exercises a kind of dictatorship which only serves to frighten liberty; it is during war that people neglect their civil and political rights, and occupy themselves only with foreign affairs; it is during war that they turn their attention from their legislators and magistrates and attach all their interests and hopes to their generals and ministers." [1]

The answer of the *Patriote Français* to this trenchant argument was that the court only made a pretense of desiring war, but in reality it did not desire it at all, as was evident from the way in which it had allowed the counter-revolution to grow and extend.[2] The fact that it had not ceased to protect the enemies of the Revolution within was good reason for suspecting that it might have some understanding with the enemies without.[3]

Inspired by this idea the demands for war continued. Brissot

[1] *Discours de Maximilien Robespierre*, December 18, 1791.
[2] Reference to the vetoes of the decrees against the *émigrés* and priests.
[3] *Patriote Français*, December 20, 1791.

was well supported. On the same day on which Robespierre made his second speech at the Jacobin Club, December 18, Roederer had argued for war, especially on the ground of self-defense, and in the Assembly the cause was now taken up by Louvet and Gensonné, who even exceeded Brissot himself in the vehemence of their demands. "We shall ask you for a scourge, terrible but indispensable," cried Louvet. "We shall ask for war. War! And instantly let France rise in arms! . . . With the swiftness of lightning let thousands of our citizen soldiers precipitate themselves upon the domains of feudalism. Let them stop only where servitude ends; let the palace be surrounded by bayonets; let the declaration of rights be deposited in the cottage. Let man everywhere, educated and delivered from oppression, regain the feeling of his early dignity, let the human race arise and breathe."[1] But in order that these somewhat extensive aims might be realized, money was necessary, and the Assembly was speedily brought down from the clouds to consider this practical necessity by a request of Narbonne for twenty millions. Of the announcement that Narbonne was to be made minister of war, the *Patriote Français* had spoken with anything but enthusiasm, and had remarked, when he took the oath of fidelity to the king and the constitution, that it was to be hoped that it was not an empty form.[2] But now that Narbonne was pursuing an active war policy, the Brissotins, although they were not altogether in sympathy with him, came to a partial agreement at least as far as a common determination to seek alliance with England and Prussia[3] and to urge a vigorous war policy against Austria. To carry out this purpose they now supported his demand for money.[4] Accordingly, on December 26, Brissot explained the action of the committees on the subject and Gensonné presented the report. There was no longer a middle ground between liberty and slavery, Gensonné declared. And, in closing his speech, he proclaimed with almost the ardor of Isnard: "The common enemy

[1] *Moniteur*, December 27, 1791. [2] *Patriote Français*, November 8, 1791.
[3] See p. 250. [4] Glagau, 78-85.

is at the gates, a general assault threatens us. Why do we dispute? Why do we fight each other? . . . Let us run to the breach to defend our ramparts or to be buried under the ruins." [1] The appeal was effective, for the Assembly voted the twenty millions unanimously.

This enthusiasm Brissot did not allow to cool, and a few days later made another speech of most belligerent temper. In spite of the fact that the king was now favoring a warlike attitude, Brissot did not hesitate to cast suspicion on the sincerity of his intentions. "You passed a decree against the rebels," he reminded the Assembly; "the king's veto made it of no effect. . . . The enemies of the Revolution have continued their threats and their gatherings; the executive power has continued its indulgence." And even when the king did take active steps, Brissot continued, he showed that he did not realize what was fitting a constitutional king, by announcing to the Elector of Trèves that *he* would regard him as an enemy instead of saying that the *nation* would regard him as an enemy. But, granted that the motive of the king might be open to suspicion, that was no reason for not declaring war. As for possible danger, Brissot was most optimistic and maintained that, although foreign nations were making warlike preparations, they were not to be feared. The English people, he declared, if not the English government, were in sympathy with the Revolution; Austria was torn by internal dissensions, Germany was really peaceable, Sweden was poor, Russia was too far away, Poland was their friend. Moreover, war was necessary for honor's sake, for external safety, for internal tranquillity; in order to establish the finances and public credit of France; in order to put an end to terror, treason, and anarchy. War was actually a national benefit, and the only calamity to be feared was not to have war. He then spoke of the diplomatic transactions, and presented the draft of a decree which included a notification to foreign powers that any help given to French *émigrés* would be regarded as an act of hostility; a demand upon the emperor

[1] *Moniteur*, December 28, 1791.

that he not only use his good offices with the German princes, but also that he send troops into Brabant to prevent all gatherings of rebels; and the recall of the representatives of France from the courts of Stockholm, St. Petersburg, and Rome.[1] The whole speech showed an utter disregard of diplomatic usage, and its entire argument may be summed up in the phrase which Brissot used with telling effect: "The French Revolution has overturned all diplomacy."[2]

Brissot was followed by Hérault de Séchelles and by Condorcet, who presented drafts of an address, setting forth in unmistakable terms the attitude of the war party toward the Rhenish princes.[3] In a burst of enthusiasm it was proposed to send this address, not only to the departments, but also to foreign powers. Cooler heads fortunately perceived the rashness of such procedure and the clause concerning foreign powers was withdrawn; but the essential part of the motion — an indictment of the French princes who were in arms against France — was carried.[4]

While these decrees were being discussed, Brissot resumed the conflict with Robespierre at the Jacobin Club and made another attempt to convince the society that war would not mean danger. As before, he drew his illustrations from America and considered actual conditions from a most optimistic and impractical point of view. There was no longer reason to fear the ministry, he argued, neither was there reason to fear the final outcome. If France was successful under despotism, what might not be expected from France now that she was free? As for the internal dangers of treason and loss of credit, treason

---

[1] *Moniteur*, December 30 and 31, 1791.

[2] In spite of his disdain for the diplomacy of the old régime, Brissot was not always consistent. When, for example, the rights of certain French citizens in Spain were involved, he was the first to make loud complaint that the *Pacte de Famille* — that is to say, the defensive alliance which had taken the place of the original compact — had been violated. But when, a few weeks later, it was pointed out that France in turn owed something to foreign powers, he was as swift to denounce that same *Pacte de Famille* as "impolitic, dangerous, and unconstitutional." *Moniteur*, January 30, 1792.

[3] *Moniteur*, December 31, 1791. [4] *Ibid.*, January 2, 1792.

was really to be desired as a means of getting rid of poison, and the prosperity of the finances depended on their putting down the rebels. Moreover, they would receive a warm welcome from the oppressed peoples against whose rulers they were contending. Finally, heroes would arise in France as in America, and if America, which was far worse off than France, was victorious, why should France too not win victory? [1]

This argument was in turn answered by Robespierre, who, in an admirable speech, very skillfully met the fallacies of Brissot's reasoning. He began by admitting that sentiment and emotion were on the side of war, and that to argue against it was to support an unpopular cause. "But," he said, — and this was the basis of his argument, — "reason is against it. Brissot's idea is beautiful, theoretically, but are we so sure of success? It is admitted that war is desired by the *émigrés*, the ministry, and the intriguers of the court, and all these factions constitute too dangerous and subtle a menace to be overlooked. America's example, as an argument for our success, is worthless, because the circumstances are different; and as for the statement that we will find a ready response among the peoples of the countries against which we fight, it is well to remember that people do not change their customs easily and that no one loves armed missionaries. The thing for us to do," he concluded, "is to set our own affairs in order and to acquire liberty for ourselves before offering it to others." [2]

A few days later, Louvet, supporting Brissot, replied to these arguments,[3] and on January 11 Robespierre spoke again.[4] In spite of Robespierre's efforts, Brissot won a signal, if temporary, victory, for the society voted to send to the affiliated clubs a circular letter prepared by the correspondence committee of the

[1] *Second discours de J. P. Brissot . . . sur la nécessité de faire la guerre.* December 30, 1791. See also Aulard, *Les Jacobins,* III, 303.

[2] *Discours de Maximilien Robespierre sur la guerre.* January 2, 1792. Aulard, *Les Jacobins,* III, 309.

[3] *Discours de Jean-Baptiste Louvet sur la guerre,* January 9, 1792. Aulard, *Les Jacobins,* III, 317.

[4] *Ibid.,* III, 318.

Jacobins, in which the arguments in favor of war were set forth and certain newspapers, including the *Patriote Français*, were recommended as patriotic. This was certainly equivalent to an approval of war, for the *Patriote Français* was belligerency itself, reporting at length speeches in favor of war and casting contempt on all arguments against it.

Meanwhile, the discussion in the Assembly shifted from the *émigrés* and their protectors, the princes, to the emperor, to whom, as head of the empire, the princes appealed. On January 14, Gensonné, in the name of the diplomatic committee, presented a report on the conduct to be pursued toward the emperor. The report declared that, inasmuch as Austria had turned the treaty of 1756 to her own profit, and since the emperor had sanctioned the encouragement of the *émigrés* by the Elector of Trèves, and had himself been responsible for the declaration of Pilnitz and the Padua circular, the ministers should be required to demand an explanation from him before February 10, and meanwhile begin preparations for war.[1] This report Brissot characterized as "remarkable for its wisdom and firmness." But to the moderate Koch it seemed most unwise, and while not censuring the war party directly, he stoutly maintained that there was ground for believing that both the emperor and the Elector of Trèves were inclined toward peace, and furthermore that they were disposed to concede all that the French nation could in justice demand.[2]

Brissot, however, would have none of such conciliatory suggestions. Even the proposal of Gensonné, that the emperor be asked for an immediate explanation of his conduct, seemed to him too mild. To ask for an explanation, he declared, puts us at the mercy of the emperor. To demand satisfaction puts him at ours. "I will not say to the emperor, with your committee," he continued, "'Will you execute the treaty of 1756?' But I

[1] *Moniteur*, January 15, 1792.
[2] *Ibid.*, January 18, 1792. See also Goetz-Bernstein, 72. The concessions of the emperor and of the Elector of Trèves certainly gave ample ground for Koch's claims.

will say to him, 'You have yourself violated the treaty of 1756. We, therefore, have the right to regard it as already broken.' I will not say with your committee, 'Will you engage not to attack France nor to assail its independence?' But I will say, 'You have formed a league against France. I, therefore, have a right to fight you, and the attack is just and necessary.' Either the emperor wants the war or he does not want it," Brissot continued. "If he wants it, it would be senseless not to forestall him; if he does not want it, he would be senseless not to forestall it by giving you, as soon as possible, the satisfaction which you have the right to expect." Then, turning to France, he demanded: "Can you fear this Austria whose people are already your friends, even though its government does hate you? Can you fear this cabinet of Vienna which Richelieu caused to tremble — Richelieu, who governed only slaves; from which Louis XIV took its most beautiful provinces; to which the timid Fleury himself dictated the laws? Should France, free, fear this cabinet?" [1]

This stirring appeal to patriotic pride produced a strong impression, but there were at least a few who were not to be blinded to the dangers of war, and the next day Mathieu Dumas counseled prudence. The burden of his plea was that if war were indeed inevitable, it ought to be waged, but that it ought not, by rash measures, to be made inevitable. What little impression Dumas's warning may have produced was immediately effaced by Vergniaud, who used all his eloquence to support Brissot. "To arms! To arms!" he cried; "citizens, free men, defend your liberty, assure liberty to mankind. It seems to me," he declared, in closing his appeal, "as though the spirits of past generations were filling the place, in order to adjure you in the name of the evils which they suffered, to preserve future generations whose destinies are in your hands. Answer that prayer: be for the future a new providence; ally yourself with the Eternal Justice which protects the French people. Then, while deserving the title of benefactors of your country, you

[1] *Moniteur*, January 19, 1792.

will also deserve the title of benefactors of the human race." [1]

These appeals to patriotism and promises of glory prevailed over the warnings of caution; and after several days of further discussion Brissot, supported by his friends,[2] succeeded in getting the substance of his motion adopted.[3] Although the time allowed the emperor for reply was extended to March 1, nothing was said of an explanation, and the form of the communication was unconciliatory enough to suit even Brissot's most radical demands. It read: "The king shall be requested to declare to the emperor that, unless he gives to the nation, before March 1, full and entire satisfaction upon the points indicated above, his silence, as well as any dilatory answer, will be regarded as a declaration of war."

Meanwhile, at the Jacobin Club, too, as well as before the Assembly, Brissot argued for war. The emperor, he asserted again, was in a state of open hostility toward France, and it was as much a matter of safety as of dignity to attack him, in case he did not give them satisfaction. The discussion there soon took the form of a personal quarrel between Robespierre and Brissot. Robespierre accused Brissot of showing approval of Lafayette, and Brissot denied that he had had anything to do with Lafayette for months.[4] After defending himself, he closed his speech with an expression of regret that the differences of opinion between patriots should injure the public welfare.[5] Whereupon Dusaulx, seizing upon the last phrase, declared that two such good patriots ought to love and esteem each other, and proposed that they show their affection by embracing each other. At this Brissot and Robespierre promptly flew into each other's arms. This dramatic demonstration naturally did not in the slightest degree change their respective opinions

---

[1] *Moniteur*, January 20, 1792.
[2] See speech of Isnard. *Ibid.*, January 22, 1792.
[3] *Ibid.*, January 26, 1792. See also Goetz-Bernstein, 84.
[4] Aulard, *Les Jacobins*, III, 331–34.
[5] *Troisième discours de J. P. Brissot sur la nécessité de la guerre*, January 20, 1792. *Ibid.*, III, 333.

in regard to the war, and within a week Robespierre made another speech against it.[1]

The struggle likewise continued in the Assembly. The victory which Brissot and the radical section of the diplomatic committee had gained in the Assembly, their opponents did not propose to regard as final. Koch, especially, persevered in his efforts to bring the Assembly back to a moderate policy and thus to avoid war. On February 1, apropos of a letter written by the Emperor Leopold, he called attention to the fact that the emperor in ordering an armament was only carrying out the will of the Diet, and that that measure did not, or, at least, need not necessarily imply the hostile intentions imputed to it. "It is only just to the emperor to say," Koch declared, "that, while the affair of the princes owning land in France was discussed in the Diet, he played the rôle of a pacificator and used all his efforts to bring the matter to a peaceable settlement." France had, indeed, no need to fear its enemies, Koch agreed, but it was wise not to seek to increase their number.[2]

The importance of Brissot's influence in these discussions is evident from the bitterness of the attacks made upon him, both from the counter-revolutionists and from the opponents of the war. As an instance of the former may be cited a caricature announced by the *Journal de la cour et de la ville*, of January 4, 1792, which represents a young man slipping up behind an old gentleman who was walking in the Palais Royal and putting his hand into his pocket. The legend beneath read: "*Brissot en mettant ses gands*" [sic], a decided reflection on Brissot's political, if not his personal, honesty. The most successful attack was that made by his fellow Jacobin, Camille Desmoulins, in his *Jean Pierre Brissot démasqué*,[3] which appeared in January, 1792. Indeed, this pamphlet is said to have made more stir than any other one pamphlet published during the Revolution.[4] Its real cause was to be found in Brissot's growing popu-

---

[1] *Troisième discours de Maximilien Robespierre sur la guerre*, January 26, 1792. *Ibid.*, III, 342.

[2] *Moniteur*, February 2, 1792.   [3] See p. 4, note.

[4] *Œuvres de Desmoulins*, ed. by Claretie, I, 251.

larity as a leader of the war party. Moreover, Desmoulins was at this time on intimate terms with Robespierre and undoubtedly wrote the pamphlet with the desire to support his friend and possibly at his instigation.[1] The occasion which called it forth was a dispute concerning the laws against gambling. Desmoulins, in the practice of his profession as a lawyer, had been engaged to defend certain persons accused of keeping a gambling-house. In spite of his efforts, his clients were convicted and sent to prison. Whereupon he placarded Paris with a complaint of the severity of the laws against gambling. Brissot was shocked at Desmoulins's apologies for gambling and promptly denounced him through the columns of the *Patriote Français* as an immoral person unworthy the name of patriot.[2]

To Brissot's denunciations Desmoulins replied by the pamphlet, *Jean Pierre Brissot démasqué*. Brissot had quite misunderstood his notice, Desmoulins declared. Its object was not to attack the law itself, but only to warn the public against a despotism of law as bad as a despotism of monarchy. After thus briefly defending his own action, Desmoulins turned all the force of his invective against his adversary. Indeed, his real purpose was to assail, and, if possible, to destroy, Brissot's reputation. His arraignment was an extremely clever piece of work and showed great skill in hitting upon Brissot's weakest and most vulnerable points. Moreover, it was as cutting in innuendo as in what it actually said. There were many things, Desmoulins began, in Brissot's past, which, in spite of his pretense of virtue, would not bear the light, and then he proceeded to drag them out. He declared, for instance, on the authority of Baron Grimm, that Brissot had been a police spy, under the old régime, in the service of M. Lenoir at one hundred and fifty francs a month.[3] To acknowledge that Brissot was a rogue was,

---

[1] Desmoulins's enmity toward Brissot dated from May, 1791, when he had taken umbrage at the patronizing tone of an article in the *Patriote Français*. For Desmoulins's reply see Claretie, *Desmoulins*, 178, note.

[2] *Patriote Français*, January 12, 1792.

[3] This pretended letter of Grimm to Volney is from Rivarol. It was published first in the *Actes des Apôtres* and was afterward reprinted by Barbier and

he declared, to give him too much credit for cleverness. "I will not say that you are a Sinon who slipped in among the patriots only to incite them to bad measures, who ranged himself with the Jacobins only to make a rear attack upon the strongest and most clear-sighted defenders of liberty. I do not believe that you are a traitor; that rôle is too odious, and you are not capable of such crime." The harm which Brissot had done, Desmoulins continued, could be satisfactorily accounted for only on the hypothesis of stupidity, and that was saying a good deal, for notwithstanding the fine title of the *Patriote Français*, Brissot alone had done more harm to the cause of patriotism and the Revolution than had all the aristocrats together. In his excessive zeal, he had advocated reforms regardless of the expediency of the moment, he had preached republicanism in season and out of season, and finally, he had stirred up the trouble which was devastating the colonies. The whole attack did much to make Brissot ridiculous. It appears to have gone practically unanswered.

The war question now entered a new phase, in which the division in the diplomatic committee became more pronounced and the debates more violent. On March 1, Delessart, the minister for foreign affairs, made a report to the Assembly of his correspondence with the emperor's ministers.[1] The moderate tone of this report displeased the war party, whereupon they demanded that the matter be referred for investigation to the diplomatic committee. The failure of the committee to make an immediate report aroused Brissot's indignation, and on March 10 he registered a formal complaint before the Assembly, charging the diplomatic committee with being determined

by Malassis in *Écrits et pamphlets de Rivarol. L'Intermédiare des chercheurs et des curieux*, January 25, 1891, xxiv, 61.

[1] *Moniteur*, March 2, 1792. See also the *Procès-verbaux* of the diplomatic committee (A. N. F⁷, 4395). On February 23 the minister for foreign affairs had reported to the diplomatic committee that the attitude of foreign powers toward France was one of hesitation; and on February 27 he reported that the emperor had declared that it had never been his intention to sustain the *émigrés*.

to let the Delessart affair drop. It was too dangerous a matter to be passed over, he protested, and asked that time be reserved for him that afternoon that he might himself take up the accusation against Delessart. It does not appear to be without significance that this indignation of Brissot's found expression on the very day after the king had dismissed Narbonne. Although, as has been pointed out, Brissot was in accord with Narbonne in that they were both working for war,[1] yet he seems to have felt that Narbonne had stolen his powder, and in the *Patriote Français* he criticized him severely and frequently. At the same time he infinitely preferred Narbonne to the rest of the ministry, who were under suspicion, and with good ground, of being reactionary. The dismissal of Narbonne thus left the Brissotins without support in the ministry. It was but natural, therefore, that Brissot should seize the occasion of the dismissal of one minister to help oust another, and so make way for an entirely new ministry.

His frank avowal of difference of opinion within the diplomatic committee on the Delessart affair provoked a heated discussion. To the aspersions cast by Brissot on the committee several members retorted that one of their number had already been chosen to make the report; that the matter had been discussed in at least four sessions of the committee; and furthermore, that Brissot knew that to be the case.[2] This assertion Brissot met with violent protests, and after an excited debate it was decreed that he be heard at two o'clock. His speech, which was of great length, was devoted to a violent attack on the emperor and a still more violent arraignment of Delessart.[3] The foreign powers were hostile in interest if not in action, he argued, and Delessart had concealed their real attitude from the Assembly, and what was worse, he had carried on negotiations with them in a very different spirit from that intended by

---

[1] Narbonne's policy was more moderate and his plans not so extensive. See Sorel, ii, 342. See also Glagau, 181. "*Brissot und die Gironde wünschten den Krieg auf jeden Fall und sobald als thunlich; dagegen war Narbonne und seine Freundschaft nicht so hitzig.*"

[2] *Moniteur*, March 12, 1792.   [3] *Ibid.*; also *Procès-verbal*, March 10, 1792.

the Assembly. He could not plead ignorance, for if he had not known how things stood, he had signally failed in his duty. On the other hand, if he had known how things stood and failed to report them, he was a traitor. The Assembly had thus wasted valuable time when war ought long since to have been declared. The emperor must be required to cease his machinations in concert with the other powers against France, and Delessart must be impeached.[1] Brissot's object, then, was to establish a charge of high treason against Delessart, based upon the minister's alleged betrayal of the interests of France, as revealed in the dispatches between the Austrian minister for foreign affairs and himself. According to Von Sybel no speech was ever "more malicious, violent, and devoid of argument,"[2] for however much Delessart, in his heart, may have been inclined to the Austrian coalition, the notes in question contained what the National Assembly had itself decreed. On the other hand, although Delessart may have stated to Austria the letter of the decrees of the Assembly, there was evidence that he had misinterpreted, whether consciously or unconsciously, their spirit. Ordinary prudence, however, might well have suggested to Delessart the wisdom of expressing the demands of the Assembly in terms of more moderation. But whatever his motive, his action was now branded by Brissot as a crime against the honor and safety of the state.[3]

So great was the effect produced by Brissot's speech that a motion was at once offered that Delessart be called immediately to the bar to answer the accusations made against him. To this extreme measure the more moderate deputies objected, and a stormy discussion ensued between the war and the antiwar parties. Several members tried to speak at once, there was

---

[1] It was not exactly impeachment in the usual sense of the term, for the effect of the action of the Assembly was not to send the accused before an upper house for trial, but to send him to the high national court at Orléans.

[2] Von Sybel, *French Revolution*, I, 432.

[3] Glagau, 143–46. Goetz-Bernstein, 139, says: "*C'est Brissot qui inaugura avec succès la politique de violence, des procédés atroces et de ces dénonciations calomnieuses dont il sera plus tard victime lui-même.*"

a wild scramble for the tribune, and such an uproar that no one could be heard. M. Becquet finally gained the attention of the Assembly long enough to remind them that they had only recently applauded some of the same communications of M. Delessart which they now condemned, and that the diplomatic committee had not felt and did not yet feel that it was ready to report on the denunciation of M. Delessart.[1] To this Brissot retorted that all the members of the diplomatic committee had declared their disapproval of Delessart. Hereupon several of the members started up to protest, and one of them, M. Jaucourt, succeeded in obtaining the floor. "The diplomatic committee," he explained, "has often had reason to suspect Delessart, but it had not been able to get proof. . . . Brissot, who has constantly refused to communicate his accusation to the committee —" He did not have a chance to complete the sentence, for this last charge brought Brissot to his feet with a prompt denial, and the lie was passed between them. Guadet, Vergniaud, and Gensonné rushed to the support of Brissot, while their antagonists pressed for adjournment. The motion for adjournment failed; and, although the suggestion of calling Delessart to the bar immediately was dropped, Brissot's motion for an impeachment was carried by a large majority, and measures were ordered for putting it in force.[2]

To read the arguments of Brissot, one would suppose that he was influenced solely by motives of patriotism and disinterested zeal; but, if Étienne Dumont is to be believed, Brissot, far from being actuated by disinterested motives, had, for the purpose of gaining control of the ministry, descended to an accusation made in bad faith. "I heard this act," wrote Dumont, "containing seventeen or eighteen counts, read in the committee. When alone with Brissot and Clavière I made some observa-

---

[1] *Moniteur*, March 12, 1792.

[2] The *Patriote Français* in its account of this debate is misleading. It even makes the statement that in all the course of the discussion, lasting two hours, not one word was said in favor of M. Delessart.

tions on the subject. I said the counts were many of them one and the same thing; others so vague that it was impossible to answer them; that they were generally artful, and calculated to excite undue prejudice and violent animosity against the accused; that some of them were contradictory; and that personal invective ought to be carefully avoided in a criminal accusation, etc. I have forgotten what else I said; but if, upon the whole, I was displeased with this document, I was indignant at Brissot's reply. Laughing at my simplicity, he said in a tone of disgusting levity: 'It is a necessary party maneuver. Delessart must positively go to Orléans, otherwise the king, who is attached to him, would replace [1] him in the administration. We must steal a march upon the Jacobins, and this act of impeachment gives us the merit of having done that which they would themselves do. This is so much taken from them. I know that the counts are multiplied without necessity, but the object of this is to lengthen the proceedings. Garan de Coulon, who is at the head of the high national court, is a nice observer of legal forms; he will proceed methodically in the examination of each separate count, and six months will elapse before Delessart will be able to get rid of the affair. I know that he will be acquitted, because there is no evidence against him; but we shall have gained our object by preventing his return to office.' 'Good God!' I exclaimed, confounded at such odious principles, 'are you so deep in party Machiavelism? Are you the man whom I once knew so decided an enemy to subterfuge? Is it Brissot who now persecutes an innocent man!' . . . 'But,' he replied, disconcerted, 'you are not aware of our situation. Delessart's administration would destroy us, and we must get rid of him at any price. It is only a temporary measure. I know Garan's integrity and Delessart will come to no harm. But we must save the country, and we cannot overcome the Austrian cabinet unless the minister for foreign affairs be a man on whom we can depend. Nevertheless, I will attend to your observa-

---

[1] *Replace* is evidently used here to mean that the king would retain Delessart in his position.

tions, and strike out the terms of invective to which you so properly object.'" [1]

In considering this charge against Brissot, it is to be taken into account that Dumont wrote his *Souvenirs* in 1799, some years after the incident in question. On the other hand, the minuteness and the character of the details are presumptive evidence of their truth. Moreover, the coincidence of the date of the fall of the Narbonne ministry and the accusations against Delessart suggests, as remarked above, an adequate motive for intrigues on Brissot's part to get control of the ministry and gives color to the charge of interested motives, if not of absolute bad faith.

Whatever his motive, Brissot succeeded in carrying his point, and on March 14 his draft of articles of impeachment against Delessart was accepted.[2] He immediately followed it up by a demand that Delessart be required to submit to the diplomatic committee all his correspondence with the envoys of France at foreign courts.[3] Such a demand shocked the conservatives, who pointed out the danger of making public negotiations regarding delicate international questions which might still be adjusted peaceably if only they were kept secret. Moreover, it would be, they declared, a violation of the constitution. To these warnings Brissot refused to listen; and, supported by Mailhe, who amended the original motion so as to include the foreign correspondence from May 1, 1789, he got his motion passed.

Whatever was the conscious motive of Brissot in assailing Delessart, the decree against the latter was followed by an entire change of ministry. The new ministry, in the appointment of which Brissot had considerable influence,[4] included Dumouriez, Roland, and Clavière, and was afterward known as the first Girondin ministry. It might better be called the Brissotin ministry. With Dumouriez in charge of foreign

---

[1] Dumont, *Souvenirs*, 378–80, given as translated in *Recollections of Mirabeau*, 310–12.

[2] *Moniteur*, March 15, 1792.   [3] *Ibid.*   [4] See p. 262.

affairs, Brissot and his friends had an active ally. Their common policy was to make war upon Austria, if possible by an alliance with other powers, but at all events war upon Austria. Their hopes were for an alliance with England and Prussia. Indeed, they had already secured the appointment of a commission to negotiate with England.[1] Talleyrand was so obviously the most capable man for the place that the Girondins, in spite of some prejudice against him, consented to his appointment, while Chauvelin[2] was made nominal head of the commission and Duroveray,[3] who was in special favor with the Girondins, was added to the legation with the title of counsel.[4] As the price of the alliance, Tobago was to be suggested, and if that were not sufficiently alluring, the Île de France and the Île de Bourbon. It was even hinted by the enemies of the Girondins that they would not stop at the surrender of fortified places, or even at the suggestion of a possible change of dynasty in France.[5] At the same time Ségur and a subordinate agent, Jarry, were dispatched to Berlin on a like errand.[6] This proposed alliance Brissot not only furthered through his influence with the ministry, but also supported in his newspaper, noting with approval Condorcet's argument that France and Prussia had in common hatred of Austria; and France and England, the liberty of the sea.[7] Despite their efforts, however, these attempts at alliance came to naught.

[1] See p. 235.

[2] Chauvelin, François, Marquis de (born 1766, died 1812). Master of the wardrobe under Louis XVI, aide-de-camp of Rochambeau in the war of the American Revolution. He was imprisoned during the Terror and released after Thermidor.

[3] Duroveray, *procureur-général* at Geneva, was banished in 1782. Later he was one of that group of men attached to Mirabeau, who helped him prepare his speeches.

[4] Dumont, *Souvenirs*, 419–20.

[5] Sorel, *L'Europe et la révolution française*, II, 336. Sorel quotes Morris, *Pellenc à Le Marck, Léouzon de Duc*. See also *Seconde annexe à la dépêche du Comte de Mercy en date du 14 janvier, 1792*, probably from Pellenc, in Feuillet de Conche, v, 124–26. Feuillet de Conche's work is, however, not to be implicitly relied upon. See also Goetz-Bernstein, 106–07, and note.

[6] Goetz-Bernstein, 113–15.

[7] *Patriote Français*, January 22, 1792.

Dumouriez, meanwhile, proceeded on the assumption that war with Austria was inevitable, and in his negotiations and in his instructions to the army did all in his power to make it so. On April 18 and 19, he communicated to the Assembly the dispatches of Noailles, the French minister at the court of Vienna;[1] and on April 20 he induced the king himself to come down to the Assembly and ask for a declaration of war. In spite of the efforts of Becquet, who made one last attempt to open the eyes of the Assembly to the perils into which they were so heedlessly rushing, Girondin influence prevailed and the decree for war was carried with but seven dissenting voices.[2]

In summing up this war policy of Brissot's two interesting questions present themselves: First, how far was it a Girondin policy? That is to say, was Brissot well supported? Were the other members of the group as eager for war as he? Second, what were their motives in adopting this policy? Was it with the idea of overthrowing the king and establishing a republic?

First, as to the policy itself. Has the belligerency of the Girondins as a whole been exaggerated? Some of their speeches certainly sounded belligerent enough — such, for instance, as the oratorical outburst of Isnard, quoted above, when he declared that the French people, having once "cast the scabbard behind them, would sheathe the sword again only when they returned crowned with the laurels of victory," and that if, in spite of their strength and courage they should be vanquished in the defense of liberty, their enemies would reign only over corpses;[3] or Louvet's proposition that their mission was to surround the castle with bayonets and place the declaration of rights in the cottage.[4] The point is to know whether, when it came to tangible measures, they were as ready to take drastic action. The evidence would seem to show that they were. Isnard certainly was eager enough in his support of Brissot's demand that the foreign princes be called to account for harbor-

[1] *Moniteur*, April 20, 1792.   [2] *Ibid.*, April 22, 1792.
[3] See p. 230.   [4] See p. 235.

ing the *émigrés*. He would not only demand an explanation, but would proceed to make war upon the *émigrés*, even though they themselves had no intention of attacking France. That their gathering on the border was a drain upon the treasury and a menace to the peace of the country was enough to provoke hostilities.[1] On the 5th of January he again argued vehemently for war, declaring that it was indispensable;[2] and on the 20th of January he approved Brissot's demand for an immediate response from the emperor, but would go even further and require the emperor to withdraw his troops and to reduce their numbers in Belgium to that number agreed on in the treaty arrangements.[3] Louvet, too, was eager for rigorous measures against the *émigrés*, while Vergniaud, like Isnard, would go even beyond Brissot. In the first place, he was for more severe measures than Brissot in regard to the *émigrés* in general, and when it concerned the action to be taken with regard to the emperor, he not only upheld Brissot's demand for an immediate response in opposition to the milder requests of the committee, but had the audacity to suggest that the emperor should be requested to forbid the white cockade in his states, and extradite such of the *émigrés* as were fugitives from justice.[4] Even Brissot, in his wildest moments, hardly went as far as this.

Gensonné and Guadet also constantly supported Brissot, though they were more moderate than he. Guadet, for example, when in December it was a question of taking immediate action against the *émigrés*, suggested that the decree be put off, since the former decree against the *émigrés* gave them till January 1 to cease their hostile manifestation; and Gensonné, while arguing that all haste be made in preparing for war, at the same time urged as a motive that this was the best way to secure peace.[5] In view also of the speeches in favor of war by

[1] *Moniteur*, December 1, 1791.   [2] *Ibid.*, January 6, 1792.
[3] *Ibid.*, January 22, 1792.   [4] *Ibid.*, January 20, 1792.
[5] *Ibid.*, December 28, 1791.

Manuel,[1] Roederer,[2] Bançal,[3] and Cloots,[4] it cannot be asserted that there was any lack of belligerency among the Girondins and Girondin sympathizers, though it is perhaps safe to say that — with the exception of Vergniaud, Louvet, Isnard, and Brissot himself — their emphasis was not so much on war alone, as on war as a means of peace.

This matter of motive suggests the second question: Did the Girondins hope by means of the war to overthrow the king and to establish a republic? The question is somewhat difficult to answer, for after the republic was once established, they were naturally anxious, in the face of suspicion of royalism, to date their republicanism as far back as they possibly could, and to claim that the desire to overthrow the monarchy and to establish a republic had long been the impelling motive of their policy. An assertion of Brissot's, for example, that without the war France would not be a republic,[5] appears at first sight to be significant, but this was made September 22, 1792, after the war was declared and the republic established, and does not necessarily imply that when he urged the war it was with the direct intention of overthrowing the monarchy. What is of importance is whether the arguments which he and the other Girondins advanced before the war was declared, were at all of this character.

[1] Manuel, Pierre Louis (born 1751). He was a member of the municipality, an orator of the Jacobins, an administrator of police, *procureur* of the Commune, and member of the Convention. He was guillotined in 1793.

[2] Roederer, Le Comte Pierre Louis. He was a member of the Constituent Assembly, and *procureur syndic* of the Department of the Seine. On the 20th of June, 1792, he warned the Assembly of the approach of the mob, and on the 10th of August protected the royal family. After the 31st of May, 1793, he retired, only to appear after Thermidor. He died in 1835.

[3] See p. 121.

[4] Cloots, Jean Baptiste du Val-de-Grâce, called Anacharsis. He was born in 1755 near Cleves, but made France his adopted country. Before 1789 he journeyed about Europe proclaiming philanthropic principles and called himself the "orator of the human race." Made a French citizen by the Legislative Assembly, he was elected to the Convention, where he continued to preach his propaganda of a universal republic. He was guillotined with the Hébartists in 1794.

[5] *Patriote Français*, September 22, 1792.

They were certainly accused at this time of republicanism, and considering the connection of Brissot, the leader of the war party, with the republican movement of the summer before, it is not to be wondered at. This accusation Brissot denied, and in his speech before the Jacobins on December 16 declared that republicanism was only a chimera brought out by the moderates to frighten worthy patriots, while the *Patriote Français* of December 6 published an article by Condorcet, which asserted that such calumnies were reiterated by newspapers in the pay of the ministers. At the same time, Condorcet plainly showed at least republican tendencies. "A true republican," he declared, "knew how to await under a constitutional monarchy the slow and sure effects of reason." "Every one who reflects," asserted a third member of the war faction, "knows that it is by no means to establish in all completeness the old régime nor on the other hand to establish a republican government that we are ready to fight." It is simply a question whether constitutional equality shall or shall not be established in France.[1]

This, indeed, was the motive most frequently adduced for the war — that France might preserve the liberty already won.[2] What business, it was asked, had the emperor to interfere in the internal affairs of France?[3] Such interference was not to be tolerated. The country must rise in self-defense.[4] "It is necessary, then," declared Brissot on January 17, 1792, "to go straight to the point and say to the emperor: 'It is our constitution which you regard with horror, it is this which you want to destroy. Either give up the idea or prepare for war.'"[5] It is to be observed, however, that it was the constitution as embodying opposition to the old régime, rather than as a perfect and final form of government, that Brissot was ready to defend so valiantly. For, at the same time that he was working with all his might to stir up foreign war in defense of the constitution, he was vigorously criticizing the party within the

[1] *Moniteur*, January 6, 1792.   [2] *Ibid.*, December 30, 1791.
[3] *Ibid.*, January 19, 1792.   [4] *Patriote Français*, December 28, 1791.
[5] *Moniteur*, January 19, 1792.

country which stood for "the constitution, the whole constitution, and nothing but the constitution."[1] He was not prepared, however, to go further and actually assail it as a whole.

What the Girondins did do was to assail the working of the constitution, as far as it concerned the executive power, and to pursue with constancy and determination the king's ministers. "The organization of the executive power," declared an article in the *Patriote Français* of November 14, 1791, "is the cause of all the disorders which affect the realm. The audacity of the seditious priests, the inertia of the courts, the apathy of the administrative corps, the insolent pretensions of the colonists, the malevolence of foreign powers, the twitchings, the convulsions, the agonies of the body politic, all these disasters are the necessary result of the criminal struggle of the executive power against the general will."[2] And on March 6, 1792, Isnard declared that the powerlessness of the executive was simply the result of its ill-will, and demanded an inquiry as to whether the ministers had done all that they ought to have done, all that they could have done, for the execution of the law.[3]

Nor did the Girondins stop with the king's ministers. Having attacked them, they proceeded with all their might to discredit the king himself. Brissot had declared, it will be remembered, apropos of Louis's note to the Elector of Trèves, that the king did not understand his constitutional position when he wrote that *he* would regard him as an enemy, instead of saying that the nation would so regard him.[4] Brissot's severe denunciation of the king for having vetoed the decree against the *émigrés* will also be remembered.[5] But not only had the king opposed the formal decree against the *émigrés*, declared the Girondins, he was actually protecting them, he had not taken prompt steps against their assembled hordes, and when he had acted he had not been in earnest; moreover, the *émigrés* knew it and were proceeding on the assumption that they might go to any length, assured that whatever steps the nation might

[1] *Patriote Français*, December 28, 1791. [2] *Ibid.*, November 14, 1791.
[3] *Ibid.*, March 7, 1792. [4] See p. 236. [5] See p. 230.

take against them would be nullified by the king.[1] The center of the counter-revolution was obviously among these *émigré* gatherings on the frontier, and the way to strike down the counter-revolution at a single blow was to make war on the *émigrés*.[2] The king might say that he wanted war, but such assertions were all pretense.[3] But whether he wanted it or not it should be declared. Whereat it was naturally retorted that there was certainly great risk in making war under a king who was really not in sympathy with it, and the danger was suggested that he might thus secure the opportunity of winning the army to his cause. At this danger Brissot scouted. There was not the slightest risk, he asserted, that a successful war would see the king at the head of a powerful army seizing his ancient crown. It is to be observed, however, that Brissot's assurance that such a thing could not happen was based, not on the virtue of the king, but on the incorruptibility of the soldiers. In fact, Brissot declared on one occasion that treason was really to be desired as a means of getting rid of the poison.[4] The above remark was not made in immediate connection with the king, but as Brissot had in previous utterances declared him to be hand in glove with the *émigrés*, and the center of the counter-revolution, he evidently believed him capable of treason. And when war was finally declared, he asserted that it alone would show who were the friends and who were the enemies of the Revolution, strengthen liberty, and unmask the perfidy of the court.[5]

The above criticism does not prove a deliberate plan to overthrow monarchy and establish a republic; it does show, however, that the Girondins did not hesitate before the possibility of such a result; that they had no abiding devotion to the constitution; and that if they were not ready to overthrow the monarchy, they were at least willing to go to the farthest

---

[1] *Patriote Français*, November 16 and 21, 1791; January 3, 1792; *Moniteur*, December 30, 1791.
[2] *Patriote Français*, December 20, 1791.
[3] Speech of Brissot at the Jacobin Club, January 20, 1792.
[4] Brissot's speech of December 30, 1791.   [5] Dumas, *Souvenirs*, 412.

extent in discrediting it. But it is to be noted that after getting control of the ministry, they had less to say about the inefficiency of the executive, though this may be accounted for in part by the fact that they were not making so many speeches, but devoting themselves more to active preparation for war.

That Brissot himself did not take an active part in the final debate does not alter the fact that the war was in a large measure his work. He had written and argued and toiled in its behalf, and he could justly look upon it as the fulfillment of his efforts as leader of the war party. It was to him "a war of the human race against its oppressors . . . the most just, the most glorious war that had ever been known."[1] He little dreamed that he had precipitated a conflict that was to drench all Europe with blood and leave France with narrowed boundaries and exhausted in strength and resources. In one sense it was, as he regarded it, the crowning point of his diplomatic career, but in its advocacy he had shown himself, both as an editor and as a legislator, impractical, extreme, and undiplomatic, and had helped to bring about conditions which were later to cause his own downfall.

[1] *Patriote Français*, April 21, 1792. Dumont, *Souvenirs*, 411, says: "*Brissot était si violent que je lui ai entendu proposer de déguiser quelques soldats en houlans autrichiens, et de leur faire faire une attaque nocturne sur quelques villages français; à cette nouvelle, on aurait fait une motion à l'Assemblée législative, et on aurait emporté à un decret de guerre l'enthousiasme. Si je n'en avais pas été témoin, je ne le croirais pas.*"

CHAPTER X

PART II

His Interests and Influence

THE period of the Legislative Assembly is notable in the history of the French Revolution for two things: the beginning of a momentous foreign war and for what was in a large part the outcome of that war — the overthrow of the monarchy. The work, however, which the Assembly was called into being to do, was simply to legislate for France, not to change its government. Indeed, any constitutional change whatever was declared to be strictly outside its province. But despite the formal agreement of all parties to accept the constitution, there were many who, while throwing themselves heartily into the legislative work of the Assembly, were not at all disposed to regard the constitutional monarchy as final, and who came to work more or less consistently for its overthrow, and for the establishment of a democratic republic. Prominent among this number was Brissot. A study, then, of his activities during the Legislative Assembly, aside from his leadership of the war party, involves a consideration of his participation in the constitutional legislation of the Assembly and also in the destruction of the monarchy. The Assembly had no sooner met than it was called upon to wrestle with knotty problems. Negroes and mulattoes were in revolt, the finances were disordered, and large numbers of priests were in a state of defiance and rebellion. The treatment of the negroes and mulattoes, together with the heated controversy concerning the jurisdiction of the Legislative Assembly over the colonies, has already been considered in connection with Brissot's work as a humanitarian. It remains to consider his attitude toward the other problems.

The financial problem, unlike the colonial question, *was clearly within the province of the Assembly*, and the existing situation demanded that immediate attention be given to it. The assignats already issued had depreciated in value, the sale of church lands had not produced the amount confidently expected, and the government was in dire straits for the wherewithal to pay its debts and even to carry on the administration. Another issue of assignats was therefore proposed. This proposition Brissot did not support with his former zeal, and the *Patriote Français*, while protesting belief in the principle involved, urged that it be not carried too far in practice. On November 8, Brissot made a speech before the National Assembly, of note on account both of its growing spirit of caution and of its democratic tendency. It would be most imprudent, he declared, for the government to plunge into further issues before ascertaining, on the one hand, the amount of the existing debt, and on the other, the value of the national property, on the security of which the assignats were issued. The government, he continued, should take into consideration the needs of different classes of its creditors, and give the preference to the claims arising from the smaller and less important of the suppressed offices and privileges, such as would come in general from the artisan class. As a further means of aiding the poor, he asked that the new issue include assignats of small denominations.[1] In the latter contention he was successful, as the value of the small assignats to the rich as well as to the poor was generally evident, but his plan for the temporary suspension of all payments over the sum of three thousand francs was voted down.[2]

While struggling with financial difficulties, the Assembly had also to deal with the problem of the non-juring priests. This refusal to take the oath to the civil constitution was regarded

[1] *Discours sur la nécessité de suspendre momentanément le paiement des liquidations au-dessus de 3,000 l., avant d'émettre de nouveaux assignats et sur les finances en général, prononcé à l'Assemblée nationale dans la séance du 24 novembre, 1791.*

[2] See Gomel, *Histoire financière de la Législative*, i, 66-67.

as seditious, and a law was therefore proposed, the purpose of which was to throw upon them the responsibility for any disturbance arising from the discussion of religious questions. In the debates on this law, Brissot took an active and able part. The larger question of liberty of the press was involved, he maintained, and there was grave danger that in trying to restrain the seditious priests, they restrict freedom in general. To denounce, for instance, a priest for having "disturbed the public order" was to check legitimate criticism and to open the way to serious limitations of freedom. Only for having expressly provoked disobedience to the laws could a man be justly held accountable. Brissot also objected to the further provision, that, if the actions, speeches, or writings of an ecclesiastic gave rise to murder, fire, or pillage, he could be prosecuted. Such prosecution was justified, he contended, only if an immediate connection could be traced. In taking this stand, Brissot appears to have been moved only by a desire for legal justice, not by any sympathy for the non-juring priests, as such. The *Patriote Français* was most rigorous in its attitude toward them, and there is every reason to believe that Brissot's newspaper, although for the time being not under his immediate direction, continued to represent his views.

Thus, on November 15, the *Patriote Français* commended Isnard's argument for the banishment of the priests and on the 30th of November heartily approved of the decree just passed, compelling the priests to take the oath immediately or run the risk of expulsion from the department in which they were resident. In taking this stand the paper was arguing on the assumption that the one important thing was to secure peace to the state and success to the Revolution, and that the religious scruples of the non-juring priests were only a pretext unworthy of consideration. "The troubles to which the seditious priests made France a prey," the *Patriote Français* declared, "are not religious troubles, they are civil dissensions. It is not a question of quarreling over dogma or even theology. . . . We have adopted unity of government; they (the non-juring priests) admit the existence of two authorities, we detest that division; we recognize the sovereignty of the people; they prostrate themselves before a higher sovereign." [1] But whatever the legislators and the press might say to the contrary, it *was* a matter both of religion and theology, and the demand of allegiance to the civil constitution of the clergy was a blow at the heart of the orthodox Catholic and a riding rough-shod over the cherished beliefs of centuries.

Besides his direct influence as a member of the Assembly, Brissot soon had the opportunity to exercise an indirect, but none the less important, influence on the progress of the Revolution through the Girondin ministry. As has been seen, he, in company with the other Girondins, had disapproved most cordially of Narbonne, not so much because of his war policy as because he had stolen their powder; and, by their constant criticism of his ministry, in which the *Patriote Français* was especially outspoken, had hastened his downfall. Brissot's precipitate attack on Delessart had further cleared the way, and, moreover, its success revealed the extent of the Girondin influence. As Dumont says, they were considered all powerful, [2] and the king, perhaps because he feared their power and saw no other way to help himself, called them to office. [3]

Not only in bringing about the appointment of a new ministry, but also in determining its personnel the leading Girondins had considerable influence, for the king, having called De Graves to Narbonne's place as minister of war, invited him to complete the ministry and De Graves turned to the party for advice. [4] Advice was precisely what they were delighted to give, and there was much running about and excited consultation. They were accustomed to meet frequently at the apartments of Vergniaud at political dinners, and it was there that the dis-

---

[1] *Patriote Français*, December 28, 1791.

[2] Dumont, *Souvenirs*, 381.

[3] "About the time that the king began to negotiate with the leaders of the Gironde an acute observer noticed that Brissot's *Patriote Français* adopted a more kindly tone in speaking of the queen." Clapham, 181.

[4] Dumont, *Souvenirs*, 381.

cussion centered. In all of this discussion Brissot was especially active. That his influence was regarded as important is evident from the fact that his advice was sought directly by De Graves and that to him was attributed Dumouriez's appointment.[1] It is to be noted, however, that this assertion was made a year later at the height of the attack of the Mountain on the Girondins, when it was to the interest of the former to make the Girondins responsible for Dumouriez's treason. Under such circumstances, it is not to be wondered at that Brissot denied that he had had any part in making Dumouriez minister. The fact remains, however, that they were closely in sympathy, on account of their common enthusiasm for war with Austria, and that Brissot in the *Patriote Français* spoke with enthusiasm of his appointment. A special obligation existed on Brissot's part toward Dumouriez if it is true, as reported, that it was on information furnished by Dumouriez that Brissot founded his report against Delessart.[2]

Whatever may be Brissot's share of responsibility for Dumouriez, it is significant that two at least of the new ministers were Brissot's close personal friends — Clavière and Roland. His long-standing friendship with Clavière, their collaboration with Mirabeau, their association in the production of works on America, and in the editorship of the *Chronique du Mois*, had given Brissot a high idea of the talents of Clavière and especially of his ability as a financier, and there is no doubt that he used all his influence in his behalf.[3] He had also been on terms of intimacy with the Rolands and was one of the most frequent visitors at Madame Roland's salon. It does not appear, however, that the first mention of Roland for minister of the interior was due to Brissot. It was suggested at one of the dinners at Vergniaud's by some one else — Madame Roland herself says

[1] *Moniteur*, April 6, 1793.

[2] Masson, *Le Département des affaires étrangères*, 146.

[3] On the 22d of March, 1792, before the list of ministers was announced, Brissot took occasion in the *Patriote Français* to refer to Clavière as a person already talked of for the position of minister of finance, and two days later loudly praised his nomination.

she does not know by whom.[1] But whoever made the first suggestion, it was Brissot who took up the matter with enthusiasm and who, on the 21st of March, presented himself at the home of the Rolands with a definite proposition. It is perhaps significant of the influence of Madame Roland that Brissot made his proposition to her rather than to Monsieur Roland himself. At all events Madame Roland replied, with becoming modesty, that while Roland appreciated the difficulties and even the dangers of the task, he felt that his zeal was equal to the responsibility, and that at least they would consider the matter. The next day Roland definitely accepted the position of minister of the interior.[2] This position, according to Brissot, was especially delicate and difficult; it was, therefore, a source of satisfaction to the friends of liberty to see it confided to firm and pure hands.[3] Brissot's confidence was not altogether shared by the critics of the Girondins, especially as Roland was a comparatively unknown man and Brissot's influence over him was evidently feared. Brissot himself, in announcing the new ministry in the *Patriote Français* of the 20th of November, had felt obliged to explain who Roland was.

Not content with having established their own adherents in the ministry, the Girondins wanted to oust De Graves. Their choice of a substitute, according to Dumont, who was consulted by Brissot on the subject, was Du Chastellet. Such a choice, as Dumont points out, showed a supreme lack of delicacy, as it involved placing among the king's responsible advisers a man who had signed the first proclamation in favor of a republic.[4] The unfitness of Du Chastellet seems to have been generally recognized and the plan fell through.

---

[1] Madame Roland, *Mémoires*, I, 67, 243. See also Perroud in *Lettres de Madame Roland*, II, 398.

[2] Madame Roland, *Mémoires*, I, 67–68.

[3] "*Brissot observa que le départment de l'intérieur était le plus délicat et le plus chargé dans les circonstances et que c'était un repos d'esprit pour les amis de la liberté que de le voir confié à des mains firmes et pures.*" Madame Roland, *Mémoires*, I, 231.

[4] Dumont, *Souvenirs*, 385.

Its failure did not deter Brissot, however, from attempting to exercise control over the affairs of the new ministry. He seems first to have undertaken to assist Dumouriez in reforming the foreign office, and to have egged him on to the dismissal of several of the heads of departments. One of the dismissed men, Hennin, afterward wrote with great bitterness of Brissot's influence in this matter, charging that it was due to him that a commission was appointed to examine their papers with the hope of finding something reprehensible; and that Brissot was moved thereto, not by zeal for official purity, but by an unholy desire to get vacant places at his disposal.[1] He had a part, moreover, as has been seen, in the appointment of the special embassy, sent to secure English alliance — being responsible especially for getting Duroveray attached to the embassy.[2] In one instance, at least, his zeal outran his discretion, when he tried to persuade Dumouriez to give a diplomatic appointment to Robert. Robert, Brissot urged, was a true friend of the Revolution, and an ardent patriot. To this Dumouriez replied that Robert was unsuited for the position, because of lack of dignity in personal appearance. To use Dumouriez's own language, he was as broad as he was high, and he (Dumouriez) would not disgrace himself by sending anywhere such a little runt. To this objection Brissot could only reiterate that "Robert had an excellent honest heart," but when Dumouriez told him that what Robert aimed at was the ambassadorship to Constantinople, he owned that he had not realized the extent of Robert's pretensions and admitted that Dumouriez was right in his refusal. Through this incident Brissot learned something of the trials of a man thought to possess influence, for he had to face an attack from Robert, who charged him with bad faith in failing to keep a promise of assistance.[3]

In another important instance Brissot and his friends at-

---

[1] Masson, *Le Département des affaires étrangères pendant la révolution*, 148, where the complaint of Hennin to the ministry dated 6th Thermidor, year V, is quoted. The length of time that elapsed may affect the validity of the testimony.

[2] See pp. 235, 250.   [3] Madame Roland, *Mémoires*, ii, 176–78.

tempted to dictate to Dumouriez. This was in demanding the dismissal of Bonne-Carrère, whom Dumouriez had established as chief director in the department of foreign affairs. Reports had been spread abroad concerning a large sum of money, of which Bonne-Carrère was in possession, and which pointed to corruption in his office. On the basis of this report Gensonné, Roland, and Brissot tried to induce Dumouriez to dismiss Bonne-Carrère, on the ground that the entire ministry would suffer in reputation. But Dumouriez was obstinate, and not only refused, but also seemed to have taken lasting offense at such interference.[1]

Over Roland the Girondin influence was greater and more lasting. In the case of Brissot, indeed, it seems to have been not mere influence but actual dictation. That he was recognized as a power behind the ministry as a whole, there is no doubt. Peltier says Brissot reigned for three months,[2] and according to Dumont he enjoyed so great an influence that it turned his head; "he no longer spoke but in oracles, and could not bear contradiction."[3]

The responsibility which Brissot felt for the government, especially after the war had begun, also affected his policy. His attitude on the subject of discipline in the army, for example, was entirely changed. Not many months before, he had declared that a thorough gradation in rank was unnecessary, that much discipline was superfluous, and that under certain conditions soldiers might even argue with their superiors.[4] But now, when the subject was discussed he spoke after an entirely different fashion. "What," he asked, "is the first means by which liberty can be made to triumph over the coalition of slaves armed against it? It is discipline. What is the second means? It is discipline. What is the third? It is discipline."[5] Again, when the subject of providing for war expenses was discussed, he gave his cordial support to Vergniaud in favor of a

---

[1] Madame Roland, *Mémoires*, I, 247–48.
[2] Peltier, *Histoire du 10 août*, I, 63.   [3] Dumont, *Souvenirs*, 404.
[4] *Patriote Français*, April 22, 1791. See p. 158.   [5] *Ibid.*, June 3, 1792.

grant of six millions to be used for the expenses of the department of foreign affairs, and denounced as unworthy the objection that such a sum might be misused — an objection which, had Brissot been in the opposition, he would surely have made himself.[1]

The commanding influence which he was felt to exert naturally made him the subject of attacks from all sides. That he was inconsistent for one thing did not escape his opponents. They seized upon various evidences of it and made them the basis of many an arraignment. Radical theories propounded by him in his early youth, chance remarks showing possible sympathy with the government of the old régime, his present connection with a government which he had formerly assailed, were all seized upon as proofs that he was a man unworthy of confidence and open to suspicion of treason to the cause of the Revolution.

One of the most bitter of these assaults was made through the columns of the *Journal de Paris*. The writer, evidently taking advantage of the fear that the attack on the status of the mulattoes might lead to an attack on slavery itself, seized upon the occasion to warn the public that it needed to be upon its guard against those who would assail the sacred right of property, notably against Brissot. That Brissot was especially dangerous was evident, he declared, from his early writings, and in proof of his assertions he proceeded to quote from Brissot's *Recherches philosophiques sur la propriété et le vol*.[2] Moreover, any man who talked as Brissot did about the "odious distinctions between rich and poor" was to be regarded with suspicion. To this attack Brissot responded promptly and with spirit.[3] The rascality of the writer, he declared, was only too evident, and showed itself in four ways: (1) by applying to a civil state what he had said of a state of nature; (2) by leaving out, or changing, the meaning of citations which showed that far from justifying theft, he condemned it; (3) by arguing from a

[1] *Patriote Français*, March 16, 1792.   [2] See p. 7.
[3] *Patriote Français*, March 8, 1792.

pamphlet printed in 1778,[1] and little known, that in 1792 he wished to overturn society; (4) by printing this article at a moment when evil-intentioned persons were alarming the French people about an alleged attack on the rights of property. His real position, Brissot declared, was evident from such a citation as this — a citation in which, by the way, he frankly admitted that he did not consider property a natural right. "Doubtless it is necessary that he who has worked enjoy the fruit of his work; without that reward for the cultivator, no harvests, no wealth, no commerce. Let us then defend and protect civil property, but let us not say it is founded in natural rights: under the pretext that it is a sacred right let us not outrage nature; let us not punish thieves so cruelly." In concluding his defense, Brissot declared with some venom that such articles as he was answering emanated from opponents of the Revolution and were paid for by the agents of the executive power.

This last shot naturally drew fire. His antagonist hotly denied that he had received any money from the executive power; reiterated his charge that Brissot *did* mean his observations on property to apply to the civil state; pointed out that Brissot contradicted himself as to the date of the publication of his pamphlet on theft, having said in one place that it appeared in 1778, and in another in 1780; declared that in any case the pamphlet was not the work of Brissot's early youth, as in 1778 to 1780 he must have been from thirty-four to thirty-six years of age,[2] and closed by answering Brissot's complaint that the anonymous writer had chosen a time of alarm for property rights to make his attack by the pertinent query: "In the name of Heaven, M. Brissot, at what time, then, *would* you invoke the respect due to property?"[3]

Before this controversy was closed, Brissot was assailed on

---

[1] Brissot in his address had given the date 1778. In this he was mistaken; 1780 was the correct date.

[2] In this he was mistaken. Brissot was born in 1754.

[3] *Journal de Paris*, March 16, 1792.

the opposite side, on this occasion not for being too revolutionary, but for not being revolutionary enough. In the issue
of March 13 of the *Journal de Paris* a writer who signed himself "F. D. P." alleged that Brissot in an essay crowned by
the Academy of Chalons, in 1780, had shown himself to be the
toady of the ministry, the apologist of the police, the friend of
kings in general, and of Louis XVI in particular, and above
all, the enemy of revolution. These allegations Brissot promptly
and hotly denied, at the same time defying the writer to sign
his name and to furnish proof of his insinuations that he had
been in the service of the police.[1] In response the writer, who
proved to be Pange,[2] accepted the defiance, at least to the extent of repeating his accusations over his signature;[3] and when
Brissot again demanded proofs that he had been in the service
of the police,[4] he only answered by inquiring why Brissot was
so violent about mere insinuations, thereby himself insinuating
that Brissot must have a guilty conscience in seeing accusation
where none was actually made.[5] At all events, Pange seems to
have offered no proof, and the matter was apparently dropped.

The success of the Girondins in bringing on the war gave a
new turn to the accusations against Brissot. They ceased to
concern themselves with the utterances of his youth and turned
upon his present policy and purpose. It was charged that he
was sold to the court, and was working for war in order to support royalty[6] and establish a protectorate. The latter charge
was made with great force at the Jacobin Club by Robespierre
and Merlin of Thionville, who seized the moment of the victory
of the war party for impugning their motives. The Girondins,
they declared, were using their influence over the court and
the ministry as false patriots and had formed a conspiracy,
with the aid of Lafayette and Narbonne, to overturn the

---

[1] *Patriote Français*, March 16, 1792.
[2] Pange, Marie François Denis Thomas de (born 1764; died 1796), belonged to an old family connected with the administration of the finances. He
collaborated in the publication of various newspapers during the Revolution.
[3] *Journal de Paris*, March 18, 1792.   [4] *Patriote Français*, March 20, 1792.
[5] *Journal de Paris*, March 25, 1792.   [6] *L'Ami du Peuple*, April 24, 1792.

monarchy and establish themselves in power. They were base intriguers, indifferent to the cause of the people. The precise object of their endeavors varied with circumstances, but the public might rest assured of one thing, it was only for their own interest that they were working.[1]

These accusations Brissot answered as follows. It could not be alleged against him, he began, that he had not been true to the cause of the people because he had not attended the meetings of the Jacobin Club with regularity. His absence was due to precisely the contrary reason, because he *had* been true to the cause of the people and as their representative had been doing his duty at the Legislative Assembly, where night sessions prevented his attendance at the Jacobin Club. Moreover, he had never ceased to defend the cause of the people and to attack their enemies in his newspaper. Then, turning to the specific points of attack, he disavowed the great influence which had been attributed to him in the formation and direction of the ministry, but at the same time stoutly maintained that it was a patriotic ministry, in whose guidance he would be proud to have a part. At this point he was interrupted by Desmoulins who by calls of *"Coquin!" "Coquin!"* precipitated a scene of great disorder. When the semblance of order was finally restored, Brissot continued his defense. He denied that he was striving to overturn royalty and to establish a protectorate, repudiated any intimacy either with Lafayette or Narbonne, declared that he had not even seen Lafayette since the 23d of June, 1791, and that if they were looking for a new Cromwell, they would not select him in a man of so little character as Lafayette. Such accusations should be signed and backed up with proofs. Then, turning to the charge against Condorcet, whose name had been especially coupled with his, and who was absent on account of illness, he launched into a panegyric of his friend,[2] and then closed his speech with

---

[1] Aulard, *Les Jacobins*, III, 518–19.

[2] "*Enfin il a fini par un panégyrique de M. le marquis de Condorcet, panégyrique qui a fait demander à plusieurs membres de la Société si M. de marquis de*

a fierce attack on Robespierre. He would not imitate his adversaries in calumny, he declared; he would not dwell on the report that they were paid for their attacks or that they maintained a secret committee by which to influence the Jacobins, but he would say that whether they wanted civil war or not they were following precisely the same line of action as those who did. As for himself he demanded no redress: having refuted the denunciations made against him, he was content to pay no further attention to them, and therefore moved that the Club proceed to the next order of business.

Brissot's hot-headed friend, Guadet, was not content, however, to let the affair drop. Brissot had scarcely finished before he rushed to the tribune with a demand that the Club take some definite action on these calumnies, at the same time paying his compliments to Robespierre in terms which provoked a scene of wild disorder, and a renewal of the accusations on both sides, till the lateness of the hour made necessary an adjournment and put a temporary end to their incriminations.[1] Far from letting the matter rest, Brissot continued his attack on Robespierre in the *Patriote Français*. "The public is divided," he wrote, "between three opinions concerning Robespierre. Some believe him a madman, others attribute his conduct to wounded vanity, others believe it can be explained only by a reference to the civil list."[2] Brissot and Guadet also printed their speeches. This gave rise to further difficulty, for when the subject was again taken up at the Jacobin Club, Robespierre declared that Brissot and Guadet had not printed their speeches as they had delivered them. He especially objected to the remarks in the preface of Brissot's speech in which Brissot

Condorcet était mort, tant on était éloigné de croire qu'on pût parler d'un homme vivant avec des éloges aussi exagérés." Delacroix, "L'Intrigue dévoilée ou Robespierre vengé des outrages et des calomnies des ambitieux," Annales révolutionnaires, i, 339. (April, 1908.)

[1] *Les Jacobins*, iii, 526–36. Note also the account given by the *Révolutions de Paris*, April 21–28, 1792. This paper took a fairly judicial attitude toward the affair, but in the main supported Brissot.

[2] *Patriote Français*, April 28, 1792.

referred to his (Robespierre's) adherents in the gallery. The result was another extremely stormy session, in the course of which Robespierre threatened to withdraw from the Club entirely, unless they would permit him to defend himself from the libels directed against him. After a prolonged scene of disorder, he finally won a slight victory, for although the Club did not pass any decree of expulsion, he did succeed in obtaining a decree that the Club did not recognize these objectionable allusions and that an address to that effect be sent to the affiliated societies. Brissot and his adherents were, therefore, at least partially discredited,[1] and a step was taken in the direction of their final defeat the following year.

They were still further discredited by their failure to achieve victories on the frontier. They had been so active in forcing a declaration of war, and so ready in their promise of quick and easy success, that their critics soon became loud in their demands for an explanation. Results, and immediate results, were demanded, and the failure to produce them was sufficient, it was urged, to give rise to the gravest suspicions. As Brissot had been a leader of the war party, it was about him that these suspicions naturally centered. "When we were discussing the great question of the war, what did M. Brissot say?" asked the *Révolutions de Paris.* "What answer did he make to his opponents? He saw only Coblenz, desired to destroy Coblenz, and claimed that if Coblenz were destroyed the Revolution would be accomplished. M. Brissot needed a campaign of only fifteen days to pacify Europe and avenge France; everything was ready, everything prepared for his vast undertaking. It is now a month since the war was declared; we have not taken a step, our armies have remained stationary." The writer then went on to paint in somber colors the general situation: "An army in frightful condition, in want of food and munitions, the frontiers undefended, the enemies of the revolution pro-

---

[1] Aulard, *Les Jacobins,* III, 548. See also *Journal des débats de la société des amis de la constitution, séance du lundi,* April 30, 1792. See the defense of Robespierre by Marat in *L'Ami du Peuple,* May 3, 1792.

tected by the courts, the condition of the army not reported by its generals." Was all this, he asked, the result of chance or conspiracy?[1] In any case, the *Révolutions de Paris* continued, they certainly owed the public an explanation of a policy that was even more tortuous and mysterious than that of Duport,[2] and Delessart, Narbonne, Duportail,[3] and Montmorin.[4]

The reply of Brissot and the other Girondins was vigorous and effective. That they were traitors they indignantly denied, but there did exist danger of treason and that danger was to be found in the counselors by whom the king was surrounded. It was these men who constituted a veritable "Austrian Committee," sympathizing with Austria and working in its interests. Even before the war had been declared, Brissot had attacked several of the former members of the ministry under this name, asserting that though they had been ejected from office and the party which they represented deposed from power, they still continued their machinations.[5]

The Girondins now instituted a more specific and violent attack, which, while directed nominally against the ex-ministers, helped to discredit royalty itself. On the 23d of May, Gensonné opened the fusillade by denouncing the "Committee" before the Assembly. He was followed by Brissot, who, in a scathing arraignment, declared that the "Austrian Com-

---

[1] *Révolutions de Paris*, May 12–19, 1792.

[2] Marguerite Louis François Duport-Dutertre was born in Paris in 1754. An advocate of *parlement* under the old régime, he was chosen a member of the electoral assembly of Paris in 1789, and later became substitute for the *procureur-général* of the Commune. From November, 1790, to March, 1792, he was minister of justice. He was guillotined in November, 1793.

[3] Duportail, minister of war under Louis XVI. He kept his post till 1792, but was many times called to the bar of the Legislative Assembly to answer accusations made against him; was finally obliged to resign and to hide in order to escape imprisonment. He died in 1802.

[4] Armand Marc, Comte de Montmorin, was born in Auvergne in 1745. Under the old régime he was sent as ambassador to Madrid and in 1787 became minister for foreign affairs, which office he continued to hold with some interruptions till October, 1791. After his resignation he remained an adviser of Louis XVI. He lost his life in the massacres of September.

[5] *Patriote Français*, March 15, 1792.

mittee" was characterized by "absolute devotion to what is called royal prerogative; by absolute devotion to Austria, by a policy of no alliance with Prussia or England, no matter how advantageous such an alliance might be; by indulgence to the real rebel *émigrés;* and by opposition to the war against the House of Austria after having provoked it." Among the active members of the committee he named the former ministers, Duport and Bertrand de Moleville.[1] Duport, he declared, used his official position to sacrifice the constitution to the executive power, while Bertrand disorganized the navy and hindered the pacification of the colonies with the purpose of keeping them under the control of the king. But the heart and soul of the "Austrian Committee" was Montmorin. As proof of Montmorin's loyalty to the king, rather than to the constitution, Brissot produced a letter to Noailles,[2] dated August 3, 1791, in which he said that the best men of the Assembly were acting in concert with the true servants of the king, in order to sustain the monarchy and restore to His Majesty the powers which are necessary if he were to govern. It was stated further that in this same letter he had declared that "within fifteen days there would be an end to the truly deplorable state of the royal family." As a further proof of Bertrand's antagonism to the Revolution, Brissot produced another letter, in this case written by an agent of the government, in which he spoke of

---

[1] Antoine François Bertrand de Moleville was born at Toulouse in 1744. An intendant of Brittany under the old régime, he became minister of marine in 1789, which office he held till March, 1792. He fled to England during the Terror, returned to France at the Restoration, and died in 1818. He and Brissot had already crossed swords, as is evident from the following: "*Lettre de M. Bertrand de Moleville, ministre de la marine, à Louis XVI au sujet de voies et moyens à employer pour diriger des poursuites contre le rédacteur et l'imprimeur de l'exécrable feuille, le Patriote Français, pour son article du dimanche précédent.*" In *Troisième recueil des pièces déposées à la Commission extraordinaire des douze,* I, 58. Bertrand de Moleville's *Histoire de la Révolution,* VII, 54, gives the text of the letter and the answer of Louis XVI. Tuetey, IV, 128.

[2] Emmanuel Marie Louis, Marquis de Noailles, was born at Paris in 1743, and died in 1822. After a career in the army he turned to diplomacy and in 1791 was sent as ambassador to Vienna. He was under suspicion by the Assembly for his sympathy with the cause of the king.

being permitted by Bertrand to serve the Count d'Artois. Bertrand, Brissot continued, was devoted not only to the king, but to the House of Austria, and had shown his devotion by concealing dispatches and by favoring the *émigrés*, and finally, with his retirement from the ministry he had not ceased his machinations, but was still working in behalf of Austria. In view of these facts, action, Brissot declared, should be taken. He therefore concluded by demanding that Montmorin should be impeached and that an investigation should be made immediately of the conduct of Duport and Bertrand. In spite of his efforts Brissot was not successful, for although his speech was ordered printed and copies sent to various committees, his motion was not carried.[1]

Within a few days Bertrand and Montmorin presented able memoirs to the Assembly, setting forth their defense. In answer to the charge that he had hindered the pacification of the colonies, Bertrand offered to produce his correspondence, and reminded the Assembly that every communication which he had received on the subject he had already submitted to them, and declared that an examination of the dates of the measures voted and of their execution would be a convincing argument that he had used all possible haste. His alleged willful disorganization of the navy he absolutely denied; the state of the navy could be fully accounted for without resorting to allegations of treason.[2]

[1] *Discours sur la dénonciations contre le comité autrichien et contre M. Montmorin.* Les Révolutions de Paris, May 19–26, in commenting upon this speech, condemned Brissot bitterly for saying, "*qu'on a reconnu l'influence du comité Autrichien dans les événemens qui ont récemment affligé la France, dans cette opposition d'un certain parti à la guerre offensive contre l'Autriche, dans les lenteurs des préparatifs de guerre, dans la communication du plan d'attaque, dans les méfiances semées entre les généraux et les ministres.*" He could hardly have been acting in good faith, Les Révolutions declared, when he wrote these lines. The Venetian ambassador wrote as follows: "*Li due discorsi non furono che due lunghe e vaghe declamazioni si promisero delle prove, ma niuna se ne portò, e perfino li piu pervenuti trovarono una tale debolezza nelli assunti, e vanità nei ragionamenti, che si formò anzi nel comune una prevenzione del contrario di quanto s'intendeva confermare.*" Kovalevsky, *Dispacci degli ambasciatori veneti*, 449.

[2] *Observations adressées à l'Assemblée nationale sur les discours prononcés par Mm. Gensonné et Brissot.*

Montmorin in making his defense contended that Brissot had been guilty of unfair play in his attack, in that his charges were based on extracts from letters which would present a different view were the whole letter given, a contention which he proceeded to support by giving the letters in full. The allusion to a concerted action between the servants of the king and the best members of the Assembly referred to the conferences between the ministers and the Assembly. As for the phrase, "servants of the king," that was a mere form of words sanctioned even in England. The deplorable condition of the royal family, soon to cease, had reference to the time of suspense when the constitution was under revision. His desire, Montmorin declared, was not to support the king against *any* constitution, but only against a constitution which left him with insufficient power. The other letter, regarding the relations of the agent of the French government with the Count d'Artois, would, he admitted, be a damaging piece of evidence were it not known that it concerned a permission given in 1789, and that immediately after the receipt of the letter the writer was removed from his position. As for his relations with Austria, Montmorin declared that far from trying to bring about war with her he had done all he could to keep the peace, and, for reasons of principle, because he believed in an Austrian alliance. But that he had concealed dispatches or favored the *émigrés*, or that since his resignation in October, 1791, he had had any part in public affairs, he emphatically denied.[1]

While the Girondins were attacking the former ministers of

---

[1] *Observations de M. de Montmorin adressées à l'Assemblée nationale sur les discours prononcés par Mm. Gensonné et Brissot dans la séance du 23 mai, 1792.*

The following declaration made by one Petit in the *Archives nationales*, C 218, 160, 118, shows how influence might be brought to bear from the galleries: "*Que le jour où M. Brissot, député à l'Assemblée nationale, a parlé sur la comité autrichien les d'Goulet et Benzelin, avoient amenés dans les tribunes de l'Assemblée trente-cinq personnes, dont le premier douze, et le second vingt-trois, a chacun desquelles ils avoient payé trois livres pour cabaler contre M. Brissot, applaudir à tout ce qui serait dit en faveur du Roi et du pouvoir exécutif et désaprouver tout ce qui seroit contre.*"

the king, they were also striving with all their might, so their enemies declared, to discredit the king and queen directly, and thus to overthrow the monarchy, and to establish a republic. This had been Brissot's motive, it was alleged, in urging foreign war, and, according to persistent report, he had for a month been seeking the same end by means of a conspiracy. A part of the plan, if a letter credited to the Count de Fersen is to be believed, was a denunciation of the queen. The plot was concocted at a supper at Condorcet's and the conspirators included Lafayette, Pétion, Brissot, the Abbé Sieyès, and Narbonne. Condorcet drew up the arraignment of the queen. Nineteen points there were, of which the most damning was that she had an understanding with the emperor and M. Delessart, with the purpose of stirring up foreign powers to attack France. In view of such a condition of affairs, it was proposed to get possession of her person, separate her from the king and from her son; then to suspend the king from his functions as an accomplice to the intriguers, on the ground that he could not be trusted to direct the operations of the army against the powers who were making war in his behalf; and, finally, to entrust the education of the dauphin to proper hands.[1] Rumors of this plot having got abroad, they were obliged to abandon it, temporarily, at least. While Fersen may have been mistaken in the definiteness of the schemes in question, he was not the only one who was confident of the existence of a republican conspiracy. Salomon speaks of a mysterious plot, whose leaders, who included Sieyès, Brissot, Condorcet, and Clavière, were accustomed to meet, now at Madame Helvetius's on the Versailles road, now at the home of a woman named D'Odun.[2] Early in March the *Ami du Roi* gave what claimed to be authentic information of a secret committee, composed of

---

[1] *Le Comte Axel de Fersen au Roi de Suède Gustave*, Bruxelles, le 24 mai (1792). Feuillet de Conches, *Louis XVI*, v, 360. The authenticity of some of Feuillet de Conches's material is very doubtful, but that contained in the latter volumes (including the 5th) is more reliable than that in the earlier volumes. See Lord Acton, *Lectures*, 364.

[2] Salomon, *Correspondance*, 386, quoted in Cahn, *Condorcet*, 322.

ardent republicans, inspired by Brissot and Condorcet, who were scheming an atrocious war against the friends of the king and of the monarchy. The Venetian ambassador, writing home in February, declared that the dominant party was working hard to bring about a public schism between the Assembly and the king, with the expectation that the king would either lose public confidence, or, that, frightened by the opposition, he would take flight and leave the power to the Assembly.[1] Dumont likewise affirms that the Girondins were working for the overthrow of monarchy,[2] and Mallet du Pan, in April, 1792, declares specifically that Condorcet, Brissot, and Sieyès had determined to dethrone the king.[3]

Whatever may have been the temper of these secret meetings, and however republican the real desires of the Girondins, they were not ready to avow themselves openly, and on May 10, Brissot, in a long editorial in the *Patriote Français*, categorically denied the existence of a republican faction. France or rather the capital, he declared, was divided into three parties, excluding the aristocrats and the counter-revolutionists. These three parties were called the *enragés*, the patriots and the moderates. None of them desired a republic, they were all under the banner of the constitution, they all had sworn to maintain the constitution, they all invoked the constitution, they all talked of liberty and equality, they all spoke the same language. There were, however, radical differences among them, and these he proceeded to state. The *enragés* recognized only the declaration of rights, swore only by that, though apparently they sustained the constitution. They wished to bring the constitution in all its parts into harmony with the declaration of rights; they were always talking of the sovereignty of the people because by this means they hoped to secure a dominating influence; and, not being able to hope for anything while order was maintained, they propagated every kind of doctrine calculated to produce disorder.

---

[1] Kovalevsky, *Ambasciatori veneti*, 399.   [2] Dumont, *Souvenirs*, 391.

[3] Mallet du Pan, *Mémoires*, I, 260.

The moderates, on the other hand, put the constitution above the declaration of rights. They wanted at all costs the maintenance of property. They looked upon the people as incapable of perfection and therefore to be kept enchained by the law forever, because they were incapable of being guided by reason. They never spoke of equality, but of the constitution.

The patriots were to be distinguished both from the *enragés* and from the moderates. They revered the declaration of rights, but at the same time they also wanted the constitution revered in every respect. They loved the people, but they did not flatter them; they loved the people, but they wanted the people to obey the law and to be punished when they did not obey it. Like the moderates they wanted peace and the maintenance of property; they wanted the reign of law, but they wanted also and first of all the reign of reason. But unlike the *enragés* and the moderates, they were not instruments in the hands of the executive power. In short, the three parties were to be characterized thus: "*Patriot*, friend of the people, friend of the constitution; *Moderate*, false friend of the constitution, enemy of the people; *Enragé*, false friend of the people, enemy of the constitution." According to these characteristics, he concluded, it was easy to see which party reasonable men ought to prefer.[1]

But whatever their ultimate purpose, the Girondins were determined, so long as the king remained on the throne, to limit his power. They accordingly called for the dismissal of the king's guard, on the ground that such action was demanded for the "maintenance of the constitution, the security of the realm, and even for the safety of the king himself." They also demanded the establishment of a camp of *fédérés* for the protection of the Assembly, and a decree for the deportation of the non-juring priests — all of which they successfully carried

[1] *Patriote Français*, May 10, 1792. It was apparently with the express purpose of combating this point of view that Robespierre established the *Défenseur de la Constitution*. Aulard, *Histoire politique*, 182.

through, and all of which Brissot supported in his newspaper.[1] These measures the Girondins considered essential to their own authority, and since they had good reason to fear the king's veto, they used all means at their command to prevent it.

Madame Roland seconded their efforts and wrote an insolent letter to the king, — in her husband's name, of course, — in which she insisted that he give his consent to the two decrees.[2] What followed is well known: the indignation of the king and queen; the dismissal of Servan, Clavière, and Roland, on the advice of Dumouriez; the king's subsequent refusal, despite Dumouriez's persuasions, to conciliate popular opinion by signing the decrees, and the resignation of Dumouriez.

With the conduct of Dumouriez in turning against them the Brissotins were naturally highly indignant. In their opinion he was nothing less than a "vile intriguer." "It is a trying thing," wrote Brissot in his journal, "for a man who has any delicacy, for a patriot who realizes how necessary union is for the prosperity of our armies, to raise the mask which covered the perfidy of a minister whom he esteemed . . . the only thing with which I have to reproach myself is not to have done it sooner. You can guess that I am speaking of the fellow, Dumouriez, who, with his protestations of patriotism, good behavior in the Vendée, and the reputation of some military talent, succeeded in seducing the patriots and in getting himself called by the people to the ministry." [3]

It was evident from his defense that Brissot was troubled lest his own reputation might suffer because of his relations to Dumouriez. He accordingly wrote an open letter to Dumouriez, published in the *Patriote Français*, of June 16, the main purpose of which was to justify himself. His only object, he declared, was to be useful to his country and he had supported Dumouriez merely as a means to that end; but his eyes ought to have been

---

[1] *Patriote Français*, May 30, 31, June 5, 7, 12, 1792.

[2] *Mémoires de Madame Roland*, I, 241. The king had accepted the decree providing for the dismissal of his guard.

[3] *Patriote Français*, June 14, 1792.

opened, if only by Dumouriez's persistence in choosing such a man as Bonne-Carrère.[1]

For his disturbance of mind Brissot seems to have had good reason, for ugly insinuations were being made against him. Certain persons were accused, in the aristocratic newspapers and in placards, of having received, without legitimate reason, large sums of money. These accusations, Brissot declared in his newspaper of June 17, while they mentioned no names, were obviously directed against him and his friends, and were inspired by Dumouriez, who knew they were false. Bonne-Carrère[2] meanwhile did not propose to let Brissot's attack on him go unanswered. According to his account, instead of having received money, Brissot was incensed because he had not, his whole ground of resentment against Dumouriez being that the latter had refused to share with him a large sum of money voted for secret expenses. This rumor, set afloat by Bonne-Carrère, is absolutely without foundation. It served, however, to widen the breach between Dumouriez and Brissot.

Meanwhile, the breach with the king was rapidly approaching a crisis. His attitude toward the decrees against the priests and the camp of *fédérés* was no secret, although the formal announcement of his veto was not made till June 19. The danger was grave, as Brissot had already pointed out. "It is no longer possible," he wrote in the *Patriote Français* of June 18, "to conceal the dangers into which the intriguers of the court precipitate the state; continued indifference would no longer be weakness, it would be treason. And the National Assembly,

---

[1] *Première lettre de Brissot à Dumouriez, Patriote Français*, June 16, 1792.

[2] Bonne-Carrère already bore a grudge against Brissot, because the latter had opposed his appointment as director general of foreign affairs. (See p. 265; also Madame Roland, *Mémoires*, I, 246–48; also *Patriote Français*, June 16, 1792; April 20, 1793.) Bonne-Carrère, says Brissot, became his enemy because he (Brissot) had exposed one of his protégés as a traitor. (Masson, *Un Diplomat*, 199.) At all events, on August 10, Brissot demanded that seals be placed on Bonne-Carrère's papers, and declared that he was not a fit person to hold the post to which he had been assigned, — that of ambassador to the United States. Seals were accordingly placed on his papers, and his appointment was revoked. (*Moniteur*, August 12, 1792.)

which can still save the country if it does act, will destroy it if it hesitates." While the Assembly still hesitated the people acted. The result was the events of June 20, when a huge mob forced its way into the Assembly, presented a petition protesting against the dismissal of the king's ministers and demanding that some action be taken against him, and then invaded the Tuileries and insulted the king and queen.

In the actual events of the day Brissot seems to have taken no part. Precisely to what extent he and the other Girondins were responsible for instigating the movement is a matter of doubt. According to the police commissioner, Sergent-Marçeau, the whole affair had been planned in the salon of Madame Roland, and Brissot, Gensonné, and Guadet were implicated.[1] Moreover, at the trial of the Girondins Chabot swore that Brissot had declared that the 20th of June had produced the effect intended.[2] But this evidence in both cases is from an unfriendly point of view and lacks corroboration. Brissot's previous attitude, however, shows that he had not shrunk from the possibility of a popular rising. As has been pointed out by M. Aulard, it was he who helped to arm the people of Paris with pikes.[3] The *Patriote Français* of October 26, 1791, gave the design of a pike, and on the 10th of February, 1792, it explained that the use of the pike was to hold the court to its duty. "While the enemies of the people were making preparations against them," it declared, "the people also made their preparations. Pikes began the revolution, pikes will finish it." As to the actual events of the day, the *Patriote Français* approved heartily of the original purpose of the demonstration, and expressed no regret at the outcome, nor did it show any sympathy with the king and queen in their distressing situa-

---

[1] *Notice historique sur les événements du 10 août, 1792, et des 20 et 21 juin précédents,* par Sergent-Marçeau. *Revue rétrospective, seconde série,* III, 342. Quoted in Biré, *La Légende des Girondins,* 73. In his deposition made June 21, Sergent does not mention Brissot. See *The Uprising of June 20, 1792,* by L. B. Pfeiffer.

[2] *Moniteur,* October 27, 1793, supplement, p. x.

[3] *Les Orateurs de la Législative,* I, 236.

tion; and when Pétion was suspended for his failure to prevent the uprising, it upheld the Assembly in quashing the suspension.[1] On the whole, it was comparatively mild in its expressions of approval, and was inclined to treat the affair lightly, comparing it to a shower which would serve to cool the air. On July 6, Brissot commented on the events of June 20 at some length. He expressed himself with caution, however; indeed, his main purpose seemed to be not to commit himself unreservedly to either side. He spoke, for instance, of the people as desiring liberty, but also law; as recognizing their duties as well as their rights; at the same time as led into excess by unworthy agitators. In the case of the national guard, there was the spirit of the rank and file to be commended, but quite another spirit among the officers was to be condemned. As for the king, he wanted the constitution, but was not sincerely reconciled with the Revolution.[2]

In taking this halfway position, Brissot but represented the general spirit of the Girondins. They had gained nothing from the events of June 20; instead of increasing their chances of a return to power under the monarchy, they had only prepared the way for the overthrow of the monarchy. They vacillated in regard to decisive action, however, but at the same time continued to attack the king. In these attacks Brissot both took an active part himself and also sustained the onslaughts of his friends. For example, he commended Vergniaud's speech of July 3, in which that famous orator struck so heavily at the king. "One passage was especially admired," Brissot wrote,[3] "that in which he traced the course which an anti-revolutionary king might follow who wanted to destroy the constitution by means of the constitution itself. Every member easily made the application, and the only thing with which M. Cambon reproached the orator was that he put in hypothesis what exists in reality."

Their attack on the king did not restrain the Girondins from

---

[1] *Patriote Français*, June 23, 1792; also July 14.
[2] *Ibid.*, July 6, 1792.   [3] *Ibid.*, July 4, 1792.

taking part in the demonstration which occurred a few days later, known as the "kiss of Lamourette," when, on the proposal of Lamourette that all who "loathed and hated the idea of a republic should rise," the deputies of the right and the left flew into one another's arms and embraced one another with rapture. Whether or not Brissot joined in this demonstration is not stated. Although the *Patriote Français* formally and enthusiastically approved of the occurrence, alluding to it as "a happy, thrice happy reunion,"[1] to Brissot himself the situation was most disconcerting. He was just on the point of making a speech against the king which this denunciation rendered most untimely. He had the good sense, however, to see that it was a mere hysterical outbreak which would not permanently influence real convictions, and that all he had to do was to postpone his speech. He, therefore, with a skillful allusion to the fraternity thus delightfully restored, begged that his intended speech might be put off till the next day, on the ground that it contained some allusions no longer fitting now that peace was restored.[2]

The next day but one he made the promised speech, but although he may have modified it in detail, in its main lines it supported the position which Vergniaud had taken a few days before. Like Vergniaud, within the limits of a single speech he attacked the monarch and upheld the monarchy. But he went even further than Vergniaud, for what the latter had only hinted and suggested, Brissot said openly. The country was still in danger, he declared, in spite of the recent reconciliation between the members of the Assembly. That reconciliation was certainly a cause for rejoicing, but it would not prevent the Prussians and the Austrians from marching against them, or Flanders and the Rhine from being threatened with invasion. "And why is the country still in danger?" he asked. "It is not that we lack troops, not that our troops are wanting in courage, that our frontiers are not better fortified, but because

[1] *Patriote Français*, July 9, 1792. The article was signed G. D. (Girey-Dupré).　　　　　　　　　　　　　[2] *Moniteur*, July 8, 1792.

our strength is paralyzed. And who is to blame for this fatal lethargy? A single man whom the nation made its chief, and whom the courtiers have made its enemy. . . . Bring together all these facts: The aversion of the cabinet of the Tuileries for hostile measures; its silence upon the coalition; its tardiness in entering Brabant; its indulgence for the rebels and the electors; the dismissal of the patriot ministers who had brought about the invasion; their replacement by creatures of the intriguers who opposed the war; the inaction of that General Lafayette who was responsible for them, for those who betrayed us; the paralyzing of the forces of Luckner; the refusal of the camp of two thousand men; the silence regarding the march of the Prussians. Consider these things and then say that there does not exist a plan of conspiracy against France, in favor of the House of Austria, against liberty in favor of the court. Say that the center of it is not to be found in that court, in the executive power, in its agents." In view of these dangers, how was the country to be saved? What measures must be taken? The country must be saved, Brissot declared, not by violent measures, but by means of the constitution. And since the constitution provided that a king who had retracted his oath should be considered to have abdicated, he demanded that a committee be appointed to investigate the king's conduct. He also proposed that the Assembly should declare enemies of the nation all those who had given or should give the king pernicious advice, and that their conduct should be investigated; that the existing ministry no longer possessed the confidence of the nation. And, finally, what is of special importance as showing Brissot's attitude toward the kind of authority afterward put in force by the Terror, he asked for the establishment of a committee of general security to examine all accusations of crimes against the general safety and against the constitution. A few days later he put the attack in more concrete form by assailing Chambonas,[1] the minister for foreign

[1] *Discours sur les causes des dangers de la Patrie, et sur les mesures à prendre, prononcé le 9 juillet, 1792.*

affairs. Chambonas,[1] he declared, had announced to the diplomatic committee that the Piedmontese and Sardinian troops arrayed against France numbered only 1200, whereas, according to Montesquieu,[2] there were 56,000. He therefore demanded that Chambonas be called on for an explanation.

Within the next few days Brissot showed a decided change of front, which gave rise to grave accusations from his enemies and much explanation then and afterwards on his own part. He first showed his change of position in his speech of July 25, in which, apropos of Gensonné's proposed action against conspirators, he again discussed measures for the safety of the state, but this time with a very different emphasis from that of his speech of July 9.[3] He now laid the emphasis not on the evil deeds of the king, but on the necessity of maintaining the constitution and the folly of establishing a republic. "There is no better means," he declared, "than regicide for making royalty eternal. No; it is not by the revolting murder of one individual that royalty will ever be destroyed. The resurrection of royalty in England was due to the punishment of Charles I; it disgusted the people and brought them to the feet of his son. If, then, these republican regicides exist, it must be confessed that they were very stupid republicans — the kind of persons whom kings might well pay for the service they render in making republicanism forever execrable. However that may be, if that party of regicides exists, if there exist

[1] Victor-Scipion Louis Joseph de la Garde, marquis de Chambonas, was born about 1750. He was the mayor of Sens at the beginning of the Revolution, and became an officer in the army. The 16th of June, 1792, he was made minister for foreign affairs in place of Dumouriez, but in consequence of denunciations presented by the Assembly he soon resigned and after the 10th of August emigrated to London. He returned to France at the Restoration, and died in 1829.

[2] Anne-Pierre, marquis de Montesquieu, was born in 1739. He was a deputy from the nobility of Paris to the Constituent Assembly and an officer in the army. In view of accusations brought against him, he had to leave France in 1792. See *Moniteur*, July 24, 1792.

[3] Gensonné's proposal was to give to the municipalities the right of arresting and examining citizens who should be accused of plots against the general safety of the state and against the constitution. *Moniteur*, July 27, 1792.

men who want to establish the republic immediately, upon the débris of the constitution, the knife of the law ought to fall upon them." [1]

The next day, July 26, he spoke again, this time apropos of a proposed letter of criticism to the king presented by Guadet. While he supported the strictures on the king's conduct contained in Guadet's letter and denounced the king as opposed to the Revolution, he counseled delay in bringing about his dethronement. "I know, gentlemen," he declared, "that if it were well proved that the king was in agreement with enemies without, not to try him, not to condemn him would be a crime of high treason against the people. But I know also that what an anti-revolutionary king would desire for the fullest possible success would be a hasty step on the part of the Assembly, a violent measure which would not have the general support of the nation. And why? Because if the king were condemned in the heat of anger, carelessly or with too great haste, the majority of the nation which desires justice for all, which desires that the enactment of justice be preceded by a severe examination, the majority, I say, might blame you, and though it might not entirely acquit the king, yet it might fail to support you in your further measures." [2]

The impression conveyed by this speech was that Brissot was opposed to dethronement. In view of his recent and vehement attacks on the king, Brissot's present position suggested that he had either changed his mind with surprising suddenness, or that he was insincere. His audience thought the latter, for there were cries of "Down with the double-faced rogue!" while one energetic spectator in the gallery, with unfortunately good aim, threw two plums at him. [3]

Various explanations of his action have been given. Ac-

[1] *Opinion de J. P. Brissot sur les mesures de police générale proposées par M. Gensonné.*

[2] *Opinion sur la marche à suivre en examinant la question de la déchéance et les autres mesures, prononcé le 26 juillet, 1792.*

[3] See Aulard, *Orateurs de la Législature*, i, 204, note. "*Il fut frappé de deux prunes [dit un journal] qu'une main vigoureuse lui avoit lancées du haut des tribunes.*"

cording to Soulavie,[1] he (Soulavie) had been asked — so he says in his memoirs — by Chambonas to try to induce Brissot by means of a bribe to moderate his efforts for dethronement, but feeling sure that this method would fail, he advised Chambonas, instead of trying to bribe Brissot, to endeavor to persuade him to give up his efforts for the dethronement, on the ground that it would injure his party. Chambonas took his advice, Soulavie adds, and succeeded.[2]

If the testimony given at the trial of Brissot is to be believed, he not only abandoned his efforts at dethronement by constitutional means, but tried to hinder the efforts of others, and when active measures were proposed attempted to put a stop to them.[3] According to Bertrand de Molleville, he demanded twelve million livres as his price for preventing the insurrectionary movement.[4] This charge, however, is absolutely uncorroborated and is a sheer absurdity.[5]

---

[1] Jean Louis Girard Soulavie was born in 1752. At the time of the French Revolution he was vicar-general of the diocese of Châlons. He became an ardent revolutionist, was one of the first priests to marry, was connected with the revolution in Geneva, and narrowly escaped the scaffold as an alleged agent of Robespierre. The latter part of his life he devoted to literary work. His best-known publication is *Mémoires historiques et politiques du règne de Louis XVI.*

[2] "*Je vous promets le secret, et vous assure que si vous prenez Brissot par la crainte de ce qui peut arriver à son parti, si la nation n'adhère pas à son opinion sur la déchéance, vous en obtiendrez par la peur ce que vous voudrez, plutôt que par des espérances . . . Je pense que si on dit à Brissot qu'il est entre deux feux, entre les Jacobins énergiques et les royalistes, et qu'il peut en manquant sa déchéance, se trouver dans le position, par exemple, des réviseurs de 1791, vous pourrez vous le gagner. Faites valoir surtout la puissance de la constitution, la minorité de ses ennemis dans le Législature, le changement tous les six mois des opinions et de l'esprit public en France, et l'incertitude de résister, en cas de déchéance, au parti d'Orléans, s'il n'en est pas l'agent; et s'il l'est l'incertitude de résister aux royalistes de 1788, réunis aux constitutionnels attachés à Louis XVI, ayant d'ailleurs Lafayette à leur tête.*" Soulavie, *Mémoires*, VI, 430–31. Chambonas's success, as far as he personally was concerned, was only partial, for, on August 4, Brissot again attacked him with the charge that he had misused the secret funds of the department of foreign affairs. *Moniteur*, August 5, 1792.

[3] *Moniteur*, October 27, 1793.

[4] See Soulavie's testimony to Brissot's incorruptibility mentioned above.

[5] *Mémoires*, II, 139.

Even at the time, his speech of July 26 created such a furor that when it was printed he tried to conciliate opinion by adding an explanatory note in which he declared that he had been misunderstood; that he was really not opposed to dethronement, but only to too great haste in bringing it about. He took this stand, he subsequently explained, because he had been brought to realize that public opinion, especially in the provinces, was not ripe for dethronement, and while striving to check too precipitate action he was using every means in his power, and especially his newspaper, to educate opinion so that it might be prepared for dethronement. This explanation of Brissot's is borne out by a dispatch of Earl Gower, who, on July 27, wrote as follows: "The Committee of Twenty-one, before whom that general [Montesquieu] was examined, had agreed to report a Project of a decree to declare that the Crown was forfeited, but upon his answering them that not only every officer but every soldier would oppose them, they desisted. This sufficiently accounts for the speech made by M. Brissot yesterday in the Assembly. It does not, however, follow that from the abortion of this scheme, his most Christian majesty is to be considered in a less dangerous situation than formerly." [1]

Deference to public opinion was, nevertheless, not the all-sufficient explanation of the action of Brissot and his Girondin friends in the eyes of their enemies, the Jacobins. The real reason, the latter asserted, was that the Girondins wanted to get themselves back into office, and, just so long as they saw any chance of doing it, they were willing to support the monarchy. Formal accusation of such intent was made against them and especially against Brissot at the Jacobin Club on August 1, by M. Anthoine.[2] The Girondins did, indeed, make a bid for position and power in the famous memoir of July 20 which Vergniaud, Gensonné, and Guadet sent to the king. After exhorting him to strengthen his own position, which they

---

[1] This dispatch was dated July 27, 1792. *Dispatches of Earl Gower*, 203.
[2] Aulard, *Les Jacobins*, IV, 169.

had themselves so successfully undermined but a few weeks before, they skillfully insinuated that the best way to do it would be to dismiss inefficient ministers and to recall to the ministry "well-known patriots." [1]

Brissot's wavering attitude not only gave occasion for attack to his enemies, but caused distress to at least one of his friends — Madame Roland. On July 31 she wrote to him complaining of his silence at the Assembly, and tried in vain to stir him to take the lead in decisive action. To her, it was a great opportunity for a great man and she ardently desired that Brissot might see and seize his chance. [2]

In the case of Lafayette, Brissot did seize his chance, and when Lafayette, in his letter read before the Assembly on the 18th of June, opposed the dismissal of the Girondin ministry and denounced the Jacobin Club, Brissot backed up his previous assertions that he was no friend of Lafayette's by a prompt and spirited attack. In spite of his own quarrels with the Jacobins, he resented Lafayette's arraignment of that body as a violation of freedom of speech and objected still more vehemently to his evident sympathy with the king. [3] After the events of June 20, this sympathy became more evident and took the form of active measures. Lafayette presumed to leave his army without permission, came to Paris, and

---

[1] See the account by Guadet, *Moniteur*, January 5, 1793. Brissot did not sign this memoir, but note his approval (see above) of Guadet's proposed letter to the king which contained much the same ideas.

[2] *Lettres*, II, 429. Whether stirred by Madame Roland's appeal or assured by the king's refusal to listen to Girondin advice that there was nothing to be gained in longer propping up the throne, Brissot spoke with open contempt on August 5 of those residents of the district of the Filles-Saint-Thomas who were opposed to dethronement. *Patriote Français*, August 5, 1792.

[3] "C'est le coup le plus violent qu'on ait encore porté à liberté, coup d'autant plus dangereux, qu'il est porté par un général qui se vante d'avoir une armée à lui, de ne faire qu'un avec son armée ; d'autant plus dangereux, encore, que cet homme a su, par sa feinte modération et par ses artifices, se conserver un parti, même parmi les hommes qui aiment vivement la liberté ; sa lettre le démasque. . . .

"Oui, tous les hommes qui idolâtrent la liberté ont dû être révoltés de cette lettre. Conserver encore quelque estime pour M. Lafayette après l'avoir entendue c'est en être indigne soi-même ? " *Patriote Français*, June 19, 1792.

after having offered his services to the royal family, appeared before the Assembly on June 28 and demanded the punishment of the instigators of the plot of June 20.[1] Whereupon the Assembly tried to pass a vote of censure against him. Again Brissot saw his opportunity and the same day he attacked Lafayette at the Jacobin Club, solemnly engaging to prove at the bar of the Assembly that Lafayette was guilty of high treason.[2] On July 29, he, with Guadet, Gensonné, and several other members of the Assembly, put on record a signed declaration containing evidence, based on statements of Marshal Luckner, that Lafayette intended to march on Paris.[3] The 4th of August Brissot tried to hasten matters by demanding a report from the committee to which the conduct of Lafayette had been referred,[4] and on August 8 he made his promised attack, and denounced Lafayette in unsparing terms. He began by saying that while he did not assert that Lafayette was actually in concert with the Austrians, he did assert that if Lafayette had been in concert with them, his actions would not have been different from what they actually were. He further declared that Lafayette had no legal right to present a petition; that he compromised the safety of the state in leaving his army; that if the Austrians were not present in large numbers he ought to have attacked them; that if they were there in large numbers it was treason to leave the army in danger; that his demand for the suppression of popular societies was an attempt on the constitution; that he had sought to intimidate and degrade the legislature and to make a Cromwell of himself; and that in view of these facts a decree of censure should be passed against him. In spite of these accusations the decree failed of enactment.[5]

[1] *Moniteur*, June 29, 1792.

[2] *Journal des débats de la Société des Amis de la Constitution, séance du jeudi, juin 28, 1792.*

[3] *Bibliothèque de la Chambre des députés ; collection des affaires du Temps*, t. 158, n. 30 bis, quoted in *Archives parlementaires*, XLVII, 268.

[4] *Moniteur*, August 5, 1792.

[5] See the *Patriote Français* of August 10, for scathing allusions to the weakness, the corruption, and the imbecility of those who voted against the decree.

Meanwhile, in regard to the king's proposed dethronement, while the Girondins were holding back, the Jacobins acted. The latter overthrew the regular municipal authorities, set up an insurrectionary commune of their own, and by its aid brought on the insurrection which culminated in the sack of the Tuileries. The insurrection once accomplished, the Girondins were not slow in pointing out that they had made it inevitable and in claiming the credit for it. To this the Jacobins retorted that though the Girondins might have had some share in preparing the way for it, when it came to decisive action it was they themselves who deserved the credit. The Girondins were, however, still in a majority in the Assembly, and since it was the Assembly which took the legal steps made necessary by the insurrection, — the suspension of the king, the overthrow of the ministry, the appointment of a new ministry, and the calling of a convention, — they might well claim that their part in the crisis was an important one.

In the hurried discussion of these pivotal measures Brissot's voice was heard several times. In order that the papers of the department of foreign affairs might be secured, he asked that seals be placed on the house of Bonne-Carrère where they were kept, and in making the motion he took occasion to allude to Bonne-Carrère as a person of detestable reputation and to remind the Assembly that he had managed to get himself appointed ambassador to the United States — an allusion which led to the passing of a further decree for the revocation of Bonne-Carrère's appointment.[1] More important than the matter of an individual ambassador was the reorganization of the ministry. Vergniaud had made a motion for such reorganization, to which Brissot objected that it should be preceded by a vote of lack of confidence in the existing ministry.[2] With the new ministry itself Brissot was greatly pleased. He evidently saw a chance for a renewal of his former influence,

---

[1] *Moniteur*, August 12, 1792. For Brissot's previous relations with Bonne-Carrère see p. 280.

[2] *Moniteur*, August 12, 1792.

an expectation which is significantly expressed in a note to Madame Roland, probably of about August 10: "I send for her husband and for Lanthenas," it read, "a list of patriots to whom places are to be given. For he ought always to have such a list before him." [1] Brissot had managed Roland before, and it was therefore natural that he should rejoice on his return to office. To the placing of Danton in the ministry it would not have been surprising if he had made some objection, but, when asked by Fabre d'Eglantine whether he was opposed to Danton, he replied that on the contrary he approved of him and that his appointment was the seal of their reconciliation.[2]

It was far, however, from being the seal of reconciliation between the Assembly and the Commune. The practical question was who was to control the power which had been taken from the king; in other words, who was to rule France till the Convention should meet. The Assembly asserted that this task was its business and its business exclusively, while the insurrectionary Commune maintained quite as vigorously that it also had a right to take part in the direction of affairs. There thus resulted a furious struggle between the Assembly on the one hand and the insurrectionary Commune on the other. The leadership in the Assembly, both in its constructive work and in its struggle with the Commune, was largely directed by the Committee of Twenty-one. This committee had grown out of a special committee organized on March 6 and 9, 1792, and known as the Committee of Twelve. On the 18th of June its members were increased to twenty-one.[3] It now became the most important committee of the Assembly and, as has been

---

[1] Quoted by Perroud (*Lettres de Madame Roland*, ii, 734, and note, app.) from a report of Brival, text corrected according to Lanthenas. See also *Correspondance*, 293. Goetz-Bernstein differs from M. Perroud in that he assigns this note to the time of Roland's first ministry. For his reasons for so doing see his *La Diplomatie de la Gironde*, 173, note.

[2] Aulard, *Histoire politique*, 219. Quoted from testimony at the trial of the Girondins. See *Moniteur*, October 27, 1793, supplement.

[3] Aulard, *Recueil des actes du Comité du Salut public*. It was also known as the *Commission extraordinaire*. *Procès-verbaux de la Législative*, August 12, 1792.

pointed out, it played a rôle analogous to that of the great
Committee of Public Safety under the Convention. Its work
was of wide scope and included measures on foreign affairs, the
provinces, the army, property, the Church, and the family.
On August 12, Brissot was added to this most important committee,[1] in which he took an active part and was at one time
its president.[2] He indorsed its action in his journal, contended
in its behalf against his old enemies, Marat and Robespierre,
presented its reports, and even when he did not appear prominently to represent it, did much to direct its course.

Among the first tasks of the Assembly was to provide against
reaction in favor of royalty. What they most feared, and with
good reason, was that Lafayette might march upon Paris. In
spite of the failure of the Assembly on August 8 to bring a decree against him, feeling had been growing. The news that he
had arrested the commissioners sent to the army brought matters to a crisis, and on August 19, urged on by the Commune,
the Committee of Twenty-one presented and secured the passage of a decree declaring Lafayette guilty of high treason.[3]
In commenting on this Brissot summed up his opinion of Lafayette with unsparing severity. "See," he wrote, "to what
a man has been brought by ambition badly directed and
sustained by little ability, an incurable spirit of intrigue, the
popularity of a courtier, ill-directed schemes, rascality without
cleverness, a policy, which, so to speak, lived from hand to
mouth, a man whom fortune persisted in making play the part
of a great personage."[4]

Another source of danger, the Assembly felt, was in the advisers of the king; and having dealt with Lafayette they next

[1] *Procès-verbaux de la Législative*, August 12, 1792.
[2] Biré. *La Légende des Girondins*, 97. Vatel, *Vergniaud*, ii, 127. Neither
writer cites his authority; considering the importance of the position, this is a
matter of note, but it is perhaps to be accounted for by the fact that the minutes of the committee after August 10 have disappeared. See Aulard, *Recueil
des actes du Comité du Salut public*, i, Introduction, p. liii.
[3] *Moniteur*, August 21, 1792.
[4] *Patriote Français*, August 20, 1792.

turned their attention to Montmorin. The preceding May accusations had been brought against Montmorin by Brissot of being devoted, not merely to the king, but to the Austrian government and the *émigrés*.[1] After the 10th of August he had hidden in order to escape arrest, but he was now discovered, and on the proposal of the Committee of Twenty-one haled before the Assembly, where Brissot reiterated his former charges against him. He charged him particularly with having entered into a treasonable correspondence with the Count d'Artois and with having failed to communicate important correspondence to the Assembly. This time the Assembly took definite action and decreed that Montmorin be sent to prison.[2]

The Assembly next proceeded to deal with the Swiss troops, a matter which demanded immediate attention because of the part which the Swiss had taken in defending the Tuileries against the mob on the 10th of August. The report of the committee was presented by Brissot, who argued that free men ought to take the responsibility of their own defense; that the agreement for the service of the Swiss in France had been made by despotic kings, less with the purpose of defending the nation against foreign powers than of defending themselves against the French people; and finally, that the action of the Swiss troops on the 10th of August made their further continuance in the service of France impossible. A decree was accordingly passed for their dismissal.[3]

While dealing with the participants in the 10th of August, the Assembly had also to justify the events of that day to foreign powers. On the suspension of the king, the representatives of almost all foreign powers had left Paris, and the temporary government thus found itself in a most embarrassing situation with respect to the governments of Europe. With a view to conciliating foreign opinion, the Assembly decreed that a

---

[1] See p. 273.   [2] *Moniteur*, August 23 and 24, 1792.
[3] *Ibid.*, August 22, 1792. Also *Rapport fait au nom de la Commission extraordinaire des Comités diplomatique et militaire le 20 août, 1792, sur le licenciement des régiments suisses au service de la France.*

defense of the events of August 10 be drawn up and sent to the powers which had declared their intention of preserving neutrality. This address, which was prepared and presented by Brissot, was an able piece of work. The bloodshed of the 10th of August, he admitted, was to be regretted, but the court alone, by ordering the soldiers to fire on the people, was to blame for it. It but precipitated the suspension of the king, which was already under consideration. That suspension was due to a long series of acts on his part, particularly in connection with foreign powers, which had made it evident beyond doubt that he was opposed to the Revolution. But although the king was suspended and a convention summoned, no anarchy existed, and the government was still being carried on in accordance with the constitution. Foreign powers, therefore, had no reason to withdraw their ambassadors from France or to break off friendly relations with her. Then turning to England he made a particularly skillful appeal. "If France has not the right to suspend the head of her executive power, we must conclude that the English are rebels and that the House of Hanover is a usurping dynasty. Surely there is no Englishman, no intelligent man, who could sustain such a doctrine. The French nation, therefore, is far from fearing a hostile attitude on the part of England; she believes in the assurances of its government, she believes in the loyalty and love of the English people, she believes that when the court of St. James shall have brought its conduct more into line with right principles it will be convinced that the French nation alone has the right, through its representatives, of passing judgment upon the fate of its first public functionary, upon the fate of its government, that no power on earth has the right of interfering in its decisions." [1]

At the same time that the Assembly was protesting against interference from without she was taking further measures to check opposition to the Revolution from within by a decree against the non-juring clergy. This decree, which was more

[1] *Projet de déclaration de l'Assemblée nationale, 5.*

rigorous than anything yet attempted, provided that all non-juring priests must leave France within fifteen days under penalty of deportation to French-Guiana. While Brissot does not appear to have actively opposed this measure, he spoke of it with some reservation and suggested that there was danger that the innocent might be punished instead of the guilty and that the priest to whom the taking of the oath was a violation of his conscience would suffer instead of the violent and dangerous anti-revolutionist.[1]

In regard to another question, concerning the Church, Brissot was more radical, namely, the decree facilitating divorce. His paper at least spoke of it in terms of unmeasured approval, as "the work of superstition overturned, the prejudices of many centuries destroyed, nature triumphant over the Church of Rome, the heavy chains of Hymen changed for garlands of flowers, morals regenerated, and conjugal fidelity established on the foundations of equality and the reciprocity of duties as well as of rights."[2]

Radical and rapid as was the work of the Assembly, it was not sufficiently so to suit the Commune, especially in its attitude toward the reactionaries. The Commune therefore proceeded to dictate to the Assembly, an interference which the Assembly naturally resented, and which led to bitter conflict. The first clash came about over the establishment of a special court, which the Commune kept demanding and which the Assembly fought step by step. As a member of the Committee of Twenty-one, Brissot was in the forefront of the fight. On the 11th of August the Assembly had taken steps toward the formation of a court-martial to try the Swiss for their part in the bloodshed of the preceding day.[3] This, however, did not satisfy the Commune, as the jurisdiction of such a court would presumably be limited to those immediately concerned with the actual violence, and did not extend to conspirators behind the scenes. On the 14th of August, therefore, the Commune

---

[1] *Patriote Français*, August 25, 1792.   [2] *Ibid.*, September 1, 1792.
[3] *Moniteur*, August 13, 1792.

sent a deputation which demanded to know what action the Assembly intended to take and added that if it did not take immediate action, they (the deputation) would wait until it did.[1] The Assembly naturally protested against such a demand, as insulting to its dignity, but at the same time it was intimidated into some concession in decreeing that each of the sections of Paris might choose two *jurés d'accusation* and two *jurés de jugement*. This halfway measure did not satisfy the Commune, and the next day the Commune again sent a deputation headed by Robespierre, which demanded in no measured terms the establishment of a special court in which the accused should be judged directly by commissioners chosen by the sections and from whose decision there should be no appeal. Brissot now came to the front and in an eloquent speech, in which he represented the Committee of Twenty-one, declared that such a court would be nothing more or less than a court-martial and as such would involve a violation of the principles of the constitution; and that, in preserving the constitutional forms of trial and at the same time in adding new jurors to be chosen directly by the sections, due provision had been made for rendering justice more impartial and more rapid. "Doubtless forms still more rapid might have been used," he admitted, "but they belong only to despotism; despotism alone can employ them, because it does not fear to dishonor itself by cruelty; but a free people desires to be and must be just even in its vengeance."[2]

One further point the committee was willing to concede, namely, that the right of appeal be done away with. The Assembly, therefore, voted in accordance with Brissot's report that the demand of the Commune for a special court be refused, but that the right of appeal be abolished. The Assembly could thus flatter itself that it had withstood the Commune. It had, however, made a vital concession, and when the Commune again reiterated its demands, it gave way and ordered the establishment of a special tribunal.[3]

[1] *Moniteur*, August 17, 1792. [2] *Ibid.*, August 17, 1792.
[3] *Ibid.*, August 19, 1792.

Brissot again came into conflict with the Commune on its action in declaring that the signers of the two petitions of the eight thousand and the twenty thousand should be declared incapable of holding any civil office or of bearing arms.[1] These petitions had been drawn up by the national guard of Paris early in the summer of 1792, in protest against the camp of *fédérés*, and represented the hostility of the bourgeois element to a democratic army. The decree of the Commune was therefore a retaliation upon the bourgeois. It was, moreover, in the eyes of the Assembly, a usurpation of power, and when the subject came up Brissot not only supported the motion that the petitions be burned, but demanded that the citizens who possessed copies of them should be asked to destroy them and that any one who should attempt to make use of them for purposes of proscription should be declared an unworthy citizen.[2]

Brissot was further aroused against the Commune by its treatment of his colleague in the management of the *Patriote Français*, Girey-Dupré. The *Patriote Français* had been most vehement in assailing the Commune, and on the 30th of August, Girey-Dupré was summoned before the Commune to answer for its strictures. Hereupon the Assembly, very angry at the assumption of such power by the Commune, not only quashed the summons, and called to its own bar the authorities of the Commune and censured them, but ordered a new municipal election and the dissolution of the Commune. The Commune, however, refused to dissolve, and continued to send out its decrees all over France and to dictate terms to the Assembly and to the Committee of Twenty-one. Brissot was highly indignant at such conduct, which he considered a base usurpation of power. "As long as the temporary commissioners," he declared, "devoted themselves to directing the revolution of the 10th of August, to pursuing the conspirators and to watching those who might be accused of being conspirators, the patriots

---

[1] See von Sybel, *French Revolution*, ii, 63.
[2] *Moniteur*, September 10, 1792.

saw, without being disturbed, the exercise of power, which, having sprung into being with the insurrection, ought to perish with it and be lost in the sovereignty of the people. But when we saw those commissioners prolong their dictatorial authority, usurp the rights of the Commune, dissolve and create again authorities which the Commune alone had the right to create and dissolve, suspend magistrates chosen and loved by the people — in short, when we realized that they were doing things which even extraordinary conditions could not justify, then, at last, good citizens opened their eyes, and perceived that they had not twice conquered liberty in order to hand it over to intriguers, and that they ought not to raise upon the ruins of royal and patrician despotism a despotism more oppressive and more hateful." [1]

The Commune, on the other hand, was supported by Marat. In a placard of August 28 he denounced "the infamous efforts of such men as Brissot, Condorcet, Vergniaud, and Guadet." They had written to all the provinces, he declared, that the National Assembly was under the knife of the Commune of Paris, and their object in so doing was to have the Convention removed from Paris to some city "gangrened by aristocracy," where, they flattered themselves, they could direct its operations to their taste. [2]

Further and more serious accusations were now brought against Brissot and the other Girondins; namely, that they were plotting to preserve the monarchy while overthrowing the monarch, and to put upon the throne either the Duke of York, second son of the king of England, or the Duke of Brunswick. The charges went all the way from an assertion that

---

[1] *Patriote Français*, August 30, 1792.

[2] "*Dans un placard du 28 août 1792* [*Chèvremont, Jean Paul Marat*, II, 96], *Marat disait que ces infâmes* [Brissot, Condorcet, Vergniaud, Guadet, etc.] *ont porté la scélératesse jusqu'à écrire, dans tous les départements, que l'Assemblée nationale est sous le couteau de la Commune de Paris dirigée par une trentaine de factieux, afin de faire choix de quelque ville gangrenée d'aristocratie, pour siège de la Convention nationale qu'ils se flattent de mener à leur gré.* Aulard, *Histoire politique*, 237, note.

the Girondins had considered these men as possible candidates for the throne of France to a direct charge of venality.[1] Of the latter there is absolutely no proof. The accusation took definite and formal shape when, on the evening of September 2, Billaud-Varennes and Robespierre denounced before the Commune a plot in favor of the Duke of Brunswick.[2] According to his own account, Brissot was charged not only with having plotted to deliver France to the Duke of Brunswick, but of having received several millions for that purpose. A search was accordingly made of his papers, but as no proof was found he was allowed to go unmolested.[3] The significance of this action lies not in the charge itself, but in the fact that it was made at the time of the massacres of September, when all suspected royalists were in imminent danger of losing their lives. That the members of the Commune should have made such a charge at this moment is an evidence that they regarded

---

[1] Pétion, in his *Discours sur l'accusation intentée contre Robespierre*, denies in reply to the reported accusation of Robespierre, that Brissot favored the Duke of Brunswick. Aulard, in his *Histoire politique* (p. 209, note), says: "*Carra, soit dans les Annales patriotiques soit à la tribune des Jacobins, avait, à mots couverts, désigné le duc d'York et duc de Brunswick, comme des candidats possibles (et acceptables) au trône de France.*" See *Acte d'accusation rédigé par Amar contre les Girondins*, 15–17. See also Paganel, who represents a moderate point of view. "*A une époque où l'existence politique de la France couroit les plus grands dangers, lorsqu'il s'agissoit de renverser le trône ou de remettre le sceptre constitutionnel dans une main puissante et protectrice, Brissot proposa aux hommes influens d'un comité qui régloit les délibérations de l'Assemblée législative, un fils de George et la constitution anglaise, sous la garantie du roi et du parlement. Ce fait est certain ; cependant il n'existe aucune preuve directe du crime de trahison.*" Paganel, *Essai historique*, ii, 232. Goetz-Bernstein, p. 276, note, quotes from Gollz to Frederick William, March 26, 1792 (Prussian archives): "*La populace devient de plus en plus insolente. . . . Cela accrédite une opinion, que pourtant je ne partage pas encore, que l'Angleterre, par Brissot et autres, paye la tribune pour maintenir la confusion en France.*"

[2] According to M. Aulard (*Histoire politique*, 253–55), the *Procès-verbaux de la commune* (ed. Tourneux, 81) does not give the names of the alleged instigators of the plot, but according to Brissot's account in the *Patriote Français* of September 4 he was one of those designated.

[3] See his own account of the matter in a letter addressed to his fellow citizens and published in the *Patriote Français*, September 4, and in the *Moniteur* of September 7, 1792. See also *Lettres de Madame Roland*, ii, 434; and Brissot, *Mémoires*, ii, 247.

Brissot with violent animosity, and that they were ready to resort to accusations which, though they may have believed, they were unable to prove.

As to Brissot's attitude toward the massacres, accounts differ. The Girondins subsequently charged the Commune and its Jacobin leaders with the responsibility and at the same time endeavored to clear themselves of all part in that responsibility. If his own statement in his *Réponse au rapport de Saint-Just* is to be relied on, Brissot used all his influence to induce Danton to put a stop to the massacres.[1] This assertion receives some support from Peltier, who was by no means an admirer of Brissot. According to his account, Brissot besought Danton to know if there were not some means of preventing the innocent from being confounded with the guilty.[2] On the other hand, according to the evidence at his trial, he was present at the house of Pétion when two of the assassins came in and drank with Pétion.[3] Desmoulins in his *Histoire des Brissotins* makes the startling insinuation that Brissot on the 3d of September had in the presence of Danton frankly expressed regret that his bitter enemy Morande had been forgotten. Such an occurrence is, however, hardly credible and lacks all corroboration. What is certain is that the Committee of Twenty-one, of which Brissot was president and in which he had great influence, took no effective action. Whether it was in a position to take such action is, however, a question.

A couple of weeks later the Legislative Assembly came to an end. Brissot's interest in the Revolution during this period, both in regard to economic and social matters and in the struggle for democracy and a republic, is perhaps best expressed in the *Patriote Français* of September 22, 1792, summing up the work of the Assembly: "When posterity shall pass in review the acts of this second assembly it will see, not without gratitude, that it has overthrown a constitutional Church built

[1] *Mémoires*, II, 247.
[2] Peltier, *Histoire de la Révolution du 10 août, 1792*, II, 489.
[3] *Moniteur*, October 27, 1793; supplement.

upon the ruins of a national religion; that it has established divorce; that it has destroyed the odious distinction which obtained between the white man and his black or mulatto fellow citizen; that it has ordered the sale of the property of the *émigrés* in small portions and the equal division of communal property; that it has torn down the aristocratic barrier raised between Frenchman and Frenchman by the title of active citizen; that it has sworn to hate and to fight kings and royalty; that it has declared with courage and sustained with firmness the war against the house of Austria, cruel enemy of the liberty of Europe and the curse of the human race; finally, pressed between despotism which was seeking to raise its head again and anarchy which was seeking to take its place, it has handed on intact and considerably increased, the treasure confided to it of national liberty." [1]

In much of this achievement Brissot had been an active participant. The part which he himself played had greatly increased his reputation; it had also increased the number of his enemies. He was both better known and better hated at the close of the Legislative Assembly than he was at the beginning. "Brissotin" had come to be a word of significant meaning. His advocacy of a war which was threatening to become disastrous, his quarrel with Robespierre, his radical measures in regard to the colonies, the attack which he had suffered at the hands of Desmoulins, and finally his conflict with the Commune, had aroused enmity against him; yet the prestige which he had won and in large measure still retained, as a leader in matters of foreign affairs, his influence on constitutional legislation, his influence as editor of the *Patriote Français*, and his official position as president of the Committee of Twenty-one gave him a place of great prominence and secured his election to the Convention.

---

[1] Quoted in Jaurès, *Histoire socialiste*, ii, 1315. That Jaurès in such a work chooses Brissot's words in which to sum up the work of the Revolution during the Legislative Assembly is in itself a tribute to the social character of Brissot's interests.

CHAPTER XI

BRISSOT AND THE CONVENTION

At the opening of the Convention, Brissot had reached the climax of his career. His leadership was recognized both at home and abroad. French newspapers of the time, for example, refer to "Brissot and Company," "Brissot and his coterie," [1] while the English *Monthly Review* for 1794 speaks of him as the leading man in France during the first months of the Convention.[2] Within a year, however, power and influence had slipped from his hands, and by the expulsion of his party from the Convention he was branded with failure. The reason for his failure is not far to seek. If he had achieved a reputation as an exponent of the war policy and as a democratic republican, he had also aroused enmity on account of his opposition to the Commune of Paris. This enmity now told increasingly against him. Moreover, he failed to perceive — and this was the main cause of his failure — that with the extension of the war there was imperative necessity of putting aside party differences and of maintaining greater centralization in government. This was the fatal mistake of Brissot and the Girondins; for their failure to see the necessity for union and centralization led to charges of federalism and royalty, and ultimately brought the party to its fall.

Brissot was elected to the Convention from three departments,[3] a decided contrast to his election to the Legislative

[1] *Révolutions de Paris*, October 27, November 3, 1792.

[2] Vol. XIII, p. 228.

[3] Of nine deputies elected from the Department of the Eure-et-Loir, Brissot was chosen the second on the 5th of September. *Procès-verbal de l'assemblée électorale du département de l'Eure-et-Loir ; Archives Nationales*, C 178 (27).

Of nine deputies elected from the Department of the Loire, Brissot was chosen the ninth on the 6th of September. *Procès-verbal de l'assemblée électorale du département du Loire ; Archives Nationales*, C 179 (43).

Of eleven deputies elected from the Department of the Eure, Brissot was

Assembly, when he had to maintain a long conflict to secure election from one.[1] The department which he actually represented — he could represent only one — was Eure-et-Loir, presumably because his election there occurred first. Not only in the elections, but in the opening days of the Convention he occupied a position of prominence, being chosen on September 21 as one of the first secretaries,[2] and on October 11 as a member of the Committee on the Constitution, and on the Diplomatic Committee.[3]

The first step taken by the Convention was the abolition of royalty. Although Brissot regretted that the motion had not been accompanied by discussion, of the action itself he enthusiastically approved. It was very difficult, he declared, for a man who for so long a time had professed republicanism to refrain from pouring out his soul on so happy an occasion. He not only rejoiced, he continued, because royalty was abolished and the yoke of the tyrants cast off, but also because it had been done by that class of citizens known as the "people." If he were asked why most partisans of republicanism were to be found among the people, he would answer it was because the people were more trustworthy, had more good sense, fewer prejudices, less calculating interest than other classes. It was the people who realized that since an hereditary king might be tyrannical, ignorant, or imbecile, hereditary royalty was unnecessary, in fact an absurdity. "What the people thought," he concluded, "the Convention did; the French are finally men, free men — Francs."[4]

Since Frenchmen were now free, the *Patriote Français* argued, in another article published the same day, it was only

chosen the seventh on the 6th day of September. *Procès-verbal de l'assemblée électorale du département de l'Eure; Archives Nationales*, C 178 (26).

[1] That he was not chosen as a deputy from Paris is an evidence of the strength of the opposition to him on the part of the Commune. See Bourne, *The Revolutionary Period in Europe*, 183.

[2] *Procès-verbaux de la Convention*, September 21, 1792.

[3] *Ibid.*, October 11, 1792.

[4] *Patriote Français*, September 22, 1792. It would hardly be suspected from this effusion that Brissot himself had counseled delay in establishing a republic.

fitting that the aristocracy of feudal titles should be abolished. *Monsieur, le sieur* implied gradations which no longer existed. Even *citoyen* suggested some distinction; it was, moreover, a sacred word, and while it might be fittingly applied to Pétion or Condorcet, to refer to Marat as *citoyen* was to prostitute the term to a base use. Republicans, the article concluded, might well imitate the Romans, and say simply Pétion, Condorcet, Paine, as at Rome people talked of Cato, Cicero, and Brutus. It was all very well for Brissot to utter pæans in praise of republicanism, but his enemies had not forgotten that his advocacy of a republic had by no means been unflagging and that in the critical months of July and August just passed, he had advised caution and even delay.

The quarrel that had developed at that epoch between the Girondins and the Jacobin supporters of the Commune now received a new and powerful impetus, since neither party needed to exercise caution for fear of giving an advantage to the monarchists. But scarcely had the decree for the abolition of monarchy been passed when the Girondins rushed to the assault. Their opponents, they cried, were forever stained with the blood of the loathsome massacres of September. It was time to set up scaffolds for the assassins and for those who provoked assassination.[1] Nor was this all. The guilty wretches had built upon their crime to make themselves masters of Paris and of all France. Masters they were and masters they strove to remain by creating a dictatorship whereby Paris could over-awe the Convention and control the nation.

To meet this danger the Girondins proposed to establish a departmental guard about Paris, consisting of delegates from the eighty-three departments.[2] The Mountain accepted the challenge and stubbornly contested every inch of the ground. They denied with indignation that they had connived at the massacres; they repudiated the charge of seeking to establish a dictatorship; but above all they violently opposed the project of a departmental guard. On this question the advantage

[1] *Moniteur*, September 25, 1792.   [2] *Ibid.*, September 26, 1792.

was distinctly on their side, for, by proclaiming themselves the
champions of the liberty of Paris, they discredited the Girondins with the people of that all-important city. Moreover, by
retorting with the counter-charge that the real object of the
Girondins was to destroy the unity of the nation by splitting
France into a score of federal republics, they rendered them
objects of undying suspicion and endless hate.[1] In this quarrel,
which raged with increasing bitterness for several weeks, Brissot spoke but seldom,[2] but in his journal he upheld his own
party with a loyalty and attacked the Mountain with a vin-
dictiveness which would have done credit to the ante-election
editorials of a modern newspaper. Whatever the Girondins
advocated was *per se* good, the views of the Mountain *per se*
bad.

The quarrel began over the question whether a man might
hold his position as minister and at the same time be a member
of the legislative body. The individual involved was Roland.
While Brissot argued against this as a principle, he did want
Roland to hold both places provisionally, and was furious with
Danton for having dragged Madame Roland into the discussion by his remark to the effect that if Roland were asked to
continue his functions as minister, the same invitation would
have to be extended to Madame Roland. Such an allusion was
both ungallant and ungracious, Brissot declared, and Danton
ought to be ashamed of himself.[3]

Meanwhile the matter of the departmental guard was again

---

[1] *Moniteur*, September 26, 1792. Although the plan for a general departmental guard was defeated, the Girondins succeeded in inducing a considerable number of *fédérés* from Marseilles to come up to Paris. This guard appeared at the bar of the Convention and proclaimed its intention of defending
Paris against the dictators. See *Moniteur*, October 22, 1792.

[2] The leadership in this quarrel passed to Buzot.

[3] "*Danton n'a pas rougi de dire que, si l'on faisait une invitation à Roland, il
falloit aussi en faire une à la femme de ce ministre, puisqu'elle aide de ses con-
seils. Ce reproche étoit infâme : c'étoit faire un crime à un ministre du bonheur de
posséder un amis, un conseiller éclairé dans sa femme. . . . Heureux, mille fois
heureux, les ministres, les fonctionnaires qui ont des épouses aussi éclairées et
aussi vertueuses : ceux-là ne risquent pas de faire de plates adresses, ou de protéger
des scélérats.*" *Patriote Français*, September 30, 1792.

taken up by Buzot, who urgently demanded such an organization. This demand Brissot commended with enthusiasm. He
again warmly approved of Buzot, when some three weeks later
the latter argued that this measure did not imply hostility to
Paris, but on the contrary furthered that unity which was for
the best interest of Paris.[1] And in describing the culminating
incident of this preliminary struggle between the Girondins and
the Jacobins — the attack of Louvet on Robespierre — he
praised the former in extravagant terms and poured his bitterest scorn upon the latter. "Louvet," he declared, "made a
speech, of which it is impossible to give an extract, because it
was all equally strong, equally fine. . . . The eloquence of the
orator was as great as his courage — and never did Cicero
show more courage when, in the Roman Senate, he challenged
the anarchist Catiline and the ambitious Antony."[2] Robespierre's speech, on the contrary, was beneath contempt.
"Robespierre spoke, — in one word we have analyzed his
speech — he spoke. He ought to have justified himself and did
not do it. When accused of having aspired to the dictatorship,
he answered that in order to aspire to it one must be a fool,
which does not prove that he did not aspire to it."[3] As for
Marat, Brissot could hardly contain himself. He begged pardon
of his readers for being obliged even to mention his name and
alluded to him as that man "whose every word was a horror,
whose every thought was a crime, every gesture a contortion,
every action an argument against Providence."[4]

The combatants in this mortal strife seized upon every coign
of vantage and delivered their blows in the political clubs as
well as in the Convention or through the newspapers. At the
Jacobin Club, it will be recalled, charges of anti-republicanism had already been made against Brissot and decisive action
had long been pending.[5] The charges were now renewed and
added to. On the 23d of September, he was accused of having

[1] *Patriote Français*, October 9, 1792. [2] *Ibid.*, October 31, 1792.
[3] *Ibid.*, November 6, 1792. [4] *Ibid.*, October 5, 1792.
[5] See p. 268.

referred to Robespierre and Danton as leaders in the Convention of a party of disorganizers and was summoned to appear before the Club to explain himself. The next day he answered by letter that he would come as soon as he had an evening when he was not occupied at the Convention.[1] The Jacobin Club, however, did not wait for his explanation, but on October 10 they took the final step and expelled him.[2] The formal accusation contained but one general charge, that of opposition to the Commune of Paris, but the circular which the Club sent out to all the affiliated societies notifying them of its action was very specific. In it they accused Brissot not only of calumniating Paris, but of having been the friend of Lafayette, of temporizing with the king, of injuring the country by bringing on a foreign war and of being at best a half-hearted republican.[3] Brissot in reply appealed to his constituents, and in a lengthy pamphlet entitled "*A tous les républicans de France sur la Société des Jacobins de Paris,*" set forth his side of the case. He began by defending his attacks on the leaders of the Paris Commune, who were now represented by the party of the Mountain. They were nothing less, he declared, than a party of disorganizers; he had preached against them and would continue to preach against them. Three revolutions were necessary, he went on, to save France: the first to overthrow despotism; the second, to destroy royalty; the third ought to overcome anarchy, and it is to that last revolution that, since the 10th of August, he had consecrated his pen and all his efforts. This was his crime in the eyes of the agitators. "These agitators or disorganizers are those," he continued, "who, while preaching theoretically an equality of departments, in fact elevate Paris above all of them; who thus elevate it only that they may elevate themselves, who wish the unity of the republic only that they may consolidate the entire republic about their little

[1] Aulard, *Les Jacobins*, iv, 327–30.

[2] The same day Pétion was replaced by Danton as president, and on November 26 Louvet, Lanthenas, Roland, and Girey-Dupré were expelled. *Ibid.*, iv, 376 and 519.

[3] *Ibid.*, iv, 377–78.

center of intrigue and from that center dominate all the departments." Then, turning to the accusation of having brought
about the war, he declared that the war had justified itself by
having overthrown royalty. As for the civil war in the colonies, that was due not to him, but to Barnave; as far as Lafayette was concerned, he had been his friend, but had been
deceived by him; and finally, as for the assertion that he,
together with his friends Vergniaud, Gensonné, and Guadet,
formed a "Brissotin" faction — that was a mere figment of
the imagination gotten up to frighten the people. This defense
naturally had little effect on the Jacobin Club; but though
stripped of his power there, he continued to be recognized
as the chief enemy of the club, at least till November. But
when during the winter of 1792–93 Buzot became more prominent, they turned their main attacks upon him.

While political strife was thus raging within, important
questions of foreign affairs were demanding settlement. The
situation was critical; war was being waged against Austria
and Prussia, but there was still a chance that by wise diplomacy
further complications might be avoided. In the discussion of
these questions Brissot was keenly interested and, as a member
of the Diplomatic Committee, took an active part.

Even in the conduct of the war the influence of the internal
strife made itself felt. Marat, for example, denounced Dumouriez for his attitude toward the Prussians and hastened to
point out that a man who had been lenient to one foe might be
lenient to another, even to the point of treason. Whereupon
Brissot, in spite of the bitterness which he had felt toward Dumouriez on account of his part in the fall of the Girondin ministry, promptly took up the cudgels in his behalf, supporting
Dumouriez's policy and defending his motives.[1] And a little
later, when Dumouriez and Pache fell into disagreement, Brissot tried to pour oil on the troubled waters. On December 2,
1792, he wrote to Dumouriez that Pache really believed in his
(Dumouriez's) talents and recognized his success. At the same

[1] *Patriote Français*, October 4, December 3, 1792, and March 1, 1793.

time he exhorted Dumouriez to pay no heed to the calumnies directed against him, but to pursue his course in the conviction that he would be righteously judged by posterity.[1]

Despite the disputes in the management of the war, which led Pache to give only a half-hearted support to the commanders, Dumouriez and the other generals won a series of victories which made France successful from the Scheldt to the Pyrenees. The question was then raised: What attitude should be taken toward the conquered territory? In the excitement of victory the members of the Convention lost their heads, and, while they gave one answer theoretically, practically they gave quite another. On November 19 they set forth in eloquent terms the revolutionary propaganda, asserting that France was ready to carry aid wherever men were seeking to recover their liberty,[2] and yet in almost the same breath they decreed the annexation of Savoy[3] and Nice[4] and the opening of the Scheldt.[5]

What was Brissot's attitude toward this revolutionary propaganda? To spread ideas of liberty had been the object of much of his pre-revolutionary writing and the motive of his numerous schemes for international organizations. He might, therefore, naturally be expected to be in the forefront in pressing a real and immediate liberty upon Europe. Indeed, it has been asserted that he surpassed all his friends in his enthusiasm.[6] This statement, however, does not seem to be borne out,

---

[1] *Correspondance*, 317–18; see also letter of December 9. *Ibid.*, p. 319.

[2] The action was taken on November 19, 1792. See the *Moniteur*, November 20, 1792.

[3] *Moniteur*, November 28, 1792.

[4] *Ibid.*, February 1, 1793. The union had been discussed as early as November 4, 1792.

[5] *Ibid.*, November 22, 1792. It is true that in some instances the inhabitants themselves of the conquered territory petitioned for annexation. It is also true that the Assembly did much to encourage such petitions. Contrary to the accepted idea that the Girondins were the leaders in the movement for annexation, Anacharsis Cloots in his *Ni Marat ni Roland* asserted that they were opposed to it. This assertion, however, is not borne out by their public utterances. See the *Moniteur*, November 20, 1792; also Sorel, *L'Europe et la Révolution française*, iii, 169.

[6] Cahen, *Condorcet*, 439.

at least in his relation to the decree of November 19. When this decree was brought before the Convention, he tried to have it referred to the Diplomatic Committee,[1] and in his newspaper he expressed himself strongly against the general terms in which it was couched and declared that this was a fault which might have been avoided if it had been referred to a committee for greater precision of statement.[2] Later, in his address *A ses Commettans*,[3] and in his *Projet de défense* when criticized for his supposed approval of the decree, he reiterated his former objections to it.[4] His objection at the time the decree was passed was certainly sufficient to warrant his later assertions that he had opposed it, but that opposition seems to have been to its wording rather than to its fundamental principle. At all events, with regard to the decree of December 15, he took the stand which might have been expected of him and expressed himself with enthusiasm. This decree declared that the revolutionary institutions should be carried into all countries occupied by the French Republic and that the sovereignty of the people and the suppression of all existing authorities should be proclaimed. According to Brissot this decree, which was to carry "war to the castle and peace to the cottage," was founded upon great principles. At the same time he tried to reconcile these principles with annexation, by pointing out — what was true only in a limited sense — that it was the desire of neighboring peoples to be united with France.[5]

---

[1] *Moniteur*, November 20, 1792.

[2] "*L'Assemblée rend enfin un décret dont il eût été sans doute plus sage de confier le rédaction à un comité : car il offre une généralité qui serait ridicule, si l'esprit du décret ne le restreignoit pas ; mais il fallait préciser cette restriction : c'est une de ces fautes dans lesquelles les assemblées tomberont toutes les fois qu'elles voudront improviser des délibérations sur des matières importantes et délicates.*" *Patriote Français*, November 20, 1792.

[3] In his address *A ses Commettans* he speaks of "*l'absurde et impolitique décret du 19 novembre, que a justement exité les inquiétudes des cabinets étrangères.*" In a note in the same address he says: "*En vain plusieurs membres en demandaient au moins le renvoi au comité diplomatique, pour rédiger de manière à ne pas blesser les puissances avec lesquelles on était en paix*" (p. 68).

[4] *Mémoires*, II, 307.

[5] "*Au nom des Comités diplomatique, de la guerre et des finances, Cambon*

The existence of opposition among the neighboring peoples to annexation offered to Brissot, however, no legitimate reason why France should refrain from annexation. "We ought not," he declared in regard to the proposed annexation of Savoy, "to pass over in silence a question which has been raised, *viz.*, whether a people whom we have delivered from despotism has the right to submit itself again to its yoke. We believe not. It is with people in society as a whole as with individuals in smaller groups; they are allowed to injure themselves, but not in such a way as to injure others. Now despotism is an evil, not only for the people who submit to it but also for others. People ought no more to be allowed to give themselves despots than individuals to keep serpents; since their neighbors ought not to suffer because of their foolish performances." [1] Nothing could more clearly express the system of liberty which France was to force on her neighbors whether they desired it or not. That, in some cases, their neighbors did not want this liberty, was only too evident, but as M. Sorel remarks, it was to be a choice between "destruction and fraternity." [2]

That the existing benighted authorities had any rights does not seem to have occurred to Brissot. The existing authorities represented despotism, and that was sufficient to deprive them of any claim to consideration. These opinions he developed in a series of reports on the subject of the relations of France to the Swiss cantons and to Geneva. The Swiss had been much irritated by the action of the Assembly in regard to the Swiss troops on account of their part in the events of the 10th of August.[3] They had refused to recognize the provisional gov-

---

fait un rapport sur la conduite que doivent tenir nos généraux à l'égard des peuples dont le territoire est occupé par les armées de la république, et il propose ensuite un projet de décret qu'on peut regarder l'organization du pouvoir révolutionnaire universel. Les grands principes de liberté et de politique, développés par le rapporteur, ont fait d'autant plus d'impression qu'il les a exposés avec cette entraînante naïveté, cette simplicité énergique qui caractérisent l'orateur de la nature lorsqu'il n'est pas corrompu et qu'il ne cherche pas à corrompre." *Patriote Français*, December 17, 1792.

[1] *Patriote Français*, September 30, 1792.

[2] Sorel, *L'Europe et la Révolution française*, III, 106.   [3] *Ibid.*, III, 121-22.

ernment, and when French troops occupied the valley of Porentruy and stirred up the inhabitants against their sovereign,
the bishop of Bâle, the cantons of Berne and Uri made open
protest and demanded the removal of the French troops. This,
Brissot argued, should not be done, as the presence of French
troops there was a measure of self-defense made necessary by
the war with the emperor, and had been provided for by previous treaties; and further, that the bishop of Bâle deserved
little consideration, as he had flagrantly violated treaties made
with France.[1] Brissot's arguments prevailed and the troops
remained. Trouble of a like nature soon arose with Geneva.
Geneva, which was a free imperial city, had in 1558 and 1584
made a perpetual alliance with the cantons of Berne and Zurich. At the time of the democratic revolution in Geneva in
1782, France, Sardinia, and the cantons of Switzerland had
intervened, established an aristocratic constitution, and provided that in case of war Geneva was to be declared neutral.

In September, 1792, the Genevese, frightened at the projects of France, called in support from Berne and Zurich. They
held that they had a right to do this on the ground that the
treaty of 1584 was not set aside by that of 1782. Brissot, in a
report on the subject, October 16, asserted that the treaty of
1584 *was* abrogated and that the Genevese had no right to call
in the troops. But while declaring that the part of the treaty
of 1782 which guaranteed the neutrality of Geneva must be
preserved, he asserted at the same time that the other part of
that treaty, that which guaranteed the aristocratic constitution, must be abandoned as unworthy of the recognition of the
French nation.[2]

Meanwhile, Montesquieu was carrying on negotiations with
Geneva, and on October 22 signed a treaty, by which Geneva
engaged to have the Swiss troops removed by the 1st of the

---

[1] *Moniteur*, October 4, 1792. He made this report in the name of the *Commission extraordinaire*.

[2] *Moniteur*, October 17, 1792. See also Sorel, *L'Europe et la Révolution
française*, III, 122–26.

succeeding January, on condition that the French troops withdraw immediately after the ratification of the treaty. The
agreement, however, had nothing to say of a proscription of the
aristocrats nor of the abrogation of the guaranty of the constitution of 1782. The 2d of November Montesquieu made another report, which, while it included some modifications in the
interests of France, still maintained the constitution of 1782.
For this failure the Convention censured Montesquieu, and on
the motion of the Diplomatic Committee, presented by Brissot
November 21, criticized the terms of the treaties, but at the
same time made the best of the situation by setting forward
the date of the evacuation of Genevese territory, not only by
the French but by the Swiss troops.[1]

While thus contending openly against aristocratic governments in Switzerland, Brissot was privately considering the
situation with regard to Spain. On November 26 he wrote in
most incendiary terms to Servan that it was necessary to declare war on Spain; that there would not be peaceful liberty for
France so long as there was a Bourbon on the throne;[2] and that
in order to assure the triumph of the Revolution and the defeat
of its enemies, Europe must be set on fire. Meantime Spanish
America must be aroused.[3] To accomplish this purpose Brissot set actively to work. He first entered into negotiations
with a young Spaniard, Marchena by name, with the idea of
stirring up revolutionary propaganda in Spain.[4] He next
turned his attention to the Spanish possessions in the new
world. The outcome of the latter undertaking was the proposed expedition of Genet to drive the Spaniards from the
Mississippi. Ever since his American travels, Brissot had been

[1] *Moniteur*, November 22, 1792.

[2] Note particularly the same expression in his letter to Dumouriez of November 28, 1792. *Correspondance*, 314.

[3] Letter to Servan, November 26, 1792. Collection Charavay; printed by
Perroud in the *Correspondance*, 312. Mallet du Pan, in his *Considérations sur la
nature de la Révolution de France*, 37, quotes from this letter. See also Brissot's
letters to Dumouriez of November 28, December 2, and 9, 1792; *Correspondance*, 314–20.

[4] See pp. 360–61; also Goetz-Bernstein, 323.

keenly interested in the western development of the United States; he had written of it at length in his *Nouveau Voyage*, had tried to advance various schemes for the sale of lands, and had been ready to risk financial investments.[1] He was now consulted as an authority on the subject, and on January 25, 1792, he was asked by the Committee of General Defense to report on the possibility of an expedition against the Spanish dependencies.[2] That there was abundant prospect of success in such an expedition he was thoroughly convinced, especially in view of the hostile attitude of the western settlers toward Spain. As to the best means of procedure, he consulted with the members of his party, as well as with Thomas Paine and the Americans whom he often met at Paine's house. His own plan seems to have been to make use of Miranda and thirty thousand troops from Santo Domingo to aid in securing the independence of Louisiana.[3] In his letter to Servan, referred to above, he spoke of Miranda's courage and genius and expressed the belief that it would be an easy matter for him to free the inhabitants of the western lands from the chains forged for them by Pizarro and Cortez.[4] It was finally decided to send Genet, an appointment for which Brissot himself was responsible.[5] Hitherto Genet's chief mission has been considered to be his efforts to fit out privateers for France and to enlist enthusiasm for his cause through popular societies; but its real importance lay in the plans by which he proposed, through the help of American frontiersmen, to wrest Louisiana from the

---

[1] See chap. IV.

[2] Aulard, *Recueil des actes de la Comité de Salut public*, II, 10, and III, 82.

[3] *Lettre à Dumouriez*, December 2, 1792; *Correspondance*, 317. See also article by Turner cited below.

[4] *Lettre à Servan*, November 26, 1792; again in *Correspondance*, 312–13. See also Brissot's own letter to Miranda dated November 11, 1792; *Correspondance*, 303–04.

[5] Otto, a former secretary in the foreign office, declared in 1797 that it was Brissot who proposed Genet as minister to the United States. (Turner, *American Historical Review*, III, 654.) See also the statement of Brissot at his trial, the *Interrogatoire*. Madame Roland makes the same assertion in *Mémoires*, I, 265–66.

hands of their common enemy and thus benefit France.[1] The persistent neutrality of the United States, however, and the fall of the Girondins at home led to Genet's recall and to the failure of an expedition which was important in its inception and origin, if not in its results.

The Genet affair had been managed by the Committee of General Defense. This committee came into existence early in 1793, on account of the growing complexity of foreign affairs, and soon began to perform the functions formerly exercised by the Diplomatic Committee. It was composed of members from several different committees and included Brissot as a representative of the Diplomatic Committee. Under its direction was carried out some of the most important work undertaken by the Convention; the army and ministry of war were reorganized, many places on the frontier were annexed and extraordinary powers were granted to the deputies on mission.[2]

With the conquest of Belgium had come the opening of the Scheldt.[3] England and Holland had been especially exasperated

---

[1] Frederick J. Turner, "The Origin of Genet's Projected Attack on Louisiana and the Floridas," in the *American Historical Review*, July, 1898, III, 650–71. Also "Documents on the Relations of France to Louisiana," 1792–1795, *American Historical Review*, April, 1898, III, 490–516. See also *Instructions to Genet*, December, 1792; in *Correspondence of French Ministers, 1791–1798*, ed. by Frederick J. Turner; *Annual Report of the American Historical Association*, 1903, II, 201–07.

[2] This Committee of General Defense was organized in accordance with a decree passed by the Assembly, January 1, 1793. It met for the first time January 4. The three sessions a week which it had arranged to hold proving insufficient for the amount of work to be transacted, daily sessions — sometimes even two sessions a day — became necessary. From January 4 to March 26, when it was reorganized, twenty-four sessions were recorded. To the reorganized committee Brissot was not elected. His work in relation to foreign affairs belongs, therefore, to the early months of the Convention. It is to be noted in passing that the Committee of General Defense was the forerunner of the great Committee of Public Safety, and the powers granted to it distinctly foreshadowed the powers afterwards granted to that committee. In this connection it is interesting to realize that Brissot, the man of all others who is often thought to have been opposed to the whole order and policy of the Committee of Public Safety, was one of the most important members of its predecessor. Aulard, *Recueil des actes de Comité de Salut public*, I, 389, 401.

[3] Proclaimed by the French ministers, November 16, 1792. See *Moniteur*, November 22, 1792.

by this action, and with reason. For this river had been closed
to seagoing vessels by the treaty of Münster and also by subsequent treaties, with the object of diverting trade from Antwerp to Amsterdam, and thus benefiting the Dutch, and it had
remained closed ever since 1648. If it were now made a free
river, both London and Amsterdam would suffer loss of trade
which would instead go to enrich Antwerp and with Antwerp
all Belgium. In his plan of defense before the revolutionary
tribunal, Brissot disclaimed having had anything to do with
this decree. It was ordered, he declared, by the executive
council without informing the Diplomatic Committee. At the
time, however, the *Patriote Français* spoke of the action with
enthusiasm, alluding to the noble destiny of France "to undo
everywhere the errors of the people and the crimes of despots." [1]

In whatever light it may have appeared to French enthu-
siasts, this "undoing of the crimes of despots" seemed to Europe an unwarrantable interference on the part of France in
the affairs of her neighbors. It was deeply resented by England
especially and was one of the causes of the war between England and France. In bringing on this war Brissot, it was alleged, had a large share — a charge which he vehemently denied. In his *Projet de défense* before the revolutionary tribunal,
he declared that both as a representative of the people and as
a citizen he had on the contrary done everything in his power
to prevent that war.[2] There is much truth in his claim, at
least as far as his attitude up to the king's trial is concerned,
but at the same time that he was talking about peace and an
alliance, he was furthering those very measures — such as the
annexations and the opening of the Scheldt — which were making war inevitable. Ever since the spring of 1792, when war
was declared against Prussia and Austria, he had been closely
connected, both through his relation to the Girondin ministry
and his membership in the Diplomatic Committee, with efforts
to secure, first, the alliance, and when that seemed no longer

[1] *Patriote Français,* November 22, 1792.   [2] *Mémoires,* ii, 308.

possible, the neutrality, of England. It was he, moreover, who together with Condorcet recommended the young Julien, who was sent to England early in the autumn of 1792 to disseminate correct information as to the situation in France, in order that war might be prevented.[1]

To prevent foreign war was, indeed, the chief ground of his argument for an appeal to the people at the time of the king's trial. The opinion that Europe was coming to take of the French Revolution, he declared, in a speech before the Convention on January 1, was not sufficiently heeded. Foreign governments would only welcome the condemnation of the king by the Convention, because it would give them the chance, which they would eagerly seize, to stir up popular feeling against the government of France. Again, there was danger that if the Convention itself made the decision, it might be accused of corruption if it were lenient to the king; of cruelty, if it were severe. The judgment of the people, on the other hand, would be sure to be just, impartial, and free from all foreign influence. Also it would show to foreign powers that the Convention was not influenced by sudden emotion, but by lofty and just principles, and, moreover, that back of the Convention was a united nation. If, therefore, the judgment of death should be pronounced, there would be less probability of war if the nation made the decision than if the Convention made it alone.[2]

Within two weeks Brissot spoke again on the war question, this time in behalf of the Committee of General Defense and in a somewhat different tone. It was a lengthy and eloquent argument that the complaints of the British government against France were not well founded, and that, on the contrary, France had just complaints to make against Great Britain and ought to take vigorous measures to repel her aggres-

---

[1] See letters of Brissot, September 15, 1792, and letter of Julien, September 19, 1792. *Affaires étrangères, Angleterre*, p. 582, f. 143; Sorel, *L'Europe et la Révolution française*, III, 141, and *Correspondance*, 299.

[2] *Moniteur*, January 3, 1793.

sion. England withdrew her ambassador after August 10, he complained. She ought to have reinstated her ambassador after the meeting of the Convention, for the action of the Convention was the sanction by all France of the deeds of the Legislative Assembly. England, moreover, had taken measures against the grain trade of France and against her assignats, and at the same time, she was not allowing Frenchmen free entry into England, and was protecting French rebels and increasing her armament. As for the complaints of England against France, the invasion of Savoy was made necessary by the hostile preparations of the king, and the annexation of Savoy was the desire of its people; and in the same way the invasion of the Low Countries was justified. If France interfered in aiding the Belgians to secure their rights, the English held Holland under the yoke of the Stadtholder. The opening of the Scheldt, he admitted, was a violation of the Peace of Utrecht and of other treaties, but it was not a violation of the principles of eternal justice. The English people did not really want war and ought to be made to understand that France did not either, but that she was being forced into it by the attitude of the English government. And finally, if worse came to worst England was not ready for war. Since the war with America she had been obliged to increase her taxes enormously and was in no position to add to them further by another war.

This speech Brissot closed by presenting the decrees drawn up by the Committee. The first of these, by its declaration of the desire to preserve harmony and fraternity with the English nation, and of intention to respect the independence of England and of her allies as long as they did not attack France, seemed to tend toward peace and to give point to Brissot's contention in his plan of defense that he did not want war and was endeavoring to prevent it.[1] The remaining propositions of the decree were, however, of a decidedly belligerent tone. The executive council was charged to ask of the English government the execution of article IV of the treaty of 1786; in

---

[1] *Mémoires*, ii, 308.

other words, to allow French citizens to reside and travel in England without the humiliating restrictions to which they had been subjected. The executive council was also to ask that Frenchmen, like other foreigners, be allowed to export grain freely from England (in accordance with the provisions of the treaty of 1786); and finally to demand a categorical answer from England as to the object of its recent armament; it being understood that if this armament were directed against France, and if the English government did not give satisfaction on all the points specified, the French government would immediately take the measures which the interest and security of the Republic demanded — in other words — declare war.[1]

Although Brissot subsequently protested that he was speaking here not for himself but for the Committee, the very fact that he gave the report and in no way protested against it lays upon him the responsibility for it. There exists, moreover, a good reason for greater belligerency on his part just at this juncture. This evidence is a letter addressed to Brissot by G. Martin, dated December 31, 1792, and apparently sent from London. The writer appears to be an agent working in the interest of France. At all events, he sends off a message posthaste to Brissot that he has just learned through a trustworthy source that there has been dispatched from London to the three courts of Berlin, Vienna, and St. Petersburg a most important note. In this note, the writer asserts, they are urged to instruct their ambassadors and agents at London to concert together immediately on plans for military operations; they are assured that there will be no trouble about subsidies, and Russia is exhorted to furnish sixty thousand troops. They are further informed that public opinion is becoming favorable to the war, and further that the approaching "catastrophe" of Louis XVI, which may be regarded as certain, will be all that is necessary to arouse public opinion to energetic action.[2]

---

[1] *Moniteur*, January 15, 1793.

[2] *Affaires étrangères, Angleterre*, 29 Supplement, 340. See Appendix A. It is true that just at this time Lord Grenville began to negotiate with foreign

This letter, which Brissot could hardly have received before January 1, and which in the natural course of events he would have received before January 12, the date of his speech, is most significant, and is in itself enough to account for his change of view. That war was now inevitable, he was convinced. He was, therefore, ready to take measures to bring about its open declaration.

The question of war was complicated by the trial of Louis XVI. That the king should be tried, and tried by the Convention, both parties agreed, and contrary to the once accepted opinion, the Girondins took an active part in urging on the proceedings. On November 6, Valazé made a report setting forth the crimes of the king, and the next day Mailhe in the name of the Committee on Legislation presented a report, arguing that the king could and should be tried by the Convention. Brissot thoroughly approved of this report and gave a lengthy *résumé* of it in the *Patriote Français*.[1] That he should approve was only to be expected, considering his own denunciations of the king at various times, and especially his speech of July, 1791, on the responsibility of the king, in which he argued along much the same line as Mailhe. The decree proposed by Mailhe was enacted and the trial began. After long debate the questions involved were finally narrowed down to three: Was Louis guilty of conspiring against the nation? Should the judgment be subject to the sanction of the people? What should be the penalty?

On the first question, Brissot, with the great majority of the deputies, simply voted "yes."[2] On the second question he had already expressed his views in his long and forcible speech of

powers as to the conditions under which a common war might be waged against France. (See Lord Grenville to Lord Whitworth, Herrmann, *Diplomatische Korrespondenzen*, pp. 346–48; also Lord Grenville to M. le Comte de Woronzow, December 28, 1792, British Museum, additional mss. 36814.) There is, however, no evidence of such definite propositions as those alleged. But whether the writer was correctly informed is not so important to the point at issue as that he communicated such a statement to Brissot.

[1] *Patriote Français*, November 8 and 9, 1792.

[2] *Procès-verbal de la Convention*, volume for January, 1793, p. 212.

January 1, in which he had argued for the appeal to the people, chiefly on account of the effect it would have on the powers of Europe in making foreign war less probable. On this occasion he did not reiterate his former argument, but, as on the previous question, simply voted "yes." [1]

In spite of the efforts of Brissot and others of the same mind, 424 members out of 767 voted against the appeal to the people. Brissot deeply regretted this decision, and on the third question — What should be the penalty? — he voted for death, but made an effort to secure postponement. Now that it had actually come to the question of the execution of the king, he saw with renewed vividness the consequences. A few days before he had been ready to force the issue by demanding a categorical answer from England as to her intentions, and by so doing to throw the onus for commencing the war upon her. Now the execution of the king would, on the contrary, give ground to foreign nations for action and would throw the onus of war on France. This he was determined to prevent. "I see in the sentence of death," he declared, "the signal for a terrible war, a war which will cost my country a prodigious amount of blood and treasure." He therefore sought some other form of punishment, a punishment which would unite as completely as possible justice and the interest of the public welfare, which would make the Convention respected by all parties, which would conciliate foreign nations, which would frighten tyrants, and would at the same time thwart the calculations of their cabinets, all of whom desired the death of Louis because they wanted to popularize the war. This punishment he found in the sentence of death, but with the suspension of execution till after the ratification of the constitution by the people. [2] On this vote, Brissot was again in a minority, the majority having voted for death.

One more attempt, however, was made to secure delay, and in this Brissot used all his efforts. That such an attempt might

---

[1] *Procès-verbal de la Convention*, volume for January, 1793, f. 212. See also *Moniteur*, January 19, 1793.   [2] *Moniteur*, January 20, 1793.

easily give rise to suspicion of royalty, he was evidently aware, for he began his speech by protesting that he was actuated not by any desire to save the king from the just consequences of his deeds, but to further the best political interests of France. The immediate execution of the king, he declared, would not further those interests, but would, on the contrary, eliminate a number of the friends of France, and increase the number of her enemies. In fact, there would be danger of a universal war. "I say more," he continued, speaking with a frankness and a realization of the danger which he had not shown before, "you have not a moment to lose in preventing it. If Louis is executed, it will be necessary to declare war to-morrow against England, Holland, and Spain, against all the tyrants of Europe; because it is inevitable on their part, not so much because they will be irritated by the death of Louis, but because all these tyrants, resolved as they are to crush our liberty, and with our liberty that of all Europe, will believe that they have found in that death a pretext in the eyes of their people. Now are you ready for this universal war? . . . Although there is every-where great disorder in our armies, although by reason of a conspiracy of which we must soon know the source, you have not even a few thousand soldiers on the Pyrenees, where at this moment there ought to be more than forty thousand French-men protecting the tri-colored flag; yet let our liberty be com-promised and you will see springing up everywhere, as out of the ground, armies, treasures, and soldiers. But to make war for a single individual! Ought we to risk the entire exhaustion of our finances, the loss of our colonies, the enervation of our commerce? Ought we to waste so much treasure and blood for a most contemptible man?" [1]

In spite of all pleas for delay, the king was condemned and executed. Brissot made no further efforts to avoid war, but

[1] *Moniteur*, January 24, 1792. During the trial the reports of the meetings of the Convention were signed by Girey-Dupré, who wrote in explanation: "*Brissot est son juge, comme représentant du peuple; il ne faut pas qu'il soit soupçonné de le juger comme journaliste.*"

instead renewed his demands for hostilities with England, declaring that war was now inevitable, but laying on England the blame for it. And on February 1, 1793, on the motion of the Committee of General Security, presented by Brissot, the Convention declared war on England and Holland.[1] For a return to his previous position, Brissot was in a measure justified. War had indeed become inevitable, but it was not only the execution of the king but the whole aggressive policy of France that had made it so, and it was Brissot who, as a Girondin, had largely directed that policy.[2]

This propaganda of political equality, which was resulting in war, had, as M. Jaurès points out in his *Histoire socialiste*, turned thought more and more to questions of social equality. "As political equality," says M. Jaurès, "became a more certain fact, it was social inequality which gave most offense. The Revolution, by the death of the king, by the universal war, assumed growing responsibilities for humanity. How could it meet these responsibilities if it did not demonstrate to all men that it truly desired the good of all, and that without leveling conditions it wished at least to assure the independence and the well-being of the entire people." [3] In this question, Brissot was keenly interested. He had realized the suspicion to which the advocates of equality would be exposed — that of being hostile to the right of property. Indeed, he had already been attacked on that ground and had vigorously defended himself. But while upholding the right of property, he was intensely democratic in his sympathies, both politically and

---

[1] *Moniteur*, February 2, 1793. For an account of the English point of view see Rose, *William Pitt and the Great War*.

[2] The Girondins meanwhile had been engaged in drawing up a constitution. Curiously enough, considering his interest in constitution-making, Brissot seems to have had very little to do with the preparation of this one. He was appointed a member of the committee entrusted with the work, but his place was soon taken by Barbaroux. Aulard, *Histoire politique*, 280. M. Aulard does not state his authority. While a member of this committee Brissot managed to have his friend, David Williams (see p. 25), invited to come over to France to aid in drawing up the constitution. Brissot, *Correspondance*, 305–06.

[3] Jaurès, *Histoire socialiste*, v, 1012–15.

socially. His democratic point of view is well summed up in an article in the *Patriote Français* of December 28, 1792, entitled *L'Égalité de fait*. In every democracy, he argued, the laws ought to destroy and prevent too great *de facto* inequality between citizens. At the same time institutions favorable to equality ought to be introduced without commotion, without violence, and with all due respect for the first of the social rights, property. "The division of land proposed by the anarchists," he continued, "or the Coblenziens, would be a fatal measure; it would be unjust, useless, and murderous: unjust, in that it would despoil the legitimate owners; useless, because the next day after the division, the indolence, the luxury of the majority would bring about again, by means of sales, the inequality of possession; murderous, in that before the division was finished, citizens would cut each others' throats; in that, again, all industry would be extinguished and that within a little while millions of citizens would perish of famine and misery."

There were other measures, he went on, which were less dangerous and at the same time more conducive to real equality. Aside from equality of inheritance between children, which he assumed was beyond question, he would propose the abolition of all inheritance in the collateral line. Property bequeathed in this way should revert to the state and should be distributed every year, in each district, to virtuous and industrious young people. There would be no injustice in this measure, he argued. To allow a man, during his lifetime, to use his property as he pleased was just, but to permit him to control it after his death was most unjust. The rights and duties of man derived their origin from the needs of the human race; a man after his death, having no more needs, could have no more rights. That a logical application of this principle would lead to the abolition of all inheritance, Brissot admitted. It was true that children were allowed to inherit the property of their fathers only by a concession of society, but since the relation between father and child was peculiarly intimate, it was a concession which society might legitimately make. The abolition of inheritance in the collateral line need therefore arouse no fear, in the minds of the cautious, of an abolition of all inheritance.

As a second step toward equality, Brissot proposed to exempt from all taxation what was necessary for the physical life of every citizen. Humanity and equity, he declared, cried aloud for such a law. Taxes should be borne by the rich; should touch only factitious needs; they should not be laid on physical necessities. The result of such a reform would be less unhappiness, less inequality.[1]

But while thus engaged in trying to further social readjustment in the interests of democracy, Brissot saw its dangers, especially when it came to practical application. In the hands of real patriots, among whom he included himself, he was convinced that democracy would not be in any respect harmful, but under the influence of interested and unscrupulous leaders, the people might easily be flattered into an undue sense of their own importance and led into excess. In fact, this had already occurred, he declared, and in an article entitled "*De la marche des agitateurs*," published in the *Chronique du Mois* of January, 1793, he tried to throw the responsibility for popular discontent upon his opponents. There was a division among the patriots, he asserted; they had fought together against royalty, but they had not the same principles. The one party "sees in the new revolution the overturning of royalty, the establishment of the republic, and in the republic the perfection of human reason, the restitution of the worthy poor to a life of comfort; they see in it a perfect equality of rights, but an equality based upon law, upon respect for property and security, upon submission to constituted authority. That is not the idea of men who, despite the fact that they possess neither talent nor virtue, dare to aspire to high position and are filled with ambition."

A striking instance of the application of theories of equality had occurred in the case of the workmen who were engaged on

---

[1] *Patriote Français*, December 29, 1792, quoted in Jaurès, *Histoire socialiste*, IV, 1010–15.

the camp for the *fédérés* at Paris. It was also a striking instance, according to Brissot, of the pernicious influence of the agitators. Under what was the virtual dictation of unscrupulous persons, these unfortunate workmen had presented a petition in which they had compared the smallness of their pay with the enormous compensation accorded to the deputies of the Convention, and had demanded that, as they both were working for the nation, their salaries should be adjusted more equitably.[1] But, although Brissot decidedly disapproved of these specific demands, he was in favor, as is evident from his proposals cited above, of greater equalization of classes.

But at the same time he was for equalization only in so far as it could be brought about without injuring the rights of any one class. For instance, apropos of a special war tax which it was proposed to lay on the rich, the *Patriote Français*[2] remarked with regret that there would be no more equality, since the taxes would no longer be the same for all in proportion to their ability to pay,[3] and a few days later the editor proposed, as a substitute, the principle of progressive taxation. Again, the *Patriote Français* approved the opposition of Barbaroux and Buzot to the forced loan of two hundred million francs from the rich,[4] and denounced the law of the maximum as involving an attack on the rights of property.[5]

It may be objected that this hostile attitude on the part of the Girondins was actuated, not so much by the nature of the measures proposed as by the fact that they were proposed by their enemies — the Mountain. This does not seem to have been true, however, in their attitude at first — whatever it may have been a few weeks later — toward the establishment of the

[1] *Patriote Français*, October 6, 1792.

[2] Brissot had by this time been forced to abandon the editorship of the *Patriote Français*, but there is no doubt that it continued to represent his policy.

[3] *Patriote Français*, March 11, 1792.

[4] *Ibid.*, May 22, 1793. See also Gomel, *Histoire financière de la Convention*, I, 485–88.

[5] *Patriote Français*, April 29, May 1, 1793.

agencies of the Terror. The *Patriote Français*, though it objected to the publicity of the votes of the jurors and the severity of the rules regulating it, offered no persistent opposition to the establishment of the revolutionary tribunal,[1] and of the establishment of the Committee of Public Safety it spoke with indifference.[2] The agencies by which the government was to be carried on seemed less important to the contending parties than did the agents, and neither party in the eyes of the other was fit to be trusted with the reins of government, — the Mountain because they were demagogues and anarchists, the Girondins because they were federalists and royalists. And now that the war problem was becoming more critical, the struggle, which had been going on since the opening of the Convention but which had been less bitter during the discussion on foreign relations and the king's trial, was renewed with violence and became a combat to the death, with no quarter.

In this combat, Brissot was one of the most active fighters. Early in February, a special attack was made on him based on a letter in the possession of the Committee of General Security, said to be signed "Brissot de Warville" and containing distinctly royalist sentiments. Brissot defended himself in his paper, declaring that he had not signed himself "Brissot de Warville" since June 19, 1791,[3] and on February 15, he reiterated his defense before the Convention. The letter, he asserted, was found among the papers of one of the committees of the Commune, was originally signed "Watteville," and some malicious person had changed "Watteville" to "Warville" and had prefixed "Brissot de." How it had come into the hands of the Committee of General Security he did not know. To this defense Bazire replied that the letter did not come from the Commune, but that it was discovered among the papers of Laporte; that the original signature was "Brissot de Warville"; that the whole signature was evidently written by the same hand and at the same time and with the same ink, and that an

---

[1] *Patriote Français*, March 12, 13, 1793.   [2] *Ibid.*, March 28, 1793.
[3] *Ibid.*, February 11, 1793.

effort had been made to erase it. After a violent dispute Brissot won a temporary victory, by securing the passage of a decree which instead of deciding the matter at once referred it to a committee for investigation.[1]

A few weeks later, the Mountain made a general onslaught on the Girondin newspapers. Jeanbon Saint-André led the attack by his speech on March 8. "On the pretext of an apparent impartiality," he declared, "like the iron bed of the old tyrant, they stretch out or mutilate to suit their taste the opinions which are set forth at the tribune. They cut the ideas of the members who displease them in order to favor one side and to present the other under the most unfavorable light. They mislead public opinion, they cruelly abuse the liberty which we accord to the press." [2] As a result of this speech it was decreed the following day "that members of the Convention who conduct newspapers must choose between the profession of journalist and that of representative of the people." [3] Brissot chose the second alternative, and from this time the *Patriote Français* was conducted under the direction of Girey-Dupré. But, although Brissot's nominal connection with the paper ceased, it continued to represent his views and to be an organ of the Girondin party.[4]

Meanwhile the failure of Dumouriez's campaign in Belgium had aroused the mob of Paris, and on March 9 they led a popular movement against the Girondins, which was the prelude of the events of May 31 and June 1. Brissot, on hearing the news, rushed off to warn the ministers of what was going on.[5] He had reason to be alarmed; for the mob, not content with the decree of the Convention against the Girondin newspapers, took the matter into their own hands and began to break the

---

[1] *Moniteur*, February 17, 1793. See also *Procès-verbal de la Convention*, volume for February, p. 246.

[2] *Moniteur*, March 10, 1793.   [3] *Ibid.*, March 11, 1793.

[4] According to the testimony of Girey-Dupré at the trial of Marat, Brissot carefully observed the law and never furnished him with any material to be inserted in the *Patriote Français*. *Bulletin du tribunal révolutionnaire*, no. 17.

[5] Louvet, *Mémoires*, ed. by Aulard, I, 77.

presses. It might naturally be supposed that the *Patriote Français* would be one of the first attacked, but for some reason, never clearly explained, it escaped and the whole movement failed.[1] But the attacks on the Girondins did not cease. Under the incentive of the Cordeliers, several of the sections of Paris denounced the Girondins to the Convention. "The evacuation of Belgium," their address declared, "is the work of an impious faction which paralyzes the Convention. The success of the enemies of France is due to the traitor Dumouriez and to the odious intrigues of the Rolands, the Brissotins, and their friends, — they ought to be gotten rid of at any price."[2]

Danton was the one man who tried with any zeal to check denunciations and substitute conciliation. He first tried to bring about greater unity of action by introducing a proposition in the Assembly on March 11, that the ministers should be chosen from that body. This to the Girondins seemed merely a move toward a dictatorship. "They [the Mountain] believed," wrote the *Patriote Français*, "that it only remained to ascend the throne, they are already dividing up among them the various branches of the executive power — Danton mounted the tribune, sure of his success; he asked that the Convention reserve to itself the right of choosing the ministers from among its own members. No one doubted that Danton wished to be first of those ministers; they doubted it still less when they heard him swear by his country that he would never accept a place in the ministry. Danton swearing by the country! The country of an ambitious man! It seems to me like an atheist swearing by the Supreme Being."[3]

At the same time Danton tried to come to some agreement with the Girondins. In the case of Garat, the minister of justice, who, though not of the inner circle, had been allied with

---

[1] Brissot in *A ses Commettans* assailed Garat, the minister of justice and a former ally of the Girondins, for not having taken steps against the conspirators.

[2] Mortimer Ternaux, *Histoire de la Terreur*, VI. 194.

[3] *Patriote Français*, March 18, 1793.

them, he seems to have met with some response. "I was always saying to the members of the two sides," writes Garat in his memoirs, "drown your hatred and your quarrels, and then you can manage everything and all will be done according to law."[1] According to Marat, Guadet also wanted conciliation and tried to flatter Danton, but all other authorities agree that it was Guadet who refused to make peace. The *Patriote Français*, now under the direction of Girey-Dupré, denied with heat the assertion that Guadet had tried to flatter Danton and declared, on the contrary, that Guadet had attacked Danton as a plotter and intriguer.[2] Brissot was also approached and, according to his testimony at his trial, he was quite willing to discuss the matter. "Several times there was a question of reunion among the patriots," he testified. "To that end I had two meetings with Danton. Robespierre had been invited to join us, but he did not come. We entered into an explanation of our principles. Danton said to me: 'We fear only one thing so far as you are concerned, that you are in favor of federalism.' I had no difficulty at all in proving to him that that fear had little ground, and we separated each satisfied with the other."[3] Brissot's attitude as reflected in these remarks appears to be rather favorable to conciliation, but it is to be observed that here he was chiefly concerned in disproving the charge of federalism. In his address to his constituents, he took a decidedly different tone and apropos of Garat's willingness to join in conciliation, spoke with vehemence of the impossibility of "establishing a permanent alliance between virtue and crime."

At all events, Danton's attempt came to naught, and when to the failure of the campaign in Belgium was added the actual treason and flight of Dumouriez, conciliation was no longer possible. Instead, the battle between the Girondins and the Mountain was waged with redoubled fury. The Mountain,

---

[1] Garat, *Mémoires sur la Révolution*, 94.
[2] *Patriote Français*, March 24, 1793.
[3] *Moniteur*, October 27, 1793, Supplement.

wild with rage, declared that Dumouriez and the Girondins had formed a vast conspiracy to restore monarchy in France and to annihilate the republicans with the Republic. On the 3d of April, Robespierre specifically charged Brissot with being implicated in the diabolical plot. "Brissot," argued the "Incorruptible," "was and is the intimate friend of Dumouriez; Brissot has never lost an occasion for defending Dumouriez; Brissot and Dumouriez together first proposed the war with Austria; Brissot and his partisans made Dumouriez commander-in-chief; Brissot holds in his hands all the threads of this wicked conspiracy. The first measure of public safety to be taken is to indict all those who are accused of complicity with Dumouriez and notably Brissot." To this attack Brissot replied on the spot, but his defense lacked cogency and ingenuousness. He denied *in toto* that he had assisted in any way in procuring Dumouriez's appointment to the ministry, and he threw the blame for the war upon the Legislative Assembly, ignoring his own part both in that body and in the Convention as an advocate of war. In his reply to the accusation of wishing to reestablish the monarchy, he omitted to mention his attitude at the crisis of the Revolution, but based his defense upon a part of his career which in no way affected existing events. "Can a man be accused of loving kings," he asked, "who was devoted to republicanism a long time before his accuser; a man who in 1782 was shut up in the Bastille for having put forth principles then frowned upon; a man who in 1788 quitted his country to go to the United States to breathe the air of liberty, and especially to prevent his children from being contaminated by the presence of a tyrant?"

The charge of treasonable complicity with Dumouriez had no real ground, but the Girondins and Brissot in particular had been in friendly relations with Dumouriez, and his desertion furnished the Mountain with exactly what they needed for a telling accusation. Only a few days before his desertion, the *Patriote Français* had praised him to the skies, and at the same time cast aspersions on the motives of the Jacobins for speaking of him with high praise. "That faction thinks," declared the *Patriote Français*, "that by unworthy flatteries it can win over to its side a man whom it fears. It flatters him because the heroes of the 2d of September do not dare to measure themselves up against the hero of the 20th of September. But this is an idle hope. Dumouriez is not going to mingle his laurels with their cypress. Dumouriez loves glory, he would not be willing to share their infamy. Dumouriez loves his country, he will save it in company with the republicans, he will not destroy it in company with the anarchists."[1] After such an outburst on the part of the *Patriote Français*, the desertion of Dumouriez was a staggering blow to the Girondins.

The opportunity was too good to be lost, and was seized by the Mountain and their adherents in the Commune. On April 8 the section of Bonconseil sent a delegation to the Convention, demanding that Brissot and his adherents be brought to trial. A few days later, Robespierre furiously attacked the Girondins, while Vergniaud, Guadet, and Pétion repelled the assault and hurled back the accusation of bad faith and treasonable intent.[2] Henceforth the struggle between the parties became more violent. The Girondins assailed Marat as the most vulnerable of their enemies and concentrated their attacks upon him. Considering the nature of his assaults on members of their party, they had good reason for indignation. For instance, such an attack as appeared in the *Ami du Peuple* of February 12, 1793, would naturally arouse their wrath: "Persons who are well informed state that Brissot is enormously rich, in spite of the airs of poverty which he affects. He is said to have invested eight hundred thousand livres in the Bank of London, and it is stated as an established fact that his wife has just acquired three fine houses in the best quarter of London."[3]

---

[1] *Patriote Français*, March 12, 1793.   [2] *Moniteur*, April 12, 1793.

[3] "*Les personnes instruites assurent que Brissot est énormement riche, malgré les airs de pauvreté qu'il affiche. Il passe pour avoir placé 800,000 livres sur la banque de Londres, et on donne pour un fait constant que sa femme vient de faire l'acquisition de trois belles maisons dans le plus beau quartier de Londres.*" *L'Ami du Peuple*, February 12, 1793.

The Girondins still possessed a majority in the Convention, and on April 13, by almost superhuman efforts, they carried a vote sending Marat before the revolutionary tribunal for trial.[1] Marat immediately retaliated, and in a letter to the Convention denounced "Dumouriez and his accomplices" in the Convention itself, — namely, Salle, Barbaroux, Gensonné, Larousse, Brissot, Guadet, Buzot, and Vergniaud, — for having demanded a decree of accusation against him. He declared, further, that he would regard the decree rendered against him as legitimate only when a like decree should be rendered against those whom he accused, and that only then would he obey the decree which put him under arrest.[2] Brissot, on his part, apparently could not let Marat alone. One of the witnesses at the trial of Marat had testified that a notice had appeared in the *Patriote Français* of April 16 to the effect that a young Englishman, who had lately come to France in order that he might enjoy the liberty there established, had committed suicide when he found that Marat had destroyed that liberty. Girey-Dupré, the editor of the *Patriote Français*, was then questioned and admitted that he had received the note from Brissot, but that the responsibility for its insertion in the *Patriote Français* was his own.[3] An attempt was then made to bring Brissot before the tribunal, but, although a note was sent to the president of the Convention, demanding that Brissot be summoned to give testimony, the Convention paid no attention to it and Brissot did not testify. The Girondins, meanwhile, waited with supreme confidence Marat's conviction. Their disappointment and dejection were correspondingly great when the tribunal acquitted Marat and the rabble bore him back in triumph to the Convention.

This was a decisive blow to the Girondins. At the same time they received another blow — an address from the sections of Paris demanding the dismissal of twenty-two Girondin members of the Convention, Brissot's name heading the list of the

---

[1] *Moniteur*, April 16, 1793.   [2] *Archives parlementaires*, LXII, 23–24.
[3] *Bulletin du tribunal révolutionnaire*, nos. 16, 17.

proscribed. This address, as well as the denunciations which Robespierre had made in his speech a few days before, Brissot hastened to answer. At the head of his pamphlet of defense, he placed a quotation from Rousseau as summarizing his own position: "I am growing old in the midst of my furious enemies, without losing either courage or patience. My only defense is to present to heaven a heart free from guile and from all evil." He then launched into a general defense, which in its efforts to throw the blame on others was hardly in keeping with the lofty tone of his text. Whatever the accusation, it was not he himself who was guilty. It was not he who had chosen Dumouriez for the ministry, it was Pétion who had recommended Miranda, it was the Convention which was responsible for the war. It was true, he admitted, that he had sustained Dumouriez as long as he had shown good principles, but since May, 1792, he had written to him only twice.[1] As for complicity with Orléans, he had advised him through Sillery to banish himself voluntarily, and had voted for his expulsion. The charge, moreover, that he had been suborned by Pitt, either to maintain the king upon the throne or to save his life, was absolutely without foundation. It was not the king but France he was trying to save. And finally, the charge of leadership on his part was, he declared, not only false but ridiculous.[2]

However true his assertions may be in the main, this last statement hardly seems consistent with his well-known activities and shows a not altogether courageous desire to sink into the background.

The acquittal of Marat and the denunciations of the sections to which the above was an answer mark the beginning of the end. Paris was now all but unanimous against the Girondins. The situation was one which demanded desperate reme-

---

[1] M. Perroud, in his *Correspondance de Brissot,* 314-20, gives three letters written by Brissot to Dumouriez within this time.

[2] *J. P. Brissot, député à la Convention, sur la dénonciation de Robespierre et sur l'adresse prêtée aux quarante-huit sections de Paris.*

dies. The Girondins decided to stake all upon a single throw, and on May 18 Guadet presented a motion that the Commune be dissolved and that the substitute delegates to the Convention be summoned to meet at Bourges. But, at the critical moment, the Girondins lost heart and abandoned their own motion for a substitute motion offered by Barère, ordering the appointment of a committee of twelve which should report on the safety of the Convention. In the composition of this committee, they won a temporary success, for all its members were Girondins, but it was not a permanent victory.

This demand for an appeal to the provinces and for the election of a new Convention gave strength to the accusation of federalism which had already been hurled at the Girondins and which from this time on was made the chief charge of their indictment. It was now skillfully used by Camille Desmoulins, who, in a pamphlet entitled *Fragment de l'histoire secrète de la révolution*, or as it was afterward called *Histoire des Brissotins*, struck quite as effective a blow as he had given a year before in his *Jean Pierre Brissot démasqué*. The attack was well timed, the facts and the illustrations were cleverly introduced, and the insinuations made with great skill. As the title implied, it was not only an attack on Brissot personally, but on the whole policy with which he was connected. At the establishment of the Republic, Desmoulins declared, all was favorable for France, despotism had been swept away, liberty had been enthroned, the arms of France were victorious, the Convention had a glorious career before it. What had prevented it from fulfilling this career? A conspiracy. That conspiracy was to be found in the Convention and Brissot was the heart and soul of it. He and the other Girondins had brought about foreign war at a time when France was ill-prepared for it. As for Brissot himself, "that Jeremiah of the 2d of September," he had showed that he was only too ready to seek personal profit from the massacres by his complaint the very next day to the Executive Council, in the presence of Danton, that "they had forgotten Morande." Brissot asserted that he had little influence in obtaining places for his friends, but, sneered Desmoulins, behold this proof to the contrary, and he gleefully commented on the letter written to Roland, in which he inclosed a list of those to whom he would like to have places given.[1] Brissot, moreover, was the accomplice of Dumouriez in bringing defeat to France and in trying to save the king, with the object of destroying the Republic. His real purpose was to divide France into twenty or thirty republics, or rather, if he could, to overturn the republican government altogether, and to set up the Duke of Orléans as monarch. The Mountain, declared Desmoulins, opposes Philippe Égalité and has opposed him at every step, but what is Brissot's position? He was a secretary in the house of Orléans, he was the author of the petition of the Champ de Mars, a petition which he obviously concerted in conjunction with Lafayette. Plainly he is an Orléanist and has been one from the beginning. And, worse than all, Brissot is in the pay of Pitt, and so guilty of the crime of treason.

The whole pamphlet showed the utmost ingenuity and, like Desmoulins's previous attack, it served to blast the credit of Brissot and of his party. Desmoulins himself is said to have spoken of it as both the precursor and the manifesto of the revolution of the 31st of May.[2]

Brissot, meanwhile, proceeded to assail the Mountain. Although his name appeared at the head of the lists of accused persons, he took little part in the final struggle in the Convention, but, like Desmoulins, waged a violent combat with his pen. Deprived of the *Patriote Français* as a means of utterance, he prepared an address in pamphlet form to his constituents. It did not, however, directly answer Desmoulins's attack. Indeed, from the date of publication of Desmoulins's pamphlet, it is extremely doubtful if Brissot had seen it at the time he launched his own address.[3] While lacking the wit and

[1] See p. 292.

[2] See *Desmoulins et Roch-Marcandier*, ed. by Fleury, i, 333.

[3] The *Avis aux lecteurs* at the beginning of Brissot's pamphlet is dated May 22. The *Société des Jacobins*, at the meeting of May 19, 1793, ordered the printing and distribution of Desmoulins's address.

brilliancy of Desmoulins's *Histoire*, it possesses clearness and
force. Its significance is twofold. Unlike many of Brissot's
political pamphlets, it dealt not with his personal career, but
with his party. It showed, however, that his own point of
view had undergone some decided changes. His purpose, he
declared, was to prove that there existed a party of disorganizers and anarchists—by which, of course, he meant the Mountain, though he did not use that word — who dominated the
Convention and the Executive Council; that that party was the
only cause of all the evils which afflicted the country, both
within and without, and that the Republic could be saved only
by the most drastic measures. Beginning with the defensive,
he asserted that the majority of the Convention — by which
he meant the Girondins, although here again he did not use
the party name — had sought to respect the law and to uphold
constituted authorities. To this end they had asked for a departmental guard, denounced Robespierre and Marat, banished
all the Bourbons, censured the massacres of September, asked
for an appeal to the people at the trial of Louis XVI, and demanded the convocation of the primary assemblies. They had
oftentimes been frustrated, however, by that party of anarchists which terrorized the Convention. These anarchists,
Brissot declared, had protected the *Père Duchêne* and Marat;
favored the law of the maximum; raised the *sans-culottes*
against the bourgeois; used the Jacobin Club as an engine of
despotism; reduced to a state of inertia the ministers, notably
Garat,[1] Pache,[2] and Monge;[3] made the revolutionary tribunal

[1] See p. 330.
[2] Jean Nicholas Pache (born 1746, died 1825) became minister of war under
the Girondins in 1792, but as he did not agree with them, was replaced in February, 1793. He allied himself with the Mountain, became mayor of Paris, was
one of the leaders in the insurrection of May 31, and for a time was allied with
Hébert, but escaped prosecution. He was subsequently arrested, but profited
by the amnesty of 1793 and retired to private life.
[3] Gaspard Monge, the celebrated French geometrician, was born in 1746.
At the instigation of Condorcet he was named minister of marine after August
10, which position he held till 1793. He was denounced as an ally of the Girondins, but escaped prosecution.

an instrument of injustice, and favored its despotism; and by asking for the expulsion of members of the Convention, had attempted the iniquity of a second Pride's Purge. As the result of their machinations, he called to witness the increase of crime, the attacks on property and security, the high price of bread, the deficit in the taxes, and the local disorders. A special and far-reaching cause for these disasters, he added, was the financial policy, and, forgetful of his own enthusiasm for the assignats, he went on to denounce their frequent and continued issue.[1] Then, turning to foreign affairs, he upheld the war with Austria, and denounced the war with England, Holland, and Spain, as due to the decree of November 19, and also to the revolutionary propaganda in general, the massacres of September, and the death of Louis. As for the allegation that he had been in large part responsible for that war, he declared that, on the contrary, he had exhausted all his efforts in trying to prevent it. But once begun, he continued, it should have been undertaken on a larger scale. Spain should have been invaded; she was defended only by the Pyrenees, which were easy to cross, and by men who were brutalized by ignorance and by slavery. Her colony across the sea, Louisiana, might have been liberated; England might have been easily and successfully attacked in the East or West Indies, or in India, or again through raising a revolt in Ireland; and the commerce of their enemies ought to have been attacked in the Mediterranean. Where the war was carried on it was a failure. This was due, he declared, not only to the mismanagement of Pache, but to the ideas of equality which had permeated the army and resulted in lack of discipline, and also in the attempt to force liberty on an unwilling people.[2]

But since these mistakes had been made, and France was

---

[1] See p. 151. It is true that he upheld a more conservative policy in regard to the later issues.

[2] On his attitude toward the decree of November 19, see p. 311; on his relation to the massacres of September, p. 301; on his speeches at the trial of the king, pp. 318–324; on his part in bringing on war, chap. ix; on discipline, p. 265.

now defeated abroad, and a prey to civil disorder within, what, Brissot asked, was the remedy? It was to be found, he declared, in putting an end to the revolutionary government. The power of the Committee of Public Safety must be checked, and a constitution established. France would be respected abroad and have peace within only when the authority of an irresponsible committee should give place to a well-ordered government based on a constitution. But, to draw up a constitution, the Convention must be free from the control of the anarchists. Various means of gaining this freedom had been suggested which Brissot took up and considered in turn. The Convention might be transferred to Versailles, but that would not do away with the passions and divisions within; the *suppléants* might be convoked in another city, but they were not very numerous and the opinion of the people could not be obtained by that means; the Convention might be increased in numbers, — that would only increase disorder; a draft of a new constitution might be presented at once to the primary assemblies, but that could hardly be done in the existing turmoil. The most feasible thing, he concluded, after stating these various objections, would be to call a new Convention, and, following the example of the American Congress in providing for federal control of the capital city, insure its perfect independence from any local interference. At all events, the immediate necessity was to provide by some means or other for the drawing up of a constitution by a free body.[1]

[1] The pamphlet was translated into English under the title: "The Anarchy and Horrors of France displayed by a Member of the Convention." The preface, by an ardent admirer of Brissot, says: "I thought I could not at this crisis do my country a more acceptable service than in laying before it the following faithful extracts from Mons. Brissot's address to his constituents. They are not the conjectures of the speculatist, nor the forebodings of the hypochondriac, they are neither the reveries of the fancy nor the effusions of malice; but a plain detail of facts, by one of the principal actors in them, a true picture of France drawn by an able artist, by one of the most capable hands in the whole Convention."

Edmund Burke took a totally different point of view. He also published an English translation of the address with a preface in which he declared that if Brissot, himself a Jacobin, could draw such a picture, the case against Jacobin-

Just here was the weak point of the Girondins. They proposed to bring about order by overthrowing the revolutionary government and establishing a constitution, and this in the face of actual and widespread civil war at home and a foreign war which was menacing their frontiers from the North Sea to the Pyrenees. And even granted that they were right, they were hopelessly divided as to the means to be used. But this was no time to talk about a constitution. If order were to be established within and foreign foes repulsed, not a constitution, but immediate action by a centralized authority was imperative. This the Mountain perceived. They perceived, too, that in the revolutionary committee they had that centralized authority, which must be backed up by force, if necessary, and force they had at their command in the Commune. Its use was precipitated by Isnard's ill-timed challenge that if any outrage should be attempted against the Convention, wanderers would soon be searching on the banks of the Seine for the ruins of Paris. The Commune responded by seizing the well-tried weapon of popular insurrection, and after an unsuccessful attempt on May 31, forced the Convention on June 2 to decree the arrest of the members of the Committee of Twelve, two ministers and twenty-two Girondins.[1]

The career of Brissot in the Convention was at an end. But

ism was forever proved. Brissot's testimony, Burke declared, was that "of a witness beyond all exception. . . . It is Brissot, the republican, the Jacobin, and the philosopher, who is brought to give an account of Jacobinism, and of republicanism, and of philosophy. It is worthy of observation that this, his account of the genesis of Jacobinism, and its effects, is not confined to the period in which the faction came to be divided within itself. In several and these very important particulars, Brissot's observations apply to the whole of the preceding period, before the great schism, and whilst the Jacobins acted as one body; — insomuch that the far greater part of the proceedings of the ruling powers — since the commencement of the Revolution in France, so strongly and so justly reprobated by Brissot — were the acts of Brissot himself and his associates. . . . A question will naturally be asked: What could induce Brissot to draw such a picture? He must have been sensible it was his own. The answer is — the inducement was the same with that which led him to partake in perpetration of all crimes, the calamitous effects of which he describes with the pen of a master, — ambition." Burke's *Works* (Boston, 1884), v, 68.

[1] *Procès-verbal de la Convention*, volume for June, 1793, p. 29.

he was only reaping what he had sown. As the chief member of the Diplomatic Committee, he had incurred much of the responsibility for involving France in a general European war; and now, since he and his party proved themselves incapable of waging a successful war, powerless to meet the danger they had invoked, because they had no settled policy, no united plan of action, they were rejected by the people, and cast out by the Convention. Such incapacity was criminal, and it involved more than their own ruin, for out of this war which they created and failed to direct sprang the Reign of Terror; and they, as the creators of the war, must bear in part the dread responsibility of having begotten the Terror.

BRISSOT AND FEDERALISM

One of the principal charges brought against the Girondins, and particularly against the Buzot wing of the party, was that of federalism. From the opening of the Convention in September, 1792, throughout the remaining months of that year, at the trial of the king, during the spring of 1793, and finally at their trial, the Girondins were accused again and again of being federalists. The term "federalism," as used in these accusations against the Girondins, meant an attempt to destroy the unity of France. In its wider significance, however, it was employed to designate the general hostility of the provinces against Paris. With federalism in this latter sense there is no doubt that the Girondins were in full sympathy. The question is, were they federalists in the guilty sense meant by their accusers? Did they plot to make France into a confederation instead of a republic, "one and indivisible"?

As early as 1789 the possibility of a confederation was suggested. Witness an editorial which appeared in the *Patriote Français* of November, 1789: "The stand which the National Assembly has taken in decreeing the division of France into a number of departments, between seventy-five and eighty, ought to remove the reproach which has been made against the partisans of the cause of the people, of wishing to divide France into a certain number of confederated republics. A confederation of eighty-five states would be a political monstrosity. A long-continued harmony between so many members of a confederacy would be a miracle."

Accusations of intention to form a confederated instead of a unified republic were again made in the republican crisis of the summer of 1791, and again Brissot came forward promptly to repudiate the charge. "What madman," he demanded, "has ever dreamed of making France into eighty-three republics? The republicans, those at least that I know, desire only a republic or a representative government of which the eighty-three departments are eighty-three fractions, coördinated one with the other, and all meeting in a common point — the National Assembly." [1] And in his speech of July 10 against the king, he reiterated the same sentiments.

A year later the struggle between the Legislative Assembly under the control of the Girondins and the Jacobin Commune of Paris again brought up the subject of the relation between Paris and the provinces, and this time it became a distinct party issue, charges being made specifically against the Girondins, of stirring up the provinces against Paris, and of striving to prevent the establishment of a unified republic.[2] And when, on the meeting of the Convention, a republic, one and indivisible, was established, the Mountain immediately raised the cry that the Girondins did not accept its unity and indivisibility, and were plotting for its destruction. This now became one of the main points of conflict between the parties. It was brought to the front again and again, and was one of the causes of the final downfall of the Girondins.

One proof of the charge, the Mountain alleged, was the effort of the Girondins to establish a departmental guard. Another proof was found in their alleged attitude toward annexa-

---

[1] *Patriote Français*, July 8, 1791, quoted by Brissot in his *Projet de défense, Mémoires*, ii, 338–39.

[2] "*Ils veulent, dit-on, arriver à un état fédératif; or* [sic] *la guerre civile peut y mener.*" Pellenc to Lamarck, June 29, 1790. Glagau, 343.

tions. This was presented with great vigor by Anacharsis Cloots, in a pamphlet entitled *Ni Marat ni Roland*. After setting forth in no complimentary terms his opinion of these two men, Cloots proceeded to report in detail sundry conversations with certain Girondins. Rebecqui, he declared, did not want Nice added to France, Buzot thought a republic could not well be larger than his own village, and Brissot considered France already too large and protested against the addition of Savoy. All of which showed, according to Cloots, opposition to the unity of the Republic on the one hand, and plans for federalism on the other.

A third alleged evidence of federalism was the attempt of the Girondins to procure a vote in favor of an appeal to the primary assemblies on the question of the punishment of the king. Such a proposition was extremely offensive to the Mountain, who believed that measures against Louis were justified on the ground of political necessity. They forthwith accused the Girondins of advocating the appeal to the people with the express purpose of stirring up division and civil war.[1] Amar repeated this same accusation at the time of the trial of the Girondins, declaring that the motive of the appeal to the people was the wish to destroy the Republic.[2]

The hostility of the Girondins to the city government of Paris constituted further proof of federalism in the eyes of their enemies. If this alone were conclusive, they would have to be pronounced guilty; for, from August 10, 1792, when the struggle between the Girondin Committee of Twenty-one began, down to the very last day of their political existence in the Convention, they were constantly at war with the authorities of Paris. Specific instances of this hostility were the accusations which they made against the Commune as responsible for the massacres of September; their attack on Robespierre for his alleged efforts to establish the dictatorship; the attack made by Buzot, January 13, 1793, on account of the action of the

---

[1] Speech of Marat, January 15, 1793. *Moniteur*, January 19, 1793.
[2] *Acte d'accusation*, October 3, 1793. *Moniteur*, October 25, 1793.

Commune in closing the theaters; the speech of Buzot, March 27, in which he declared that the representatives were only ambassadors [1] from each part of the Republic; the inopportune threat of Isnard, when he declared that if anything happened to the Convention, people would soon be searching along the Seine to find where Paris had once stood; and finally, the numerous attempts to appeal to the provinces, either by the convocation of the primary assemblies or by the removal of the Convention from Paris.

The Girondins, it was further alleged, did not confine themselves to words, but were stirring up the provinces to actual revolt. Point was given this accusation by the protests and addresses against Paris which began to come in as early as October, 1792. On the 20th of this month, the administrators of the Department of Calvados sent an address to the Convention in which they called down maledictions upon whatever part of the Republic should try to rule the whole.[2] On January 2, 1793, this department made another address to the Convention. "You are represented as exposed to the axe of the executioner," they wrote. "Paris, the cradle of liberty, is filled with proud and bloody agitators. . . . The citizens of Calvados in their impatience rise up, they hasten to inscribe their names in the civic registers, they want to set out to avenge your menaced liberty. . . . They propose to sustain the work of their representatives or die." [3] Within a day or two the administrative Department of the Haute-Loire issued an appeal in terms quite as emphatic. "Citizens," they cried, "the agitators of Paris and the enemies of the Revolution are constantly conspiring against it by flattering the people into believing that Paris is practically the exclusive sovereign of the republic of which it is only the eighty-fourth part. It permits itself to dictate decrees to the Convention at its pleasure, and thus prevents it from giving us a good constitution. The only means of remedying these abuses is to organize a departmental force

---

[1] This was in his speech of March 28, 1793. *Moniteur*, March 30, 1793.
[2] *Moniteur*, October 21, 1792.   [3] *Patriote Français*, January 8, 1793.

which shall be able to protect our legislators and make the law effective." [1] These appeals the Mountain regarded as attacks on the indivisibility of the Republic and a direct evidence of federalism, and when the appeals were backed by open insurrection the Mountain saw again the hand of the Girondins and triumphantly asserted that there was undisputed proof of federalistic design.

In the course of this struggle the Girondin party had become more and more divided, but it was the Buzotins, not the Brissotins, who led the movement of the provinces against Paris. Brissot, however, had been, and still was, too prominent a figure to escape popular wrath and official condemnation. Accusations were brought against him personally, as well as against his wing of the party. These were reiterated at the time of his expulsion from the Jacobin Club in October, 1792, and in his address "*A tous les républicains de France*" he defended himself again, referring to his protests in the summer of 1791 against the suspicion of supporting a federated republic. He had convinced Danton, he declared, that he did not hold federalist principles, but, in spite of his protests, Robespierre continued to accuse him. As for the alleged evidence against him that he had praised the *Fédéralist*, it fell to the ground because that work was not in favor of a confederate government, but distinctly against it.

In regard to the accusation made later, by Anacharsis Cloots, that Brissot, apropos of proposed annexations, had said that France was already too large to be governed as a unit,[2] Brissot replied that he had been quite misunderstood, and that the only basis for the statement which he was alleged to have made was his opposition to Cloots's scheme for a universal republic, concerning which he had said that in case France were to be extended beyond the limits prescribed for her by nature, the ideal was not a universal republic, but a girdle of federated republics. Was it not unfair, he asked, to judge him by a single remark like this, taken out of its context?

[1] *Moniteur*, January 8, 1793.   [2] Cloots, *Ni Roland ni Marat.*

In spite of Brissot's attempted repudiation of these charges, they continued to be made against him, and when twenty-one of the Girondins were finally brought to trial, the indictment was against "Brissot and his accomplices." It was charged that he had advocated a departmental guard, at any rate, till the last, when he argued for an appeal to the primary assemblies in preference; that he had objected to annexation; that he led the demand for an appeal to the people during the trial of the king; and that he lent the influence of his newspaper to the attacks against Paris. In his *Projet de défense* he therefore devoted considerable space to a reply to these accusations. It was but a reiteration of his former protest on this subject. He declared that, far from being a federalist, he had attacked federalism even before the existence of a republic, and in support of his assertions, pointed to his attitude in 1791. When at that time a republic was proposed, and when the cry was raised that France was too large for a unified republic, and that a federated republic meant danger from internal anarchy and from foreign foes, he was one of the first to recognize the danger and to protest that no one had any intention of so dividing France. In answer to the charge that he had favored a departmental guard, he laid stress on the fact that, as soon as he realized that the project for such a guard was provoking serious discord, he promptly opposed it. The accusation of having calumniated Paris he repudiated with indignation.

The Girondins, as a party, were quite as emphatic in their defense. That their efforts to raise a departmental guard were an evidence of federalism, they flatly denied. They had no intention whatever, they declared, of using the proposed departmental guard to destroy the unity of the Republic; on the contrary, they had demanded it for the very purpose of securing that unity.[1] It was the same motive, they protested, which influenced them to advocate an appeal to the provinces at the time of the king's trial, and later an appeal to the primary assemblies to elect another Convention, and which finally led

[1] Speech of Buzot, September 25; *Moniteur*, September 26.

them to raise the provinces in armed insurrection against Paris. This defense is borne out by the fact that no department raised troops for the defense of its own territory; no department declared itself independent: they were only acting together and for the common interest. According to M. Dauban, the movement, instead of being federalistic, was but the equivalent of the departmental movement of 1848, when the national guards from all over France came to fight the insurgents of Paris.

The origin, however, of the charge of federalism is clear enough. In the first place, many of the Girondins were federalists in theory; in the second place, their attitude toward the provinces gave abundant color to the accusation of hostility to Paris. Buzot, for example, in his memoirs, frankly acknowledged such belief and appealed in support of it to the theories of sundry eighteenth-century philosophers and to the example of the United States.

Further, Buzot declared, in the course of an argument with Cloots, that since a man's patriotism consists not so much in love of the land on which he lives as in the love of the citizens with whom he lives, there could be little common enthusiasm for the country between men separated by hundreds of leagues. Smaller divisions were, therefore, necessary.[1] But while repudiating federal ideas, Buzot used the phraseology of federalism and in the same breath spoke of the deputies as ambassadors from the different parts of the Republic. Gorsas, another Girondin, in his newspaper, the *Courrier des Départements*, demanded with surprise and indignation why federalism should be regarded as a crime, and referred his readers to the *Esprit* of Helvetius.[2] And Brissot, while not advocating federalism for France, was always holding up the United States as having an ideal form of government.

But to assert that the Girondins believed in federalism is one thing; to explain what they meant by it is quite another.

---

[1] *Mémoires de Madame Roland*, i, 107–08.
[2] *Courrier des Départements*, October, 1792, quoted by Biré, 350–51.

It may be said that as the federal system of the United States was their inspiration and the model which they would have liked to see followed in France, one has only to study that system in order to understand their position. But it is extremely doubtful if they themselves understood the federal government across the water. To them it was undoubtedly much more like a confederation than a federation, and if they had attempted to copy it in France, they would probably have developed a highly decentralized organization.

In addition to their theories, there was the further suspicious fact that their attitude toward the provinces was, to put it mildly, not out of harmony with their theoretical beliefs. That attitude may be explained without reference to federalism. It was a natural outcome of the situation in the summer of 1792. In fact, at that time, when the overthrow of the king was under consideration, they went so far as to suggest the advantages of federalism and began to sound public opinion on the subject, but they did little more than suggest it. While they were still hesitating and temporizing, the Jacobins, together with the Commune of Paris, carried through the insurrection of August 10. The events which followed, though they may be explained quite apart from any connection with federalism, gave color to the accusation that they were still working for that particular form of government. Irritated at what they considered too great an extension of the power of Paris, the Girondins naturally looked to the provinces, which, as a matter of course, were inclined to be jealous of Paris. This led to the renewal of the struggle under the Convention; the Girondins, on the one hand, seizing the opportunity afforded by the events of the first weeks of September to accuse the Mountain of responsibility for the massacres; and the Mountain, on the other, seizing upon the alliance between the Girondins and the provinces to accuse the latter of wishing to divide the Republic and to establish a federal system of government. Although the Girondins stoutly maintained that when once the Republic was established they abandoned any federative plans they might have had, it was natural that the Mountain should doubt their assertion. Thus, the origin of the charge of federalism is evident enough, but the alleged proof brought forward by the Mountain in support of it is absolutely insufficient. As is generally recognized, the Mountain, although they succeeded in expelling the Girondins from the Convention and in securing their conviction, really failed to prove the case against them.

What is clear, however, is that despite their abandonment of federalism as a form of government, the policy of Brissot and the other Girondins was decentralizing in tendency. Witness Brissot's attitude in the summer of 1789. "It is time," he wrote, "that the Parisians renounce the idea that the provinces ought to be sacrificed to them. That despotism which all the realm used to see in Paris . . . is no more. The bond which is to unite Paris to the provinces can no more be a bond of slavery, but of fraternity." [1] Later, he disapproved of the plan of Maluet for the dependence of local authorities on the monarch.[2] And again, his proposition for a council composed of representatives of the departmental guard and for an appeal to the provinces at the time of the king's trial and later in an effort to renew the Convention, were evidences of a policy of decentralization. In short, the Girondins represented as a whole the system of strong local government established by the constitution of 1791 rather than the centralization which had culminated in Louis XVI. But not only was the whole trend of French history against them, but France was now at war, and in time of war to adopt and follow a policy of decentralization, which would with difficulty have had a permanent success only in time of peace, did not show far-sighted and wise statesmanship. It was because of this lack of practical ability and of their ill-considered efforts at decentralization at a period when centralization was needed, and not because of any attack on the unity of the Republic, that they so signally failed.

[1] *Patriote Français*, August 7, 1789.
[2] *Ibid.*, February 23, 1790. This may have been, however, largely objection to the power of the king, as such, rather than to centralized government.

CHAPTER XII

THE events of the last weeks of May showed the fatal weakness of the Girondins. The latter, it is true, realized the growing strength of the Mountain, but, although they foresaw the issue, they were unable to do anything to avert it. As Brissot pathetically put it, they discussed much, but they could come to no conclusion.

It was no longer a question primarily of political principles, but of personal safety, and the danger was daily becoming more imminent. As early as the 19th of May, Brissot wrote to a friend that they were suffering torturing anxiety; that people were saying that enough cooks and cab drivers had been decapitated; that it was the heads of the deputies which ought to come off now; and that such threats had so terrified the deputies that half of them were afraid to sleep at home, lest they might be arrested during the night.[1] Some of them took refuge at the home of Meillan, possibly because it was situated in a quarter of the city where there was more Girondin sympathy.[2] Brissot fled there on the 31st of May, and Vergniaud, Gensonné, Guadet, and others soon joined him. In momentary fear of arrest, they dared not go to bed on the night of June 1, but passed the night in their chairs, getting what sleep they could. The next morning they gathered together as many of their friends as they could reach and tried to agree on a plan of action. Some were for going to the Assembly; others thought that too hazardous and proposed that they draw up a declara-

---

[1] Letter of Brissot, May 19, 1793. *Correspondance*, 338.

[2] "*Plusieurs des proscrits s'étaient réfugiés chez moi. Je logeais dans un hôtel vaste et presque inhabité à portée de la Convention et dans un quartier où les bons citoyens conservaient encore de l'influence. . . . Pétion, Brissot, Guadet, Salles, Gensonné, et quelques autres cédèrent enfin à nos instances et consentirent d'attendre dans cet asile le résultat de la séance.*" Meillan, 52.

tion of principles; but despite the gravity of the crisis they could come to no decision. Instead of doing anything definite, they spent the time discussing the relative dignity of suicide or death on the scaffold; but even here they could not agree. While they were in the midst of this discussion, the brother of Rabaut Saint-Étienne rushed in, wildly excited, crying out that the Convention was no more and calling on the deputies to save themselves. The instinct of self-preservation at once asserted itself, and without waiting to decide either on a common form of death or a common line of action, the deputies, with few exceptions, sought safety in precipitate flight.[1]

The futile efforts and misdirected energies of the Girondins in opposing needed centralization may arouse contempt, but their sufferings in flight and imprisonment cannot fail to awaken sympathy. The politician sinks into the background; one sees rather the human being in a crisis which involves his personal safety and his very life. This is emphatically true of Brissot. He fled with the rest from the home of Meillan, and his thoughts turned at once toward Chartres, his native city, as a place of refuge, but he was unable to leave Paris at once, because of the lack of ready money.[2] Where he hid in Paris is not known, but by June 4 he had managed to get away, and by the 5th he had reached Versailles. Here, at the home of one Beau, he met a friend and admirer named Souque,[3] who courageously determined to accompany him in his flight.[4] They

---

[1] Brissot, *Mémoires*, ii, 216.

[2] *Lettre de Barbaroux aux Marseillais*, cited by A. Duchâtellier, *Histoire de la Révolution en Bretagne*, i, 407. *Lettres de Madame Roland*, ii, 734, note.

[3] Examination of Souque before the council general of the Department of the Allier. *Correspondance*, 341–46. Souque had known Brissot at the Jacobin Club. He escaped the guillotine, but was left in prison till the 9th Thermidor. He afterward served in various affairs under the Directory, and in 1819 was elected a member of the *Corps Législatif*. He was also known as a dramatic author of some repute. See Vatel, *Charlotte Corday et les Girondins*, ii, 249, note.

[4] According to the examination before the council general of the Department of the Allier, business interests were in part responsible for Souque's determination to accompany Brissot, as he had been connected with the army in the Department of the Eure-et-Loir.

accordingly set off together toward Chartres. Here Brissot was destined to be bitterly disappointed.[1] "I hoped," he wrote in his memoirs, "that my reputation and the services which I had rendered to liberty would make me welcome. The first man I saw was a friend of twenty years' standing: he trembled and was embarrassed; he urged me to flee immediately, promised to come back to see me again, but did not appear. Those whom I met afterward, while they showed more courage, gave me the same advice. I could certainly apply to myself that passage: '*In patriam venit et sui eum non receperunt.*'"[2]

Saddened by what seemed to him the basest ingratitude, he departed from Chartres in despondency, feeling that if his own city refused to receive him, there was no refuge left. But to wander about aimlessly for any length of time was not possible, and learning that some of the deputies had gone toward Orléans, he and Souque turned their steps in that direction.[3] Under such circumstances, it is small wonder that the forests through which Brissot passed seemed very alluring, and that he longed, as in the days of his youth, to return to a life of nature. "How I regretted," he wrote in describing his feelings, "that I could not bury myself and hide forever from those men for whom I had sacrificed all, and who had not hesitated to sacrifice me. The more wild, sad, and lonely Nature appeared, the more she pleased my soul."

The state of opinion in Orléans was not reassuring, and finding that "Maratism" was in the ascendant, he and Souque decided speedily that no safety was to be found there. They therefore continued their weary journey in the direction of Gien, Nevers, and Moulins. To their dismay, they found that whenever they passed through a village, they had to stop, show their passports, and answer embarrassing questions. Souque seems

---

[1] The support which Brissot had received from Chartres came largely from the Jacobin Club there, and his expulsion from the Jacobin Club at Paris would naturally influence the local Jacobin Club against him.

[2] Brissot, *Mémoires*, ii, 216.

[3] Examination of Souque before the council-general of the Department of the Allier. *Correspondance*, 341–46.

to have been more astute and to have shown more practical sense than Brissot. At all events, he tried to arrange their journey so that they might reach Moulins at an early hour and thus run less risk of being detained. But Brissot, who was overcome with fatigue, insisted on stopping at a little inn a couple of leagues from Nevers for a good night's rest. This upset Souque's calculations, and, in consequence, they did not arrive at Moulins till noon. Instead of the single sleepy guard whom Souque counted on hoodwinking, the local authorities were numerous and wide awake.[1] Disaster followed for both Souque and Brissot.

According to their custom, Souque went alone to the police with their passports.[2] This was a wise precaution, since Brissot, widely known as he was, might be recognized, and his passport, which represented him as a Swiss merchant, Ramus by name, of Neuchâtel, Switzerland, be challenged.[3] But fate, which had treated him kindly so far, failed him on this occasion. The suspicion of the police officer whose business it was to *visé* the passports was aroused, and Brissot was obliged to present himself in person before him. He was then shown an order from the minister of the interior, forbidding the acceptance of any Swiss certificates, except such as were signed by Barthélemy, ambassador of France in Switzerland. Brissot's objection, that this order could not possibly apply to him, since his passport antedated it by two months, was not favorably received, and the officer continued to press him with questions, which he did his best to answer satisfactorily. But the officer refused to be satisfied, and would do nothing without consulting the mayor, who wished to consult the district, and the district in turn carried the matter to the department. Brissot was accordingly called before the departmental council. He was naturally much disturbed lest he be

---

[1] Brissot, *Mémoires*, II, 221–22.

[2] See note of M. Perroud, *Correspondance*, 339.

[3] Ramus was the son of a Swiss pastor of Neuchâtel, Switzerland, and was in the employ of Beau at whose house Brissot stopped at Versailles.

recognized, but he put a brave face on it and stoutly maintained that he was a Swiss merchant. But to support his assertion he soon found was not so easy. Where were his papers? he was asked. He had none. Where were his trunks? He was traveling without any. Who were his correspondents? Without hesitation he named several important houses, and trying to brazen it out, he offered to stay at Moulins till the authorities should assure themselves of his identity. Whereupon one obstinate member of the council proposed that in the meantime he be kept in prison, a proposition to which Brissot vehemently objected, and demanded instead that he be allowed to remain under guard at the inn. After much discussion, it was finally decided that he be placed provisionally in a state of arrest, and that the conveyance in which he and Souque had arrived be examined. Meanwhile, the prospect of imprisonment brought Brissot to his senses. He realized how impossible it would be to conceal his identity for any length of time, and, that by revealing it, showing himself, as he put it, "invested with the sacred character of representative of the nation," he might escape actual imprisonment. Accordingly, when he was brought before the *comité de sûreté générale*,[1] he confessed who he was.[2] In defense of his action, he declared that had he felt that the decree against him represented the real desire of the legislators, his respect for the law and for the Convention would have prevented his flight, but his conviction that the decree against the deputies had been passed under duress, and that the Convention had no force at its command wherewith to prevent the massacre of the victims, persuaded him that he was justified in fleeing and in taking every possible measure for his safety, even to the deceit of traveling under a false passport. In conclusion, he asked that his case be referred to the Convention.[3] When the committee of public safety thus reported the result

---

[1] M. Perroud, in a footnote, explains that this committee was more properly called the *comité de surveillance*, and that in its *procès-verbal* it calls itself the *comité de salut public*. *Mémoires de Brissot*, ii, 222.

[2] *Procès-verbal du comité de salut public. Correspondance*, 346–49.

[3] See *Correspondance*, 346–49.

of their examination to the council of the department, the latter declared that Brissot was under the safeguard of the law and the loyalty of the citizens of Moulins, and that he should be treated with the respect due to a representative of the nation. It also decreed that Brissot and Souque should be kept under guard by the municipality at the inn.

Souque was also examined. From the stress laid on questions as to the motives which actuated Brissot and himself to go to this or that department, the examiners were evidently suspicious that Brissot and Souque were engaged in fomenting a conspiracy against the Convention.[1] They were unsuccessful, however, in forcing from Souque any incriminating admissions. Neither had the committee of public safety found any incriminating papers among the effects of Souque and Brissot and nothing worse than two English pistols.[2]

The suspicious attitude of the administrators apparently represented popular opinion, for a mob gathered under the windows of the inn and hooted at Souque and Brissot as traitors. This mob Souque had to brave, in going to appear before the departmental council, and on his return he found it still waiting for him with insults and threats of the guillotine. According to Brissot, it was a critical and dangerous situation. With great difficulty Souque managed to get through the mob and up to the room where Brissot was waiting for him. Pale and speechless, he threw himself upon Brissot's neck, crying that their last moment had come. Whereupon the mayor declared that he could not answer for what might happen, and that the only way to appease the mob was for Brissot and Souque to be put in prison. At which Brissot promptly appealed to the decree of the Convention which placed the deputies under arrest in their own homes, and declared that he would go to prison only under force. The procureur of the commune, who was present, sympathized with Brissot and

---

[1] *Interrogatoire prêté pardevant nous administrateurs composant le conseil général du département de l'Allier, juin 10, 1793. Correspondance,* 341–46.

[2] *Procès-verbal du comité. Correspondance,* 346–49.

harangued the mob so successfully that they were persuaded to disperse.[1]

It is to be noted that it was only Souque who was examined directly by the council of the department. This body, after having learned through their committee of public safety who Brissot really was, respected his position as representative of the people and confined their investigation to Souque.[2] They took heed, moreover, to Brissot's request and decreed that the department send to the Convention all the papers involved and await its instructions. Brissot also sent a letter to the Convention, in which he set forth the reasons why he considered himself justified in his flight. He had hesitated at first, as flight seemed to him unworthy of a representative of the people; but as the Convention was no longer free, it had ceased to represent the people. The most potent cause of his flight, however, was fear of arrest, and here he was justified on the ground of self-preservation. After thus defending himself, he went on to demand in the name of justice that he be not condemned without being heard in his own defense, and above all that his companion, Souque, be released.[3]

The Convention did not look with favor upon Brissot's appeal. In their estimation, he had added to the crime of conspiracy the guilt of using a false passport and thus forfeited all claim to consideration, and should be committed to prison like

---

[1] Brissot, *Mémoires*, ii, 223–24.

[2] *Extrait du procès-verbal de la session extraordinaire du conseil du département de l'Allier.* Given in the *Correspondance*, 350–51.

[3] The letter is quoted in full in Vatel, *Charlotte Corday et des Girondins*, ii, 248. The *Moniteur* gives it only in part. Marat published it with the following comment: "*Tout le monde sait que Brissot, l'ancien espion de police, l'âme damnée de Lafayette, de Narbonne, de Bailli, l'agent de Louis Capet, le complice de Dumouriez, et l'âme damnée de la faction des hommes d'état qui ne cessent pas de machiner pour le rétablissement de la royauté, en feignant de vouloir la République, est l'un des 35 meneurs mis en état d'arrestation. Tout le monde sait qu'il a pris la fuite il y a cinq jours, pour aller machiner en Suisse, au moyen d'un faux passeport dont il s'était pourvu d'avance. Tout le monde sait qu'il a été arrêté par la municipalité patriote de Moulins; mais tout le monde ne connoît pas la lettre qu'il vient d'écrire à la Convention, la voici mot pour mot, on y verra que ce vile intrigant est aussi plat que perfide.*" L'Ami du Peuple, 14 juin.

any other criminal. One member declared that there did not exist a dungeon sufficiently black to shut up such a conspirator. The matter was finally settled by a decree, passed on the recommendation of the Committee of Public Safety, that Brissot and Souque should be brought to Paris.[1]

Meanwhile Brissot was becoming a cause of civil dissension in the Department of the Allier, and the administrators were only too glad to get rid of him.[2] Two events, in particular, accelerated their zeal. In the first place, the district of Gannat drew up an address in behalf of Brissot, which it sent to the department. This was read to the departmental council in its session of June 17, and provoked a sharp reprimand. The department, it was stated, thoroughly disapproved of the address because it opposed the decree of the Convention, placing the twenty-two members under arrest; because it was opposed to the arrest of Brissot; and finally because the example set by the district of Gannat was likely to disturb the peace and unity of the department.[3] The department decreed, moreover, that the action of Gannat be communicated to the Committee of Public Safety.

That Brissot should be held responsible for stirring up the district of Gannat was but natural. If his own account is to be accepted, he was an "accessory after the fact," and knew nothing of the action of the district till after it had been taken.[4] But he certainly was indiscreet. The address, it seems, was brought to him by an officer of the department, one Descombes.[5] Brissot, evidently pleased by this sympathy, was

---

[1] Aulard, *Recueil des actes du comité de salut public*, IV, 578.

[2] The temper of Brissot's captors is well shown by the account of his arrest and examination given in a personal letter by one of the members of the tribunal, Royer by name. While agreeing with the official account as to fact, it is distinctly hostile to Brissot. A. N., AD. XVIII[c], vol. 241.

[3] *Procès-verbal des séances de l'assemblée administrative du département d'Allier. Séance du 17 juin, 1793.* See also for the whole subject Louis Biernawski, *Un département sous la Révolution française. L'Allier de 1789 à l'an II.*

[4] This defense of Brissot's is given in his *Réponse au rapport de Saint-Just, Mémoires*, II, 263–65.

[5] Brissot gives the name as Lescombes, but it appeared in the *procès-verbal* as Descombes.

imprudent enough to write an answer, in which he defended his position and thanked the district of Gannat for its action.[1] He was soon made aware of his indiscretion by the mayor of Moulins, who hastened to warn him that the action of the district of Gannat had stirred up great indignation. Whereupon Brissot offered to make what reparation he could by writing on the spot to Descombes, begging him to suppress the letter. This last letter, instead of being sent, as Brissot trusted it would be, was promptly turned over by the mayor to the committee of general security. The result was an examination of Brissot's papers.[2] Popular opinion against Brissot now expressed itself by a demand by the *Société populaire*, addressed to the council of the department, that in view of the disturbances to which his presence was giving rise, he be sent away as soon as possible. The department accordingly decreed that rapid measures be taken to "direct Brissot toward Paris."[3]

As for the district of Gannat, it soon had reason to regret its enthusiasm in Brissot's behalf, for the Convention called to its bar the officers of Gannat and ordered that the seat of the district administration be transferred from Gannat to Saint-Pourçain. This decision naturally provoked consternation at Gannat and frantic appeals for pardon. The 25th of June the citizens of Gannat sent an address to the Convention, protesting that they were guilty of no counter-revolutionary design, that their village had been calumniated, and that they had no intention of marching against Moulins.[4] The 26th of June, the *procureur-syndic* of the district of Gannat appeared before the council of the department to explain the action of the district.[5] The 27th the council general of Gannat appointed a special committee to make further explanations.[6] The 3d of July the administrators appeared before the bar of the Convention, and by making humble apology and retracting their

---

[1] See *Correspondance*, 358–60.   [2] Réponse, *Mémoires*, ii, 263–65.
[3] *Procès-verbal des séances de l'assemblée administrative du départment de l'Allier, June 18, 1793.*
[4] District du Gannat, *Correspondance*, June 25, 1793.
[5] *Procès-verbal*, referred to above.   [6] Gannat, *Conseil-général*, 263–64.

action, were able to secure their personal reinstatement and the reëstablishment of Gannat as the head of the district.[1]

The very next day after the popular society of Moulins, stirred by the Gannat incident, had urged Brissot's departure, another evidence of sympathy in his behalf came to light, and made more desirable still his speedy departure from Moulins. This was the arrival in Moulins of a young Spaniard, named Marchena, who declared that he had made the journey expressly to see Brissot. Being brought before the officers of the municipality, he gave a straightforward account of himself — an account which agrees very closely with Brissot's subsequent explanation of their relations.[2] It seems that Marchena, having been banished from Spain on account of his revolutionary views, had been obliged to flee from his country. He had settled at Bayonne, where he had connected himself with the Jacobin society. A speech which he had delivered in August, 1792, against royalty and on the organization of the Republic, brought him to Brissot's attention. The latter saw in him a person likely to be useful in preparing the revolution in Spain, and accordingly invited him to come to Paris and presented him to Lebrun. The decline of the Girondin party apparently put an end to Marchena's activities in this matter, but not to his devotion to Brissot, and he now voluntarily came to Moulins prepared to share Brissot's imprisonment and misfortunes. In addition to his sympathy with Brissot, the municipal authorities found him guilty of the more tangible charge of traveling under a false passport. The council general accordingly decreed his imprisonment till he could be brought before the committee of public safety of the department.

This arrest, following so closely on the heels of the Gannat

---

[1] *Biernawski*, ii, 363–64. The incident was made much of as showing that Brissot was a dangerous conspirator. Billaud-Varennes, in a speech delivered the 15th of July, said: "*Pendant un résidence de quelques jours à Moulins, Brissot a presque réussi à y réaliser la guerre civile.*" *Discours sur les députés de la Convention, mis en état d'arrestation, par son décret du deuxième juin prononcé dans la séance du quinzième juillet, 1793*, p. 24.

[2] Brissot, *Mémoires*, ii, 226, 265–66; also *Extrait des minutes déposées au secretariat de la municipalité de Moulins*, printed in *Correspondance*, 361–68.

affair, now brought matters to a crisis. The department, without waiting for directions from Paris, passed a decree which provided that Brissot should start the next day, the 20th; that he should be accompanied by a civil commissioner appointed for the purpose, and by two national guards; that he should make the journey in a four-seated carriage; that another civil commissioner should go ahead in the conveyance in which Brissot had arrived in Moulins; that Souque and Marchena should be sent to Paris accompanied by two national gendarmes, but that they should be separated from Brissot by a distance of several hours; that the execution of these measures should be entrusted to the municipality of Moulins, and that for this purpose the necessary funds should be advanced by the department.[1] These decrees were, however, unnecessary, as the municipality, having in the mean time received notice from Paris of the decree of the Convention ordering the transfer of Brissot, had proceeded to immediate action.

There were many details to be arranged: what route should be followed; how many horses would be needed to start with; where, and how, fresh horses could be obtained along the route; where conveyances could be found; who should be chosen to accompany the prisoners; what the expense would be, etc. An interesting complication arose concerning a conveyance. It was reported that a certain citizen, Faucompre by name, whose father was an *émigré*, possessed a carriage suitable for the purpose. The question of ownership thus became important, for, if the carriage were the property of an *émigré*, it could be taken for the service of the Republic, otherwise not. The municipality in perplexity appealed to the department, which decided that, as the father and son lived together, the carriage might be considered as belonging to the father, and so subject to confiscation. The department also, on request of the commune, advanced three thousand francs for necessary expenses.[2]

---

[1] *Assemblée administrative du département de l'Allier*, June 19, 1793.

[2] *Registre des délibérations prises par le conseil général de la commune de*

All these measures seem to have been taken with great haste, for, on the evening of the 19th, the very day on which the decree of the Convention reached Moulins, the authorities started their prisoners. It was a cavalcade of some importance, one rider going in advance to provide for the change of horses, then three carriages, one each for Brissot, Souque, and Marchena, accompanied by civil commissioners and gendarmes.[1] The moment of departure was a trying one for Brissot. It had been announced for seven o'clock in the evening, and by three o'clock the square was full, while the windows and roofs of adjacent buildings were covered with spectators. Although no actual violence seems to have been offered, there were shouts, "To the guillotine." But Brissot appears to have been prepared for insults and to have received them with at least outward calm. As far as Montargis, he met with evidences of curiosity rather than of antagonism, but there he had a most unpleasant experience. Hostile crowds gathered round and drew hideous and suggestive caricatures on the sides of his carriage. "Nothing," he declared, "could be more like a dance of cannibals around their victim attached to the fatal stake than the sight of those monsters announcing to me with a jubilant air the approaching guillotine."[2] His fears were naturally aroused as to the reception he might meet at Paris, but his arrival there seems to have occasioned no outbreak.

He reached Paris on the 22nd of June, and on the decree of the Committee of Public Safety, he was taken temporarily to the mairie, where it was decreed that he should remain pending the action of the Convention.[3] He seems to have confidently expected that he would soon be transferred to his own home,[4] but the next day, in accordance with a decree of the Convention placing him under arrest, he was taken to

Moulins, 19-20 juin, 1793. Also Procès-verbal des séances de l'assemblée administrative du département de l'Allier, 20 juin, 1793.

[1] Registre des délibérations prises par le conseil général de la commune de Moulins, juin 19, 1793.

[2] Mémoires, ii, 228.

[3] Recueil des actes du comité de salut public, v, 44.   [4] Mémoires, ii, 228.

the Abbaye,[1] where he remained till the 6th of October, when he was transferred to the Conciergerie.[2]

Meanwhile a deputation of his escort presented themselves to the Convention. They seemed to feel that Moulins deserved some reward for making so notable a capture and asked the Convention for an advance of 150,000 francs for the provisioning of their city, but beyond the reference of their request to a committee they received little encouragement.[3]

The Convention now turned its attention to the expelled Girondins, and on July 8, Saint-Just, in the name of the Committee of Public Safety, presented a report upon the deputies who, by the decree of June 2, had been placed under arrest. While assailing the faction as a whole, the arraignment was directed against Brissot especially. "There exists," he declared, "a conspiracy to establish tyranny and the old constitution. The conspirators did their best to preserve the monarchy in the summer of 1792, even to the extent of proposing the Duke of York or the Duke of Orléans as rulers if they could not keep Louis XVI himself upon the throne; and when they failed, they calumniated Paris and have ever since been trying to divide the Republic. In this conspiracy, Brissot has played the part of a Monk — and has intrigued both in internal and in foreign affairs, first to save the king, and then to reëstablish royalty and to divide the Republic. Witness his actions and his words: he showed great attachment to the monarchy, he even declared, if there exist men who intend to establish a republic upon the ruins of the constitution of 1789, the knife of the law ought to fall upon them like the partisans of Coblenz. When, in spite of such threats, the king was suspended, Brissot demanded that he be well treated. He attacked those who defended the 10th of August and brought it about; he made a fine protest of indignation against the massacres of September, but at the time he was glad enough to profit by the

---

[1] *Procès-verbal,* June 23, 1793.

[2] Brissot, *Mémoires,* ii, 272; note, by M. Perroud.

[3] *Registre des délibérations prises par le conseil général de la commune de Moulins, 1 juillet, 1793* and *Moniteur,* June 25, 1793.

shedding of blood, and inquired eagerly whether one of his personal enemies had been assassinated; he used his influence against peace in October, 1792, and, besides, threatened the Convention with the arms of England and Spain; and to gain influence in America, had his brother-in-law appointed vice-consul-general at Philadelphia. At the time of the king's trial he endeavored to save him from execution, and then, when it was too late to save him personally, he conspired with Dumouriez in favor of royalty; and finally he tried to raise civil war against Paris and to get the aid of Dillon in proclaiming the son of Louis XVI king and his mother regent. The conspiracy was directed from Saint-Cloud, where Madame Brissot received the conspirators in the former royal palace, where they planned the destruction of the Republic." [1]

In his prison cell, Brissot prepared an answer to these charges — an answer which was both able and eloquent.[2] He now learned for the first time, he declared, the nature of the charges made against him and his friends; but although they now knew of what they were accused, Saint-Just had failed to produce the written evidence which he promised. Moreover, many of the accusations concerned matters of opinion, and it was contrary to law to judge a deputy for his opinions. The general charges of royalty and federalism, he asserted, were manifestly absurd, as they mutually contradicted each other, and, as for the latter, the departmental movement burst forth after and not before the 2d of June, and, as shown by the oath taken by the rebels against the Convention, was not for the purpose of destroying but of preserving the unity and indivisibility of the Republic. Having thus dealt with the charges against the Girondins as a whole, Brissot then turned to the points in which

---

[1] *Moniteur*, July 18, 19, 1793.

[2] M. Perroud sees no reason to doubt the genuineness of this defense. One internal evidence of great weight in its favor, he points out, is the curious mistakes in proper names in the Montrol edition — mistakes which can most reasonably be accounted for on the supposition that the matter was printed from a manuscript of Brissot's which the editor had difficulty in deciphering. See *Mémoires*, ii, 232; note by M. Perroud.

he himself was especially assailed, and took up his own personal defense. He had been compared to Monk, but his character and that of Monk, he declared, far from offering points of resemblance, presented only antitheses. "Monk was a courtier, and I have always hated courts from the bottom of my heart; Monk commanded armies, and I am a stranger to the art of war; Monk was powerful, and I am powerless; Monk was ambitious, and I have no ambition, not even for glory; Monk changed his party, and I have invariably kept to that of the Republic; Monk was made a duke as the price of his treason, and I should always have the fear of the scaffold before me if I should be base and stupid enough to commit treason; for, in the eyes of kings, I have committed a crime that they never pardon: I have condemned a king to death; I have dared to say that a king deserves death as I dared to advance the idea that it would be impolitic to make him suffer it." His enemies, Brissot continued, asserted that he had defended monarchy; let them cite a single passage from his works before as well as after 1789, where he had upheld it. As for the special phrase cited, in which he called down the knife upon any one daring to propose a republic, it was taken from its context, and was, as a matter of fact, included in that speech of July 26 which was approved by the Assembly, as was evidenced by the fact that they ordered it printed. "In short," Brissot declared with indignation, "it is with a phrase uttered in 1792 under the old constitution that they try to prove that under the Republic in 1793, I wanted to reëstablish royalty." [1]

The reason why the Girondins were in favor of suspension instead of dethronement, Brissot went on to say, was not because they were seeking to preserve royalty, but because suspension was the way to avoid a regency and to bring about a total change in the form as well as in the personnel of government. It was alleged against him, as though it were a crime, that he asked after the 10th of August that the king be treated

---

[1] This does not seem quite accurate, as it was to show that Brissot was attached to the monarchy in the summer of 1792 that these words were cited.

with humanity; he did not remember making such a request, but granted that he did, would cruelty be a republican virtue? In any case, he showed his opposition to royalty by his proposition for the dismissal of the Swiss troops and by the address to foreign powers, which was his own work. He could not be accused of calumniating Paris, for he never attacked the disorder and anarchy which there prevailed without carefully explaining that he was not attacking Paris as a whole, but only the evil forces therein. The Morande incident he emphatically denied. On the contrary he tried, he asserted, to induce Danton to put a stop to the massacres and used all the means in his power to have those responsible punished. He never heard of the propositions for peace referred to; in fact, no diplomatic committee existed at the date in question. The war was due, in the first place, to the action of the *émigrés* and the electors; the appeal to the people was not for the purpose of saving the king, but to avoid civil dissension and to take from foreign powers all pretext for interference by making them see that the judgment of the king was the wish of the nation.

He himself was in no way responsible for the war with England. On the contrary, he did all he could to prevent it. The real cause was England's own conduct. That he had any understanding with England or America, he emphatically denied, and to adduce the appointment of his brother-in-law to a post in Philadelphia as a proof of the latter connection, was a sheer absurdity. The charges of complicity with Dumouriez and Dillon were likewise without foundation. In the case of Dillon, the date of the alleged plot precluded any possibility of guilt on his part, as he was already under arrest at Moulins. He had fled, moreover, not to conspire, but because he believed that the Convention was not free.

But absurd as these charges were, the height of absurdity was reached, Brissot declared, in the accusation that the conspiracy was directed in the salon of Madame Brissot in a once royal palace. All that the tale of the royal palace amounted to was that Madame Brissot had for a time rented two rooms in the apartment of the concierge of the palace. As for the political salon, Madame Brissot lived in absolute seclusion, devoted to the education of her children and caring for her household, without even the aid of a servant. To penetrate into his one refuge from political life and to drag his private and personal relations into publicity was nothing short of an outrage. If they insisted on a scrutiny of his private life, they would find the most democratic simplicity, if not actual poverty — in itself an answer to the calumny that he profited by the Revolution to enrich his family.[1]

The writing of this eloquent defense occupied much of his time during the month of July. Counting the forty-five days of his imprisonment, referred to above, from the 10th of June, he must have finished it about the 8th of August.[2] It was written at the Abbaye, where he had been imprisoned since the 23d of June.[3] Madame Roland was one of the prisoners there at the time of Brissot's arrival. The next day she was removed,[4] she herself thought, on account of the fear of the authorities of communication between them, but according to Sophie Grandchamp, the friend of Madame Roland, it was because Madame Roland occupied the one cell which was considered a proper place of confinement for Brissot.[5] In spite of the removal, they managed to establish communication through Mentelle,[6] Bosc,[7] and Champagneux,[8] and it appears to be in part, at least, due to Madame Roland that Brissot was instigated to write his memoirs.[9] This production he turned over a few weeks before his condemnation to his friend Mentelle,[10] who, knowing how keenly Madame Roland would be interested, offered to let her see the manuscript. She, however, realized

---

[1] *Réponse au rapport de Saint-Just, Mémoires*, ii, 230–71.
[2] *Mémoires de Brissot*, ii, 271; note by M. Perroud.
[3] See p. 363.   [4] *Mémoires de Madame Roland*, ii, 351, and note.
[5] *Ibid.*, ii, 485.   [6] See p. 17.   [7] See p. 121.
[8] The former assistant of Roland in the ministry of the interior.
[9] *Mémoires de Brissot*, i, ix. See also *Lettres de Madame Roland*, ii, 734.
[10] *Édition de Montrol*, preface, xix, *et seq.*

the danger of loss or confiscation, and wrote back to Mentelle that unless a copy existed, she was unwilling to run the risk.[1] During this time, too, he also wrote what he called a "legacy to his children."

While engaged in writing these memoirs and last messages to his family, he was also making appeals to the Committee of Public Safety and to the Convention. The day after his incarceration at the Abbaye, he wrote to the Committee, enclosing a letter which he asked to have read to the Convention, and begging at the same time to be allowed to see his wife. Such permission was granted, he wrote, when he was imprisoned in the Bastille under the old régime, and the régime of liberty surely would not be more severe. On the 24th[2] and again on the 27th of June, he wrote asking to be given a hearing. Marat was not condemned unheard, he argued; would they do less for him? He also begged again for permission to see his wife, his mother-in-law, and his sister-in-law. And on June 30 he once more begged the Convention for permission to see his sister-in-law on necessary business.[3] These demands were apparently answered only in part, for, although the Committee of Public Safety, on July 3, granted him permission to communicate with his mother-in-law and his sister-in-law, nothing was said about his wife.[4] Thus separated from those who were dearest to him and tortured with crushing anxiety as to their future and his, Brissot dragged out the weary weeks of his imprisonment.

According to his enemies, he was still engaged in fomenting conspiracy against the Convention — a charge which he vehemently and indignantly denied.[5] "The people ask you for

---

[1] "*Je ne veux point voir les cahiers de B. que lorsque vous en auriez un double, il y a toujours du danger dans les transports, et il ne faut pas risquer une perte irréparable.*" *Lettres de Madame Roland,* II, 527.

[2] See *Bib. nat., fr. nouv. acq.* 307.

[3] *Correspondance,* 369–72.

[4] *Receuil des actes du comité de salut public,* v, 153. The 9th of August, Madame Brissot herself was put under surveillance. *Notice sur la vie de Brissot,* in *Correspondance,* lxvi.

[5] This seems to be apropos of a report, made by Barère to the Convention

bread," he wrote to Barère the 7th of September, "you have promised them my blood. Thus you order my death even before I am brought to trial. . . . Ah! if my blood could bring abundance and put an end to all divisions, I would shed it myself immediately. In order to excuse that sanguinary phrase, you imagine that I am conspiring in my prison, you imagine that I have said, '*Before my head falls, heads will fall in the Convention !*' . . . Yes, I conspire with my triple locks and my triple bars! I conspire alone or with the philosophers of antiquity who teach me to bear the wrongs which I suffer for the cause of liberty, that cause of which I shall always be the apostle." [1]

Meanwhile the Convention was preparing to bring Brissot and the other accused Girondins to trial. After several attempts had been made to hasten the procedure,[2] the general indictment against them was finally presented, on October 3, by Amar. This, the decisive act which brought the Girondins before the revolutionary tribunal, consisted of forty-five distinct counts. It repeated many of the charges of Saint-Just's report, but was longer, more detailed, and more sweeping. It presented Brissot as the head and front of the Girondins and the most culpable member of that faction. There existed a conspiracy, Amar declared, against the liberty and safety of the French people, and Brissot was one of its leaders. This Brissot, who was an agent of the police and a base intriguer

the 5th of September, on the danger of a rising in Paris. It was followed by a demand that Brissot and several others be brought at once before the revolutionary tribunal. *Moniteur*, September 6, 1793.

[1] The letter given is in Vatel, *Charlotte Corday et les Girondins*, ii, 250–51; also in *Correspondance*, 376–78.

[2] The 26th of July the Convention decreed that the Committees of General Security and Legislation be required to present, with as little delay as possible, the act of accusation against Brissot. The 19th of August the public prosecutor asked for the papers and acts of accusation against Brissot. Whereupon the Convention sent a request to the Committee of General Security to make its report in three days. August 25, the public prosecutor complained that he had not yet received the papers, and on October 1 the Committee of General Security was again asked to report immediately. See the *procès-verbal* of the Convention on these different days.

under the old régime, began his career in the Revolution as a member of the *Comité de Recherches* of the Commune of Paris, in which he acted as the agent of Lafayette. Even when Lafayette, in April, 1791, showed his sympathy for the king and made pretense of resigning the command of the Parisian guard, Brissot continued to support him and declared in the *Patriote Français* that the retirement of Lafayette would be a public calamity. Brissot, moreover, was always an enemy of popular societies and showed himself at the Jacobins only at times of crisis. The first occasion was in the month of April, 1790, when, under the pretense of philanthropy, he inaugurated a plan which was to end in the ruin of the colonies; the second occasion was in March, 1791, when, in criminal collusion with Lafayette, he prepared the way for the day of the *Champ de Mars*, in order to give Lafayette a chance to assassinate the patriots. The third occasion was in January, 1792, when he came to preach war with the purpose of hindering the Revolution and destroying liberty.[1]

On his election to the Legislative Assembly, Brissot allied himself openly with the deputies of the Gironde and tried, together with them, to usurp a useful popularity, by defending the cause of the people on occasions of slight importance, although they abandoned it often enough in times of crisis. They were the agents of the court in trying to bring about war at a time when France was in no way prepared for it. With traitorous intent they supported Narbonne, lauding him to the skies, and getting him sent to the army, contrary to all law, before he had rendered his accounts as minister. Brissot and Condorcet came forward in their newspapers as the defenders of Dietrich, who was convicted of complicity with Lafayette and of having worked to deliver up Strasbourg. Brissot and the mob tried to prevent the 10th of August and treated with the king. Brissot gave the king advice pernicious to liberty, as is proved by a letter in his hand addressed to Louis XVI, in possession of the *Comité de Surveillance*, in which his signature

---

[1] *Moniteur*, October 20, 27, 1793.

is scratched out. Moreover, he showed not only in his secret correspondence, but also in public speech, his attachment to monarchy, when he declared, on June 26, that the knife of the law ought to fall on those who desired a republic. At the same time he was responsible for the newspaper entitled the *Républicain*, published in March, 1791 (*sic*), and for the petition which led to the butchery of the *Champ de Mars*. But in July of 1792, when people wanted a republic, he tried to save royalty, and after the 10th of August he tried to mitigate the king's imprisonment by having him placed at the Luxembourg. He was one of those who attacked the leaders who had brought about the 10th of August; he and other agents of the English faction had a part in planning the Belgian campaign, in which Dumouriez let the Prussians retire. They wanted to receive the Duke of Brunswick at Paris; they planned to flee with the king and the Legislative Assembly beyond the Loire. Brissot appealed to the people to save Louis XVI; he then proposed a declaration of war with England after having tried to prevent it; he conspired with Dumouriez, proposed a national guard around Paris as a base of federalism, stirred up rebellion against Paris; when arrested at Moulins he was probably on his way to Lyons to foment further rebellion; and finally, if he were not in actual alliance with Pitt, it was curious that he and Pitt were working for precisely the same things — the overthrow of the Republic, the destruction of Paris, the ruin of the French colonies, and the arming of all Europe against France.

In his cell in the Conciergerie, Brissot thus learned from this report what charges were to be made against him when he should be brought before the bar for trial. He accordingly began at once a *Projet de défense devant le tribunal révolutionnaire en réponse au rapport d'Amar*.[1] It was an able and lengthy

---

[1] *Mémoires*, ii, 272–306. In the first paragraph he speaks of his rigorous captivity of four months. M. Perroud notes: "*L'arrestation de Brissot est du dixième juin. C'est donc vers le dixième octobre, à la Conciergerie, où il avait été transferé le sixième, qu'il dut commencer ce projet de défense.*" *Ibid.*, ii, 272, note.

defense which he drew up,[1] a final and supreme effort to clear himself from the charge of treason and to prove that he was a sincere patriot, and, above all, a true lover of liberty.

"France and Europe have resounded for some time," he declared, "with the alleged conspiracy of thirty-two deputies against the Republic." They accused him of being at the head of it. But, he continued, he had long waited with impatience for them to give definite details of these crimes. And, in the meantime, calumniators were profiting by their silence to stir up public opinion against them. Unless, then, they spoke out in their defense, there was danger that people think them powerless to defend themselves. "I am therefore going to refute," he declared, "all the facts alleged against me in the reports of Saint-Just and Amar. I shall prove that there is not one of them which is not absolutely false. In order to prop up their absurd accusation, they have ransacked all my past life; I thank my adversaries, for my entire life has been devoted to liberty and will bear witness to my love for it." Of this love, all his early works bore witness, he maintained. His *Théorie des lois criminelles*, his *Bibliothèque philosophique*, denounced the crimes of kings and ministers; his *Correspondance politique* and his *Tableau des sciences et des arts en Angleterre* were written to inoculate France with the principles of the English and American constitutions; *l'Histoire philosophique d'Angleterre* to show to the French people the course which they ought to pursue to break their fetters; his *Lettres à Joseph II* exhorted a tyrannized people to reconquer their rights. In short, there was not a single one of his works which did not have for its object "to avenge humanity, liberty, and reason from the outrages of despotism." His journey to America was undertaken in order that he might learn how to bring about a like revolution in France, and to find a place of abode for his family in a new country, in case it should be necessary to abandon hope of

---

[1] It was nearly twice as long as his answer to Saint-Just. He naturally repeated some of his arguments, as this defense was not only an answer to Amar, but to all the denunciations made against himself.

such a revolution at home; and on his return to France, he embarked on the dangerous career of a journalist, in order that he might daily combat the prejudices, the abuses of despotism and aristocracy.[1]

"I, accused of royalism in 1793!" he continued; "I, who offered myself on eleven successive ballots for the place of deputy to the Legislative Assembly, to be overwhelmed with thousands of libels only because of my known republicanism.

"I, who wishing to combat every kind of aristocracy, that of color as well as that of nobility, published so many works in order to raise to the level of the white colonists that valuable class of mulattoes who form the bulwark of our colonies and who will save them from the hand of our enemies.

"I, who in 1789 dared to be the first and only one to maintain that the Constituent Assembly had not the right to make a constitution without the approval of the people — a truth which was recognized only after the establishment of the Republic in 1792.

"I, who at the time of the flight of the king and when the most ardent patriots trembled at the mere name of a republic, tried on several occasions, and especially in my speech of July 10, 1791, to reconcile them to the republican régime and to induce them at least to establish an executive council named by the people and independent of the king.

"I, who during the Legislative Assembly, worked, talked, published with the one purpose of diminishing the royal prerogative, of preventing its fatal effects, of unmasking the treason of the ministers, and, since the king would not maintain liberty, of bringing about the Republic by a second revolution."

After thus defending his general principles, Brissot took up, one by one, the specific charges against him. He denied that he had ever been a spy or had had any nefarious connections with England. He was not married to an English woman, as was alleged, and his stay in England in 1783–84 for the pur-

---

[1] Note that he puts forward his democratic principles as an evidence of republicanism.

pose of studying English institutions was a flimsy basis for the charge of conspiracy in 1793. As for his alleged complicity with Lafayette, what connection, he asked, had his relations with him in 1790 with a conspiracy in 1793? He had been deceived in Lafayette, he admitted, but surely Lafayette's part in the American Revolution and Washington's admiration for him were good reasons for believing that Lafayette was a sincere friend of liberty and republicanism. He himself, however, had never sought his favor,[1] his election to the first municipality of Paris was not due to Lafayette's protection; moreover, as a member of that municipality, he had worked against the royalists, had tried to prevent action against the instigators of the riots of October 5 and 6, and had opposed the plans of Lafayette, and after the 17th of July he had openly denounced him. He was not responsible for the petition which led to the massacre, and as soon as Lafayette showed his true colors by firing on the public, he (Brissot) attacked him in his newspaper. That in spite of these attacks, he went about openly in the streets of Paris, while the other enemies of Lafayette were hiding, was not an evidence, as was alleged, that he had a secret understanding with Lafayette, but was, on the contrary, a proof of his own bravery and fearlessness. Moreover, since that time, he had never ceased to denounce him.

Another charge laid at his door was responsibility for the war with Austria. But war was a matter of honor, and was inevitable, and if he did wage war, he had the support of the entire nation. Moreover, war was declared on April 20, and his last speech on the subject was delivered the 9th of January; it was plain that other influences must have been at work. He was also charged with being allied with the court. But he had had no personal relations with the royal family; he had always been their enemy; and while they had tried to put off the war, he had been for it.

He was likewise charged with responsibility for the disasters

---

[1] But see page 162 for his efforts to get money out of Lafayette for the cause of popular societies.

in the colonies. Such an accusation must concern itself, he declared, only with his opinions, for he had never had any part in the administration of the colonies, and had never had any correspondence with any one there. As for his opinions, they were both patriotic and republican. They were not only not the cause of the disasters of Santo Domingo, but those disasters could be attributed only to violation of the principles which he defended; in fact, his opinions could not be criticized without condemning with him all those who had sustained the same principles and the three national assemblies which had sanctioned them. The real cause of the civil war was the perfidy of the agents of the government, the aristocracy of the whites, the vacillation and inconsistency of the Constituent Assembly, while the revolt of the blacks was due to the counter-revolutionists in alliance with the counter-revolutionists of Spain and England. His approval of the commissioners, Santhonax and Polverel, now under decrees of accusation, was charged against him. To be consistent, like accusation would have to be brought against all the Jacobins, and, in any case, waiving the question of their guilt, he had never had any correspondence with them.[1] That he had been paid a sou for his opinions by Pitt or by any one else, he indignantly denied.

Another accusation laid upon him was that he was responsible for the war with England. On the contrary, he had, he declared, done all that he could to prevent war with England. Witness his opposition in July, 1792, to the proposition for a Batavian legion which would have alarmed England and Holland; his efforts as member of the Diplomatic Committee to engage Delessart to enter into negotiations with the court of St. James, his furtherance of the embassy of Chauvelin and Talleyrand. The real responsibility for the war with England rested on the authors of the decrees of November 19 and December 15 and of the annexation of Belgium and other conquered countries, also on the enemies of the appeal to the people. And for

[1] M. Perroud points out that there exists a letter written by Santhonax to Brissot. See *Correspondance*, 331–34.

these measures he was in no way, he declared, responsible; he had no part in opening the Scheldt, which was ordered by the executive council without informing the Diplomatic Committee; he opposed the decree of November 19, protector of insurrections, since he strongly urged that it be sent back to the Diplomatic Committee to be drawn up in such a fashion as not to alarm neutral powers; he repeatedly warned the partisans of annexation, and especially of the annexation of Belgium, that they would draw upon France the arms of England; in his different expressions of opinion on the trial of the king, he gave constant warning that if he were condemned without having the judgment ratified by the people, France would be exposed to a rupture with England. For all these reasons he disclaimed all responsibility. Then, taking up his speech of January 12, — and here he was on firmer ground than in some of his preceding assertions,[1] — he reiterated his arguments on that occasion against war; and finally coming to the speech after the execution of the king, in which he proposed the formal declaration of war, he pointed out that there he was speaking not personally, but in the name of the Committee, and that in any case the action of the English government had by that time made war inevitable.

This eloquent plea stops abruptly, and it is evident that he was called to trial before he had had time to finish it. The prospect of the trial gave further opportunity to Brissot's opponents, and while he was thus defending himself, renewed accusations continued to pour in against him. On the 29th of September a deputation of the French colonies denounced the writings and speeches of Brissot as the cause of the disasters of the colonies and asked that prompt measures be taken to bring him to justice.[2] Ruelle, *chargé d'affaires* in the Netherlands, accused him of having removed from the papers of the Diplomatic Committee the complaint which he (Ruelle) had made against the

[1] There was some truth in Brissot's assertion, in so far as he stood for less precipitation, but his claims here are not in accord with his exuberant rejoicing at some of these measures.

[2] *Procès-verbal de la Convention*, September 29, 1793.

minister Lebrun.[1] A letter addressed to the public accuser, signed Guisat, suggested that Charles Théveneau Morande, being an enemy of Brissot and at the same time *au courant* with the intrigues of the British government, might be able to give valuable testimony. Another citizen wrote that a former general of the Army of the North had certain information to give against Brissot in regard to his correspondence with Dumouriez and his intrigues in Holland.[2] Unsigned communications entitled "*À ajouter à l'affaire de Brissot*" and "*Notice sur Brissot*,"[3] professed to give proof of his alleged conspiracy with England to ruin the colonies. All these are further evidence of the animosity against him.[4]

On the 15th of October he was brought before the revolutionary tribunal for a preliminary examination. The questions put to him involved the accusations already made either in the formal decrees or in the recent personal denunciations, and his answers were reiterations of his innocence and an emphatic denial of all the charges from first to last. At the beginning of the examination he was asked to name a lawyer for his defense and chose Chaveau Delagarde.[5]

This preliminary examination was followed by the trial which began on October 24. As in Amar's accusation, so in the trial, Brissot occupied the chief place, and, as the most prominent of the accused, had a special chair.[6] Fourteen witnesses were called, the testimony of ten of whom concerned Brissot.[7]

---

[1] *A. N.*, W 292, *dossier 204, 2e partie, pièce* 73, 74. See also *Procès-verbal de la Convention*, July 30, 1793.

[2] *A. N.*, W 292, *dossier 204, 3e partie, pièces 6 et 10.*

[3] *A. N.*, F7, 4443, no. 18.

[4] *A. N.*, AA54, 1509, no. 46. Appendix C.

[5] *Interrogatoire de Jacques Pierre Brissot, Archives nationales*, W 292, *dossier 204, 5e partie*. Printed in the *Correspondance*, 378–85. "*Chaveau Delagarde dut au début de la Révolution avoir des liaisons avec Brissot (voir deux lettres de lui au Patriote Français des 15 fev. 1790 et 25 sept. 1791)*." *Lettres de Madame Roland*, II, 532, note.

[6] Aulard, *Histoire politique*, 404.

[7] The records of the trial are preserved at the *National Archives* at Paris, W 292, *dossier 204, Affaire des Girondins*. The account given there is, however, very brief. See also the *Moniteur* of October 27, 1793, Supplement; the *Bulletin du tribunal révolutionnaire* and the *Révolutions de Paris*.

The ten were Pache,[1] Chaumette,[2] Destournelles,[3] Hébert,[4] Chabot,[5] Montaut,[6] Fabre d'Eglantine,[7] Bourdon,[8] Desfaix,[9] and Duhem [10] — all of the party of the Mountain. Their charges, on the one hand, and Brissot's defense, on the other, are for the most part reiterations of the accusations and answers already made. Indeed, practically every charge which had been brought forward was repeated, but the so-called testimony in support of these charges consisted more of mere assertions than of definite proof, and was often either vague or trivial. In addition to what had previously been adduced,

---

[1] Jean Nicolas Pache (born 1746, died 1823) was made minister of war under Girondin influence in 1792, but went over to the side of the Mountain and was put out of the ministry. He became mayor of Paris and was one of the instigators of the insurrection of May 31.

[2] Pierre Gaspard Chaumette (born 1763, died 1794) was closely connected with the Commune of Paris, was the author of some of the most revolutionary measures and was the friend and supporter of Hébert, with whom he was executed.

[3] Louis Deschamps Destournelles (born 1746, died 1794) was elected minister of public contributions by the Convention in 1793 and was a member of the Commune of Paris.

[4] Jacques René Hébert (born 1755, died 1794) was a famous demagogue, the editor of the *Père Duchesne*, and a member of the insurrectionary Commune of Paris of August 10. He was guillotined in 1794.

[5] François Chabot (born 1759, died 1794) was a deputy to the Legislative and to the Convention, and was one of the most advanced revolutionists. He was condemned to death and executed with Danton and Desmoulins in the spring of 1794.

[6] Louis de Maribonde Montaut (born 1754, died 1842) was a deputy to the Legislative and to the Convention and was a most bitter enemy of royalty. He defended the massacres of September and stirred up prosecutions against the royalists and contributed to the fall of the Girondins.

[7] Philippe François Nazaire Fabre d'Eglantine (born 1755, died 1794) was a deputy from Paris to the Convention and a friend and ally of Desmoulins and Danton. He had a certain reputation as a poet and man of letters. He was condemned to death with the Dantonists.

[8] Léonard Bourdon (born 1758, died 1815) was a member of the Convention and one of the most advanced of the party of the Mountain.

[9] François Desfaix (born 1755, died 1794) was a famous orator at the Jacobins, took the initiative in a number of prosecutions, and was executed with the Hébertists.

[10] Pierre Joseph Duhem (born 1760, died 1807) was a deputy to the Legislative and to the Convention. He was a most implacable enemy of printers and journalists and was one of the instigators of the insurrection of May 31.

the testimony and the defense may be summarized as follows: As a member of the *Comité des Recherches* of the Commune, Brissot had tried to impede the revolution, and, to this
end, had protected Bailly and Lafayette; he had tried to form
a secret club in order to neutralize the influence of the Jacobins; he was in part responsible for the disasters of the colonies,
as was evident from the fact that he had given Santhonax a
secret mission; he had praised and upheld Narbonne, and when
Delessart, seeing through the plans of Narbonne, helped to
bring about his dismissal, Brissot attacked Delessart; in his
attack on the Austrian committee, he was both vacillating and
equivocal; he had great influence over the Girondin ministry
and named the agents of the diplomatic service, as was evident
from Robert's complaint against Brissot for failing to name him
to the post at Constantinople; under the Legislative Assembly,
he allied himself with Marat and they together introduced
measures against the king, and then withdrew them the next
day, in order to sell themselves more dearly. He did not want
monarchy overthrown, and therefore he was pleased with the
action of June 21; and when told by Chabot that it had put
off liberty by three centuries, retorted that it would produce
what they had expected, namely, the return of the ministry.
On the 8th of August, at an assembly in the rue d'Argenteuil,
Brissot had rushed in and announced with breathless dismay
what he called most incendiary proposals at the Jacobins.
After the 10th of August, he had been much concerned for the
safety of Capet and had tried to have him kept at the *hôtel
de justice*. The Committee of Twenty-One, after the 10th of
August, had rejected the eighty-four stars in the new seal, sig-
nifying unity, which proved that they had ideas of federalism.
On the 11th, Brissot, at the home of Pétion, had practically
made threats against the representatives of the Commune.
He had used his influence to control the elections to the Convention, and in particular he had written a letter to the electoral body of Beaugency to induce them to choose Louvet.
At the epoch of the massacres, he had calumniated Paris in

the interest of Pitt, in order to arouse English sentiment against France. These massacres he had spoken of in the newspaper of Gorsas as "just and terrible," and worse than that, he was at Pétion's when the assassins came in, their hands covered with blood, and when Pétion drank with them. He had insulted Montaut when, at the king's trial, the latter had voted for death and accused Brissot of humanity toward the tyrant; he had proposed sending troops against Spain when war had not yet broken out with that nation, his real purpose being to use them for a sectional war. And, finally, he was engaged in the conspiracy against Paris; and as evidence of his interest and influence in this conspiracy, it was alleged that he had not told what he knew about the revolt in the Vendée and that a letter of his (apparently the address to his constituents) had had much weight in stirring up feeling at Bordeaux.

In answer to these charges, Brissot made the following defense. He denied that as a member of the *Comité des Recherches* he had tried to hinder the Revolution, or that he had protected Bailly and Lafayette, and in support of his contention, offered to produce a certificate of approval from the municipal government. The secret and suspicious club to which Chabot referred was a perfectly innocent meeting, whose nucleus was the deputation from the Gironde drawn toward Brissot by their common interest in the colonies. As for Santhonax, although he had spoken well of him, he had never given him any secret mission to the colonies. In his attack on the Austrian committee, he had perhaps gone too far and had made charges which he was unable to substantiate, but that was because Chabot himself had withheld certain papers which were needed to complete the proof. As to his influence on the ministry, Robert was mistaken in thinking that he (Brissot) had any great weight; he did interest himself in behalf of Genet, but when he gave advice it was because it was asked for. He was not a monarchist; on the contrary, he did all he could to discredit the supporters of monarchy, Montmorin and Delessart; he was opposed to dethronement only so long as public

opinion was not ripe for it; the specific instance of the meeting
in the rue d'Argenteuil he did not remember; his interest in
the place of abode for the king after the 10th of August was
only that he might be near the Assembly, and he did not
threaten the representatives of the Commune. He did, he admitted, write a letter to the president of the electoral club
recommending Louvet, but he did not intend it to be read to
the Assembly. The reference to a comment in the journal of
Gorsas on the days of September he did not remember, and
while he did not deny being at Pétion's, he did deny that any
one came in while he was there with his hands covered with
blood. He did not remember having insulted Montaut, but
was quite sure that he (Brissot) had never voted against a decree in favor of humanity. The troops which he was charged
with wishing to use against Paris were really intended for use
either against Spain directly or for a naval attack on Mexico.
He had not withheld information on the Vendée; even if he
had information, it was the business of the ministry to announce it. His address of May 26 he did indeed sell openly
at the door of the Convention, but he had not sent it to Bordeaux. That he was a monarchist, a federalist, or a traitor to
the Revolution or to his country, in the pay of Pitt or of any
one else, he vehemently and indignantly denied.

In considering the value of his defense and the charges to
which it was a reply, it must be remembered in the first place
that the records of the trial are untrustworthy. The meager
procès-verbal preserved at the Archives does not give the testimony, and the details furnished by the *Moniteur* and the *Bulletin du tribunal révolutionnaire* were presented by the enemies of
the Girondins and in the most hostile spirit. For example,
in the account in the *Moniteur* and the *Bulletin*, the evidence
of the witnesses is given in full, while the replies of the accused
are frequently summarized. But even taking the records at
their face value, many of the charges were manifestly absurd
or, as was stated above, based on unworthy evidence. Further,
the witnesses were not only prejudiced and interested persons,

but avowed and special enemies, and several of them had had a part in the expulsion of the Girondins — witnesses whose testimony in any court which made the slightest pretense of justice would be heavily discounted. Moreover, no effort was made to secure an impartial jury; on the contrary, it was made up by the committees of the Assembly, and was composed of the most violent members of the Mountain. Consequently, Brissot and the other Girondins were virtually condemned before they were tried.

It does not appear that Brissot had an opportunity to make use of the defense he had prepared. According to the notes of Chaveau Delagarde, he was condemned unheard, without a chance to make a final defense either personally or through his advocate.[1] According to Miss Helena Williams, who, however, is by no means reliable, he defended himself with such eloquence that not only his colleagues, but even the chairmen of the hostile committees were almost overcome by it.[2] But taking the account in its worst possible light, the only reasonable or important charges from which Brissot did not clear himself are his opposition to the 10th of August and his passive attitude toward the massacres of September. But granting that he did not want the insurrection and that he made no objection to the massacres, that does not prove that he was an anti-revolutionist.

---

[1] "*Je fus chargé de défendre dans cette affaire notamment Vergniaud et Brissot, et par une singularité qui n'appartient qu'à elle seule et que personne peut-être n'a pas encore jusqu'à présent observée, ces infortunés ont été condamnés sans avoir été défendus ni par eux-mêmes ni par leurs défenseurs.*" Quoted in Vatel, *Vergniaud*, ii, 426.

[2] She may refer to his reply to each witness in turn, while Delagarde seems to refer to the absence of a final summing up. "*Brissot, comme on sait, se défendit avec tant d'éloquence devant le tribunal révolutionnaire, que je fus frappée de l'effet surprenant que son discours produisit sur son collègue Lasource, comme lui accusé, et qui venait passer les soirées dans la chambre de la prison du Luxembourg, où nous étions alors tous enfermés. Il m'assura que l'auditoire, composé cependant de Jacobins, fut ému jusqu'aux larmes, et que le chef du jury révolutionnaire, Antonelle, était agité de convulsions nerveuses, qui le secouaient sur son siège. J'en avais presque pitié, me dit Lasource, il vaut bien mieux mourir.*" Williams, *Souvenirs de la Révolution Française*, 23.

The jurors, however, thought differently. The trial had commenced October 24. By October 29 the Convention became impatient. It had already decreed that there should be no general defense;[1] it now passed a decree to the effect that when the jurors of the revolutionary tribunal felt that they were "sufficiently informed," they might ask to have the trial closed.[2] This suggestive measure seems to have had the desired effect, for on the next day, October 30, the jurors declared themselves sufficiently informed, retired to deliberate, and the same day returned a verdict of guilty.[3] It was a solemn scene when the jurors came in with their verdict. If Villate[4] is to be believed, Camille Desmoulins, who was present, was almost overcome. According to Villate he was seated quite near the jurors' bench, and when the jury filed in, he rushed forward to speak to the foreman, M. Antonelle. Something in Antonelle's face stopped him and he exclaimed: "My God! I am sorry for you! This is a horrible day!" And when he heard the declaration of the jury, he lost all control of himself, crying aloud: "My God, my God, it is I who kill them, it is my *Brissot dévoilé*." As the accused filed in to hear the verdict, every one turned toward them. There was absolute silence. When the prosecuting attorney reached the fatal words, "punishment of death," Desmoulins all but fainted, and, although he wanted to get away from the terrible scene, was powerless to move. Brissot also was nearly overcome, Villate continued; "his arms dropped limply at his side, and his head fell forward on his breast. Gensonné, pale and trembling, asked to be allowed to speak on the application of the law. Boileau, in astonishment, threw up his hat, crying, 'I am innocent'; and turning passionately toward the people, invoked their aid. The accused sprang to their feet. 'We are innocent; people, you are deceived,' they cry. The people remain motionless. The gendarmes force the

---

[1] *Procès-verbal de la Convention*, September 26, 1793.

[2] *Moniteur*, October 30, 1793.

[3] *Ibid.*, October 27, 1793, Supplement.

[4] Villate (or Vilate; born 1768, died 1795) was a juror of the revolutionary tribunal. He is not altogether reliable.

people to sit down. Valazé draws from his breast a dagger which he thrusts into his heart; he falls over backward and expires. Sillery lets fall his two crutches, his face full of joy, and, rubbing his hands, cries out, 'It is the happiest day of my life!' The late hour, the lighted torches, the judges, and the public, worn out with the long session, — for it is midnight, — all give to that scene a sombre, imposing, terrible character." [1]

The statement that the condemned Girondins, in the forlorn hope of bringing about a rescue, threw assignats to the crowd in the courtroom, rests on good authority, but the incident is almost incredible. The *procès-verbal* says nothing of such an incident, nor does Villate, just quoted. On the other hand, it is given both in the *Bulletin* and in the *Moniteur*. [2]

Of that last night there remain few authentic details. The famous last banquet does not rest on contemporary evidence and has been shown to be a matter of legend rather than of fact. [3] Riouffe says that they kept up their courage well and spent the night in singing. [4] They were allowed confessors. Brissot, however, did not avail himself of the opportunity, though, when some of his friends expressed surprise, he hastened to assure them that he believed in eternal life in another world. [5] He

[1] Villate, *Mystères de la mère de Dieu dévoilés*, chap. XIII.

[2] See also *Les Révolutions de Paris*, no. 213, and an accompanying illustration. "*Le Moniteur et le Bulletin du tribunal révolutionnaire prétendent que les Girondins, pour exciter les assistants à se soulever en leur faveur, leur jetèrent des assignats, en criant: 'A nous, mes amis,' et que l'auditoire, indigné, ne répondit que par les cris de 'Vive la République!' Cette assertion est fausse. Vilate, qui assistait aux débats, n'en parle pas, et le procès-verbal de l'audience, conservé aux Archives de l'Empire, IV. 292, dossier 204, est également muet sur cet incident, qu'il eût assurément noté, s'il s'était passé.*" Campardon, *Le Tribunal révolutionnaire de Paris*, I, 158, note.

[3] See Granier de Cassagnac, *Histoire des Girondins, et des massacres de September*, I, 47; and Biré, *La Légende des Girondins*, 416–20. It is, of course, possible that they had a last meal together, but that it assumed the character which the legend has imputed to it is hardly possible. Lasource and Sillery, two of the alleged participants, were not at the Conciergerie at all.

[4] Riouffe, *Mémoires d'un détenu*, 65. Riouffe was a writer of some reputation. At first carried away by the principles of the Revolution, he turned against the Terrorists and was imprisoned.

[5] See the account of the Abbé Lothringer in the *Républicain français* of 6 fructidor an V (August 23, 1797); also Biré, 420, and Vatel, *Vergniaud*, II, 330.

could not help feeling keen anguish at the thought of parting from his family and anxiety for their future support, as is evident from the pathetic and yet brave letters which he wrote to his wife, mother-in-law, brothers, and sisters;[1] but at the same time he was strengthened by the firm conviction that he was dying for his country, and that some time he would be vindicated. He had already written to his family that death seen near at hand and looked at in a philosophical spirit lost all its horrors.[2] And he seems to have kept up his philosophic spirit to the last. On the testimony of a fellow prisoner, "he was grave and thoughtful, he had the air of a sage struggling with misfortune, and if he showed more concern than the others, it was only for his country."[3]

By the afternoon of the 30th he realized that the end was indeed near, and in anguish of spirit wrote his last farewell to his wife. "I see, my dear Félicité," he cried, "that my last hour has come. Unless I am greatly mistaken, they are going to give the verdict to-day. Perhaps I shall have the misfortune of not being able to see you again; yet I would give everything to be able to. If this happiness is refused, bear the blow with courage. You owe it to our children; watch over them; look out for them. Keep some of my notes to show to them some day. They will say: 'This is the writing of a father who loved us, and better than us loved the public good, for he sacrificed himself and has been sacrificed for it. . . .'

"Adieu, my loved ones, wipe away your tears. Mine are wetting this paper. But our separation will not be eternal."[4]

The next day the condemned were taken in carts to the place of execution. As they left the Conciergerie, they joined in singing the *Marseillaise*.[5] Even the hostile court admitted that they preserved their self-control to the last. The Executive Council, well aware of the importance of the occasion and of

---

[1] *Correspondance*, 388–93.

[2] *Mémoires*, I, 9. For the position of his family during these terrible days, see pp. 403–05, and *Lettres de Madame Roland*, II, 683.

[3] *Riouffe*, 60.   [4] *Correspondance*, 394.   [5] *Bulletin*, 64.

the danger of disorder, had taken due precautions.[1] Such measures were indeed required, for in spite of the bad weather[2] a larger crowd than had gathered on such occasions for years lined the streets and filled the windows all along the line of march.[3] Through this crowd, amid hostile cries of "*Vive la République*," "*À bas les traîtres*," the sad procession made its way from the Conciergerie to the Place de la Révolution. Here Brissot and the other condemned Girondins went bravely to their death.[4]

[1] *Recueil des actes du comité de salut public*, VIII, 119–20.
[2] *Révolutions de Paris*, no. 213, p. 148.
[3] *Bulletin*.
[4] They were buried at the cemetery of the Madeleine, as is attested by the undertaker's bill. See Vatel, *Vergniaud*, II, 337.

CHAPTER XIII

BRISSOT'S FAMILY LIFE

In one of his essays, Robert Louis Stevenson says that wherever there is a philosopher, there is a suffering relative in the background. This was certainly true of Brissot, and the suffering member of his family was his wife. Although she held no salon and played no part on the political stage, she was an active force behind the scenes, a presence indispensable to Brissot and the silent victim of his political misfortunes. A brief study of this personal aspect of Brissot's life renders vivid the heavy price in poverty, suffering, and sorrow paid by the family of a revolutionist, and at the same time it furnishes a picture of one of the most interesting women of the Revolution.

It was in 1778 at Boulogne, where he was engaged in work for Swinton, that Brissot first made the acquaintance of the young woman who was later to become his wife. In spite of a wide circle of friends and the *entrée* to the homes of some of the best families of the town, including relatives of Sainte-Beuve, he was lonely and unhappy. "My heart had been longing for some time for a special attachment," he wrote afterward in looking back on this period of his life. "It seemed to me that I was wandering about in space, and when I would come back at night to my solitary abode, I was always discontented with my lot. I needed another self and I did not find it."[1] While in this mood he met the woman who was to become his "other self" — Félicité Dupont. She was the daughter of a Madame Dupont, the widow of a merchant.[2] He seems to have been strongly drawn to her from the first, but as she was already

---

[1] *Mémoires*, I, 166.

[2] Phillips, an English writer of the time and a friend of Brissot, says that the mother of Mademoiselle Dupont kept a lodging-house at Boulogne, frequented chiefly by English people. *Biographical Anecdotes of the Founders of the French Republic*, II, 6.

engaged, he concealed and repressed his emotions and sought distraction in a whirl of social life and in passing attachments which left him only vain regrets.[1]

This distracting and unsatisfactory life at Boulogne soon came to an end. Swinton, Brissot's employer, became interested in other literary projects and found him no longer necessary. He was therefore obliged to throw himself once more into the whirlpool of Paris. He found life lonesome, and in his solitary walks in the Luxembourg, his thoughts turned back to the pleasant hours he had passed with Swinton's family at Boulogne, and the idea occurred to him that a marriage with Swinton's eldest daughter would be rather attractive. He therefore wrote to Swinton, but was promptly rejected as a most undesirable *parti* — a rebuff which injured his pride rather than his heart. He had frankly admitted that the girl in question had her faults. Indeed, it is quite evident that the charms of the daughter were much less seductive than the possibilities of a business alliance with her father.[2]

But he soon found consolation in his trials and disappointments through the geographer Mentelle. This connection, among many other things, he owed to Madame Dupont. She was a friend of Mentelle and had commended Brissot to him. The latter responded with promptness and cordiality. He went to call on Brissot soon after Brissot's arrival in Paris, invited him to his house and introduced him to his friends. A keen memory of his own early struggles made him most sympathetic with the young journalist, and Brissot found in him not merely a profitable means of extending his acquaintance among literary men, but a lifelong friend.[3]

Best of all, at the house of Mentelle, he found Félicité Dupont, who had come up to Paris to finish her education. The freedom with which he was received there gave him abundant opportunity for pursuing her acquaintance, and as she had broken her engagement, there was now no further obstacle to his suit. To his great joy she responded to his affection and

---

[1] *Mémoires*, i, 167.   [2] *Ibid.*, i, 177–78.   [3] *Ibid.*, i, 185–86.

they soon became engaged. The two years of their engagement were the happiest of his life. Félicité shared his intellectual interests, which at this time were largely along the line of scientific pursuits. They read and studied and went to Fourcroy's lectures on chemistry together, and then spent their evenings in going over the lessons of the day. Félicité was especially interested in medicine and devoted herself to such studies in natural philosophy as would prepare her to be a good mother to her children.[1] At the same time she used her influence to get Brissot to study anatomy. The dream of his life, he felt, was realized; he had found at the same time a good wife and a good comrade. Moreover, she sympathized not only with his intellectual interests, but with his weaknesses, and when he confessed to her an old *liaison* and the existence of a child, she forgave the past and even thought of receiving the child into their home and bringing it up as their own.[2]

Although he was hardly in a position financially to marry, his confident expectations of success in the *Lycée de Londres* led him to take the step; and on September 17, 1782, he and Félicité were quietly married at Paris.[3] At that time Félicité was employed as a kind of governess under the direction of Madame Genlis for one of the daughters of the Duke of Chartres.[4] As it seemed imprudent for Brissot to take his wife over to England till he had managed to lay at least the foundation for his *Lycée*, it was decided that he should go alone and that she should continue her work. Moreover, while their financial resources were so precarious, it would be well for her not to abandon her means of livelihood. It was for this reason, apparently, that the marriage was kept secret.[5]

The parting was hard, but buoyed up by his never-failing hope of success, Brissot started off for London, while Félicité went back to her work. Her position was not altogether pleasant. She was subjected to certain conditions which did not

---

[1] *Mémoires*, I, 185–86. [2] *Correspondance*, 35–39.
[3] *Archives du département de la Seine.* See also *A. N. F¹ᵃ*, 570.
[4] Afterward the Duke of Orléans. [5] *Mémoires*, I, 300.

seem suitable, but when she complained to Madame Genlis the matter was speedily adjusted. But in spite of Madame Genlis's kindness, or perhaps because of it, she could not gather up sufficient courage to tell her of her marriage. It therefore fell to Brissot to communicate the news. He did not hesitate to combine business with personal matters and utilized the opportunity, while writing to Madame Genlis of his marriage, to send her a copy of one of his works, and a prospectus of the *Lycée de Londres*, and incidentally to solicit for the *Lycée* her influence with Vergennes. Madame de Genlis responded kindly, though she was obviously displeased by the marriage, and could not help showing her displeasure to Félicité.

Meanwhile Brissot was clamoring for his wife in London, and as she was no longer well nor happy in her work, it seemed best from every point of view for her to give up her position. Although Madame de Genlis was displeased at the time, she showed her good will toward Félicité and wrote to her on several occasions in a most friendly spirit. But with the severance of their professional relations, all close personal connection came to an end. In spite of this fact, this early relation was of some lasting importance, as it was afterward made the basis of the charge that Brissot was intimately connected with the House of Orléans.[1] Thus, after nearly a year of separation since their marriage, Félicité went to London in July, 1783, to join her husband and to begin her real married life.[2] It lasted only ten years, but those ten years were destined to be full of hardship and suffering. The promise of a life of comradeship forecasted by the period of their engagement was not fulfilled, though not through the fault of Félicité, but because of Brissot's growing absorption, first in his literary and philanthropic schemes, and then in the Revolution. As the wife of a penniless man of letters and a political leader, she had much to endure both before and during the Revolution, in poverty, privation, and loneliness.

---

[1] *Mémoires*, ii, 12–14.

[2] See article by M. Perroud, "*La Famille de Madame Brissot*," in *La Révolution française* for September, 1910.

It seems that Brissot was not able even to go to meet her at Dover, though whether this was because he could not afford the expense or the time does not appear.[1] He apparently took her at first to the place where he had been living on Brompton Road,[2] but on the establishment of his *Lycée*, he moved his personal residence to the house which he had rented for the society, 26 Newman Street. But they were scarcely installed in their new abode, when troubles began to come thick and fast. Desforges, who had put up the money for the *Lycée*, came to stay with the Brissot family and proved to be a most undesirable addition. ·Violent, quick-tempered, vindictive, and avaricious, were some of the epithets applied to him by Brissot, while he on his side tried to persuade Brissot that Félicité was suspicious, imperious, and entirely lacking in charm, a quality much needed in attracting strangers to such an establishment as they were trying to found. Brissot was naturally indignant. The reason for such an outburst, he declared, was simply that Desforges expected and demanded to be taken into the very bosom of the family and was piqued to find himself treated merely as a business associate.[3] This was but the beginning of difficulties. Permission to send his publication into France was temporarily suspended; and he foolishly added to his burdens by starting another publication, *Le Tableau des Indes*. Neither the *Tableau de l'Angleterre* nor the *Lycée* prospered,[4] he had used up all the funds advanced by Desforges, who refused to give him any more; he could not therefore avail himself of a favorable opportunity of securing a place of meeting for the *Lycée*, and in order to save what he had already put in, he determined to start out for France to secure more funds.

In the midst of all these difficulties, Félicité's first child was born, April 25, 1784,[5] and when the baby was only a few days old and Félicité was still very ill, Brissot was seized for debt

---

[1] See letter of Brissot to Bentham, July 8, 1783. Bentham Papers, III, British Museum; additional manuscripts, ff. 324; printed in the *Correspondance*, 64.
[2] See letter addressed to him at that place by his brother. *Correspondance*, 51.
[3] *Mémoires*, I, 345.   [4] *Ibid.*, I, 389–92.
[5] See *Récompense nationale*, *A. N.*, F[la] 570.

and hurried off to prison.[1] Fearing the effect on her if she knew the real state of the case, he allowed himself to be taken away without letting her know what had happened, leaving strict injunctions with his sister-in-law to make excuses for his absence. After a short imprisonment he was able to satisfy his creditors temporarily, and to get back to his family, but the growing embarrassment of his finances made him feel that a journey to France in quest of funds was imperative. This separation caused Félicité keen suffering. In his desire to spare her Brissot tried to conceal his most crushing anxieties, and only succeeded in hurting Félicité, who, probably not realizing their desperate financial condition, felt that for her husband to go off on business, leaving her unprotected and ill, showed a most woeful lack of sympathy and tenderness.[2] According to Brissot's own admission, she certainly needed protection, for Desforges, who remained behind, took occasion to harass and annoy her. Physical weakness, combined with torturing mental anxieties, soon reduced her to such a state that she was scarcely able to care for the little Félix. But this was not all. Brissot had not been long in Paris when he was arrested and thrown into the Bastille. Torn with anxiety as to what was befalling his wife at home, and fearing that the sudden news of his calamity might be fatal to her and their little son, he almost reached the point of desperation.[3] It was in this crisis that his mother-in-law came to the rescue;[4] and without waiting for the ordinary boat, ventured to cross the Channel in a little skiff with only a single sailor, in order to get to her daughter before she should receive the news by post. In spite of all the precautions taken by Madame Dupont in breaking the news to her daughter, Madame Brissot was for the time being completely crushed by it.[5] She rallied speedily, however, and set to work in her husband's behalf. She came over to Paris, and "to her active measures," as Brissot says in his memoirs, "as much as to his own innocence," he owed his release.[6]

---

[1] *Mémoires*, I, 392.   [2] *Ibid.*, I, 395.   [3] *Ibid.*, II, 5–7.
[4] See p. 44.   [5] *Mémoires*, II, 6–7.   [6] *Ibid.*, II, 14–23.

In ordinary times, as well as at epochs of crisis, Madame Brissot was a true helpmate to her husband, not only in the practical affairs of life, but also in his literary undertakings. As is evident from her studies during the period of her engagement, she was by no means ignorant or petty in her interests. She had a fair education, which included some knowledge of English. She even engaged in translation, and the year before her marriage, published a translation into French of a work by Robert Dodsley, entitled *Manuel de tous les âges, où Économie de la vie humaine.* The original of this work purported to be an ancient Indian manuscript found among the papers of the Grand Lama, and was somewhat after the style of the Book of Proverbs. The following year she got out a translation of another work, called *Nouveau précis de l'histoire d'Angleterre depuis les commencements de cette monarchie jusqu'au 1783.* This was a tiny volume, a kind of compendium of history designed especially for children, containing much geographical information and arranged by reigns. After her marriage she assisted her husband in the translation of a history of England, which appeared under the title of *Lettres philosophiques et politiques sur l'histoire de l'Angleterre depuis son origine jusqu'à nos jours, traduites de l'anglais.*[1]

Now, however, she had no time or strength for anything but her family and her domestic duties. Besides Félix, two other children were born, Edmé Augustine Sylvain, March 13, 1786,[2] and Jacques Jérôme Anacharsis, March 31, 1791.[3] With three children to care for, and very little money to do it on, life was hard indeed for Madame Brissot. Her husband's enterprises absorbed instead of producing money, and, from the beginning of the Revolution, politics completely engrossed his attention.

---

[1] A second edition was published in London in 1790, in which Brissot appears as the translator. In the preface he does not mention his wife's help, but the catalogue of the *Bibliothèque Nationale* cites it as her work.

[2] *Ville de Paris, Paroisse de la Madeleine, ville l'Évêque. Extrait du registre des actes de naissance de l'an 1786.* Bib. Nat., *Papiers de Roland,* vol. III, *fr. nouv. acq.* 9534, f. 322.

[3] Bib. Nat., *Papiers de Roland, fr. nouv. acq.* 9534, f. 392, and A. N., F[1a] 570.

They grew more and more apart, and the difficult task of making both ends meet fell upon her shoulders. In her humble apartment in the rue de Grétry, she struggled on, doing much of the housework herself, helping to entertain her husband's friends, and going without real necessities. To add to her troubles, their house became a kind of *entrepôt* for persons about to emigrate to the New World,[1] and they were not always the most agreeable guests. Apropos of one of these guests, a certain Marquis de Wahody,[2] who was always making up his mind to go to America and yet never starting, she wrote: "Such people may be classed with those philosophers who, I believe, are disciples of whomsoever can help them, with no idea that there are any limits, who are always pursuing chimeras, seeking happiness and never finding it, looking for repose in indolence, always on the watch for a chance to play a leading part. Such is our Pythagorean, always proclaiming that he is ready to give up comforts, yet always making himself comfortable; never wishing to bother anyone, yet often asking for things which are not in the house, milk, for instance, and expressing astonishment that you cannot procure it in Paris whenever you happen to want it."[3]

As a refuge from all this weariness and as a means of getting her husband out of the turmoil and dangers of political life, Madame Brissot often thought of emigration to America. The 19th of January, 1790, she wrote to her brother that she was preparing to join him in America, and asked him for a list of things which she ought to bring with her from Europe. "I rejoice," she added, "that the Revolution is over, but every day I have reason for distress because of anxiety for my husband."[4]

But unfortunately for Madame Brissot, the Revolution was not over, and as Brissot became more and more absorbed in it, life grew still harder for her. Her health became so fragile that she could not care for the three children alone, and she was

[1] *Correspondance*, 242–45.

[2] Valady is probably intended. See *Correspondance*, 244; note of M. Perroud.

[3] *Correspondance*, 242–45.   [4] *Ibid.*, 248.

often worn out with fatigue and worry.[1] "Up to this moment," she wrote to her brother in America, "I have had to exercise such economy that I fear my health will be permanently affected by it. I feel the necessity of living differently, of having good service, of being well housed, of getting good air, especially of having country air in the summer. This last has become indispensable, and even this enjoyment costs money. . . . I do not yet know where to go in the country this summer. While waiting, I go every day to M. Pétion's, the mayor of Paris, who has a charming garden out on the boulevard near us."

The disposition of her children and the means of providing them with a proper education was another source of anxiety. She was evidently sorely troubled by the traits of character which they showed. "Félix," she confessed sadly to her sister, "is not any too obedient, very lazy, and does not know much. . . . They are children about whom there is nothing extraordinary, except their very bad disposition, yet I hope they are going to be sensible and good." Their inexplicable disposition, she admitted with humiliation, might be due in part to the fact that she had done too much for them. But if she were in part responsible, her husband, she declared, was also to blame. He was so wrapped up in political affairs that he paid no heed to the education of the children, and did not assist her at all in bringing them up. He could not or would not give any time to teaching, and private tutors were expensive. The result was both sad neglect for the children and her own growing alienation from her husband, a sad realization, as she put it, of a closer attachment to her children than to him.[2]

But though shut away by her family cares from much contact with people, Madame Brissot was a keen judge of character. She estimated Desforges at his true worth, much to his discomfort,[3] saw through the pretensions to virtue and self-sacrifice of the Marquis de Valady,[4] and weighed with discrimination the value of the would-be emigrants who stopped

[1] *Correspondance*, 283–84.
[2] *Ibid.*, 328.
[3] *Mémoires*, I, 345. Also see p. 391.
[4] See p. 394.

at her home on their way to the New World.[1] To Brissot, enthusiasm for emigration seems to have been a sufficient passport, but to Madame Brissot's more discerning mind mere
enthusiasm did not seem sufficient guarantee of a good pioneer.
As an instance of her shrewd judgment, note a letter to her
brother in America in which she sets forth the character of
certain newcomers he is likely to receive. The Messrs. Vallots
had just bought some land of the Scioto Land Company, she
writes, and her brother would better be informed of what
manner of men they were. One was a jeweler out of work; the
other had been employed by the *Patriote Français*, but he could
not get on with Madame Dupont,[2] was brusque, possessed of
no great intelligence, and liked to take it easy. Since these
brothers had no way of establishing themselves in France, it
had occurred to another brother of theirs and to Brissot that
it would be a good thing to send them to America. The older
was rather narrow-minded, and not at all good-looking, but
he was not likely to do any harm, except through stupidity.
The younger was better-looking, but very egotistical, and moreover, likely to disagree with his brother.

Having thus described the character of these prospective
emigrants, Madame Brissot went on to give her brother some
shrewd practical advice. In case the younger brother did fall
into difficulties, the elder brother, she argued, would be very
likely to attempt to get rid of him by proffering his services to
Monsieur Dupont. Let the latter by no means accept. The
case of the young Mentelle was different, she continued. He
had disappeared from home, and as nothing had been heard
from him in three months, it was not improbable that he might
turn up in America, and if so, she counseled her brother to receive him. Although the youth in question had not showed himself particularly industrious, she felt that his faults were those
which kindly counsel and good surroundings might remedy.[3]

---

[1] *Correspondance*, 242–45.
[2] Brissot's mother-in-law, who had charge of the office. See p. 123.
[3] *Correspondance*, 242–45.

Such was the discerning character of Madame Brissot's advice. It bears out Madame Roland's statement that she had much tact and judgment.[1] That Madame Brissot always looked at matters with sound practical sense is evident from this correspondence with her brother and sister in America. When, for instance, her brother showed a growing attachment for some one who seemed to her unsuitable as his wife, she gave her sister shrewd advice how to check the matter; and when her sister Nancy's marriage was under consideration, she did not forget the practical problem involved, and reminded her that if her marriage took her away from her brother, there would be an added difficulty for both of them in the way of domestic service.[2]

On this occasion of her sister's proposed marriage, Madame Brissot offered her advice which showed an understanding sympathy and at the same time revealed a wisdom which seems to have been born not only of knowledge of the world, but also of sad experience on her own part. Nancy had evidently written telling her of her growing affection for a certain man and of her determination to put him to a year's proof. Madame Brissot replies that while she commends her sister's resolve to remain indifferent, she cannot help but doubt her firmness. In fact, she suspects that she is already too much taken with the stranger's good qualities to listen to any counsel. Yet she needs to remember that man is fickle; that if she looks for unaltering happiness, she is sure to be disillusioned; her husband will have his own interests in which she will not share, and she will undoubtedly feel herself neglected. Above all, there will surely be discord and unhappiness if the husband neglects his children, or if husband and wife are not in harmony on the education of the children. "May my example," Madame Brissot wrote in sadness and weariness, "put you on your guard against the rocks which you are surely going to encounter."[3]

---

[1] *Correspondance*, pp. 268–69. Also *Mémoires de Madame Roland*, I, 198. Madame Roland speaks of her with infinite esteem and respect.
[2] *Ibid.*, 326–28.   [3] *Ibid.*, 329.

In her shrewd judgment of character in general she clearly discerned the weakness of her husband. In a single word, which at the same time betrayed her own suffering, she summed it up. "I confess," she wrote, "that I have not the strength to consent to sacrifice my husband for — I will not say my country — but for a race of men who will be stronger than he."[1] That Madame Brissot herself was stronger than her husband in many ways, one cannot but suspect. In sane and penetrating judgment she certainly showed herself his superior. Brissot's fatal optimism was constantly leading him into difficulty, while Madame Brissot's ability to realize that there was a possibility of failure as well as of success gave her better balance and made her a safer guide. Brissot seems to have had some appreciation of this. "Oh, my Félicité," he wrote, "your whole soul is as pure, as strong as that of those celebrated women like Cornelia and Portia, who were well educated and on an equality with their husbands. Like them, you know how to scorn the grandeur, the pleasures, the fatal vanities of the world; like them, you know how to place your happiness in that of your husband; like them, you know how to inspire him to virtue by your example; with him you seek the truth; sometimes your eye, more fortunate than his, discovers it; it is often from you that he draws that noble courage which characterizes his writings; your severe criticism purifies them and makes them more useful."[2]

His wife's family also was devoted to Brissot. From the time of his marriage he seems to have been the center of their interest, and with *his* fortunes the entire family prospered or suffered. He used his influence in their behalf, and they in turn aided and encouraged him. With his brother-in-law, François Dupont, he was on terms of special intimacy. The residence of the latter at Boulogne put him in a position where he could be very useful to Brissot in his enterprise in connection with the *Lycée*. From a lively correspondence carried on between them at the epoch of Brissot's London residence, it would

[1] *Correspondance*, 248.   [2] *De la Vérité*, 241.

appear that Brissot looked upon Dupont for aid in getting his publications conveyed into France, and also in securing information as to the condition of commerce in various parts of Europe. And on the other hand, Brissot helped Dupont by looking after the payment of his obligations and by furthering his ambition towards a place in the diplomatic service.[1] They evidently regarded America as affording a good opening. In May, 1783, Dupont wrote to Brissot: "I told him [Swinton] that I had put off my journey to America till next year, and that I ought not to set out without having the position of consul or secretary interpreter of the embassy; that it is not too soon to set about it now, and that he might perhaps aid me through Monsieur de Beaumarchais. I will write to Monsieur to get him to present a memoir in my behalf to Monsieur de Vergennes. . . . If you present one for me, do not forget to mention the languages."[2] Meanwhile, Dupont having become engaged in business which took him to Germany and eastern Europe, an American consulship began to look less attractive and the possibility of a position in the Levant suggested itself instead.[3] Such plans came to nothing, and by the beginning of 1789 he was established in America near Philadelphia, not as consul but as an American farmer.[4] Brissot gave him letters of introduction to his personal and business friends, who received him with much cordiality, gave him helpful advice, and invited him to their homes.[5] But it was three years before Brissot could do anything for him in the way of political preferment. Finally, after the 10th of August, 1792, he succeeded in having him made vice-consul of France at Philadelphia.

For making this appointment Brissot seems to have been much criticized. It was an evidence of nepotism, his opponents declared; the position was very important and gave opportunity for working much good or ill to France, and it showed

[1] *Correspondance*, 45, 50–53.   [2] *Ibid.*, 53.   [3] *Ibid.*, 87–90.
[4] *Lettres de Madame Roland*, ii, 217, note.
[5] Letters were sent to him in care of Brissot's friend, Miers Fisher. See the Craigie Papers in the collections of the American Antiquarian Society and the Scioto Papers in the collections of the American Historical Society.

that he was in close connection with the government of the United States.[1] In meeting these criticisms, Brissot called attention to the insignificance of the position and the impossibility of his deriving from it any influence upon American affairs; and while admitting that he did secure the appointment for his brother-in-law, he declared that this was the one and only case where he used his position to seek advancement for any member of his family. Moreover, no one need charge him, even in this single instance, with giving an appointment regardless of merit, for Dupont was eminently suited for the position. His brother-in-law, he declared, was a republican in principle; indeed his chief motive for emigrating to the United States was his hatred of the monarchical form of government; moreover, he had a wide commercial experience and an extended acquaintance, spoke several languages, including English, and what was of great importance, he possessed public esteem and confidence.[2]

Besides a brother-in-law, Brissot's marriage gave him three sisters-in-law to whom he was deeply attached.[3] Of the eldest, Marie Thérèse, little seems to be known; the second, Julie Henriette, was with Brissot and his wife in London in 1783 for a time. Later she assisted Brissot in the office of the *Patriote Français*. Of the third sister, Marie Anne, commonly called Nancy, Brissot seems to have been especially fond. He evidently saw a good deal of her in her girlhood, during the period of his engagement with Félicité, and while conversing on the sciences with the latter, delighted in trying to influence and develop her young sister. "Already," he wrote later in speaking of this period of her youth, "she showed that strength of character which she has since developed." After his marriage

---

[1] In a note to Brissot's *Mémoires*, ii, 257, M. Perroud quotes from Desmoulins's *Histoire des Brissotins* to show how the facts were twisted. "*Comment ne serions-nous pas affamés?*" asked Desmoulins, — perhaps with the irony of intentional exaggeration, — "*comment nous viendrait-il des grains d'Amérique? qui est-ce qui est consul-général de France? C'est le beau-frère de Brissot.*"

[2] *Mémoires*, ii, 256–57.   [3] *Ibid.*, i, 301.

she went over to London to live with her sister Félicité and Brissot,[1] and then later went to join her brother François in America. She was evidently very attractive, and the question of her marriage was a source of much anxiety to her family at home. In the eyes of her family no one seemed quite good enough for her,[2] and her brother was much relieved when what he feared was a possible engagement came to nothing. Later she married a M. Aublay and went to London to live.

But if Brissot was attached to his brother-in-law and to his sisters-in-law, it was with his mother-in-law with whom the bond was closest, and on whom he constantly relied. She seems to have been a woman of energy and ability, to whom all her children turned for advice and help in all the affairs of life, both business as well as personal. It was to her, in the first place, that he owed the introduction to Mentelle, which in turn meant the *entrée* to the best literary and scientific circles of Paris and the opportunity for a closer acquaintance with Félicité. It was she who, at the time of his marriage, advanced the ready money necessary for establishing his *Lycée*, took him back to Boulogne with her and started him on his English ventures with encouragement and sound advice. It was she again who received his business partner, Desforges, on his way through Boulogne, and when the enterprise failed, helped Brissot out of dire straits by a substantial present. It was she who, on the news of Brissot's imprisonment in the Bastille, risked great danger in crossing the Channel in order that she might break the news to her daughter.[3] When the *Patriote Français* was founded, it was she who took charge of the office.[4] It was her advice which was looked to in difficulty, and when Félicité was disturbed and perplexed by Brissot's neglect of their children and at the division which had developed between herself and her husband on the subject, it was she to whom the wife turned for help, sure that she would understand the situation and would be able to heal the breach and bring Brissot to a

[1] See article by M. Perroud referred to above. [2] *Correspondance*, 307–08.
[3] *Mémoires*, i, 300–01, 343, 393; ii, 56. [4] *Correspondance*, 242.

more reasonable attitude of mind.[1] And finally, during Brissot's imprisonment, it was she to whom he wrote his last letters and who took care of the family after his death.[2]

It was only when death was imminent that, at last, Brissot fully realized — what he had only had glimmerings of before — that he had neglected his family, and in the last few weeks of his life, he poured out his soul in what he called "*Un Legs à mes enfants.*" After setting forth the object and aims which had actuated his own life and begging his children to profit by his mistakes, he gave utterance to a last cry of vain regret — he could not quite bring himself to say for his political career, but for the trouble and grief it had brought to his family, whom, though he had neglected, he loved. "It is painful, indeed," he wrote, "for a man of tender feelings, for a good husband, a good father, to separate himself from those he loves, and, I confess it, my children, this is the thought which has often overcome me, which had made me shed burning tears. To leave you so soon! You whom I have scarcely seen, you whom my occupations have prevented my taking care of, bringing up myself! To leave you at the moment when, breaking my political bonds, I was going to devote myself to your education, and to deserve your tenderness by showing myself your father! Above all, to leave my wife, who, since our marriage, has known, in her alliance with me, only the sorrows of persecution or the privations of solitude. . . . To leave her at the moment when I was planning to adopt a line of conduct which would secure for us a sweet domestic life! Yes, these thoughts are heartrending. . . . But calling to my aid the counsels of philosophy, I console myself by the thought that my children will find in their mother a teacher capable of guiding them in the paths of austerity, in good character; that my Félicité will find

---

[1] *Correspondance*, 284. Madame Dupont, like Félicité, seems to have been well aware of Brissot's weak points. Just as he was starting for America she wrote him: "*Tenez votre jugement en suspens, mon cher, tant que vous ayez vu et entendu par vous-même. Qui vous connaîtra ce faible en abusera et vous rendra souvent injuste.*" — *Correspondance*, 191.

[2] Article by M. Perroud referred to above.

in her own soul, nourished from her youth in the principles of reason, strength sufficient to support this frightful blow; that all her family, that her generous mother, that her loving sisters and her worthy brother will form but one family, one soul, where will be graven the image of a man whose most ardent desire was to make them happy." Then, with a note of hope, he adds, "I still believe that all public spirit is not lost, that gratitude dwells in some hearts and that generous friendship will pay a public debt, will come to the rescue of a family whose interests I have perpetually sacrificed to the public good." [1]

As has been said, the family at the moment of Brissot's death was under the care of his mother-in-law. The situation was harrowing, for it was not only the imprisonment and execution of her son-in-law which she had to endure, but also heartrending anxiety for her daughter, Madame Brissot, who had been imprisoned. She seems to have borne the burden manfully; at all events, she appears to have been able to keep from Brissot the news of Madame Brissot's whereabouts, so that he was able to die in ignorance of the fate impending over his wife. [2]

After the arrest of her husband, Madame Brissot had been threatened by angry crowds which gathered about her abode at Saint-Cloud and had been obliged to seek other refuge for herself and her children, but she was soon discovered and placed under arrest by the committee of general security of the municipality of Saint-Cloud. [3] Her case was then taken up by the National Committee of General Security, who put her under arrest at the Hôtel de Necker, rue de Richelieu, under the care of the citizen Courtois, discharged the commissioners from Saint-Cloud and decreed that, since her journeys and absences made her an object of suspicion, she be brought before the Committee for examination. [4] Her examination took place on

---

[1] *Un Legs à mes enfants, Mémoires*, I, 10–11.
[2] See article by M. Perroud referred to above.   [3] *A. N.*, 4443, no. 18.
[4] *Extrait du registre des arrêtés généraux du comité de sûreté générale. A. N.*, AF[II] 286. Tuetey, VIII, 32, 65–66.

August 11, when she was closely questioned as to Brissot's political relations and her own connection with them.[1] She was asked why she had left Paris to retire to Saint-Cloud? who were the persons whom she was accustomed to see at Saint-Cloud? did she know that the concierge at whose lodging she lived was a relative of Gensonné? had she not received proscribed deputies? what had become of her husband's books and papers? when had she last visited England? where had she gone on her last absence from Paris? how much money had she sent over to England? where had she invested it? what correspondence did Brissot maintain with Englishmen or other foreigners? what was the nature of the correspondence which Brissot had with Roland and with Madame Roland? what was the nature of the correspondence of Brissot with Pétion and the other proscribed deputies? had she ever seen any agent of England, or of any other enemy, come to speak with Brissot? did she not know that Brissot was on intimate terms with Dumouriez? In answer to these searching inquiries, Madame Brissot replied that she had gone to Saint-Cloud because it was her custom to spend a part of every year in the country on account of her health; that she did not know that the concierge was related to Gensonné; that her last journey was to Chartres and that she fled there to escape the hostile invectives which she heard under her windows after her husband's arrest; that it was nine years since she had been in England; that she had never sent any funds there or invested any anywhere else. Of her husband's political relations or of his correspondence she knew nothing whatever; she had never heard of any alliance with Dumouriez; Guadet was the only one of the proscribed deputies whom she had seen, and she certainly had never received any of them at her house.

This general denial was apparently not satisfactory to the Committee, for she was still kept under surveillance. However, either because the Committee became less rigorous, or on account of the kindness of heart of the officer to whom she was

[1] *Correspondance,* 373–76.

entrusted, she was allowed to go about and to talk with friends whom she met, while the officer kept at a distance. But even this small measure of liberty allowed her provoked the discontent of the people, and complaint was made by certain women that undue favoritism was being shown and that the wife of a poor man would not have been so treated — a significant evidence of the popular feeling toward the Girondins.[1]

Whether this hounding of poor Madame Brissot resulted at once in curtailing her liberty does not appear, but at all events, on the 30th of October, on the order of the Committee of General Security, she, with her child (probably the youngest), was put in prison at La Force.[2] Here she remained till the 19th of the following February, when she was released by order of the same Committee.[3]

Though the record of these weeks is a blank, the loneliness and torturing anxiety which she suffered can readily be conceived. On her release she had to face the problem of providing for her family. It was a weary struggle, and had she not been able to take advantage of the turning tide of public opinion in favor of the Girondins, she must have succumbed. Emboldened by this changing attitude, she made request in May, 1795, for the restoration of her husband's papers,[4] — a request which after some delay was finally granted.[5] A few months later she ventured to put in a claim for herself and for her children for the losses she had sustained because of the persecution of which she and her husband had been the victims. Immediately after the fatal 31st of May, she wrote, her husband and she had been obliged to separate and to abandon their home, which was closed by the government. She had been obliged to wander

[1] *Rapport de l'observation, La Tour-La-Montagne, A. N.,* F[7] 36883.

[2] *Extrait du registre des mandats d'amener du comité de sûreté générale, A. N.,* AF[II] 289; Tuetey, VIII, 3367.

[3] *Lettre par le concierge adjoint de la maison de la Petite Force, Paris, 1er ventôse, an II* (February 19, 1794). See *Correspondance,* 397.

[4] *Requête de la veuve de Brissot, A. N.,* W 292, M 204 (2e *partie*); Tuetey, VIII, 566.

[5] *Correspondance,* 401.

about for several months, seeking a refuge for herself and her children, till she herself was imprisoned. The journeys which she had made, the apartments which she had been obliged to rent in different places, caused her unusual expenses, which she was able to meet only with the generous aid of relatives and friends. And when, finally, she was able to reclaim her furniture and her husband's library, she received only a part of it and that part was in bad condition. She perceived with grief that a large part had been stolen, spoiled or lost. She had had made, she added, an appraisal by a competent authority. Besides this loss there were the expenses which she had been obliged to undergo, which brought the whole amount to 80,510 francs.[1] This sum she begged the government to reimburse. To this request the government acceded in part, by ordering the payment of 50,000 francs "for the property which had been taken from her during the imprisonment of her husband." The other expenses it was evidently unwilling to make good.[2]

This was in September, 1795. The next month the general trend of opinion in favor of the Girondins was evidenced by the action of the Convention. Those proscribed deputies who had succeeded in escaping were re-admitted to the Convention, and those to whom it was too late to make reparation received the recompense of being honored as "martyrs of liberty." On the 3d of October, 1795, a special celebration was held in their memory. Every member of the Convention wore crape on his arm; a funeral urn was set up in the hall bearing the inscription: "To the magnanimous defenders of liberty, who died in prison or upon the scaffold during the tyranny"; and the President made an eloquent address in which he recalled the services rendered to liberty by the martyred representatives of the people, "their constant courage and their tragic end."[3]

---

[1] Note the amount; it was evidently reckoned in the depreciated paper currency. For example, three tablecloths were estimated at 2500 francs. The list included underclothing, dresses, table-linen, ornaments, household furniture, wine, and books. *Correspondance*, 402–07.

[2] *Correspondance*, 408.

[3] *Procès-verbal de la Convention*, October 3, 1795.

The next year more tangible reparation was made by the government of the Directory. The 26th of April, 1796, the Council of Five Hundred decreed that, "considering that Valazé, Pétion, Carra, Buzot, Gorsas, Brissot, members of the National Convention, are of those representatives of the people, who, after having coöperated to establish liberty and to found the Republic, sealed it with their blood, and died victims of their devotion to the country and of their respect for the rights of the nation," the widow of each of them should have a pension of two thousand francs a year for herself, and a pension of two thousand francs a year for each of her children till he should have reached the age of fifteen years.[1] In accordance with this decree, Madame Brissot was given a pension. Thus, support of his family, which in his dying moments he had felt confident would in some manner be provided for, was in part, at least, undertaken by the government.[2] But even with this help it was with much difficulty that Madame Brissot managed to get along. She was thoroughly weary of the struggle, but somehow or other a means of support must be found, and in 1799, with her mother and sisters, she attempted to establish a school at Versailles. An announcement under the heading, "*Éducation de famille sous la direction de citoyenne Cléry, veuve Dupont, à Versailles, rue du Peuple français, no. 4*," in which they set forth in the most alluring terms at their command the advantages of their establishment, appeared in the *Décade philosophique*. Their experience of the world, the success of Madame Dupont with her own children, the good location, the fine air, and beautiful gardens are all pictured as making their school especially desirable. A note, apparently by the editor of the *Décade*, adds that it may interest the public to know that the citizens Dupont and Cléry are the mother-in-law, widow, and sisters-in-law of Brissot.[3]

[1] *Résolution du conseil des Cinq-Cents, 7 floréal, an IV*, quoted in Vatel, *Charlotte Corday et les Girondins*, II, 27.

[2] *Récompense nationale, 9 floréal, an IV*, A. N., F1a 570.

[3] Article by M. Perroud referred to above. See also *Correspondance*, 418–19.

The project does not seem to have succeeded, and Madame Brissot was obliged to ask help from the government. She seems to have considered the possibility of obtaining a subsidy for a school (probably the one referred to above); but when this fell through she tried to get a place as directress in one of the hospitals, a position which she sought rather because it was the only thing available than because she felt any special fitness for the work. Indeed, she frankly confessed in a private letter that she much preferred educational work, and that after her long struggle with misfortune she felt as though she were recovering from an illness and doubted her adequacy to the task.[1]

She finally appears to have found a means of livelihood in a reading-room or bookshop which she maintained at no. 7 rue du Commerce, Paris, while she and her mother lived around the corner on the rue de Furstenburg.[2]

While seeking government employment for herself, she had also applied to the government for aid in the education of her children. On one occasion she asked for a place for her youngest son in the *Collège des Colonies*. Two of her sons had been placed at Saint-Cyr, but as one of them preferred the marine service, she asked that a scholarship given to the first be transferred to the second. She was evidently disturbed as to the condition of one of them, at least, for she added that she would prefer to have the amount of the scholarship in money, "because if there are characters whom public education improves, there are others whom it develops too rapidly before their judgment has been cultivated."[3]

The second son, Silvain, seems to have had something of his father's restlessness and independence, and his manifestations of the latter were not always well judged. While a pupil at the *École polytechnique*, it is reported that he refused to take

[1] *Correspondance*, 422–24.
[2] *Bib. Nat., Papiers de Roland*, iii, *fr. nouv. acq.* 9534, f. 392.
[3] Letters of Madame Brissot to various ministers, noted in the catalogue of the *Collection Charavay*. See also *Correspondance*, 418, 421, 424–25.

the oath to the emperor — a refusal which, considering that he was a *pensionnaire* of the government, was decidedly ill-advised and which naturally led to his prompt retirement from the school. "All the pupils were solemnly convoked to take an oath of fidelity to the emperor," wrote Miss Helena Williams, who declares that she relates this episode on the authority of the boy's grandmother from whom she heard it the next day. "The president called the boys one by one. When the turn of the young Brissot came: 'You swear,' said the president, 'fidelity to the emperor?' The young man answered with a firm voice, 'No.' The president, as you may well imagine, was absolutely taken back by this brusque declaration, and the whole company was stupefied with astonishment. Finally they ventured to ask Brissot what was the reason for his refusal. 'I am too young,' he answered, 'to pass judgment on political matters; what I know is that my father died on the scaffold for the Republic, and I am a republican.'" [1]

Whether on account of this episode, or for other reasons, is not clear, but in 1816, Silvain went to America.[2] Here he seems to have met failure at every turn. From the tone of his letters one cannot help but suspect that it was, in part at least, his own fault. François Dupont had been struck by the liberty, the democracy, of the new country. What especially impressed Silvain were the crude manners, the lack of ceremony, the paucity of means of amusement. His constant lament is his lack of funds; he needs two hundred francs a month, he has only one hundred twenty; he has borrowed money, he hopes his mother will pay it; can she not send him more soon? He is giving French lessons as a means of livelihood, he ought to be studying English, but time is lacking for it; there are too many French people in New York, he ought to get away in order to have better opportunities for acquiring English, but, as he already owes money at his boarding-house, he cannot leave.

[1] Helena Williams, *Souvenirs*, 23–24. She is not always reliable.
[2] He was for a time at Guadaloupe. Letters to his mother and his grandmother. *Correspondance*, 434–40.

These are some of his laments and must have been trying news for his mother at home.

He did finally manage to get down to New Orleans, where he fell in with relatives of his mother's family, who secured for him a place on a Louisiana plantation. His stay here, however, was short. He complained that he was shut off from all that made life worth while; he wrote unfortunate articles for the New Orleans newspapers which stirred up trouble; and finally he quarreled with his employer. He then returned to New York, whence he wrote to his mother with bitter upbraidings for not sending him money. His sad straits, though he himself may have been responsible for them, cannot fail to arouse sympathy. He was practically penniless and friendless. He finally secured a position at Albany as a teacher of mathematics and French in a school there, but the school was a poor affair, his room was cold and cheerless, and he could not collect his salary. In this desperate situation he fell ill and died on March 16, 1819.[1] The eldest son, who had sought a career in the marine, died in Santo Domingo; while the youngest son, Anacharsis, the only one who was anything of a success, became a farmer in the Department of the Yonne.[2]

No one of her three children was apparently of any help to Madame Brissot. They all were, on the other hand, a source of care and anxiety. Silvain especially, with his only too evident failures and his constant and petulant demands for money, occasioned his family much distress. Finally, worn out with

---

[1] Letters of Silvain Brissot, *Correspondance*, 434–44. The notice of his death was sent to Madame Aublay (Nancy Dupont) by Miers Fisher. *Ibid.*, 444.

[2] Nauroy, *Curieux*, no. 29, May, 1886. "*Le troisième fils de Brissot, Jacques Jérôme Anacharsis, naquit à Paris le 31 mars, 1791; il paraît avoir aimé les voyages, je le trouve officier de hussards sous l'empire, propriétaire au hameau du Val Saint-Étienne, commune de Veron (Yonne) en 1818, marchand de vins en gros à Paris, chaussée de Ménilmontant, no. 57, en 1827, contrôleur général de la navigation de la Seine avant 1854, demeurant à Corbeil (Seine-et-Oise) en 1854; tout cela ne l'a pas empêché d'écrire les ouvrages cités dans l'Intermediaire,* XVIII, p. 436. (For another record of his activities, see *Correspondance*, 431–33.)

her anxieties and disappointments, she died on January 4, 1818, one year before Silvain, and was buried at Père Lachaise, at the expense of her sister Nancy, now Madame Aublay.[1] She died as much a victim of the Revolution as though she had met death on the scaffold, and her life was one of its unseen and unnoticed tragedies.

[1] See article by M. Perroud referred to above.

CHAPTER XIV

BRISSOT'S GENERAL POLICY AND CHARACTER

In summing up Brissot's part in the French Revolution, the questions naturally arise: What were his general principles? What was his relation to the Girondins as a party? How far was he a typical Girondin?

The long-accepted view of the policy of the Girondins has, within the last few years, been shown to be mere tradition and legend. They were reputed to be federalists, royalists, aristocrats, but opponents of bloodshed and advocates of mercy. Recent investigation has made evident on the contrary that they were republican in policy, democratic in spirit, and quite as sanguinary as the Mountain; and if it has not been proved that they were not federalists in *any* sense of the word, proof is lacking that they were federalists in the sense meant by the Mountain.[1] This change, which has taken place regarding the conception of the party as a whole, applies likewise to Brissot. The same ideas were imputed to him as an individual, and they are likewise disproved.

He was the friend of the Duke of Orléans, it was asserted, and in July, 1791, he was working in favor of the House of Orléans and not at all for a republic; and when the real republicans were forced to flee, he walked the streets of Paris unmolested. Further, he was a warm personal friend of Lafayette and continued to be even after Lafayette began to show his royalist sympathies. He delayed the establishment of the Republic for the sake of keeping his friends in office, tried to stop the insurrection of August 10 and attempted to betray France to the Duke of Brunswick. When once the Republic was proclaimed, he worked as hard to overthrow it as he had to prevent its establishment. He deliberately brought on foreign war

[1] Aulard, *Histoire politique*, 395, 402.

when he knew the country was not ready for it; tried to save the king by an appeal to the people; and was hand and glove with the traitor Dumouriez. Finally, from the very beginning of the Revolution he used his influence in colonial affairs with the one purpose of stirring up the colonies to revolt.

These were the charges. As to their justification: in regard to several charges it must be admitted that Brissot's defense was rather weak; for instance, his freedom from arrest in the reaction which immediately followed the flight to Varennes is not explained, and he certainly showed his approval of Lafayette, up to the very eve of the massacre of July 17. But concerning the real substance of the charge that he was an Orléanist, or that he did not want a republic at all, there is no proof. On his own admission he did delay the establishment of a republic in the summer of 1791, but only because he did not think the time ripe for it, and even in July, 1792, he feared that the revolt might be premature. The claim that his hesitation was due only to expediency is borne out by his writings. Ever since his journey to the United States he had not ceased to laud the glories of a republic. And in the face of his repeated assertion that a republic was an ideal form of government, to assert that he was opposed to a republic, *per se*, is in itself an absurdity. He certainly did everything in his power, by his attack on royalty and on the ministry, to render the position of the monarch untenable, and to bring monarchy to its downfall. All claim that he tried to overthrow the Republic after it was once established is equally without ground. On one point, indeed, he failed to clear himself, for, in spite of his efforts to disprove all connection with Dumouriez, Brissot's correspondence and the support which he gave Dumouriez in his paper seemed to indicate cordial relations up to the last. But of any traitorous designs of his own toward the Republic there is not a shred of reliable evidence.

A second misapprehension concerning the Girondins is that they regarded with horror the shedding of blood. Their enemies, however, did not hold any such views regarding them, and at the trial of the Girondins, they attempted to fasten upon Brissot in particular approval of the massacres of September. It must be admitted that in this case they succeeded fairly well. In answer to the accusations Brissot declared that he had never ceased to denounce the massacres. But the point was, when did he begin? He asserted, it is true, that he had begged and prayed and implored Danton to put a stop to the massacres, but apparently he did not mention this appeal till the summer of 1793. At all events, his references at the time to the massacres show no particular horror. Far from denouncing them, he echoed Roland's mild remark: "Yesterday [Roland is speaking of September 3] was a day over the events of which it is perhaps necessary to draw a veil." [1] It is to be remembered however, that the Girondins were then in danger themselves, and it would have required extreme courage to make any protest. Brissot's general attitude at this period, however, if it may be judged by the action of the Committee of Twenty-one, of which he was president, and in which it must be supposed he had some influence, was not one of clemency. For under the direction of that committee drafts of laws were presented suppressing the right of appeal, ordering arrests, and extending the punishment of death. Further, although Brissot with the other Girondins was a bitter enemy of the men who afterward directed the government of the Terror with all its horrors of bloodshed, it must be remembered that he did not shrink from that foreign war which in large part made the Terror necessary; but that, on the contrary, it was he who was largely responsible for it.

As for Brissot's connection with federalism, it has already been shown that, although he was strongly inclined to federalism in theory, proof is lacking that he tried to put federalism into practice or to break up the unity and indivisibility of the Republic.

Finally, it was charged that the Girondins were undemocratic; that they held themselves apart from the multitude;

[1] *Patriote Français*, September 5, 1792.

that they were the aristocrats of the Revolution; or, as expressed by some modern socialists, that they were the very personification of the bourgeois element in bitter hostility to the proletariat.[1] A special charge was brought against Brissot in this connection, that he was an enemy of popular societies. On one occasion, it is true, he had written that people needed to be on their guard, that clubs, like old tools, became blunt and rusty. But this remark was inspired by the fact that he was just then assailing the monarchical club, not because it was a club, but because it was monarchical. Indeed, he was careful to add that clubs should be checked only when they were bad; when they were good they should be fostered, for they performed a most useful function in helping to create public opinion and in keeping watch over public functionaries. It was precisely from public officials who objected to this inconvenient censorship, he declared, that much of the criticism of the clubs emanated.

The accusation of opposition in general to democracy is likewise without foundation. Indeed, in summing up Brissot's part in the French Revolution, the one word which best characterizes his policy is *democratic*. From his earliest days he was the antagonist of arbitrary and despotic government in all its forms, and the upholder of the rights of man. A declaration of these rights, he maintained, when that subject was discussed, was as necessary to a constitution as was a foundation to a house. It was in no sense, he added, with emphasis, a granting of rights, — no power on earth could do that, — but merely a statement of what inevitably existed. In the interpretation of these rights he stood for the most thoroughgoing equality. No titles of nobility; participation by every one in municipal government; no distinction between active and passive citizens ; population the sole basis of representation ; a direct method of election for members of the legislative body; no life tenures for judges; admission of women and of passive as well as active citizens to popular societies; the abolition of

[1] Kropotkin, *La Grande Révolution*, 457.

primogeniture, no social forms to indicate distinctions between classes; and finally, the immediate extension of the principles of the Revolution to the colonies, at least to the extent of recognizing the civil rights of the mulattoes, and the ultimate abolition of slavery: these were some of the measures which, as has been seen, he regarded as imperative if there were to be anything like *real* equality.

But Brissot was the champion not only of "the people," as a whole, but of the poor especially. While he held certain abstract theories of socialistic tendency, in practical politics he was certainly not a socialist in the present use of the term. He was emphatically opposed to state control in economic matters and vehemently protested against the suspicion of cherishing a desire to attack property.[1] Yet at the same time he was in favor of various measures which might be said to be socialistic in character, tending to the advantage of the poor and to minimizing the differences of opportunity between rich and poor, as, for instance, the issuing of small assignats, the abolition of the octrois, the prohibition of bequests in the collateral line, and the exemption from taxation of the necessities for physical life.

Liberty, too, as well as democracy, was to be extended as rapidly and as thoroughly as possible. In economic questions he stood for liberty by upholding freedom of trade. Liberty of the press he not only claimed as an abstract right, but also took the lead in seizing it for himself by establishing the *Patriote Français* in defiance of a rigorous censorship. He was also the ardent champion of those hitherto despised classes whose liberty had been so greatly restricted, — Jews, Protestants, and actors.

In order that these rights might be preserved he maintained further the necessity of the fullest extension of the sovereignty

---

[1] It is largely because of his support of the right of property that he is assailed by such writers as Kropotkin. See *La Grande Révolution*, 457. "*Il faut lire Brissot pour comprendre tout ce que préparaient les bourgeois alors pour la France, et ce que les Brissotins du vingtième siècle préparent encore partout où une révolution va éclater.*"

of the people. It was for this end that he stood for the limitation of the king's power by a suspensive instead of an absolute veto, by checking his authority in declarations of peace and war, by prohibiting his choice of a ministry from the legislative body, and then by making the ministry which he did choose responsible to that body. Further, in order that the will of the people might be carried out more promptly, he would have but one chamber instead of two; he would give the suffrage to all; and he would not put a new constitution into effect till it should have been submitted to the people. He was in fact but too ready to regard the voice of the people as the voice of God, even when it was raised in violation of constituted authority and international agreements, as in the case of the annexation of Avignon. Even the risings of the mob — "popular movements" in his euphemistic phrase, "were to be expected and desired among a people who are not yet freed, especially among a people a large share of whom are excluded from making of the laws."

The rights which he was working to secure in these various ways he would not limit to France, but would extend to all mankind. His patriotism was not French, it was cosmopolitan. To spread the principles of the French Revolution among the oppressed everywhere was a good reason, it seemed to him, for making war on despotic governments. As M. Aulard says: "He was not an exclusive patriot; the Revolution, in his view, ought to be made for the profit of all oppressed nations, of all humanity whatever its race; for the profit of the negro as well as of the white man.[1]" In short, in spite of his advocacy of war, it may fairly be assumed that were he alive to-day, he would find his most congenial place among the supporters of universal brotherhood.

So far, then, Brissot's policy, except that he was rather more cosmopolitan than the rest, seems to be typically Girondin, and therefore, as M. Aulard has shown of the party in general, very like the policy of the Mountain to which it has been thought

[1] Aulard, *Orateurs de la Révolution*, i, 233.

to be diametrically opposed. The only real difference between the Girondins and the Mountain, M. Aulard maintains, was that the Mountain wanted Paris to have the supremacy over the departments during the war, and that the Girondins were opposed to such supremacy. If this distinction be true, Brissot was again a typical Girondin, for, from July, 1792, until the time of his trial, he never ceased to attack what seemed to him a rank usurpation of power by the capital city.

But this distinction given by M. Aulard is based only on the policy of the respective parties. M. Faguet, in his criticism of M. Aulard, goes one step further and points out a temperamental difference.[1] According to M. Faguet, the real difference between the Girondins and the Mountain lay not so much in a clear-cut divergence of opinion on the political questions of the time as in a fundamental difference of character: the Girondins were "men of principle," and the Jacobins "opportunists." In the case of Brissot this is evidently true, at least as far as his colonial and foreign policies were concerned. His guiding principle in regard to the colonies was that the slave trade should be abolished and rights of citizenship given to the mulattoes. To these principles he persistently clung, in spite of all warnings of the disasters to which too precipitate action must inevitably lead. Even when the prophesies of the planters were fulfilled and frightful insurrection broke out, he would not believe that it was due in any degree to the extreme measures which he himself had been instrumental in instituting.

The question of the war was a still more marked instance of adherence, on the part of Brissot and of the other Girondins as well, to a fixed principle, in utter disregard of circumstances. Despotism was an evil, he argued; therefore despotism must be attacked; diplomacy was an agency of despotism; therefore all diplomacy must be disregarded. And when the opponents of these radical ideas suggested that before beginning the attack on despotism it might be well to consider the resources for such an attack, and that in the question of diplomacy it was worth

---

[1] *Revue de Deux Mondes*, August 15, 1901, 5th period, IV, 631–59.

while, simply as a matter of policy, not to offend diplomatic etiquette, he went so far as to declare that such ideas savored not only of cowardice but of actual anti-revolutionary tendency. The suggestion that the circumstances of the case were to be considered, he scorned as a positively traitorous idea.

The hypothesis that Brissot and the Girondins were "men of principle" does not, however, adequately account for their attitude in respect to the other subjects of accusation. What principles can be discovered in their uncertain attitude toward the dethronement of the king and the establishment of the Republic, or in their passive acquiesence in the massacres of September, or in their divided opinion on the trial of the king, or even in their persistent opposition to Paris? The full antithesis to "men of circumstances," as applied to the Mountain, is not "men of principle." Something more is needed to cover the whole case. It is true that the Girondins were "men of principle" in so far as they were idealists, but they did not always have ideals, and where they failed to have ideals they did not substitute a feasible policy. Like the Mountain, they were sometimes guided by circumstances, but unlike the Mountain, they were not well guided. In other words, they were unpractical.

In this respect again Brissot was a typical Girondin. There is no doubt that he was a thorough republican in theory; but when it came to the crisis he failed to take a decisive stand, and during the critical fifty days from June 20 to August 10, when the overthrow of the monarchy became an urgent question, he did not seem to know what course to take. While claiming to support the monarchy, he attacked the king with such violence as to make the continuance of the monarchy impossible. Moreover, at the trial of the king his idea apparently was to get rid of responsibility by appealing to the people, and in the so-called federalist movement, while he was constant in his hatred of Paris, he was unable to unite his party in any feasible scheme for joining the provinces against it.

In so far he was a typical Girondin. How far was he really

the head of the group? He certainly was a leader of the Girondins in the sense that he was one of the most prominent of their
number, a person of definite influence and position within the
party. This opinion was universally held at the time;[1] the
conviction was expressed by his enemies when they fastened
the term "Brissotin" to one wing of the party; the fact is admitted in all the writings of his friends; it comes out in the trial;
it was recognized by the Buzot faction; and it is apparent in
the ranks of impartial spectators like Dumont.

Just who were included among the Brissotins it is somewhat
difficult to state, especially as the term was variously used and
amid shifting political affiliations: sometimes meaning the special adherents of Brissot in his war policy; sometimes the
supporters of the Girondin ministry; sometimes the leaders in
the opposition to the Commune of Paris in August, 1792; and
finally, after the opening of the Convention, that faction of the
Gironde which was less actively engaged in the federalist controversy, in contrast with the Buzotins who led the struggle.
Gensonné, Guadet, Clavière, and Valazé, and for a time Roland, Condorcet, and Vergniaud, might perhaps be most
properly classed as Brissotins.

That the Brissotins kept together as well as they did was due
partly to the fact that they were accustomed to meet frequently, in informal gatherings or clubs, to talk over their ideas
and to lay out a plan of action in the Assembly — according
to their enemies, to intrigue, to hatch plots. Their first gatherings were held four times a week at Madame Roland's, where
it was Brissot who introduced the other deputies.[2] Number 5
Place Vendôme, the apartment of a woman named Odun,[3] the
homes of the banker, Biderman,[4] of Valazé[5] and Buzot,[6] were

---

[1] Note, for instance, Les Révolutions de Paris, November 5, 1792: "Brissot
n'est pas sans talents, sans mérite, mais jamais conception hardie ne sortira de
son cerveau. . . . Après lui, les plus dangereux de son parti sont Guadet, Vergniaud, Gensonné. . . . Quels sont les autres? Buzot, Barbaroux, Kersaint, etc.
Voilà ce qu'on appelle, à bon droit, Brissot et sa coterie."

[2] Mémoires de Madame Roland, i, 63.

[3] Dumont, Souvenirs, 374.   [4] Ibid., 266.   [5] Moniteur, May 24, 1793.

[6] Thermomètre du jour, n. 526, June 9, 1793. That meetings were held at
Buzot's was denied by Madame Roland. See her Mémoires, ii, 57.

places of frequent meeting. Brissot, it was asserted, was most assiduous in his attendance, and was the heart and soul of these gatherings. While admitting that such gatherings took place, Brissot denied that they were devoted to intrigue or that he was a frequent attendant. That he was the chief of the party he also denied. "I, chief of a party!" he exclaimed. "I, a solitary man, knowing scarcely forty members of the Assembly, appearing rarely at the tribune, frequenting neither clubs, nor sections, nor committees!"[1] Nor was he generally acknowledged as a leader by the Girondins most closely associated with him. As one writer puts it, "Brissot's authority was neither avowed by himself nor recognized even by those who, nevertheless, did nothing without consulting him." It remains true, however, that from the autumn of 1791 to the publication of Desmoulins's *Histoire des Brissotins*, the term "Brissotin" was freely and frequently used, with the obvious implication of leadership and authority.

Such a position he could not have obtained had he not been a person of strong character. But what his character was is a question on which most divergent views are held. He has been judged to be everything, from a rogue and a scoundrel to a saint and a martyr. The former opinion is that of his most violent opponents among the members of the Mountain. In their denunciations he appears as a man of great subtlety, a political intriguer, constantly scheming for his own benefit, and utterly careless of the means by which he obtained his end.[2] A more impartial view is that of Dumont, but even he agrees with the Mountain in considering Brissot an intriguer. Dumont's judgment is all the more valuable because he had originally a high opinion of Brissot, an opinion which he maintained till the Delessart episode. "From that time," he writes, "Brissot fell in my estimation. I did not come to a rupture with him, but my friendship weakened with my esteem. I had

---

[1] *Patriote Français*, April 20, 1793.

[2] For a consideration of Brissot's character see Aulard, *Histoire politique*, 405.

formerly known him candid and generous; he was now insidi-
ous and persecuting. If he had any qualms of conscience — for
Brissot was both a moral and a religious man — they were al-
layed by the pretended necessity of saving the state. It is in
times of political faction that we see illustrations of the correct-
ness of the ideas of Helvetius upon what constitutes virtue.
Brissot was faithful to his party, but a traitor to integrity."[1]
"Brissot was one of those men," Dumont says on another occasion, "in whom party spirit prevailed over right and justice;
or rather, he confined right and justice to his own party. He
had more of the zeal of the monk than any man I ever knew.
Had he been a Capuchin he would have doted upon his staff
and his vermin — a Dominican, he would have burned heretics
— a Roman, he would have proved not unworthy of Cato and
Regulus. But he was a French republican, who had determined to overthrow the monarchy; and to accomplish this
object he hesitated not to calumniate, to persecute, and to perish himself upon the scaffold."[2]

M. Aulard, on the other hand, calls attention to an opinion
held even by some men of the Mountain — to the effect that
Brissot was lacking in partisanship. Cloots, for example, in his
pamphlet, *Ni Marat ni Roland*, said that as for Brissot he never
knew a man less *brissotin* than he. And when Danton wanted
to annoy Brissot he would say: "Brissot, you are a *brissotin*."[3]
Buzot bears like testimony. "He was," says Buzot, "so little
adapted by nature to intrigue that the mere suggestion of dissimulation or anything underhand was a punishment to him.
We used to make fun sometimes of his simplicity, of his good
nature, and we would say in fun: 'Of all possible Brissotins he
is the least *brissotin*.'"[4] According to Girey-Dupré, he lived
like Aristides and died like Sidney.[5] Clarkson says of him:
"Brissot was a man of plain and modest appearance. His

---

[1] Dumont, *Souvenirs*, 380. The translation is that of the *Recollections*, 312.
[2] *Ibid.*, 357; *Recollections*, 295.
[3] Aulard, *Histoire politique*, 405.   [4] Buzot, *Mémoires*, 16.
[5] Brissot, *Mémoires*, ed. by Montrol; Preface, iii.

habits, contrary to those of his countrymen in general, were domestic. In his family he set an amiable example, both as a husband and as a father. On all occasions he was a faithful friend. He was particularly watchful over his private conduct. From the simplicity of his appearance and the severity of his morals, he was called 'The Quaker'; at least in the circles which he frequented. He was a man of deep feeling. He was charitable to the poor, as far as his slender income permitted him. But his benevolence went beyond the usual bounds. He was no patriot in the ordinary acceptation of the word; for he took the habitable globe as his country and wished to consider every foreigner as his brother." [1] Madame Roland testifies to the same effect. "Brissot's simple manner," she says, "his frankness, his natural ease seemed to me in perfect harmony with the austerity of his principles. . . . He is the best of men, a good husband, a tender father, a faithful friend, a virtuous citizen."[2]

Madame Roland might have added that he did not suffer from too lowly an appreciation of his own virtues. But if his writings betray a decided tendency to self-glorification, they have at the same time every mark of simplicity and earnestness, and tend to bear out the opinion of Brissot's friends rather than that of his enemies. His actions, however, are not quite so consistent with disingenuousness and perfect uprightness. For instance, he was ready to use in the cause of the Revolution the same despotic means which he had attacked as among the greatest evils of the old régime, and his conduct toward Delessart is not above question. But that he ever betrayed the colonies or sold his vote or his influence, either to the court or to any foreign power, though repeatedly alleged, is absolutely without proof. It is tolerably certain that on one occasion, at least, money was offered him. "There are many persons now living," wrote an English contemporary of Brissot in 1798, "who know that during the spirited animadversions of Brissot on the cabals at court which he denominated *Austrian Committees*, a

[1] Clarkson, *History of the Abolition of the Slave Trade*, II, 165–66.
[2] *Mémoires*, I, 197.

hundred thousand livres were tendered as the price of either
his silence or his friendship; and that, living in a garret into
which he ascended by four flights of stairs, and having a wife
and three children depending on his stipend as deputy and the
trifling produce of his newspaper, he declined the offer without
noise or ostentation."[1]   A more striking evidence of Brissot's
incorruptibility was the Soulavie episode. Shortly after the
20th of June, 1792, it will be remembered,[2] Soulavie was offered
eight hundred thousand francs by Chambonas, the minister of
finance, with which to win over Brissot to the side of the court,
but declined to undertake the commission, as he was sure that
it would be utterly useless. Brissot would repulse him, he declared, at the mere suggestion.[3] This is all the more convincing
because Soulavie was opposed to Brissot politically and disliked him personally.

Far from amassing a fortune, he lived and died poor. He may
not have been a saint, but he certainly was not a rogue. The
truth lies between these extremes. He was an enthusiast — an
erring and self-deceived one sometimes, but he was not a hypo-
crite. As Lescure says of him: "There was in his life more than
one error, more than one fault, but there was nothing criminal."[4]

The testimony of Brissot's friends, however, is more convincing evidence of his moral character than of his fitness for
leadership. According to Madame Roland, he was "confident
even to imprudence, happy, naïve, ingenuous as a boy of fifteen;

---

[1] Phillips, *Biographical Anecdotes*, 13.   [2] See p. 287.

[3] Chambonas: "*Vous voyez donc que cet homme (Brissot) est intéressé. Il faut
donc que vous vous chargiez de le gagner. On ne demande pas qu'il quitte ses opinions, mais simplement qu'il suspende son plan de déchéance. Nous avons à votre
disposition cent mille livres. Si cette somme ne suffit pas, offrez quatre cent mille
livres, puis cinq cents. Allez jusqu'à huit cents; mais ne pasez pas, c'est la limite
de nos pouvoirs; mais il faut qu'il adopte notre projet d'ajournement de la déchéance. . . .*" Soulavie: "*Si j'avais quelque lueur, quelque espérance de réussir,
je me dévouerais à votre commission; mais je dois vous dire qu'une telle ouverture
suffira pour que Brissot me repousse.*" Soulavie, *Mémoires historiques*, VI,
429–30.

[4] Brissot, *Mémoires*, ed. by Lescure; Preface, ii.

he was made to be companion of wise men and the dupe of rogues." He was a good judge of men, she adds, but he did not *know* men at all.[1] Brissot's mother-in-law evidently held the same opinion, for, just as he was starting for America, she wrote warning him that he would be likely to meet men more subtle than he, and exhorting him to be on his guard.[2]

Pétion says of him that he was the embodiment of disinterestedness; that he allowed people to use his ideas without giving him any acknowledgment; that his only thought was to be useful.[3] "I have known Brissot from his infancy," Pétion declared on another occasion; "I have seen him in those moments when the very soul shows itself, when a man abandons himself without reserve to friendship, to confidence; I have known his disinterestedness, I have known his principles; I protest to you that they are pure. Those who make of him the head of a party have not the slightest idea of his character; he is a man of intelligence and learning; but he has neither reserve nor the faculty of dissimulation, neither the attractive personality nor the *spirit de suite* which make a party leader, and what will surprise you is that far from leading others, he is very easily imposed upon."[4]

Phillips, the Englishman referred to above, who evidently wrote from a friendly point of view, describes Brissot as "a votary of true Philosophy whenever he heard her voice or clearly understood her principles; but those principles were not familiar to his mind; they were not always of his own acquisition; and the simplicity and integrity of his heart induced him to confide in others with blind credulity."[5] In summing up

[1] *Mémoires*, i, 197. Meilhan in his memoirs (p. 99), confirms this: "*Quiconque a connu Brissot doit savoir que personne n'était moins propre à former un parti. C'était un homme de cabinet, studieux, sédentaire, d'une société douce et paisible, mais dépourvu de l'audace sans laquelle on n'est jamais chef en aucun genre. Il avait même une facilité de caractère qui le plaçait à la suite des autres plutôt qu'à leur tête.*"

[2] *Correspondance*, 191.   [3] *Notice sur Brissot*, in Vatel. Vergniaud, ii, 240.

[4] *Discours de Jérôme Pétion sur l'accusation intentée contre Robespierre, non prononcé mais imprimé en novembre, 1792.* Quoted by Vatel, *Charlotte Corday et les Girondins*, ii, 219, note.

[5] Phillips, *Biographical Anecdotes*, ii, 15.

Brissot's career, Phillips says again: "As a politician, his heart was better directed than his head — he wanted knowledge of mankind. His reason was therefore misled by his imagination; and his credulity and reliance on the pretensions of others rendered him totally unfit for any important share in the administration of national business." [1] In short, as Bailleul [2] says, he was not a man of the world. [3]

Brissot also lacked an imposing physical presence. He was short in stature, slight in frame, and stooped a little in the shoulders. Nor was he blessed with ease of manner. He says himself that he was very timid, very awkward, especially when he appeared for the first time among strangers. [4] This stiffness, moreover, was not merely a question of manner; it was indicative of one of Brissot's most dominant characteristics. He did not know how to adapt himself to people, and as a consequence was always getting into quarrels and disputes. [5] He adopted fixed standards of morality, and with a narrow puritanism went about applying them without tolerance and without sympathy. The single word which perhaps best describes his character is rigidity.

But if Brissot was not altogether fitted for leadership, he was perhaps more so than the other Girondins. His prominence may in fact partially be accounted for by a process of elimination. Condorcet was not emotional enough, could make no popular appeal; Vergniaud was too indolent, too much of a dreamer; Buzot was too headstrong; Gensonné, too aloof; Guadet lived too much in the present. Brissot, on the other hand, whatever his limitations, did possess certain qualities which made for success and leadership. For one thing he had

[1] Phillips, *Biographical Anecdotes*, II, 20.

[2] Jacques Charles Bailleul (born 1762, died 1843) was a French politician, member of the Convention, and an opponent of Robespierre and Danton. As a signer of the protest against the arrest of the Girondins, he was himself arrested and thrown into prison, but escaped execution.

[3] *Examen critique de l'ouvrage posthume de Madame de Staël.*

[4] *Mémoires*, I, 272.

[5] Note his quarrels with his father, Swinton, Linguet, the father of Fanny Burney, Desforges, Morande, etc.

not only abounding faith in every cause to which he was devoted, but also indefatigable industry in working for it himself, and in making others work. While his executive ability may not have been of the highest order, he certainly was possessed of considerable skill. In short, the qualities which he showed in his early writings continued to be his striking characteristics and explain in large measure both his success and his limitations. His boundless ambition, his tremendous earnestness, and his never-failing optimism enabled him, in spite of his ingenuousness and rigidity, to inspire confidence. At the same time, the defects of his qualities account for his failure. His tremendous earnestness was accompanied by no saving sense of humor, his ambition led him into large plans of which he did not count the cost, and his optimism did not take account of insurmountable obstacles. But though he failed because he lacked the power to adapt himself to circumstances, to realize that it was "not a theory but a condition" by which France was confronted, to perceive at the supreme crisis that the war, which he himself had so large a part in bringing on, demanded immediate centralization in government; yet he stands out among his contemporaries for his high ideals and for a passion for liberty, which, as Garat says, was with him nothing short of a religion. "His eyes," to quote a modern writer, "were fixed on the map of Europe, while others saw only their club or their section." [1]   In a word, while he embodies the spirit of the Revolution in his insistence on the liberty of the individual and on the rights of man, he also foreshadows the new spirit of the nineteenth century — as interpreted by Mazzini in his stirring essay on *Faith and the Future* — in his belief in a larger brotherhood and in his faith in liberty, not for the individual alone, but for humanity.

[1] Aulard, *Orateurs de la Révolution,* i, 224.

APPENDIX

APPENDIX A

LETTERS BY AND TO BRISSOT

Letter of Brissot to Jefferson

(Jefferson Papers, 1st series, vol. 2, Library of Congress. Copy.)

CHANCELLERIE D'ORLÉANS
ce 3 janvier, 1787.

MONSIEUR

J'ai l'honneur de vous adresser ci-joint les questions sur les fonds publics des États-Unis, dont je vous ai parlé. Vous m'avez fait espérer ainsi que M. de Crèvecœur, que vous pourriez en vous adressant au *treasury board* du Congrès, nous procurer une réponse complète & exacte sur tous les points.

Cette réponse est singulièrement importante pour fonder le crédit des États-Unis & je ne doute point que mon digne ami Clavière avec son ami d'Amsterdam ne parviennent à leur établir un grand crédit quand une fois ils auront des lumières suffisantes sur leur situation. Vous voudrez donc bien, Monsieur, mettre ces questions au nombre de vos dépêches prochaines & me faire parvenir ou à M. Clavière la réponse aussitôt qu'elle sera dans vos mains.

(Signed)   BRISSOT DE WARVILLE.

Questions sur les fonds publics des États-Unis.

On suppose que le Congrès des États-Unis d'Amérique met quelqu'importance à leur établir un bon crédit en Europe. Ils ne peuvent y trouver que de grands avantages. La grande affaire des Américains est sans contredit es défrichements & ces défrichements demandent toujours plus de numéraire parcequ'ils le repandent sur une plus grande etendue de pays. Il sera donc avantageux aux Américains de donner à leur papiers un tel crédit qu'il puisse se placer dans les États de l'Europe où l'argent est très abondant & dans ceux où le commerce peut les admettre; car ces papiers pourroient venir chercher l'argent Européen de plusieurs manières, soit, directement & par voye d'emprunt, soit indirectement & en retour de fournitures Européennes lorsque les productions Américaines ne suffiroient pas au moment même pour les payer. La constitution républicaine est de toutes celle qui favorise le mieux un crédit public; & sous ce point de vue les États-Unis ont droit au crédit le plus etendu puisqu'il s'appuie sur un sol immense, fertilisé par la liberté.

Mais dans ce moment soit par la malice de leurs ennemis, soit par les difficultés qui s'élevent entre eux sur leurs dettes et leurs régulations intérieures on ne peut pas encore faire naître en Europe, en faveur des Américains une confiance générale; une infinité de faits, vrais ou faux ou mal représentés, donnent des ombrages perpétuels; & font croire à beaucoup de gens que les Américains eux-mêmes ne sont pas encore persuadés de l'importance de leux crédit au dehors, on ne connoissent pas toute l'étendue des égards dûs au maximes qui fondent & maintiennent le crédit public.

Il seroit donc très nécessaire d'avoir tant de la part du Congrès que de la Chambre de la trésorie, toutes les instructions nécessaires pour se former des idées justes sur l'état présent des dettes Américaines intérieures et extérieures; sur la manière dont elles sont considérées en général & en particulier, par la réunion des États & par chacun d'eux individuellement & pour juger s'il y a des dettes dont le remboursement soit considéré sous des degrès différens de certitude.

Les fonds [stocks] Américains se devisent en effets continentaux & effets particuliers à chaque état. On désire sur les premiers d'avoir leur liste, leur origine, la capitale, la forme, le terme de remboursement s'il y en a — par qu'il est payé — quand, comment, ou quels sont ceux qui ont cours dans le commerce? s'il y a qui soient reçus aux payements des taxes ou qui servent à ce payement? Est-il du des arrérages & en quelle quantité? sur quel objet chaque emprunt ou fond continental est-il hypothéqué?

Les mêmes questions sont à répondre sur les fonds particuliers à chaque état & s'il y en a de ceux-ci qui soient reçus dans tous les états, on désire d'en avoir la liste; comme aussi de connoitre ceux qui n'y sont pas reçus & quelle en est la raison? On désireroit aussi d'avoir la liste des prix aux quels tous les différents effets Américains se négocient actuellement & la distinction de ceux dont le rembours prochain est le plus probable.

Enfin cette question regarde plus particulièrement le Congrès.

On demande quel intérêt le Congrès accorderoit à des particuliers qui lui prêteroient de l'argent à la condition de ne'n pouvoir être remboursé qu'en fonds de terres appartenantes au Congrès & dans le cours d'un certain nombre d'années, que le Congres désigneroit & qui ne devroit pas être trop court.

Si de pareils emprunts pouvoient avoir lieu ils exigeroient la détermination d'une certaine étendue de terres avantageusement situées pour le commerce & la culture, lesquelles seroient réservées pour acquitter ces emprunts, en déterminant d'avance la manière dont les porteurs de ces effets pourroient en prendre possession.

Si une telle idée peut s'appliquer à un plan quelconque, d'une exécution sûre, et facile & qu'il soit possible de lui donner une forme séduisante pour ceux qui cherchent à varier d'emploie de leur argent, il ne seroit pas impossible que cette manière d'emprunter ne réussit en Europe surtout si le produit de tels emprunts servoient à acquitter des parties de dettes étrangères, parce qu'alors ils donneroient lieu à des traites entre des particuliers & les états mêmes à qui le Congrès à des avances à rembourser.

Mais il faudroit que les plans de tels emprunts arrivassent en Europe avec des pleins pouvoirs aux ambassadeurs du Congrès de traiter & même de pouvoir admettre certaines modifications & y engager le Congrès s'ils s'en présentoient de convenables aux préteurs sans être nuisibles aux intérêts des États-Unis.

Daniel Parker to Andrew Craigie

(Craigie Papers, iii, 111. American Antiquarian Society, Worcester, Mass.)

HAVRE DE GRÂCE, June 2, 1788.

MY DEAR SIR:

I have much pleasure in the present opportunity of introducing to your acquaintance Monsr Brissot de Warville, a French gentleman of the most respectable character and connections, his views in going to America are principally to obtain a perfect knowledge of the funds and the land in the western Territory. The representations that he will make to his friends in Europe will determine them respecting the purchase of the Funds, — as he is a literary man and his pursuits having been confined to that line, he will pass unsuspected in America of having any design to buy the Funds. He will communicate with you freely on the subject, if he should recommend them to his connections they will make large purchases, all of which he proposes to confine entirely to you and Col. Duer. He is a gentleman that merits all confidence that you will give him all the information in your power [sic]. I shall leave it with you to settle with him such terms as you may think, proper, my great object has been to prevent a competition in the purchases. I have no doubt but I shall soon form an arrangement with M. de Warville's friend here for a large purchase of those funds in which you will be interested so that we shall be all united in one general interest. You will find M. de Warville to possess true republican sentiments and great knowledge in the affairs in Europe, of France in particular.

I must pray you to give him all the attention and assistance in your power and to make acquainted [*sic*] with all your friends in congress.

I am most faithfully your friend and ser't,

(Signed)   DAN. PARKER.

Andrew Craigie to Daniel Parker

(Craigie Papers, I, 27. American Antiquarian Society, Worcester, Mass. Copy.)

NEW YORK, Dec. 3, 1788.

MY DEAR FRIEND:

This will be handed to you by our friend M. de Warville who will make it his first business to see you on his arrival to communicate the arrangements that have been made with him. Since my acquaintance with this Gentleman I have had such proofs of his amiable disposition and candor that I feel the most perfect confidence in his character. He has formed the best connections in this country, and is highly respected by our first Characters, and as he has acquired great knowledge of affairs here you will receive from him much useful information.

I hope and believe you will receive full satisfaction from the explanations M. de Warville will give and with the power from Col. D. and myself you will be able to settle the arrangement to your mind.

I am yours,
(Signed)   A. CRAIGIE.

Brissot de Warville to Colonel William Duer

(Scioto Papers. New York Historical Society, New York City. Written in English.)

FALMOUTH, Jan. 15, 1789.

DEAR COLONEL:

We are arrived here after a long, tedious, and stormy passage of 41 days. I thought I could fly immediately to London, but the road is obstructed by the vast quantity of snow so I am obliged to stay one day more here. Arriving here we have been told very strange news which shall certainly have a great influence over this world and bring some revolution. The insanity of the king of Great Brit., the death of Spain's, the declining authority of his cousin's of France, I believe that all these circumstances will pave the way to the prosperity of my good friend the American. Clouds are gathering here: they are or they shall be, at least, if you are wise, quickly over in your continent. Nothing is yet determined about the restrictions annexed to the regency. However, it is certain the Prince of Wales will be regent and of course it is very likely there will be a great change in the ministry. Pitt has reassumed a great popularity in defending the right of the people. Considering the effect of the revolution respecting America, I am inclined to believe that you'll be more favorably treated by the future ministry who shall be consisting of men whose liberality of ideas and affection toward America are unquestionable.

What I have picked up here respecting France is that the king has fixed the way of convocating and of organising the States-General — they must be very numerous. So much the better. The French comptroller seems in distress. So much better too. We shall have a better competition for the debt.

Adieu my dear friend. Rely upon it, I shall play the devil to despatch all our business as fast as possible and to send you intelligence. Tell Dr I thank him for his letter of credit, but I've not had any occasion for it. My best compliments to him. Remember me to your ladies and depend on my everlasting friendship.

(Signed)   DE WARVILLE.

Please to send the inclose [sic] to my brother-in-law, M. Dupont, wherever he may be. I'll be obliged to D^r. Craigie to mention my arrival with my compliments to Mr. Barett.

Andrew Craigie to Brissot

(Scioto Papers. New York Historical Society, New York City.)

NEW YORK, 24 Jan. 1789.

MY DEAR FRIEND:

It was a month or five weeks after your departure before you were suspected of having left America and it has caused considerable speculation among those whom you would suspect to be most curious on this occasion. I hope long before this you are happy with your friends in France and begin to think of returning to America. I am this day informed by a letter from my friend Porter at Alexandria that your brother is arrived at Norfolk in Virginia. I hope in a few days to have the pleasure of seeing him in N. Y.

I now forward to you a power of attorney and copy of this deed of this land which I am interested in and wish you to have sold. This tract is about 140 miles from the city of New York and about the same distance from the city of Philadelphia within a quarter of a mile of the River Susquehannah [sic] where it is navigable for boats of 20 to 30 and (sometimes) 50 barrels. The produce of the country sells nearly as high as in the city and the soil is good. A French crown or six *livres* per acre is the lowest price which the proprietors can receive. I suppose a much higher price may be procured for it, as I am informed that land in the vicinity of it has lately been sold for three and some for five dollars per acre. The proprietors will allow you one half of all you can get above the six *livres*, but in case it sells for only six *livres* per acre they will allow you a handsome compensation for your trouble. . . .

Securities have risen since you left here. Notes bearing interest from the first Jan. 1788 have been sold for 5/3.

Wishing you and your plans all possible happiness and that sometime we may have the pleasure to see you again in this country,

I remain, my dear Sir,

Your affectionate friend,

(Signed)   ANDREW CRAIGIE.

Our friend the Colonel is well and has lately written to you.

Brissot to Colonel William Duer

(Scioto Papers. New York Historical Society, New York City. Written in English.)

PARIS, 31 January, 1789.

I've written to you, my excellent friend, from Falmouth. I hope you have received my letter. The roads were very bad so I was detained much longer I expected. Mr. Parker was not in London. I overreached him at Dover, we crossed the British Channel and went together to Paris; I availed myself from the length of the way and the leisure we had, to sound his disposition respecting our speculations and projects. I communicated to him the general plan of association. His lecture seemed not to me operate forcibly on his mind. He told me he saw many difficulties in forming such an association, in dividing the shares; moreover he had entered into many engagements he ought to fulfill. However he promised me to make an attempt. I reminded him that you had furnished him with information, that you had assisted him and of course you were entitled to some benefit. He answered me it was his interest to give you a share in the profits either of his own bargain or of the general association, were it conveyed into execution.

We have since seen Mr. Van Staphorst in Paris. He seems not averse to an association and a partner to Mr. Stadninski I have met just now assured me the latter was in the same disposition. That association cannot be settled but in Amsterdam, where I hope to be with Mr. Parker in a fortnight. As to my friend Clavière, he is always satisfied with the solidity of the speculation and he'll come into. However there are many modifications to make in the plan. Rely on the equity of Mr. Clavière and on my zeal for your concern and this of Dr. Craigie.

Respecting the transfer of the foreign debt, Mr. Parker confessed to me that some while ago he with Mr. Laurent de Couteux had given a plan to Mr. Necker to get that transfer and he hoped to succeed. He did not give to me any details about it. I told him that there was another plan for redeeming that debt, formed by Mr. Clavière, approved by you, from which immense advantages might derive to the Society which should carry it into execution, that we were determined to apply to the French court, but that we might suspend our own application, on the condition that, if Mr. Parker obtained the transfer from the ministry, he should enter into a general association with us and on equal footing, that he should bind himself in writing. He agreed, but as the consent of Mr. Laurent de Couteux is required, we are to settle with him that point. The minister, probably on account of his various and pressing affairs, has not given any answer. However the circumstances seem favorable to get the transfer.

As to the loan Mr. P. told me that it would not proceed but in Holland, that he did not see any difficulty to succeed if, chiefly, the new congress looked determined to appropriate to the payment of the interest a part of the impost he is to raise.

We have not yet conferred about the Illinois lands, the other matters being much more important, so any information about the progress is postponed till the next letter.

I come now to the purchase of the $109350 certificates. Very likely you are already acquainted by Mr. Seton and Dr. Craigie that the bills have not been accepted, with the motives of the refusal, and the bond of the payment. I tried everything in my power to have them accepted from my friend who was first inclined to accept them. But after considering the matter he told me: Suppose I pay those bills, suppose you empower to transfer in my name that debt, the power going to America may be lost, the certificate coming back may be lost; Mr. Seton may die. Many difficulties may arise about the transfer in my name. In those circumstances my property shall be uncertain and not at my disposal for a long while and meanwhile I shall be deprived from 6000 stirling at a time when the money is so scarce and so valuable. Moreover I cannot sell those funds without having the certificate in my name. without being able to transfer it immediately to the purchaser. It therefore seems necessary that I get it previous to accepting. I shall bind myself to pay at his reception.

So your friends in America cannot have any doubts about the payment since you have paid them in cash at least 5% of the purchase.

I could not make any reply to those forcible arguments and so I acceded to the plan proposed by Mr. Clavière stated in the letter I've sent to Messrs. Seton and Craigie. I was chiefly inclined to adopt it, considering that Mr. Seton was not entitled to require any damage, having not advanced any money, the bills not being protested, and the payment being ascertained. So my dear friend send as fast as possible the transfer in the name of Mr. Clavière and the bills shall be paid immediately. . . . (The next paragraph is illegible on account of a tear in the paper.)

Don't miss any occasion to write to me. The money is scarce here, high paid, credit stagnant, tho' the writs for the General states are despatching. Believe me for life your good friend.

(Signed)   BRISSOT DE WARVILLE.

CHEZ M. CLAVIÈRE. HÔTEL LA
COMPAGNIE D'ASSURANCE. RUE
DE RICHELIEU.

P.S. Please to present your ladies with my humble respects, my compliments to Dr. Craigie and you'll oblige me to forward that letter to Mr. Dupont whose I don't know the direction.

Brissot to Colonel William Duer

(Scioto Papers. New York Historical Society, New York City. Written in English.)

PARIS, April 28, 1789.

DEAR FRIEND: —

I am quite amazed not to have received any line from you since I have left America. Have you forgotten one of your best friends. I am waiting with impatience for your answer about the transfer of the certificates.

I see very often here Parker and Haskell. No confidence can be put in Parker. What is certain is this, that he looks for monopolizing the sale of American funds in Europe; and he looks very cool about sharing the profits with his friends in America. He has played so many tricks here that he has created a diffidence about the American funds. There is very little chance for Haskell to sell now his certificates here, but probably he'll find a market in Holland. That requires only some time. I have not any doubt that when the disturbances shall be settled here, the debt funded and the national credit restored, it will be possible to bring some moneyed people in a speculation upon your funds and lands. But now it is quite impracticable. We must then have patience for putting in execution the schemes we have planned. On this very circumstance I'll spend the whole year here.

I suppose now that Clavière's transfer is coming here. We'll do the best for disposing of it. The elections are going very briskly. I've failed to be elected in my own country and they talk of me for being a representative for Paris. Shall I succeed, God knows, but I don't care very much. Though I believe there will be a good constitution, it shall be by far inferior to yours. I do beseech you my friend write me some time about the progress of your new government and believe me forever your everlasting friend,

(Signed)   BRISSOT DE WARVILLE.

No. 1 GRÉTRY.

G. Martin à Monsieur Brissot

(Affaires Étrangères. 31 Décembre, 1792. Angleterre — 29 — Supplément fo. 340. Original.)

Affaires secrètes.

COMPATRIOTE: —

Je m'empresse de vous faire part d'un avis que j'ai reçu il y a quelques heures et sur lequel vous pouves [sic] compter, l'ayant eu d'une personne en qui j'ai la plus grande confiance, qui la mérite par des preuves incontestables que j'en ai eue [sic] et qui a luimême chiffré la pièce dont je vais vous parler. Notre ami commun le connoit et saura qui je veux dire. Cette pièce n'est rien moins qu'une déclaration et réquisition envoyée d'ici aux trois Cours de Berlin, Vienne et Pétersbourg, — par lesquelles après leur avoir témoigné l'accord le plus complet sur leurs idées, leurs vues et leurs projets au sujet de la France, dont il est de la dernière importance d'arrêter les progrès d'une manière effective, les sollicite respectivement d'envoyer les instructions et les pouvoirs les plus amples à leurs ambassadeurs ou envoyés ici, et en outre de faire passer à Londres sans perdre de tems un Militaire Entendu afin de concerter en commun les operations convenables en les assurant qu'aussitôt qu'on aura pris les mesures definitives et frappé les premiers coups, il n'y aura aucune difficulté sur les subsides, puisqu'on est déterminé à agir de la manière la plus vigoureuse, et qu'on en sent l'absolue nécessité. En attendant toutes les Puissances doivent ne négliger aucun moyen de donner à leurs forces toute l'extension possible, en recrutements, augmentation, approvisionnements, etc., et la Russie doit agir de manière à pouvoir fournir un corps de soixante mille hommes s'il est jugé nécessaire, en le rapprochant autant qu'il lui sera possible, et que sa situation en Pologne lui facilitera pour une partie, et l'autre s'avancant au dehors de la Baltique, pour être transportée par mer et escortée par une flotte angloise, qui ne trouvera aucune opposition dans les mers du Nord. Cette note repond aux sollicitations de ces Puissances et à la connoissance qu'elles avoient donné de l'état de leurs finances qu'elles représentent comme un peu épuisées, dans un moment où la prudence les empêche d'ajouter ouvertement de nouvelles taxes. Toute mesure ultérieure est renvoyée à des moments plus favorables, la seule chose dont on doive et puisse s'occuper c'est d'écraser l'ennemi commun, qui n'a d'autre ressource que de porter le trouble et le desordre partout, sans s'embarrasser des conséquences, puisque leur banqueroute est inevitable et des efforts bien concertés l'ameneront immédiatement, et mettront leurs ennemis intérieurs en état de se déclarer sans crainte, et avec succès, puisqu'on a raison de croire par une infinité de communications sures qu'ils sont beaucoup plus nombreux qu'on ne pense en général. Il y a ensuite une infinité d'autres détails et de pièces auxquelles on renvoye et on finit en demandant les mesures les plus promptes, et en observant qu'il ne convient pas de vouloir paroitre se méler des affaires intérieures, du moins en commençant, que cela convient surtout à ce pays, où il importe de menager l'opinion publique, dont on est assuré et qu'il ne faut pas aliener — que tout a contribué dernièrement à la rendre favorable, et que la Catastrophe de Louis XVI à laquelle on s'attend et qu'on regarde même comme assurée achevera d'exalter les esprits et de les porter aux mesures les plus énergiques, que L'Angleterre en attendant fera les préparatifs les plus étendus, et tout ce qui dependra d'elle pour assurer le succès d'une entreprise, que l'intérêt de l'humanité rend indispensable. On a fait partir deux paquebots avec les mêmes dépêches l'un pour la Hollande et l'autre pour Hambourg, et on a envoyé en même tems des dépêches aux Cours de Lisbonne, de Madrid et de Turin.

L'importance de cette Communication me fait courir tous les risques pour vous la faire parvenir, faites en l'usage que vous croires le plus convenable en evitant de me compromettre. Je desire beaucoup qu'on use de clémence envers le Roi, quand la Justice et l'humanité ne l'exigeroit pas, la politique la plus saine devroit y déterminer, et la Convention doit se prononcer, et ne pas craindre les Maratistes et leurs semblables. Je suis persuadé quelle sera soutenue par les départements — il seroit grand (temps?) de lui bannir et de le faire transporter en Angleterre, en gardant son fils pour ôtage, qu'auroit on à craindre, il est nul par luimême, et n'aura jamais la confiance des Emigrants et de ceux qui les soutiennent. Après cette mesure qui auroit l'effet le plus grand sur cette nation il en est une autre sur laquelle je ne hésiterois pas, et qui seroit de se rendre maître de la

Hollande. Comme je pense qu'il ne seroit pas difficile, en fesant [*sic*] naître de ces occasions qui ne manquent jamais, et en étant préparé à profiter des premières hostilités pour s'avancer. Cette mesure est hardie, mais elle est nécessaire, et si on ne s'y décide pas, je crains bien qu'on ne s'en repente quelque jour, la saison pourra même favoriser un pareil dessein, car on doit s'attendre à de fortes gelées cette année, qui est la cinquième depuis que nous n'en avons pas eu de considérables. Il y va du salut de l'Empire, du bonheur du monde, et dans de grands dangers, il faut de grandes mesures. S'il est quelque chose en quoi je puisse être utile, comptes toujours sur moi. Bien des choses à notre ami commun, j'enverrai le manteau et la chaine de montre dans deux ou trois jours. Montrés [*sic*] lui cette lettre, il vous en dira son avis. Tout à vous.

G. Martin.

31 Decembre.

Noël part aujourd'hui pour la Haye. Il faut trouver quelqu'autre moyen de me faire parvenir sûrement vos lettres, ce qui me paroit difficile, mais vous pourriés [*sic*] les adresser à quelqu'un pour moi et me le faire sçavoir par la poste à qui.

APPENDIX B

LIST OF MEMBERS OF THE SOCIÉTÉ DES AMIS DES NOIRS

THE following list of members of the *Société des Amis des Noirs* is found at the *Archives Nationales*, AD. xviii, C 115, at Paris. The paper has neither date nor signature, but from the epithet applied to Lameth[1] it must have been as late as 1790, and from the epithets applied to Mirabeau and Robespierre, the author was probably an anti-revolutionist.

Tableau des Membres de la Société des Amis des Noirs

1. Brissot de Warville,
   rue d'Amboise, no. 10.
2. E. Clavière, administrateur de la Compagnie royale d'Assurance sur la vie,
   rue d'Amboise, no. 10.
3. Le Marquis de Beaupoil Saint-Aulaire au Temple.
4. Brack, Directeur général des Traites,
   rue de Grammont, no. 2.
5. A. S. Cerisier,
   en Bourbonais.
6. Duchesnay, Censeur royal,
   rue des Bernardins, no. 37.
7. Le Marquis de Valady, c'est lui qui a fait révolter le régiment des gardes françoises, à Londres.
8. Dufossey de Bréban, Directeur de la Régie générale
   rue de Grammont, no. 19.
9. De Bourge,
   rue des Filles du Calvaire, no. 16.
10. Madame la Marquise de Baussans,
    Place Royale.
11. J. J. Clavière, Négociant (rue Coq-heron) au Parlement d'Angleterre.
12. Roman, Négociant rue Coq-heron au Parlement d'Angleterre.
13. De Montcloux, fils, Fermier Général,
    rue S. Honoré, no. 341.

[1] Supplément aux procès-verbal Colonies, tome I, Traité des nègres, parti II.

14. De Montcloux de la Villeneuve, Conseiller à la Cour des Aides,
    rue S. Honoré, no. 341.
15. Madame Poivre,
    rue Feydeau, no. 22.
16. De Trudaine, Conseiller au Parlement,
    rue des Francs Bourgeois, no. 39.
17. De Trudaine de la Sablière, Conseiller au Parlement,
    rue des Francs Bourgeois, no. 39.
18. Malartic de Fonda, Maître de Requêtes,
    passage des Petits-Pères, no. 7.
19. Le Roi de Petitval, Régisseur général,
    passage des Petits-Pères, no. 7.
20. L'Abbé Colin,
    au Presbytère de S. Eustache.
21. Du Rovray,
    en Irlande.
22. Short, Secrétaire de l'Ambassade des États-Unis d'Amérique,
    près la grille de Chaîllot.
23. De Pilles, ancien Procureur des Comptes,
    rue de Grammont, no. 19.
24. Le Marquis de Condorcet, Secrétaire perpetuel de l'Académie
    des Sciences. Membre de l'Académie Françoise,
    hôtel de la Monnoie.
25. Charton de la Terrière,
    en Amérique.
26. Kornman,
    rue Carême.
27. Blot, Controleur de la marque d'or,
    à Lyon.
28. Esmangard, fils, Conseiller au Parlement,
    rue des Capucins, no. 22.
29. Dieres, Conseiller à la Cour des Aides,
    rue Jacob.
30. Des Faucherets,
    rue de Paradis.
31. Gramagnac, Docteur en Médicine,
    hôtel de Lussan, rue Croix des Petits-Champs.
32. Lanthenas, Docteur en Medicine,
    rue Thevenot, no. 31.
33. Du Vaucel, Fermier Général,
    rue neuve des Mathurins, no. 1.
34. Gallois, Avocat au Parlement,
    rue des Petits Augustins, no. 24.

35. Le Marquis de Mons,
    rue neuve des Petits-Champs, no. 26.
36. L'Abbé Guyot, Prévôt de S. Martin de Tours,
    rue Traversière, no. 35.
37. Pigot,
    à Genève.
38. Le Baron de Dietrick,
    rue Poissonière.
39. Lavoisier, Fermier Général,
    à l'Arsenal.
40. Bergerot, Directeur des Fermes,
    hôtel des Fermes.
41. Biderman, Négociant,
    à Bruxelles.
42. De Pastoret, Maître des Requêtes,
    rue des Capucines, no. 74.
43. Cottin, fils, Banquier,
    Chaussé d'Antin, no. 8.
44. D'Audignac, Directeur de la Régie générale,
    rue de Choiseul.
45. Le Comte de la Cépede,
    au Jardin du Roi.
46. Munier de Montengis,
    à l'hôtel Royal des Invalides.
47. Madame Clavière,
    rue d'Amboise, no. 10.
48. Le Chevalier de Boufflers,
    hôtel de Rohan, rue de Varenne.
49. Gougenot, Receveur général de la Régie générale,
    rue de Choiseul.
50: Petry, Directeur des Fermes,
    hôtel de Longueville, rue S. Nicaise.
51. De Saint-Alphonse, Fermier Général,
    rue S. Honoré no. 423.
52. Fortin,
    rue de Choiseul.
53. Henry, Avocat au Parlement,
    rue Saint-Jean-de-Beauvais.
54. Le Prince Emmanuel de Salm,
    rue de Grenelle, faubourg S. Germain, no. 231.
55. Duport, Conseiller au Parlement,
    rue du Grand-Chantier, hôtel du Port-frais, no. 2.
56. Segretier.

57. Soufflot, Inspecteur des Bâtimens de Sainte-Geneviève,
   à Sainte-Geneviève.
58. Agasse de Cresne,
   rue Pavée Saint-André-des-Arts, no. 12.
59. Servat, Agent de la ville de Bourdeaux,
   boulevart Montmorency, vis-à-vis le Pavillon.
60. Croharé,
   rue de la comédie françoise, au coin de la rue des Cordeliers.
61. Le Comte de Valence,
   rue Chausee d'Antin, no. 170.
61.[1] Hocquart de Tremilly, Avocat Général de la Cour des Aides,
   rue neuve des Petits-Champs, no. 71.
62. Le Comte Charles de Lameth, dit le Général des Annonciades,[2]
   et de la milice bourgeoise de Pointoise,
   cul-de-sac-Notre-Dame-des-Champs.
63. Le Chevalier Alexandre de Lameth,
   même demeure.
64. Le Chevalier Théodore de Lameth,
   même demeure.
65. Le Marquis du Châtelet,
   hôtel de Brissac, quai des Théatins.
66. Le Comte de Rochechouart,
   rue de Grenelle, faubourg S. Germain, no. 99.
67. Molliens, premier Commis des Finances,
   rue de la Michaudière.
68. Bergon, premier Commis des Finances,
   rue de la Michaudière.
69. De Sannois, Fermier Général,
   hôtel des Fermes.
70. Le Vicomte de Ricey,
   rue de ———.
71. Benoit de Lamothe, Sous-chef de la comptabilité de la Régie
   générale,
   rue neuve Saint-Eustache, no. 21.
72. Leroy de Camilly, Payeur des Rentes,
   rue S. Marc, no. 23.

[1] The mistake here is in the original numbering. There are two 61's.

[2] Lameth, as member of the *Comité des Recherches* to which he was elected in 1720, was obliged to make a visit by night to the convent of the *Annonciades* to arrest M. de Barentin, an accused minister who had taken refuge there. This visit was made the subject of ridicule by the royalists and furnished the occasion for a comic poem beginning, —

> "*Je chante ce héros de milice bourgeoise,*
> *Orateur à Paris, général à Pontoise.*"

73. Dupleix de Mezy, Conseiller au Parlement,
    rue des petites Écuries du Roi.
74. Vallou de Villeneuve, Sous-chef de la Régie générale,
    rue S. Joseph.
75. Le Marquis de la Feuillade,
    rue des Marais.
76. De Moulan, Receveur général des Finances,
    rue de Clichy.
77. Le Marquis de S. Lambert.
78. De Vayne.
79. De l'Etang.
80. Savalette de Lange.
81. Le Marquis de Pampelune.
82. Desissarts.
83. L'Abbé Sieyès, le Député.
84. L'Abbé Lageare.
85. Doizan, fils du Fermier général.
86. De Boullongne.
87. Le Sage.
88. Le Roy.
89. L'Abbé Coulon.
90. Gougenot de Croissy.
91. De Missy.
92. Bertrand des Brus.
93. Lescallier.
94. Marquise de Condorcet.
95. My-lord Daer.
96. L'Abbé Noél.
97. Le Baron de Buest.
98. Messent.
99. L'Abbé Louis.

Associés Etrangers

1. L'Abbé Piatoli,
   boulevard de Richelieu, chez Madame la Princesse Lubor-
   miska.
2. Clarkson, négociant,
   à Dublin.
3. Siodier, négociant,
   à Genève.
4. Dumont,
   à Londres.
5. Mazzey.

Associés correspondans regnicoles.

1. De Souligné. Directeur des Fermes,
   à Lyon.
2. De Suilly, Gentilhomme,
   à Orleans.
3. Pétion de Ville neuve, Avocat,
   à Chartes.
4. D'Autroche (Cher),
   à Orleans.
5. Le Marquis de Gronchy,
   à Meulan.
6. M. le Duc d'Aiguillon.
7. M. le Comte de Mirabeau, dit le Flambeau de la Provence,
   comme Robespierre la Chandelle d'Arras.[1]
8. M. Cottin, Député de Nantes.

---

[1] According to the *Dictionnaire Larousse* the nickname *Chandelle d'Arras* was applied to Robespierre by the *Actes des Apôtres*, a royalist journal which ridiculed him as a provincial lawyer lost among distinguished orators. The *Flambeau de la Province* probably came from the same source.

APPENDIX C

ACCUSATION AGAINST BRISSOT IN CONNECTION WITH THE COLONIES

(*Archives Nationales.* AA 54, 1509. 2, no. 46.)

Notices sur Brissot

BRISSOT a été l'agent de l'engleterre [*sic*] pour ruiner les Colonies Françaises.

Brissot connoissoit le génie des hommes de couleur et l'esprit public des colonies. il [*sic*] sçavoit que pour agiter les Colonies, il suffisoit de metre [*sic*] en mouvement les passions de ces deux classes d'hommes que l'encien [*sic*] régime avoit placés à de grandes distances. C'est pour cela que le 15 fevrier 1790. No. CXCI il applaudit à Joly de Fleury qui demanda à la Commune de Paris qu'elle sollicitoit auprês de l'assemblée Constituante L'admission des hommes de Couleur dans son sein. Brissot appuya cette petition à la Commune dont il étoit membre.

Brissot dit dans son No. 233, 29, Mars., 1790, que ne pas admetre les députés des hommes de couleur au sein de l'assemblée Constituante: C'est préparer la ruine de la Colonie.

Dans son No. 594, 25 Mars 1791. Brissot dit que l'assemblée nationale ne doit pas balancer de prefferer [*sic*] aux blancs les hommes de Couleur dont les vertus fairont [*sic*] un jour la regeneration et la prosperité des Colonies.

Dans son No. 664, 3, Juin 1791, il se pleint [*sic*] de ce que le Comité Colonial n'a pas provoqué de l'assemblée nationale le décret d'admission des députés des hommes de couleur.

Dans son No. 816, Novembre 4, 1791, sachant que les Commercans du Havre preparaient des secours pour S[ain]t Domingue; il les accuse de n'y porter des secours que pour aider les blancs à opprimer les hommes de couleur.

Dans son No. 820. Novembre 8, 1791, il dit que les détails donnés sur l'assemblée Coloniale de S[ain]t Domingue de la revolte des esclaves ne sont que mensonge. il dit que cette revolte n'est qu'un pretexte pour appeller les Anglois au Cap.

Dans son No. 834, 22, Novembre 1791, il dit que les desordres de Saint Domingue sont une manœuvre de cette Colonie pour se rendre indépendante. Il les attribue encore à la cruauté des blancs envers leurs esclaves.

Dans son No. 850. 8. Decembre 1791 — il dit que les blancs ont revolté leurs nègres pour se rendre indépendante et ne pas payer leurs dettes.

Dans son No. 208 — Mars 4, 1791 — il accuse l'assemblée provinciale du Nord de S[ain]t Domingue de vouloir se rendre indépendante.

Dans son No. 557, 16 — Fevrier 1791 — il dit si les colons entendent bien leurs intérêts ils se soumetront quoique certainement on ait comis une injustice à n'entendre pas leurs représentans: mais s'ils sont bons français, ils oublieront cette injustice.

Dans son No. 935 — Mars. 2, — 1791, il dit que les mulatres n'ont lassé les municipalités que parcequ'elles étoient le repaire de l'aristocratie.

Dans son No. 955, Mars 22, 1792, il attenne le tableau des desordres de St. Domingue, il en accuse l'orgueil des blancs, leur obstination à ne pas accorder l'activité politique aux hommes de couleur, il en accuse enfin l'assemblée Coloniale.

Dans son No. 961, 28. Mars 1792, il dit que la Province du Nord de S[ain]t Domingue est perdue par l'obstination de l'assemblée Coloniale à restituer aux hommes de couleur l'activité politique.

Dans son No. 967, 1 Avril 1792, il dit on remplit les papiers publics de funestes nouvelles sur la situation de S[ain]t Dominque. Nous ne devons cesser de metre [sic] le public en garde contre les mensonges dont la france est imbue. On sçait que nos princes les Colons ont toujours dans leur poche quelques lettres de commende, [sic] justement arrivant du Cap et bonnes on mcauvais [sic] suivant le besoin.

Dans son No. 979, 15 Avril 1792, il dit que le decret du 15 May n'est pas la cause des malheurs de S[ain]t Domingue mais bien l'orgueil des blancs.

Dans son No. 1022, 26 May, 1792, il fait l'apologie de Blanchelande et autres chefs des Conspirateurs et une diatribe attroce [sic] contre l'ass[emblée] Coloniale.

Dans son No. 1022, 28 Mars 1792, il applaudit à une lettre de S[ain]t Domingue qui annonce la coalition de 15000 hommes tant blancs que mulatres qui marchent contre le Ville du Port au Prince, il applaudit encor [sic] à l'incendie de l'habitation du patriote borel. [sic]

Dans son No. 1075, 20, Juillet, 1792 — il rapporte une lettre qu'il dit venir de S[ain]t Domingue qui fait l'apologie de Blanchelande et autres contre revolutionaires pendant qu'elle distille le venim sur les patriotes.

Dans son No. 1096, 10. Aout, 1792, il fait l'éloge de la loi du 4 Avril 1792 — qui suivant lui pouroit seule rammener [sic] l'ordre à S[ain]t Domingue.

Dans son No. 1112 — 26, Aout 1792, il fait l'éloge de Blanchelande et des autres chefs de la contre révolution.

Dans son No. 1187, 9, Novembre 1792, il fait l'apologie de Blanchelande.

Dans son No. 1273, 5 Fevrier 1790, il accuse les petits blancs d'avoir égorgé et pillé les maisons du Cap.

Dans son No. 233, 29, May 1790, il insere son discours sur la necessité d'établir à Paris une société pour l'abolition de la Traite.

Dans son No. 327, Juillet, 10, 1790, il pretent [sic] qu'on peut écrire sur les nègres sans aucun danger parce-qu'il[s] ne savent n'ont [sic] pas le tems de lire.

Dans son No. 1026, 1er Juin 1792, il dit que les malheurs de S[ain]t Domingue frappent l'Angleterre bien plus que la france.

Dans son No. 1263, 26, Janvier 1793, il dit que les Colons blancs se reffugient dans la nouvelle engleterre [sic] dont ils ne peuvent manquer de corrompre les moeurs en y emmenant leurs fantaisies et leurs esclaves.

Dans son No. 1263, 26, Janvier 1793, il nie que l'assemblée Coloniale ait le droit que lui ont attribué l'assemblée Constituante et celle [sic] legislative celui de prononcer sur le sort des esclaves.

Dans son No. 1270, fevrier 2, 1793, il insere un pamphlet qu'il dit être de Villete. Ce pamphlet adresse á la Convent[ion] Nationale dit donnés à vos nègres la liberté: vous couvrirés [sic] la terre de combatans, qui sçauront la deffendre [sic] il ne vous en coutera qu'un decret.

Le 27. Octobre 1792, Brissot dit que — Talien a tort de proposer l'envoy de secours à S[ain]t Domingue il dit que Talien ignore que les Espagnols n'ont dans cette contrée que 3000. hommes pendant que la patrie française est deffendue par dix mille hommes de troupes reglées et vingt mille mulatres.

Dans son No. 1004, 10. May — 1792, il dit qu'il n'existe aucune faction républicaine; que c'est un phantome [sic] que les moderés ont créé pour aigrir les patriotes. [The following sentence is illegible.]

Dans son No. 1209, 27. Novembre 1792, il dit que la Convention doit sevir contre la rebellion de l'ass[emblée] Colo[niale] qui a envoyé en france trois Commiss[aires] pour presenter à la sanction un decret sur l'esclavage.

Affaire de sa lettre à la Constitua[nte]

l'affaire de Geng^t. *D.*

APPENDIX D

BRISSOT'S ELECTION TO THE LEGISLATIVE ASSEMBLY

THE following table explains Brissot's struggle for election as a deputy from the department of the Seine to the Legislative Assembly. It shows his successive defeats, the names of those who defeated him, and his final victory. It will be noted that the election had to be by the absolute majority of the electors. For the details of the struggle see Chavaray, *Assemblée Electorale de Paris, 1791–92*, pp. 137–227.

Deputy.	Date.		Ballot.	Total.	Brissot.	Candidate Chosen.
First	1 Sept.		First	802	10	
	1	"	Second	821	2	Garran de Coulon
Second	2	"	First	687	130	Lacépède
Third	3	"	First	739	163	
	3	"	Second	814	179	Pastoret
Fourth	4	"	First	709	153	
	4	"	Second	725	138	Cerutti
Fifth	5	"	First	698	100	
	5	"	Second	799	82	Beauvais de Préau
Sixth	5	"	First	733	112	
	6	"	Second	609	32	Bigot de Préameneu
Seventh	6	"	First	756	33	
	6	"	Second	773	18	
	6	"	Third	694	0	Gouvion
Eighth	7	"	First	722	15	
	7	"	Second	759	9	Broussonet
Ninth	7	"	First	663	142	
	9	"	Second	662	198	
	9	"	Third	752	305	Cretté de Palud
Tenth	9	"	First	719	180	
	9	"	Second	644	168	
	10	"	Third	769	263	Gorguereau
Eleventh	10	"	First	697	96	
*	12	"	*Second	652	137	
	13	"	Second	653	256	
	13	"	Third	757	352	Thorillon
Twelfth	13	"	First	725	254	
	14	"	Second	692	302	
	14	"	Third	641	409	*Brissot*

* Annulled.

APPENDIX E

LETTER RELATING TO CONNECTION OF BRISSOT WITH WAR WITH ENGLAND

(Affaires Étrangeres. Le 19. Septembre l'an 1er. de l'égalité. Angleterre — 582. f°. 182. Original. Paris.)
1ère division.

Jullien fils au Ministre des Affaires Étrangères

PARIS — ce 19. 7bre l'an 1er de l'égalité.

MONSIEUR,

Je reçois dans ce moment une lettre d'Angleterre qui me prouve que la mesure que je vous ai proposée et qu'ont appuyée M[essieu]rs Brissot et Condorcet est plus que jamais urgente et nécéssaire. On intercépte presque tous les paquets venant de france, c'est à dire qu'on veut epaissir le bandeau jetté sur les yeux du peuple Anglais et le conduire ensuite plus aizément à cette guerre qu'il ne pourroit jamais consentir s'il était éclairé. Sur l'invitation de M[onsieur] Brissot et d'un de mes amis M[onsieur] Eury à qui vous aviez paru témoigner le désir de me voir pour que j'achevâsse de vous donner les renseignements que j'avois pu prendre, je me suis présenté plusieurs fois chez vous, — sans jamais pouvoir vous parler, les occupations multipliées de votre place me font assez sentir l'impossibilité où vous étes de recevoir tous ceux qui s'adressent à vous. Cependant le motif qui m'a conduit me parait ainsi qu'à tous ceux à qui je l'ai communiqué d'une grande importance. Quel a été mon étonnement d'entendre dire à l'un de vos secretaires à qui vous comptiez différer jusqu'après les premières opérations de la convention nationale la mesure proposée. Ce seroit perdre absolument l'effet qu'on peut en attendre. Je suis, Monsieur, dans le langage de la liberté et de l'égalité qui ne sauroit être étranger au ministre de Citoyens égaux et libres.

Votre Concitoyen, frère et ami,

JULLIEN *fils*.

Et au Verso: Au Ministre des Affaires Étrangères, à Paris.

BIBLIOGRAPHY

BIBLIOGRAPHY

I. MANUSCRIPT MATERIAL

THE papers of Brissot, after the death of Madame Brissot, remained in the hands of their son Anacharsis. After some years he confided them to the publisher Ladvocat, who, in turn, passed them on to M. Montrol, who used them as the basis for his publication of the memoirs of Brissot. The "portfolio," as this collection of papers is called, must certainly have contained correspondence and other material not utilized in the memoirs, but what has become of these manuscripts is a matter of uncertainty. It seems that they were in 1865 in the possession of the son of M. Montrol, who was unwilling to relinquish them.

Apart from this portfolio Anacharsis probably kept a portion of the correspondence for himself. At all events, his widow appears to have given some of the letters to M. Faugère, copies of which are to be found among the Roland papers at the *Bibliothèque Nationale*, at Paris; the widow of Brissot's grandson also possesses a part of the family correspondence, and there exist numerous other letters in different places. All of this scattered correspondence, which includes letters written by various members of his own and his wife's family, together with a number of documents pertaining to the arrest and trial of Brissot, has been collected and published by M. Perroud in his recent edition of the *Correspondance et Papiers de Brissot*, but the "portfolio" is still undiscovered. The Brissot manuscripts, then, are for the most part either included in the *Correspondance* or are not accessible.

There is one exception, however. Since the publication of the *Correspondance* there has been discovered among the Craigie Papers in the collection of the American Antiquarian Society at Worcester, Massachusetts, and among the Scioto Papers in the collection of the New York Historical Society, a considerable collection of letters to and from Brissot and concerning him, dealing chiefly with his relations with American speculators. Possibly these letters may have some connection with the sixty-five letters to Brissot by Americans announced in the Charavay Catalogue of 1858. A list of the letters in this recently discovered material and a list of other manuscript sources not contained in M. Perroud's collection are given below.[1]

[1] See the *Étude critique* by M. Perroud, prefixed to his edition of Brissot's memoirs, xiv; also the *Correspondance*, avertissement, 450–57.

A. Archives Nationales (Paris)

1. In carton " Tribunaux révolutionnaires — affaire des Girondins." (*W 292, dossier 204*)

Lettre des commissaires et des colons de Saint Domingue au Comité de sûreté générale, 26 septembre, 1793. Original signé. *A. N.*, W 292, no. 204 (2ᵉ partie), pièce 68; Tuetey, viii, 3335.

> A denunciation of Brissot as responsible for the troubles in Santo Domingo and also of Milcent, one of his alleged agents.

Lettre de citoyen Ruelle, ci-devant chargé des affaires de France aux Pays-Bas, au Comité de sûreté générale, 24 juillet, 1793. Original signé, *A. N.*, W 292, no. 204 (2ᵉ partie), pièce 74; Tuetey, viii, 3210.

> An accusation that Brissot had removed an important document from the papers of the Diplomatic Committee, namely, a complaint against the ex-minister Lebrun.

Lettre du citoyen Ruelle, ancien chargé des affaires de France, aux Pays-Bas, à l'accusateur public près le Tribunal révolutionnaire, 8 octobre, 1793. Original signé, *A. N.*, W 292, no. 204 (2ᵉ partie), pièce 73; Tuetey, viii, 3360.

> A renewed statement of the same accusation.

Lettre du sieur Tresset, fils, rue de Cléry, hôtel de France, à l'accusateur public du Tribunal révolutionnaire, 7 brumaire, an II (28 octobre, 1793). Original signé, *A. N.*, W 292, no. 204 (3ᵉ partie), pièce 6; Tuetey, viii, 3415.

> Calls attention to the desirability of summoning Morande as a witness against Brissot, especially in regard to his relations with the British government.

Déclaration faite par devant François Joseph Denizot, juge au Tribunal révolutionnaire par Pierre François Page, 28ᵉ jour du 1er mois de l'an II (19 octobre, 1793). Original signé, *A. N.*, W 292, no. 204 (5ᵉ partie), pièce 6; Tuetey, viii, 3383.

> An accusation that Brissot was acting as the agent of England in his colonial policy.

Avis de M. Collombel, député de la Meurthe, au Comité de Salut public, 7 brumaire, an II (28 octobre, 1793). Original signé, *A. N.*, W 292, no. 204 (3ᵉ partie), pièce 10; Tuetey, viii, 3413.

> A charge that Brissot was guilty of complicity with Dumouriez.

Lettre de Varlet, électeur de la section de Droits, apôtre de la liberté, au citoyen Fouquier Tinville, accusateur public du Tribunal révolutionnaire, 8 brumaire, an II (29 octobre, 1793). Original signé, *A. N.*, W 292, no. 204 (3ᵉ partie), pièce 5; Tuetey, VIII, 3419.

A request to be called as a witness in the trial of Brissot.

2. *Other Material at the Archives Nationales*

Lettre de M. Brissot de Warville à M. Buisson en date du 10 avril, 1789. Copie, *A. N.*, V,[1] 551.

An explanation by Brissot of his use of Buisson's name as a person to whom he might send subscriptions for the *Patriote Français*.

Lettre de M. Maissemy à M. Buisson, 13 avril, 1789. Copie. *A. N.*, V[1], 551.

Commends Buisson for having disclaimed responsibility for the distribution of the prospectus of Brissot's journal.

Lettre de M. de Maissemy, lieutenant général de la libraire, proposant l'interdiction de la feuille périodique, intitulée le *Patriote Français*, ou journal libre, impartial, et national, par une société des citoyens qu'annonce sans permission aucune Brissot de Warville, arrivé au dernier degré de l'audace enhardie par impunité; avec lettre circulaire aux inspecteurs de la presse des provinces. Tuetey, I, 2862.

Annulation de la société projetée entre M. Brissot de Warville et le libraire, Buisson, pour la publication du *Patriote Français*, 17 septembre, 12 novembre, 1789. Minutes, *A. N.*, V[1], 553; Tuetey, II, 2902.

Lettres de félicitation des Sociétés des Amis de la Constitution de l'Yonne et de Saint-Denis et de plusieurs électeurs du district de Lyon pour la choix de Brissot, 19, 20, 28 septembre, 1791. Originaux signés, *A. N.*, B,[1] 11; Tuetey, I, 3033.

The occasion was his election to the Legislative Assembly.

Comité diplomatique (assemblée législative), Procès-verbaux, rapports, adresses, avis, etc. *A. N.*, F⁷, 4395.

Brief summary.

Rapport de police au sujet des menées de la cabale des Narbonne, Brissot et Fauchet, des conciliabules chez M. de Sillery, et de la discussion orageuse chez le maire de Paris entre Robespierre, Brissot, Legendre, Guadet et Claviere. 3 avril, 1792. Original, *A. N.*, F⁷, 4386.

"D'après Bertrand de Moleville, *Histoire de la Révolution de France*, VIII, 229. Brissot, l'abbé Fauchet, Isnard, Vergniaud, et Guadet figurent parmi les députés dont on avait voulu, en novembre 1791, acheter la voix et l'influence moyennant un subside mensuel de 6,000 livres pour chacun d'eux." Tuetey, *Répertoire*, IV, 163.

Déclaration du sieur Joseph Petit, practicien, reçue par le sieur Jean Pierre Civet, commissaire de police de la section du Faubourg-St.-Denis, portant . . . qu'il a été dénoncé par les sieurs Goulet et Beuzelin, payés comme lui, pour cabaler contre Brissot le jour où celui-ci devait parler sur le Comité autrichien, 5 juin, 1792. Copie conforme, *A. N.*, C 218, no. 160, 118; Tuetey, IV, 439.

Procès-verbal des séances de l'assemblée electorale du département d'Eure-et-Loir à Dreux, 2–9 septembre, 1792. *A. N.*, C 178.

Procès-verbal de l'assemblée electorale du département du Loiret à Beaugency, à partir du 2 septembre, 1792. *A. N.*, C 179.

Procès-verbal de l'assemblée electorale du département de l'Eure à Bernay à partir du 6 septembre, 1792. *A. N.*, C 178.

> This and the two preceding titles deal with Brissot's election to the Convention.

Proposition faite par l'un des membres du Comité révolutionnaire des 48 sections séant à la Commune sur les objets suivant . . . que l'on arrête le nommé Raimond, mulâtre confident de Brissot et de Pétion qui doit avoir la correspondance secrète de Brissot, relative aux colonies et avec l'Angleterre, ainsi que celle de Pétion, rien n'empêchant d'ailleurs de s'emparer des papiers de ces deux faux mandataires chez eux, si on les y trouve, 31 mai, 1793. Minute non-signé, *A. N.*, BB³ 80; Tuetey, VIII, 2683.

Extrait des rapports et déclarations reçus au Bureau de surveillance de la Police, signalant les faits suivants: . . . le bruit s'était répandu en même temps que, le 30 mars, Brissot s'était présenté aux barrières et qu'on l'avait empêché de sortir, mais que le Maire avait donné des ordres pour que ce député eût le passage libre, ce qui mécontente le public. 31 mars, 1er avril, 1793. Extrait et original signé (2 pièces), *A. N.*, AF^{IV}, 1470; Tuetey, IX, 497.

Extrait des rapports et déclarations reçus au Bureau de surveillance de la Police, signalent les faits suivants: . . . Il existe, dit-on, les lettres, écrites par Dumouriez à Brissot, recommandant de tâcher d'envoyer, en qualité de commissaires dans la Belgique, Robespierre et Marat parceque c'est le seul moyen de s'en défaire. 6 avril, 1793. Extrait et original signé (2 pièces). *A. N.*, AF^{IV}, 1470.

Extrait des rapports et déclarations reçus au Bureau de surveillance de la Police, signalant les faits suivants: . . . D'après certains rapports Brissot aurait envoyé des millions à Philadelphie, cette assertion se trouve confirmée par trois témoins qui, le 30 avril, ont déposé contre Brissot et Guadet au Tribunel révolutionnaire. 1er mai, 1793. Copie, *A. N.*, AF^{IV}, 1470; Tuetey, IX, 545.

Déclaration du sieur Gillet, secrétaire du Comité révolutionnaire de la section de l'Unité, signalant l'hotel de Patriote Hollandais, rue des Moulins comme logeant nombre de députés, entre autres, Pétion, Brissot, Guadet, qui ont quitté leur domicile habituel et sont venus y chercher un refuge. Sans date (2 juin, 1793). Original signé, *A. N.*, BB³, 80 (dos. 3); Tuetey, VIII, 2834.

Dénonciation contre le nommé Bouquét, frère de Guadet, que Roland a nommé régisseur du château de Saint Cloud, chez lequel réunissaient 3 fois par semaine Brissot, Vergniaud, Gensonné, Pétion, Buzot, etc., et contre la femme de Brissot qui a logé assez longtemps dans le chateau qui demeure rue des Ursulines, à Saint Cloud, et chez laquelle doivent trouver des papiers importants, 3 juin, 1793. Original signé, *A. N.*, BB³, 72; Tuetey, VIII, 3027.

Lettre écrite à Brissot par son frère datée du 5 août, 1793. *A. N.*, F⁷, 4443, no. 18.

> Contains a message from Genet.

Arrêté du Comité de sûre é générale, applaudissant aux mesures de sûrété prises par le comité de surveillance et de salut public, à l'égard de la femme de Jacques Pierre Brissot, 9 août, 1793. Extrait du registre des arrêtés généraux du Comité de sûreté générale. *A. N.*, AFᴵᴵ, *286; Tuetey, VIII, 3265.

> Provides for bringing Madame Brissot before the Committee of General Security.

Arrêté du Comité de sûreté générale, décidant que la citoyenne Dupont, femme de Jacques Pierre Brissot, restera en état d'arrestation à l'hotel de Necker, rue de Richelieu, 9 août, 1793. Extrait du registre des arrêtés généraux du Comité de sûreté générale. *A. N.*, AFᴵᴵ, *286; Tuetey, VIII, 3266.

Notices sur Brissot, *A. N.*, AA⁵⁴, 1509.

> Found among the papers pertaining to the Colonial Committee; without date or signature. It consists of a long series of accusations against Brissot — in almost every case followed by a citation from the *Patriote Français* — denouncing him as responsible for the troubles in the colonies. See appendix C.

À ajouter à l'affaire Brissot. *A. N.*, F⁷, 4443, no. 18.

> Unsigned and undated. It consists of a number of charges, including complicity with Lafayette, opposition to the insurrection of August 10 and support of the civil war in the colonies.

Pétition de la Société des Amis de la Liberté et de l'Egalité de Versailles à la Convention nationale, réclamant le prompt jugement de Brissot, et de ses infâmes complices, retardé par on ne sait quelle politique timide ou lenteur funeste, le peuple entier demandant par leurs voix le châtiment de ce traître 7 septembre, 1793. Originaux signés de MM. Charbonnier, président et Bocquet secrétaire (2 pièces). *A. N.*, F⁷, 4443; Tuetey; VIII, 3311.

Rapport de l'observateur La Tour-La-Montagne, annonçant que . . . Un ouvrage nouveau de Brissot est sous presse et va paraître au premier jour; c'est, dit-on le testament politique de cet homme dangereux; le libraire Marat, au Palais Royal, cour des Fontaines, s'est chargé de l'impression et de la distribution de cet ouvrage, dont on attend sans doute un grand effet. 13 septembre, 1793. Original signé, *A. N.*, F⁷, 3688³; Tuetey, IX, 1296.

Rapports de l'observateur La Tour-La-Montagne, signalant les faits suivants: La citoyenne Brissot avec son fils se promène dans Paris, accompagnée d'un gendarme, s'arrête fort souvent, parle à beaucoup de monde, et le gendarme reste à distance. Des femmes, ont dit, en murmurant: 'en ferait-on autant pour une pauvre marchande.' 27 septembre, 1793. Originaux (2 pièces), *A. N.*, F⁷, 3688³; Tuetey, IX, 1433.

Lettre de M. Fouquier-Tinville, accusateur public du Tribunal révolutionnaire, au président de la Convention nationale, annonçant l'écrou à la Conciergerie des députés Brissot, etc. 7 octobre, 1793. Original signé, *A. N.*, C 273, no. 692; Tuetey, VIII, 1729.

Arrêté du Comité de sûreté générale, portant que le concierge de la petite maison de la Force recevra la nommée Dupont, femme Brissot et son enfant. 22ᵉ jour du 1er mois de l'an II (13 octobre 1793). Extrait du registre des mandats d'amener du Comité de sûreté générale. *A. N.*, AFᴵᴵ, *289; Tuetey VIII, 3367.

Récompense nationale, 9 floréal, an IV. *A.N.*, Fᴵᴬ, 570.

The record of the pension providing for Brissot's wife and children.

Inventaire de toutes les pièces trouvées sur la table de Brissot lorsque le décret qui le met en etat d'arrestation lui a été signifié à la maire. *A. N.*, F⁷, 4443, no. 18.

B. Affaires Étrangères (Paris)

Lenoir au Comte de Vergennes. Le 4 mai, 1783, Paris. Aff. étrangères, Angleterre, 542, f. 183. Original.

Note faite à la hâte. Le 21 avril, 1783, à Londres. Aff. étrangères, Angleterre, 542, f. 79. Minute.

Compte rendu à son Excellence Monsieur le comte D'Hadmer . . . par le Sr. Receveur. Le 22 mai, 1783, à Londres. Aff. étrangères, Angleterre, 542 f. 278. Minute.

This and the three preceding titles concern the efforts made to apprehend the authors of certain libels, with which Brissot was suspected of having some connection.

Despatch of Chauvelin, minister plenipotentiary of France, to
Lebrun, minister of foreign affairs, London. 29 September, 1792. Aff.
étrangères. Correspondance politique, vol. 582, p. 255.

> A commendation of the note drawn up by Brissot and sent by the
> Legislative Assembly to foreign powers shortly after the 10th of August.

Jullien fils, au Ministre des affaires étrangères. Paris le 19 fevrier,
l'an 1ᵉʳ de l'égalité. Aff. étrangères, Angleterre, 582, f. 182. Original.

> A report from a young man whom Brissot had recommended as a suit-
> able person to help cultivate in England a public opinion favorable to
> France.

G. Martin à Monsieur Brissot. 31 dec. 1792. Aff. étrangères, Angleterre, 29, supplément, f. 340. Original. Affaires secrètes.

> A letter giving secret information as to the supposed intentions of Ger-
> many, Austria and Russia toward France. Of considerable importance in
> connection with Brissot's attitude toward foreign war. The writer was
> probably not altogether correctly informed. See note, p. 320.

C. District and Municipal Archives at Moulins and Gannat

Registre des délibérations prises par le conseil général de la commune de Moulins. 19 juin, 1 juillet, 1793.

Délibérations du conseil municipal de Gannat, 27 juin, 5 juillet,
1793.

Procès-verbal du conseil général du district de Gannat, juin 27,
1793.

> This and the two preceding titles deal with events at Moulins and
> Gannat in connection with Brissot's arrest and imprisonment.

D. Manuscript Department of the Library of Congress at Washington, D.C.

Letter of Brissot to Thomas Jefferson, Jan. 3, 1787. In Jefferson
papers, letters from T. Jefferson, 1st series, vol. 2, 1786–87.

> A letter of inquiry on the public funds of the United States. See Ap-
> pendix A.

Letter of Brissot to Washington. New York, Aug. 10, 1788. In
Washington papers.

> A letter written to enclose the letter of introduction to Washington
> given by Lafayette to Brissot. At the bottom of the sheet a translation
> of Brissot's letter has been made in another hand.

Letter of Washington to Brissot. Mount Vernon, Aug. 28, 1788. In Washington papers.

> An acknowledgment of the above.

Letter of William Short to Brissot. Amsterdam, Nov. 29, 1790.
Letter of William Short to Brissot. Dec. 26, 1790.

> This and the above concern information which Brissot has furnished Short on the action of the Assembly, with regard to the duty on American tobacco. Short also speaks of the trade in oil. The two letters, particularly the latter, are almost illegible.

Letter of William Thornton to Brissot. Philadelphia, Nov. 29, 1788. In the Thornton Papers.

> A long account of Thornton's plans for the transportation of American negroes to a settlement in Africa, at Sierra Leona.

Letter of Brissot to Thornton. Paris, June 17, 1789. In the Thornton Papers.

> An acknowledgment of the above.

Letter of Clavière, honorary President of the *Société des Amis des Noirs*, to Dr. Thornton, June 16, 1789. In the Thornton Papers.

> Clavière writes that while the *Amis des Noirs* approve of Dr. Thornton's scheme in the abstract, they feel that public opinion is not yet ripe for action.

E. American Antiquarian Society, Worcester, Massachusetts

Daniel Parker to Andrew Craigie, Havre de Grace, June 2, 1788. Craigie Papers, iii, 111.

> Introducing Brissot and commending him as likely to be useful in their plans for speculation.

Andrew Craigie to D. Parker, July 27, 1788. C. P., i, 4.

> Announcing the arrival of the Cato with Brissot, and stating his intention of interesting him in American speculations.

Andrew Craigie to D. Parker (copy), New York, Oct. 29, 1788. C. P., i, 22.

> This and following all deal with the schemes for speculation in the American debt and in Western lands.

William Duer to D. Parker, Nov. 5, 1788. C. P., ii, 52.

Andrew Craigie to D. Parker (copy), New York, Dec. 3, 1788. C. P., i, 28.

Andrew Craigie to François Dupont (copy), Feb. 2, 1789. C. P., I, 25.

François Dupont to Andrew Craigie, Philadelphia, Feb. 9, 1789. C. P., II, 1.

François Dupont to Andrew Craigie, Feb. 9, 1789. C. P., II, 2.

Andrew Craigie to François Dupont (copy), Feb. 17, 1789. C. P., I, 32.

François Dupont to Andrew Craigie, Philadelphia, Feb. 20, 1789. C. P., II, 4.

Andrew Craigie to François Dupont, New York, Feb. 26, 1789. C. P., I, 33.

François Dupont to Andrew Craigie, March 15, 1789. C. P., II, 5.

Andrew Craigie to François Dupont (copy), New York, May 4, 1789. C. P., I, 34.

C. Gore to Andrew Craigie, Boston, May 5, 1789. C. P., II, 89.

François Dupont to Andrew Craigie, Philadelphia, May 14, 1789. C. P., II, 7.

François Dupont to Andrew Craigie, Philadelphia, July 15, 1789. C. P., II, 10.

Thomas Porter to Andrew Craigie, Alexandria, Va., May 5, 1790. C. P., II, 143.

Andrew Craigie to Joel Barlow (copy), New York, May 24, 1790. C. P., I, 60.

Andrew Craigie to Joel Barlow (copy), New York, June 16, 1790. C. P., I, 64.

François Dupont to Andrew Craigie, Philadelphia, June 20, 1790. C. P., II, 2.

François Dupont to Andrew Craigie, Philadelphia, July 4, 1790. C. P., II, 9.

Andrew Craigie to François Dupont (copy), New York, July 21, 1790. C. P., I, 71.

Andrew Craigie to François Dupont (copy), New York, Sept. 29, 1790. C. P., I, 89.

F. NEW YORK HISTORICAL SOCIETY: SCIOTO PAPERS

1. Letters written by Brissot

Brissot to Wm. Duer, Falmouth, Jan. 15, 1789.

This and the following have to do with the speculation in which he was engaged with Craigie and Duer.

Brissot to Wm. Duer, Paris, Jan. 31, 1789.
Brissot to Wm. Duer, April 28, 1789.

2. *Letters to or concerning Brissot*

François Dupont to Brissot, Berlin, July 26, 1783.

Deals with the business affairs of the Dupont family.

Account of Brissot with Andrew Craigie, dated Dec. 3, 1788.

In connection with the speculation.

François Dupont to Brissot, Paris, Sept. 15, 1788.

Announces that he was just on the point of starting for America.

Miers Fisher to Brissot, Philadelphia, Nov. 25, 1788.

This letter and the next concern Brissot's departure for France.

Miers Fisher to Brissot, Philadelphia, Dec. 11, 1788.
Miers Fisher to François Dupont, (undated).

This letter and the next deal with personal matters and announce the arrival of a Frenchman recommended by Brissot.

Miers Fisher to François Dupont, Philadelphia, Oct. 21, 1789.
Andrew Craigie to Brissot, New York, Jan. 24, 1789.

This and the following deal with the speculation in the American debt.

David Maitland to Brissot, London, Feb. 10, 1789.
Andrew Craigie to Brissot, June 13, 1789.
Miers Fisher to Brissot, Philadelphia, Nov. 12, 1789.

Personal matters.

Joshua Gilpin to Brissot, Philadelphia, April 28, 1790.

This and the next two letters concern paper moulds which Brissot was to procure for Gilpin in France.

Joshua Gilpin to Brissot, Philadelphia, May 3, 1790.
Joshua Gilpin to Brissot, Philadelphia, Oct. 7, 1790.
Miers Fisher to Brissot, Philadelphia, May 1, 1790.

This and the following concern a possibility of Brissot's return to America.

Miers Fisher to Brissot, Philadelphia, July, 5, 1790.
Andrew Craigie to Brissot, May 24, 1791.

This and the following deal with the land speculation in which Brissot was engaged.

Thomas Porter to Brissot, Alexandria, July 12, 1790.
Andrew Craigie to Brissot, Aug. 31, 1790.
Andrew Craigie to Brissot, New York, Sept. 12, 1790.
Andrew Craigie to Brissot, New York, Oct. 6, 1790.

F. de Bayard to Brissot, Philadelphia, Nov. 2, 1790.

An expression of gratitude for kindness shown him by Miers Fisher, to whom he had been recommended by Brissot.

Miers Fisher to Brissot, Philadelphia, Nov. 2, 1790.

Introduces Wm. Temple Franklin, a grandson of Benjamin Franklin, who is to execute a commission for Robert Morris, to sell land in New York State.

Thomas Porter to Brissot, New York, May 1, 1791.

On financial matters.

Jacob Shoemaker to Brissot, April 22, 1791.

Comments on the French political situation and denounces slavery.

Jacob Shoemaker to Brissot (undated).

Same subject as above.

Jacob Shoemaker to Brissot, Sept. 9, 1791.

On the state of public credit.

Joshua Gilpin to Brissot, Philadelphia, March 15, 1791.

On business connected with the sending of paper moulds.

Jacob Shoemaker to Brissot, Nov. 20, 1791.

Criticizes Brissot's *Nouveau Voyage.*

Letter to Brissot (unsigned), Bensalem, Nov. 20, 1791.

It begins "Cher Frère et Chère Sœur," and is evidently from François and Nancy Dupont. On family matters.

Letter to Brissot (unsigned), Philadelphia, Nov. 28, 1791.

It begins in the same manner as the above and is evidently from the same persons. Informs Brissot of the criticism which his *Nouveau Voyage* has aroused in America.

De Nancrede to Brissot, Boston, May 1, 1791.

A note of introduction.

Miers Fisher to François and Annette Dupont, Dec. 11, 1791.

On family matters.

Jacob Shoemaker to Brissot, Philadelphia, May 16, 1792

Hopes that Brissot has not taken offense at the criticism on his book.

Letter to Brissot (unsigned), Sept. 5, 1792.

Expresses desire of seeing him in America.

Miers Fisher to Anne Dupont, Nov. 11, 1793.

> Expresses regret that he can render him no assistance on account of the epidemic.

Letter to Brissot (unsigned), Jan. 20, 1793.

> Comments on French political affairs.

Miers Fisher to Anne Dupont, Veuve Aublay, Philadelphia, May 28, 1797.

> Congratulates her on being at home again.

Letter addressed to Madame Aublay (unsigned and undated).

> Apparently from Madame Brissot, urging her to return to France.

Miers Fisher to Anne Dupont, Bensalem, Sept. 18 (year ?).

> Condolences on the death of her brother-in-law.

G. Miscellaneous

Proceedings of the Committee for the abolition of the slave trade. 1787–1819. 3 vols. British Museum, manuscripts, 21254–56.

> Contains information as to the relations between Brissot and the *Amis des Noirs* with the London society.

Lettre de M. de Comte de Mirabeau à M. le Cont^{lle} G^{nl}: Paris, 30 mai, 1785.

> Concerns the payment of the work on the Banque de St. Charles. The letter is the property of the late M. Paul Arbaud, of Aix in Provence. For a copy of it the writer is indebted to Professor F. M. Fling, of the University of Nebraska.

Brissot, notes inédites sur l'Amérique.

> These notes are in Brissot's own hand, unsigned and undated. They are the property of M. Charles Vellay of Paris.

Letter of Brissot to the Convention from the Abbaye. July 24, 1793. *Bib. Nat.*, Fr. nouv. acq., vol. 307.

> Asking for a hearing.

Letter of Lord Grenville to M. le Comte de Woronzow, Dec. 20, 1792. In correspondence of Lord Grenville. British Museum, additional Mss. 36814.

> Concerning a possible alliance of England with Austria, Prussia, and Russia against France.

II. PRINTED MATTER

A. Brissot's Own Works

Le Pot-pourri, étrennes aux gens de lettres (par Brissot de Warville et N. F. Gaillard). London, 1777.

> A collection of satires on the bar, the press, the theatre, contemporary customs, etc.; but directed chiefly against individual men of letters, who are attacked openly by name.

Testament politique de l'Angleterre. Philadelphia [Amsterdam], 1780.

> Published anonymously. It purports to be an original production "found among the papers of the late Lord Littleton," but from the account of the publication given in Brissot's memoirs (i, 137), it was evidently his own work. A satire on the policy of England, especially with regard to her colonies.

Politick Testament van England. Amsterdam. 1781.

> A Dutch translation of the preceding.

Lettre de Brissot (1er fevrier, 1780) à M. Doyen sur *son Histoire de la Ville de Chartres.*

> Extract from the *Journal Encyclopédique*, April, 1780. Noted by M. Perroud in his edition of Brissot's memoirs.

Recherches philosophiques sur le droit de propriété et sur le vol considérés dans la nature et dans la société. Chartres, 1780.

> Reprinted in vol. vi of the *Bibliothèque Philosophique*. An argument that in a state of nature there is no such thing as exclusive property. It was made the basis of a bitter attack on Brissot in 1792.

Théorie des loix criminelles. 2 vols. Berlin, 1781.

> First submitted to the Economic Society of Berne in competition for a prize on the best means of reforming the penal code, but published without waiting the result of the competition. Meanwhile it was submitted in modified form for a prize offered by the Academy of Chalons-sur-Marne. The first volume treats of the means of lessening crime; and of the reformation of the criminal law with a view to making the punishment fit the crime and lessening the severity of the punishment. The second volume deals with the reform of the procedure in criminal trials.

Théorie des lois criminelles, . . . nouvelle edition précédée d'une lettre sur l'ouvrage par le Président Dupaty et suivie du Sang innocent vengé ou Discours sur les réparations dues aux accusés innocents. 2 vols. Paris, 1836.

> The editor frankly acknowledges making notes and changes.

Les Moyens d'adoucir le rigueur des loix pénales en France, sans nuire à la sûreté publique, ou Discours couronnés par l'Académie de Chalons-sur-Marne, en 1780, suivis de celui qui a obtenu l'accessit (par J. E. D. Bernardi) et des extraits de quelques autres mémoires présentés à la même Académie. Chalons-sur-Marne, 1781.

> A slightly modified form of the first part of the *Théorie des lois criminelles*. Another edition with considerable additions was published in the *Bibliothèque philosophique*, vol. VI.

Le Sang innocent vengé, ou Discours sur les réparations dues aux accusées innocents. Couronné par l'académie des sciences et belles-lettres de Chalons-sur-Marne, le 25 août, 1781. Berlin et Paris, 1781.

> Reprinted with explanatory notice and reply to the attack in the *Mercure* of August 3, 1782, in the *Bibliothèque philosophique*, vol. VI. Again reprinted in the second edition of the *Théorie des lois criminelles*, 1836, vol. II.

De la Suppression de la peine de mort. Ouvrage couronné par l'académie de Chalons-sur-Marne, en 1780, réimprimé par A. Brissot. Lille, 1849.

> Consists of brief extracts from the preceding work, from that part dealing with the suppression of the death penalty.

Un Indépendant à l'ordre des avocats, sur la décadence du barreau en France. Berlin, 1781.

> At first published anonymously. When attributed to Brissot, he did not deny the authorship. Republished with *Réflexions Préliminaires*, in the *Bibliothèque Philosophique*, vol. VI.

(Indépendance des Anglo-Américains démontrée utile à la Grande-Bretagne. Lettres extrait du Journal d'Agriculture, avril et mai, 1782. In political pamphlets.)

> Published anonymously. It is attributed by the catalogue of the Library of Congress to Brissot; but as it contains criticism on Rousseau not in harmony with Brissot's other writings, it seems hardly possible that it can be his.

De la Vérité ou Méditations sur les moyens de parvenir à la vérité dans toutes les connoissances humaines. Neuchâtel, 1782.

> A consideration of the different kinds of reasoning by which one may arrive at the truth, and of the kind of government and climate best suited to the search.

Bibliothèque philosophique du législateur, du politique, du jurisconsulte, 10 vols. Berlin et Paris, 1782-85.

> Consists of reprints of several of Brissot's earlier works (*Moyens de prévenir les crimes en France; Le Sang innocent vengé; Recherches philoso-*

phiques sur le droit de propriété et sur le vol, and *De la Décadence bu barreau françois*), speeches, essays, memoirs, codes and constitutions from all parts of Europe and from the United States. In some cases they are given entire and sometimes in extracts or *résumés*.

Lettres philosophiques sur St. Paul, sur sa doctrine politique, morale, et religieuse et sur plusieurs points de la religion chrétienne considérés politiquement. Traduit de l'anglais par le philosophe de Ferney, et trouvées dans le porte-feuille de M. V., son ancien secrétaire. Neuchâtel, 1783.

> An argument against the writings of St. Paul on the ground that they contain contradictions, improbable stories and vicious doctrines, and that they show a spirit of marked intolerance. Among these vicious doctrines Brissot places foremost that of predestination and the resurrection of the body.

[The same.]   Chartres, 1774. (?)
[The same.]   Hamburg, 1782.

Le Philadelphien à Genève ou Lettres d'un Américain sur la dernière révolution de Genève, sa constitution nouvelle, l'émigration en Irlande, etc., pouvant servir de tableau politique de Genève, jusqu'au 1784. Dublin, 1783.

> A defense of the democratic party in Geneva.

Correspondance universelle sur ce qui intéresse le bonheur de l'homme et de la société. Vol. i, Neuchâtel, 1783. Vol. ii, Londres, 1783.

> An effort to bring about reform under color of a correspondence between savants. It was a part of his plan to include translations of German works. A large part is obviously Brissot's own work.

Lettres sur la liberté politique, adressées à un membre de la Chambre des Communes d'Angleterre, sur son élection au nombre des membres d'une association de comté; traduites de l'anglais en français par le R. P. de Rose-Croix, ex-Cordelier. Avec des notes de l'abbé Pacot, auteur de l'histoire des Pays-Bas, théologien, conseiller aulique etc. Seconde édition. Liège, 1783.

> Attributed to Brissot. It is in fact a translation of the work of David Williams, a criticism of the English government under George the Third. The notes, which contain many sarcastic comments on the French government, are probably from Brissot's own pen.

Journal du Licée (sic) de Londres, ou Tableau de l'état présent des sciences et des arts en Angleterre. 2 tomes en 1. Paris, 1784.

> The Journal was planned to include: (1) discoveries in physics, chemistry, and anatomy; (2) discoveries in the arts; (3) book reviews; (4) cata-

logue of novelties; (5) plays; (6) reports of judicial decisions and all that concerns the political and civil constitution of England; (7) notices of meetings of different societies.

Tableau de la situation actuelle des Anglais dans les Indes orientales, et de l'état de l'Inde en général. Paris, 1784.

An effort to present an impartial picture of India, and to create a public sentiment which should demand just government and more freedom of trade. A most opportune subject, as England, having just lost her American colonies, was giving more attention to her possessions in the East.

L'Autorité législative de Rome anéantie ou Examen rapide de l'histoire et des sources du droit canonique. Chartres, 1784.

An argument to show that the legislative authority of Rome rested on a slight foundation, since the Holy Scriptures contained almost nothing on dogma or discipline, the decrees of the councils were not infallible and many decrees of the Popes false, and the authority of the Fathers often doubtful. Published anonymously.

[The same.]   1785.

Rome jugée ou l'autorité législative du pape anéantie, pour servir de réponse aux bulles passées, nouvelles and futures, du pape, etc. Paris, 1791.

A new edition of the preceding, published at the time of the formation of the civil constitution of the clergy and directed especially against the Pope. Brissot's name appears in this edition.

Un Défenseur du peuple à l'Empereur Joseph II, sur son règlement concernant l'émigration, ses diverses réformes, etc. Dublin, 1785.

An argument in favor of emigration. Published anonymously.

Seconde lettre d'un défenseur du peuple à l'Empereur Joseph II, sur son règlement concernant l'émigration, et principalement sur la révolte des Valaques, où l'on discute à fond le droit de révolte du peuple. Dublin, 1785.

Mackintosh, W. Voyages en Europe, en Asie, et en Afrique . . . commencées en 1777 et finis en 1781 . . . suivis des Voyages du Colonel Capper dans les Indes . . . en 1779. (Traduits par Brissot.) 2 vols. Londres et Paris, 1786.

Brissot's name does not appear on the title-page. In the preface he gives his idea of the functions of a translator as follows: "Il y avait des répétitions, je les ai élaguées; des longueurs, j'ai abrégé; des idées peu claires, j'ai éclarci; des faussetés, j'ai les ai réfutés dans les notes; en un mot j'ai tâché de conserver dans cet ouvrage tout ce qui pouvait être instructif, intéressant, amusant, pour les Français."

[The same.]   1792.

Examen critique des voyages dans l'Amérique septentrionale, de M. le Marquis de Chastellux; ou lettre à M. le Marquis de Chastellux, dans laquelle on réfute principalement ses opinions sur les Quakers, sur les nègres, sur le peuple et sur l'homme. Londres, 1786.

> A defense of the morality and religious and political dogmas of the Quakers and of the ability and rights of the negroes.

A translation of the same. Philadelphia, 1788.

Mon mot aux académiciens. 1786.

> In his *Bibliographie de Brissot* (Mémoires I, xxxii) M. Perroud says: "Je n'ai pu retourner cette brochure en faveur du magnétisme animal et du somnambulisme; mais elle a sûrement existé, car les *Mémoires secrets* du 18 juillet 1786 l'annoncent, sous ce titre: Un mot à l'oreille des académiciens et disent que c'est un écrit 'vigoureux.'"

Dénonciation au public d'un nouveau projet d'agiotage ou Lettre à M. le Comte de S——— sur un nouveau projet de Compagnie d'assurances contre les incendies à Paris, sur ses inconvéniens, et en général sur les inconvéniens des compagnies par actions. Londres, 1786.

> Brissot's name does not appear on the title-page. His argument is based on the following grounds: (1) Fires are less frequent at Paris than at London, whose example in the matter of insurance it is proposed to follow; (2) the premiums at which the company proposes to insure would not make it worth while; (3) it would be difficult for the owner of a house to apportion the expense among his tenants; (4) the city government will feel less responsibility in preventing fires; (5) claims for damages will give rise to disputes; (6) and in the case of this particular company the promoters hope to make a monopoly of it and by connecting it with a water company in which they are already interested, they hope to raise the price of the stock of both companies.

Seconde lettre contre la Compagnie d'assurance, pour les incendies à Paris et contre d'agiotage en général, adressée à MM. Perrier et Compagnie. Londres, 1786.

> The title-page bears this quotation from Rousseau: "On commence par mettre le feu à la maison pour faire jouer les pompes." Chiefly an attack on M. Perrier, the author of the prospectus of the proposed company, and a reply to his argument for connecting the fire insurance company with the water company.

Lettres philosophiques et politiques sur l'histoire de l'Angleterre depuis son origine jusqu'à nos jours traduits de l'anglais. (Brissot translator.) 2 vols. London, 1786.

> In the *Biographie Universelle* of Michaud it is stated that these are the famous letters attributed to Lord Lyttleton. This is a mistake. They are

instead a translation of *A History of England in a Series of Letters from a Nobleman to his Son*, by Oliver Goldsmith, published anonymously in 1774. The notes are by Brissot. According to the preface he allowed himself considerable liberty in making the translation. The translation has been attributed to Madame Brissot, but Brissot says nothing to indicate that it was not his own work.

De la France et des États-Unis, ou de l'importance de la révolution de l'Amérique pour le bonheur de la France, des rapports de ce royaume et des États-Unis, des avantages réciproques qu'ils peuvent retirer de leurs liaisons de commerce, et enfin la situation actuelle de États-Unis, par Étienne Clavière et J. P. Brissot de Warville. Londres, 1787.

> An argument against the mercantile theory and for greater freedom of trade, especially for closer commercial relations between France and the United States; on the ground that the United States needed the manufacturers of France, and France the natural products of the United States. The work is dedicated to the American Congress and to the friends of the United States in both hemispheres.

[The same.] Reprinted in 1791 as vol. III of the *Nouveau Voyage dans les États-Unis*.

Considerations on the relative situation of France and the United States of America, translated from the French. London, 1788.

> A translation of the above.

Commerce of America with Europe. London, 1794.

> Another translation of the above. Published as the second volume of the translation of the *Nouveau Voyage*.

[The same.] A Dutch translation of the above. Amsterdam, 1794.

> Published as the second volume of a Dutch translation of the *Nouveau Voyage*.

Lettre à l'auteur du *Mercure politique* par les auteurs du traité intitulé *De la France et les États-Unis*. Bouillon, 1787.

> A defense in answer to certain charges that had been made in the *Mercure Politique* of June 30, 1787, regarding statements contained in *De la France et des États-Unis*, relative to Warren Hastings. Brissot evidently believed in his guilt.

Point de banqueroute ou Lettre à un créancier de l'État, sur l'impossibilité de la banqueroute nationale et sur les moyens de ramener le crédit et la paix. Londres, 1787.

> Published anonymously. An argument against a declaration of bankruptcy on the following grounds: (1) That it would degrade not only the

sovereign and the ministers, but also the entire nation before the world; (2) England was worse off than France, but did not declare bankruptcy; (3) there would be no confidence in the treaties of peace and of commerce made by France; it would injure both foreigners and Frenchman who had lent to the state; (5) there would be a general upset to financial conditions; and (6) a bad moral effect would result.

[The same.] London, 1787.

Point de banqueroute ou Lettres à un créancier de l'État, sur les conséquences de la révocation des deux impôts, relativement à la dette nationale. Seconde partie. Paris, 1787.

> A defense of *Parlement* for its refusal to register certain proposed taxes, and a defense of France for taking the side of the republican party in Holland.

Point de banqueroute ou Lettres à un créancier de l'État, sur l'impossibilité de la banqueroute nationale, et sur les moyens de ramener le crédit et la paix. Nouvelle edition, augmentée de trois autres lettres sur la dette nationale considerée relativement à la révocation des deux impôts, à la guerre de Holland et à celle de Turquie. Londres, Oct. 1787.

> A republication in a single work of the two preceding pamphlets.

[The same.] London, 1788.

Observations d'un républicain sur les différens systèmes de l'administrations provinciales, particulièrement sur ceux de MM. Turgot et Necker, et sur le bien qu'on peut en espérer dans les gouvernemens monarchiques. Lausanne, 1788.

> A severe criticism of the plans both of Necker and of Turgot, on the ground that they did not go to the root of the matter, and a frank statement of disbelief in the efficacy of reform under a monarchy.

[The same.] Paris, 1789.

Lettre à l'Empereur sur l'atrocité des supplices qu'il a substitués comme adoucissement à la peine de mort. Bruxelles, 1787.

> Brissot's name does not appear on the title-page. He praises the emperor for having abolished the death penalty, but censures him for having substituted that of branding.

Réponse à une critique des lettres d'un cultivateur américain, des Quakers, etc., faite par l'auteur anonyme des Recherches sur les États-Unis. April, 1788.

> The critic whom Brissot attacks was M. Mazzei, an Italian who had lately visited the United States. A defense of Crèvecœur, particularly of his attitude toward the negroes and the Quakers.

Discours sur la nécessité d'établir à Paris une société pour concourir avec celle de Londres, à l'abolition de la traite et de l'esclavage des nègres; prononcée le 19 fevrier, 1788, dans une société de quelques amis rassemblés à Paris, à la prière du comité de Londres.

> This address, though not signed, is undoubtedly by Brissot.

A translation of the same. In Clarkson, Thomas, An essay on the impolicy of the African slave trade. Philadelphia, 1788.

Le Moniteur. [Par Condorcet, J. P. Brissot de Warville et Clavière.] 1788.

> Published anonymously. The catalogue of the *Bibliothèque Nationale* at Paris, and the article on Brissot in the *Biographie Universelle*, by Michaud, attribute it to Brissot, Clavière, and Condorcet. Its point of view does not, however, seem in harmony with the general attitude of these men. See Perroud, *Mémoires de Brissot*, i, xlvi.

Le Patriote Français, ou Journal libre impartial et national, par une société de citoyens. 16 mars, 1789.

> The prospectus of the Journal.

Plan de conduite pour les députés du peuple aux États Généraux, 1789. [Paris, 1789.]

> A discussion, in much detail, of the rights and duties of the States-General. Its most significant features are its support of monarchy and its argument that the business of the States-General does not include the making of a constitution.

Discours prononcé par M. Brissot de Warville, à l'élection du district de la rue des Filles-Saint-Thomas, le 21 avril, 1789. [Paris, 1789.]

> An argument that the electors should be instructed on the following points in order that they in turn might instruct the representatives: that they make a declaration of rights; that they consider the means of establishing a free constitution; that they provide provisionally for the urgent needs of the state.

Trois mots aux Parisiens sur la nécessité de publir les noms des candidats.

> M. Perroud, in his *Bibliographie de Brissot* (*Mémoirs de Brissot*, i, xxxiii), notes: "Petite brochure qui parut en mai 1789, quelques jours avant l'élection de Paris."

Précis adressé à l'assemblée générale des électeurs de Paris, pour servir à la rédaction du cahier des doléances de cette ville. [Paris, 1789.]

> An appeal to the electors of Paris to adopt some system in drawing up their statement of grievances, to confine themselves to essentials and not to wander into useless details.

Observations sur la nécessité d'établir dans les différents districts et dans l'assemblée générale des électeurs de Paris, des comités de correspondance avec les députés de Paris aux États-Géneraux, suivies d'un récit de quelques faits arrivés dans l'élection du District-des-Filles-Saint-Thomas. 1789.

> Brissot's argument was to the effect that by keeping in existence some machinery for concerted action the people of Paris would be better able to exert influence upon the States-General.

Le Patriote Français. [No. 1. Paris, 6 mai, 1789.]

> An account of the opening of the States-General and a discussion of the cahier of the third estate at Paris.

Lettre de M. Brissot de Warville aux souscripteurs de journal intitulé "Le Patriote Français." [12 mai, 1789.]

> An explanation of the delay in the appearance of the Patriote Français.

Scrutin de l'election de Paris ou Lettre de M. B. de W. à un électeur, mai, 1789.

> Noted by M. Perroud in his Bibliographie de Brissot.

Mémoire aux États-Généraux sur la nécessité de rendre dès ce moment la presse libre, et surtout pour les journaux politiques. 1789.

> A plea for freedom of the press on the ground that it was a natural right.

No. 1er L'Ombre de J. P. Brissot aux législateurs français, sur la liberté de la presse ou Extrait fidèle d'un imprimé ayant pour titre "Mémoire aux États-Géneraux sur la nécessité de rendre dès ce moment la presse libre," par J. P. Brissot de Warville. Publié avec quelques notes par T. Dethier de l'Ourthe. Paris, an VII.

> An effort to turn to practical use the earlier writings of the Revolution.

Réflexions sur l'admission aux États-Généraux des députés de Saint Domingue. [Paris, 1789.]

> An argument against the admission of the deputies on the ground that the number was too large, that their election was neither free nor valid, and that their admission would injure the cause of the mulattoes.

Projet d'une déclaration des droits de la Commune pour servir au plan de municipalité de la ville de Paris.

> Noted by Perroud in his Bibliographie de Brissot.

Discours prononcé au district des Filles-Saint-Thomas, le 21 juillet, 1789, sur la constitution municipale à former dans la ville de Paris.

> Given in part in Lacroix, Actes de la Commune de Paris.

Le Patriote Français, journal libre, impartial et national par une société de citoyens, et dirigé par J. P. Brissot de Warville. 8 vols., 28 juillet, 1789-2 juin, 1793.

> See chapter IV.

Motifs des commissaires pour adopter le plan de municipalité qu'ils ont présenté à l'assemblée générale des représentants de la Commune, lus à l'assemblée générale . . . suivis du projet du plan de la municipalité. Paris, août, 1789.

> An explanation of the plan for a city government.

Adresse de l'assemblée générale des réprésentants de la commune de Paris présentée à l'assemblée nationale. 10 oct., 1789.

> This address, which was drawn up by Brissot, was occasioned by the transfer of the National Assembly to Paris after the events of October 5 and 6.

Observations sur le plan de la municipalité de Paris suiviés du plan original et d'une déclaration des droits des municipalités. Paris, [15 nov., 1789].

> A defense against the accusation of giving the municipality too much power.

Opinion de J. P. Brissot de Warville sur le question de savoir si Paris sera le centre d'un département de dix-huit lieues de diamètre ou s'il formera seul un département en lui joignant une banlieue de deux ou trois lieues. Paris, Dec., 1789.

> An argument in favor of the latter alternative on account of the unique character of the city.

Mémoire sur les noirs de l'Amérique septentrionale lu à la Société des Amis des Noirs le 3 janvier, 1790. Paris, 1790.

> An account of his observations during his recent journey to America, dealing with what had been done (1) against slavery; (2) against the importation of slaves; (3) for freedom; (4) for the education of the negro.

Adresse à l'Assemblée Nationale pour l'abolition de la traite des Noirs, par la Société des Amis des Noirs. 5 février, 1790.

> The address appears to have been the work of Brissot, at that time president of the society.

Discours sur la rareté du numéraire et sur les moyens d'y remédier, prononcé à l'assemblée générale des représantants de la Commune de Paris, le 10 février, 1790. Paris, 1790.

> An attack on the methods of the *Caisse d'escompte* and an argument for its more rigid control by the government.

Motion sur la nécessité de circonscrire la vente des biens ecclésiastiques aux municipalités dans leur territoire etc.; présentée à l'assemblée générale des représentants de la Commune de Paris. 22 mai,
1790. Paris, 1790.

> An argument to show that the municipalities were to get an unduly
> large benefit from the unrestricted sale to them of church lands.

Rapport sur la lettre de M. de Bourges au Comité de Constitution,
concernant l'affaire des juifs, fait par M. Brissot de Warville à l'assemblée générale des représentants de la Commune de Paris, le 29 mai,
1790. [Paris, 1790.]

> An argument in favor of giving the rights of active citizens to the Jews.

Discours sur la vente des biens ecclésiastiques et sur les nécessité
de l'attribuer, pour Paris, au seul bureau de ville, à l'exclusion des
sections etc.; prononcé à l'assemblée générale des représentants de la
Commune de Paris, le 14 juin, 1790. [Paris, 1790.]

> A plea for centralization in city government.

Rapport dans l'affaire de MM. D'Hosier et Petit-Jean, lu aux
Comités de recherches de l'Asemblée nationale et de la municipalité
de Paris, le 29 juillet, 1790. Paris, 1790.

> A defense of the alleged despotic action of the committee.

Another edition with a covering title containing the words, "Projet de contre-révolution par les somnambulistes ou rapport," etc.

A Stanislas Clermont . . . sur le diatribe de ce dernier contre les
Comités de recherches et sur son apologie de Madame Jumilhac et des
illuminés. Paris, 1790.

> This and the following, a defense of the committee àpropos of the same
> subject as the above.

Réplique de . . . à Stanislas Clermont, concernant ses nouvelles
observations sur les Comité de recherches, sur les causes des troubles,
les folliculaires, le long Parliament d'Angleterre, M. Necker, etc.
Paris, 1790.

Lettres à M. le Chevalier de Pange sur sa brochure intitulée "Réflexions sur la délation et sur le Comité de recherches." Paris, 1790.

> A defense of the *Comité de recherches*.

Discours prononcée à la section de la Bibliothèque dans son assemblée générale du 24 octobre, 1790, sur la question du renvoi des ministres. [Paris, 1790.]

> An appeal to the people to demand the dismissal of the ministry.

Lettre de J. P. Brissot à M. Barnave, sur ses rapports concernant les colonies, les décrets qui les ont suivis, leurs conséquences fatales; sur sa conduite dans le cours de la Révolution; sur le caractère des vrais démocrates; sur les bases de la Constitution, les obstacles qui s'opposent à son achèvement, la necessité de la terminer promptement. Paris, 1790.

> An attack on Barnave's colonial policy and an argument to the effect that the troubles of the colonies were due to the laws of March and October, 1790, and that unless these laws were changed the colonies would become independent, or would pass under the government of some foreign nation.

Réflexions sur le nouveau décret rendu pour le Martinique et les colonies le 29 novembre, 1790, pour servir de suite à la lettre à M. Barnave. [Paris, 1790.]

> A criticism of the decree which provided for sending out to the colonies commissioners and troops.

Réflexions sur l'état de la Société des électeurs patriotes, sur ses travaux, sur les formes propres à faire de bonnes élections . . . lues à l'assemblée de cette société dans la séance du 21 décembre, 1790. Paris, 1790.

> A discussion of the best methods of voting.

Liberté de la presse, précis pour J. P. Brissot contre M. Bexon, se disant représentant de la municipalité de Remiremont. Paris, 1790.

> A defense of the freedom of the press apropos of the accusations of libel brought against Brissot by the municipality of Remiremont.

J. P. Brissot au libelliste, Louis-Marthe-Gouy.

> A denial of the allegations of Gouy and a promise to answer them.

Réplique de J. P. Brissot à la "Première et dernière Lettre de Louis-Marthe-Gouy," défenseur de la traite des noirs et de l'esclavage. Paris, 1791.

> A defense of his own policy with regard to the slave trade and a most vituperative attack on Gouy.

Affaire de Tobago. Réponse de J. P. Brissot aux lettres insérées dans le *Journal de Paris*, par MM. Dillon . . . et Henrion [de Flozelles] . . . sur les réclamations des planteurs de Tobago. [Paris, 1791.]

> Concerns the decision of a court by virtue of which certain planters, whom these writers defended, escaped paying their debts.

Nouveau Voyage dans les États-Unis de l'Amérique septentrionale [fait en 1788]. 3 vols. Paris, 1791.

> Volume III consists of the work previously published by Clavière and Brissot: "De la France et des États-Unis."

New travels in the United States of America performed in 1788. Translated from the French. Dublin, 1792.

> A translation of the above.

[The same.]   2 vols. London, 1792.

[The same.]   2 vols. London, 1794.

> This edition contains a sketch of the life of Brissot, said to be by Joel Barlow, who translated the *Voyage* from the French. It includes a portrait of Brissot and an appendix. M. Perroud, in his *Bibliographie de Brissot* (*Mémoires*, I, xxxviii, notes: "Cette vie, traduite séparément en anglais, a été publiée en 1798. Note de Villenave dans l'article de *Biog. univ.* de Beaulieu."

[The same.]   Boston, 1797.

Nieuwe Reize in de Vereenigde Staaten van Noord-Amerika. . . . Uit het Fransch vertaald en met eenige ophelderingen en bijvoegselen vermeerderd. 3 deel. Amsterdam. [1794.]

Reise durch die vereinigten Staaten von Nord Amerika im Jahre 1788 aus dem Französischen mit der kurtzen Lebensgeschichte des Verfassers und mit einigen Erläuterungen und Zusätzen vermehrt von Theophil Frederik Ehrmann. Durkheim an der Haard, 1792.

Nya resa genom Nord-Americanska fristaterna år 1788. Från franska originalet sammendregen . . . af Johan R. Forster. Öfwersatt från tyskan. Stockholm, 1799.

Discours sur la question de savoir si le roi peut être jugé, prononcé à l'assemblée des Amis de la Constitution, dans la séance du 10 juillet, 1791. Paris. [1791.]

> An argument in favor of holding the king responsible for his misdeeds. Made at the time of the republican crisis after the flight to Varennes. One of Brissot's most noted speeches.

A Discourse upon the question whether the king shall be tried. Translated by P. G. de Nancrede. First American edition, Boston, 1791.

> A translation of the above.

Discours prononcé par M. Brissot à l'assemblée des Amis de la Constitution le 10 juillet, 1791, ou Tableau frappant de la situation actuelle des puissances de l'Europe. [Paris, 1791.]

> An extract from the above address.

Recueil de quelques écrits principalement extraits du "*Patriote Français*," relatif à la discussion du parti à prendre pour le roi, et de la question sur le républicanisme et la monarchie. Paris, 1791.

> A collection of several important articles which had previously appeared in the *Patriote Français*.

Réponse de J. P. Brissot au second Chant du Coq. [Paris, 1791.]

> A denunciation as libelous of a poster in which he had been assailed.

Discours sur les conventions, prononcé à la société des Amis de la Constitution, séante aux Jacobins, le 8 août, 1791. [Paris, 1791.]

> A plea for fixed, periodic conventions which should be independent of the executive and legislative branches of the government.

Réponse de Jaques Pierre Brissot à tous les libellistes qui ont attaqué et attaquent sa vie passée. Paris, 1791.

> An account of his early life and a defense of the charges made against him in connection with his candidacy for election to the Legislative Assembly.

The life of J. P. Brissot, deputy from Eure and Loire to the national convention, written by himself and translated from the French. London, 1794.

> A translation of the above.

Aux Électeurs du département de Paris.

> Noted by M. Perroud in his *Bibliographie de Brissot* in connection with the elections to the States-General. But it appears rather to be the pamphlet published in connection with the Théveneau de Morande controversy. Aug. 26, 1791.

Réplique à Charles Theveneau Morande. Paris, 1791.

> A reply to further attacks. See the preceding work.

Dernier Mot de J. P. Brissot sur un nouveau libelle de Morande et sur les autres libelles, adressé aux électeurs de Paris. [Paris, 1791.]

Discours sur la nécessité de maintenir le décret rendu le 15 mai, 1791, en faveur des hommes de couleur libres, prononcé le 12 septembre, 1791, à la séance de la société des Amis de la Constitution. [Paris, 1791.]

> A protest against any reconsideration of the decrees in favor of the mulattoes.

Discours sur l'utilité des sociétés patriotiques et populaires, sur la nécessité de les maintenir et de les multiplier par-tout, prononcé le 28 septembre, 1791, à la séance de la société des Amis de la Constitution. [Paris, 1791.]

> Emphasizes the need of such societies to keep watch over the administration and to discuss and prepare the way for good laws.

Discours sur l'organisation des comités, destiné à être prononcé à l'Assemblée nationale le 12 octobre, 1791, prononcé aux Jacobins le 14 octobre. Paris, 1791.

> An argument in favor of having as few committees as possible.

Discours sur les émigrations et sur la situation de la France relativement aux puissances étrangères, prononcé le 20 octobre, 1791, à l'Assemblée nationale. Paris, 1791.

> An argument that in meting out punishment to the *émigrés* a distinction should be made between the princes and the public functionaries on the one hand, and private citizens on the other.

Discours sur un projet de décret relatif à la revolte des Noirs, prononcé à l'Assemblée nationale, le 30 octobre, 1791. Paris, 1791.

> An expression of doubt as to the reported revolt and a plea for the rearming of the mulattoes.

Discours sur la nécessité de suspendre momentanément le paiement des liquidations au-dessus le 3,000 l. avant d'émettre de nouveaux assignats, et sur les finances en général, prononcé à l'Assemblée nationale dans la séance du 24 novembre, 1791, [Paris, 1791].

> A criticism of the loose management of the finances and a plea for the issue of assignats of small denominations.

Discours sur les causes des troubles de Saint-Domingue, prononcé à la séance du 1er décembre, 1791. Paris, [1791].

> An argument that the revolt was caused by the mulattoes and negroes being deprived of their rights.

Projet de décret, relatif à l'emploi des troupes destinées pour Saint-Domingue. Paris, 7 dec., 1791. [Paris, 1792.]

> A plea for sending to the colonies commissioners and troops who were to be subject only to the orders of these commissioners, that is to say that they could not be used by the whites against the negroes and mulattoes.

Sociéte des Amis de la Constitution séante aux Jacobins à Paris. Discours sur la nécessité de déclarer la guerre aux princes allemands qui protègent les *émigrés*, prononcé le 16 décembre à la Société. [Paris, 1791.]

> One of Brissot's speeches in the controversy with Robespierre on the war question.

Discours de J. P. Brissot, député, sur les dispositions des puissances étrangères relativement à la France, et sur les préparatifs de guerre ordonnés par le Roi, prononcé à l'Assemblée nationale, le 29 décembre, 1791. [Paris, 1791.]

> An argument in favor of war.

Société des Amis de la Constitution, séante aux Jacobins à Paris. Second discours de J. P. Brissot, député, sur la nécessité de faire la guerre aux princes allemands, prononcé à la société dans le séance du vendredi 30 décembre, 1791. [Paris, 1791.]

> Another of his speeches in the controversy with Robespierre.

Lettre de J. P. Brissot à M. Camus, député à l'Assemblée nationale, sur différents abus de l'administration actuelle des finances, suivie d'une dénonciation concernant la même administration. Paris, 1792.

> Brissot attacks especially a claim supported by Camus of the Duke of Orleans to a *dot* promised by Louis XV to the daughter of the regent.

Discours de J. P. Brissot, député de Paris, sur la nécessité d'exiger une satisfaction de l'Empereur et de rompre le traité du premier mai, 1756, du 17 janvier, 1792. [Paris, 1792.]

> A vehement argument in favor of war.

Société des Amis de la Constitution séante aux Jacobins à Paris. Troisième discours de J. P. Brissot . . . sur la nécessité de la guerre, prononcé à la Société du 20 janvier, 1792. [Paris, 1792.]

Discours sur la nécessité politique de révoquer le décret du 24 septembre, 1791, pour mettre fin aux troubles de Saint-Domingue; prononcè à l'Assemblée nationale, le 2 mars, 1792. [Paris, 1792.]

> An argument that the decree of September, 1791, taking away the civil rights of the mulattoes, and not the decree of May, 1791, which gave them these rights, was the cause of the revolt.

Discours sur l'office de l'Empereur du 17 février, 1792, et dénonciation contre M. Delessart, ministre des Affaires étrangères, prononcé à l'Assemblée nationale, le 10 mars, 1792. (Paris, 1792.]

> A denunciation of the Emperor as well as of M. Delessart.

Discours de MM. Brissot et Guadet, députés à l'Assemblée nationale, prononcés à la séance de la Société des Amis de la Constitution, le 25 avril, 1792. [Paris, 1792.]

> Chiefly an attack on Robespierre.

Discours sur la dénonciation contre le Comité autrichien, et contre M. Montmorin ci-devant ministre des Affaires étrangères prononcé à l'Assemblée nationale, à la séance du 23 mai, 1792. [Paris, 1792.]

> An attack on the government with regard to its policy in foreign affairs on the ground that it was under the influence of persons really devoted to Austrian and anti-revolutionary interests.

Lettres de J. P. Brissot à M. Dumouriez, ministre de la guerre [16, 17 juin, 1792]. [Paris, 1792.]

A bitter denunciation of Dumouriez apropos of his part in causing the fall of the Girondin ministry.

Discours de J. P. Brissot, . . . sur les causes des dangers de la patrie et sur les mesures à prendre; prononcé le 9 juillet, 1792. [Paris, 1792.]

An argument in favor of pronouncing the country in danger, decreeing the responsibility of the ministers, punishing the generals who try to control the assembly, and selling the property of the *émigrés*.

Opinion de J. P. Brissot, . . . sur les mesures de police générale proposées par M. Gensonné, prononcé le 25 juillet, 1792. [Paris, 1792.]

An argument in support of the measures proposed by Gensonné but less hostile to the king than some of Brissot's previous speeches.

Opinion de J. P. Brissot, . . . sur le marche à suivre en examinant la question de la déchéance et les autres mesures, prononcée le 26 juillet, 1792. [Paris, 1792.]

This speech, like the preceding, rather more moderate than that of July 9.

Discours de J. P. Brissot . . . sur les dénonciations relatives au général Lafayette, prononcé le 10 août, 1792. [Paris, 1792.]

The date was really August 8. Brissot fully supports the attack on Lafayette.

Projet de déclaration de l'Assemblée nationale aux puissances étrangères redigé par J. P. Brissot. [Paris, 1792.]

A protest against breaking off all relations with France on the part of neutral governments on account of the suspension of the king.

Rapport fait au nom de la Commission extraordinaire, des Comités diplomatique et militaire, le 20 août 1792, sur le licenciement des régiments suisses, au service de la France, par J. P. Brissot. [Paris, 1792.]

An argument based chiefly on the events of August 10 in favor of disbanding the Swiss regiments.

Rapport fait à la Convention nationale au nom de la Commission extraordinaire et du Comité diplomatique sur les réclamations des cantons de Berne et d'Uri, relativement à l'évacuation des défilés de Porentruy le 3 octobre, 1792. Paris, [1792].

An argument that the French had a right to occupy these passes.

Rapport et projet de décret concernant l'introduction, dans la ville de Genève, de 1600 Suisses des troupes de Berne et de Zurich, présentés au nom de Comité diplomatique le 16 octobre, 1792. Paris, [1792].

An argument that such introduction of troops was a violation of existing treaties.

À tous les Républicains de France, sur la Société des Jacobins de Paris. Paris, 1792.

Written at the time of his explusion from the Jacobin Club; a defense of his policy and an attack upon the majority of the Jacobins as a party of disorganizers.

[The same.] Reprinted by the *Patriote Français*, 29 octobre, 1792.

[The same.] Reprinted with pamphlets of Kersaint and Lanthenas. (November, 1792.)

Rapport fait à la Convention nationale, au nom du Comité diplomatique, sur la négotiation entre Genève et la République de France, et sur la transaction du 2 novembre, 1792, le 21 novembre. Paris, 1792.

An argument to show that Geneva had violated the guaranteed neutrality.

Discours du citoyen Brissot à la Convention nationale concernant la République de Genève, extrait du *Moniteur* du 22 novembre, 1792. [Paris, 1792.]

An extract from the above report.

Dernier mot sur Clootz. In Réponses au Prussian Clootz, par Roland, Kersaint, Guadet et Brissot. [Paris, 1792.]

A defense against accusations of federalism.

Discours sur le procès de Louis, prononcé à la Convention nationale, le 1er janvier, 1793. [Paris, 1793.]

An argument for an appeal to the primary assembly.

Rapport fait au nom du Comité de défense générale, sur les dispositions du gouvernement britannique envers de France, et sur les mesures à prendre, prononcé à la Convention nationale, dans sa séance du 12 janvier, 1793. Paris, [1793].

A denunciation of England's treatment of France and an argument in favor of war.

Report of the Committee of General Defense on the dispositions of the British government towards France, and on the measures to be taken. Addressed to the National Convention of France. . . . Also the second report on a declaration of a war with England. . . . To which is added the Protests entered upon the journals of the Lords and House of Parliament against a war with France, etc. London, 1793.

> Includes a translation of the preceding report.

Rapport sur les hostilités du roi d'Angleterre et du Stathouder des Provinces-Unis, et sur la nécessité de déclarer que la Républic française est en guerre avec eux, au nom du Comité de défense générale. [Paris, 1793.]

> An argument that war was now inevitable, and that it was the desire, not of the English people, but of the English ministry.

Exposé de la conduite de la nation française envers le peuple anglais et des motifs qui ont amené la rupture entre la République française et le roi d'Angleterre, précedé du rapport prononcé par Brissot au nom de Comité diplomatique et du discours de Ducos, 12 janvier, février, 1793. [Paris,] 1793.

> Includes the *Rapport fait au nom de Comité de defense générale* and the *Rapport sur les hostilités du Roi d'Angleterre.*

J. P. Brissot, sur la dénonciation de Robespierre, et sur l'adresse prêtée aux 48 sections de Paris. [Paris, 1793.]

> A defense against the change of being allied with Dumouriez and Morande and of being suborned by Pitt.

À ses commettans sur la situation de la Convention nationale, sur l'influence des anarchistes et les maux qu'elle a causée, sur la nécessité d'anéantir cette influence pour sauver la République. Paris, [1793].

> An attack on the Mountain and a defense of his own position.

The Anarchy and horrors of France displayed. By a member of the Convention. Extracts from J. P. Brissot's address to his constituents, with a preface. [London, 1793.]

> A translation of part of the above.

J. P. Brissot to his constituents on the situation of the national convention. London, 1794.

> Another translation of the above. A portion of the speech is also translated in an appendix to Burke's preface to the address.

Mémoires de Brissot . . . sur ses contemporains, et la Révolution française, publiés par son fils [A. Brissot] avec des notes et des éclaircissements historiques, par M. F. de Montrol. 4 vols; vols. i–ii, Paris, 1830; vols. iii–iv, Paris, 1832.

> See below.

[The same.]   Notes by M. de Lescure.   Paris, 1877.

Scarcely more than a reprint of the preceding.

[The same.]   Mémoires publiés avec Étude critique et notes par M. Perroud. 2 vols. Paris, [1910].

When M. Perroud undertook his new edition, the Montrol edition had long since been regarded with suspicion, some critics even holding that it was entirely apocryphal. But M. Perroud, in his *Étude Critique*, proves beyond doubt that Brissot did leave memoirs, but that the edition of M. Montrol consists largely of interpolations. As M. Montrol seems to have agreed with the publishers beforehand to produce four volumes, it was not strange that he had to resort to padding. Of the 1300 pages of the edition of 1830 M. Perroud finds that 600 pages were taken from other works, though for the most part from those of Brissot himself; that another 100 pages are suspicious, and that still another 100 consist of letters, written or received by Brissot. What remains forms the basis of this new edition. It consists of two parts: the first covering the period of his childhood and youth; the second consisting of his account of his arrest and two *projets de défense*. Even though the gap includes the most important period of his life and the time of his greatest political activity, the memoirs as they stand, thus critically edited, furnish one of the most valuable sources for a study of his career.

Correspondance et papiers précédés d'un avertissement et d'un notice sur sa vie par M. Perroud. Paris, 1912.

See above, preliminary note under manuscript material.

B. Controversial Matter

As indicated by the heading a large portion of the following material is intensely partisan, and was written in the heat of the conflict. For the most part it concerns either Brissot's character or some phase of his policy and involves both his uprightness as a man and his wisdom as a politician.

1. *Pamphlets, Addresses, Contemporary Criticisms*

Baillie.   L Anti-Brissot; par un petit blanc de Saint-Domingue. [Paris.]

An attack on Brissot's colonial policy.

Basire, Claude.   A. J. P. Brissot.   [1792.]

Accounts for the whereabouts of a certain letter for which Brissot had charged him with being responsible.

Bergasse, Nicholas. Déclaration . . . au sujet d'un article inséré dans le journal *Patriote* de M. Brissot de Warville. [Paris, 1790.]

> Concerns an alleged plot to convey the king to Rouen. Bergasse denied that he had any part in such a plot, even if it existed.

Bertrand de Moleville, Antoine François. Histoire de la Révolution de France. 14 vols. Paris, 1801–1803.

> Contains material on the relations between the author and Brissot, who were political enemies. Written from the point of view of an aristocrat. Intensely partisan.

—— Observations, adressées à l'Assemblée nationale. . . sur les discours prononcés par MM. Gensonné et Brissot dans la séance du 23 mai. [Paris, 1792.]

> Reply to accusations made against the Austrian committee.

Bonne-Carrère, Guillaume. Exposé de la conduite de Brissot depuis le commencement de la Révolution, jusqu' à ce jour [5 septembre, an II]. [Paris, 1794.]

> A defense of the part he had played in the Revolution. He was a bitter enemy of Brissot.

Burke, Edmund. Preface to the address of M. Brissot to his constituents, translated by the late William Burke, Esq., 1794; vol. IV. In Burke's works, 9 vols. Boston, 1839.

> Burke asserts that the address of Brissot is simply a condemnation of the Revolution out of the mouths of the revolutionists themselves.

Camus, Armand Gaston. Lettre de . . . à M. Brissot, 26 mars, 1791. Paris, 1791.

> A protest to the effect that Brissot, without sufficient proof, had made accusations in regard to the management of the finances.

Chabot, François. A. J. P. Brissot. [Paris, 1792.]

> An accusation that Brissot tried to hinder the Revolution of August 10, and on the other hand did nothing to hinder the massacres of September.

Champagneux, L. A., ed. Œuvres de MM. J. Ph. Roland, . . . précédées d'un discours préliminaire. 3 vols. Paris, year VIII.

> The preface gives some details about Brissot's manuscripts, but as they are based on hearsay evidence, they are to be taken with caution.

Chastellux, Marquis François Jean de. Voyage . . . dans l'Amérique septentrionale, dans les années 1780, 1781, et 1782. 2 vols. Paris, 1786.

> A work which, on account of its criticism of the Quakers and negroes, was sharply criticized by Brissot.

Claviére, Étienne. Adresse de la Société des Amis des Noirs, à l'Assemblée nationale, . . . dans laquelle on approfondit des relations politiques et commerciales entre la métropole et les colonies, etc. Paris, 1791.

> A statement of the principles of the *Amis des Noirs* and a plea for the extension of civil rights to the mulattoes.

Clermont-Tonnerre, Cte Stanislas, Marie Adelaide de. Réflexions sur l'ouvrage intitulé "Projet de contre-révolution par les somnambulistes, ou rapport dans l'affaire de MM. Dhosier et Petit-Jean, lu aux comités de recherches de l'Assemblée nationale et de la municipalité de Paris, le 29 juillet, 1790, par J. P. Brissot." Paris, 1790.

> An attack on the *Comité des Recherches* of the Commune of Paris, on the ground that its methods savored too much of the old regime.

—— Nouvelles observations sur les comités des recherches. Paris. [1790.]

> A reply to Brissot's answer to the above.

—— Sur le dernière réplique de J. P. Brissot, . . . de 14 octobre, 1790. Paris, 1790.

> A continuation of the same controversy as the above.

Courtois, Edme Bonaventure. Lettre à l'auteur du *Patriote Français* [signé: Courtois, commandant de la garde nationale d'Arcis-sur-Aube, 20 août, 1791]. [Paris, 1791.]

> A letter approving the attitude of Brissot in the crisis of July, 1791.

Desmoulins, Camille. Jean Pierre Brissot démasqué [1 février, 1792]. [Paris, 1792.]

> An arraignment of Brissot's whole life, up to 1792, with special emphasis on his war policy.

—— Sociéte des amis de la liberté et de l'égalité séante aux ci-devant Jacobins, Saint Honoré, à Paris. Fragment de l'histoire secrète de la Revolution. [Paris, 19 mai, 1793.]

> An attack on Brissot and his political adherents, on the ground that they were advocates of royalty and federalism.

—— Histoire des Brissotins ou Fragment de l'histoire secrète de la Révolution et des six premiers mois de la République. [Paris,] 1793.

> The same work as the preceding, printed by order of the Jacobin society.

Desmoulins, Camille. The History of the Brissotins, or part of the history of the Revolution, and of the first six months of the Republic, in answer to Brissot's address to his constituents. Printed at Paris by order of the Jacobin Club, and dispersed by their corresponding clubs. London, 1794.

A translation of the preceding.

—— Œuvres recueillies et publiées d'après les textes originaux et précedées d'une étude biographique et littéraire, par J. Claretie. 2 vols. Paris, 1874.

Duluc, Perisse. Lettre de . . . à M. Brissot, auteur du *Patriote Français*, sur les assignats. Paris, 1790.

An answer to Brissot's objection that his (Duluc's) former opposition to the assignats prevented his being an efficient member of the committee charged with their emission.

Dumouriez, C. F. P., Général. Sur les troubles des colonies en réfutation des deux discours de M. Brissot . . . 1er et 3me décembre, 1791. Paris, 1791.

Dutrône La Couture, Jacques François. Adresse aux François, contre la Société des Amis des Noirs.

Garran de Coulon, J. P. Rapport sur les troubles de Saint-Domingue. 4 vols. [Paris, 1797–99.]

Favorable to the cause of the negro.

Genlis, Madame de. Précis de la conduite de . . . depuis la Révolution, suivi d'une lettre à M. de Chartres et de réflexions sur la critique. Hambourg, 1796.

Contains an account of Madame de Genlis's relation to Brissot and to his wife, which does not agree with Brissot's own account. Madame de Genlis is, however, not to be trusted.

Gouy d'Arcy, Jean Louis Marthe de. Première et dernière lettre de . . . à Jean Pierre Brissot, auteur d'un journal intitulé *Patriote Français*. Paris, le 10 janvier, 1791. [Paris, 1791.]

A somewhat coarse invective against Brissot, on account of his advocacy of the negro and the mulatto. Gouy d'Arcy was one of the leading deputies who represented Santo Domingo.

[The same.] Another edition. Paris, 1791.

—— Fragment d'une lettre de L. M. de Gouy, . . . adressé à ses commettans ou Seconde fustigation de J. P. Brissot. [Paris, 1791.]

On the same subject as the above.

Kovalevsky, Massimo. I Dispacci degli ambasciatori veneti alla corte de Francia durante la rivoluzione. Turino, 1895.

> Valuable observations as to state of public opinion, as seen by ambassadors in little sympathy with it.

Louvet de Couvray, Jean Baptiste. Société des Amis de la Constitution. Discours sur la guerre, prononcée à la Sociéte, le 9 janvier, 1792. [Paris.]

> A speech in ardent support of Brissot's war policy.

Malassis, A. P. ed. Écrits et pamphlets de Rivarol, recueillis pour le première fois, et annotés par A. P. Malassis. Paris, 1877.

> Contains what purports to be a *Réponse de M. le Baron de Grim, chargé des affaires de S. M. l'Imperateur de Russie à Paris, à la lettre de M. Chassebœuf de Volney,* in which occurs the accusation that Brissot was a police spy in the pay of M. Lenoir. Not reliable.

Mallet du Pan, J. Considérations sur la nature de la Révolution de la France, et sur les causes qui en prolongent la durée. Londres et Bruxelles. [1793.]

> Contains criticisms of Brissot and the Girondins from a hostile point of view.

Manuel, L. P. La Police de Paris dévoilée. 2 vols. Paris, l'an second de la liberté. [1791.]

Marivaux, J. C. Martin de. Lettre de . . . à l'auteur de la diatribe intitulée "Lettre de J. P. Brissot à M. Barnave, sur ses rapports concernant les colonies, 31 décembre, 1790." [Paris, 1790.]

> An attack on Brissot, not merely on account of his colonial policy, but also for alleged monarchical sentiments.

Mirabeau, Comte de. De la Caisse d'escompte. [Paris?] 1785.

—— L'Analyse des papiers anglais. 102 nos. 4 vols. 1787-88.

> Served as an organ for the *Amis des Noirs.* "*Le titre de cette feuille,*" *dit Brissot, qui eut fait un des rédacteurs,* "*était un marque à la faveur duquel Mirabeau répandait des vérités hardies.*"

Montmorin, Saint Héreme C. A. M. de. Observations de M. de Montmorin adressées à l' Assemblée nationale, sur les discours prononcés par M. Gensonné et Brissot, dans la séance du 23 mai, 1792. [Paris.]

> A denial of the accusation brought against him and a defense of his policy.

Moreau de Saint-Méry, M. L. E. Considérations presentées aux vrais amis du repos et du bonheur de la France à l'occasion des nouveax mouvemens de quelques soi-disant Amis des Noirs. Paris, 1791.

> No title-page. Another copy has title-page with above and "Paris, 1791," and one extra page at the end, with a brief justification of Moreau de Saint-Méry's personal conduct.

M . . . J. Avis d'un député à ses collègues; sur le discours de M. Brissot, lu à la séance du 30 octobre, 1791, concernant une revolte de nègres à Saint-Domingue, signed J. M. . . . l'. Paris, 1791.

> A criticism of Brissot's colonial policy.

Paganel, Pierre. Essa historique et critique sur la Révolution française. 3 vols. Paris, 1815.

> Written from the point of view of a member of the Plain. On the whole, friendly to the Girondins, though opposed to Brissot's colonial policy. (La 1ere édition fut enlevée entière par l'ordre de l'ancien gouvernment en 1810, et détruite en totalité en 1813.)

Pange, M. le chevalier de. Réflexions sur la délation et sur le comité des recherches. Paris, 1790.

> A severe attack on the methods of the Committee; with special reference to their pursuit of M. Besenval.

Peltier, Jean Gabriel. Histoire de la Révolution du 10 août, des causes qui l'ont produite; des événements qui l'ont précédée, et des crimes qui l'ont suivie. 2 vols. Londres, 1795.

> Includes the events leading up to the Revolution of August 10 and the results, as well as the events of the day itself. From the point of view of a royalist and reactionary.

Phillips, Richard. Biographical anecdotes of the founders of the French Republic. 2 vols. London, 1788.

> Contains an interesting and sympathetic sketch of Brissot, evidently based on first-hand information. Published anonymously, attributed to Phillips.

Pons, F. R. J. de. Observations sur la situation politique de Saint Domingue, 27 novembre, 1790. [Paris, 1790.]

> A defense of the slave trade on the ground that it was necessary for the existence of the French colonies.

Robert, François. A ses frères de la Société des Amis de la Constitution, de la Société fraternelle et du club des Cordeliers. [Paris.]

> An explanation of why he did not receive an appointment as ambassador to Constantinople. Throws light on Brissot's influence with the Girondin ministry.

Robespierre, Maximilien. Société des Amis de la Constitution. Discours de . . . sur le parti que l'Assemblée nationale doit prendre relativement à la proposition de guerre annoncée par le pouvoir exécutif, prononcé à la société le 18 décembre, 1791. [Paris, 1791.]

> A speech against Brissot's war policy.

—— Société des Amis de la Constitution. Discours de . . . sur la guerre prononcé à la société des Amis de la Constitution, le 2 janvier, 1792. Paris, 1792.

> Another speech in opposition to war.

—— Société des Amis de la Constitution. Troisième discours de . . . sur la guerre, prononcé . . . dans la séance du 26 janvier, 1792, l'an quatrième de la liberté. Paris, 1792.

> Third speech in opposition to war.

—— Réponse aux discours de MM. Brissot et Guadet, du 25 avril, 1792, prononcé à la Société des Amis de la Constitution. Paris, 1792.

> A continuation of the attack begun by Robespierre. April 4.

Roland, de la Platière, J. M. Lettre à Brissot de Warville. Lyon, 1er mars, 1790. [1790.]

> A friendly protest that Brissot had written of conditions in Lyons in such a way as to make Roland responsible for views which he did not hold. Throws light on relations between the two men.

Rousseau, Le Comte, de. Discours de . . . prononcé le 12 fevrier à l'assemblée de la Commune, sur les opinions de MM. Kormann et Brissot de Warville, relatives à la caisse d'escompte. Paris, 1790.

> A defense in opposition to Brissot's attack of the *caisse d'escompte* in its relations with the national treasury.

Rouyer. Historique de l'arrestation de Brissot. Le citoyen Rouyer, commissaire national du tribunal du district de Moulins et membre de la Société populaire au citoyen Vidalin, deputé à la Convention nationale par le département de l'Allier. [Moulins le 11 juin, 1793.] In Convention nationale. Récits de la Révolution A. N. A.D. xviiie 241.

> An account drawn up by an eye-witness and in a hostile spirit.

Saint-Cyran, M. J. Réfutation du projet des Amis des Noirs sur la suppression de la traite des nègres et sur l'abolition d' esclavage dans nos colonies. [Paris] 1790.

De Salm, La Princess Constance. Notice sur la vie, les ouvrages de Mentelle. Paris, 1839.

The most valuable part of this work is a series of extracts from a manuscript of M. Mentelle in which is included an appreciation of Brissot.

Sergent-Marceau, A. F. Notice historique sur les évènements du 10 août et des 20 et 21 juin précédants. In the *Revue retrospective*, second series, iii, 328–46.

From the point of view of a participant, and of a Montagnard.

Tarbé, C. Réplique à J. P. Brissot sur les troubles de Saint-Domingue; prononcée à l'Assemblée nationale le 22 novembre, 1792. Paris, 1792.

A defense of the policy of the colonial committee and an attack in turn on Brissot's colonial policy.

Théveneau de Morande, Charles. Réplique de . . . à Jacques Pierre Brissot sur les erreurs, les oublis, les infidélités et les calomniés de sa réponse. Paris, 1791.

Part of the attack made upon Brissot at the time of his candidacy for the Legislative Assembly.

—— Lettre aux électeurs du département de Paris sur Jaques Pierre Brissot. Paris [3 septembre], 1791.

See preceding title and note.

—— Supplément au No. 25 de *L'Argus Patriote*. Paris, 6 septembre, 1791.

See above.

Vernay. Lettre à M. Brissot de Warville sur ses Réflexions importantes relatives aux élections futures des municipalités contenues dans le supplement du no. clxiv de son journal intitulé *Le Patriote Français*. Lyon, 1790.

An attack on Brissot for having inserted in the *Patriote Français* an article advising against the election to municipal office of all persons connected with the old regime.

Vilate, Joachim. Les Mystères de la Mère de Dieu dévoilés. Paris, l'an III.

Contains some details with regard to the trial and last hours of the Girondins. Not altogether reliable.

Avis d'un député à ses collègues, sur le discours de M. Brissot, lu à la séance du 30 octobre, 1791, concernant une révolte de nègres à Saint-Domingue.

A severe criticism of Brissot's position.

Adresse à l'assemblée nationale.

Sets forth the dangers to French commerce of the abolition of the slave trade. The signers include the names of deputies from Marseilles, Bayonne, Bordeaux, Nantes, Rochelle, Saint-Malo, Havre, Dieppe, Dunkirk and Lille.

Amis des Noirs, Société de. Adresse à l'Assemblée nationale pour l'abolition de la traite des noirs, par la Société des Amis des Noirs de Paris. 20 février, 1790.

Signed Brissot, president, Le Page, secretary. While pleading for the abolition of the slave trade the society protested against the assumption that they were working for the *immediate* abolition of slavery. Throws light on the purposes and aims of the society.

Seconde adresse à l'Assemblée nationale, par la Société des Amis des Noirs. 9 avril, 1790.

Adresse aux amis de l'humanité par la Société des Amis des Noirs sur le plan de ses traveaux. 4 juin, 1790.

An outline of the methods and work of the Society, signed by Pétion as president and Brissot as secretary.

Adresse de la Société des Amis des Noirs à l'Assemblée nationale, à toutes les villes de commerce, à toutes les manufactures, aux colonies, à toutes les sociétés des amis de la constitution; adresse dans laquelle on approfondit les relations politiques et commerciales, entre la métropole, et les colonies, rédigée par Clavière.

A special plea for the extension of civil rights to the mulattoes and a general statement of the principles of the society.

Tableau des membres de la Société des Amis des Noirs.

Without date or signature. In *Supplément aux procès-verbal de l'Assemblée nationale, colonies, tome* i; *traite des nègres, partie* ii. *A. N.*, AD^XVIII, C. 115. Of considerable value, as showing the growth and personnel of the *Amis des Noirs.*

Lettre aux Bailliages de France. [1 dec., 1789.]

An attack on the *Amis des Noirs* on the ground that it was an anti-patriotic society.

Réglements de la Société des *Amis des Noirs.*

Drawn up by Condorcet. Printed in article by Léon Cahen, "*La Société des Amis des Noirs et Condorcet,*" in *La Révolution Française,* June, 1906.

Circulaire de la Société de la liberté et de l'équalité, séante aux ci-devant Jacobins de Paris, rue Saint-Honoré. Paris, 1792.

An explanation, sent to the affiliated societies, of the reasons for the expulsion of Brissot.

Considérations présentées aux vrais amis du repos et du bonheur de la France à l'occasion des nouveaux mouvements de quelques soi-disant Amis des Noirs. [1790.]

Dénonciation de la secte des Amis des Noirs, par les habitants des colonies françaises [signé: Les Colons assemblées en l'hôtel de Mas-siac.]

Découverte d'une conspiration contre les intérêts de la France.

> Without date or signature. A violent attack on the *Amis des Noirs*. In the same series as the above. They both throw light on the importance of the Society.

Le Diable dans un bénitier et la Métamorphose du gazetier cuirassé.

> An attack on the police methods of the old régime. For his alleged col-laboration with Pelleport in the authorship of his pamphlet, Brissot was imprisoned in the Bastille in 1784. It has never been finally settled as to who was really the author.

An inquiry into the cause of the insurrection of the negroes in the island of Santo Domingo. London, 1792.

> An English attack on Brissot's colonial policy.

Flower of the Jacobins, containing biographical sketches of the characters at present at the head of affairs in France, dedicated to Louis XVI, king of France and Navarre. Third edition. London, 1793.

> Attacks on Monsieur Égalité, Pétion, Merlin, Dumouriez, Chabot, Carra, Gorsas, Danton, Marat, Condorcet, Robespierre, and Brissot.

Lettre à MM. les députés des trois ordres, pour les engager à faire nommer par Les États Généraux, à l'exemple des anglais, une com-mission chargée d'examiner la cause des noirs [signé: Un ami des Noirs]. [Mai, 1789.]

> An argument against the slave trade.

Lettre de M. . . . à M. Brissot de Warville, président de la Société des Amis des Noirs. [Paris.]

> "*Par les députés extraordinaires des manufacturiers et du commerce, en faveur du maintien de la traite.*"

Lettres de la Société des Amis des Noirs à M. Necker avec la ré-ponse de ce ministre. Juillet, 1789.

> A protest against certain statements regarding the slave trade, made by Necker in his address at the opening of the States-General.

Lettres des diverses Sociétés des Amis de la Constitution, qui réclament les droits de citoyen actif en faveur des hommes de couleur des colonies [8 mars, 17 avril, 1791]. [Paris.]

For the most part letters addressed to the *Société des Amis de la Constitution*, at Angers, in response to the circular sent out by that society, announcing its plan to present a petition to the National Assembly in favor of the mulattoes.

Liste des ouvrages sur la traite et l'esclavage. [Paris.]

The same list which was published in the *Patriote Français* of May 7, 1790.

Un Mot sur les Noirs, à leurs Amis.

An argument in favor of slavery, and an attack on the *Amis des Noirs*, on the ground that they were unpatriotic and that they were working against the real interests of France.

Observations du Mercredi, 15 décembre, 1790.

Opinion de M. Brissot sur quelques idées de M. A. Lameth. 1790.

A criticism of Brissot's objections to certain remarks of Lameth on the relation of the ministry to the legislative body.

Observations sur un ouvrage de M. Brissot de Warville, 7 décembre, 1790.

A quotation from a letter by Brissot with warm commendation of his patriotic principles.

Observations sur un article du journal de M. Brissot de Warville, concernant une protestation contre les assignats.

Unsigned and undated. Evidently by Bergasse, whose name is written in the margin. On a previous occasion Bergasse had expressed surprise that Clavière should uphold forced assignats. The present pamphlet is an answer to Brissot and a further criticism of the dangers of the proposed assignats.

Observations pour servir de réponse aux objections de M. Brissot contre la convocation actuelle des assemblées primaires dans son opinion du juillet 26. [Paris, 1792.]

A protest against the suspicion expressed by Brissot, that the partisans of the king were favoring the convocation of the primary assemblies, in the hope that once called they could be intimidated into taking action favorable to the king.

Perfidie du système des Amis des Noirs. [Nantes, ce 23 février, 1791.]

The address closes thus: "Ils sont les vœux unanimes et universelles de tous les citoyens et individus de la ville de Nantes et tels ne peuvent qu'être ceux de tous les bons et sensés Français."

Réflexions sur la despotisme qu'exercent à Saint-Domingue les commissaires nationaux civiles, Polverel and Santhonax. Dénonciation de ces mêmes commissaires par le citoyen sans-réproche, homme de couleur, affranchi du citoyen Page, homme blanc et commissaire de Saint-Domingue.

> Allegations against Brissot and the Girondins to the effect that they had upheld the policy of Polverel and Santhonax.

Réponse des députés de Saint-Domingue aux inculpations de M. Brissot, adressé le 5 décembre à M. le président de l'assemblée nationale.

Répresentations à MM. Brissot, l'abbé Audrin, Chabot et les autres députés détracteurs du pouvoir exécutif. [Paris, 1792.]

> Unsigned and undated. A protest against attacks on the king's ministers. The way to restore dignity to the existing government, the writer argued, was not to insult its first agents.

Sur les troubles des colonies et l'unique moyen d'assurer la tranquillité, le prospérité et la fidelité de ces dépendances de l'empire, en réfutation des deux discours de M. Brissot du 1er et 3me décembre, 1791.

> An argument that the troubles of the colonies were due to the agitation of the slavery question.

Vie privée et politique de Brissot. Paris, l'an II.

> A violent attack on Brissot, written, apparently, after his arrest at Moulins, June 10, 1793, and just before his trial. It compares him with Tartuffe. The pamphlet contains a picture of Brissot.

Vie secrette et politique de Brissot. Paris, l'an VI.

> A duplicate of the preceding, but with a different title-page.

2. Memoirs and Letters

Bailleul, Jacques Charles. Examen critique de l'ouvrage posthume de Mme. la Baronne de Staël ayant pour titre, "Considérations sur les principaux événements de la Révolution française." 2 vols. Paris, 1818.

> Contains an appreciation of Brissot and the Girondins from the point of view of a man who had occupied the position of a moderate in the Convention. It also gives an account of the origin of the term "Brissotin."

Barbaroux, Charles Jean Marie. Mémoires inédites de Pétion et Mémoires de Buzot et de Barbaroux. Dauban, C. A., ed. Paris, 1866.

> Dauban is thoroughly in sympathy with the Girondins.

Bertrand de Moleville, Antoine François. Mémoires particulières pour servir à l'histoire de la fin du règne de Louis XVII. 2 vols. 1816.

> Throws light on the attitude of supporters of the king towards Brissot.

Crèvecœur, Saint John de. Letters from an American Farmer. London, 1782.

> A work of great interest, because of its influence upon Brissot.

Delacroix, J. L'Intrigue dévoilée ou Robespierre vengé des outrages et des calomnies des ambitieux. [Paris,] 1792.

> Contains an attack on Brissot as an adherent of Lafayette. The partisanship of the writer is evident from the title.

Dumont, Étienne. Souvenirs sur Mirabeau et sur les deux premières assemblées législatives, ouvrage posthume publié par J. L. Duval. Paris, 1832.

> Contains interesting comments on the attitude of Brissot on various occasions, which are, however, to be taken with some caution.

—— Recollections of Mirabeau and of the two Legislative Assemblies of France. London, 1832.

> A translation of the above.

Garat, Le Comte, D. J. Mémoires sur la Révolution, ou exposé de ma conduite dans les affaires et dans les fonctions publiques. Paris, l'an III.

> Garat was a friend and at the same time a critic of the Girondins.

Genlis, Madame la comtesse de. Mémoires. In Barrière, Bibliothèque des Mémoires, xv. 1846.

> Unreliable.

Louvet de Couvrai, Jean Baptiste. Mémoires sur la Révolution Française. F. A. Aulard, ed. 2 vols. Paris, 1889.

> Edited from a more unbiased point of view than the previously published memoirs of other Girondins.

Mallet du Pan, Jacques. Mémoires et correspondance de . . . pour servir à l'histoire de la Révolution Française, recueillis et mis en ordre par A. Sayous. 2 vols. Paris, 1851.

> Hostile to Brissot.

Meillan. Mémoires. Paris, 1823.

> Favorable to the Girondins.

Riouffe, H. Mémoires d'un détenu pour servir à l'histoire de la tyrannie de Robespierre. Paris, l'an III.

Gives information as to Brissot's last days in prison.

Roland, Madame Marie Jeanne Phlipon. Lettres publiées par Claude Perroud. In Collection de documents inédits sur l'histoire de France. 2 vols. Paris, 1900–02.

In "*Collection de documents inédits sur l'histoire de France, publiés par les soins du ministre de l'instruction publique.*" A work of most thorough scholarship; contains much material upon Brissot and his relation with the Roland group.

—— Mémoires. Publiés par Claude Perroud. 2 vols. Paris, 1905.

A work of the same character as the above; also contains much information as to Brissot.

Soulavie, J. L. G. Mémoires historique et politiques sur le règne de Louis XVI. 6 vols. Paris, 1801.

Not in sympathy with Brissot.

Williams, Héléne Marie. Souvenirs de la Révolution française. Traduit de l'anglais [par C. C.]. Paris, 1827.

Miss Williams was in sympathy with the Girondin policy and a personal friend of many of them. She gives various details as to the family of Brissot, but her accounts are not to be relied upon.

—— Lettres sur les événements qui se sont passés en France dépuis le 31 mai, 1793, jusqu'au 10 thermidor. Traduites de l'anglais. Paris.

See above.

3. Newspapers

Only those are cited which especially concern Brissot.

Les Actes des Apôtres. November, 1789, to October, 1791. (311 nos., 11 vols.) L'an de la liberté 0.

L'Ami du peuple. Ed. par Marat. Sept. 12, 1789, to July 14, 1793.

This and the preceding extremely hostile to Brissot.

L'Ami du Roi. Parts 1–4. Paris, 1790–92.

Motto: *Pro Deo, Rege et Patria.*

Annales politiques, civiles et littéraires, du dix-huitième siècle ouvrage périodique, par M. Linguet. 19 vols. Londres et Paris, 1777–91.

Decidedly polemic in character, twice suppressed. Brissot was for a brief time connected with this journal.

L'Aniti-Brissotin. Journal du soir. Du 117 nos. 1er brumaire, an II, à 27 pluviôse, an III.

Upholds the system of the Terror.

Le Babillard. Journal du Palais-Royal et des Tuileries. 116 nos. [June 5, to Oct. 7, 1791. Paris, 1791.]

This journal and its successor, Le Chant du Coq, bitterly hostile to Brissot.

Le Babillard et le Chant du Coq. Nos. 117–38. Oct. 8, to Oct. 30, 1791. Paris, 1791.

" Le Chant du Coq semblait n'avoir été créé que pour mener un campagne acharnée contre Brissot."

La Chronique du mois ou les cahiers patriotiques de E. Clavière, C. Condorcet, L. Mercier, A. Auger, J. Oswald, N. Bonneville, J. Bidermann, A. Broussonet, A. Guy-Kersaint, J. P. Brissot, J. Ph. Garran de Coulon, J. Dussaulx, F. Lanthénas, et Collot d'Herbois. 5 vols. Nov. 1791, to July, 1793.

La Chronique de Paris. 8 vols. Aug. 24, 1789, to Aug. 25, 1793.

Moderate, inclined to the side of the Girondins.

Le Courrier des départements. 47 vols., ed by Gorsas. July 5, 1789, to May 31, 1793.

It appeared under the successive titles of Le Courrier de Versailles à Paris, Le Courrier de Paris dans les Provinces, Le Courrier de Paris dans les 83 départements, Le Courrier des IXXXIII départements, Le Courrier des départements.

Courrier de l'Europe, gazette anglo-français, par Serre de Latour, Morande. Brissot, le comte de Montlosier; 32 vols. Londres et Boulogne, 1776–92.

" Un des recueils les plus importants à consulter, non seulement pour l'histoire politique, mais encore pour l'histoire morale et littéraire du siècle dernier. Intéressant surtout pour l'histoire des colonies anglais." Hatin, Bibliographie, 74.

Gazette nationale ou le Moniteur Universal, du 24 novembre, 1789.

One of the most valuable sources for the debates in the successive Assemblies.

Le journal général de la cour et de la ville. 15 vols. Sept. 15, 1789, to Aug. 10, 1792.

> Hostile to Brissot.

Journal de Paris. 87 vols. Jan. 1, 1777, to Sept. 30, 1811.

> Inclined to be hostile.

Le Mercure, 1672–1853.

> During the Revolution, and since, called the *Mercure de France*. From 1789 to 1792 of the party of constitutional monarchy.

The Monthly Review, or Literary Journal, enlarged. 108 vols. London, 1790–1825.

> Contains criticisms of certain of Brissot's works; more or less friendly.

Le Républicain, ou le Défenseur du gouvernement représentatif par une société des républicains [par Condorcet, Thomas Paine et Achille Duchatelet]. [Paris, 1791.]

> The newspaper which represented the sudden and short-lived republican movement of the summer of 1791.

Les Révolutions de France et de Brabant. 86 nos. Nov. 28, 1789, to July, 1791.

> Critical, rather than hostile. On several occasions, however, Desmoulins expressed hearty approval of Brissot's conduct.

Les Révolutions de Paris. 18 vols. July 12, 1789, to Feb. 28, 1794.

> At first rather in sympathy with Brissot, but it did not hesitate to assail him particularly for his part in municipal affairs, and as the Revolution progressed criticized him more and more severely.

Le Thermomètre du jour. 7 vols. Aug. 11, 1791, to Aug. 25, 1793.

> "An implacable enemy of nobles, priests, and kings."

C. COLLECTIONS OF DOCUMENTS

Aulard, François Alphonse. La Société des Jacobins. Recueil de documents pour l'histoire du club des Jacobins de Paris. 6 vols. Paris, 1889–97. In Collection de documents relatifs à l'histoire de Paris pendant la Révolution française, publiée sous le patronage de Conseil municipal.

—— ed. Recueil des actes du Comité de salut public avec la correspondance officielle des représentants in mission. 20 vols. 1889–1910.

Challamel, Augustin. Les Clubs contre-révolutionaires, circles, comités, sociétés, salons, réunions, cafés, restaurants et librairies. Paris, 1895.

Charavay, Étienne. Assemblée électorale de Paris. 18 novembre, 1790, à 15 juin, 1791. Paris, 1890.

—— Assemblée électorale de Paris. 26 août 1791, à 12 août, 1792. Paris, 1890.

Chassin, Ch. L. Les Élections et les cahiers de Paris en 1789. 4 vols. Paris, 1888–89.

Funck-Brentano, Frantz. Les Lettres de cachet à Paris. Étude suivie d'une liste des prisonniers de la Bastille. [1659–1789.] Paris, 1903.

Hatin, Eugène. Bibliographie historique et critique de la presse périodique française. Paris, 1866.

Lacroix, Sigismund. Actes de la commune de Paris pendant la Révolution, publiés et annotés par Sigismund Lacroix. 7 vols. 1er série. 25 juillet, 1789, à 8 octobre, 1790. Paris, 1894–1898.

Mavidal, J., et Laurent, E. Archives parlementaires de 1787 à 1860. Recueil complet des débats législatifs et politiques des chambres françaises. Première série [1787 à 1799]. Paris, 1879–

> The editing of this work is not of the highest order. It supplements the information found in the *Moniteur*, but it is to be used with some caution.

Robiquet, Paul. Le Personnel municipal de Paris pendant la Révolution, période constitutionelle. Paris, 1890.

Bulletin du tribunal criminel établi par la loi du 10 mars, 1793, pour juger sans appel les conspirateurs. 8 vols. Paris, 1793.

> Contains reports of the trial, drawn up naturally in a spirit hostile to the Girondins.

Procès-verbal de l'Assemblée nationale [législative]. 16 vols. Paris, 1791–92.

Procès-verbal de la convention nationale. 74 vols. Paris, 1792. An IV.

Supplement aux procès-verbal de l'assemblée nationale. Colonies. Tome i. Traites des nègres. Part ii.

Browning, Oscar, ed. The dispatches of Earl Gower, English ambassador at Paris from June, 1790, to August, 1792, to which are added the dispatches of Mr. Lindsay and Mr. Monro, and the diary of Viscount Palmerston in France during July and August, 1791. Cambridge, Eng., 1885.

> Contains comments on several of Brissot's speeches.

D. General Works

Aulard, F. A. Histoire politique de la Révolution française. Paris, 1901.

Very suggestive as to the Girondin policy in general.

—— L'Éloquence parlementaire pendant la Révolution française. Les Orateurs de la Législative et de la Convention. 2 vols. Paris, 1885–86.

Contains an interesting and suggestive sketch of Brissot.

Avenel, H. Histoire de la presse française depuis 1789 jusqu'à nos jours. Paris, 1900.

Beaulieu, Claude François. Essais historiques sur les causes et les effets de la Révolution de France. 6 vols. Paris, 1801–03.

From the royalist point of view.

Belote, T. T. The Scioto Speculation and the French Settlement at Gallipolis. In University studies, published by the University of Cincinnati; series ii; vol. ii, 103. Cincinnati, 1907.

Biré, Edmond. La Legende des Girondins. Paris, 1881.

Extremely hostile to the Girondins and to the Revolution.

Biernawski, Louis. Un Département sous la Révolution française, L'Allier de 1789 à l'an III. Moulins, 1909.

Contains material on arrest of Brissot.

Buchez, P. J. B., et Roux, P. C. Histoire parlementaire de la Révolution française ou Journal des assemblées nationales dépuis 1789 jusqu'en 1815. 40 vols. Paris, 1834–38.

Especially valuable for the clues which it gave to the contemporary journalistic opinion.

Bourne, H. E. The Revolutionary Period in Europe, 1789–1815. New York, 1904.

A brief but scholarly treatment of the whole period.

Cahen, Léon. Condorcet et la Révolution française. Paris, 1904.

Valuable information on relations between Condorcet and Brissot. Well documented.

Campardon, Émile. Le Tribunal révolutionaire de Paris. Ouvrage composé d'après les documents originaux conservés aux Archives de l'Empire, suivi de la liste complète des personnes qui ont comparu devant le tribunal. 2 vols. Paris, 1866.

> Gives an account of the trial of the Girondins. Hostile to the tribunal and in sympathy with the accused.

Charpentier, ( ). La Bastille dévoilée ou Recueil de pièces authentiques pour servir à son histoire. 3 vols. Paris, 1789–90.

> *Par Charpentier, d'après Barbier. Par Louis Pierre Manuel, d'après M. Girraud.* [Note in catalogue of *Bibliothèque Nationale*.] Contains a statement that Brissot received the keys of the Bastille.

Claretie, Arsène Jules. Desmoulins, Lucile Desmoulins, étude sur les Dantonistes, d'après des documents nouveaux, et inédite. Paris, 1875.

> Contains information as to the relations of Brissot and Desmoulins.

Clarkson, Thomas. The History of the Rise, Progress, and Accomplishment of the Abolition of the African Slave Trade, by the British Parliament. 2 vols. London, 1808.

> One of the most valuable sources for the history of the *Amis des Noirs*.

Cornillon, J. Le Bourbonnais sous la Révolution française. 3 vols. Moulins, 1889–91.

> Contains information on conditions at Moulin at time of Brissot's arrest.

Crèvecœur, Robert de. Saint John de Crèvecœur, sa vie et ses ouvrages [1735–1813]. Paris, 1883.

> Gives interesting information as to the relations of Brissot with Crèvecœur.

Dard, Émile. Un Acteur caché du drame révolutionaire, le général Choderlos de Laclos, acteur des "Liaisons dangereuses," 1741–1803, d'après des documents inédits. Paris, 1905.

> Contains information as to the part played by Brissot in the republican crisis of July, 1791.

Duchatellier, A. R. Histoire de la Révolution dans les départements de l'ancienne Bretagne. 6 vols. Paris, 1836.

Feuillet de Conches, F. Louis XVI, Marie Antoinette et Madame Elizabeth. Lettres et documents inédits. 6 vols. Paris, 1864–73.

> Much of the material contained in the first two volumes is of doubtful authenticity. The last four volumes are less open to question.

Fleury, Ed. Camille Desmoulins et Roch Marcandier. 2 vols. Paris, 1851.

Made up largely of quotations, not very critical, favorable to Desmoulins.

Gallois, Léonard. Histoire des journaux et des journalistes de la Révolution française, 1789–96. 2 vols. Paris, 1845–46.

Contains a suggestive sketch of the *Patriote Français.*

Glagau, Hans. Die französische Legislative und der Ursprung der Revolutionskriege, 1791–92. Berlin, 1896. In Historische Studien.

Based in part on the Austrian archives.

Goetz-Bernstein, H. A. La Diplomatie de la Gironde. Jacques Pierre Brissot. Paris, 1912.

A thorough and well-documented study.

Gomel, Charles. Histoire financière de l'Assemblée constituante. 2 vols. 1896–97.

—— Histoire financière de la Législative et de la Convention. 2 vols. 1902–05.

Goupil, Paul. La Propriété selon Brissot de Warville. Thèse pour le doctorat. Paris, 1904.

Emphasizes Brissot's inconsistency and his debt to Rousseau.

Granier de Casagnac, A. Histoire des Girondins et des massacres de Septembre d'après les documents officials et inédits. 2 vols. Paris, 1860.

One of the first studies of the Girondins from a comparatively unbiased point of view.

Guadet, Joseph. Les Girondins, leur vie privée, leur vie publique, leur proscription et leur mort. 2 vols. Paris, 1861.

As the title suggests, — a eulogy.

Hatin, Eugène. Histoire du journal en France. Paris, 1846.

Includes information on the beginnings of the *Patriote Français.*

Hérissay, Jacques. Un Girondin, François Buzot. Paris, 1907.

A successful attempt to make vivid the personality of Buzot.

Herrmann, Dr. Ernst. Diplomatische Correspondenzen aus der Revolutionszeit, 1791–97. Gotha, 1867.

Abstracts and translation of dispatches dealing largely with the outbreak of war.

Jaurès, J. La Constituante, 1901. La Législative, 1902. La Convention; 2 vols.; 1903. In *Histoire Socialiste*, 1789–1900, sous la direction de Jean Jaurès et collaborateurs.

Contains material indicating Brissot's interest in economic matters. From the point of view of a socialist.

Kropotkin, Pierre. La Grande Révolution, 1789–93. Paris, 1909.

Attacks the Girondins on the ground that they represent the bourgeois point of view in hostility to the proletariat.

Lomenie, Louis Léonard, et Charles de. Les Mirabeaux, nouvelles étudies sur la société française au 18ᵐᵉ siècle. 5 vols. Paris, 1885–91.

Throws light on the early relations between Brissot and Mirabeau.

Masson, Frédéric. Le Département des affaires étrangères pendant la révolution, 1787–1804. Paris, 1877.

Based on documents.

Mathiez, A. Le Club de Cordeliers. Paris, 1910.

Mills, Herbert Elmer. The Early Years of the French Revolution in Santo Domingo. Poughkeepsie, 1892.

Monin. L'État de Paris en 1789. Paris, 1881.

Morellet, L'Abbé Andre. Mélanges de littérature et de philosophie du 18ᵐᵉ siècle. 4 vols. Paris, 1818.

Contains a criticism of some of Brissot's literary work.

Pallain, G., ed. La Mission de Talleyrand à Londres, en 1792. Paris, 1889.

Information on Brissot's attitude toward foreign affairs.

Pfeiffer, L. B. The Uprising of June 20, 1792.

A scholarly study.

Robiquet, Paul. Théveneau de Morande. Paris, 1882.

Throws light on one of Brissot's most bitter adversaries, and on the libelists of the old régime, with whom Brissot came in contact during his stay in London in 1784.

Rose, J. H. William Pitt and the Great War. London, 1911.

Sagnac, Ph. La Législation civile de la Révolution française. Paris, 1890.

Seligman, E. La Justice en France pendant la Révolution française. Paris, 1901.

Sorel, Albert. L'Europe et la Révolution française. 8 vols. Paris, 1885–1904.

Sybel, H. von. The French Revolution. 4 vols. London, 1867–69.

Ternaux, Mortimer. Histoire de la Terreur, 1792–94, d'après des documents authentiques et inédits. 7 vols. Paris, 1862–69.

> Contains documents bearing on Brissot.

Vatel, Charles. Charlotte de Corday, et les Girondins, pièces classées et annotées. 2 vols. Paris, 1864–72.

> Contains a *Notice sur Brissot*, by Pétion, of special value on many points of his early life. Pétion apparently derived much of his information directly from Brissot himself.

——— Vergniaud, Manuscrits, lettres et papiers, pièces pour la plupart inédites. 2 vols. Paris, 1873.

> Contains several important documents bearing on Brissot, not accessible elsewhere.

Vaultier, F. Souvenirs de l'insurrection normande dite du fédéralisme en 1793, publiées pour la première fois, avec notes et pièces justificative, par M. Georges Mançel. Caën, 1858.

Wallon, Henri Alexandre. Histoire de Tribunal révolutionaire de Paris, avec le journal de ses actes. 6 vols. Paris, 1880–82.

> Favorable to the Girondins.

——— La Révolution de 31 mai et le fédéralisme en 1793, ou la France vaincue, par la commune de Paris. 2 vols. Paris, 1886.

Washington, George. Writings, ed. by Ford. 14 vols. New York, 1889–93.

Wilberforce, R. I. and S., editors. Life of William Wilberforce, by his sons. London, 1838.

E. MAGAZINE ARTICLES

Aulard, François Alphonse. Formation du parti républicain. In *La Révolution Française*, for 1898, XXXV, 296–347.

Bourne, Henry E. American Constitutional Precedents in the French National Assembly. In the *American Historical Review*, April, 1903, VIII, 466–86.

Cahen, Léon. La Société des Amis des Noirs et Condorcet. In *La Révolution Française*, June, 1906, pp. 481–511.

Chamberland, ( ). A propos de Brissot [le conventionnel né à Chartres en 1754]. In Procès-Verbaux de la Société archéologique d'Eure-et-Loire. [Chartres.] 1901, X, 121–23.

Denos, G. Étude sur la maison dite de Brissot à Chartres. In Procès-verbaux de la Société archéologique d'Eure-et-Loire. [Chartres,] 1901, X, 163–69.

Faguet, Émile. Une histoire de la Révolution française. In *La Revue des Deux Mondes*, 1 août, 1901, fifth period, IV, 631–59.

Manning, W. R. The Nootka Sound Controversy. In the *Annual Report* of the American Historical Association, 1904.

Perroud, A. Brissot de les Rolands. In *La Révolution Française*, mai, 1898, XXXIV, 403–22.

—— La Famille de Madame Brissot in *La Révolution Française*, LIX, 270–74, Sept. 14, 1910.

—— Sur l'authenticité des Mémoires de Brissot. In *La Révolution Française*, août, 1904, XLVII, 121–34.

—— Un Projet de Brissot pour une association agricole. In *La Révolution Française*, mars, 1902, XLII, 260–65.

Sorel, Albert. Un Général diplomate. In *La Revue des Deux Mondes*, juin 15, août 1, août 15, 1884, third period, LXIV, 302–32, 575–606, 789–829.

Turner, Frederick J. The origin of Genet's Projected Attack on Louisiana and the Floridas. In the *American Historical Review*, July, 1898, III, 650–71.

—— Documents on the Relations of France to Louisiana, 1792–95. In the *American Historical Review*, April, 1898, III, 490–516.

L'Intermédiaire des Chercheurs et des Curieux. Article signed G. D., Oct. 10, 1891, XXIV, 777.

Gives information as to the descendants of Brissot.

L'Intermédiaire des Chercheurs et des Curieux, XXIII; 707; XXIV, 62. Inquiry signed L. C. Answer signed Maurice Tourneux.

Inquiry and answer covering an alleged letter of the Baron Grim, asserting that Brissot had been a police spy.

The Monthly Review, XXXVI, 593, and VI (enlarged series), 531–43.

Book reviews of *De la France* and *Le Nouveau Voyage*.

INDEX

INDEX

Abbaye (prison), 363, 367-368.
Actes des Apôtres, 107, 120, 212 n., 217, 243 n., 447 n.
Adams, John, 25, 69, 74.
Adams, Samuel, 75.
Adelaide, Madame, 21 n.
Albany, 410.
Alembert (d'), 13, 19 n., 21.
Alexandria, 435.
Allais, 162.
Allier, Department of the, 352-353 notes, 356-357 notes, 358-359 notes, 361-362 notes.
Alsace, 227 n.
Amar, 369, 371, 372, 377.
America. *See* United States.
Ami du Peuple, 119-120, 224 n., 271 n., 333, 357 n.
Ami du Roi, 217, 234 and n., 276.
Amis des Noirs, Brissot's part in founding, 1-2, 40, 67, 96; connection with like societies in America, 78; addresses of, sent to municipal assembly, 105-106; mentioned, 121; incentive to organization of, 182-184; assistance given to, by Mirabeau, 183-185 and n., 193-194 and notes; first meeting of, 184-185; first president of, 185; efforts of Brissot to secure members for, 186; assistance given to, by Lafayette, 186-187; connection of, with Condorcet, 187; constitution of, 187-188; condition of, during Brissot's absence in America, 189; address of, on opening of the States-General, 189 and n.; relation of, to abolition of slave trade, 189-190, 197-199; letter of, to deputies, 190; assistance of Clarkson to, 190-194 and notes; plans of, 191-192; opposition to, of *Club de Massiac*, 194, 196; relation of, to States-General, 195-201 and notes; relation of, to admission of deputies from Santo-Domingo to States-General, 195-196 and notes; relation of, to admission of mulattoes to rights of citizenship, 196-197, 200-201, 208-212; relation of, to self-government of colonies, 196, 199-201; efforts of Brissot to interest the municipal government of Paris in work of, 197, 198 n.; attitude of, toward immediate abolition of slavery, 198; address of, to National Assembly, 198 and n., 200, and n.; attitude of, toward decrees of March 8 and October 12, 1790, 199-203; opposition to, 203-205, 212-215; attitude of, toward decree of May 15, 1791, 206-212; accusations against Brissot as leader of, 212-215; Brissot's reputation as leader of, 217; list of members of, 442-447.
Amsterdam, 317, 436.
Andover, 69 n.
Angers, Jacobin Society of, 206.
Anthoine, 288.
Antiquarian Society Papers, quoted, 66, 71, 72, 73, 85, 221, 399 n., 433-434.
Antonelle, 382 n., 383.
Antwerp, 317.
Arbaud, M. Paul, 34 n.
Argental (d'), 21 and n.
Argenteuil, rue d', 379, 381.
Argus Patriote, 217-218.
Artois, Count d', 274-275, 294.
Assembly, National (first), mentioned, 98, 102-104, 109-110, 118-119, 121 n., 123-124, 132, 139-145, 147-149, 153-154, 156, 158, 168, 170-171, 180, 191, 197-210, 212, 217.
Avignon, 142, 143 n., 417.
Aublay, M., 401.
Aublay (Madame). *See* Dupont, Nancy.
Auger, 120 n.
August 10, work of Assembly after, 293-302.
Aulard, F. A., quoted, 56 and n., 78 n., 125 n., 161, 175, 194 n., 232 n., 281, 300 n., 324 n., 417-418, 422, 427 n.

Austria, 236, 239–240, 250–251, 272, 275, 284, 302, 317, 339, 374.
"Austrian Committee," 272–275 and notes, 379–380, 423.
Auvergne, 272 n.

Babillard, Le, 217, 218 n., 222 and n.
Baillard, 426 and n.
Bailly, 96, 104, 138, 179, 357 n., 379–380.
Bâle, 313.
Bançal des Issarts, 121 and n., 144 n., 151, 161, 172, 175 n., 202 n., 253.
Barbaroux, 324 n., 327, 334.
Barbier, 243 n.
Barentin, 445 n.
Barère, 336, 368 n., 369.
Barett, 435.
Barlow, Joel, 86.
Barnave, 42 n., 135, 181, 200, 201 and n., 202, 213 n., 309.
Barthélemy, 354.
Bastille, imprisonment of Brissot in, 24, 27, 29, 32–33, 368, 392; mentioned, 97 and n., 98, 203, 332, 368.
Bayonne, 360.
Bazire, 328.
Beau, 352, 354 n.
Beaugency, 379.
Beaulieu, 219 and n.
Beaumarchais, 30 n., 53, 399.
Beaupoil Saint-Aulaire, 186 and n.
Beauvais de Préau, 451.
Beccaria, 45, 56.
Becquet, 247, 251.
Belgium, 252, 316–317, 329–331, 375.
Bentham, Jeremy, 25 and n., 391 n.
Benzelin, 275 n.
Bergasse, Nicholas, 37 and n., 38 and n., 152.
Berlin, 54, 250, 320, 439.
Bernardin, de Saint Pierre, 186, 197 n.
Berne, 22, 313.
Berne, Economic Society of, 14.
Bertrand de Moleville, 141 and n., 273–274 and notes, 287.
Besançon, Academy of, 19 n., 20 n.
Beverly, 69 n.
Bexon, 140.
Bibliothèque, Section of. *See* Municipality.
Biderman, 120 n., 420.
Bigot de Préameneu, 451.
Billaud-Varennes, 300, 360.

Blanchelande, 209, 449–450.
Blot, 7 and n., 8, 39, 121, 151.
Boileau, 383.
Bonconseil, Section of, 333.
Bonne-Carrère, 265, 280 and n., 291 n.
Bonneville, 120 n., 121 n.
Bordeaux, 152, 162, 203 and n., 213, 380–381.
Bosc, 121 and n., 122, 367.
Boston, 69 and n., 71–72, 74–75.
Bouille, Marquis de, 158–159, 169 n.
Boulogne, 14–16, 387 and n., 388, 398, 401.
Bourbon, 314.
Bourbon, Ile de, 250.
Bourdon, 378 and n.
Bourges, 336.
Brabant, 237, 284.
Brach, 186 and n.
Breteuil, 30 n., 32.
Brienne, 51, 187.
Brissot, Jacques Pierre, reasons for writing the life of, 1–3; reputation at the beginning of the Revolution, 1; reasons why biography has not been written, 1–3; early writings permeated with revolutionary doctrines, 2; parentage, 4; birth, 4 and n.; name, 4 and n.; baptism, 4; love of study and reading, 4–6, 7; interest of mother of, in his studies, 4–6; opposition of father of, to education of children, 4–5, 6; brothers and sisters of, 4 and n., 5; schooling, 5–6; choice of legal profession, 6; treatise of, on canon law, 7; *Rome démasqué,* 7; essay on theft and property, 7; study of languages, 7; thoughts of marriage, 7–8, 16; religious experience, 8–10; reading of Rousseau, Voltaire, and Diderot, 8–9; conversion to deism, 9; *Lettres philosophiques sur la vie et les écrits de Saint Paul,* 9 and n., 25, 41–42, 120 n.; opposition to family on matters of religion, 9–10; aspiration for a career in Paris gratified, 10–11; addition of "de Warville" to name, 10 and n., 11; arrival in Paris, 11 and n.; life in Paris, 11–14; plans for presentation of plays in foreign languages, 11; devotion to a literary career in company with

Guillard, 11–12; difficulty in gaining livelihood, 12; *Le Pot pourri*, 12; threat of *lettre de cachet*, 12; illness, 12; plans for reform of laws and legal institutions, 13–14, 19–21; *Théorie des lois criminelles*, 13–14, 18–19; 45–47 and notes, 52, 54 *n.*, 55, 372; *Testament politique de l'Angleterre*, 13; *Pyrrhonisme universelle*, 13; writings on laws and political institutions, 13, 18–20, 25, 36–37, 49–55; employment by Swinton on the *Courrier*, 13–15; dismissal by Swinton, 15; *Réponse a tous les libellistes*, quoted, 14, 30, 32–33, 49, 53–54, 68, 220–221 notes; unsuccessful application to father for aid, 15–16; return to Paris, 16; work for Linguet, 16; death of father, 17; legacy from father, 17; insanity of mother, 17; scientific study, 17; interest in Marat, 17; resumption of study for the bar and final abandonment of a legal career, 18; winning of prizes on subject of legal reform, 19–20; *S'il était dû des indemnités*, 19; *Quelles pourraient être en France les lois pénales*, 19; *Des funestes effets de l'égoisme*, 19 *n.*; *Un Indépendant à l'ordre des avocats*, 19, 47 *n.*, 52, 55 and *n.*, *Biblothèque philosophique*, 19 *n.*, 20, 36, 44–46 and notes, 49–50 notes, 52, 55 and *n.*, 57, 133 and *n.*, 372; *De la Vérité*, 19–20, 52; *Histoire universelle de la legislation criminelle*, 20; establishment and failure of the *Lycée*, 20–21, 25–30, 33 and *n.*, 219; journey to Switzerland, 21; engagement, 18, 389; marriage, 22–23, 389; *Le Philadelphien à Genève*, 22, 25, 50 *n.*, 52; connection in London with libel writers, 23–24; acquaintance in London with men and women of note, 24–26; joined in London by wife, 25, 390–391; trouble with Desforges, 25, 30, 391; *La Correspondance*, 26, 29, 52, 53 *n.*, 54, 113, 372; *Tableau exact des sciences et des arts en Angleterre*, 26, 54, 372, 391; *Tableau des Indes*, 26, 52–53; birth of a son, 26, 391–392; arrest for debt and release, 27, 391–392; departure for France, 27, 392; arrest and imprisonment in the Bastille,

27, 392; *Lettre aux électurs*, 28 *n.*, 220 *n.*; *Journal de Lycée*, 29; *Réplique de Brissot*, 29, 220, 221, 222 notes; accusations against of implication in libels, 30–33; release from Bastille through efforts of friends, 32, 392; accusation of responsibility for *Le Diable dans un bénitier*, 30–32, 321; help received from Clavière and from mother-in-law, 33; birth of second child, 33 and *n.*, 395; financial difficulties, 34; collaboration with Clavière in work for Mirabeau, 34; work for Mirabeau, 34–36; collaboration in *Caisse d'escompte*, 34; collaboration in the *Banque de Saint Charles*, 34; trouble with Mirabeau over manuscript, 35 and *n.*, *L'Autorité législatire de Rome anéantie*, 36, 41, 147; translation of *Travels in Europe, in Asia, and in Africa*, 36 and *n.*; *Un Défenseur du Peuple à l'Empereur Joseph II*, 36 and *n.*, 53 *n.*, 55; *Lettre à l'Empereur sur l'Atrocité des supplices*, 36 and *n.*, 55, 372; *L'Examen critique des royages dans l'Amérique septentionale de M. le Marquis de Chatellux*, 36 and *n.*, 52, 55 and *n.*, 59–60; interest in scientific studies, 37 and *n.*; plans for the *Société Gallo-Américaine*, 37; *Dénonciation au public d'un nouveau projet d'agiotage*, 37 and *n.*; *Seconde lettre contre la compagnie d'assurance*, 37 and *n.*, connection with Bergasse in political reform, 38; work for the Duke of Orlèans, 38–39; *Point de banqueroute*, 37 and *n.*, 50 *n.*, 51, 53 *n.*, 183; *Lettres philosophiques et politiques sur l'histoire de L'Angleterre*, 37 and *n.*, 372, 383; *Un mot aux académiciens*, 37; *De la France et des États-Unis*, 37, 48 and *n.*, 52, 55 and *n.*, 63–66 and notes, 69, 90, 121; attitude toward republicanism and dethronement, 38, 128, 165, 253–255, 269, 181, 276–292, 363–366, 371–374, 379–380, 412–413, 419; threat of *lettre de cachet*, 39; visit to England and Holland, 39 and *n.*; *Recherches philosophiques sur la propriété et le vol*, 43–44, 46 *n.*, 266–267; work against the slave trade, 40, 59–60;

influences seen in early writings, 41; subjects of early writings, 41–48; *Moyens d'adoucir en France la rigueur des lois pénales*, 45–47 and notes, 49; *Le Sang innocent vengé*, 45–47 and notes, 55; writings on the United States, 48–50; *Observations d'un républicain*, 50, 148, 164; ideal for universal brotherhood, 52–53, 419, 427; trouble with the censorship, 53–416; opinion concerning rights of Jews, 53, 146, 416; anonymous publications, 54; style of writing, 56; significance of early writings in connection with later career, 57–58; criticism of writings of by *Monthly Review*, 66 n.; journey to America, 66–90; *République à Stanislas Chermont*, 68 n., 84 n.; *Nouveau Voyage*, 69 n., 70–84 notes, 90 n.; reasons for publication of *Nouveau Voyage*, 88, 90, 315; relation to federalism, 90, 172, 342–356, 379–380, 412, 414, 419; return to France, 91; at opening of the States-General, 91–96; failure of election to the States-General, 95–96; work as a municipal politician, 91–112; *Plan de conduite*, 92–94, 124, 135, 148, 165; *Observations sur la nécessité d'établir . . . des comités de correspondance*, 93 and n., 127 n.; *Discours prononcé au district des Filles-Saint-Thomas*, 94 n., 100 n.; *Précis adressé à l'assemblée générale des électeurs de Paris pour servir à la rédaction des doléances de cette ville*, 94 n., 95; *Motifs des commissaires pour adopter le plan de municipalité*, 99; *Observations sur le plan de municipalité de Paris*, 99 n.; *Opinion . . . sur la question de savoir si Paris sera le centre d'un département*, 101 n.; opinion on questions of finance, 102–104, 147–149, 151–154, 265–266, 359 and n.; opinion on ecclesiastical questions, 102–103, 111–112; 144–147, 259–261; 296; *Motion sur la nécessité de circonscire la rente des biens ecclésiastiques aux municipalités*, 103, 111 n.; *Discours sur la rareté du numéraire et sur les moyens d'y remédier*, 104 n., 152 n.; interest in development of local govern-

ment, 105; *Discours prononcé à la section de la Bibliothèque dans son assemblée générale . . . sur la question du renvoi des ministres*, 104 n.; *Réflexions sur l'état de la Société des électeurs patriotes sur ses travaux, sur les formes propres à faire de bonnes élections*, 105 n.; *Rapport dans l'affaire de MM. Dhosier et Petit-Jean*, 108 n.; *A Stanislas Clermont*, 108 n., 109 n.; *Réplique à Stanislas Clermont*, 109 n.; *Lettre à M. le Chevalier de Pange*, 109 n.; work as editor of the *Patriote Français*, 113–181; *Discours sur l'organisation de comités*, 119 n.; *A tous les républicains de France*, 121 n., 346; *Discours sur les conventions*, 133 n.; opinion on foreign affairs, 142–143, 295; attitude toward democracy, 159–165, 180–181, 259, 324, 325–327, 414–417; attitude toward women, 162; attitude toward socialistic ideas, 162–163, 416; *La profession de foi sur la monarchie et sur la républicainisme*, 173–175; *Discours sur la question de savoir si le roi peut être jugé*, 175–177 and notes, 231 and n.; attitude toward Lafayette, 180, 193 and n., 224, 241, 268–269, 276, 289, 296, 308–309, 337, 357 n., 370 and n., 378–380; relation to the *Société des Amis des Noirs*, 182–215; *Discours sur la nécessité d'établir à Paris une société pour concourir avec celle du Londres, à l'abolition de la traite et de l'esclavage des nègres*, 185; *Mémoire sur les noirs de l'Amérique septentrionale*, 189 and n.; *Réflexions sur l'admission aux États-Généraux des députés de Saint-Domingue*, 196 and n.; *Discours sur la nécessité de maintenir le décret rendu le 15 mai 1791 en faveur des hommes de couleur libres*, 207 and n.; election to the Legislative Assembly, 216–224, 451; accusations against at time of candidacy, 217–223; comments made on election of Brissot, 224; address on receiving the election, 224–225; position of in the Legislative Assembly, 225–226, 258; *Discours sur l'organisation des comités*, 226 and n.; elected one of secretaries of the Legislative Assembly, 226; membership in Diplomatic Committee of Legislative Assembly, 226–227, 229, 375; advocacy of foreign war, 230–257; relation to Jacobin Club, 232–234, 236; *Discours sur la nécéssité de déclarer la guerre*, 233 and n.; *Second discours sur la nécéssité de faire la guerre*, 238 n.; *Troisième discourse sur la nécessité de la guerre*, 241 n.; attacks on, because of his advocacy of war, 242–244 and notes, 271–272; attack on Delessart, 243–249 and notes, 261–262, 375, 379–381; efforts to obtain foreign alliance, 256, 317–318; *Réplique à la première ct dernière lettre de Louis Marthe Gouy*, 254 and n.; *Discours sur la nécessité de suspendre momentanément le paiement des liquidations au-dessus de 3000 l.*, 259 n.; opinion on ecclesiastical questions, 259–261; opinion on financial questions, 259 and n.; leader of Girondins, 261–266 and notes, 281–291, 419–421; attitude on discipline, 265–266; attacks on, 266–272, 280 and n.; attack on "Austrian Committee," 272–275 and notes, 379–380; *Première lettre à Dumouriez*, 280; wavering attitude toward monarchy, 280–291, 412–413, 419; attitude toward events of June 20, 281–282 and notes; *Discours sur les causes des dangers de la patrie ct sur les mésurcs à prendre*, 284 n.; *Opinion sur les mésures de police générale proposées par M. Gensonné*, 286 n.; *Opinion sur la marche à suirre en examinant la question de la déchéance et les autres mésures*. 286 n., attitude toward events of August 10, 291–292, 294–295, 363, 379–381, 412–483; attitude toward second Girondin ministry, 292 and n.; work as member of the Committee of Twenty-one of the Legislative Assembly, 292–294 and notes, 296, 298, 301–302, 414; attitude toward Swiss troops, 294 and n.; address to foreign powers, 295; *Projet de déclaration de l' Assemblée nationale*, 295 n.; attitude toward the Commune of Paris, 296–303 and notes; accusation against, of plotting to put upon the throne the Duke of York or the Duke of Brunswick, 300 and n., 363, 412; accusation of, for connection with the massacres of September, 301, 380–381, 413–414; election to Convention, 303–304; member of the Committee on the Constitution, 304, 324 n.; member of the Diplomatic Committee, 304, 316–317, 342, 376; attitude toward the abolition of royalty, 304, 305, 332, 363, 379–380, 412–413; opposition to centralization, 306–307, 350; support given to Buzot against Jacobins, 307; *A Tous les républicains de France*, 308; support given to Dumouriez, 310, 413; attitude toward revolutionary propaganda and annexations, 310–312 and notes; *A ses Commcttans*, 311 and n.; attitude toward Swiss cantons and Geneva, 312–314; attitude toward Spain, 314; attitude toward Spanish America and furtherance of Genet's expedition, 314–316 and notes; member of the Committee of General Defense, 316 and n., 318–320; attitude toward Committee of Public Safety, 316 n., 328; attitude toward opening of the Scheldt, 316–319, 376; attitude toward war with England, 317–324, 439–441, 452; attitude on king's trial and death, 317–318, 321–324, 419; attack on, as alleged royalist, 328; attacks on, as leader of the Girondins, 328–332; attempt of Danton to conciliate, 331; attack on, for alleged conspiracy with Dumouriez, 332–333; accusation of having accumulated wealth, 333 and n.; attack on Marat, 334; defense against attacks of sections of Paris and of Robespierre, 335; *Sur la dénonciation de Robespierre et sur l'addresse prêtée aux quarante-huit sections de Paris*, 335 n.; attack on Mountain in pamphlet, *A ses Commcttans*, 337–341 and notes; accusation of being an Orléanist, 337, 412–413; expulsion from the Convention, 341–342, 350–352; refuge at house of Meillan, 351–352; flight from Paris to Versailles, 352; flight in company with Souque to Chartres, 352; cold reception at Chartres, 353; flight toward Orléans, 353; arrest and examination at Moulins, 354–355; confession of identity, 355; appeal to the Convention, 356–358; connection with district of Gannat, 358–359; help offered to by Marchena, 360; hostile demonstration against at Moulins, 356–357; transportation back to Paris, 361–362; imprisonment at Paris, 362–363; arraignment with other Girondins by Saint Just, 362–364; answer to arraignment of Saint Just, 364–367; responsibility of Brissot for war, 366, 370–371, 374–376; appeals while in prison to the Convention, 368–369; indictment of, by Amar, 369–371; relation to colonial policy, 371–375, 379–380, 413–418, 448–450; *Projet de défense*, 371–376; accusations against, 376–377, 448–450; prominence in trial as leader of the Girondins, 377; preliminary examination, 377; choice of lawyer, 377; witness against, 378; testimony against at trial, 379–380; defense at trial, 380–381; value of defense, 381; verdict against, 383–384; last hours and execution 384–386 and notes; family life, 387–403; proposal for hand of Swinton's daughter, 388; relation with wife's family, 398–402; in general principles a typical Girondin, 412–419; difference from other Girondins in wider outlook and greater cosmopolitanism, 417, 427; in regard to the other Girondins how far a leader, 419–421; divergent views as to fitness for leadership, and character, 421; appearance, 426. *See also Amis des Noirs*, Municipality, *Patriote Français*, and United States.

Brissot, Edme, Augustine, Sylvain, 393, 408–410.

Brissot, Félix, 393, 399, 410.

Brissot, Jacques, Jérôme, Anacharsis, 393, 410 and n.

Brissot, Madame. *See* Félicité.

Brissotins, 225, 235, 249, 301–303, 309, 330; *Histoire de*, 336–337, 420–422.

Bristol, 69 n.

Britain, 318.

Brookfield, 69 n.

Brother-in-law, Brissot's. *See* Dupont, François.

Broussonet, 120 n., 451.

Brunswick, Duke of, 299, 300 and n., 371, 412.

Buisson, 114 and n., 115.

Bulletin du tribunal révolutionnaire, 381, 384.

Bunker Hill, 231.

Burke, 218, 340–341 notes.

Burney, Fanny, 24, 426 n.

Buzot, 126, 171, 186, 306 n., 307, 327, 334, 342, 344–345, 348, 420, 422, 426.

Buzotins, 346, 420.

Cahen, 188 n.

Caisse d'escompte. See Brissot.

Calas case, 21 n.

Calonne, 34 n., 35 and n., 61 and n.

Calvados, Department of, 345.

Cambon, 282, 311 n.

Cambridge, 69 n., 74.

Cambridge, University of, 183.

Camus, 153 and n.

Capet. *See* Louis XVI.

Carolina, North, 84.

Carra, 184.

Cazenove, 66 n., 67 and n.

Cercle social, 161, 172.

Cerutti, 451.

Chabot, 281, 378–380.

Chalons-sur-Marne, Academy of, 19, 287 n.

Chambon, 17.

Chambonas, 284–285, 287 and n., 424.

Champagneux, 151 and n., 367.

Champ de Mars, petition of, 177–179, 337, 370–371.

Champs Élysées, 164.

Channel, the English, 27, 401, 436.

Chant du Coq, 217 and n., 218 n.

Charavay, 68 n., 217 n., 218 n.

Charles I, 285.

Chartres, mentioned, 4–7, 10, 39, 94, 186 n., 220, 222 and n., 223, 352–353.

Chartres, Duke of, 21 and n., 32–33, 389.

Chassé, 145.

Chastellux, Marquis de, 36 and n., 52, 55, 59–61, 67, 77, 79, 183.
Chaumette, 378 and n.
Chaveau de la Garde, 138 n., 377 and n., 382 and n.
Chauvelin, 250 and n., 375.
Chester, 69 n.
Châtelet, 96, 138.
Choderlos de Laclos, 166, 177–178 and n.
Chronique de Paris, 120.
Chronique du Mois, 120 and n., 262, 326.
Clarkson, Thomas, 185 and n., 190–194, 422.
Claretie, 218 n.
Clavière, Étienne, relation to Brissot, 22 and n.; financial assistance given to Brissot, 34; collaboration with Brissot in work for Mirabeau, 34 and n., 35 and n.; collaboration with Brissot in De la France et des États-Unis, 48, 55 n., 63–66 and notes, 90; connection with Société Gallo-Américaine, 61–63; connection with Brissot in American speculation, 66–67, 72–73, 89, 431, 437–439; connection with Brissot at opening of States-General, 91; connection with Chronique du Mois, 120 n.; connection with Patriote Français, 121; connection with republicanism, 169, 171, 276; connection with the Amis des Noirs, 184–185, 191–192, 205–206, 442; in the ministry, 249, 262 and n., 279; mentioned, 247, 420.
Clermont, 172.
Clermont-Tonnèrre, Stanislas, 68 n., 108 and n., 109 n., 165–166.
Cleves, 253 n.
Clive, 72 n.
Cloots, 253 and n., 310 n., 344, 346, 348, 422.
Coblenz, 233–234, 271, 363.
Collot d'Herbois, 120 n.
Colons Blancs, Club de. See Massiac, Club de.
Comité de Recherches. See Municipality; also Paris.
Committee of Public Safety, 293, 340.
Committee of Twenty-one. See Legislative Assembly.
Commune, struggle of, with Legislative Assembly, 292, 296–302 and notes; struggle of Brissot against, 296–302 and notes, 308, 328, 333.
Conciergerie, 363, 371 and n., 384 n., 386.
Condorcet, connection with Amis des Noirs, 184 n., 187–188, 191, 212, 443; attitude toward republicanism, 251, 276–277; mentioned, 19 n., 32, 120 n., 154, 171–172, 180, 213 n., 221, 237, 250, 269. and n., 270 n., 299 and n., 305, 318, 338, n., 420, 426, 452.
Confédération des Amis de la Vérité, 161.
Constantinople, 264, 379.
Constituent Assembly, 19 n., 113, 124, 182, 207, 223, 253 n., 285 n., 373, 375.
Conti, Prince de, 32 and n.
Convention, election of Brissot to, 303–304; general position of Brissot in, 303; membership of Brissot in Diplomatic Committee of, 304, 342; membership of Brissot in Committee on the Constitution, 304; abolition of royalty by, 304–305; struggle in, between Girondins and Mountain (Jacobins), 305–308; attitude of, toward revolutionary propaganda, 310–312 and notes; attitude of, toward Swiss cantons and Geneva, 312–314; attitude of, toward Spanish America and Genet's expedition, 314–316 and notes; Committee of General Defense of, 315, 316 and n., 318–320; Committee of Public Safety of, 293, 315 n., 358, 362–363, 368; attitude of, toward opening of the Scheldt, 316–319; attitude of, on king's trial, 318, 321–324; discussion of war question by, 318–324; Committee of General Security of, 324, 328, 369 n., 403, 405; final struggle in, between Girondins and Mountain supported by Commune of Paris, 351; Committee of Legislation of, 369 n., mentioned, 20 n., 25 n., 117, 123, 125 n., 141, 153 n., 181, 186 n., 238 n., 253 n., 293, 299, 302, 305, 306 and n., 307–308, 310–311, 314, 316 and n., 318, 319, 321–324, 329, 332–339, 345, 347, 349–351; 355, 356–359, 361–364, 366, 368, 370, 377, 378 n., 383, 426 n., 440, 450.

Copenhagen, 34.

Cordeliers, 166 n., 179 n., 330.

Corps Législatif, 352 n.

Courrier des Départements, 120, 348 n.

Courrier de l'Europe, 13–15, 24, 27, 219.

Courtois, 403.

Craigie, Andrew, 66 and n., 71–73 and notes, 85 and n., 89–90 notes, 433–438.

Cretté, de Paluel, 451.

Crèvecœur, Saint John de, 59–61, 63, 67, 70 n., 186, 431.

Danton, connection with Brissot, 138, 166 n., 173, 186 n., 221, 292, 301, 306 and n., mentioned, 2, 104, 308 n., 330–331, 366, 378 n., 414, 422, 426 n.

Dard, 179 and n.

Dauban, 348.

Daverhoult, 230–231.

De Bourges, 191.

De Graves, 261–263.

Delacroix, 97 n.

Delaunay, 32.

Delaware, 82.

Delessart, attack of Brissot on, 244–249 and notes, 261–262, 272, 379–380, 420.

De Moustier, 69, 70 n.

De Pons, 213 n.

De Saint-Étienne, 125 and n.

Descombes, 358 and n., 359.

Desfaix, 378 and n.

Desforges, 25–30, 219–221, 391–392, 401, 426 n.

Desmoulins, Camille, Jean Pierre Brissot démasqué, 4 n., 124, 218 n., 242–244; Histoire des Brissotins, 336–337 and n., 338, 421; connection with Brissot, 139, 167–168, 269, 301–302, 383, 400 n.; Révolutions de France et de Brabant, 119, 138, 167 and n., 169 and n., 176 and n., 384 n.; mentioned, 378 n.

Destournelles, 328 and n.

Dhosier, 108 and n.

Diderot, 8, 56.

Dietrich, 371.

Dillon, Arthur, 203–204, 364, 366.

Directory, 352 n., 407.

Dodsley, 393.

Dover, 391, 436.

Droz, 20 n.

Du Barry, Madame, 13, 30 n.

Du Chastellet, 171 and n., 172, 263.

Du Crest, Marquis, 38–39.

Duer, William, 66, 69, 72–73 and notes, 85 and n., 433–436, 438.

Duheim, 378 and n.

Dumont, Étienne, 91 and n., 95 n., 171 and n., 172 n., 247–249, 261, 263, 265, 277, 420–422.

Dumas, Mathieu, 240.

Dumouriez, 249, 251, 262, 264–265, 279–280, n., 285 n., 309–310, 314 n., 329, 332, 335, 337, 357 n., 364, 366, 371, 377, 404, 413.

Dupont, Félicité. See Félicité.

Dupont, Francis, 79 n., 84, 85 and n., 89 n., 398–401, 409, 435, 438.

Dupont, Julie Henriette, 400.

Dupont, Madame, kindness to Brissot, 16, 387–388, 401; loan of money to him, 23, 33; assistance to Brissot in gaining release from the Bastille, 27; bearer of news to Félicité, 27, 392, 401; help in the office of the Patriote Français, 123, 396; relied on by Félicité, 401–402; care of family after Brissot's imprisonment, 403; project of, for a school, 407; opinion of, concerning Brissot, 402 n., 425.

Dupont, Mademoiselle. See Félicité.

Dupont, Marie Thérèse, 400.

Dupont, Nancy (Madame Aublay), 397, 398, 400–401, 411.

Dupont de Nemours, Lomémie, 35 n.

Duport, 136, 272 and n., 273–274.

Duportail, 272 and n.

Duroveray, 22 and n., 250 and n., 264.

Dussaulx, 120 n., 241.

Electoral Assembly, 223–244 and n.

Élie de Beaumont, 21 and n.

Émigrés, attitude of Brissot toward question of, 227–232, 236, 252, 255–256.

England, 15, 20, 23, 36, 37 n., 39, 40 n., 49, 54, 61, 73, 117, 143, 151, 176, 182 and n., 184, 186 n., 191, 214, 220, 221, 235, 250, 273 and n., 275, 285, 295, 299, 316, 318–320, 323–324, 339, 364, 366, 373–376, 389, 404.

Eure, Department of the, 303 n., 304 n.

Eure-et-Loir, Department of the, 303 n., 304 n, 352 n.
Europe, 271, 294, 302, 310, 314, 317, 318, 322, 323, 371, 372, 399, 427, 433.
Eury, 452.

Fabre d'Eglantine, 292, 378 and n.
Faguet, M., 418.
Fairfield, 69 n.
Falmouth, 85, 436.
Faucompre, 361.
Federalism. See Brissot; also Girondins.
Félicité, acquaintance of, made by Brissot, 15-16, 387; engagement to Brissot, 18, 387-389; marriage to Brissot, 22-23, 389; relation to Madame de Genlis, 23, 388-389; life in London, 26, 391-392; birth of first child, 26; news broken to, of Brissot's imprisonment in the Bastille, 27, 392; necessity of frugal life for, 34; literary work, 37, 393 and n.; interest in the United States as possible place of abode, 81-82, 89, 394, 396; opinion of, concerning the Patriote Français, 123 n.; arrest of, 368 n.; accusations against, in connection with Brissot's arrest and trial, 364, 366-368; letters of Brissot to, 385; part in Brissot's career, 387; efforts to secure release of Brissot from Bastille, 392; birth of second and third children, 393; difficulties and privations, 394-396; character of, 395-398; alienation from husband, 395; troubles of, with children, 395, 408, 411; pension given to, and to children of, 407; opinion of, concerning Brissot, 398; appreciation of, by Brissot, 398, 402-403; flight of, after arrest of Brissot, 403; arrest and examination of, 403-404; imprisonment of, 405; efforts of, to obtain from government reimbursement of losses, 406; attempt to establish a school, 407; application of, to government for aid, 408; maintenance of reading-room by, 408; death and burial of, 410-411.
Ferri, 61 n.
Fersen, Count de, 276 and n.
Feuillet de Conche, 250 n., 276.

Filangieri, 48, 56.
Filles-Saint-Thomas, 289 n. See also Municipality.
Fisher, Miers, 69, 88, 89 n., 399 n.
Flanders, 283.
Foreign war. See War.
Foucroy, 398.
France, 235, 237, 240, 242, 246, 249-250, 253 n., 254, 257, 273, n., 274 n., 285 and n., 292, 294-296, 305, 310, 311-314, 316-324, 335-337, 340, 341 n., 370-372, 376, 380, 391-392, 412, 417, 427, 433-435.
France, Isle de, 250.
Franklin, Benjamin, 57, 69, 78, 184.
Franklin, Temple, 69.
French Scioto Company. See Scioto Company, French.

Gallo-Américaine Société, 37, 61-63 and notes, 70 n.
Gannat, 358-360.
Garat, 19 and n., 330-331, 338, 427.
Garran de Coulon, 120 n., 208 n., 248.
Gébelin, 7.
Genet, 90, 314-316, 380.
Geneva, 22 and n., 25, 53, 250 n., 287 n., 312-314.
Genlis, Madame de, 21 and n., 32, 33 and n., 389-390.
Genlis-Sillery, Madame de. See Genlis, Madame de.
Gensonné, 208 and n., 211, 220, 235, 239, 247, 252, 265, 272, 274 n., 275 n., 281, 285 and n., 286 n., 288, 290, 309, 334, 351 and n., 383, 404, 420 and n., 426.
Gerle, 145.
Germany, 236, 399.
Gibbon, 24.
Gien, 353.
Girey-Dupré, 123 and n., 283 n., 298, 308 n., 323 n., 329 and n., 331, 334, 404, 422.
Girondin ministry, 22 n., 261-266 and notes; Brissot's influence on, 289, 309, 317, 379.
Girondins, Brissot's connection with, 1-3, 181, 225, 261, 268, 272-278, 282-291, 324, 412-423; belligerency of, 251-257, 418-419; attitude of, toward republicanism and dethronement, 253-255, 276-291, 412-419; attack of, on "Austrian

Committee," 272–276 and notes; responsibility of, for events of June 20, 281 and *n.*, 419; accusation against, of plotting to overthrow the republic, 299, 305 and *n.*, 412; struggle of, with Commune, 301–302, 305, 333; opposition of, to centralization, 303; efforts of, for a departmental guard, 305–306 and notes; struggle with party of the Mountain (Jacobins) during the Convention, 305–309, 327, 333, 342, 351; attitude of, toward revolutionary propaganda, 310; attitude of, toward death and trial of the king, 321; attitude of, toward war with England, 324; constitution drawn up by, 324 *n.*; newspapers of, attacked, 329; *Patriote Français*, organ of, 329; attempt of Danton to reconcile with Mountain, 330–331; attack on, on March 9, 329–330; accusations against, on account of Dumouriez's failure and desertion, 329, 333; accusations against, of federalism, 336–337, 342, 350, 412; attitude toward centralization, 350; expulsion of, from Convention, 342, 350, 352; report of Saint-Just on, 363–364; defense of, by Brissot, 364–365; report against, by Amar, 369–371; trial of, 377–382; verdict against, 383–384; last hours and execution, 384–386 and notes; reaction in favor of, 405–407; summary of general policy of, 411–417; comparison of, with party of the Mountain, 418–419; question of leadership of, by Brissot, 419; mentioned, 1–3, 117, 120, 121 *n.*, 123, 166 *n.*, 171–172, 184, 210–211, 214, 249, 251, 253, 261, 263, 265, 281 and *n.*, 282, 288, 289, 291, 292 *n.*, 299, 307, 309, 317, 318 *n.*, 382, 405.

Goetz-Bernstein, 292 *n.*
Gorguereau, 451.
Gorsas, 348, 381.
Goulet, 275 *n.*
Gouvion, 451.
Gouy D'Arsy, 203 and *n.*, 204 *n.*
Gower, Earl, 181 *n.*, 288.
Grandchamp, Sophie, 367.
Grégoire, 121, 202.
Grenville, Lord, 320 *n.*

Grétry, rue de, 393.
Griffin, 69.
Grimm, 342 and *n.*
Guadaloupe, 409 *n.*
Guadet, 208 and *n.*, 210–211, 225, 247, 252, 270, 281, 286, 288, 289 *n.*, 290, 299 and *n.*, 309, 331, 333–334, 336, 351 and *n.*, 404, 420 and *n.*, 426.
Guiana, French, 296.
Guillard, 8, 11–12.
Guy-Kirsaint, 120 *n.*

Hambourg, 440.
Hamilton, Alexander, 69, 84.
Hancock, General, 69, 75.
Hanover, House of, 295.
Hartford, 69 *n.*
Harvard, 74.
Haskell, 438.
Hastings, Warren, 36.
Haute-Loire, Department of the, 345.
Havre, 71, 83.
Heath, General, 69, 75.
Hébert, 338 *n.*, 378 and *n.*
Hébertists, 253 *n.*
Helvetius, 120 *n.*, 348, 422.
Helvetius, Madame, 276.
Hennin, 264.
Hérault de Séchelles, 186 and *n.*, 237.
Holland, 39, 40 and *n.*, 50, 53, 85, 316, 319, 323–324, 337, 375, 377, 438, 440–441.
Horeau, 6–7.
Hudson River, 81.
Hungary, 53.

Illinois Company, 82 *n.*, 89.
India, 61, 339.
Indians, 65, 80.
Indies, East, 36, 81, 339.
Indies, West, 182, 389.
Intermédiare (l') des chercheurs et des curieux, 244 *n.*
Ireland, 339.
Isnard, 230, 235, 241 *n.*, 251–252, 255, 260, 341, 345.
Ivernais (d'), Sir Francis, 22 and *n.*

Jacobin Club, attacks on Brissot at, 268–271, 288, 289; attack on Lafayette at, 290; expulsion of Brissot by, 307–309; mentioned, 121 *n.*, 160, 173, 175–176 and notes, 177–179,

194, 222 n., 223, 226 and n., 231 n., 232 and n., 233–239, 241, 289, 307, 309, 338 n., 352 n., 353 n., 379.

Jacobin Party, accusation of guilt of massacres of September, 305; struggle with Girondins during the Convention, 305–309, 334–350, 362 n.

Janvier, M., 10.

Jarry, 250.

Jaucourt, 247.

Jaurès, 302 n., 324.

Jay, John, 84.

Jeanbon, Saint-André, 329.

Jefferson, Thomas, 66 n., 186, 431.

Jesuits, 60.

Jews, 53, 102, 134, 146, 416.

Joly, 197, 448.

Joseph II, 36 and n., 53 n., 55.

Journal de Paris, 55 n., 61 n., 120, 266–268 and notes.

Journal général de la cour et de la ville, 104 and n., 120, 217–218, 219 n., 228, 242.

Julien, 318 and n., 452.

Jumilhac, 108–109.

June 20, attitude of Brissot toward events of, 281–282.

Kentucky, 118.

Kerolio, 138 n.

Kersaint, 420 n.

King, Rufus, 84.

Kirwan, 24, 33.

Koch, 226, 229–231, 239 n., 242.

Korman, 37 n., 38 n.

Kropotkin, 416 n.

La Blancherie, 20 and n.

Lacépède, 451.

Laclos. See Choderlos de Laclos.

Lacretelle, Pierre Louis, 19 and n.

Lafayette, connection of Brissot with, 179–180, 186, 191, 193 and n., 224, 241, 268–269, 276, 289 n., 290, 293, 308–309, 337, 357 n., 370, 374 and n., 379–380, 412–413; mentioned, 63 n., 65 n., 68 n., 80 n., 97 and n., 125, 157, 159, 162, 167 and n., 169 and n., 287 n.

La Force, 405.

La Harpe, 21 and n.

Lameth, Théodore, 160, 181, 445.

Lamourette, 283.

Lanthenas, 120 n., 121 and n., 122, 140, 151, 160–162, 186, 202 and n., 292 and n., 308 n., 443.

Laporte, 328.

Lasource, 382, n., 384 n.

Laurent de Couteux, 437.

Lavoisier, 154.

Law, 153.

Lebrun, 360, 376.

Legislative Assembly, Committee of Twenty-one of, 292, 296–302 and notes, 344, 379; struggle of, with Commune, 292, 296–302 and notes, 379–381; action of, against Lafayette, 293, 379–380; action of, toward Swiss troops, 294 and n.; action of, toward foreign powers after August 10, 294; attitude of, toward nonjuring clergy, 296; opinion of Brissot of work of, 301–302; mentioned, 25 n., 28, 117–118, 123–124, 175 n., 181, 186 n., 207, 208 n., 216–217, 223–229, 231, 239, 241–242, 244–247, 251, 253 n., 258–259, 261, 269, 272 n., 273–280, 282, 285 n., 286 n., 288–299 and notes, 301–303 and notes, 317, 332, 370, 373, 378 n., 379.

Lenoir, 31–32.

Leopold, 342.

Le Page, 122, 123 n.

Levant, The, 399.

Linguet, 11, 113, 426 n.

Lisbon, 440.

Loire, 303 n.

London, first visit of Brissot to, 15; location of Lycée, 20; Brissot's life in, 24–33; mentioned, 30 n., 161 n., 172 n., 214 n., 218–219, 285 n., 317, 320, 333, 389–390, 400–401, 434, 436.

Lons-le-Saunier, 160.

Louis XIV, 228, 240.

Louis XV, 30 n., 103 n., 153.

Louis XVI, 30, 141, 149, 177, 250 n., 255–268, 272 n., 267 n., 273, 320–324, 338–339, 344, 350, 357 n., 363–364, 370–371, 380–381, 440.

Louisiana, 315, 316 n., 339.

Louvet, 235, 238 and n., 251–253, 307, 308 n., 381.

Loyseau, 32.

Lubersac, 186 and n.

Luxembourg, 382 n., 388.

Luckner, Marshal, 290.

Lycée. See Brissot.

Lyons, 39, 151, 222, 223 n., 371.

Macaulay, Mrs., 26.
Mackintosh, 36.
Madéleine, cemetery, 386 n.
Madison, James, 69, 84.
Madrid, 52, 272, 440.
Mailhe, 249, 326.
Maissemy, 114 n.,116 n., 137.
Malassisin, 244 n.
Mallet du Pan, Jacques, 22 and n., 36, 277, 314 n.
Malouet, 131, 172.
Maluet, 350.
Mansfield, 24, 33, 182.
Manuel, 116, 253.
Marat, 2, 17, 104, 138–139, 224, 261 n., 293, 299 and n., 305, 309, 329 n., 331, 333–335, 338, 344, 357 n., 368, 379.
Marchena, 314, 360–361.
Marie Antoinette, 30–31.
Marseilles, 306 n.
Martin, 320, 439, 441.
Martinique, 198.
Massachusetts, 69, 75.
Massacres of September. See September massacres.
Massiac, Club de, 194, 196, 199.
Mathiez, 179 n.
Maty, 24.
Maury, L'Abbé, 147.
Mayenne, 20 n.
Mazzei, Philippe, 61 n.
Mediterranean, 339.
Meillan, 351 and n., 352, 425.
Mentelle, 16–18, 25, 32, 367, 368.
Mercier, 120 n.
Mexico, 381.
Mercure, Le, 19 and n., 21 n.
Merlin of Thionville, 268.
Middleton, 69 n.
Mifflin, Warren, 69.
Mirabeau, Gabriel Riqueti, Count de, relation to Clavière, 22 n.; relation of Brissot and Clavière to, 34 and n., 35 and n.; trouble with Brissot over manuscript, 35 and n.; work by Brissot for, 36; connection of Brissot with, in municipal affairs, 101; establishment of newspaper by, 113 n.; difference of opinion between Brissot and, on constitution, 126, 128–133, 143–144; opinion of, on foreign affairs, 142–143; opinion of Brissot on death of, 144; assistance given to

Amis des Noirs by, 183–185 and notes, 193–194 and notes, 202; mentioned, 221, 250 n., 442.
Miranda, 316 n., 335.
Mississippi River, 81, 314.
Mohawk River, 81–82.
Monge, 338 and n.
Monin, 96.
Moniteur, Le, mentioned or quoted, 97 n., 101 n., 117, 123 n., 130 n., 138 n., 141 and n., 196, 206 n., 209–211 notes, 215 n., 228–233 notes, 235–237 notes, 239–242 notes, 244–245 notes, 247 n., 249 n., 251–252 notes, 254–256 notes, 280–281 notes, 283 n., 285 n., 287 n., 290–291 notes, 293–294 notes, 296–298 notes, 301 n., 305–306 notes, 310–311 notes, 313–314 notes, 316 n., 318 n., 320 n., 322–324 notes, 329 n., 333–334 notes, 344–347 notes, 357 n., 364 n., 369–370 notes, 383–384 notes, 420 n.
Monk, 363, 365.
Montaigne, 136.
Montargis, 362.
Montaut, 328 and n., 380–381.
Montesquieu, 41, 45, 49–50, 56, 285 n., 288.
Montesquieu (General), 313–314.
Monthly Review, 303.
Mont Jura, 161.
Montmorin, 219, 272 and n., 275 and n., 294, 380.
Montrol, 10 n.
Morande, Théveneau de, 24, 28–32, and notes, 218–219 and notes, 301, 336, 366, 377, 426 n.
Moravian Brethren, 150.
Moreau de Saint-Méry, 204–205.
Morris, Robert, 73 n.
Mosneron, 198 n.
Mother-in-law, of Brissot. See Dupont, Madame.
Moulins, 353–356, 359, 360–363 and notes, 371.
Mountain, Party of the, hostility between, and Girondins, 305–306, 327–333; attack of, on Girondins because of Dumouriez's failure and treason, 329–333; attack, of, on Girondin newspapers, 329 and n., 334; attempt of Danton to reconcile with Girondins, 330–331; final struggle with Girondins, 334–342;

mentioned, 2-3, 117, 186 *n.*, 262, 308, 378 and *n.*, 382; comparison of, with Girondins, 417-419.

Municipality of Paris, Brissot's connection with district of the Filles-Saint-Thomas of, 93, 94-95 notes, 100 *n.*, 221; plan of Brissot for committees of correspondence of, 93 and *n.*, 97-98; Brissot, president of the Filles-Saint-Thomas of, 97-98; Brissot's part in building up permanent organization for, 98-101; Brissot's ideas on relation of, to central government, 99-101; Brissot's ideas on relation of, to departments, 101; Brissot's part in administration of, 102; relation of, to events of October 5 and 6, 102, 106-107; Brissot's opinion on sale of church lands to, 102-103, 111; Brissot's opinion on relation of, to the *caisse d'escompte*, 103, 111; relation of Brissot to the section of the *Bibliothèque* of, 104 and *n.*, 222; appeal in Brissot's section of, for dismissal of ministry, 104 and *n.*; attempt of Brissot to interest, in cause of negro, 105, 106, 111; support of Brissot of democratic faction of, 104; relation of Brissot to *Comité des Recherches* of, 106-110, 112, 118, 157, 370, 380; opinion of Brissot on balance of power between central council and districts of, 110-111; end of Brissot's active part in, 111-112.

Münster, Treaty of, 317.

Nancy, 158-159.
Nantes, 152, 162, 203, 204 *n.*
Napoleon, 1, 22 *n.*, 216.
Narbonne, 233, 235, 245, 261, 268-269, 272, 276, 357 *n.*, 376, 379.
National Assembly. *See* Assembly, National.
Necker, 50-51, 115, 148-149, 164, 190 and *n.*, 191-192, 437.
Negro, support of, by Brissot against strictures of Chastellux, 59-67; interest of Brissot in condition of, in the United States, 78-80. *See also* *Amis des Noirs*, and United States.
Netherlands, 376.
Neuchâtel, 22, 54, 354 and *n.*
Nevers, 353.

Newark, 69 *n.*
Newburyport, 69 *n.*
New Hampshire, 84.
New Haven, 69 *n.*
New Jersey, 82.
New Orleans, 410.
New Rochelle, 69 *n.*
New York, 67-68, 69 *n.*, 72 *n.*, 75, 77, 214, 409-410, 435.
New York Historical Society Papers, quoted, 79 *n.*, 221, 434-439.
Nice, 310, 344.
Noailles, 251, 273 and *n.*
Nolleau, 10.
Nootka Sound, 143 and *n.*
Norfolk, 435.
North Sea, 341.
Nouveau Voyage, 61 *n.* *See also* United States.

Odun (d'), Madame, 276, 420.
Ogé, 202-203, 206 *n.*, 214.
Ohio, 88.
Ohio Company, 85.
Orléans, 246 *n.*, 248, 335, 353.
Orléans, Duke of, 23 and *n.*, 33 and *n.*, 38-39, 95, 153, 287 *n.*, 363, 389 *n.*, 390, 412-413.
Oswald, 120 *n.*

Pache, 309-310, 338 and *n.*, 339, 378 and *n.*
Pacte de Famille, 143, 237 *n.*
Padua Circular, 239.
Paganel, 208 and *n.*, 215 *n.*, 225 and *n.*
Paine, Thomas, 63 *n.*, 121, 171, 305, 315.
Palais-Royal, 219, 242.
Pampeluna, 186 and *n.*
Pange, Chevalier de, 109 and *n.*, 268 and *n.*
Paris, attack of, on Girondins, 334-335, 341-350; mentioned, 10-11, 14-17, 52, 54, 67, 72, 214-215, 220 *n.*, 222 and *n.*, 223, 243, 272-273 notes, 283 *n.*, 297, 299, 304 *n.*, 306 and *n.*, 307-308, 338 *n.*, 343-350, 352, 353 *n.*, 358, 362, 366, 368 *n.*, 370-371, 374, 378 *n.*, 381, 388 *n.*, 392, 394-395, 401, 404, 408, 412, 418-420, 436. *See also* Municipality.
Parker, Daniel, 66 and *n.*, 71-72 notes, 73, 83, 433-434, 436-438.

Parlement of Paris, 18, 51.

Pastoret, 451.

Patriote Français, establishment of, by Brissot, 2, 96, 113, 416; quoted, 87–88, 101 and n., 102, 104–105 notes, 113–149 and notes, 152–154, 156, 158–177 and notes, 179–181 notes, 186 n., 197 n., 200–201 notes, 211 n., 214 n., 216–217, 219, 223 n., 225 n., 227 n., 230–235, and notes, 250 n., 253–259 notes, 260–263 and notes, 265–266 notes, 268 n., 270 n., 272–273 notes. 274 n., 278–282 notes, 283 and n., 289 and n., 290 n., 293 and n., 296 and n., 300 n., 304 and n., 306–307 notes, 309, 311 and n., 312 n., 317, 321 n., 326–331 notes, 333 and n., 343 n., 345 n., 350 n., 412 n.; struggle of, with censorship, 113–116, 137–138; comparison of, with other journals, 113; first and second prospectus, 114; interest of, in municipal affairs, 118; organ of the *Amis des Noirs*, 118, 194–195, 197 and n., 201 n., 202–207 and notes; interest of, in the United States, 118–119, 125, 130–133, 137, 142, 152, 164, 176; style, 119–120; relation of, to other journals, 120; assistance of collaborators in, 121–122; assistance of family in, 123, 196, 400–401; financial support of Le Page in, 122; partnership of Girey-Dupré in, 123; responsibility of Brissot for, 123–124; opinion of, on the declaration of rights and on the constitution, 124–136; opinion on question of one chamber or two, 126–127; opinion on the veto, 127–130; opinion on right of declaring war and making peace, 130–131; opinion on choice of the ministry, 130–132; opinion on methods of amendment, 132–133; opinion on extent of suffrage, 133–134; opinion on basis of suffrage, 134–135; support of, of rights of Jews, Protestants, and actors, 134, 146; opinion on submittal of constitution to the people, 135–136, 180; opinion on judicial system, 136–137, 156–157; opinion of freedom of the press, 137–138; opinion on freedom of speech, 138–140; accusation of, for libel, 140; forced abandonment of, by Brissot, 141, 329 and n.; opinion on administration of National Assembly, 141–142; opinion on Avignon, 142; opinion on ecclesiastical questions, 142–147, 260–261 and notes; opinion of, on Nootka Sound, 143; opinion of, on financial questions, 147–153, 359 and n.; interest of, in economic matters, 54; opinion of, on events of October 5 and 6, 157–158; opinion of, on affairs of Nancy, 158–159; opinion of, on military discipline, 159; interest of, in democracy, 159–165; attitude of, toward popular societies, 160, 162; opinion of, on republicanism, 165–177; opinion of, on flight to Varennes, 168–169; opinion of, on qualifications for electors, 180 n.; reputation of Brissot as editor of, 181, 217; advocacy by, of foreign war, 233–235 and notes, 256–257; recommended as patriotic by Jacobin Club, 239; attack of, on Desmoulins, 243 and n.; criticism by, of Narbonne, 245; attitude of, toward republicanism, 254–255, 277–278; attack of, on Robespierre, 270 and n.; attitude of, toward Dumouriez, 279–280 and notes; attack of, on court, 280; design of pikes given by, 281; approval by, of "kiss of Lamourette," 283; attitude of, toward Lafayette, 293; support by, of Legislative Assembly against the Commune, 296–302; summary by, of work of Legislative Assembly, 301–302; attitude of, on abolition of royalty, 304 and n., 305; support by, of Girondins against Mountain, 306 and n.; support by, of Buzot against Jacobins, 307; attitude of, toward the revolutionary propaganda and annexations, 311 and n.; attitude of, toward opening of the Scheldt, 317; alleged support of Lafayette by, 320; attitude of, toward trial and death of Louis XVI, 321; attitude of, toward social democracy, 325–327; attack on, as Girondin newspaper, 329 and n.; under direction of Girey-Dupré, 331; attitude of, toward treason of Dumouriez, 332–333; organ of Girondins, 329; attacked in connection with trial of Marat, 324; attitude toward federalism, 342.

Pelleport, 23–24, 27, 31–32.

Peltier, 265, 301.

Pennsylvania, 49, 77–78, 82–84.

Père Duchêne, Le, 119, 338, 378 n.

Perroud, M. Claude, quoted, 4–5 notes, 10 n., 15 n., 24 n., 33 n., 87 n., 121, 122–123 notes, 150 n., 292 n., 314 n., 335 n., 354–355 notes, 363–364 notes, 367 n., 371 n., 375 n., 400–403 notes, 407 n.

Pétion, source of information on Brissot's childhood, 6, 7 and n.; assistance given by, to Brissot in founding a *Maison philanthropique,* 39; efforts of, to secure election of Brissot to States-General, 94; assistance given to Brissot in the *Patriote Français,* 121; agreement with Brissot on the constitution, 131, 134–135; mentioned or quoted, 6–7 notes, 11 n., 14 n., 24 n., 28 n., 30 n., 34 n., 39, 56 n., 66–67 notes, 84 n., 121 n., 140, 143, 168, 169 and n., 176, 180, 191, 202, 221, 276, 282, 301, 305, 308 n., 333, 335, 351 n., 379–381, 395, 404, 425.

Petit, 275 n.

Petit-Jean, 108 and n.

Philadelphia, 69 n., 75, 78, 119, 364, 366, 379, 435.

Philippe Egalité, 337.

Philips, James, 62 and n.

Phillips, Richard, 425–426.

Pigott, 138 n., 151, 186 and n.

Pilnitz, Declaration of, 239.

Pinkard, Dr., 183.

Pitt, William, 218, 335, 337, 371, 375, 380–381, 435.

Poitiers, 186 n.

Poland, 236.

Polverel, 375.

Pope, the, 142–147.

Porentruy, 313.

Porter, 435.

Portsmouth, 69 n.

Price, 24.

Priestly, 24, 33.

Protestants, 53, 416.

Providence, 69 n.

Prudhomme, 119.

Prussia, 235, 250, 273, 309, 317.

Pyrenees, 310, 339, 341.

Quakers, 59–61, 67, 77–80, 146, 151, 161, 182–183, 186 n.

Ramus, 354 and n.

Rebecqui, 344.

Receveur, 24, 31–32.

Recherches, Comité de. See Municipality.

Remiremont, 139.

Républicain, Le, 371.

Restoration, the, 273 n., 285 n.

Révolutions de France et de Brabant, 119–120, 229.

Révolutions de Paris, 106 n., 107, 108 and n., 119–120, 197 and n., 270 n., 271, 272 and n., 274 n., 303 n., 420 n.

Rhine, 227, 283.

Rhode Island, 82–83.

Richelieu, 240.

Riouffe, 384 and n.

Riverol, 243–244 notes.

Robert, 166 and n., 177, 264, 379, 388.

Robespierre, antagonism between and Brissot, 232 and n., 234–235, 237–239 and notes, 241–242 and notes, 243, 268–271 and notes, 278 n., 293, 297, 302 n., 303, 307–308, 335, 338, 344; mentioned, 2, 140, 168–169, 180–181, 287 n., 331, 426 n., 442, 447 n.

Robert, Dubayet, 215.

Rochambeau, 250 n.

Rochefoucauld, Duke of, 191, 193 n.

Roederer, 253.

Rohan, Cardinal de, 231.

Rolands, assistance in attempting to found a *maison philanthropique,* 39; assistance in attempting to found the *Société agricole,* 89, 151; connection with *Patriote Français,* 121–122 and notes, 262; mentioned, 7 n., 33 n., 330. *See also* Roland, Madame; Roland, M.

Roland, Madame, assistance of, on the *Patriote Français,* 121–122 and notes, 134–135 and notes; connection with Brissot, 161–162 notes, 168–170 and notes, 178 and n., 180 and n., 262–265 and notes, 367–368 and notes, 404, 420 and n., 422; opinion of, concerning Brissot, 424–425; opinion of, concerning Madame Brissot, 397; opinion quoted, 144 n., 150 n., 151, 168–170 and notes,

175 n., 176 and n., 180 n., 202 n., 206 and n., 219, 223 and n., 262–265 and notes, 279, 280 n., 281, 289 and n., 292 n., 300 n., 306, 315 n., 352 n., 367 and n., 368 n., 399 n., 420 n., 423 and n.

Roland, M., connection with Brissot, 121, 161–162, 249, 262–263, 265, 279, 292 and n., 306, 337, 404, 414, 420.

Rome, 237.

Rousseau, 8, 41–44, 56, 75, 150.

Royer, 358 n.

Ruelle, 376.

Ruhl, 231.

Russia, 84, 236, 320, 439.

Rye, 69 n.

Saint-Cloud, 108, 159, 167, 364, 404–405.

Saint-Cyr, 408.

Saint-Cyran, 213 and n.

Saint-Denis, 223 n.

Saint-Just, 301, 363–364, 371 n., 372.

Saint Paul, 9 and n., 25, 41–42.

Saint-Pierre, Bernardin de, 32–33.

Saint Petersburg, 237, 320, 439.

Saint-Pourçain, 359.

Sainte-Beuve, 387.

Salem, 69 n.

Salle, 334, 351 n.

Saloman, 156, 276.

Santhonax, 375 and n., 379–380.

Santo Domingo, 192, 195–196, 199, 208–210, 212–215 and notes, 315, 375, 410, 448–450.

Savoy, 22, 310, 312, 319, 344.

Scheldt, 310, 316–317, 319, 375.

Schuyler, 84.

Scioto Company, 70 n., 73 and n., 79 n., 85–89 and notes, 221, 396.

Scioto Company, French, 87–89.

Ségur, 250.

Seine River, 345.

Seine, Department of the, 101, 253 n.

Seinie, Countess de, 94.

Sens, 285 n.

September, massacres of, 300–302; connection of Brissot with, 300–302, 362–364; responsibility for, 305, 366, 414.

Sergent Marçeau, 281 and n.

Servan, 279, 314 and n.

Seton, 437–438.

Sharpe, Granville, 183.

Shays' Rebellion, 159.

Sieyès, 136, 138, 144, 276–277.

Sillery, Marquis de, 21 n., 384 and n.

Slavery and the Slave Trade, opposition to, 78–80, 84; recognition of, by Constitution of United States, 84. See also Amis des Noirs.

Société agricole, 89, 150–151, 161.

Sorel, 250 n., 312.

Soulavie, 287 and n., 424 and n.

Souque, 352 and n., 353–358, 361–362.

Spain, 81, 143, 237 n., 313–315, 323, 339, 360, 364, 375, 380–381.

Spencer, 69 n.

Springfield, 69 n.

Stadinski, 66 n., 67 and n., 426.

Stadtholder, 319.

States-General, principles of Brissot in regard to, 93; connection of Brissot with elections to, 93–96; draft of a cahier for, 93–96; failure of Brissot to secure election to, 95 and n.; mentioned, 52, 74, 85, 115–117, 125, 137, 153 and n., 158, 165, 186 n., 188, 196 and n., 216–217, 435.

Stockholm, 237.

Strasbourg, 227, 320.

Swinton, 13–16, 24, 27, 113, 219, 387, 399, 426 n.

Sweden, 236.

Switzerland, 21, 314, 354, and n., 357 n.

Sybel, von, 246.

Talien, 450.

Talleyrand, 152–153, 162, 250, 375.

Tarbe, 208, 211.

Terror, the, 2–3, 250 n., 273 n., 284, 328, 414.

Thermidor, 250 n., 253 n., 264 n., 352 n.

Thomassin, 108.

Thorillon, 451.

Thouret, 136.

Tobago, 250.

Toulouse, 20 n., 273 n.

Toussaint l'Ouverture, 212.

Tremondrie, 201 n.

Trenton, 69 n.

Trèves, Elector of, 236, 239 and n., 255.

Tuileries, 164, 284, 291, 294.

Turgot, 35 and n., 50–51, 103, 164.

Turin, 440.

United States, reasons for Brissot's journey to, 40, 61; interest of Brissot in, 48–50, 59–90, 372; influence of, on Brissot, 49; admiration of Brissot for, 49–50; efforts of Brissot to obtain means for a journey to, 61; argument of Brissot for close relations with, 63–66; opportunity for journey to, 66; employment of Brissot by speculators in American debts and lands, 66–67, 72–73, 85–89; contract of Brissot for journey to, 67, 72–73; purposes of journey, 67–68; questions of Brissot concerning, 68; fitness of Brissot for investigation of, 68–70; limitations of Brissot as an investigator, 70; general attitude of Brissot toward the, 70; experiences of Brissot during voyage to, 71; visit of Brissot to Cambridge and John Adams, 74; visit to Hancock, 74; opinions concerning Samuel Adams, 74; journey of Brissot to New York, 75–76; opinion of Brissot on stage-coaches in, 76; opinion on inns in, 76; opinion on position of women in, 76; opinion of growing luxury in, 76–77; relation with Quakers in, and opinion of, 77–78; opinion on forms of worship in, 77–78; visit to Franklin in, 78; interest in condition of negro in, 78–80; interest in economic problems of, 80–82; interest in western expansion of. 80; interest in, as a possible place of settlement, 81–82; criticism of paper money of, 82–83; admiration for liberty and equality in, 83–84; acquaintance with distinguished citizens of, 84; attitude toward new constitution of, 84; departure from, 85; interest in land companies in, 85–89; account of journey to, published in *Nouveau Voyage*, 88–90; settlement of relations in, 89; subsequent influence of, upon Brissot, 90, 150–151, 176, 310, 413; influence of, seen in *Patriote Français*, 117–119, 125, 130–133, 137, 142, 152, 176, 181, 227; influence of, on Brissot in connection with war, 238; influence of, on *Amis des Noirs*, 189; influence of, on Brissot's plan for expedition to Spanish America, 315–316; alleged influence of, on federalistic ideas of Brissot, 349; alleged understanding of Brissot with government of, 364–366; plans of Madame Brissot for emigration to, 394–395; settlement of François Dupont in, 399; alleged close connection of Brissot with, 400 and *n.*; residence of Silvain Brissot in, 409, 410; correspondence in regard to speculation in the debt of, and in land, 431–439; mentioned, 280 *n.*, 291, 332, 348. 364, 372. *See also Gallo-Américaine Société*, and *Nouveau Voyage*.

Uri, 313.
Utrecht, Peace of, 319.

Valady, Marquis de, 184, 394 and *n.*, 395.
Valazé, 321, 384, 407, 420.
Vallots, 396.
Vancouver Sound, 143.
Van Staphorst, 436.
Varennes, 168, 413.
Vatel, 30.
Vellay, Charles, collection of papers of Brissot, 67 *n.*, 68 *n.*, 87 *n.*, 89 *n.*
Vendée, 279, 380, 381.
Vergennes, 13, 399.
Vergniaud, 102, 225, 240, 247, 252–253, 261–262, 282–293, 288, 299 and *n.*, 309, 333–334, 351, 382 *n.*, 420 and *n.*, 426.
Versailles, 106 *n.*, 115, 191, 276, 340, 352, 354 *n.*, 407.
Vienna, 240, 251, 273 *n.*, 320, 439.
Villar, Noël, 20 and *n.*, 21, 23.
Villate, 383–384 and notes.
Villefranche, 39.
Vingtain, 32.
Virginia, 69, 84.
Volney, 240 *n.*
Voltaire, 8, 13, 41–42, 45, 56, 146.

War, foreign, opposition to, 229–235; letters from England concerning, 439–441. *See also* Brissot.
Warren, 231.
Warville, de, 10 and *n.*, 11, 163 *n.*, 220, 221 and *n.*, 328, 431, 435, 438–439.
Washington, 68 *n.*, 69, 79–80, 97, 118, 231.

Washington, Mrs., 80.
Wethersfield, 69 *n.*
Wilberforce, 183, 190 *n.*
Williams, David, 25 and *n.*, 26, 49, 324 *n.*
Williams, Helena, 382, 409

Wilmington, 69 *n.*

Yonne, 223 *n.*, 410 and *n.*
York, Duke of, 299, 300 and *n.*, 363.

Zurich, 313.

𝕮𝖍𝖊 𝕽𝖎𝖛𝖊𝖗𝖘𝖎𝖉𝖊 𝕻𝖗𝖊𝖘𝖘

CAMBRIDGE . MASSACHUSETTS

U . S . A

CPSIA information can be obtained
at www.ICGtesting.com
Printed in the USA
LVOW10s1536260617

539313LV00060B/1488/P